President by Massacre

Recent Titles in
Native America: Yesterday and Today
Bruce E. Johansen, Series Editor

President by Massacre

Indian–Killing for Political Gain

~

Barbara Alice Mann

NATIVE AMERICA: YESTERDAY AND TODAY
Bruce E. Johansen, Series Editor

An Imprint of ABC-CLIO, LLC
Santa Barbara, California • Denver, Colorado

Copyright © 2019 by Barbara Alice Mann

Library of Congress Cataloging in Publication Control Number: 2019018375

ISBN: 978–1–4408–6187–1 (print)
     978–1–4408–6188–8 (ebook)

23 22 21 20 19   1 2 3 4 5

This book is also available as an eBook.

Praeger
An Imprint of ABC-CLIO, LLC

ABC-CLIO, LLC
147 Castilian Drive
Santa Barbara, California 93117
www.abc-clio.com

This book is printed on acid-free paper ∞

Manufactured in the United States of America

Contents

❦

Series Foreword

~

[handwritten notes:]
Jackson 7R 1829-1837
Harrison 9R 1841
Taylor 12R 1849-1850

In *President by Massacre*, Barbara Alice Mann provides a brilliant dissection of Native Americans' forced removal, the spread of slavery, and the establishment of oligarchy as the United States' standard style of governance during the first half of the nineteenth century. Her tools are the papers and writings on the foreign and domestic actions of three U.S. presidents: Andrew Jackson, the seventh; William Henry Harrison, the ninth; and Zachary Taylor, the twelfth.

While existing histories usually examine the policies of these three men in isolation, Professor Mann seeks common threads in a context of broader economic and social history—how it was, for example, that the forced labor of African American slaves by Taylor's presidency was harvesting cotton from lands that had been occupied by Native peoples who had been dispossessed on the Trail of Tears and other forced marches under Jackson's Removal policies barely a generation earlier, all driven by the popular ideology of Manifest Destiny supported by a pseudoscience of racial superiority.

DREAMS AND NIGHTMARES

All of this was accomplished by self-declared "populists" who enriched themselves as oligarchs by speculating in Indian land and profiting from black labor in what Professor Mann describes as a new caste system under the cover of "democracy." Thus, writes Dr. Mann, racism became the *deus ex machina* of the American Dream—manufactured from Native American and black nightmares.

All of this should ring a modern bell for students of history. Consider, for example, the billionaire Donald J. Trump, also a land speculator, who rails against immigrant labor while profiting from it, meanwhile representing himself as a populist defender of the "forgotten" white working class. Adolf Hitler, likewise, was an appreciative student of United States' westward expansion, declaring that the Volga River (in what was then the Soviet Union) would become known as Germany's Mississippi.

Mann's synthesis of this history is unique in the academic world, but she rejects any claim that no one has ever pointed out the confluence of Indian massacre and dispossession, black slavery, and presidential oligarchy. She argues that both Native peoples and African Americans recognized the connections from the beginning, by providing mutual shelter and making common cause. Many of the Seminole, for example, who evaded Jackson's pursuit as an Indian-fighting general before he was president, were of mixed descent—Native peoples and escaped slaves.

Far from what Mann calls the "American fairy tale of 'brave pioneers' of modest means venturing alone into a 'hostile wildernesses' " served us by some popular historians—this is a rough ride down a rocky road. It is going to rend many heretofore firmly implanted popular preconceptions.

As Professor Mann states in her Introduction, "Although not often examined in tandem, genocide, slavery, and oligarchy arose as the major, mutually reinforcing factors in the runaway expansion of the United States from 1783 through 1850. The studied oblivion of that mutuality relates, perhaps, to the fact that the most influential actors in 'opening' the land to Euro-settlement were also the elite slave-holders now celebrated as early heroes of the Euro-American saga.... Notwithstanding, based on their oligarchic wealth and high governmental positions, they stood to profit handsomely from dispossessing Indians of their land while spreading African slavery across it in 'pursuit of happiness.' The cognitive dissonance occasioned by these disjointed truths has prevented an exploration of their seedy aspects."

Professor Mann describes how these three presidents, Jackson, Harrison, and Taylor, parlayed their militarily mounted land grabs into "Indian-hating" political capital with the electorate, to accelerate the transfer of much of the Mississippi Valley, in a scathing review of a century during which Native Americans were largely seen as enemies to be absorbed or exterminated under the aegis of Manifest Destiny, a set of assumptions that economic necessity and God's will required Indigenous peoples' banishment from their homelands. Jackson, especially, made himself rich by speculating in the real estate that was being seized from its Native American owners. He also speculated in slaves, the second-most valuable asset, after land, in the United States of his time.

As Professor Mann asserts, "None of the extant works on any of the three presidents examines their actions sequentially or dynastically in terms of land seizure from Indians and the associated expansion of slavery. Allusions to land expansion are president-specific, usually brief, and couched in terms of 'Manifest Destiny.' None of them present the history of Indian genocide and African slavery as existing in tandem for tangible, political and economic reasons." Cherokee lands in the 1820s, for example, became cotton plantations worked by imported African slaves within a generation.

Many of the standard histories of these presidencies do not fully treat Indian policy, despite the fact that Native nations were a major subject of statecraft at the presidential level through several hundred treaties. Arthur M. Schlesinger Jr., for example, published the *Age of Jackson* with only incidental reference to Jackson's pivotal role in removal of the Cherokees on the Trail of Tears. There was no "happiness" on the Trail of Tears.

UNCOMFORTABLE HISTORICAL TRUTHS

Speaking of uncomfortable historical truths producing cognitive dissonance, Adolf Hitler admired Manifest Destiny. We have it in his own words, in his designs for the race law of the Nazi state. As Hitler imagined the future, Germany would deal with the Slavs much as the North American settlers had handled the American Indians. Hitler, as he killed the Jews, said that it was "the world's proven indifference to the fate of the Apaches that gave him the confidence that he would get away with it."[1] And, one might add, to pursue the policy with a horrid Teutonic efficiency. Timothy Snyder described how Hitler compared the twentieth-century German thrust eastward across Europe to United States' expansion westward during the nineteenth century, saying "the East was the Nazi Manifest Destiny."[2] Hitler, himself, said that the Volga (River), in Russia, would become Germany's Mississippi River.

In 1928, within two generations after the massacre at Wounded Knee closed the frontier (1890), James Q. Whitman found Hitler admiring how the Americans had "gunned down the millions of Redskins to a few hundred thousand, and now keep the modest remnant under observation in a cage."[3] In *Mein Kampf*, Hitler described the United States as nothing less than "the one state" that has made progress toward the creation of a "healthy" racist order worthy of emulation in Germany's own Nuremberg laws.[4] Roland Freisler, who was known as the "hanging judge" of the National Socialist People's Court, said that as a model U.S. jurisprudence would "suit us perfectly."[5]

In *President by Massacre*, Professor Mann provides Indigenous perspectives on the three presidents' rhetoric and policies from archival records and oral histories of Native nations at which they were directed, including the Muskogee (Creeks), Seminole, Shawnee, Sauk, and Meskwaki (Fox), to contribute a unique account that compares and contrasts two very different worldviews. While many biographies exist of each president, no other author has applied rigorous scholarship to their records in relationship to Native peoples. In her introduction, Mann argues that to cling to airy god talk about the confiscation of North America is to downplay the role of early America's well-placed elites. Using political, economic, and military methods, they seized "fresh" Indigenous lands and then traded heavily in slaves to work those lands—all in pursuit of oligarchic wealth.

For more than twenty years, Dr. Mann has been providing a corrective (and often searing) account of what some historians still blandly call the "westward movement," in thirteen books, including (for our series), *George Washington's War on Native America* (2005), *Daughters of Mother Earth* (2006), and *The Tainted Gift* (2009). She also has played a major role in documenting the origin date of the Haudenosaunee (Iroquois) Confederacy (1142 CE), about five hundred years before the older consensus in academia. She is among the most notable thinkers in contemporary Native American studies.

For these reasons, I am honored to welcome Barbara A. Mann's *President by Massacre* to our series Native America: Yesterday and Today.

Bruce E. Johansen
Series Editor
Frederick W. Kayser Research Professor
School of Communication
University of Nebraska at Omaha

NOTES

1. Gopnik, 2012, 115.
2. Snyder, 2012, 160.
3. Whitman, 2017, 9.
4. Whitman, 2017, 2.
5. Whitman, 2017, 160.

Introduction: Chosen Oblivion

∽

> History would be a wonderful thing—if only it were true.
> —Leo Tolstoy

*A*lthough not often examined in tandem, massacre, slavery, and oligarchy arose as the major, mutually reinforcing factors in the runaway expansion of the United States from 1783 through 1850. Many Euro-Americans resist seeing this truth put as bluntly as this, for the survival of their ideomythology requires them to sidestep the contiguity of these factors. White-'splainin' has slipped lately as the only acceptable approach to history, allowing this text openly to address the massacre-slavery-oligarchy interface. It explores how the slaughter of one people supported the enslavement of another, with both crimes perpetrated by a third, its elite enriching itself by intertwining both offenses.

Indigenous America has long pointed to these confluences. The Iroquois League had fingered slavery as the engine of invasion since the eighteenth century at least, one reason that the League, in particular, worked against settler slavery whenever it could. Escaped African slaves were freed, should they make it to Iroquoia. The eighteenth-century Seneca adoptee Mary Jemison recounted that one such African couple was granted land to farm. When she returned to Gardeau Flats, New York, in the famine occasioned by the genocidal Sullivan-Clinton attacks of 1779, it was to this African couple that she turned for aid.[1]

The League was hardly alone in its analysis of and opposition to settler slavery. In 1780, when the Shawnee homeland defense committee stopped a barge of squatters navigating down the Ohio River, they found a slave among the passengers. The Shawnee made a point of taking all of her mistress's goods, giving them to the slave, now freed, and then forcing the mistress to wait on the African woman.[2] One of the mightiest arguments of Lenape war advocates was that co-operation with the settlers would soon leave the Indian dupes enslaved, "harnessed to the plough and whipped to work."[3] In 1811, when *Tecumseh* called on the Muskogee of Alabama to join his cause, he warned that, unless the settlers were pushed out, they would soon enslave or massacre all of the Muskogee.[4]

Africans long apprehended the confluence of invasion and slavery, as well. It was one reason that Africans fought with the British against the Revolutionaries in the American Revolution. Having outlawed importing slaves to English lands in 1772 under the Mansfield Decision, the British were far ahead of American colonists on this burning issue, and the Africans knew it.[5] So did the Indians. It is hardly a secret that the Seminole nation was primarily a coalition of Muskogee and escaped Africans allied in a joint resistance to the U.S. invasion of Florida. It was, at bottom, why Andrew Jackson made a point of attacking them in the First Seminole War.[6]

Settlers on the ground were well aware of this confluence, too. The British Proclamation of 1763 and the Fort Stanwix Treaty of 1768 both stuck in the settler craw for cracking down on land seizure, and worse, the British made good on their pledge to drag off settlers who violated the proclamation and the treaty.[7] It was not for nothing that, in the Declaration of Independence, Thomas Jefferson included the charge against George III of "raising the conditions of new Appropriations of Lands"—that is, that Britain was scrutinizing "deeds" and not allowing the settlers to seize territory from the Indians, at will.

The studied oblivion of the massacre/land seizure/slavery axis in most Western texts relates to the fact that the most influential actors in "opening" the land were also the elite Indian-killers and slaveholders now celebrated as heroes of the Euro-American saga. The cognitive dissonance occasioned by these simultaneous truths prevents an exploration of their seedy aspects. Notwithstanding, based on wealth and high governmental positions, the settler elites stood to profit handsomely from dispossessing Indigenous nations of their land to spread African slavery. The results still reverberate. After all, as started under the Dutch and operated until emancipation, Wall Street was America's major slave and slavery-driven market.[8]

In looking at expansionism, mainstream American histories have traditionally treated the settler rush from "sea to shining sea" as a plebeian venture undertaken by rugged, small farmers for democratic reasons of landed independence. Should Manifest Destiny be mentioned, it is blamed on populism, with the discussion quickly deflected to the busy "settlers" acting as Adam Smith's seething mass of individuals, each working for private gain in blissful oblivion of, yet beautiful harmony with, the rest and all as guided by the "invisible hand" of the settler god to produce the economic symphony of classless Euro-American wealth.[9] Thus neatly side-stepping genocide and slavery, official history tidies up the roles of well-placed elites, their not-so-invisible hands stretched across years of consistent, goal-driven effort, strategizing political, economic, and military methods of seizing new Indigenous lands to be worked by their African slaves.

For territorial expansion to work, Smith's masses had to undulate on cue, for the elites, alone, lacked the numbers required to overrun the land. The need for disposable, lower-class aid required elites to cough up an incentive sparkling enough to entice their lesser European counterparts to die for them. The induce-ments they hit upon were the promise of guaranteed, if modest, land wealth enjoyed as members of the highest racial caste. Most Euro-peasants lusted for land of their own because they associated it with the familiar European system of landed wealth, whereby they might ape the lifestyles of the gentry. Landholding was, then, the first draw that the elites dangled before the mass of incoming, dispossessed Europeans in America, even if they had to work off an indenture, first, to "get theirs."

The second inducement for Euro-peasants was even greater: the grant of undis-puted upper-caste status in America. Here, the rationale for aristocracy was reworked to privilege all Europeans, everywhere. To accomplish this, it had to do a bit of violence to the old European model of aristocracy. As first articulated by Plato, humanity existed in four grades possessing, in descending order, souls of gold, silver, bronze, or iron. The upper, golden few were inherently and, even, supernaturally superior to all others, their golden essence acquired through birth, alone. (Plato, himself, admitted that the story was a con to justify the ruling class of his republic.)[10] Useful as golden kingship had been in Europe, once colonial-ism became central to the Western European economy, elites had to accommo-date a more encompassing ranking of humanity than Plato's, at least at the geographic endpoints of their trade routes.

Enter, Western science. Plato's old quadripuntal rankings evolved into the race theory that justified colonialism. As first floated by the baron of Montesquieu in 1748, race was connected to the four directions, becoming the personality expression of any group's geographical location, but by the 1758 (tenth) edition of his famed *Systema Naturae*, Carolus Linnaeus had biologically tied the sup-posed four races to the equally supposed four geographical locales, in a fairly clear hierarchy of worth, with Europeans placed at its pinnacle.[11] Then, from 1790 to 1795, Johann Friedrich Blumenbach cemented the intrinsicality of race by improving on Linnaeus. He rendered race an immutable fact of biological inheritance that followed one to any spot on the earth.

Blumenbach accomplished this new and improved ranking of "the races" in a descending order of "degenerations," flattering Europeans as the first generation, the pure "Caucasian" (by whom he very literally meant the people living around the Caucasus Mountain range). The first degeneration from the Caucasian yielded the second rank of humanity, the Asians and "Malays" (the latter, a group that Blumenbach invented out of whole cloth to separate Africans from Europeans by two, not one, declension). The second degeneration from the Caucasian sank Africans and Indigenous Americans into a third rank as irretrievably subhu-man.[12] Blumenbach became the standard of nineteenth-century "race science," from which there was no appeal, stimulating the school of "polygenesis," which postulated the third rank, anyway, as a separate species from the European.[13]

Race "science" thus created an inescapable caste system. In essence, it just updated Plato's original system by granting golden souls to *all* Europeans, if only they lived abroad. As such, it became the animating force behind American Manifest Destiny, for the inherently superior Euro-American settler, of whatever class, "deserved" the land and the labor of others. Thus widening the pool of privilege to include all "white men" formed the backbone of Jacksonian Democracy. Due to its undoubted benefits to Euro-colonists living in a triracial space, racism became the *deus ex machina* of the American Dream.

The birth-caste of race transformed all Euro-peasants into the natural, biological superiors of every Indian and every African in sight. Now, here was an inducement of no mean gratification to its beneficiaries: caste membership in the master race. The birthright to rule constituted quite a wish fulfillment for former Euro-peasants, a bone thrown to them by oligarchs, enticing poor settlers to become the cannon fodder of elite expansionism. The rise of the United States was, then, inextricably connected with the rise of America's racial caste system.

A class system nevertheless obtained in the United States as well, so its elites needed a myth as powerful as racial caste to support its continuing devotion to class distinctions. It arose as the fetching new theory of a "natural aristocracy." In the seventeenth century, Europeans growing rich through trade, not birth, had begun demanding social face, a quotidian sort of recognition for the stars of literature, science, philosophy, or trade who, although born outside of traditional golden lineages, were undeniably "superior." To avoid the collapse of the Euro-class system, class privilege was extended to this new "natural aristocracy" as stars, despite their nonnoble birth.[14]

The Christian god, not Plato, had to justify this leap, so in 1656, James Harrington articulated a "natural Ariftocracy diffus'd by God throut the whole Body of Mankind."[15] The pragmatic result of Harrington's suggestion was to accommodate mercantilist pretensions to grandeur, creating a crass aristocracy made of money. A century later, *déclassée* American *société* eagerly glommed on to the salving notion of a "natural aristocracy," as enthusiastically canvassed by Thomas Jefferson and John Adams.[16] Thus rationalized (at least for the natural aristocrats), elites of class remained safely aristocratic even as they lay embedded within the caste of race. Most of this sort of aristocracy were southern slavers who, following the lead of John Taylor of Caroline (ancestral relative of Zachary Taylor), scorned northern upper-crusters as playing governmental systems for personal benefit.[17] As in all hierarchical systems, everyone had to hate someone.

Thus, for all the populist repudiation of British-style aristocracy that energized discussion in early America, instead of rooting out the notion that some people were born biologically better than the rest, American ideology split the proposition into two parts: racial caste and moneyed class. Racial caste widened the pool of those who could claim to have been well-born. If in Europe, the myth claimed that some few persons were of a preternaturally higher quality than the mass of Europeans, then in America, the legalized fiction became that all "whites" were naturally superior to the biologically degenerate Indians and Africans. Still, even as caste status was granted to all settlers, the moneyed class system remained in place, resting solely on one's ability to secure and keep money. Moneyed class privileged those who already had wealth and rigged the system to help them keep it, but it also welcomed any and all who showed that they could acquire new wealth, thereby pretending that the system was classless.

American Empire - modeled on Rome

The economic system underpinning America's money-based classes was the raid. In Europe, the aristocracy originated in raiding cultures with this or that warlord's commando gang hitting in one-off raids. Eventually, warlords' successes strapped them to particular locales, where they continued to ransack their targets but, now, in low-intensity, permanent raids. Thus sustainable as feudalism, raiding later formed the essence of colonialism, soon dressed up as the "triangle trade." The primary beneficiaries of North American colonialism were the British elites, who sufficiently annoyed the American colonists that their Revolution rejiggered the benefits to fall to themselves. After 1783, the raiding intensified against African labor and Indigenous land and its assets.

To understand American expansionism, then, one must first understand that the new U.S. oligarchs were simply emulating the raiding economy of the European oligarchs, hence the self-comparisons of their early Republic to "imperial" (raiding culture) Rome, or should the commentator have been feeling particularly frisky, those other raiders, the Anglo-Saxons.[18] Antebellum Congressmen and intellectuals, alike, continually imagined America as the "modern" Rome, in expostulations as well as warnings, in art as well as architecture, and in virtue as well as vice.[19] The public did draw the line at Horatio Greenough's 1841 sculpture of George Washington, but only because Greenough had given the General a Zeusian body that was clearly naked under a thin toga that had slid carelessly down around his lower waist, awakening Puritanical outrage.[20]

Raiding cultures "conquer," justifying their seizures as righteous, if the loot is but taken in a "just war," one in which it is possible to assign the origin of the conflict to the population targeted for conquest. Albeit as old as the Roman Empire, itself, the U.S. "rights" by "Discovery" and "Conquest" were formulated legally by Rome's successor, European Christianity, in a series of four papal bulls, those of 1095, 1179, 1245, and 1493. Pope Urban III started off the justifications with the 1095 Council of Claremont, specifically to justify the First Crusade. This was THE bull that rationalized all the rest by removing any property rights from "infidels," so that if property had been seized by a "Christian," then that theft was lawful.[21]

During the Third Crusade in 1179, the Lateran Council of 302 bishops with Pope Alexander the III at their head prohibited the sale of any arms to "Saracens," because those arms could then be used to kill Christians, that is, the targets of Christian attack were not allowed to defend themselves.[22] As Crusading progressed to colonization of the "Holy Land," outright theft of non-Christian domains followed in 1245, with Pope Innocent IV asserting the legality of Christians invading the land of "infidels" to seize it in "just wars," defined as Europeans "defending" Christianity.[23] Just why the Christian god could not defend himself was left unaddressed.

Once these principles against Middle Eastern and North African Islam were in place, it was an easy jog over to the "pagan" Americas, rationalizations in tow.[24] Retrofitted to the "New World," they were famously codified by Pope Alexander VI in his three papal bulls of 1493, *Inter caetera, Inter caetera II,* and *Inter caetera divinai*, which granted the supposed rights by "Discovery" and "Conquest" in the Americas.[25] The spoils of such "just" warfare typically included conquered land, parceled out to one's soldiers, and foreign captives, dragged home as slaves.

A little cutting here and a tad of tucking there reshaped the old bulls for British Protestant usage by adding that, although the North American Indians had "occupation" rights, the land belonged to "Christians" as soon as the invaders "improved" whatever land that they were seizing by putting up a rickety fence or a rude lean-to.[26] This reasoning culminated Thomas Jefferson's legal arguments for land seizure. Yes, he conceded, the Indians were "the prior occupants" of America who held "the right of the soil," but the United States could take the land from them either by "their free consent, or by the right of conquest in case of a just war."[27] ("Free consent" meant the highly questionable "treaties.") All of these methods and rationales, as plied by America's brand-new oligarchy, flowed directly from the legal fictions supplied by old *inter caetera* aggression.

Once America's peasant armies had carved out a chunk of territory, the land was allocated exactly according to *inter caetera* prescription, under "land warrants," which served as the primary pay of the militiamen and soldiers. Class demarcations were unabashedly observed as U.S.-commissioned officers, whose ranks were reserved to the upper classes, received lands in the thousands of acres, as opposed to common soldiers, who received between 160 and 320 acres.[28] Already living in the Europeanized east, many veterans sold their land warrants to large-scale land speculators for pennies on the dollar. At this point, the land usually wound up in the hands of speculators to sell to incoming Euro-peasants for a tidy profit, sometimes double- or triple-selling the same parcel. Those glorified in Euro-American history as "pioneers" were originally acknowledged in primary documents to have been "squatters," because either they had not been part of a formal or militia army or they had not purchased the land from the Euro-American government or a U.S.-empowered speculator.[29] In the end, an oligarchic few prospered at the complete expense of the former Indian proprietors, not to mention the life-draining expense of the slaves dragged in from Africa to work the land. Moneyed elites likewise prospered at the expense of their own peasant class, whom the oligarchs openly despised as lowlifes, even as they fed off their Brownshirt services to the budding empire.

This process has been obscured by nearly all official histories, which—however they may dissimulate—still work from the "Great Man" premise of history to foreground one prominent actor as *sui generis*. Thus, William Henry Harrison's actions are isolated from those of Andrew Jackson, just as Jackson's actions are isolated from those of Zachary Taylor, even though each of their behaviors aided and buttressed those of the others. To read official histories, however, these men were all slogging about in unrelated political swamps. Some of this misdirection might arise from a sheer inability to see the forest while counting leaves on individual trees, but the rest looks mightily like chosen oblivion. Eyes tightly closed and fingers in the ears, the oblivion chants, "I can't hear you!"

The narrative today, that race is a moral failing of individual racists to be rooted out through public shaming, simply works to maintain the racial caste system because it misidentifies the problem, leading people to look in the wrong direction for a remedy. Far from a perceptual problem of individuals, racism confers material benefits on Euro-Americans of any social position, with the caste system remaining hard at work on behalf of Euro-Americans. Unlike the sophisticates who plead innocent by inability to fix the situation, racists are naive enough to celebrate their racial caste privilege out loud, potentially unmasking the game for all its beneficiaries. Far from feeling shame, racists tout their righteous anger at the prospect of their socioeconomic advantage being canceled, allowing "minorities" to be "given" an equal shot at "white" prosperity.

A primary thrust of this work, then, is to tell the story of the massacre of Indians and the spread of chattel slavery as historical correlatives in the service of building an American oligarchy. It will examine the overall pattern of wealth extraction, as the operation of elite status enabling and guiding further bloody land and asset seizure, allowing the spread of slavery. Moreover, this book holds that, however covertly, American oligarchic formations were recognized and legitimized at the time as acts of empire-building. I have a sneaking hunch that many historians have looked away from this fact accidentally on purpose, to sidestep the culpability of modern Euro-Americans in continuing to enjoy the fruits of the historical crimes of massacre and slavery. Too close a look might, for instance, call into question their land rights and inherited privilege.

This book also quizzes rather than accepts the analyses that triumphed at the polls between 1800 and 1850 and then segued whole into the "American" story. In testing the claims of yore, it looks to all available sources, including non-U.S. sources. Attention is paid to the cultural perspectives and active analyses of Indians regarding U.S. land seizure and Africans regarding slavery. It taps British, French, and Spanish sources, as well as the notations of stray observers on the ground, who often only fragilely grasped what they witnessed. Finally, this work recognizes that Euro-American historians, themselves, have learned perspectives that have colored and altered the way that their histories have been prepared and purveyed.

This book is divided into three parts following the succession of renowned "Indian fighters" turned presidential candidates: William Henry Harrison, the ninth president; Andrew Jackson, the seventh president; and Zachary Taylor, the twelfth president. I realize that this is not a perfect schema because, for instance, although elected after Jackson, Harrison actually held federal office before Jackson, while Taylor was as famous for his land-grab from Mexico as for his actions in the Black Hawk War and Second Seminole War. Notwithstanding such difficulties, each man took a cue from the fables of "white" rights to Indian lands, while slavery followed these men around like a puppy.

Part I, Chapter 1 delves into the background and connections of William Henry Harrison (1773–1841), the first governor of the Northwest Territories. Harrison forced land- and asset-grabbing treaties that were repudiated by the Indigenous nations involved while working to sidestep federal law to allow slavery, especially in his adopted home in modern-day Indiana, activities that also helped obscure his connection to the Burr Conspiracy. Part I, Chapter 2 examines the Tecumseh resistance, the primary obstacle to the seizure of the Old Northwest for intensive settlement, in the cultural and historical context of the Great Lakes Woodlanders. Part I, Chapter 3 details the war against the Tecumseh resistance under cover of the U.S. War of 1812.

Part II, Chapter 4 examines the background of Andrew Jackson (1767–1845) as a land speculator, slave trader, and elite plantation owner, as supported by connections with high officials, as well as his incessant push to acquire Muskogee lands in Alabama, partially to wipe his participation in the Aaron Burr plot from public memory. Part II, Chapter 5 explains Muskogee history and culture, particularly in terms of the civil war that erupted between the Tecumseh-allied resistance and the settler-accommodating assimilationists of the Muskogee, as well as Jackson's utilization of the Muskogee civil war as a pretext for his Creek War (1813–1814). Part II, Chapter 6 details Jackson's murderous war on the Muskogee, which killed all but perhaps a dozen of the 5,000 Muskogee traditionalists, under the cover of the U.S. War of 1812, enabling Jackson to grab all of modern-day Alabama.

Part III, Chapter 7 scrutinizes the deep connections to plantation slavery of Zachary Taylor (1784–1850), whose family had been illustrious Virginians since 1650, and his choice of a military career, the first half of which earned him a high reputation as an "Indian fighter." Part III, Chapter 8 looks at Taylor as a combat officer "defending" against "Indian attack" in the entirely unwarranted Black Hawk War (1832). This chapter uses the cultural and historical context of the Sauk and the Meskwaki peoples in examining the destruction wrought on them in the Black Hawk War. Part III, Chapter 9 examines Taylor's role from 1838 to 1839 in the Second Seminole War, particularly his movement to the central Battle of Okeechobee and his use of vicious dogs. The culture and history of the Seminole peoples being attacked, as well as the damage wrought on them, is examined, particularly in the panic that the Seminole instilled in the slave South by giving quarter and citizenship to escaped slaves, who openly fought "white" Americans in the conflict.

Finally, a short conclusion considers the expiration date of Euro-American oblivion of Native American and African American stories.

NOTES

1. Seaver, 1824, 74–75.

2. Girty, Draper Manuscripts, Reel S-17, 194.

3. Heckewelder, 1971, 116.

4. Satz, 1979, 38.

5. Countryman, 1996, 49–50.

6. Richardson, 2008, 389; Jaynes, 2005, vol. 1, 738–39; for Jackson, USS, 1847, no. 222, vol. 3, 2; Porter, 1964, 427–29.

7. Sullivan, 1921, Mohawk Speech, vol. 3, 705–06; Corry to Johnson, vol. 3, letter 5/13/1762, 737–38; Johnson to Lords of Trade, vol. 3, letter 8/1/1762, 837–51; Ritenour *et al.*, 1912, 303; Reynolds, 2015, 111, 117–18.

8. Farrow *et al.*, 2005, 20, 82, 92, 125; Singer, 2008, 1–2, 28, 30, 51.

9. Smith, 1776/1804, vol. 1, 349.

10. Plato, 1985, 415a–415e.

11. Montesquieu, 1862, 203–204, 217; Linneaus, 1758, vol. 1, 20–22.

12. Blumenbach, 1806, vol. 1, 71–72; Blumenbach, 1795, 191–92, specific to Caucasians, 286, 28990.

13. Ricard, 1999, 36–40.

14. Harrington, 1737, 47, 57, 138.

15. Spelling and punctuation in the original. Harrington, 17–37, 47.

16. Jefferson, 1907, vol. 13, 396; vol. 14, 1, 6.

17. Wilson, 2014, 394.

18. For example, comparison to Rome, Parton, 1870, vol. 2, 366, 537–41 passim; 548; for example, Anglo-Saxons, Fitzhugh, 1854, 266–67; generally, Richard, 1994.

19. Allen, 2008, 24, 29, 32, 42–43.

20. Allen, 2001, 174; photo, 175.

21. Turner, 1994, 78.

22. Davenport and Paullin, 1917–1937, no. 254, 11.

23. Miller, 2011, 855.

24. Newcomb, 2008.

25. For *Inter caetera*, *Inter caetera II*, and *Inter caetera divinai*, Miller *et al.*, 2010, 12–13.

26. Miller, 2006, 19.

27. *ASPIA*, 1832, vol. 1, 13.

28. For the "squatter" to "pioneer" shift, Oberly, 1990, 9–10.

29. Buss, 2011, 42–44, 51, 64–67.

PART I

~

William Henry Harrison, 1773–1841, Admin., 1841

CHAPTER 1

~

Dodging Well and Becoming Conspicuous: William Henry Harrison

Although most modern Americans seem to have forgotten as much, taken as many now are with "exalted" lineages and rumors of personal descent from "royal" bloodlines, such claims were pure anathema at the founding of the country. To be called "aristocratic" was to be insulted. Any Americans in danger of being pronounced elite, including Thomas Jefferson and John Adams, were at pains to support a cloying distinction between an "artificial" and a "natural" aristocracy, showcasing American republicans as the natural aristocrats.[1] The non-elite public was not buying into this "natural" logic but continued to scorn those it found "aristocratic." Cognitive dissonance reigned.

Consequently, in his 1824 political biography of William Henry Harrison, Moses Dawson went out of his way to downplay Harrison's descent from one of Oliver Cromwell's generals, not to mention from his father, Benjamin Harrison, whose American Revolutionary services occasioned his 1782 ascent to the governorship of Virginia. Instead, Dawson pegged away at Harrison's personal merit, insisting that "his own conduct," not his "being descended from an opulent and respectable line of ancestry," was the cause of his rise. Indeed, Dawson seemed almost distressed that Harrison was not more humbly descended than he was. The public, Dawson cried, would "more readily give credit" to Harrison had he been "the son of a wretch the most wicked," because "there must be more merit due" to the spawn of "a vitious [vicious] parent" than of one who had set him a good example. Respect for sheer lineage was a "relic of ancient barbarism," that is, of British aristocracy, and repulsive "in a republican country," where the point was "for every man to be accountable for his own actions." To hold otherwise, Dawson mused, was to indulge in the "antirepublican" sentiments of "aristocratical or monarchical governments."[2]

Notwithstanding Dawes's flawless recital of his political catechism, given not only Harrison's descent but also the mighty manipulators supporting Harrison from childhood on, there was never the slightest suspense about his making good. With his father, Benjamin Harrison, a signatory of the Declaration of Independence and one of the twelve wealthiest men in Virginia, owning the enormous Berkeley slave plantation in Virginia, Harrison was born with a mouthful of silver spoons.[3] His grandmother, Anne Carter Harrison, was the daughter of the phenomenally wealthy planter Robert "King" Carter, owner of 1,000 slaves.[4] In his will, Benjamin Harrison bequeathed slaves along with land to his descendants.[5] Because the eldest son inherited, as the third son, Harrison was marked for a medical career, studying first with Dr. Andrew Leiper in Richmond and later with the famed Dr. Benjamin Rush in Philadelphia. There, upon the death of Harrison's father, the wealthy and powerful "Financier of the American Revolution," Robert Morris, stood as young Harrison's guardian ad litem.[6] This was a can't-miss send-off into life.

As suggested by his cousin, Virginia governor Richard Henry Lee, Harrison rejected medicine in favor of a military career (typically reserved to the second son). Despite lacking any military background, Harrison instantly obtained a U.S. Army ensignship, because President George Washington considered Lee's suggestion the petition of "a friend."[7] Besides, Washington had shared quarters with Benjamin Harrison in Philadelphia during the heady days of the Continental Congress.[8] Revolution or not, then, the British system of "preferment" through moneyed "connections" remained alive and well in the early Republic.

Harrison's meteoric rise in the military was partly connected to his solid relationship with General James Wilkinson, who rose to the command of the U.S. Army and later to the governorship of Louisiana Territory, using his lofty positions to act as a double agent of the Spanish government against U.S. interests.[9] Their relationship started in 1792, when Wilkinson stepped in to save the young ensign from a serious military misstep.[10] Harrison had scandalously first whipped a civilian for drunkenness and next the man's friend for objecting, resulting in Harrison's arrest and a brouhaha of national proportions for the army.[11] Notwithstanding the trouble—indeed, in the midst of it—Wilkinson promoted Harrison to lieutenant, "mentioned" him "in favorable terms" to President Washington, and selected the youth to conduct Mrs. Wilkinson to Philadelphia.[12] As historian Robert Owens put it, the two "seem to have gotten along well."[13] Perhaps the men recognized the connivance gene in each other, for certainly, Harrison was later drawn into the Burr Conspiracy by Wilkinson.

Almost immediately after the whipping fracas, Harrison landed strategically with General Anthony Wayne.[14] Probably because the lieutenant was always sober, reasonably educated, unabashedly upper crust, and had already creditably managed a "small command" in "the Western country" in 1791, Wayne appointed Harrison as an aide-de-camp in June 1792, in command of a company of infantry.[15] In his official report on the all-important Battle of Fallen Timbers in 1794, Wayne named Harrison among his "faithful and gallant Aids-de-camp."[16] (Also singled out for praise were "Brigadier General Wilkinson" and Captain Solomon van Rensselaer, the Rensselaers later being important to Harrison.)

Seriously injured by "the falling of a tree" on August 2, Wayne watched the battle from a distance, so he depended on his officers for accounts of the action.[17] All he could personally have seen of Harrison was from behind the lines, running the officers' messages back and forth.[18] Never one to let a political opportunity slip past, however, Harrison used Wayne's praised presence at the Battle of Fallen Timbers when he stood in 1799 for the representative to Congress from the Northwest Territories.[19]

The whiff of martial danger aside, the oligarchic connections going on there were intense, leaving the schizophrenia of Harrison's log-cabin "everyman" impersonation at odds with reality, especially given Harrison's marriage into the generously landed family of "Judge" John Cleves Symmes. At this time, the largest landowner of the area typically became the area's judge. Under an early ruling by U.S. chief justice John Marshall, such territorial judges were not constitutional but rather congressional appointments. Qualifications were those of character as determined by elitist standards. Thus, from 1787 to 1804, territorial judges "were appointed for good behavior," primarily the good behavior of being wealthy.[20]

Like Harrison's own father, Symmes had been active in the American Revolution as a Continental Congress delegate from New Jersey and, ultimately, a member of the state's Supreme Court. The Symmeses hobnobbed with William Livingston, another American Revolutionary from New Jersey, who wound up not only as governor of that state but also as father-in-law to Symmes, who married Susannah ("Sukey") Livingston. Sukey had high connections of her own, as sister-in-law to John Jay, president of the Continental Congress and, eventually, the first chief justice of the U.S. Supreme Court.[21] Symmes's in-laws, the Livingston family, owned slaves.[22] Cashing in, Symmes became the proud possessor of the "Symmes Patent" in southwestern Ohio, although no Indians had agreed to its loss.[23] First claimed in 1787, deeded in 1788, and formally patented in 1792, the patent's terms were revised and finalized in 1794, after Wayne's victory, when the Indians no longer had a choice in the matter.[24] The original patent was for 1,000,000 acres, belonging to Symmes and his two partners, Jonathan Dayton and Daniel Marsh.[25] Under the Doctrine of Discovery, as retooled by the British and adopted by the United States, putting up a Western-style house, barn, or even, fence was called "improving the land," demonstrating that, unlike the Indians, the settlers knew how to use the land properly, thus making its expropriation legal.[26]

Symmes immediately began selling small farms in the area to eager settlers without much regard to whether the land was actually *in* his patent. Worse, like most of the land-warrant speculators, including William Cooper (founder of Cooperstown and father of James Fenimore Cooper), Symmes played dirty.[27] Cooper and Symmes sold and resold the same shares multiple times without all the bother of informing the original purchaser(s).[28] This occasioned considerable hollering from both the people defrauded and the U.S. Treasury office (it turned out that Symmes had failed to pay the government for the whole acreage), so once the noise died down, Congress reduced the land grant to the 311,682 acres north of the Ohio River that Symmes had actually paid off.[29] The reduced acreage was deeded to Symmes by act of Congress in 1792, in exchange for veterans' land warrants, which became objects of intense speculation.[30] The scandal surrounding the Symmes patent was well known, as was the fact that, in 1799, Harrison maneuvered congressionally to allow Symmes to keep as much of the land as possible.[31]

Additional trouble erupted in 1792, when Symmes attempted to sell parcels legally belonging to *Gallegina Uwati* (ᏍᏓᏴ ᎤᏩᏘ, "Elias Boudinot," Cherokee) even as both men undertook to defraud the Miami and Shawnee of Ohio.[32] Meantime, Symmes went bankrupt in trying to establish Symmes City, another boondoggle, because the soldiers guarding the land for him decamped precipitously to follow their commander, himself chasing a "black-eyed girl" who preferred Cincinnati to a settler mudhole in the backwoods.[33] Between the lawsuit, which *Gallegina Uwati* won, and the army's desertion, which aided no one, Symmes City collapsed.

Scion of the Virginia elite Harrison might have been, but he was still the third son, not the heir to Berkeley Plantation. Portionless young men married up, even when that required sidling past the prospective father-in-law. Knowing the game (having used it himself), Symmes was less than thrilled when, in 1795, Lt. Harrison offered marriage to his elegant daughter, Anna ("Nancy"). Having been the local judge pulled into Harrison's 1792 whipping scandal, which had led to the arrest of Harrison, Symmes was disgusted and, most probably, chagrined by the proposed connection.[34] Unsurprisingly, then, on June 22, 1795, Symmes grumbled to his friend (and Harrison's guardian) Robert Morris that, although Harrison had "understanding, prudence, education, & resource in conversation," along with "£3,000 property," he had "no profession but that of arms." True, Symmes needed "assistance" in his own business "arrangements," but it was the help of a lawyer, not that of a soldier.[35] Harrison must have realized the tenuous ground he was on, so he embellished his credentials, for in another letter to Morris in December 1795, Symmes referred to the lieutenant, who would not be promoted for two more years, as "Captain Harrison."[36]

Similarly, Harrison's questionable boast of £3,000 might have related to a Berkeley land deal of 1793. Because of Symmes's relationship with Morris, he might have learned that Harrison *père* had left 3,000 acres of Virginia real estate to William Henry Harrison, who promptly sold them to his elder brother, Benjamin, for five bonds valued at £100 each, along with a one-eighth interest in a Kentucky land speculation, which never paid off, all secured by a £1,000 bond, which had paid nothing since 1786.[37] On the one hand, in 1793, £500 was equivalent to $2,255 (not the $5,000 that Harrison claimed in an undated will, ca. 1835).[38] On the other hand, in 1799, one acre of Berkeley land sold for $20.[39] Had Harrison sold his Tidewater land on the market, he could have realized upward of $60,000 for his 3,000 acres. Symmes fretted to Morris on June 22, 1795, that Harrison had no farm in Kentucky (perhaps in reference to the Kentucky land speculation). In short, Symmes smelled a rat. Consequently, as of June 22, 1795, Harrison had "not yet received an answer" to his marriage proposal, Symmes told Morris, "at least, not from me."[40]

Worse, Symmes might have heard through Morris that Harrison had been rejected as a suitor twice before, in an age when a father had as much say in the matter as his daughter. In 1791, Harrison had proposed to a Philadelphia "belle," Sarah Cutler (possibly the daughter of the brass-foundry owner Samuel Cutler) and been rejected.[41] Next, in 1793, Harrison aspired to Morris's own eldest daughter, Hetty, but that also came to naught, for in 1795, Hetty married James Marshall, brother of John Marshall, soon-to-become chief justice of the U.S. Supreme Court.[42] These two rejections might well give pause to the third father approached by Harrison.

Either furtively or through Symmes's refusal to be present, Nancy Symmes and Harrison married on February 28, 1796, while Judge Symmes was away from home.[43] Scorning the wedding, as a "run away match," that is, an elopement, Symmes griped to Silas Condict, a wealthy member of the New Jersey elite, that Harrison had been "bred to no business" that Symmes could use.[44] On March 2, 1796, Symmes moaned to Morris that Harrison could "neither bleed, plead, nor preach," in reference to three of the four professions thought fit for aristocratic younger sons—medicine, law, and the church, respectively.[45] The military was the fourth profession, but bleeding on the battlefield was not valued by Symmes. Probably knowing that Harrison had, against Morris's better judgment, jettisoned the safe bleeding of medicine for the dangerous bleeding of the army, Symmes wished that Harrison could at least plow.[46] As it was, the best he could hope for was that Harrison could "dodge well a few years," evading bullets long enough to "become conspicuous," that is, famous.[47]

Dodge, Harrison did, but despite apocryphal stories that Harrison wormed his way into Symmes's good graces, Symmes ostracized the young couple for the next fifteen years.[48] Clearly, his loathing of tipplers did not translate into an automatic esteem for teetotalers.[49] When Symmes did finally break down to accept his daughter's invitation to visit the Harrisons at Grouseland in 1811, Symmes's change of heart had less to do with Christian charity than with financial failure.[50] His chaotic dealings and sloppy accounting had finally caught up with him, his house now lost to fire, and his fortune, to bankruptcy. Symmes died in poverty in 1814.[51]

At first, Harrison attempted to settle down in North Bend, Ohio, setting up a four-room cabin on 160 acres given to him by Symmes.[52] Ironically enough given the whipping scandal, to earn a living in 1797, Harrison bought a large distillery operation near Cincinnati for $600. (Distilleries were cynically used in the fur trade.[53]) What happened to this distillery is unclear, but Harrison attempted to unload it on Judge Jacob Burnett of Cincinnati, who refused the offer.[54] In the 1831, as "The Pledge" (against alcohol consumption) gained social ground, Harrison repudiated his distilling venture, claiming to have seen the light, but more likely because he could not make a go of it.[55]

Clearly no Yankee trader, after marrying up, Harrison's unabashed method of financial ascent was through government, regarded as a birth right by scions of Founders & Sons. Resigning from his captaincy in 1798 to enter politics, he returned only briefly to the military (as a newly anointed general) during the

War of 1812, but this did not stop him from parlaying his Indian-fighting credentials into public office. Beginning politically as secretary of the Northwest
Territories (1798–1799), Harrison moved up to representative of the Territories
(1799–1800) and then to territorial governor of Indiana (1801–1813). The
presidency always lurking in the back of his mind as his ultimate goal, Harrison
climbed from congressional representative from the Northwest Territories
(1816–1819) to senator in the Ohio House (1819–1821) and then to U.S. senator
to Congress from Ohio (1825–1828), before finally becoming the U.S. ambassador to Columbia (1828–1830), fully intending to leap from there to the vice
presidency and, at last, to the presidency (1841). Throughout, Harrison was
frankly motivated by salary, from his $1,200 annual salary as secretary of the
Northwest Territories (worth $22,416 today) and his $2,000 per annum as governor of Indiana Territory (or $36,300 today) to his $9,000 annual salary as
"Envoy Extraordinary and Minister Plenipotentiary" to Columbia (worth
$244,190 today).[56] With justice, John Quincy Adams fingered Harrison's crass
"thirst for lucrative office" as "absolutely rabid."[57] Harrison apparently viewed
public office as his form of *citoyen oblige (à lui)*.

During the territorial portion of his career, Harrison managed to become
embroiled in the Burr Conspiracy, which raged from 1805 to 1807. Although
for obvious reasons, crucial evidence on the Burr Conspiracy went missing while
what survived remains fragmentary, the conspiracy clearly involved many sur-
prisingly high-level, well connected personae, resulting in a constitutional crisis
of no mean proportions. Starting in 1804, then vice president Aaron Burr used
his connections in Washington, DC first, in March, to have his brother-in-law,
Joseph Brown, named secretary of the Louisiana Territory, and then pushing for
Wilkinson as governor of the Louisiana Territory.[58] On March 11, 1805, unaware
of Burr's plans, Jefferson appointed Wilkinson, governor of Louisiana Territory,
as a reward for his services as a general.[59] A notorious grafter, Major General
James Wilkinson was most probably drawn into the plot by Burr's initial bribe
of his posting as governor.

In April 1805, replaced as vice president during the second Jefferson
Administration, Burr swung into action on his plan, making contacts as he crisscrossed the "west," indelicately enough, in synch with a wax exhibit of his fatal,
1804 duel with Alexander Hamilton.[60] Burr's travel plan was to gather up
supporters and co-conspirators, and in that capacity, he met with any number of
officials and leading citizens. The goal of Burr's scheme was to carve an independent
empire out of western lands, of which he was to be the head.

Creating new countries out of mid–North America was hardly a new thought.
In 1788, Arthur St. Claire put down an attempt by Kentuckians to break away
from the United States.[61] From 1793 to 1794, another breakaway attempt was
mounted by Kentuckians to negotiate independently for the navigation rights to
the river that they "so ardently pant[ed] for."[62] In November 1795, Lieutenant
Harrison was confidentially dispatched by General Wayne to quiet, once and
for all, this French-inspired scheme "for the conquest of the Spanish province
of Louisiana."[63] In 1803, settlers "on the Spanish side of the Mississippi" were

"very much Divided in Sentiment on the score of becoming American citizens . . . lest their Slaves should be liberated."[64] Certainly in 1805, the British minister to the United States assured his superiors (on information from Burr) that the Louisiana Territory intended to break from the United States.[65] Indeed, the western territories were generally presented at this time as hungering to break free of the eastern states to form their own countries.[66] Thus, Burr did not just wake up one day in 1804 to invent breakaway schemes over breakfast.

Details of the Burr Conspiracy remain murky. By some accounts, the grand plan was, with Great Britain's aid, to seize "Louisiana" from the United States, although at Burr's 1807 trial, Wilkinson specified the target as Mexico.[67] What, precisely, "Louisiana" meant to people at the time is a matter of doubt. Texas was then in northern Mexico, bordering the Louisiana Territory, with some Americans under the impression that the Louisiana Territory extended to the Rio Grande.[68] According to Wilkinson's unreliable testimony at the Burr trial, Burr had arranged for a small army of 7,000 men, 500 of whom had a flotilla of boats, along with up to "12,000 stands of arms."[69] The 500 were to proceed down the Allegheny, presumably navigating the Ohio and Mississippi Rivers, winding up at New Orleans. There, the plan was there to seize equipage from the military and funds from the United States Bank, therewith to mount an invasion of Spanish-held northern Mexico (Texas). Boats at the Allegheny were readied, while "schooners" were on contract along the Gulf Coast.[70] Wilkinson gingerly omitted the information that the British, in cahoots with Burr, were to meet the army at New Orleans with the schooners to give the breakaway project their "naval support."[71] This plot was stopped only in 1806 when Wilkinson chickened out, betraying Burr to Jefferson. Then, a miracle transpired. Magically, Wilkinson shape-shifted from co-conspirator to gallant disrupter of treason, offloading all the blame onto Burr.[72]

If I had to guess, which I do not, I would suggest that the planned robbery of the United States Bank at New Orleans, where the government had around $2,000,000 on deposit, in combination with Wilkinson's last-minute realization of his intended second-fiddle status to Burr, were what finally moved Wilkinson to extricate himself from Burr's grip.[73] Burr's letter to Wilkinson of July 29, 1806, activating the plot, revealed—apparently for the first time—that Wilkinson was to "be second to Burr only" in the new empire.[74] Second? Seizing the United States Bank in open league with England was a lot of risk to take, just to set up Burr as emperor and Wilkinson as Burr's fall guy.

Wilkinson most probably reflected, as well, on the loss of his secret emoluments from Spain necessarily resulting from a seizure of Texas. From September, when the plot swung fully into action, till November, when he blew the whistle on it, Wilkinson took a time-out to rethink everything. As the military commander in New Orleans, might he carry out the plan without Burr? In that case, how was he to keep the Spanish emoluments inflowing? If he pulled out entirely, how might he legally save, without incriminating, himself? Once he had figured out the last option on October 21, 1806, Wilkinson wrote Jefferson about what was afoot and began arresting, not joining, Burr's militia. Burr's abortive arrest and grand jury hearing in Kentucky in December 1806 could only have spurred Wilkinson's resolve.[75]

The trial testimony, the depositions, and the remaining letters of the principals indicate Wilkinson's keen involvement from the start. For instance, Burr and Wilkinson used a cipher, which Wilkinson testified had been created militarily between 1795 and 1796. Not only would Wilkinson have had to supply it but also it included a code for New Orleans, a centerpiece of the conspiracy but not of U.S. territory until 1803.[76] Wilkinson is known to have actively altered documents, so it is strongly suspected that he deliberately flubbed his decoding of the July 29, 1806, letter for purposes of self-exculpatory testimony at Burr's trial and then again, in 1811, at his own inquiry.[77]

Harrison was drawn into this hot mess by his old superior, Wilkinson. When the two first communicated about it is unknown but conjecturable. Wilkinson's letter of September 19, 1806, is generally cited as the starting point, but it was demonstrably not. First, the year of the September 19 letter was not 1806, as editor Logan Esarey incorrectly had it in the standard, 1922 *Governor's Messages*. The year was, instead, 1805, as corrected in the 1993 Clanin typescript from the manuscripts of Harrison's documents.[78] The adjusted date matters greatly, given Burr's peregrinations through "the west" in 1805, gathering up co-conspirators.

In his deposition regarding the Burr Conspiracy, Captain George Peters remembered a conversation he had with Wilkinson in mid-April 1805, about a "canal" project "on the Indiana shore," for which Wilkinson "expected" to meet with an "interested" Governor Harrison.[79] Burr's flotilla would have needed the canal around the Ohio River falls in Indiana at Jeffersonville, across the river from Louisville, Kentucky.[80] The canal was a project that Harrison had first pitched to Jefferson, most probably in all innocence, in early August 1802, the flattering town name of "Jeffersonville" an inducement to approve the town.[81] By the time the canal project hit Congress, however, Harrison's innocence was questionable.

The project was communicated to the Senate on January 28, 1805, by Representative Jonathan Dayton, with a resolution to convene a commission on its siting submitted by the Senate on January 24, 1807.[82] Dayton was a Burr co-conspirator and, not unimportantly, Judge Symmes's land-patent partner.[83] It is hardly coincidental, then, that in March 1805, Burr visited the site of the proposed canal.[84] In a letter of September 26, 1805, to Wilkinson, Burr mentioned Harrison and Dayton in the same sentence, concerning a now-missing letter from Dayton.[85] Burr then directly mentioned the canal project in a letter from Cincinnati dated October 7, 1805, sent to an unnamed but identifiable recipient. Burr mentioned "your deserted Village" as being "really gloomy."[86] The Symmes patent included Cincinnati, while Dayton, Ohio, named for Jonathan Dayton, was incorporated in 1805. It sits forty-four miles north of Cincinnati, strongly indicating that the unaddressed recipient of this letter was U.S. representative Dayton, who pushed the canal project in Congress.[87]

On June 7, 1805, Harrison wrote to Wilkinson from Vincennes. Of this crucial letter, little survives. A tiny excerpt from it was read into testimony at the Burr trial by Wilkinson. In it, Harrison begged Wilkinson not to "receive" any "impressions relative to the people of St. Louis, from Major Bruff." The "bare idea of his [Bruff's] being in your confidence would frighten some of them out of their senses," Harrison added cryptically, for reasons he would "hereafter explain."[88] Major James Bruff was in military command of Upper Louisiana until the new governor Wilkinson relieved him of duty later that same June. Bruff caught wind of what was afoot and organized stiff opposition to Wilkinson in the army.[89] Bruff's obstruction is probably why Wilkinson expressed dismay to Burr in September 1805 that his officers "did not seem to be taking so readily to the Mexican idea."[90] As for St. Louis, it was a center of the Burr Conspiracy, being Wilkinson's headquarters as governor of Louisiana.[91] Thus, Bruff was body blocking the Burr Conspiracy, angering Wilkinson, who had Bruff court-martialed.[92]

What the rest of Harrison's message concerned was redacted as too sensitive to read aloud in open court, but Burr's lawyer demanded, under the rules of evidence, that either the full letter be read into the record or the excerpt be withdrawn from the record. The U.S. attorney blocked that plea, however, arguing that the rest of the letter was "entirely private and confidential," with no further reference to Major Bruff (just then, the topic of testimony). Directly addressing the judge from the witness box, Wilkinson pleaded that the letter's contents were so "sacredly confidential" to him that he would "go to jail rather than produce it" in full. The judge then ruled that the extract be withdrawn from evidence and told trial note-takers to "erase" all references to the extract. They did not erase them, so the extract was later published as a footnote to the trial testimony.[93]

Here, editor Esarey made another critical mistake, misidentifying Wilkinson's letter to Harrison of September 19 as the letter that Wilkinson had refused to produce in full at the trial. It was not the letter in question. What Wilkinson had refused to read aloud was Harrison's letter of June 7, 1805.[94] The June 7 letter exists in Clanin in a larger fragment than what was read into the trial record. It contains a request that Wilkinson find positions for two destitute men, but it hardly seems likely that this commonplace request for patronage was worthy of jail time to protect.[95] The rub clearly lay in the destroyed portion of the letter, yet a second letter of June 7, 1805, likewise by Harrison, might contain a clue as to what the destroyed portion of Wilkinson's letter concerned. In this letter, Harrison pleaded with Albert Gallatin, then U.S. secretary of the Treasury, not to hire Wilkinson's nephew, Dr. Joseph Wilkinson.[96] Harrison further referenced the Jouett family, Detroit in-laws of the doctor.[97] Disparagement of close relatives is something that Wilkinson might well have wished to conceal from public record in open court.

Esarey's misidentified letter of September 19, 1805, was not the Bruff message but something else entirely, being a letter of introduction for Burr, addressed to Harrison from Wilkinson. The contents of this letter of introduction begged Harrison to dump Benjamin Parke, Harrison's ally in bringing slavery to Indiana, in favor of sending Burr, instead, to the U.S. Congress as the territorial representative. Interestingly, five times, this short letter used the word, "boon."[98] Not inconsequentially, Burr's July 29, 1806, cipher letter to Wilkinson used similarly overblown "boon" language—"The gods invite us to glory and fortune; it remains to be seen whether we deserve the boon"—suggesting that what Wilkinson signed to Harrison was actually composed by Burr.[99] Be that as it may, Harrison had already put Parke in prime position to advance his own schemes for introducing slavery into Indiana. Perhaps making Benjamin Parke, not Aaron Burr, Indiana's U.S. representative, was the major reason that Harrison was not dragged even further into the Burr affair than he was. If so, it shows that Harrison's commitment to slavery was stronger, even, than his friendship with Wilkinson.

Despite its authorship, Burr acquired the September 19 letter from Wilkinson while he was in St. Louis.[100] He needed Harrison. Having inspected the Indiana canal site in March on his way west to St. Louis, Burr realized Harrison's importance to the project, hence the letter from Harrison's dear old friend Wilkinson introducing Burr to Indiana's governor on his way back east.[101] After meeting Harrison in Vincennes, on September 26, 1805, Burr informed Wilkinson that they had "gone round about," leaving Burr so sure of Harrison's "good will" as to repose his "entire belief" in it. Burr felt "more & more pleased" with Harrison, who was to tell Wilkinson about the now missing letter from Jonathan Dayton, further enhancing the circumstantial evidence that the gloomy-village letter of October 7, 1805, was directed to Dayton and that the topic was how the canal fit into Burr's conspiracy.[102]

Burr certainly regarded Harrison as in the loop of the conspiracy, for he included him in his green-light notifications once the plot was in motion. On October 24, 1806, even as his flotilla was moving down the river to New Orleans, Burr wrote to Harrison from Lexington, informing him that Andrew Jackson had alerted the militia of Western Tennessee and suggesting that Harrison do the same with the militia of Indiana, in regard to a war with Spain, which Burr claimed was imminent.[103] Burr also notified Wilkinson, twice. "On or about the 8th of October," Wilkinson told the court, he first received Burr's letter in cipher.[104] The second delivery of this same cipher message had a cover letter dated September 27, 1806.[105] Wilkinson had been in St. Louis at the time he received the first cipher letter from Burr but did not arrive in New Orleans until November 27, 1806, at which point, he began arresting conspirators.[106] During this interim, Burr would reasonably have believed that Harrison had moved (he had not) and that Wilkinson was still with him (he was not).[107] Whether Harrison and Wilkinson had conferred on their mutual refusal to move is unknown but seems likely.

Burr contacted Harrison again on November 27, 1806—the very day of Wilkinson's arrival in New Orleans, the moment that Burr would have learned of Wilkinson's betrayal. The purpose of Burr's second letter to Harrison was to clear his name. Disclaiming any "designs to attempt a separation of the Union," let alone "connection with any foreign power," Burr asked for Harrison's "active support," perhaps in dispelling the rumors or, more darkly, in destroying incriminating letters. Burr acknowledged his involvement "in an extensive speculation" and his association with "some" of Harrison's "intimate and dearest friends," including "some of the principal officers of our government."[108] These lines to Harrison might even have carried ominous undertones. Not incidentally, Burr later tried to blackmail former co-conspirators, and his co-conspirators did the same. In 1806, Wilkinson even attempted to blackmail the Mexican viceroy;[109] someone acting for Burr attempted to blackmail Andrew Jackson in 1812;[110] and a major Burr conspirator, Harmon Blennerhassett, attempted to blackmail Burr in 1813 by threatening to publish an exposé of the affair, using the letters and data he had on hand.[111]

After the Burr Conspiracy crashed and burned, Harrison was viewed with grim suspicion by many in the public. His friendship with Wilkinson was no secret, nor was his involvement in the Ohio River canal project. Neither did it escape notice that, on April 3, 1807, Harrison wrote a character reference for militia major Davis Floyd, an energetic participant in the Burr Conspiracy. In the letter, Harrison downplayed Floyd's part in the plot, by portraying Floyd as a "dupe of the artful and mischievous" Burr.[112] To the public, this just proved that Harrison knew both of Floyd and of his part in the conspiracy. It was also public knowledge that, at an 1813 dinner in New York, Harrison had declared that, should he be so inclined, he could "(by discovering a secret of Wilkinson's) destroy him."[113] In 1813, "discovering" meant "revealing."

In a wistful defense of Harrison published in 1834, based on "confessedly conjectural" conclusions that Harrison and Wilkinson had both been falsely accused, Kentucky historian Mann Butler claimed that Harrison had "rebuffed" Burr's approach because Burr had spoken insultingly of Wilkinson as a secret-spilling chatterbox. A second, proxy approach made on Burr's behalf to Harrison by Captain Robert Wescott, who had married Burr's niece, likewise failed, Butler maintained. He portrayed Harrison as stoutly declaring that, if Burr's "schemes were inimical to the government of the United States, he would exert his utmost endeavors to have him hung."[114] Of course, nothing of the sort had occurred, and the noble intention to overturn the plot was well known to have been uttered by Major Bruff, not Harrison, who instead faded as far as possible into the wallpaper, once the conspiracy imploded.

In regard to Harrison's uncharacteristic reserve, once the Burr plot was upended, it is worth noting that the Symmes circle was keeping close tabs on Burr's 1807 trial and Wilkinson's court-martial, which did not start until 1811 and resumed in 1815 (as interrupted by the War of 1812).[115] Writing from Chillicothe, Ohio, on January 11, 1808, Judge Symmes noted that "No Burr nor Blannerhasset" had appeared in the stalled federal court.[116] Perhaps this was said in relief that nothing seemed afoot in Wilkinson's case, for Symmes pretty certainly knew of Dayton's involvement and, quite possibly, of Harrison's. Ten years later, when Blennerhassett did publish the material he had, he directly named Harrison as a conspirator, in company with other high officials including Jefferson, Jackson, and Wilkinson.[117] If the involvement of Jefferson was highly unlikely, then that of the latter two was certain.

More generally discussed than the Burr affair is Harrison's interface with slavery, albeit scholars largely soft-pedal its juicier aspects, taking Harrison's apologia at face value. In 1822, Harrison preposterously proclaimed himself friendly to abolition, with supporters presenting him as noncommittal on slavery in 1840. The claim of outright abolitionism rested on one, greasily misleading address published in 1822, during Harrison's run for Congress as the representative from Ohio. The subsequent uncertainty regarding his position came, not from Harrison, but from the Whigs of 1840, who were desperately attempting to attract the northern abolitionist—without losing the southern slavery—vote in their presidential campaign, for which Harrison was their candidate.

Harrison's 1822 claim came in answer to charges that he was pro-slavery. His entire defense rested on his having joined what he styled an "Abolition Society" in Richmond in 1790, when he was seventeen years old.[118] Harrison offered a certificate from a fellow Society member, "Judge Gatch" (the noted evangelist, Philip Gatch), to prove his claim, insisting that he had never enslaved anyone or owned slaves, although he said that he had "been the means of liberating many slaves," a transparent lie.[119] A circuit-riding Methodist minister who freed his own slaves in the 1780s, Gatch moved to the "North-western Territory" in 1798. Late in life, Gatch became an associate judge of Clermont County, near Cincinnati.[120]

Thus, during Harrison's Ohio congressional bid, having a testimonial from the known abolitionist judge Gatch would have represented a political coup for Harrison, as far as attracting the abolitionist vote in Ohio. The proof fell short of the claim, however, for Gatch's deposition presented the Richmond group as a simple, Quaker-founded "Humane Society." Although it favored gradual emancipation, its activities raised not a single Virginia eyebrow.[121] Indeed, multiple Richmond socialites belonged to it, and "its principles were not understood to be at all in conflict with the rights guaranteed to the owners of slaves."[122]

Harrison's slip-sliding claim to abolitionism backfired on him. Vocal as Ohio abolitionists might have been in 1822, they were not in the majority.[123] Ohio's famed prohibition on slavery in its 1803 Constitution had squeaked through the Convention by only one vote, with "free" Ohio immediately thereafter enacting vicious Black Codes.[124] Moreover, in the 1820s, the anti-slavery Federalist Party collapsed, leaving Ohio abolitionists facing hard times, given the high numbers of slave-state migrants to Ohio.[125] The putative Federalist tie-in hurt Harrison in other ways, besides. Federalists were scorned as elitist bankers by hardscrabble Ohio farmers, who were just then in a fury over the financial "panic" (depression) of 1819–1822, which was popularly attributed to shifty-eyed Federalist bankers. Thus, Harrison's opponent, James Gazlay, won by "successfully pinning the label of aristocrat" on Harrison.[126] Given his social pedigree, Harrison was undeniably aristocratic, which was enough to sink his bid.

The other claim, that of Harrison's ambivalence toward slavery, owes to his second presidential run. While arguing in 1840 for "Abolition Petitions," Vermont representative William Slade declared his intention of supporting Harrison as the Whig candidate for president, despite acknowledging that he did not actually know Harrison's views on slavery. "I do know, however," Slade continued, "that they cannot be worse than those of his competitor," Martin Van Buren. At least,

Harrison would not vow "in advance, that he would exercise the veto" on legislation for abolition, Slade declared.[127] Every word of Slade's promotion of Harrison was based on wishful thinking, not fact.

Slade had not been paying attention, or Harrison's position on slavery would have been quite clear to him. Born a slave master on his father's Virginia Berkeley slave plantation, Harrison remained a slave master on his 300-acre Indiana plantation, Grouseland, which had been specifically built to house slaves. Indiana tax records for 1808 show Harrison as owning 128 slaves, a number that dwindled to thirty-two by 1830.[128] This diminution had more to do with his poor economic situation after his ambassadorial failure than with any change of heart regarding slavery. In 1830, a healthy male slave was fetching around $400, or nearly $10,000 in today's dollars.[129] Harrison was raising cash by selling slaves.

In 1835, Harrison dashed any lingering doubt about his position at a dinner speech he gave in Vincennes, Indiana. Here, he ominously warned "emancipators" not to start anything, for free states had no right to impose their abolitionist will on slave states. He likened the abolitionists to the "followers of Tecumseh" and the "Scythian hordes of Attila or Alaric." Any attempt to force abolition would, he warned, plunge the country into a devastating war.[130] The point here is not prescience. The Nullification Crisis of 1828–1832 led by South Carolina claimed that the states, not the federal courts, were empowered to decide the constitutionality of federal laws.[131] Far from precognition about the Civil War, then, the point here is that, one year before his first presidential run, Harrison was publicly endorsing states' rights to slavery. During that run, he went out of his way to repudiate his 1822 tract, by correcting the record: the Richmond group was just a "Humane Society," as Gatch had said, and not the abolition society that he had earlier claimed.[132]

In fact, Harrison worked diligently to bring slavery to the Old Northwest, using his governorship of Indiana Territory to weasel slavery into the law. Appointed governor of Indiana on May 12, 1800, Harrison held plenary powers.[133] As provided for in the act of May 7, 1800, territorial governors appointed their own councils, which provided a list of names from which the governor picked his own sitting judges as well as territorial representatives to the U.S. Congress.[134] The governor and his appointed judges, by majority vote among them, created the civil and criminal laws, modeled on those of the original states, as were "best suited to the circumstances" of their territory.[135] With such latitude, governorships were very much dictatorships, so Harrison had every hope of prevailing in his slavery quest.

The *bête noir* of Harrison's effort was Article VI of the Northwest Ordinance of 1787, which declared, "There shall be neither slavery nor involuntary servitude in the said territory, otherwise than in the punishment of crimes," although a "fugitive" from "labor or service" in other states could be "reclaimed" by his or her owner.[136] Harrison was not the first to resent this clause. In 1787, the political bellwether, translator, and trader, Bartelémi Tardiveau assured President Washington that Article VI was "obnoxious," not to mention, illegal, as an ex post facto prohibition against slavery. Tardiveau pushed Congress on behalf of the French slaveholders of Vincennes to have Article VI repealed.[137] In October 1802, Harrison assembled a convention in Vincennes, of which he was the president, to draw up a petition to suspend Article VI, which he duly sent to Congress.[138] After consideration in March 1803, Congress declared that enough settler labor was entering Ohio that a relaxation of the slavery rule was "inexpedient."[139]

The congressional ruling was clear, but that did not stop Harrison from obviating Article VI through a war on syntax. On September 22, 1803, his legislature adopted a law redefining slavery as a contract of indenture in "A Law concerning Servants." Under this law, "negroes and mulattoes," carefully lumped in with other noncitizens by way of disguise, were "under contract to serve another" and thus "compelled" to finish out their term of contract.[140] It was under this statute that Harrison famously prevented two slaves in Indiana, Peggy and George—whom Harrison carefully styled "indentured servants"—from being sold "without their consent" during an 1804 estate liquidation of a Virginia couple.[141] In importing Peggy and George into Indiana as slaves, the owners had omitted the required step of registering them as "indentured servants."[142] Returning Peggy and George as slaves would expose Harrison's fancy sidestep of indenture, so he had to act.

In 1805, as the court case to return George and Peggy to their "owners" loomed, George quickly indentured himself to Harrison for eleven years, thus securing his (delayed) emancipation.[143] Not playing ball by indenturing herself, Peggy languished in the custody of the estate's agent until 1806, when the court released her, but with the proviso that her owners could still lay legal claim to her as a runaway.[144] In 1808, the plucky Peggy sued the slave catcher for unpaid wages backdating to 1804, but unsurprisingly, she lost her case.[145] As recently as 2012, this episode has been glossed in Harrison's favor as his fighting "fiercely" to keep the pair out of slavery, but that interpretation ignores Harrison's need to support the credibility of his 1803 "indentured servant" dodge. It was Peggy who "fought fiercely" for her own freedom.[146]

On February 17, 1804, Harrison tried again for a federal waiver of Article VI, this time embedding the slavery request among seven others sent to Congress as the Indiana State Convention's petition declaring, among other requests, that the majority of Hoosiers wanted Article VI to be suspended in Indiana.[147] The House of Representatives sent what was characterized as Harrison's "letter" to a subcommittee, which during the first session of the eighth Congress endorsed suspending Article VI "in a qualified manner for ten years," allowing U.S.-born slaves to enter the Territory, while barring "the importation of slaves from foreign countries." It also provided that male children of such slaves be freed at twenty-five, and female children at twenty-one years of age.[148] The measure languished in limbo.

Harrison needed his own man in Congress. Enter, Benjamin Parke. Joined at the hip to Harrison on the slavery agenda, Parke became the first Indiana representative to the U.S. Congress, serving twice, in the 1805 and 1807 terms.

In 1806, the Indiana Legislative Council (run by Harrison) and Indiana's House of Representatives again papered the U.S. Congress with "sundry resolutions," still pushing for a suspension of Article VI, as requested in the 1804 petition under legislative consideration.[149] The recommendation to allow "qualified" slavery was finally referred to the first session of the ninth Congress on February 14, 1806.[150] Even with Parke present, however, the proposal to obviate Article VI was defeated (62 Nays to 55 Yeas) when it came to the floor for a vote.[151]

Undaunted, on November 26, 1806, Harrison signed another territorial law on slavery, this one cleverly disguised as "An Act concerning Executions." It provided that, as property of an executed felon, "negroes and mulattoes" could be sold and forced to serve the "residue" of "their time of service," under the pretense that their enslavement had been an "agreement of servitude" under the September 22, 1803, law.[152] This language of servitude alluded to Leviticus 25:8–13, wherein servants' terms of service could run fifty years. At a time when Euro-setters were quite aware of their bible, the allusion was more evocative than it sounds today.

Harrison's next assault on Article VI was frontal. On September 17, 1807, he signed "An Act concerning the Introduction of Negroes and Mullattoes into the Territory," which directly allowed slave-owning migrants to bring their "Negroes and Mullattoes" into Indiana, where the people would remain slaves, notwithstanding Article VI, thereby eliminating any more George-and-Peggy headaches.[153] The act also established that any children "born of a parent of colour, owing service or labor by indenture" would "serve the master or mistress of such parent, the male until the age of thirty, and the female to the age of twenty-eight years."[154]

On February 12, 1807, Parke introduced resolutions of the Legislative House of Representatives of the Territory of Indiana to suspend outright Article VI of the Northwest Ordinance. The suspension would aid "emigration" to the state, as most incoming settlers were from slave states, and after all, not that many slaves would be involved. "The abstract question of liberty and slavery is not involved in the proposed measure," the resolution intoned because it would merely legitimize the slaves already in Indiana.[155] Meantime, the Indiana legislature sent its newest, July 13, 1807, pro-slavery push to George Clinton, the slavery-accommodating, second vice president to Jefferson. "Slavery is tolerated in the Territories of Orleans, Mississippi, and Louisiana," insisted the territorial legislature, so what was the holdup in Indiana?[156] This appeal was, however, quickly followed by an October 10, 1807, counterpush from Indiana abolitionists, disputing the claimed popularity of slavery in Indiana.[157] At that point, Indiana ended its quest to suspend Article VI, for with Harrison's "servant" laws specifying their application to "Negroes and Mullattoes," no one could have been in doubt that de facto slavery was permitted in Indiana.

In 1827, his term of U.S. senator from Ohio about to end with no renewals in sight, Harrison needed to line up his next, lucrative public office, for whenever out of office, he fell on hard times. Not only was his business acumen poor—he already owed around $19,000 to the United States Bank[158]—but that of his sons was even worse. His eldest son, John Cleves Symmes Harrison (Symmes), was a convicted embezzler, sacked from his government job in Vincennes for having stolen $12,803.63, the rough equivalent of $325,000 today.[159] Symmes died in 1830, before he could pay off the debt, leaving Harrison to take in his widow and six children.[160] Harrison's second son, William Henry Harrison Jr., smelled just as ripe as his elder brother, or perhaps a bit more so, as a habitual drunkard. He neglected his duties as a lawyer, failed at farming, and died at thirty-eight, also leaving his father to assume the burden of his family and to pay off his debt. Harrison *père* found himself unable to come up with the final $6,000 of that liability.[161]

Harrison thus needed the dependable, steady income of government employment to keep him afloat. Given Harrison's social standing, such political buoyancy was certain, but the vice presidency, on which he had pinned his hopes, fell through despite the prior assurances of political movers and shakers.[162] The animosity of the rival Henry Clay faction, which "universally ridicule[d] his pretensions," was not to be overcome in 1828.[163] The vice presidency denied him, Harrison next set his cap at the ambassadorship of Gran Columbia, a composite of modern-day Venezuela, Ecuador, Panama, and Columbia.[164] When that also fell through, on February 28, 1828, Harrison trolled for appointment as major general of the U.S. Army, but harboring "strong objections" to Harrison, President John Quincy Adams reconditely hoped that Congress might save him from openly refusing the appointment by abolishing the position, as it did.[165]

Disgruntled at losing the major generalship, Harrison immediately reinstated his push for the ambassadorship.[166] His petitions for the post made Adams queasy, for he could see where a Harrison appointment tended. On May 6, 1828, Adams noted that, although Harrison possessed an "active and lively" mind, that mind was ultimately "shallow," giving Adams pause about promoting this "political adventurer" to an international post, where he could do some real damage. Although "not without talents," Adams found Harrison "self-sufficient"—that is, not needing the Christian god—as well as "vain, and indiscreet" in using Columbia, "very earnestly," to plump his vita in anticipation of the 1832 vice presidency, all in all, a less-than-glowing testimonial from a perceptive contemporary.[167]

On May 20, 1828, Adams was still struggling with the petition, privately fearing that Harrison wanted the ambassadorship "much more" than it wanted him or than it was "wanted by the public interest."[168] Worse, refusing to wink at African slavery, Adams ripped Harrison's "slave-driving, Jeffersonian school" of politics, which Harrison had illegally carried into Indiana.[169] Publicly, however, Adams lay his reluctance about the ambassadorship on doubt that Columbia even required a U.S. ambassador, hoping again for an abolished post to save him from an awkward refusal. Privately, Adams realized that Harrison's motivation was the salary with little thought as to his duties, should he land the office.[170] For his part, Harrison was every bit as uncomplimentary about Adams, having earlier lashed out at him as an airy intellectual, a "disgusting man to do business [with]. Coarse, *Dirty*, and clownish in his *address* and *dress* and stiff and abstracted in his opinions, which are drawn from books exclusively."[171] Clearly, Adams and Harrison did not get along.

Finally, besieged regularly by every Harrison booster in Washington, DC and needing the few political "friends" he had left, Adams relented on May 22, 1828, formally nominating Harrison to the seat of "Minister Plenipotentiary to the Republic of Columbia."[172] Alas for blind boosterism, Adams should have heeded his doubts, for Harrison is today reputed to have been the "worst United States envoy to Bogotá in the history" of U.S.–Columbian "bilateral relations."[173] South American historians seem far more aware of this than U.S. historians, who typically gloss over Harrison's Columbian debacle, but it is an important indicator of Harrison the man, his temper and his judgment.

Harrison assumed his post in February 1829, after leisurely travels to his station.[174] With Gran Columbia sitting at the crossroads of international trade and intrigue, Harrison's boss, his old nemesis Henry Clay as secretary of state, forbade him from mixing in Columbian partisan politics, although it remained standing U.S. policy for its South American diplomats to be on the alert for any European efforts to set up Latin American monarchies.[175] Harrison was supposed to appreciate the delicate balancing act to keep economic and imperial rivals— say, England—at bay, while securing Gran Columbia to U.S. interests. England was debating how deeply to involve itself in Columbia, despising it as one of South America's "political shadows, without form or substance," resulting from what the British high command saw as "the misfortune of having gained their independence too soon."[176] There was frank, high-level analysis of the financial fallout should Great Britain "interfere" on behalf of "the bondholders of the government of Columbia."[177] The United States could easily have taken advantage of this situation.

It is, however, highly doubtful whether Harrison grasped the mighty forces at play, let alone his opening for negotiations, for the United States also looked down on Latin America. Columbia had been seen as property not polity, since the Monroe Doctrine of 1823 articulated U.S. imperial dreams. Consequently, as the very existence of Gran Columbia hung in the balance, Harrison acted with bombastic abandon. He failed disastrously to oversee his embassy staff, chattered irresponsibly in public, and for his grand finale, gravely insulted *el Presidente*, Simón Bolívar.

As his first act of signal bad judgment, Harrison appointed his eighteen-year-old son, Carter Bassett, as his embassy attaché and the equally juvenile Edward Tayloe, another elite son of Virginia, as his secretary of legation, with Rensselaer van Rensselaer (son of his old acquaintance Solomon van Rensselaer) joining the group as attaché in June 1829.[178] Carter and Tayloe immediately took to meddling in Columbian politics, at which game they were easily played by a British double agent, Dabney Overton Carr. A young "crack brained" Virginian of distinguished descent, who had been disgraced and disinherited by his father, Carr served in the employ of Bolívar's trusted general, Daniel O'Leary, himself a double agent, working for British interests in Columbia.[179] Carr wormed his way into Ambassador Harrison's good graces via his Virginia credentials and faux friendship with Carter Basset, making Harrison appear to be part of the over-throw plot against Bolívar.[180] For his pains, Carr was killed during the Córdova revolt against Bolívar.[181]

In his next questionable act, Harrison helped untoward appearances along through indiscretion. British spy talk in Columbia had Bolívar planning to crown himself king, gossip that Bolívar ardently repudiated but which Harrison fully believed and passed along to Andrew Jackson's secretary of state, Martin Van Buren, on March 27, 1829.[182] Oblivious of Great Britain's part in the scheme, Harrison became close with the intricately scheming James Henderson, the British consul-general in Bogotá, whose daughters, Margaret and Mary Packer, Carter and Tayloe eagerly wooed.[183] Harrison saw no problem with this close relationship, even as Henderson assiduously stirred the political pot of Columbian instability, making Harrison and crew his patsies.

Thus playing both ends against the middle, Henderson moved in close contact with José María Córdova-Muñoz, the head of the anti-Bolívar rebels—himself courting another Henderson daughter, "pretty Fanny"[184]—even as British agent O'Leary circuitously urged a crown for Bolívar, pushing the Earl of Aberdeen, via British colonel Patrick Campbell, for British aid in the project.[185] On January 20, 1830, to sink the disinformation about a royal lineage in formation, Bolívar wrote an open letter to the Columbian people, earnestly declaring, "*Nunca, nunca, os lo juro, ha manchado mi mente la ambición de un reino que mis ene-migos han forjado artifisiosament para perderme en vuestra opinion.*" (Never, ever, I swear to you, has the ambition of a kingship, which my enemies have artificially cooked up to sink me in your opinion, crossed my mind.)[186]

Blithely incognizant of it all, at a brunch in August 1829, Harrison gabbed heedlessly about monarchical tyrants, instancing Napoleon, to demonstrate his contempt for monarchy, a story circulated by the Córdova rebels spreading the rumor that Bolívar lusted after a crown.[187] In addition, Harrison dropped incau-tious remarks to Henderson's wife, to the effect that Columbian soldiers should "cut the throats of their damned oppressors."[188] This, despite being aware enough of a plot against Bolívar to describe it to van Buren in a letter of September 14, 1829.[189] Heaven only knows what Carter Bassett and Edward Tayloe blabbed to the Henderson girls, who were clearly aware of events. In con-trast to the boys, however, so self-controlled were the girls that no "indiscreet expression escaped the lips of one of them," even upon the death of Córdova, a man whom they had known, entertained, and flirted with.[190]

Thus, instead of dangling aid to Bolívar that would have benefited the United States while enticing Bolívar's goodwill away from England, Harrison so com-pletely soured Bolívar on the United States that the *el Presidente* grumpily eschewed the states as an insalubrious model. In his famous August 5, 1829, *Carta de Guayaquil* (letter from the Port of Guayaquil, Columbia), Bolívar observed that the United States "*parecen destinados á plagar la América con miserias a nombre de la Libertad!*" (seems destined to plague [Latin] America with miseries in the name of Liberty!)[191] A month later, Bolívar told General O'Leary, the British agent ensconced in his inner circle, that "*Yo pienso que mejor sería para la*

América adoptar el Corán que el Gobierno de Los Estados Unidos" (I think it would be better for [Latin] America to adopt the Q'ran than the Government of the United States), snidely adding, "*aunque es el mejor del mundo*" (even though it is the best in the world).[192] Bolívar was pretty clearly thinking of Harrison in this jibe.

It is probable that Bolívar was thinking of Harrison throughout this last letter, for immediately prior to the ridicule, he had been making fun of "*la nueva nobleza*," the vaunted natural aristocracy, into which Harrison was an inductee. "*Nadie sufriría sin impaciencia esta miserable aristocracia cubierta de pobreza é ignorancia y animada de pretensiones ridiculas*," he snarled. (Nobody could suffer without impatience this miserable aristocracy, enveloped in poverty and ignorance and animated by ridiculous pretensions.)[193] Given Bolívar's palpable ire in the Guayaquil letters, one wonders whether he found Harrison a disgusting man to deal with, coarse, dirty, and clownish in address and dress. What is certain is that Harrison lacked any fluency in Spanish (his education was in Latin and Greek classics), let alone diplomatic experience for the international post, unless his arm-twisting "treaties" with the various Indigenous nations of the Old Northwest counted.[194] If so, it should be noted that his style there had helped bring on the Tecumseh War.

By the fall of 1829, frantic talk had erupted among top Columbian officials regarding Harrison's involvement in an assassination plot against their members, traced to the youth contingent of Harrison's coterie.[195] In his later, self-serving spin on his Columbian ouster, Harrison did not deny the anti-Bolívar meddling but off-loaded everything onto his son and Tayloe.[196] He never did catch on to Carr. Not believing that any diplomat could be as clueless as Harrison, Bolívar's government alleged that Harrison, himself, was up to no good, implicating him as well as Carter Bassett in the Córdova rebellion.[197] Although ultimately clearing Harrison, the government of Columbia angrily sent him and his crew packing on October 19, 1830.[198] Luckily for face-saving deflections, Jackson had recently won the presidency, allowing Harrison to explain his ignominious ejection from Columbia as Jackson's having recalled him in favor of his own crony, Thomas P. Moore of Kentucky.[199]

Intensifying the chaos, Moore immediately began vilifying Harrison to Columbian officials.[200] Moore's hints to Columbian officials of a forthcoming, unfriendly publication by Harrison led the Columbian government to allege that the ambassador planned, upon his return to the United States, "to open a newspaper warfare" against Columbia and Bolívar.[201] In December 1830, the stacked ineptitude of both Harrison and Moore led their lesser but better U.S.–Columbian colleague, John M. Macpherson, to hope that the United States "at some *future day*" might create "some kind of diplomatic school, where the rudiments, at least, of the profession" would be "taught."[202] Indeed.

Harrison's sole Columbian "achievement," as it were, came on September 27, 1830, exactly one day after Moore took over. This grand finale of Harrison's international missteps came in the form of a profoundly insulting public letter that Harrison addressed to Bolívar. Crowing about the exemplary "fame of our Washington," Harrison lifted him up as an exemplar and, by way of contrast, simultaneously likened Bolívar to Napoleon.[203] Written to a very sick man just two months before he died and couched as a principled rebuke of Bolívar for falling off the republican wagon, the letter excoriated *el Presidente* for establishing himself as a dictator. Harrison smugly lectured him on those "qualities of the hero and the general" required for public service, while scolding him for supposedly trying to cajole Great Britain into backing his scheme to establish a royal line in Columbia.[204]

Harrison's remarks were stunningly oblivious of the pickle that Bolívar faced just then, for surrounded by double-dealers, he was quite ill (most probably dying of arsenic poisoning), Gran Columbia was falling apart, and European powers were licking their lips in anticipation of a partitioning feast.[205] Scrambling to hold his fractious country together, Bolívar had essentially declared martial law to put down the military revolt led by Córdova.[206] The effrontery of Harrison's letter was, therefore, acute not only in view of Harrison's own questionable behavior—during both the Burr and the Córdova conspiracies—but also in light of the Shays rebellion at home. In 1786, President Washington had, himself, famously moved in a rather tyrannical and very military way to put down a tax rebellion staged by Daniel Shays of Western Pennsylvania, undercutting Harrison's Washington example.[207]

Once home, Harrison immediately published this letter in pamphlet form (copies of which he sent twice to Adams and once to Henry Clay), opening the "newspaper warfare" that Columbian officials had feared.[208] Harrison's inaccuracies mattered little, however, as his musings on generals and heroes had always been propaganda aimed at his home constituency, in anticipation of his presidential runs. The meme of General Washington was meant to invoke the meme of another great general— say, one who had fought at Tippecanoe or Thames. Harrison's excoriation of Bolívar did ultimately prove helpful at home in burnishing his credentials as a Man of the People but not until his 1840 presidential bid.[209]

To recover from his aristocratic birth, the Burr Conspiracy, his introduction of slavery into Indiana, and, at least in upper-level governmental and political circles, knowledge of the hash that he had made of U.S. diplomacy in Columbia, it was imperative to Harrison's future presidential runs to deflect attention away from his money-grubbing lust for office and onto an ideomythology that the voting public cherished. If slavery was divisive, then the credentials that got a man elected attached to land seizure, through coerced treaties and outright warfare against the "savages." For these, Harrison depended on the earliest part of his career, to which we now return, his treaty-making, Indian-fighting, log-cabin governorship of the Northwest Territories.

NOTES

1. Adams, Adams, and Jefferson, 1959, 398.
2. Brackets mine. Dawson, 1824, 1–2.
3. Gunderson, 1993, 3; Williams and Gianetti, 2017, 198–99; Perling, 1947, 73.
4. Hardy, 1911, for Carters, 109–10; for Benjamin Harrison, 284.
5. "Will of Benjamin Harrison," 1895, 124–31.
6. Goebel, 1926, 18; Owens, 2007, 14; Hildreth, 1840, 8; Rappleye, "Financier" sobriquet, 2010.

7. Harrison, 1939, Harrison to Brooks, letter 7/20/1939.

8. Owens, 2007, 6, 14–15; Perling, 1947, 74.

9. Jacobs, 1938, double agent, 80–81, 104, 130, 133, 135, 137, 152, 205–6, 273; for governorship, 215.

10. Carter, 1934–1975, Sargeant to Wilkinson, vol. 3, letter 6/4/1792, 376–77; Gunderson, 1993, "William Henry Harrison," 7–8.

11. Ibid., Sargeant to Symmes, vol. 3, letter 6/4/1792, 377–78; Sargeant to St. Clair, letter 6/19/1792, 400; Sargeant to St. Clair, letter 6/30/1792, 402–4; Sargeant to Wilkinson, letter 6/4/1792, 376–77; Sargeant to Symmes, letter 6/13/1792, 379–80; Sargeant to Judges, letter 8/7/1792, 382–83; Jacobs, 1938, 125.

12. Quotation, Goebel, 1926, 39; Jacobs, 1938, 127; Owens, 2007, 17–18; Gunderson, 1993, 8.

13. Owens, 2007, 17.

14. Gunderson, 1993, 9.

15. For Harrison in 1791, see Harrison, 1831, "small command," 4, "Western Country," 3. The "Cox" whom Harrison mentioned is almost certainly Isaac Cox, who settled in Harrison County, West Virginia, along Kincheloe Creek (the creek that Harrison mentions fording), which was the "Western Country," abutting Ohio, at the time. Lowther, 1911, 333–34; for Harrison's 1792 appointment, "General Wayne's Orderly Book," 1905, "General Orders," 10/16/1792, 396; Gunderson, 1993, 11, 13–14.

16. *ASPIA*, 1832, vol. 1, 491.

17. Nelson, 1985, Wayne to Wayne, letter 9/10/1794, 261; "General Wayne's Orderly Book," 1905, vol. 34, entry 8/3/1794, 541; Pratt, 1997, 7–8.

18. Harrison, Harrison to Brooks, Manuscripts Collection, New-York Historical Society, letter 7/20/1839.

19. Gunderson, 1993, 19.

20. Curtis *et al.*, 1864, *United States v. Guthrie*, 17 H. 284, 1854, 514.

21. Jay, 2010, 219–20.

22. Ibid., "Abbe," 42, 60, 65, 88, 91, 106, 133, 135, 147–49, 151, 153, 159, 161–62, "Wealthy," 112.

23. Dawson, 1824, 4; Gunderson, 1993, 5; Mann, 2004, 147–64.

24. Mann, 2004, 179–83.

25. McBride, 1909, 50–54; Badollet and Gallatin, 1963, "J. C. Symmes's Patent," 1811, Appendix, 13.

26. Cohen, 2010, 864, 860–67; Miller, 2006, 3; Miller *et al.*, 2010, 3–9; Madison *et al.*, 1962–1991, vol. 7, 310.

27. Franklin, 2007, 304–6.

28. McBride, 1909, 50–54; Symmes *et al.*, 1926, 19–20; Symmes to Drayton, letter 8/10/1796, 181–82; Symmes to Drayton, letter 3/5/1804, 189; Drayton to Symmes, letter 9/26/1789, 235–36.

29. USCSB, 1795, 83–84; Gallatin, 1811, 14.

30. Carter, 1934–1975, "Grant of Lands to Symmes," vol. 2, 5/5/1792, 394–95.

31. Symmes, 1926, note 256, 187; Carter, 1934–1975, "Patent Issued," vol. 2, 496–98; Esarey, 1922, Harrison to Constituents, vol. 1, letter 5/14/1800, 15; *ASPPL*, 1834, vol. 1, no. 70, 115; no. 72, 115–9.

32. Symmes, 1910, *The Trenton Circular*, "To the Respectable Public," 95.

33. Harrison, 1867, 9–10.

34. Carter, 1934–1975, Symmes to Sargeant, letter 6/30/1792, 402–4.

35. Symmes *et al.*, 1956, Symmes to Morris, letter 6/22/1795, 98.

36. Ibid., Symmes to Morris, letter 12/22/1795, 77; for promotion to captain, Cox, ed., 1908, note 5, 100.

37. Gunderson, 1993, 12–13.

38. Ibid., note 28, 26.

39. "Enclosure, Schedule of Property," Item b, Founders on Line, accessed January 3, 2018.

40. Symmes to Morris, 1956, letter 6/22/1795, 98.

41. Goebel, 1926, 19; "Portrait of Sarah Cutler Dunn" by Gilbert Stuart, RISD Museum, Museum Appropriation Fund 31.273, accessed January 3, 2018.

42. For Harrison's aspiration, Gunderson, 1993, 15; for Hetty Morris's marriage, Oberholtzer, 1903, 265–66.

43. Cayton, 1996, 167.

44. Symmes *et al.*, 1956, Symmes to Condict, letter 2/28/1796, 103.

45. Ibid., Symmes to Morris, letter 3/2/1796, 82.

46. For Morris, Gunderson, 1993, 3.

47. Symmes to Morris, 1956, letter 3/2/1796, 82.

48. Hess, 2016, 227.

49. Symmes *et al.*, 1956, Symmes to Boudinot, on drinkers, letters 1/12/1792 and 1/15/1792, 97.

50. Ibid., Anna Harrison to Symmes, letter 2/7/1811, 147; for Symmes's visit, xxiv.

51. Ibid., 13–16, 21; house fire, 23. A similar house fire took the residence of a young James Fenimore Cooper, heir to the Cooper's fortune, and it was apparently a case of arson, which looks to have been a go-to method revenge on the rich. The Cooper fire was set by a settler angry at having been defrauded by Cooper *père*, getting posthumously even via the son, Franklin, 2007, 390.

52. Harrison, 1867, 7.

53. Sayre, 2017, 184–85.

54. Cox, 1908, Harrison to Findlay, letter 7/18/1800, note 5, 100. Noted Ohio jurist, Burnett created the Ohio Constitution and was an associate justice of the early Ohio Supreme Court, *National Cyclopaedia of American Biography*, 1901, 155.

55. Burr, 1840, 257–58.

56. For secretarial pay, see Cleaves, 1990, 26; for Indiana governor, see Esarey, 1922, vol. 1, note 1, 194; for Minister Plenipotentiary to Columbia, see Clay, 1959–1993, Clay to Harrison, vol. 7, letter 5/29/1828, 308.

57. Adams, 1874–1877, 530.

58. For Brown, see Kline, 1983, vol. 2, letter 3/18/1805, 911, 918; Carter, 1934–1975, Burr to Jefferson, vol. 13, letter 3/10/1805, 97; commission of Joseph "Browne," Jefferson to Madison, letter 4/6/1805, 99,–100; Brown to Jefferson, 114; for Wilkinson, see Ford, 1920, Wilkinson to Burr, letter 5/23/1804, 82–83.

59. Carter, 1934–1975, Jefferson to Madison, vol. 13, Commission 3/11/1805, 98–99; Wilkinson to Madison, letter 4/7/1805, 114–15.

60. Lewis, 2017, 58.

61. Carter, 1934–1975, St. Clair to Jay, vol. 2, letter 12/13/1788, 166–70.

62. Smith, 1882, St. Clair to Secretary of State, vol. 2, for quotation, letter (no month, no year), 1794, 327; also see St. Clair to Shelby, letter 11/7/1793, 320–21; St. Clair to Secretary of War, letter 12/7/1793, 321–25.

63. Harrison, 1939, letter 7/20/1839, 3.

64. Carter, 1934–1975, Davis to Breckinridge, vol. 7, letter 10/7/1803, 124.

65. Kline, 1983, Merry to Harrowby, "Most Secret," letter 3/29/1805, 927–30.

66. Wilkinson was told by a co-conspirator of Burr that "the people of the Territory were ready to join" the conspiracy, *ASPMA*, 1861, 549; Wilkinson, 1816, Clark to Wilkinson, letter 9/7/1805, Appendix XXXIII, n.p.

67. *ASPMISC*, 1834, vol. 1, no. 230, 540.

68. Kline, 1983, vol. 2, note 3, 818.

69. *ASPMA*, 1832, vol. 1, 540; for "stands of arms," 554.

70. *ASPMISC*, 1834, vol. 1, 540.

71. Beveridge, 2005, Burr to Wilkinson, vol. 3, Cipher letter 7/29/1806, Appendix D, 614; Lewis, 2017, 107, 114; Kline, 1983, Merry to Harrowby, "Most Secret," vol. 2, letter 3/29/1805, 927–30.

72. *ASPMA*, 1832, vol. 1, 486, et seq.

73. For deposits in United States Bank, Lewis, 2017, 3.

74. Beveridge, 2005, vol. 3, 614.

75. Burton, 1951, 737; for date of Wilkinson's letter to Jefferson, *ASPMISC*, 1834, Jefferson to the U.S. Senate, vol. 1, no. 217, letter 1/22/1807, 468.

76. *ASPMISC*, 1834, vol. 1, 543.

77. Lewis, 2017, 10–11; *ASPMISC*, 1834, vol. 2, no. 280, 79–127; *ASPMA*, vol. 1, no. 100, 268–95.

78. For the letter as misdated, compare Esarey, 1922, vol. 1, 197, to Clanin, 1993, Reel 2, Image 183. Esarey took the letter from Parton, 1892, vol. 2, 50. A close reading of the text shows that Parton had correctly if inconspicuously given the year as 1805, but haste could have confused a reader as to the year.

79. Wandell and Minnigerode, 1925, 43; Wilkinson, 1816, Appendix LXVII.

80. Kline, 1983, vol. 2, note 4, 935.

81. Carter, 1934–1975, Harrison to Jefferson, vol. 7, letter 8/6/1802, 66–67; same letter given as Esarey, 1922, Harrison to Jefferson, vol. 1, letter 8/8/1802, 51, and note 1, 51. Given Esarey's proven mistakes, I trust Carter on the date. The town of Jeffersonville associated with the canal around the falls is located across the Ohio River from Louisville, Kentucky; Jefferson replied, noting the "honor" Harrison offered in naming Jeffersonville after himself, Jefferson, 1907, Jefferson to Harrison, vol. 9, letter 2/27/1803, 368; Carter, 1922, Jefferson to Harrison, vol. 7, letter 2/27/1803, 89.

82. *ASPMISC*, 1834, vol. 1, no. 188, communication, 1/28/1805, 419; no. 208, resolution, 3/21/1806, 453–54; and no. 224, submission, 1/24/1807, 479.

83. Kline, 1983, vol. 2, esp. 923, 985–86; but also multiple instances recorded in Kline.

84. For visit, see Lewis, 2017, 58.

85. Kline, 1983, Burr to Wilkinson, vol. 2, letter 9/26/1805, 940.

86. Ibid., Burr to unnamed recipient, vol. 2, letter 10/7/1805, 942.

87. Steele and Steele, 1896, for 1805 founding, 83; named for Jonathan Dayton, 21.

88. Brackets mine. *ASPMA*, 1832, Harrison to Wilkinson, vol. 1, Extract, letter 6/7/1805, 580.

89. Jacobs, 1938, 218, 226.

90. Wandell and Minnigerode, 1925, 47.

91. For St. Louis, see Lewis, 2017, 58, 63, 110, 191, 213; for St. Louis as Wilkinson's headquarters, 15.

92. Italics in the original. *ASPMISC*, 1834, vol. 1, 571–74.

93. *ASPMA*, 1832, vol. 1, 581.

94. For Easary's misleading footnote, see Esarey, 1922, note 1, 198.

95. Clanin, 1993, Reel 2, Image 211.

96. His relatives were the influential Dodemead family, whose daughter Alice married Dr. Wilkinson, while her sister, Elizabeth, married Charles Jouett; Burton, 1917, 39–40.

97. Clanin, 1993, Reel 2, Image 209; for Wilkinson family tree, see chart, in "Wilkinson," n.d. Harrison knew Charles Jouett as an Indian Agent, first in Detroit, 1802–1805, and later in Chicago, 1805–1811, and again, 1815–1818; Esarey, 1922, vol. 1, note 1, 181.

98. Clanin, 1993, Wilkinson to Harrison, Reel 2, Image 348, letter 9/19/1806; and Esarey, 1922, vol. 1, 197–98.

99. Beveridge, 2005, 615.

100. Jacobs, 1938, 222–23.

101. "Editorial Note" in Kline, 1983, vol. 2, 922, 924.

102. Kline, 1983, Burr to Wilkinson, vol. 2, letter 9/26/1805, 940; Burr as meeting with Harrison on return leg of journey, Melton, 2001, 85.

103. Clark, 1809, notes, 16.

104. Lewis, 2017, 171; *ASPMA*, 1832, vol. 1, 539.

105. *ASPMA*, 1832, vol. 1, 541.

106. Ibid., vol. 1, 541.

107. Kline, 1983, vol. 2, 1007.

108. *ASPMA*, Burr to Harrison, vol. 1, letter 11/27/1806, 201.

109. Cox, 1918, 194.

110. Moser *et al.*, 1980–2013, Thompson to Jackson, extortion attempt, vol. 2, letter 7/3/1812, 309; Thompson to Jackson, letter 9/30/1812, 322.

111. Blennerhassett and Safford, 1864, Blennerhassett to Burr, letter 4/16/1818, 550–52.

112. Esarey, 1922, Harrison to Williams, vol. 1, letter 4/3/1807, 205.

113. Brackets mine. Article 1: "Review of Wilkinson's Memoirs," note a, 17. Brackets mine.

114. Butler, 2010, note *, 319–20; for Wescott as marrying Burr's niece, Lewis, 2017, 74. Barbara Alice Mann is absolutely unrelated to the Mann Butler family.

115. *ASPMISC*, 1834, vol. 2, no. 280, 79–127; Records relating to the 1811 and 1815 courts-martial of Wilkinson, M1523, National Archives Identifier 301659, Record Group 153: Records of the Office of the Judge Advocate General (Army), 1792–2010; Jacobs, 1938, 266.

116. *ASPMA*, vol. 1, Symmes to Brown, letter 1/11/1808; Symmes *et al.*, 1956, 130; The charges at the Burr trial listed "Blannerhasset Island" in Wood County, Virginia, as the site from which Burr's little army was to have set out, "Burr's Conspiracy—Trial at Richmond, Virginia," in 486.

117. Blennerhassett and Safford, 1864, Blennerhassett to Burr, letter 4/16/1818, 551.

118. Todd *et al.*, 1847, 133.

119. Ibid., whole address, 135–39; Goebel, 1926, 18, 76.

120. M'Lean, 1854, 91–96; as judge, 163.

121. Todd *et al.*, 1847, citing Judge Gatsch, 133; contents of Gatch's certificate, 135; Goebel, 1926, 18.

122. Todd *et al.*, 1847, 135.

123. Middleton, 2005, 80.

124. Ibid., Convention, 27–37; Black Codes, 42–73.

125. Ibid., 28, 44.

126. For quotation, Cayton, 1986, 135; for bank claim, Greve, 1904, vol. 1, 574.

127. Slade, U.S. 26th Congress, 1st Session, vol. 8, no. 6, 1/7/1840, 856.

128. Hodge, 1902, 82.

129. Barnett and Burkett, "The Forks of the Road Slave Market at Natchez," accessed December 26, 2017.

130. Todd *et al.*, 1847, 136–37.

131. Harrison certainly thought about the Nullification Crisis, Harrison, 1908, Harrison to Findlay, letter 12/2/1832, 79–80. His son, William Jr., also wrote of "these times of *Nullification* and bombarding from *valourous* sons of South Carolina," indicating that the topic was spoken of in his circle, in Harrison, 1908, Harrison Jr. to Findlay, letter 2/16/1833, note 34, 80.

132. Goebel, 1926, 358.

133. Esary, 1922, vol. 1, note 1, 194.

134. USC, 1845, Chapter 41, vol. 2, "An Act to Divide the Territory," 5/7/1800, 58–59.

135. USC, 1800, 249.

136. Ibid., 255–56.

137. Smith, 1882, Tardiveau to St. Clair, vol. 2, letter 6/30/1789, 118.

138. Esarey, 1922, vol. 1, "Proclamation," 11/22/1802, 60–61; "Resolution," 12/25/1802, 61–62; "Petition," letter 12/28/1802, 62–67; Harrison to [Randolph], 67; Carter, 1934–1975, Jefferson to Harrison, vol. 7, letter 2/27/1803, 89, and note 5, 89–90.

139. *ASPPL*, 1834–1861, vol. 1, no. 76, 146.

140. Philbrick, 1930, "A Law concerning Servants," vol. 21, Law Series, vol. 2, quotation, 42; entire law, 42–46.

141. Esarey, 1922, "Proclamation," 4/6/1804, vol. 1, 94–95.

142. Dunn, 1888, 237.

143. Ibid., 313.

144. Ibid., 237–38.

145. Esarey, 1922, vol. 1, note 1, 95.

146. Collins, 2012, 34; repeated, note 34, 130. Collins notes that the 1803 "Law concerning Servants" would be read as "a cynical attempt to maintain slavery," 34, but then glosses the George and Peggy case to refute that reading of the law. Collins also leaves the misimpression that Peggy was released immediately in 1804, 34.

147. Esarey, 1922, "Second Report on Petition," vol. 1, 91–93; Harrison's message was read into the record in, USC, 1834, 1023.

148. USC, 1834, 8th Congress, "Indiana Territory," 1023–24.

149. *ASPMISC*, 1834, vol. 1, no. 229, 10th Congress, 1st Session, 485.

150. *ASPMISC*, 1834, vol. 1, no. 203, 450–51.

151. USC, 1834, 1st Congress, 8th Session, 1035.

152. Indiana Territory, 1807, quotations, 189; whole law, 187–89.

153. Philbrick, 1930, 523–26.

154. Ibid., paragraph 13, 526.

155. *ASPMA*, vol. 1, no. 222, 9th Congress, 2nd Session, 477–78.

156. Ibid., vol. 1, no. 229, 484–85.

157. *ASPMISC*, 1834, vol. 1, no. 229, 485–86.

158. Goebel, 1926, 294.

159. Cox, "Selections from the Torrence Papers, IV," 1908, Harrison to Findlay, letter 12/7/1830, 72. Harrison refers to his "second son." John Cleves Symmes was his first living son and his second son was William Jr., but it was John Cleves Symmes against whom the lawsuit was filed.

160. Bonney, 1875, vol. 2, 36; Hess, "Harrison," 226. In 1831, Congress gave Clarissa Harrison eighteen additional years to pay off $9,258.08, as secured by a real estate lien, in

U.S. Executive Documents, 25th Congress, 3rd Session, vol. 4, Doc. 177, "Balances Due," 2/9/1839, 2.

161. Harrison, 1908, Harrison to Findlay, letter 12/2/1832, 78–79, note 30, 77–78.

162. "Selections from the Torrence Papers, III," 1907, Harrison to Storer, letter 1/17/1828, 118–19.

163. Ibid., Neville to Findlay, letter 3/4/1828, 120.

164. Adams, 1874–1877, vol. 7, entry 1/9/1827, 223.

165. Ibid., "strong objections," vol. 7, entry 2/28/1828, 454; abolished, 454, 456; entry 4/11/1828, 504, 505; entry 4/14/1828, 506, 507; entry 4/19/1828, 513.

166. Ibid., vol. 7, entry 5/6/1828, 530, 531; entry 5/17/1828, 544; entry 5/19/1828, 546, 547; vol. 8, entry 5/20/1828, 3, 4.

167. Ibid., vol. 7, entry 5/6/1828, 530.

168. Ibid., vol. 8, 4.

169. Ibid., vol. 10, 457. Here, Adams was expressing disgust with John Tyler, the one-month vice president who had just assumed the presidency upon the death of Harrison.

170. Ibid., vol. 7, entry 5/17/1828, 544; realization of actual reason, entry 5/6/1828, 530.

171. Italics, brackets, and capitalizations in the original. Cox, "III," 1908, Harrison to Findlay, letter 1/24/1817, 107.

172. Ibid., vol. 8, entry 5/22/1828, 6.

173. Drexler, 1997, 30.

174. Moreno de Angel, 1977, 543; Goddard, 1841, 17.

175. Moreno de Angel, 1977, Brunch, 510; Clay and U.S. policy, 544.

176. *Despatches*, 1867–1880, Head to Wellington, vol. 6, letter 1/19/1830, 428.

177. Ibid., vol. 5, letter 4/21/1829, Wellington, "Memorandum," 586–87.

178. Bonney, 1875, vol. 1, 438–39; Adams, 1874–1877, vol. 8, 211–12; Goebel, 1926, 256; Bonney, 1875, vol. 1, 527; de Angel, 1977, 543.

179. de Angel, 1977, 543, 548; Bonney, 1875, vol. 1, 525, 530–31; vol. 2, 25–26. For disgrace, see de Angel, 1977, 548; for Carr as "crack brained," Bonney, 1875, vol. 1, 531; for identity, see Carr, 1894, 306, entry 2939; for O'Leary's employ, Bonney, 1875, vol. 1, 531; for O'Leary as British agent, de Angel, 1977, 557, and Brown, 2012, 46–47.

180. Adams, 1874–1877, vol. 8, 189–90, 211; Herring, 2008, 161; Bonney, 1875, vol. 1, 526, 530; vol. 2, 4; Loveman, 2010, 104; Goebel, 1926, 285–88.

181. Bonney, 1875, vol. 2, 32–33.

182. Moreno de Angel, 1977, 544.

183. Bonney, 1875, vol. 1, 504, 517; Moreno de Angel, 1977, 427–28; Goebel, 1926, 263.

184. de Angel, 1977, 410, 419; Bonney, 1875, vol. 1, 410, 531; for "pretty Fanny," 429; Bonney, 1875, Fanny was thirteen at the time, vol. 1, 531.

185. *Despatches*, 1867–1880, Wellington to Aberdeen, letter 7/19/1829, vol. 6, 28; Aberdeen to Wellington, letter 12/8/1829, vol. 6, 315; Moreno de Angel, 1977, 546; Brown, 2012, 46–47.

186. Monsalve, 1916, vol. 2, open letter 1/30/1830, Bolívar, 311.

187. Moreno de Angel, 1977, 510.

188. Goebel, 1926, 284.

189. de Angel, 1977, 515.

190. Bonney, 1875, vol. 2, 12; de Angel, 1977, 428.

191. For "country of Washington," Hall, 1836, 301; for la *Carta de Guayaquil*, translation, mine and brackets mine, Monsalve, 1916, vol. 2, 245.

192. Translation and brackets mine; Monsalve, 1916, vol. 2, letter 9/13/1829, 251.

193. Translation mine; Monsalve, 1916, vol. 2, letter 9/13/1829, 247.

194. For college education in Latin and Greek classics, see Manuscripts Collection, New-York Historical Society, Harrison to Brooks, letter 7/20/1839, 3; Collins, 2012, 69; for Spanish, as he handed over the ambassadorship, formally introducing his successor to the Columbian government on 9/26/1829, he spoke in English, not Spanish, according to eyewitness, van Rensselaer, in Bonney, 1875, van Rensselaer to van Rensselaer, vol. 1, letter 11/17/1829, 524.

195. Moreno de Angel, 1977, 548, 550–51.

196. Adams, 1874–1877, vol. 8, 211–12; Goebel, 1926, 256, 287; Moreno de Angel, 1977, 547–52.

197. Bonney, 1875, vol. 1, 525–26.

198. Moreno de Angel, 1977, 560; Goebel, 1926, 285, 287–88; Hess, 2016, 232.

199. Adams, 1874–1877, vol. 8, 189–90. In his memoirs on 3/13/1829, Adams was less clear than Jacksonian historians on the exact genesis of Harrison's recall, vaguely noting that Harrison had been "superceded," Adams, 1874–1877, vol. 8, 112; also see Drexler, 1997, 31; and Goebel, 1926, 270–71; Bonney, 1875, van Rensselaer to van Rensselaer, vol. 1, letter 11/17/1829, 524.

200. Bonney, 1875, vol. 2, 14, 30, 33–37 passim.

201. Ibid., vol. 2, 19.

202. Italics in the original. Bonney, 1875, vol. 2, 37.

203. Hall, 1836, "fame of our Washington," 308, Napoleon, 302; for brunch, de Angel, 1977, for brunch, 510.

204. Goddard, 1841, 18; for the text of Harrison's letter, see Hall, 1836, 301–8.

205. For arsenic poisoning, see Keiger, 2010, accessed February 19, 2018.

206. Adams, 1874–1877, vol. 8, 190. Although Adams doubted Harrison's claim to have seen a letter involving the British foreign secretary, George Hamilton-Gordon ("Lord Aberdeen"), there was in fact a series of letters involving Bolívar, Columbia, and Great Britain: "Petición," to Aberdeen, Minister of Foreign Relations, in *Coleccion de*, 1829, 193–96; *Despatches*, 1867–1880, Wellington to Aberdeen with instructions for Campbell, vol. 6, letter 7/19/1829, 28; Aberdeen to Wellington, letter 12/8/1829, pulling away from Bolívar's proposals, through Campbell, apparently, in *Despatches*, 1867–1880, vol. 6, 315; Adams incorrectly doubted Britain's involvement, Adams, 1874–1877, vol. 8, 212. Also see Goebel, 1926, 275–79; Brown, 2012, 47.

207. Hoagland, 2006, 213.

208. For Harrison sending the pamphlet to Adams, see Adams, 1874–1877, vol. 8, 211; for Harrison sending the pamphlet to Clay, in Clay, 1856, Harrison to Clay, letter 4/11/1830, 258.

209. Collins, 2012, 68–69.

CHAPTER 2

◠

"Defrauded and Cheated": The Build-up to the Tecumseh War

As the first governor of the Indiana Territory, Harrison was still in the heady days of his career, initially appointed to the position by President John Adams in 1800 at age twenty-seven, with the appointment renewed by President Thomas Jefferson in 1803, 1806, and again, by President James Madison in 1809.[1] On February 8, 1803, Jefferson simultaneously appointed Harrison a U.S. treaty commissioner (with a $6 per diem attached).[2] Then, as war loomed, Harrison assumed a U.S. Army commission as brigadier general on August 22, 1812, promoted from there to major general on February 27, 1813, giving up his governorship only upon receiving the second commission.[3] In the heat of the War of 1812, Kentucky state officials, by eager acclamation, made Harrison a brevet major general of its state militia—a move that they soon lamented.[4] These successive positions marked the high point of Harrison's career, providing the credentials through which he acquired all other offices and the platform for his presidential bids.

What Harrison did in these thirteen years are also the deeds for which Euro-American histories extol him today. If to accomplish praise, these accounts must downplay his involvement in the Burr Conspiracy, his illegal expansion of slavery into Indiana, and his botched Columbian ambassadorship, then to complete their accolades, they necessarily recast his land-fleecing treaties by underhanded tactics and his later outright massacre of the Indians who objected to it all as the sad but unavoidable effects of U.S. expansion, the "need" for which is never quizzed. Instead, Harrison is breezily styled an "Indian fighter" and *Tecumseh*'s movement, "Red Muslimism," but the facts on the ground were less glorious than advertised.[5] If Harrison flubbed military leadership, then the Indians were neither "red" nor "Muslim" but a Homeland Defense Committee against settler aggression.

By and large, the Algonkin-language peoples of Indiana, whose lands Harrison busily expropriated, were the Miami, close relatives of the Illiniwek (Illinois Confederacy) peoples. Gabriel Dreuillettes in 1657–1658 originally parsed out the Miami peoples as the "Ouinipegouek" or "Crane People," named for the cry of the crane, with the same Crane People rendered as "Atchatchakangouen" by Claude Alloues in 1672–1673. Alloues also listed the Kilatika, Mengakonkia, Pepikokia, Piankeshaw, and Wea as Miami, while naming the "Kakachiouek" or Kaskaskia, "poueteouatami" or Potawatomi, and "Kikaboua" or Kickapoo as being in the vicinity, too.[6] The languages these neighbors spoke were mutually intelligible, even though Kickapoo derived from a Shawnee base.[7] The Pepikokia were later cross-identified with either the Wea or the Piankeshaw, the names of two of their original five, seventeenth-century towns, while the Kilatika were renamed "Eel River Indians" by the settlers.[8] Settlers habitually (re)named people this way, either for their clan towns or in botched translations. Thus, to the settlers pushing west, the Mengakonkia, Pepikokia, Piankeshaw, and Wea wound up as just the "Piankeshaw" or "Wea."

The Kaskaskia and Kickapoo are often presented by nineteenth-century authors as not *really* Miami, but throughout the earliest records, they were listed as Miami. Thus, their "independent" status begins to look less like a natural fact than like a treaty-making ploy, as it certainly was for Anthony Wayne at the Greenville Treaty talks.[9] If the Kaskaskia hung with the Illiniwek, without necessarily being Illini, then the Kickapoo aligned with the Sauk and Meskwaki ("Mesquaki"), without being Sauk or Meskwaki, but Miami-confederated.[10] In 1730, the Kickapoo peoples entered a permanent peace with the Illiniwek without joining that confederacy.[11]

Of these nations, the "poueteouatami" (Boodewaadamig) or Potawatomi people are the outliers, not being Miami or Illini but, instead, members of the Three Fires Confederacy, along with the Anishinabe ("Chippewa") and the Ottawa. By 1778, the Potawatomi peoples had established a permanent presence along Indiana's Tippecanoe River.[12] In Harrison's period, the Ottawa of the Three Fires occupied modern-day, lower-peninsula Michigan, extending into northwest Ohio, with the thousand-strong Potawatomi reaching into Indiana along the settler-desired Wabash River, while the populous Anishinabe stretched as far west as Minnesota and as far east as Ontario.[13] Following Michigan's *Keekaukaumeeōāngee* (St. Joseph River) down to the Maumee River, and then following the Maumee into Indiana, the Three Fires were spreading south, until U.S. invasion pushed them back north.[14]

Settler propaganda notwithstanding, it was not warfare but intermarriage that was the most common outcome of migratory mingling. For instance, the Three Fires' Potawatami speaker at the Greenville Treaty talks in 1794 was *Mtamins* ("New Corn"), a Potawatomi adoptee (from the Sauk).[15] *Mihšihkinaahkwa* is presented as Kilatika, although his mother was Mohegan.[16] Similarly, *Tecumseh* might have been recorded as Shawnee, but his mother was actually Muskogee, an important connection facilitating his entrée into southeastern councils.[17] Attempting the same with settlers, the Miami intermarried there too. A captive-cum-adoptee of the Kilatika Miami known as *Apekonit* ("Carrot Top"), William Wells married *Mihšihkinaahkwa's* ("Little Turtle's") daughter, *Manwangopath* ("Sweet Breeze"). Wells became so Kilatika as to have gone out on the war trail with them, although he later returned to settler society. As Indian agent at Fort

Wayne, Wells regularly riled the United States by standing up for the Miami peoples.[18] Intermarriage was a traditional method of quelling strife but its resulting multidimensional identities simply confused the settlers, who preferred slimming all down to one, easily grasped, identity.

Based on ancient, complex spiritual systems, Woodlanders developed advanced, democratic governmental structures based on the gift economy. Each group had its own capital, such as the Wea capital of *Ouiatanon* (near modern-day West Lafayette) or the Kickapoo capital of *Masanne*, which sat across the Wabash River, a little north of *Ouiatanon*, the doubled towns in a twinned relationship.[19] The Miami had their confederated capital at *Kiihkayonki* or *Kekionga*, at modern-day Fort Wayne, Indiana, now situated over *Kekionga*.[20] Similarly, St. Louis displaced old *Cahokia*, capital of the Illini people, as Vincennes displaced the central Piankeshaw town of *Chippecoke*.[21]

All Indigenous systems stood as conscious reflections of the sacred, Twinned Cosmos, consisting of Blood (—) and Breath (|), also indigenously referred to as "Water" and "Air."[22] The Twinship was the most profound organizing principle of Indigenous America, even as monotheism became the most profound organizing principle of Europe. Under the Twinship, "one" (as either — or |) is a fraction (½), with what Westerners see as "two" being the first complete quantity (+). Like all North American Indian groups, the Miami had Blood clan halves (moieties) reflecting the Cosmic Twinship, but Europeans were more intent on displacing the Miami than on recording their culture ethnographically, so that the Miami clan moieties were very little noted, and then, only in a form more garbled than were the national names.[23] Lacking an understanding of the Twinship principle, Western scholars mixed and matched groupings, but unscrambled, the Kickapoo had Prairie-style, doubled moieties (⚌) common to Plains peoples, in the ceremonial Kickapoo Berry (Blood), Eagle (Breath), Raccoon (Blood), and Tree (Breath). The only groupings recorded for the Potawatami are likewise garbled, with the spatial three (Δ), common to national (Breath) governmental councils (Younger, Elder, Firekeeper) recorded as clans (Blood), instead.[24] With the primary settler chronicles as sloppy and half-literate as this, parsing out the original Blood clan and Breath national halves of the Indiana peoples is very challenging today.

North American matriarchy also derives from a Twinship base, with brother-sister linkages typically dominant. Despite the anthropological rumor that Miami clan descent followed the male line, it did not.[25] Until recently Western, male anthropologists mischaracterized matrilineage using masculinized terms, presenting a convoluted descent line through the sister's brother. In the Miami system, mother's brothers were all "uncles," while "daughters" of "uncles" were "mothers." Thus, anthropologists presented the descent of a male youth as "unilateral in the male line through one's mother's brother," but this is just descent through the common mother of both the brother and sister in question.[26] Moreover, all Miami children clung to the mother, the people living matrilocally.[27] This sister-brother parallelism in a matrilocal residence system is a very common matriarchal pattern, which is why old sources recorded that there were "also female chiefs, both of war and of the village."[28]

Governmentally, nations coalesced in large, populous, mutually reinforcing confederacies like the Miami, the Three Fires, and the Illiniwek Confederacies. Consequently, at the 1794 Greenville Treaty council, the Three Fires spoke, one after the other—Ottawa, Anishinabe, and Potawatomi—and were, in return, addressed as a unit by Anthony Wayne.[29] The Twinned Cosmos was also replicated in councils, echoing the legal Twinship of the Iroquois, with doubled "Father" (Breath ‖) and "Mother" (Blood =) halves (⚌) organized into interactive, national (male +) and clan (female +) councils, operating on a gift economy of expanding alliances.[30] In space-related Breath councils, younger "nations" interacted with outsiders, say treaty commissioners, on the advice and consensus of elder "nations," taking time for travel and consultation with elders.[31] Speedy deliberations were regarded as immature and troublesome.

The individual confederacies also entered into UN-style collectives (⚌ ⚌ ⚌). Thus, well before the arrival of the Europeans, the Three Fires Confederacy had entered into a collective with the confederated Miami nations, jointly planting a white poplar as their Tree of Peace to seal the deal.[32] These UN-style collectives could be quite extensive. At contact, for instance, the Iroquois League, or Six Nations Confederacy, had sixty-one affiliated nations.[33] Europeans emphasized the mutual-defense clauses of these collectives, but gifting economics and diplomacy were the primary Indigenous glue.

Although western texts disproportionately emphasize warfare as an Indigenous focus (it was actually a settler focus), Woodlanders preferred to stay out of the way of their enemies. Thus, when the Miami settled briefly at *Meearmeear Wüküegon* ("Fort Miami" at Roche De Bout on the Maumee River), they quickly departed to avoid trouble with the Iroquois League, because it was Seneca land.[34] In 1772, when the Lenape and Mahican moved into southeastern Ohio as a refuge from Philadelphia-area militias, they found the Miami along their Muskingum River lands.[35] Again, no fighting ensued. Instead, at a large council, the Lenape and Mahican recounted to the Miami their traditions of Muskingum environs to such perfection, that the Miami agreed that land was Lenape and vacated the area.[36]

The confederacies primarily existed as extended gifting circles. Ordinarily, the gift economy worked locally, but when something was not available in the local circle—for instance, copper from the Anishinabe of Michigan—the extended circle acquired it.[37] Similarly, white and purple wampum beads, made from whelk or quahog shells found on the eastern Atlantic coast, were obtained by the Anishinabe peoples of the continent's interior. Abalone shell beads, obtainable only from the west coast, showed up in eastern Cherokee beading.[38]

The gift economy was distinct from the exchange economy of the settlers, in that there was no equivalency of value required or implied. The basis was good will, not good deals. It was commonplace for rich groups to give generously to poor groups, who were expected to return the favor once back on their feet. Europeans clearly did not understand this system, typically terming it "bribery" or "charity." They viewed the gifts expected at any council with a jaundiced eye, explaining why Henry Dearborn, secretary of war, instructed Governor Harrison at an 1802 council to give only "medals" (to U.S.-"friendly" Indians) or, better, cold hard cash that could be spent on goods in Vincennes, thus dumping the money back into the settler economy. Harrison was also to wrestle the Piankeshaw, Kickapoo, and Kaskaskia into giving away some of their own annuities to the Sauk.[39]

However heavily ingrained in settler meta-myths as loosely knit hunters and gatherers, Indigenous Woodlanders were large-scale farmers. The extensive acreage under Indigenous cultivation was noted by all early travelers, starting with Jacques Cartier in 1541, explaining why settlers always attacked at harvest time and reported spending days cutting down crops (to starve out the Indians).[40] Thus it was in late August, 1791, that then colonel James Wilkinson destroyed "at least 430 acres of corn" during an attack on the Miami peoples of Indiana.[41] Settlers also scouted Indian farmlands well in advance of moving on them. In June 1795, the United States having just seized Ohio, ensign Thomas Bodley scouted out Indiana. Among other things, Bodley reported that the Potawatomi and Wea peoples, one mile up from the mouth of the Tippecanoe River, had 200 acres under cultivation.[42]

Although the official narrative of governmental America presented—and still presents—its noble intentions of pristine honor toward the Indians, this myth is belied by the facts. Invasion masqueraded as the spread of "civilization" to stateless "savages." Thus, whereas the U.S. Constitution posited Indigenous confederacies as sovereign nations, neither Harrison nor officials in Washington, D.C. seemed to grasp this. Pursuant to the Doctrine of Discovery, U.S. officialdom viewed them, instead, as conquered, disorganized pagans whose lands were forfeit, as advised by President Washington in a 1783 policy letter to Congress.[43] Treaty commissioners in the Old Northwest demonstrably behaved in accordance with this attitude.[44]

The greatest pretense of good will dated to the first Trade and Intercourse Act (1 Stat. 137 [1790]) which, continuing through its multiple iterations into 1834, maintained that the U.S. government would prevent the theft of Indian land and crimes against Indians.[45] In fact, however, any settler could squat on any Indian land, and any squatting settler could commit any crime against any Indian and never be removed, seldom be arrested, never be convicted. As early as 1787, in what became Indiana, Bartelémi Tardiveau, the French trader and translator, calmly recorded that "all" settlers had "an equal interest in establishing the maxim that 'no injury done to an Indian [wa]s punishable.'"[46] The Intercourse Acts cloaked crime with legal fiction.

From 1795 to 1797, the French social critic François-Alexandre-Frédéric, duc de la Rochefoucauld-Liancourt, traveled across the new United States. After reciting the 1796 Intercourse Act, he noted that, although "*sage et juste dans sus dispositions*" (wise and just in its provisions), the statute was "*loin d'être punctuellment éxecutée*" (far from being punctiliously executed). In the western U.S. settlements, he found "*le plus mauvaise espèce de toute l'Amérique et à peu-près du monde entire*" (the very worst sort [of people] in all of America, and very nearly in the whole world). The settlers were there for "*l'avidité*" (greed), looking to sate "*le desire et le projet de les piller*" ([their] desire and intention of pillaging them [the Indians]). "*Les sentimens, et jusque à l'idèe de le honnêteté et de le humanité lui [étaient] inconnu*" (The sentiments and even the idea of honesty and humanity [were] unknown to them).

Disgusted, Rochefoucauld-Liancourt averred that frontier settlers were *"touts des hommes pillards et féroces"* (all looting and ferocious men). Consequently, there were *"ni dénounciteurs, ni témoins, ni jurys, ponr le procès qui devrais être fait à l'habitant qui commettait un délit, ou un crime, contre un Indien"* (neither accusers nor witnesses nor juries in cases that ought to be pressed against a settler who committed an offense, or a crime, against an Indian). He concluded that the settlers, *"sur-tout celui des frontiers, ne crois pas pleu que l'Indien est un homme, que certain colons de Antilles ne croyent qu'un nègre appartient à l'espèce humaine"* (above all, those on the frontier no more believe an Indian to be a man than certain West-Indian planters believe a Negro to belong to the human species).[47]

Harrison essentially shared Rochefoucauld-Liancourt's estimate of the situation but without the moral shock. After detailing examples of wanton acts in an 1801 letter to Henry Dearborn, Governor Harrison jested that "it was not but too evident that a great many of the Inhabitants of the Fronteers consider the murdering of Indians in the highest degree meritorious."[48] Like all territorial governors, Harrison shrugged off such crimes, as though boys would be boys, and nothing could be done to stop them, although governors held the law entirely in their hands. Even when directly ordered by the president to arrest and prosecute murderers, sentencing somehow never materialized, with failures attributed to legal technicalities preventing action.[49] In fact, however, governors did nothing because settlers were achieving governmental goals by eliminating Indians, so that carefully crafted language coddled the commando behaviors.

While Harrison was governor of Indiana Territory in the spring of 1801, for instance, a respected Indian family, including "a woman and some children," was killed for $50 worth of fur and other goods.[50] Although one of the murderers was apprehended in 1802, the locals "rising" against the authorities forced his temporary release. Reapprehended, the culprit broke jail. Moreover, instead of punishing all the "white men" who had not only committed but also boasted of "their exploit," Harrison weaseled them off the hook because the crime might have occurred in Indian, not U.S., territory. He then used this excuse to survey and claim Indian lands. (Settler rumor had it that the Indians later executed the culprits.)[51]

In another instance of October 1802, a settler in a drunken rage with "an Indian in Clarke county" sought out his sleeping adversary and bludgeoned him to death. The murderer was quickly arrested, the evidence against him, incontrovertible. Notwithstanding, when he was put on trial and "proved guilty," the jury "brought in a verdict of 'not guilty' in a few minutes," despite the fact that the murderer was generally despised in town as a disgrace to decency. The verdict came pursuant to a principle repeated like a mantra: "no white man ought in justice to suffer for the murder of an Indian."[52]

As the well-oiled citizenry depleted Indian numbers by murder, U.S. officialdom undercut the Indigenous cultural core by:

- sending in Indian agents and missionaries to disrupt cultural systems;
- establishing "factories" (trading posts) intentionally running up large Indian debts;

- building settler roads over Indigenous roads and then claiming exclusive U.S. rights to them;
- building U.S. forts at and around Indigenous capital cities; and
- deliberately separating confederated nations, interacting with them individually.

Once an area's confederacy was thus softened up, the United States forced concession treaties and, when the Indians showed any sign of organizing opposition to invasion, took military action.

As wedges, first into Indigenous lands were always the Indian agent and the missionary (sometimes, one in the same). Under the 1793 Intercourse Acts, "temporary" Indian agents (made permanent in 1834) were set up as "civilizers" of Indians in the next-eyed lands. Lyman William was appointed on July 14, 1801, as the main, "Temporary" agent for the Northwest Territories, headquartered in Detroit. His orders from Henry Dearborn were to "teach" the Indians "industry," meaning Euro-style, menial work and habits of obeisance to settler authority, and to make them crave the "comfort and convenience in civilized life." The list of work to be imposed forced spinning and weaving on women and farming on men.[53] Clearly, this plan obviated long-standing Indigenous cultural patterns, whereby only women farmed, while men tended the forest.

The Indian subagent appointed and instructed to set up his office in Fort Wayne, Indiana, was William Wells. On March 1, 1793, he received his initial appointment with vague orders to promote "civilization among the friendly Indians," that is, force them into Euro-socioeconomic and religious systems.[54] From 1796 to 1802, Wells went from "Temporary Resident" agent to "Temporary Agent" in 1802 and again in 1804, with explicit orders to build a "factory" (trading post) at Fort Wayne.[55] Unfortunately, as *Apekonit*, Wells's personal history boded ill for him among the profoundly racist settlers of Indiana. Thus, when Wells was thrust together with a crooked missionary sent by the president, all the settler prejudices ginned up at once in a witches' brew, to excoriate the first and support the second.

Obviating the establishment clause of the Constitution, President Thomas Jefferson sent in the lead missionary on a $6,000 grant of federal monies (worth over $120,000 today). Baltimore Quaker William Kirk descended on Fort Wayne in June 1807, with a bevy of submissionaries to set up work on "the Wabash." Understanding, however, that the ultimate plan was a massive transfer of their assets to settler coffers, the Miami peoples of Indiana promptly rejected Kirk and the horse he rode in on.[56] In April 1808, *Tenskwatawa*—the "Shawnee Prophet"—directly articulated the Indigenous analysis: impoverishment was the goal of missionary efforts to "civilize" them. It forced Indian men to become small farmers, thus neatly disempowering both the female farmers and the male forest-keepers. Worse, everyone now had to live in "praying" towns, meaning that they had to purchase goods from settlers instead of producing what they needed.[57] Meanwhile, their land was confiscated as "surplus."

Western texts speculate that Wells deliberately scuttled Kirk's plan to "civilize the Indians," presumably to push himself forward for the missionary job (and the $6,000). Harrison so informed the War Department, although it was *Tenskwatawa*'s resistance that was repudiating Kirk.[58] Wells replied that Kirk was a grifter, spending $3,000 of his $6,000 on illicit purposes immediately as he hit Fort Wayne, while "creating jealousies and sowing the seeds of Discord" among the Indians.[59]

Like all U.S. officials, Harrison indulged the scowling contention that the simple-minded Injuns were necessarily being "controlled" by some "white man" lurking in the woodpile, and if it was not *the Spanish, the French*, THE BRITISH!, then it was a U.S. official.[60] Here, Wells was fingered as the agitator.[61] In his 1803 report, Harrison alleged that Wells and his father-in-law *Mihšihkinaahkwa* had "control entirely" of the Miami, while exercising "considerable influence" over the Potawatomi.[62] Harrison's gripe misleads modern students. *Mihšihkinaahkwa* was not a Miami chief in the way as he is presented in Western texts. He was a Kilatika chief but only a speaker of the Confederacy.[63]

Harrison's spite and bile was wide of his mark. Wells was an Indian agent, and Indians despised them. In 1803, the Miami knew that Wells had served as a scout and then an interpreter for the United States. "[Y]ou all well know that he is a bad man," the Shawnee *Wampomshuwah* ("Alexander McKee") told the Miami, "taking and killing your men, women and children."[64] It was the Potawatomi who beheaded Wells for his failed attempt at evacuating settlers from Fort Dearborn to Fort Wayne in 1812.[65] Certainly, the Potawatomi did not see Wells as their tool. Meantime, *Mihšihkinaahkwa* was the great war chief who had turned back the settlers more than once. If he suffered any disfavor, it was because he had actually invited the original U.S. trading post into Indiana at Fort Wayne, in 1802.[66]

The Miami also hated trading posts without coaching. In 1808, *Tenskwatawa* took on the settler exchange economy foisted on the people through the government's "factories." Promising cheap manufactured goods, the president urged the Indians to "form one large village," while pinky swearing that, *honest*, it was not a ploy to throw them into debt, for it was "not his wish to buy the Indians Land." Nevertheless, said *Tenskwatawa*, the "man at vincennes [Harrison] and the one at Fort Wayne [Wells] and the one at Detroit [William] was always persuading Indians to Sell their Land," becoming "great men by cheeting the Indians."[67]

Tenskwatawa hit the nail on the head. The official purpose of the trading posts was to force land sales. In a letter of February 27, 1803, to Harrison, President Jefferson articulated this twist on trade. The furs and leathers of commerce required Indians to overhunt the land. Knowing this, Jefferson reasoned that the resultant "decrease of game" would force the Indians into peasant-style farming. Once confined to the "culture of a small piece of land," the Indians would "perceive how useless to them" their "extensive forests" were and "be willing to pare them off ... in exchange for necessaries for their farms and their families." Consequently, the United States should "push" its "trading uses" and run "influential individuals run into debt," because desperate Indians became "willing to lop [debts] off by a cession of lands."[68] The process of creating debt peonage has never been more succinctly stated than this.

Having made first entry with missionaries, Indian agents, and trading posts, Indiana settlers began cutting roads, as Harrison noted in a letter of 1802.[69] Despite "pioneer" mythology, settlers were not cutting roads from scratch in a "wilderness" but adapting preexisting Indian roads to their own purposes. Daniel Boone is thus credited with "opening" the 600-mile "Wilderness Road" west through Kentucky into Indiana, whereas he had just renamed the "War Trail of Nations," in settler usage since 1775.[70] The same expropriation was applied to the "Kaskaskia Trace," another Indigenous thoroughfare.[71] It forked, veering either down to the Kaskaskia town of *Tshipkoheēoāngee* (near Vincennes) or moving further west as the "St. Louis Trace," both destinations of high settler interest.[72] In 1778–1779, George Rogers Clark located the "Kaskaskia trace," permanently stamping it U.S. property.[73] Another popular Indigenous thoroughfare into Indiana was the Miami Trail, terminating at *Kekionga*, known to settlers since 1679 as the portage site between the headwaters of the Maumee River at *Kekionga* and *Chippecoke* ("Vincennes") on the lower Wabash River.[74] The Miami Trail was thus followed into Indiana from Ohio by Josiah Harmar in 1790, James Wilkinson in 1791, Arthur St. Clair in 1792, and Anthony Wayne in 1794.[75]

So commonplace was this method of road-establishment that John Gibson, secretary of the Northwest Territories on July 23, 1807, relayed Harrison's orders for old-time settler John Severn to guide Captain William Hargrove to and along a "blind trace," that is, a decayed Indian road, marking a settler road that could "easily be followed without a guide."[76] There were in Indiana, alone, over a dozen, lesser known Indian roads taken over for settler usage as post roads, such as the "Buffalo trace" from Fort Recovery (Fort Winchester), Ohio, to Vincennes.[77] In this way, all major Indian routes went "postal," and as early as 1802, Harrison directly connected new roads to the importation of settlers.[78]

U.S. postal roads (easily convertible to military purposes) were constructed almost immediately as Indiana became a territory. By 1800, one ran from northwestern Kentucky at the Ohio River to Fort Massac (near modern-day Metropolis, Illinois).[79] In November 1803, mail-carrying expenses were figured over a post road to Fort Massac.[80] In August 1801, Congress approved a road over the old Kaskaskia trace, from Vincennes through Kaskaskia to Cahokia (then, eight miles outside of St. Louis).[81] In February 1805, President Thomas Jefferson received the postmaster general's detailed study of the fastest and best highway placements, from Washington, D.C. to "St. Lewis," Detroit, and New Orleans.[82] Unsurprisingly, in May 1806, the Gallatin authorized building:[83]

1. a road from St. Louis through Vincennes and on to Dayton, Ohio (on August 14, adjusted to Cincinnati);
2. a road from Kaskaskia to Vincennes, intersecting the first road;
3. a fork from the first road, running west of the Indian boundary down to the "North bend on the Ohio River";

4. another fork from the first road, running from Vincennes to the falls of the Ohio River; and
5. a road from Kaskaskia to Lexington, Kentucky.

All these roads cut directly into and through Miami territory. It belatedly occurred to someone that the Miami might object to them, so provisos were added to the original order in 1806 to obtain Indian visas, yet the surveyor was to "Explore the country on both sides of the present Indian boundary line," without venturing too conspicuously into Indian territory.[84]

The public also got into the act, requesting post roads in 1804 and 1806, but not successfully until 1807, when petitioners pointed out that Forts Wayne and Dearborn (Chicago) included garrisons, yet no letter delivery system. Thus, "publick dispatches of great importance" were sometimes left in limbo for months, with the potential "injury" to the public "easily foreseen by the most superficial observer." The remedy was to connect the nearest post office in Ohio with one to be established in Fort Wayne, with correspondence for Fort Dearborn sent through Fort Wayne.[85] Because no war, with either the Miami or the British, was afoot in 1807, the implied national security concerns here bespeak a settler mindset of perpetual hostilities.

Miami permission for the U.S. roadbuilding turned out not to be so easily procured as Harrison had claimed in 1802.[86] The Miami balked, especially, at the proposed "stations" every twenty-five or thirty miles (soon morphing into a tavern every ten miles) from Louisville through Vincennes to St. Louis.[87] As convivial as taverns may sound, they formed public meetinghouses, military headquarters, and popular muster points for militias.[88] Militia drinking got so predictably out of hand, that the 1806 Indiana Act Regulating Militias was amended in 1810 to prohibit "ardent spirits or strong waters" within two miles of the muster—unless a regular tavern on the muster grounds was selling the booze![89] This last provision might seem self-defeating, but taverns were lucrative perquisites granted to friends of Harrison like Spier Spencer, who were not only officers but also proprietors of the local taverns.[90]

The history of illegal squatting somehow turning into land ownership had led the Miami to conclude that the U.S. roadbuilding existed because the settlers had "resolved to destroy" the Miami, so as to "take possession of their lands," as chiefs frankly informed Harrison in 1802. Harrison brushed off this fear as British propaganda working on weak minds.[91] Dearborn's response to the allegation was to send Indian agents onto Miami land as "superintendents," to act as spies, cultural disrupters, and economic manipulators, placed directly under Harrison's control.[92] Dearborn left unexplored by what right the United States legally supervised the internal affairs of a sovereign state, but perhaps it was the effect of racism working on weak minds.

On the plea of stopping squatters from selling lands they did not own, in 1802, Harrison opened communications with the secretary of state and Congress on the matter of Who Owned the Land.[93] This seemed not to be the Miami, however, for in a succeeding letter to Dearborn, Harrison presented the problem as the need for settler security from Indian attack on the roads being cut through "the

Territory."[94] However Harrison obviated the fact of Indian ownership, the Indians were having none of it. On February 23, 1802, Dearborn wrote Harrison, annoyed that the Lenape and Shawnee were complaining "loudly" of settlers "killing" their game and stealing their horses.[95] By 1807, the Indians were forcefully stopping settlers like the Larkins family from traveling through their country, killing Larkins while taking the wife and five children captive. Harrison ordered a militia patrol of "the old Indian trace," but his treaty relations with the Lenape on the line, he did not demand release of the prisoners.[96] Given such incidents, a burning question around roads became whether Indians were "punishable" by settlers for a "murder committed on their own lands."[97] Specious as this question may seem given national sovereignty, it was central to U.S. roadbuilding, because all of the roads ran smack through Miami lands. These roads trucked in increasing numbers of settlers (and their slaves) by the tens of thousands (see Table 2.1).

Table 2.1   Population of Indiana Territory/State (1657–1825)

Year	Settlers	Africans	Miami[a]	Total by Years	
				Settlers	Indians
1657–1658	<50	<20	>24,000	<70	>24,000
1700			16,000		16,000
1720			6,400		6,400
1788	12,205[b]		5,160	12,205[b]	5,160
1800	2,375[c]	163[c]	≅1,000	2,538[c]	≅1,000
1810	23,890	630[e]		24,520	
1815	63,897[d]		1,700	63,897[d]	1,700
1817			1,400		1,400
1820–1825	147,718	1,420[e]	1,400	149,138	1,400

[a] The Miami counts include the Wea, Piankashaw, Eel River, Pepikokia, Kickapoo, Kaskaskia, Mascouten, Uomamik, as well as the Miami, proper, at Kekionga (Fort Wayne), as counted up by missionaries, traders, and other Western interlopers. The usual count was by "warriors," a settler category that assumed that every male between fifteen and fifty was a soldier. The "warrior" population was then counted as one- fourth of the total population, so that multiplying the "warrior" count by four yielded the whole population. All Indian population statistics are official settler guesstimates.

[b] This is the total of settlers entering the Northwest Territories as a whole.

[c] Indiana Territory included Illinois. This count separates Indiana from Illinois, as per John Gibson, secretary of the territory. Total for the whole territory was 5,641.

[d] Undifferentiated as to racial status.

[e] Free and slave.

Table 2.1 shows the shrinkage of the Miami population in tandem with the growth of the settler population.

Sources: Birbeck, 1906 162; *Executive Journal, Indiana*, 1900, 83; Jablow, 1974, 25; Krzywicki, 1934, 461; Thornbrough, 1957, vol. 19, no. 3, 85–86.

Simultaneous with roadcutting was fort building. Typically, forts were built at or near Indian towns and not infrequently as retreads of prior forts. The French Fort Ouiatenon sat at the Wea Miami capital of *Ouiatenon*, 1719–1720, while in 1702 and again in 1730–1732, the French put Fort Vincennes at the Piankeshaw capital of *Chippecoke*.[98] Under *Pontiac*'s strict "no forts" policy of 1763, Fort *Ouiatenon* was burned to the ground, but the British built Fort Sackville at the much-abused *Chippecoke* in 1777. The Americans seized Sackville during the Revolution, rechristening it Fort Vincennes. Thereafter, it became Fort Knox, used as a staging ground against *Tecumseh*.[99] The French set up Fort Miami at *Kekionga* in 1715, so that in 1794, Anthony Wayne simply segued it into Fort Wayne.[100] As settlers rushed west to the Potawatomi land of *Checago*, they erected Fort Dearborn in 1803 at Chicago.[101]

By 1801, the Northwest Territory was getting up eight forts in the Old Northwest.[102] By 1803–1804, the list had grown in sophistication and specifics.[103] Additional forts were erected over the next few years. Clearly, the settlers were gearing up for a fight well in advance of the War of 1812.[104] By the outbreak of the Tecumseh War in 1811, the Indiana Territory was well supplied with at least thirty forts, from major U.S. Army stations to settler militia posts (see Table 2.2). To these were added any number of ad hoc settler militia forts, many poorly recorded or but briefly mentioned, often with little information concerning them now known.[105]

With U.S. roads, army posts, trading posts, Indian agencies, and missions boxing in the Miami militarily, Harrison felt that the advantage was now his, so he began pressing in 1802 for land-concession treaties. Historian Robert Owens is onto something in attributing Harrison's idea of treaty making to having observed Anthony Wayne's Greenville Treaty negotiations in 1794.[106] Probably, because the Greenville Treaty transferred 11,808,409 acres from the Ohio Indians to the settlers, it became the standing model for U.S.–Indian land relations, from 1795 to 1871.[107] Harrison outdid his mentor. All told in six years, Harrison had helped the United States to almost 33,400,000 acres of confederated Miami and Potawatomi, and Sauk and Meskwaki land. (See Table 2.3.)

Of course, this land was immediately available to speculators like Harrison. While still a territorial representative, Harrison had altered the rules of the game to favor speculators. Originally, individuals had to purchase public lands at 4,000 acres a crack, but Harrison personally forced through a law allowing sales by whole section (640 acres) or half-section (320 acres).[108] In spring, 1800, the Harrison Land Act was passed and signed, and settlers could purchase 320 acres of land in the Northwest Territories for $2 per acre.[109] In 1804, an amendment shaved that again to 160 acres.[110] Importantly, the Harrison Land Act initialized the sale of public land on credit, with one-fourth down and the balance to have been paid off in four years.[111] This made the land eminently affordable, and sales, quick and easy.

Throughout his terms as governor, Harrison speculated like mad, paying "*hush money*" to some while threatening the incorruptible, stimulating complaints to the U.S. government.[112] In 1810, U.S. surveyor Nathaniel Ewing complained bitterly

Table 2.2 Forts of the Old Northwest Heading into the Tecumseh War of 1811

Dates	Fort Name	Location	Usage	Notes
1794–1815	Fort Adams	Rockville, Ohio	Supply depot, blockhouses	Rebuilt in 1812
1790–1814	Fort Amanda	Auglaize River, near St. Mary's, Ohio	Supply depot and boat building	Unnamed post 1790–1794, built atop old Ottawa town; named in 1812 rebuild
1812–1813	Fort Ball	Tiffin, Ohio	Supply depot, 500 men possible	Plagued by disease over winter of 1813; many desertions
1784–1816	Fort Barbee	St. Mary's, Ohio	Supply depot and blockhouse	Rebuilt 1812
1804–1826	Fort Belle Fontaine	Across MI River from Alton, Illinois, 15 mi. from St. Louis	Main fortification, Louisiana Territory	Built on swampy ground; in 1810, relocated to Belle Mont
1811	Fort Boyd	At mouth of Vermilion River, Indiana Territory	Blockhouse	Burned by U.S. troops upon retreat, weeks after building
1811	Fort Branch	Gibson County, Indiana Territory	Blockhouse	Settler militia fort
1794–1815	Fort Brown	At mouth of Little Auglaize River, Ohio	Supply depot guarded route	Rebuilt for War of 1812
1811	Fort Bruce	Bruceville, Indiana Territory	Settler fortification	Built by militia major William Bruce
1804–1815	Fort Cuivre Peoria, Illinois	Near modern-day Peoria	Settler blockhouses	Built by Cuivre Settlement militia
1803–1836	Fort Dearborn	Chicago, Illinois Territory	Blockhouses, barracks	Potawatomis burned, 1812

Dates	Name	Location	Type	Notes
1801–1826	Fort Detroit	Detroit, Michigan Territory	Main fortification	Surrendered to British, 1812; reauthorized by the United States in 1801
1811–1818	Half-Way Fort	Half-way between Forts Harrison and Knox, Indiana Territory	Blockhouses, bastions, barracks	Also called "Fort Gill"; a gill was a quarter of a pint of liquor, the amount rationed to soldiers
1811–1818	Fort Harrison	Terre Haute, Indiana Territory	Main fortification	Staging ground, Battle of Tippecanoe, 1811
1791–1818	Fort Jefferson	Modern-day Fort Jefferson, Ohio	Blockhouse	Settler Militia rebuild, 1810
1794–1814	Fort Jennings	Modern-day Fort Jennings, Ohio	Blockhouse	Rebuilt for War of 1812
1759–1815	Fort Kaskaskia	Near modern-day Chester, Illinois	Main fortification	French built, 1759; British till 1778; 1803, U.S. rebuilt; 1807, militia use; abandoned After War of 1812
1787–1816	Fort Knox I & II	Vincennes, Indiana Territory	Main fortification	Rebuilt 1811 nearby first fort
1803–1815	Fort Ledgerwood	Modern-day Carlisle, Indiana	Blockhouse	Settler militia fort, used in War of 1812
1769–1815	Fort Loramie Loramie, Ohio	Modern-day Loramie, Ohio	Supply depot	French trading post; rebuilt as U.S. fort 1795 and 1812

(continued)

Table 2.2 (Continued)

Dates	Fort Name	Usage	Location	Notes
1796–1812	Fort Mackinac	Main fortification	Michilimackinac, Michigan Territory	Recommissioned by the United States in 1801; fell two weeks into War of 1812
1808–1813	Fort Madison	Main fortification	Modern-day Fort Madison, Iowa	U.S. Army, Control point for Louisiana Territory
1794–1814	Fort Massac	Fortification	Near modern-day Metropolis, Illinois	The United States reauthorized in 1801; original French fort, 1750
1793–1841	Fort Piqua	Supply depot	A few miles north of modern-day Piqua, Ohio	By 1811, used as Indian agency headquarters
1811	Fort Robb	Blockhouse	Gibson County, Indiana Territory	Settler militia fort
1811–1816	Fort Turman	Fortification	Terre Haute, Indiana Territory	Settler militia fort
1805–1815	Fort Vallonia	Blockhouse	Modern-day Vallonia, Indiana	Settler militia fort; rebuilt in 1810
1794–1819	Fort Wayne	Main fortification	Fort Wayne, Indiana Territory	Built by Wayne, reauthorized by the United States in 1801
1794–1815	Fort Winchester	Supply depot	Modern-day Defiance, Ohio	Old Fort Defiance, rebuilt 1812 as Fort Winchester

| 1807–1894 | Newport Barracks | Modern-day Newport, Kentucky | Barracks | Across Ohio River from Cincinnati; replaced Fort Washington at Cincinnati; 1811 U.S. staging grounds |

Table 2.2 shows the primary forts extant in the United States at the opening of the Tecumseh War and their locations.

Sources: **Fort Adams**, Carter, 1934–1975, vol. 7, 94; Slocum, 1905, vol. 7, 94; Brown, 1875, 27; Tucker, 2014, vol. 1, 139, 206, 996; **Fort Aikman**, Allison, 1896, 172; **Fort Amanda**, Johnson and Schneider, 2017; McAfee, 1816/1919, 170; Slocum, 1905, 28, 289; **Fort Ball**, McAfee, 1816/1919, 382; Meek, 1909, 96; Gilpin, 2012, 157; Brown, 1875, 26–27; **Fort Barbee**, McAfee, 1816/1919, 157, 170; **Fort Belle Fontaine**, Buckley, 2002, 29–30; **Fort Boyd**, Gilpin, 2012, 14–15, 19; Allison, 1986, 164, 320; Payette, 2010, "American Forts, East: Indiana"; **Fort Branch**, Allison, 1986, 172, 320; **Fort Brown**, Slocum, 1905, 28, 502; Gilpin, 2012, 178; **Fort Bruce**, Allison, 1986, 319; Esarey, 1922, vol. 3, 219; Allison, 1986, 319; **Fort Cuivre**, Carter, 1934–1975, Bruff to Wilkinson, vol. 13, letter 9/29/1804, 57; **Fort Dearborn**, Carter, 1934–1975, vol. 7, letter 10/1/1807, note 10, 115; "Petition to the Postmaster General from the Residents of Fort Wayne," 477; Jouett to Secretary of War, letter 12/1/1807, 496; McAfee, 1816/1919, 113–16; Tucker, 2014, vol. 1, 223; Brown, 1875, 9; **Fort Detroit**, McAfee, 1816/1919, 71–72, 105; Tucker, 2014, vol. 1, 224; ASPMA, 1832–1861, Dearborn to Congress, Document No. 46, vol. 1, Attachment B, 12/23/1801, 156; **Half-Way Fort**, Payette, "American Forts, East: Indiana," 2010; **Fort Harrison**, Carter, 1934–1975, Secretary of War to Harrison, vol. 8, letter 9/18/1811, 133–34; Brown, 1875, 7–8; Tucker, 2014, *Encyclopedia of the Wars*, vol. 1, 227–28; **Fort Jefferson**, Wilson, 1914, vol. 1, 579; **Fort Jennings**, McAfee, 1816/1919, 157, 163; Slocum, 1905, 284; **Fort Kaskaskia**, as U.S. rebuilt, Carter, 1934–1975, Dearborn to Stoddard, vol. 7, letter 2/19/1803, 85–86; Hauser, 2000, 66–68; **Fort Knox I and II**, Carter, 1934–1975, Secretary of War to Lyon, vol. 7, letter 4/4/1803, note 13, 117; Tucker, 2014, vol. 1, 229; ASPMA, 1832–1861, Document No. 46, as "Fort Vincennes," vol. 1, 156; Smith, 1903, 61–68; as Fort Knox I, II, and III, Allison, 1986, 87–90 passim, 318; **Fort Ledgerwood**, Sullivan County Historical Society, 1884, 470, 636; Payette, 2010, "American Forts, East: Indiana"; **Fort Loramie**, Hurt, 1996, 207–9; Woehrmann, 1971, vol. 24, 232; Brown, 1875, as "Fort Laramie," 27; **Fort Mackinac**, Slocum, 1905, 272; Tucker, 2014, vol. 1, 223; ASPMA, 1832–1861, Document No. 46, as "Michilimackinac," vol. 1, 156; Brown, 1875, 6; **Fort Madison**, Jackson, 1966, 1–62; Jung, 2016, 201–33; **Fort Massac**, Carter, 1934–1975, "Petition to Congress by Inhabitants of Fort Massac," vol. 7, 254–56; Slocum, 1905, 183, 342; McAfee, 1816/1919, 270; ASPMA, 1832–1861, Document No. 46, vol. 1, 156; **Fort Piqua**, Slocum, 1905, 380, 388; Woehrmann, 1971, 232; **Fort Robb**, Allison, 1986, 172, 310; **Fort Turman**, Goodrich and Tuttle, 1875, 399–400; Brown, 1875, 28; Sullivan County Historical Society, 1884, 808; **Fort Vallonia**, Allison, 1986, 243–45, 249, 254, 318; Gilpin, 2012, 196–97; The Federal Writers' Project, 2014, 369; **Fort Wayne**, Tucker, 2014, vol. 1, 237–38; Brown, 1875, 13; ASPMA, 1832–1861, Document No. 46, vol. 1, 156; **Fort Winchester**, Carter, 1934–1975, Petition to Congress of the Democratic Republicans of Wayne County, as "Fort Defiance," vol. 7, letter 12/6/1804, 241; McAfee, 1816/1919, 170; Brown, 1875, as "Fort Defiance," 13–14; Gilpin, 2012, 155, 157; Slocum, 1905, 476; **Newport Barracks**, ASPMA, 1832–1861, Document No. 46, as "Fort Washington," vol. 1, 156; Tucker, 2014, *Encyclopedia of the Wars*, vol. 1, 237; Thomas, 1992, "Newport Barracks," 680.

Table 2.3 Treaties between the United States and Indian Nations of Ohio, Indiana, Illinois, and Wisconsin (1795–1809)

Date	Treaty Title[a]	Nations	Ceded Acres	U.S. Acquisitions	Sale in Dollar ($)	Plus Annual Annuity
8/20/1795	Greenville Treaty (Anthony Wayne)	Wyandot, Lenape, Shawnee, Ottawa, Chippewa, Miami, Potawatomi, Kilatika, Wea, Kickapoo Piankeshaw, Kaskaskia	11,808,409	902 miles various portages; British army posts at Detroit, Chicago, and Michilimackinac plus surrounding land; Fort Vincennes, Indiana; Fort Massac, Illinois; Mackinaw and "De Bois" (Bois Blanc) Islands in Lake Michigan; 150,000 acres in Illinois to George Rogers Clark *et al.*	$20,000	$9,500
6/7/1803	First Treaty of Fort Wayne (William Henry Harrison)	Lenape, Shawnee, Potawatomi, Kilatika, Wea, Kickapoo, Piankeshaw, Kaskaskia	2,038,400	Fort Vincennes and adjacent land; 42 miles at salt springs, Ohio and Wabash Rivers; road, Vincennes to Kaskaskia, Indiana; road, Vincennes to Clarksville, Indiana	0	150 bushels salt plus right to locate the two roads[b]
8/7/1803	Treaty with the Eel River, etc. (William Henry Harrison)	Kilatika, Wyandot, Piankeshaw Kaskaskia, "Kickapoo through their Kilatika Representatives"	2,038,400[b]	Two road lines set, as per first Treaty of Fort Wayne)	0	0

Date	Treaty	Tribes	Acres	Price	Purpose	Terms
8/13/1803	Treaty with the Kaskaskia (First "Treaty of Vincennes") (William Henry Harrison)	Kaskaskia, Cahokia, Michigami	8,911,850	$580.00	Fix Kaskaskia boundaries; right of United States to distribute annuity among select families and "suitable sum for the great chief"	$1,000 in cash or goods; 100 acres for chief with house and fencing provided; 1,280 acres reserved for living; first load of goods delivered free of charge; $100/year for seven years for Catholic priest
8/18/1804	Treaty with the Delawares (William Henry Harrison) DISPUTED	Lenape (Delawares)	1,910,717	$800	Road from Vincennes to Falls of Ohio River; all land between Ohio and White Rivers; return of (allegedly) stolen horses; road between Vincennes and "Clark's Tract"	$100 for Catholic priest plus $300 to build church; debt forgiveness; $300 for ten years plus one time $400 in implements and animals; United States to pressure Piankeshaw to recognize Lenape right to Miami land
8/27/1804	Treaty with the Piankeshaw (John Gibson)	Piankeshaw	Not specified	$700	Land for road from Vincennes to Falls of Ohio River	$200 for ten years in goods, money, provisions, or animals
11/3/1804	Treaty of St. Louis (William Henry Harrison)	Sauk, Fox	14,803,520	$2,234.50	22 miles for fort at Wisconsin River and safe passage for U.S. personnel	$600/Sauk; $400/Fox in goods, animals, and implements
8/21/1805	Treaty of Grouseland (William Henry Harrison)	Lenapes, Potawatomi, Miami, Kilatika, Wea, Piankeshaw	1,910,717[c]	$4,000.00	Renegotiated the disputed 8/18/1804 "Treaty with the Delawares," as Miami land on which Lenapes were guests, not proprietors	$600/Miamis; $250/ Kilatika; $250/Wea; $500/ Potawatomi for ten years only

(continued)

Table 2.3 (Continued)

Date	Treaty Titlea	Nations	Ceded Acres	U.S. Acquisitions	Sale in Dollar ($)	Plus Annual Annuity
12/30/1805	Second Treaty with the Piankeshaw (William Henry Harrison)	Piankeshaw	2,676,921[d]	Land between Wabash River and Kaskaskia land, Vincennes, and ceded Kaskaskia land	$1,100.00	$300; United States reserved right to distribute among individuals, at will;1,280 acres to Piankeshaw reserved for living and hunting
9/30/1809	Second Treaty of Fort Wayne (William Henry Harrison)	Miami, Kilatika Lenape, Potawatomi	2,900,000	"Supplementary" renegotiation of Treaty of Grouseland	0	$500 supplemental to Miami in animals for three years; plus a permanent addition of $200/year to Miami; $100/year to Wea; and $100/year to Kilatika if they cajoled the Kickapoo into accepting Article 9 of the Treaty of Grouseland
9/30/1809 (Actual signing date 10/5/1809	Supplementary Treaty with the Miami, etc.	Miami, Kilatika, Wea	2,900,000[e]	"Supplementary" additions to Second Treaty of Fort Wayne	0	Additional $500 in domestic animals for two years plus an "armoree" for Indian use at Ft. Wayne; if they cajoled the Kickapoo to confirm Article 9 of the Fort Wayne Treaty, a permanent, extra $200 to the Miami and $100 to Wea and Kilatika

Date	Treaty title[a]	Tribe	Acreage	Terms	Annuity	Additional
10/26/1809	Treaty with the Wea (William Henry Harrison)	Wea	2,900,000[e]	Wea assent to "Supplementary" renegotiation of Treaty of Grouseland	$1,500	$300 supplemental to Wea plus permanent addition of $100/year if they cajoled the Kickapoo into accepting Article 9 of the Treaty of Grouseland
12/9/1809	Treaty with the Kickapoos (William Henry Harrison)	Kickapoo	138,240	(1) Ratified Article 9 of the Treaty of Grouseland; (2) Additional land cession	$800	(1) Permanent additional annuity of $400 in goods; (2) one time $100 plus $700 in goods

[a] Standard, abbreviated Treaty Titles.

[b] Acreage already ceded in the first Treaty of Fort Wayne.

[c] Land "ceded" in disputed Treaty with the Delaware.

[d] Acreage number recorded in Monnette. Bateman et al. recorded acreage as 2,676,150.

[e] Land ceded in second Treaty of Fort Wayne.

Table 2.2 lists the eleven treaties orchestrated by William Henry Harrison between 1803 and 1809, leading into the Tecumseh's War. Although Harrison did not lead the Greenville Treaty negotiations, he was Anthony Wayne's aide-de-camp and learned his approaches to U.S.-Indian treaty making from that experience.

Sources: For treaties: Kappler, 1904, vol. 2, Treaty of Greenville, 39–45; (1st) Treaty of Fort Wayne, 63–64; Treaty with Eel River, etc., 66; Treaty with the Kaskaskia, 67–68; (1st) Treaty of Vincennes, 70–72; Treaty of St. Louis, 74–77; Treaty with the Piankeshaw, 72–73; Treaty of Grouseland, 80–82; (2nd) Treaty of Vincennes, 89; Treaty of Fort Wayne, 103; Treaty with the Weas, 103–4; Treaty with the Kickapoo, 105; ASPIA, 1832, vol. 1, Greenville Treaty, No. 69, 562–63; (1st) Treaty of Fort Wayne, No. 104, 688; Treaty with Eel River, etc., No. 104, 688; Treaty with the Kaskaskias, No. 104, 687; Treaty of Grouseland, No. 108, 696–97 and No. 126, 761; (2nd) Treaty of Vincennes, No. 112, 704–5; Treaty of Fort Wayne, No. 126, 761–62; Supplemental Treaty with the Miami, Kilatika, and Wea, No. 126, 762; Treaty with the Weas, No. 126, 762; Treaty with the Kickapoos, No. 127, 762–63; for acreages: Bateman et al., 1916, vol. 1, 294–95; Monette, 1846, vol. 2, notes 1–11, 521–22.

of his shady dealings to Secretary of the Treasury Albert Gallatin, noting that Harrison was deeply in debt, flailing to stay afloat and retaliating against Ewing's having challenged his speculations.[113] The U.S. representative from Indiana Territory Jonathan Jennings declared himself "a foe to all intriguing and speculating men in office," in which category he pointedly included Harrison. Publishing a very specific list of detailed complaints about Harrison's swindles, Jennings fought unsuccessfully against Harrison's reappointment as governor in 1809.[114] Harrison's scams against fellow settlers paled in comparison with his scams against Indians, however.

Having been at Wayne's side throughout the Greenville Treaty council, Harrison absorbed all of Wayne's tricks, using them in his own treaties between 1803 and 1809. Wayne's first dirty trick had been to include as signatories two nations, the Piankeshaw and the Kaskaskia, that had never been present, a fact attested to by Harrison, himself, in 1802 and 1803.[115] In 1974, after examining the handwritten Greenville Treaty for the Indian Claims Commission, David Bond Stout concluded that the Piankeshaw and Kaskaskia were most likely scrawled in after the document was signed.[116] Wayne, himself, mentioned that he had altered the treaty text after its signing.[117]

A second, commonly used dirty trick was to claim that anyone showing up was a duly anointed speaker of his nation, as Wayne did at Greenville. First, Wayne anointed a Kickapoo as the Kaskaskia speaker, despite having no conceivable right, this side of racist ideology, to appoint negotiators, let alone, for a nation not their own. This did not stop Wayne from also appointing a Wea to speak for the Piankeshaw.[118] A third dirty trick was to distribute alcohol during the negotiations to befuddle the Indian negotiators, as Robert Owens has shown that Wayne did.[119] By contrast, simultaneously with these negotiations, Wayne issued order after order to keep liquor out of the hands of his own soldiers.[120]

A fourth dirty trick Wayne employed was to lie outright. Wayne presented the Jay Treaty between Great Britain and the United States to the Indian counselors as a *fait accompli*, which it most certainly was not and, at the time Wayne did this, looked as if it might never be. Notwithstanding, to impress upon the Indians the futility of looking to Great Britain for aid, Wayne read aloud to the delegates proposed articles one and two, calling for the destruction of British forts of Detroit, Niagara, St. Clair (Michigan), and Michilimackinac (subsequently re-established).[121] Even once a partial version of the highly contentious Jay Treaty had been begrudgingly signed by the United States in 1796, it favored Great Britain.[122] Clearly, the withdrawal of the British was hardly the settled matter that, as a negotiating tactic, Wayne presented it to have been at Greenville.

The final dirty trick employed by Wayne was the threat of U.S. violence, should the Indian nations not agree to his terms. Although Wayne was less blatant about it than had been the commissioners at earlier coerced treaties, it was painfully obvious that attacks would follow, should the treaty not be accepted.[123] In fact, this was the only reason that *Tarhe* ("The Crane," Wyandot), the primary leader of the peace faction at Greenville, had agreed to dicker. Had the U.S. Army not been lurking in the background as a cudgel, it is highly doubtful that Wayne could have secured the treaty. It should not escape remark, although it almost always does, that all Indian Affairs were handled through the U.S. Department of War (now Defense), not the U.S. Department of State, as with all other foreign relations.

Harrison absorbed all of Wayne's ploys, using them in negotiating his own treaties. Jefferson even recommended Wayne's old trick of naming, willy-nilly, this or that "chief" as the proprietor of the land in play, regardless of his actual national status.[124] Harrison knowingly misrepresented facts of who had rights over which land. Treaty minutes also show him distributing drink at sticky points in the talks. In a variation on threats, Harrison "bullied or bribed" selected, malleable chiefs into going along with a deal, while buying land from people unconnected to the land in question. He threatened to withhold annuities due, unless reluctant chiefs played ball.[125] By such means, between 1803 and 1809, counting the Wea "supplement" of 1809, Harrison's tricks resulted in twelve treaties for Indiana land, as summarized in Table 2.3, Treaties between the United States and Indian Nations of Ohio, Indiana, Illinois, and Wisconsin. Collectively, these treaties led the Miami peoples into the Tecumseh War in 1811, demonstrating that the War of 1812 was more about Indian land seizure than about British impressment of sailors.

In close cahoots with Jefferson, Harrison received his secret marching orders in a "sacredly" confidential letter of February 27, 1803, touching off his treaty-making success with Jefferson's "unofficial and private" plan of action. Even to his co-conspirator, Jefferson felt compelled to preface his tactical advice with the cant of "perpetual peace with the Indians." Fine words out of the way, Jefferson described a diabolically sequential method of dispossessing the Indians of their lands, and even their lives, should they object. Starting from the inaccurate premise that Indians were hunters, Jefferson proposed to whittle down Indians lands till the only option was small-scale, yeoman farming, the better to force transfers of their "extensive forests" to the settlers. To accomplish this, federal trading posts would sell items to the Indians cheaply, to drive U.S. competitors out of business but mostly to run up Indian debt to be paid off in land, while the influx of immigrants would either encourage assimilation or force the Indians west of the Mississippi River.[126]

Moreover, fear was to be a tool. U.S. "strength" against Indian "weakness" was "now so visible," said the president, that the Indians "must see" that the United States had "only to shut [its] hand to crush them," thereby showing that settler "liberality" came from "motives of pure humanity," or, in other words, that settlers could kill them all at will. The cost of any nation's resistance to all this benevolence called for the immediate seizure of that nation's land followed by forced removal to the west. Once the Mississippi River was overrun by the United States, the land could be successively claimed by first picking off the weakest and smallest nations, buying them out. The purchases would circumscribe the boundaries of the large nations, progressively hemming them in, presumably to be picked off one-by-one, as he suggested that Harrison do in Indiana Territory with the Kaskaskia, Potawatomi, and Kickapoo. Closing by reiterating that his letter was "private and friendly" and not to "control" anything coming through "official channels," Jefferson cautioned Harrison to keep the letter to himself, recognizing "how improper" it would be to reveal its contents to the Indians.[127] Jefferson's consciousness of anything but "motives of pure humanity" is palpable in this final admonition.

Harrison followed Jefferson's plan to the letter.

Jefferson's nomination of Harrison as a treaty commissioner did not come till 1803, but that did not stop Harrison from opening negotiations for his first Treaty of Fort Wayne in 1801.[128] This treaty came partly because the Kickapoo and Piankeshaw had not actually treated at Greenville but more because of a tasty salt spring in their possession, "perhaps the very best ... from the Alleghany Mountains to the Mississippi."[129] As such, it was craved by the settlers, who used massive quantities of salt as their only food preservative.[130] The Piankeshaw openly worried that any boundary was the opening salvo for a land grab, so they refused to go to Vincennes as ordered in December 1801, with the Kilatika chief *Hibou* (also, *Meshingomesia, Ozandiah,* "Owl") preventing another meeting in 1802.[131]

In February 1802, Dearborn handed Harrison a gift: on February 10, Lenape ("Delaware") and some Shawnee delegates were in Washington, D.C., complaining "loudly" about wild, lawless settlers.[132] Dearborn asserted that they requested Harrison to arrange a lessee for the salt spring that was apparently occasioning the squatting. They also, said Dearborn, wished for a border to be drawn to demarcate their land, thoroughly, and to make land grants to their interpreters (this last item sounds fairly fishy).[133] In a letter to Jefferson dated January 17, 1803, Dearborn also claimed that they had offered to deed over the salt mine, in exchange for annuities.[134]

There was a small problem with this plan. The Lenape had no land rights in Indiana. The Miami had loaned a tract of White River land to some landless Lenape converts in February 1802, with the loan mysteriously transmuting into a "grant" in U.S. papers.[135] (Thomas Jefferson testified that he had been personally informed by *Aupaumut* and *Mihšihkinaahkwa* that the Miami had permanently granted land, so long as the Lenape never tried to "alienate" it.[136]) On March 25, 1802, Harrison let Dearborn know that the Lenape and the Shawnee cadre there had no right either to lease the spring or to cede the land. Instead of treating with the Miami groups for a lease to a private company, which would jack up prices to locals while returning nothing to the government, Harrison proposed having the Miami cede the land, outright, to the United States.[137] By April 23, Dearborn gave Harrison the go-ahead to suspend the extant lease on the salt spring to explore the cession to "public land."[138] By June 17, seeing that the U.S. government and the Illinois and Wabash Company were in a proprietary tussle over the deed, Dearborn sent in a surveyor.[139] How any of this would calm Miami fears was left unstated.

On August 12, 1802, Jefferson informed Dearborn that Harrison planned "easily" to acquire the "French grant" to Vincennes and environs (where the salt lick was), advising Dearborn "to leave matters very much" to Harrison's discretion.[140] This "French grant" became a major bone of contention, for the Miami solemnly maintained that no such grant had ever been made.[141] Notwithstanding, also on August 12, Harrison summoned Kaskaskia, Kickapoo, Wea, Kilatika, Piankeshaw, and Potawatomi speakers to Vincennes, ostensibly to reassure them of his goodwill but actually to force a land treaty, including the salt spring. Those who came did not show till September 12, tardiness being a Woodlands sign of displeasure, leaving Harrison to open talks on the September 17 with a scowl. He pretended to "relinquish all claim to lands" around Vincennes, even as he laid out the boundaries of the land that he intended to take, dangling a bribe to attendees while warning them away from war.[142]

The speakers countered that they had expected land usurpation to be on the table, but they "earnestly besought" Harrison not to demand the cession. The Lenape war chief, *Buckongehelas*, dressed Harrison down "with vehemence" for land grabbing. The Shawnee agreed with him, and both delegations immediately left the talks. The Wea speaker, Lapoussier, assured him that no gift of the land around Vincennes had ever been made to the French, although the French had warned them that, should the Americans arrive, things would go badly for the Miami. To be sure, said Lapoussier, Indians were regularly killed in Vincennes, and when they passed Americans on its street, they had "to turn [their] eyes aside," yet the Miami had kept the peace of Greenville.[143]

Harrison somehow prevailed but by what means is unrecorded. He signed the "treaty" based on these talks on September 17, 1802, in the presence of *Mihšihkinaahkwa* (Kilatika) and *Pinšiwa* ("Wildcat," "John Baptiste Richardville," Miami), both of whom refused to sign. *Panisciowa* ("Jean Baptiste Ducoigne," Kaskaskia) and *Wonongasea* ("Five Medals," Miami) did sign, along with several nonchiefs.[144] The account of these talks as produced by Moses Dawson in 1824 gave Wells equal credit with Harrison for turning the tide in Harrison's favor, as the parties agreed to sign the treaty cessions later at Fort Wayne (when the Miami and the Potawatomi went for their annuities).[145] This seems unlikely, however, as Wells's father-in-law *Mihšihkinaahkwa* had refused the treaty. Moreover, on November 2, Dearborn received Harrison's "treaty," but he did not accept it. For "want of authentic documents," Harrison had to "resort to a new convention."[146] This is one of the few, highly irregular treaties not accepted as clean and just by the U.S. government, because alarmed by what had just transpired, the chiefs quickly and mightily protested to Washington, D.C., both Harrison's tactics and the falsity of the supposed "treaty."

On January 17, 1803, an angry Dearborn demanded an explanation of the hanky-panky from Harrison, although this letter, containing a record of the chiefs' complaint, is mysteriously missing from the record.[147] From Dearborn's account to Jefferson, however, the Kaskaskia, Kilatika, Piankeshaw, and late-arriving Kickapoo had not actually agreed to much of anything, so they forthwith repudiated the 1803 Fort Wayne Treaty.[148] On February 21, 1803, the Lenape and Miami were again complaining "loudly" that Harrison took much more land than just a bit on either side of the river, not to mention their salt spring, regarding which they had agreed to no more than a one-year lease.[149] Dearborn's demand and the chiefs' complaint can, however, be inferred from Harrison's reply. They are that Harrison had:

1. gotten the participants drunk before he treated with them;
2. dealt with ringers, whom he knew would do his bidding;

3. dickered with nations that had no right to cede the land in question; and
4. ignored that individual nations of the Confederacy could not make treaties that were binding on the entire Confederacy.

Not liking to have to defend himself because of Indian complaints, Harrison waited till March 3 to reply, blaming the time elapsed on bad mail delivery, although other Harrison-Dearborn correspondence in the intervening period was not interrupted.[150]

Interestingly, in his rambling, scrambling letter of self-defense, Harrison did not deny having produced "ardent spirits" for the delegates but self-righteously insisted that he had not distributed the alcohol until after the deal had been reached. Harrison did not directly address the charge of using ringers but, instead, spleneti-cally accused William Wells and Mihšihkinaahkwa of stirring up the Kekionga Miami against the treaty. How this was possible is unclear, because Harrison also claimed that 90 percent of the Miami "utterly abhor[red]" Wells and Meshikiniquak, who were Eel River Kilatika, not Kekionga Miami. Still furious at having been stood up at his intended Fort Wayne signing, at which some representatives arrived late, and others, not at all, Harrison also lambasted Hibou, claiming that he was personally responsible for no one having shown up. Although a Kilatika Miami, Hibou was a political rival of Mihšihkinaahkwa. Clearly, Harrison had tried to play Kilatika factions off against one another, and they did not appreciate it.

Against the charge that he had treated with the wrong people, Harrison con-tended that neither the Miami nor the Potawatomi had any claim to the land in question, because it had been ceded by the Lenape and Piankeshaw, and anyhow, it was French land (that is, about to be covered under the Louisiana Purchase). Harrison heatedly disputed that the Kekionga Miami elders had to approve of anything contracted by the Piankeshaw and Kaskaskia, falsely insisting, in the lat-ter case, that they were part of the Illini, not the Miami, Confederacy and that the Kaskaskia lived in mortal dread of the Potawatomi (whom Harrison seemed to think were part of the Miami Confederacy).

Harrison was also palpably angry with Wells for pointing out that neither the Piankeshaw nor the Kaskaskia, as individual member nations of the Miami Confederacy, could make a deal that was binding on the Confederacy. It was his right, Harrison countered, to treat with any nation that had been at the Greenville Treaty. (The Kaskaskia had not so been.) Harrison's deflections aside, the land had never actually belonged to either the Lenape or Piankeshaw but to the Miami and Potawatomi.[151] Harrison's scattergun, self-contradictory defense was more intent on obfuscating facts than on exercising logic.

Harrison could not fully defend himself because Jefferson's secret orders to break up the Miami and Three Fires Confederacies were "sacredly" confiden-tial.[152] Dearborn was not in on Jefferson's orders, however, so the January-to-February brouhaha dented Harrison's armor with Dearborn. This context puts Jefferson's February 1803 nomination of Harrison as a treaty commissioner in a new light. Jefferson was supporting Harrison, and once he had Senate confirma-tion of Harrison's commission on February 8, he effectively took control of

Harrison out of Dearborn's power.[153] Everyone governmental got the message. By the time Harrison did reply to Dearborn's scolding, commission in hand, he already knew the outcome of the rumpus. I suspect that Harrison contacted Jefferson instantly upon receipt of Dearborn's letter, accounting for his delay in answering Dearborn, although the surviving correspondence gives no indication about this, either way.

Harrison still had the land to grab, especially the salt lick, so he got up the Fort Wayne council of 1803 to pursue the matter. Whereas the 1802 treaty council had kept fairly extensive minutes, the 1803 council cagily produced hardly any record. Dawson claimed that Harrison threatened those groups thinking about not showing up with not receiving their annuities because he would give the goods, instead, to those who did attend.[154] The scant official record has the Fort Wayne council opening on June 1, 1803, with the express purpose of resuming "the proceedings" of "October last." (It had been held in September.) The talks still did not go smoothly. On June 4, Harrison harangued the delegates, pursuing his claim that the Greenville Treaty had already handed over their land (it had not), while warning them not to listen to "foreign emissaries." By June 5, "chiefs" still present evaded any decision. On June 6, the Kickapoo arrived, but whether that was before or after the chiefs had agreed to surrender their rights to the "Lands claimed about Vincennes" was not revealed.[155] The first Treaty of Fort Wayne, signed on June 7, 1803, was the first "legitimate" cession of Miami land. It ensured that Harrison grabbed the coveted salt spring, along with 2,038,400 acres of Miami territory.[156] *Buckongehelas* was listed as a signatory, along with two Shawnee, *Pashsheweha* and *Ketchkawhanund*.[157]

Not much was said at the time, or later, about this treaty, because it redounded little credit on Harrison but resulted in considerable later difficulty for the president, secretary of the treasury, Congress, and surveyor general in cleaning up the mess.[158] Furthermore, instead of being disciplined for his part in bringing forward Miami complains, William Wells was given a raise, just ten months after Harrison's self-defense, which had carefully cast aspersions on Wells.[159] In light of all this, Harrison's October 29, 1803, letter of gushing gratitude to Jefferson for reappointing him governor takes on new meaning. Assuring Jefferson that "nothing more of your plan" remained but to tackle Illinois, Harrison worked to set up his next treaty.[160]

Eight months after the screaming died down, the motive behind Harrison's salt-spring urgency snapped into clear focus: the salt company was making a killing, undercutting its competitors by producing "superior" salt while lowering its price to levels that "diffused a general joy Amongst the Citizens of this Territory." By way of showing Jefferson that the fracas had been worth the trouble, Harrison enclosed a sample of the salt.[161] As always with Harrison, hanky-panky flowered, here around the ownership and operations of the salt spring. With official records cryptic and/or strategically missing, what happened is unclear but was obviously untoward.[162] Thereafter, the land around the salt spring was exempted from public sale, being leased, only, by the government, but in 1809, the joke was on Harrison, as the spring was found to lie in Illinois Territory and was thus transferred to a rival treasury.[163]

Harrison now found himself caught between annoyed officials in Washington, D.C. and greedy constituents in Indiana. On December 28, 1802, contending that "the quantity of lands in the Territory open for settlement" was insufficient, the Vincennes Convention had demanded more Indian land.[164] These opposing interests left Harrison pitted against Washington, D.C., so to satisfy appearances in Washington, D.C. and *l'avidité* in Vincennes, he appointed "chiefs" to reaffirm the 1803 Fort Wayne Treaty, in the "Treaty with the Eel River, Etc.," signed August 7, 1803.[165] Little record of the "Eel River" treaty exists, beyond Jefferson's submission of it, in train with companion treaties, on October 31, 1803.[166] Although originally listed as a "supplement" to the 1803 Treaty of Fort Wayne, it now appears in the record as an independent treaty.[167] Its purpose was to force the Kilatika to recognize Article 4 of the Fort Wayne Treaty. Article 4 conceded land on either side of the Vincennes fork, to Clarksville and to Kaskaskia, and agreed to the construction of taverns and ferry ports.[168]

The signatures on the Eel River treaty are worth examining. It claimed to speak for the Kilatika, Wyandot, Piankeshaw, Kaskaskia, and Kickapoo, yet no nations were listed by the signatures, so the national identities of *Akaketa*, *Puppequor*, "Pedagogue," and *Saconquneva* are unknown and that of "Black Dog," barely traceable. *Makatewelama* ("*Chien Noir*," French for "Black Dog") was listed in 1804 as a "Piankeshaw chief" and appeared again on an 1805 treaty (as *Macatiwaaluna*), but he is otherwise invisible.[169] The only names of known personages are *Katunga* ("Charley"), Lapoussier (also Laboussier), *Panisciowa* ("Ducoigne"), *Wabakinklelia* ("Gros Blé" "Big Corn" in French, usually rendered, "Gros Bled"), and *Ohequanah* (also, *Chiquia*, "Little Eyes"):

- *Katunga* was a son of *Mihšihkinaahkwa*. Titles of office passed through the grandmother line to a maternal nephew, so *Katunga* was not a Kilatika lineage chief, although Harrison presented him as such.[170] Neither of the actual Kilatika chiefs appears as signatory.
- Laboussier was a speaker of the Wea who clearly did not speak for any of the named nations.[171]
- *Panisciowa* ("Jean Baptiste Ducoigne," Kaskaskia) was a proud wearer of U.S. medals, the "half-breed" son of a French father and a Kaskaskia mother, so well known to U.S. officials, that Jefferson suggested using him, by name, to Harrison.[172] *Panisciowa* did not speak for all Kaskaskia but just for his family.
- *Wabakinklelia* was the lineage name of one French-aligned Piankeshaw faction from the 1720s that continued as a U.S.-aligned faction in the 1800s.[173]
- *Ohequanah*, Wea, signed this and the 1809 Fort Wayne Treaty and documentedly spied for Harrison in 1811 during the Tecumseh War. He did not speak for any of the treaty-named nations.[174]

This treaty, then, forms a perfect example of Harrison's gaining signatures from naïfs and ringers.[175]

Ignoring Dearborn's 1802 warning not to be too land-greedy, while mindful of his constituents' demands, Harrison followed up the Eel River Treaty by turning his eyes to the Kaskaskia.[176] In 1802, Harrison had already boasted to Jefferson that lands between the Kaskaskia, Ohio, and Mississippi Rivers could be "easily obtained." Jefferson urged a system of bribery be tried first, so as not to irritate either the French settlers (who claimed the land) or the Kaskaskia (whose land it was).[177] Ruminating further in 1803, Jefferson noted that, the Cahokia "being extinct," the United States was "entitled" to their land (at a "small" purchase price) by America's "paramount sovereignty" and by the Kaskaskia's being "reduced to a few families."[178]

Jefferson aside, the Kaskaskia were still very much in existence, hence Harrison's treaty of August 13, 1803.[179] In March 1803, Dearborn ordered an army post established in Kaskaskia.[180] Little other fanfare attended this treaty conference, and Harrison barely did more than send the final treaty to Dearborn in September and notify Jefferson of it in October. Nevertheless, it netted the United States 8,911,850 acres, thanks to bribes granted to "the great chief" and Harrison ringer, *Panisciowa*.[181] Looking like a payoff, Article 3 promised a house with a "sufficient" fence for the "great chief." The United States also agreed to pay to build a church and bring in a priest.[182] No one needed to add that "christianization" always helped to divide a people, but someone should have addressed how direct U.S. support of the Catholic church was legal under the First Amendment.

The Lenape were next in the spotlight. Harrison had not forgotten that the Lenape delegates sent to Washington, D.C. had registered complaints against him over his 1802 treaty.[183] Jefferson and Dearborn were as little pleased with the Lenape as Harrison, for by the spring of 1804, the three of them were talking of removing the Lenape west of the Mississippi, to somewhere vaguely in Missouri.[184] The removal plan related to the traditional history of the Lenape peoples, which thanks to Moravian missionaries, was fairly well known to early U.S. officials. A little before the French arrived, eastern Lenape sent a delegation back west to reestablish relations with their western brethren, not to be confused with their *Oubaché* (Wabash) relations. In the seventeenth century, the eastern Lenape told the French missionaries that traveling home required a journey of seven years, "for they lived a great way towards the sun-setting," that is, west of the Mississippi River.[185]

Although they had lived (probably) on the Western Great Plains around 3,000 years before, the Lenape had no burning desire to return west now and were clear about the matter when invited by their Plains cousins to join them in their war against the Osage.[186] Hearing of this exchange, however, Harrison realized that the Lenape were vulnerable, and he pounced. Under the U.S. governmental threat of deportation, the Lenape negotiated a deal for temporary annuities in exchange for moving from Vincennes to an enormous tract of land between the lower White River fork and the Ohio River in Indiana. Bearing the signature of *Buckongehelas*, this deal became the Treaty with the Delawares (1804). Another signatory was *Alimee* ("George White Eyes"). The White Eyes lineage was from Ohio, with the original "George White Eyes," *Quequedegatha*, a Moravian-allied Lenape who abdicated his civil office to become a war chief in 1778.[187] Lenape titles passed through the female line, and once abdicated, not resumed, so how legitimate *Alimee* was as a civil chief is debatable. Harrison obviously included Article 5—a very ungracious acknowledgment that the land really belonged to the Piankeshaw—at Lenape insistence, but it was obviously through gritted teeth.[188]

With this underhanded "Delaware Treaty," Harrison accomplished the hidden goal of setting allies at odds, for formerly friends, the Lenape and Piankeshaw were now quarreling. The 1,910,717 acres of land ceded was indisputably Piankeshaw, and the Piankeshaw intended to keep it.[189] The Miami rescinded the Lenape land grant, under its original caveat, never to sell. Consequently, on June 27, 1804, nine days after the Delaware Treaty was signed, Jefferson demanded that Harrison find a way to take the Piankeshaw land just ceded by the Lenape.[190] Harrison's letter of May 1804, eliciting this advice is not extant, but Article 5 of the Delaware Treaty gives insight into his thinking. Because of the Piankeshaw's "obstinately refusing to recognize the title" of the Lenape to the land ceded, Harrison agreed to negotiate with the Piankeshaw to "endeavor to settle the matter"—amicably, of course.[191]

This being an emergency, just eleven days after the treaty with the Delaware was signed, the Treaty with the Piankeshaw, 1804, bought off the signatories with ten years' worth of annuities and $700 outright. Interestingly, Secretary John Gibson signed the treaty, not Harrison, with Gibson informing Secretary of State James Madison that the treaty had been his doing, alone.[192] This suggests a Piankeshaw refusal to deal with Harrison. Gibson's treaty was really a sop to calm everyone down, buying the small amount of land required to cut the U.S. highway between Vincennes and the Falls of the Ohio River, while conceding that the Kaskaskia had had no right to cede the Piankeshaw land in the Kaskaskia treaty. It is unclear whether the Piankeshaw thought that the treaty was returning their 1,910,717 acres of land, but it did not. Also unclear is whether the signatories represented the Piankeshaw. They included French-derived, U.S. go-to men, *Wabakinklelia* (*Gros Blé*, or Big Corn) and *Makatewelama* ("*Chien Noir*," or "Black Dog"), along with the usual untraceables.[193]

The Treaty of St. Louis came in 1804, after long maneuvering that involved Cahokia. Following settler agitation, 1800–1802, to push west to Illinois, Congress empowered entry with a U.S. post office at Cahokia and a road from Vincennes to Cahokia. By 1803, settler courts were operating there.[194] Captain Amos Stoddard was dispatched on February 19, 1803, to establish a Fort Kaskaskia, and two days later, Harrison was instructed to begin treating with the area Indians.[195] Meantime, Harrison notified Dearborn that the "Sackees [Sauk], a considerable nation," were feeling left out of the U.S. gift-giving, portraying the cause as regret at having cold-shouldered the Greenville Treaty. Now, they "were extremely desirous to be put on a footing with the other tribes." Accordingly, Harrison wished to meet with area nations and, with specific reference to the Sauk, extend the Greenville Treaty to include them.[196]

The Sauk were not so much desirous of a U.S. interface as they were concerned that the United States had given gifts to their enemies, the Osage, with whom they were then at war. Major Bruff interpreted the Sauk reaction as sheer jealousy, but presenting gifts to one group to the public exclusion of the other meant that the giver had taken sides with giftee over the giftless.[197] Thus, to the Sauk, it looked as though the United States had just entered the war on the side of the Osage in order to forestall the powerful Osage from next turning on the United States. In 1804, the Sauk did not yet understand that settler customs differed from Sauk customs.[198]

Neither did the settlers yet understand Woodlander customs, for in 1804, Dearborn ordered St. Louis Indian agent Pierre Chouteau to secure the peace with all the nations of the Illinois Territory, while favoring the Osage.[199] This was a self-defeating quest, especially if the idea were to capture the fur trade from the Spanish, now that the Louisiana Territory was in U.S. hands. Favoritism toward the Osage was also puzzling, because the Sauk regularly brought in $60,000 worth of furs annually as compared to the Grand and Petit Osage's $43,000, the Lakota's $15,000, and the Omaha's $10,000.[200]

This comedy of errors explains why the Sauk replied by dragging the U.S. flag "at the tails of their horses" (within excrement range), enraging the militia.[201] It also explains Sauk hunters tossing settler scalps at their chiefs, directing them to "go cry with the whites." The militia presented the speech as a taunt, but civil chiefs were responsible for keeping the peace, while visiting to cry with those injured was a peace-making move appropriate to opening communications. The Sauk idea was to force the United States not to side with the Osage by demonstrating that the Sauk could be dangerous, too. Grasping a bit of this, Bruff kept track of the "1150 warriors" of the "Sockeys and Reynards" (Sauk and Meskwaki).[202]

The urgency behind the Sauk and Meskwaki Treaty of St. Louis came pursuant to a congressional resolution of 1800, authorizing copper prospecting on Lake Superior, with Harrison learning of a "considerable" Sauk deposit in 1802.[203] Squatters began mining immediately. Beguiling the Sauk to acquire the deposit was obviously on Harrison's mind, because in the letter to Dearborn, immediately before his copper announcement, Harrison hoped that the Sauk could receive a $500 advance on a prospective annuity.[204] In June 1804, Jefferson instructed Harrison to offer an annuity of "five or six hundred dollars" to the Sauk and Meskwaki.[205] All that remained was a pretext on which to force a U.S.-favorable treaty.

An opportunity arose when four settler men were killed along the "river Cuivre [Copper]" around this time relative to the U.S. copper-fever, although it is usually elided with the Sauk-Osage war, still ongoing in spring.[206] Two separate incidents made the settlers cry. First, in the spring of 1804, a fledgling copper-mining camp called Cuivre Settlement held a dance, to which the Sauk were invited. Libation flowed freely. While dancing with the daughter of Sauk chief *Quashquame*, a miner groped her, and perhaps worse, forcing her to flee the dance. A male relative of the woman (not *Quashquame*, who was dead drunk just then) waylaid the groper, tomahawking him, thus prompting the demand that the killer be delivered up to U.S. justice.[207] Second, on September 6, 1804, three settlers were killed by four Sauk, setting off a militia panic of fort building on the "river Cuivre."[208] In later histories, the two incidents somehow merged into one, with historians citing four settlers killed and incorrectly attributing all deaths to the hunting-lodge incident.[209]

Hot on the trail of the suspects, Amos Stoddard's militia entered the Sauk capital of Saukenuk, where one man, a "prominent member of the tribe," surrendered himself "as a *peace offering* for his nation," to convince the militia to leave the Sauk alone.[210] Although innocent of any murders, in another Woodlands custom, he took the place of a culprit. *Makataimeshekiakiak* ("Black Hawk," Sauk) was later clear that the hostage went to St. Louis because of the one man killed, presumably at the dance, not because of the three killed at the hunting lodge.[211] This indicates either that the Sauk were responsible for but one of the deaths or that the primary Sauk chief *Quashquame* knew of but one death. Because they were having no luck nabbing the actual suspects, impatient to return with somebody in custody, Stoddard's militia took the "peace offering," imprisoning him in the St. Louis guardhouse.[212] Despite having this man in custody, Bruff demanded that the chiefs produce "those Murderers," for either a civil or a military trial.[213] Interestingly, this indicates that Bruff knew that the man in custody was innocent.

Harrison left out of his official story of the St. Louis Treaty that he began by offering the Sauk a deal that they could not refuse. *Quashquame* reported that Indian agent Pierre Chouteau came "several times" to his "camp," pressuring him into ceding land on the promise that Harrison would release the hostage in exchange.[214] Accordingly, a delegation headed by *Quashquame* went to St. Louis solely for the purpose of securing the hostage's release.[215] Arriving with another Sauk chief, one Meskwaki chief, and one "warrior," nation unnamed, *Quashquame* eventually acceded to the ransom demand, with the signatories on the St. Louis Treaty neatly matching the number cited: *Layauvois, Pasepaho, Quashquame, Outchequaka,* and *Hashequarhiqua*.[216] Only when it became clear that he had signed away land did *Quashquame* realize that he had been duped.[217]

Quashquame had X-ed the agreement on the understanding that the Sauk and Meskwaki still owned their land.[218] Worse, the hostage, whose release was the Sauk point of the bargain, was killed, instead. On May 27, 1805, Harrison attributed the shooting to a "Centinel," characterizing the circumstances as a prison break.[219] A year later, Harrison referred to the "Centinel" by name as "Mr. Hammond," so he certainly had more information than is currently on record.[220] The presidential pardon of the hostage promised to *Quashquame* had been sent in February, Harrison told Dearborn, arriving two months after it was sent. This 1805 letter reads as if Harrison were under pressure from Washington, D.C. to explain what the devil had happened. Delayed mail was Harrison's go-to excuse for mishaps, but even two months late, the pardon would have arrived in Vincennes on or around April 1, and if "immediately forwarded," as Harrison claimed, would easily have arrived in St. Louis by May 1, the very day the Sauk was killed.[221] (Chouteau's messengered letter of May 22 had arrived in Vincennes on May 27.[222])

Importantly, Harrison was in Vincennes, not St. Louis, at the time of the murder. Thus, he had information regarding the shooting from someone else. In his labored explanation to Dearborn, Harrison attached two letters, one from Chouteau dated May 22 and one from Benjamin Parke dated May 25.[223] Copies of those letters do not now exist in the files. Harrison's 1922 editor Esarey did not include Harrison's list of the enclosures but suggested an unrelated letter of May 22 from Chouteau. The 1993 editor of Harrison's letters suggested that two extant letters, the one from Chouteau and the other from Benjamin Parke dated May 25, 1805, were those in question. I doubt these suggestions. First, the suggested letters simply do not fit the bill. Second, it was not at all unusual for officials to write two, consecutive letters on the same day, rather than toss a confidential matter into a letter on other business. Third, I have come across more than one instance of sensitive documents mysteriously disappearing, so I wonder whether the actual letters were sanitized from the record.[224]

The suggested Chouteau letter of May 22 addressed the Lakota, not the Sauk. Another letter from Chouteau, in French, dated May 31 did speak of the Sauk. Chouteau had been on the point of sending them annuity goods, but as they had evacuated their capital, Saukenuk, he feared that they were gearing up for war, supposedly due to the murder of the Sauk hostage. Had Chouteau sent the annuity boat, *"infailliblement"* (undoubtedly) its crew would have fallen *"la Victime d'une Vengeance injuste et barbare"* (victim to an unjust and barbarous vengeance). Instead, he sent an interpreter to the Sauk, hoping to reconcile them to news of the death.[225] This letter (which does not appear in Esarey) sounds like a follow-up to the now-missing enclosure, for it presumes knowledge not in evidence. The original letter would have informed Harrison of Hammond's murder of the hostage.

The May 25, 1805, letter that Clanin offered as Parke's missing enclosure addressed another matter entirely, a murder committed by a Lakota man. The Lakota turned him in, requesting mercy, and Parke wanted to release him, as the Lakota would return him upon U.S. request. Saying that "the subtleties of our law" evaded the Indians, Parke brought up the Sauk hostage, grumpily alluding to "the fellow lately escaped" and lamenting that the United States had "played the fool" in that matter.[226] Again, this sounds like a follow-up, not the substantive letter, itself.

As attorney general of the Indiana Territory, Benjamin Parke was in St. Louis during the murder, before the Lakota arrived, to deal with legal issues surrounding the imprisonment of Indians under U.S. law.[227] Most likely, the presidential pardon had been sent with him from Vincennes. Parke would immediately have realized the legal implications of the Sauk's death and known that, if Hammond had shot the Sauk during a jail break, then there was no legal problem. Unfortunately for the prison-break scenario, the government would have had the man's body immediately to hand rather than found almost a month later, "near St. Louis," with holes in his head from buckshot.[228] The fact that these events occurred immediately before the Lakota brought in a man to hand over to the St. Louis authorities is no doubt why Harrison termed their arrival "at this particular time" as "certainly an unfortunate circumstance," for the murder was something likely to invite Lakota distrust of U.S. officials.[229]

In his capacity as governor of the Louisiana Territory, James Wilkinson was also a belated source on the killing. He informed Dearborn that "150 Chiefs & warriors of the Sauk" were awaiting his arrival in St. Louis, which he expected to reach, himself, on July 2. Meanwhile, Chouteau had brought with him "three *grand* Chiefs" to meet him in advance at Fort Kaskaskia, suggesting exigence.[230]

A "few days" after his arrival in St. Louis, Wilkinson "held a council" with the Sauk and Meskwaki to explain how and why their man "was shot by a Sentinel, when attempting to make his escape." Wilkinson claimed that the "great Spirit" required blood for blood, so a Sauk man had to die. He then handed the victim's brother the presidential pardon and told him to keep it as a warning against "Bad Deeds," cold comfort to a grieving brother.[231]

U.S. state documents are not the only sources on this affair, however. A settler account stated that the "murderer was released, according to promise" but "was immediately shot down, presumably by a relative of the white man whom he had killed."[232] The reason for the presumption was left unstated. In 1922, Esarey opined that the man had been shot "more probably by a personal enemy" than by the sentinel, apparently based on the settler version of events.[233] In his account, *Makataimeshekiakiak* clearly stated that "their friend was led out of prison," officially. The hostage then "ran a short distance and was shot."[234] It was not unusual for North American Indians to run long distances in races, in ceremonies, as messengers, or whenever they were in a hurry, so running did not indicate fleeing. Thus, if official accounts feature a jailbreak, then Sauk and settler accounts have the man released and shot on his way home. Both versions cannot be true, unless the shooter, Hammond, was the "Centinel" as well as a relative of the slain groper.[235]

The problems with the Treaty of St. Louis, signed on November 3, 1804, went well beyond the murder of the innocent hostage.[236] Uncredentialed by their nations as treaty counselors, the chiefs were never empowered to sell 14,803,520 acres of land but solely to lease a tidbit of land on either side of the Mississippi River to ransom out the hostage.[237] Harrison clearly knew what he was doing in this land grab, for despite his interdictions against giving Indians liquor, the delegation was stinking drunk, conference-long. Although some historians off-load the blame for that onto Chouteau, the drinking could only have occurred with Harrison's knowledge and assent.[238] Returning to Saukenuk, shamefaced in their "fine coats" and "medals," but without the hostage, the five were reviled.[239] *Quashquame* was impeached and demoted from a primary to a very minor chief, with *Makataimeshekiakiak*, formally a minor chief, elevated to his place as primary.[240] Meanwhile, in March 1805, Treasury Secretary Gallatin ordered surveys of Sauk and Meskwaki land to begin.[241] On November 6, 1805—three days after the treaty was signed—Wilkinson announced that the copper load's location had been found, although it had clearly been known before to miners.[242] U.S. officials might have hurried from this shady deal in 1805, giggling over their cleverness, but it would return to haunt the United States in the Black Hawk War.

Given the high tensions running through the Indian nations following Harrison's frenzy of treaty-making, Jefferson wanted Harrison, "with as little delay as possible," to meet with the Miami and Pottawatomi chiefs to smooth out the rough patches created by his "Dellaware" deal.[243] Most of the Miami nations were still fuming over it, and Jefferson wanted the Lenape actively noising about Harrison's underhanded methods "severely reprimanded." As for the Miami and Potawatomi, Jefferson suggested buying the chiefs off with "two or three hundred dollars" to "quiet their minds."[244] There was more to Indian dismay leading into the Grouseland council than Lenape telling tales out of school, however, for the United States was preparing to survey lands it claimed under the Greenville Treaty. The Sandusky and Maumee areas of Ohio were part of that treaty, but the lands of "Chikago" were never included, and the chiefs well knew it.[245] The Indians also knew that surveying in Indiana was set to begin in July.[246] As usual, Harrison blamed all the resistance on *Meshinkinoquak*, personally.[247]

Jefferson's order led to the Treaty of Grouseland (1805), held at Harrison's lavish estate of Grouseland, then just outside of Vincennes. After acquiring 300 acres of Miami land in 1801, between 1802 and 1804, he constructed what he called "Harrison House" but what is today known simply as Grouseland.[248] A $20,000 slave plantation (or $4,000,000, today and perhaps why Harrison pestered Jefferson for a "small" raise in 1805[249]), Grouseland was built in partial replication of his birthplace, the thousand-acre Berkeley slave plantation owned by his father in Charles City, Virginia, but also with possible nods to Johnson House, the lavish estate of Sir William Johnson, the Revolutionary-era British Indian agent.[250] Grouseland's over-the-top opulence was meant to intimidate Indians and impress settlers, while covertly encouraging slavery in Indiana Territory.

John Gibson ordered "the principal chiefs" to Grouseland in June 1805, where their "Father" had only their "interest and happiness" at heart.[251] Indians use fictive kinship in titles of office, but there are rules to the usage. "Father" (Uncle, actually) was traditionally accorded based on who had arrived in a place first.[252] Competence was also required. "What kind of father are you?" *Sadekanakte* (Onondaga) demanded of seventeenth-century French governor Frontenac. "You deal with us whom call us 'children' as if we were hogs."[253] In Indiana, the Miami at Kekionga were the "Father" nation of the group, so the United States' "Father" language was equally insulting.[254] Moreover, *Mihšihkinaahkwa* balked at the order to appear immediately, because Indians took consultation time to consider requests properly.[255] Although this request was the sort of exchange that Harrison indicted as obstructionism, *Mihšihkinaahkwa* did have to consult, for Woodland confederacies were not top-down organizations but democracies. Moreover, *Mihšihkinaahkwa* was struggling to maintain his own position in the Miami Confederacy, which Harrison was working to undermine, in favor of more malleable actors.

The spoilers were *P'Koum-Kwa* ("Peccan," "Pakuan") and *Pinšiwa* ("Wildcat," "John Baptiste Richardville"). Born to a chief's lineage at Kekionga, *P'Koum-Kwa* was a close relative of *Mihšihkinaahkwa* and a maternal uncle of *Pinšiwa*. It was *P'Koum-Kwa* who took over as principal chief in 1812 following the death of *Meshikinoqua* and signed the second treaty of Greenville (1815). *P'Koum-Kwa*'s (and *Mihšihkinaahkwa*'s) nephew, *Pinšiwa* was the son of the lineage-titled *Tacumwah* (*Mihšihkinaahkwa*'s sister) by a French nobleman turned fur trader. An assimilated fur trader and a wealthy man, *Pinšiwa* saw his interests as aligned with the settlers'. He became chief later on.[256] *P'Koum-Kwa* and *Pinšiwa* were both in bed with Harrison, so it is hardly surprising that, in this family feud, Harrison presented them as the *real* "Miami" chiefs, supporting them even as he undercut

Mihšihkinaahkwa.[257] Consequently, after *Mihšihkinaahkwa* had told Gibson to wait while he consulted others, *P'Koum-Kwa* confided to Gibson that he was perfectly ready to go forward immediately.[258]

Wells attempted to aid his father-in-law, *Mihšihkinaahkwa*, by demanding that Harrison's men, John Gibson and Francis Vigo, show their authorization to call the Grouseland conference and announcing that *Mihšihkinaahkwa* was misunderstood when he replied that he had to consult others.[259] Not waiting, Harrison's men proceeded to visit the Kilatika, Potawatomi, and other nations, arm-twisting "enemies" including *Hibou*, while cultivating supporters including *Pinšiwa* and *P'Koum-Kwa*. That May after the death of the Lenape chief, *Buckongahelas*, who had signed the offensive treaty, Gibson and Vigo also courted the Lenape, assuring them that Harrison was troubled by their claims never to have sold any land and complaints that Harrison "had defrauded and cheated them." The Lenape refused to budge from their contentions.[260]

By June 1805, these various nations were on their way to Fort Wayne for annuities and, no doubt, also to consult with *Mihšihkinaahkwa*, who agreed that everyone would be in Grouseland by August, yet reiterating his demand to see Gibson and Vigo's authorization to contact the individual Miami nations directly (a grave violation of confederated procedures intended to divide the Confederacy).[261] A testy confrontation ensued with Vigo and Gibson after Wells assured the Lenape that they had sold their "right" but not Miami land. Clearly, the atmosphere around the Grouseland conference was tense, as each side stiffened its position.[262] Worse, the British seized the opportunity to send encouragement to the Miami, as Harrison vented his spleen against Wells.[263]

By August 10, 1805, the various nations were gathered at Grouseland, while a preliminary *tête-à-tête* between Wells and Harrison purportedly cleared the air between them, while Harrison increased grants to *Mihšihkinaahkwa* for his readiness to dicker.[264] Announcing that he "observed the most exact neutrality" in the talks, Harrison made it clear to the Lenape that the United States would withdraw its "guarantee" of protection and annuities if they did not cave, forcing the Miami into line with the United States. Harrison's growling came just as the western Lenape had been enlisted by the Sauk and Mesquaki to join them in the war with the Osage, with the western Lenape now inducing the Indiana Lenape to join them in the venture.[265] The Potawatomi heavily repudiated the treaty, however, with their war chief *Main Poc* sneering that *Wenameck* was not authorized to sign and was "not fit" to mend *Main Poc*'s moccasins.[266]

Next, the Piankeshaw attempted without success to force an increase in the annuities promised them for their 1804 treaty, so the Miami switched to pressuring Harrison into a good price for the land in the Grouseland treaty. Although Harrison later consoled Dearborn that the price he paid for the land was "greater than [he] could have wished," in his account of the talks to Jefferson, he crowed at having paid "about one cent per acre"—for land he could turn around and sell to settlers at $6 per acre.[267] Pointedly excluding the Piankeshaw from the Grouseland treaty annuities, Harrison was forced to include the Potawatomi (perhaps in exchange for *Checago*). In the end, Harrison sealed the land deal that he had been working on since the Delaware Treaty was first noised about in 1802.[268] The Treaty of Grouseland was signed on August 21, 1805.[269] *Mihšihkinaahkwa* was a signatory.

Dearborn found the treaty "highly satisfying and pleasing."[270] Somehow or another, even as smiles raced around Washington, D.C. and Vincennes over the great acreage acquired in two short years, no U.S. official seemed to grasp why the Illinois and Indiana nations might be feeling unfriendlier by the day. Over 1805, Harrison muttered darkly about "Greater exertions" made (by Britain) to "poison the Minds of the Indians" against the United States. If the "Sauk" were quiet, then the Kickapoo remained "as insolent as ever," he griped.[271] Meantime, settlers were preying unconscionably on the now-helpless Kaskaskia and stealing from the Kickapoo, committing assault, and driving them from their own fields.[272] Why the British would have been necessary to alert the Indians to these current events was left unexplained.

Harrison boasted that he could secure the remaining Piankeshaw lands "easily," as soon as he had the president's instructions. By November 1805, apparently receiving Jefferson's go-ahead, he hoped "soon" to "close a bargain" with the Piankeshaw for the land remaining between the Wabash and the "Kaskaskia purchase" of 1803.[273] On November 29, he was tapping his toe impatiently, awaiting the arrival of a vital Piankeshaw chief to "negociate" the deal.[274] By December 28, Harrison confessed negotiating with the Piankeshaw had proved more challenging than expected, although he had finally brought them to "reasonable terms," with a treaty about to be signed.[275] Arms were so sufficiently twisted that on January 1, 1806, Harrison forwarded the treaty to Jefferson, touting it as "highly advantageous" to the United States and not a "bad bargain" for the Piankeshaw (even though he had "forgotten" to include a negotiated stipulation). What the Piankeshaw thought of the "bargain" was not recorded, but it is recorded that only three, French-aligned Piankeshaw signed this significant treaty: *Wabakinklelia* ("*Gros Blé*"), *Makatewelama* ("*Chien Noir*"), and the untraceable *Pauquia* ("Montour" probably the "Nontour" X-ing on the original treaty).[276]

Contrary to Harrison's conspiracy theories, the nations of Indiana saw for themselves what was happening. Thus, when in 1808, *Tenskwatawa* laid out his five-point plan for foiling invasion, they listened. First, the Indians had to implement border control to keep out the illegal immigrants. Second, Indigenous poverty was a settler-engineered condition. Its cure was to refuse to engage with the U.S. trading posts, because then the settlers had no pretext of debt with which to force land concessions. Third, as united in a pan-Indian movement, the Indians were to "watch the Boundary line" between Indian lands and the lands already usurped. Fourth, should a "white man put his foot" over the line onto Indian land, the Young Men were to put that foot right back again where it belonged. *Tenskwatawa* asserted that the Indians "unanimously agreed" to work with him to "remove the cause" of their dispossession.[277] This speech constituted a warning shot over the bow of the *USS Ship of State*, but Harrison ignored it, to resume wheeling and dealing in 1809.

In March 1809, James Madison took over presidential duties from Thomas Jefferson and performed a little housekeeping at the Fort Wayne Indian agency.

Wells was handed his walking papers, as his old enemy John Johnston took over the post, with orders to be especially attentive to the disgruntled Miami.[278] It did not help. By April 15, gossip was that Johnston had "intrigued" against Wells to grab his job, a not-unlikely circumstance.[279] With Wells gone, and *Tenskwatawa* and *Tecumseh* making themselves central to local affairs, Harrison incredibly resumed treaty councils, perhaps to demonstrate to the new president his continuing worth as governor.[280]

A concession that the Miami forced on Harrison at Grouseland stipulated that the Miami, Kilatika, and Wea "still consider themselves as one nation," so that no one of them could "dispose" of land that they held "in common."[281] Although the article was violated forthwith by the second Piankeshaw treaty, this provision returned to center stage in 1809, when Harrison attempted an end run around the Kickapoo, Wea, and Kilatika at the second Treaty of Fort Wayne. Not able to ram his demands though without their signatures, to make it legal, he was forced to treat with all three throughout 1809.

When Miami chiefs arrived at Fort Wayne for their June 1809 annuities, Harrison worked on them to proceed to Vincennes by August to hash out a deal with Harrison.[282] In July 1809, Harrison urged the new secretary of war, William Eustis, not to place a fort in Wea county but to cancel it in return for the Wea's ceding their land along the "Vermillion" River.[283] This, even as he assured Eustis that the Indians were now riled up enough to side with the French against the United States. (Earlier in the same letter, he had blamed British "intrigue" for the unrest.[284])

Receiving Eustis's authorization to "extinguish" the Miami title to the Vermilion River, Harrison proceeded to Fort Wayne, arriving on September 15, 1809.[285] The western Lenape arrived on September 18, and Harrison entered into a secret deal with them to persuade the Indiana Lenape to return west with them. (They did not go west till 1818.[286]) On September 19, Harrison refused a Potawatomi request for liquor.[287] With the Miami ringers *Pinšiwa* and *Wonongasea* missing, the Miami under *Mihšihkinaahkwa* and *Hibou* informed Harrison on September 20 that they refused to part with "another foot" of territory. Dismissing this as a bargaining tactic, Harrison greased the wheels with liquor, handing out two gallons to each nation on September 23.[288] It is worth pausing a moment to look at what had just transpired. In six days, Harrison obliterated two of his most ardently claimed positions: first, not to allow the western and Indiana Lenape to combine forces and, second, not to distribute liquor to the Indians, having forbidden any such sales on August 23, 1809.[289] Instead during this council, he put Western and Indiana forces together and then passed out generous amounts of liquor, around 218 gallons of whiskey distributed to 1,390 Indian delegates over two months.[290]

Nevertheless, the Miami stood firm. Irked, Harrison spun out smears of the British. Tension mounting to the point that tomahawk threats now broke out among the Indian factions, as a Potawatomi chief sided with Harrison. The "bad words" were not put behind them until September 28, when speaking for the Miami, *Hibou* announced that they might sell some land—for the same price of

$2 per acre as settlers would pay for it—but they offered only land that they did not own near Fort Recovery, which was in Ohio and already covered under the Greenville Treaty of 1795. The whole offer was an obvious mockery of Harrison's treaty process.[291] ("Knowledge" of the "value of land is fast gaining among the Indians," Harrison had lamented to Dearborn in 1805.[292])

At this, Harrison attempted to turn the tide his way by calling on *P'Koum-Kwa*, who passive-aggressively repeated Harrison's words at the Grouseland treaty, that he had never intended to buy land from people who did not own it. Because the Potawatomi did not own the land in question, said *P'Koum-Kwa*, they had no business entering the present discourse. Grievance after grievance now poured out of the Indian delegates. To extract an agreement to his current land-cession proposal, Harrison was forced to "promise immediate satisfaction" of all the grievances. At that point, it was all over but the X-ing of the treaty, which was accomplished on September 30, 1809, for Senate ratification on January 2, 1810.[293] Harrison declared victory and distributed annuities.[294]

There remained the little matter of the Kilatika and Wea, however, for the Kilatika had not signed at Fort Wayne and the Wea had not even come to the treaty conference. Harrison traveled to a town on "Raviere [Petit]" (the Mississinewa River) to confer with the Kilatika, where he acquired the signatures of significant Miami chiefs, including *Hibou, Mihšihkinaahkwa*, and *P'Koum-Kwa*, as well as that of the Shawnee chief, *Monakwanee* ("Silver Heels"). This treaty is practically never mentioned, except as a "supplement" to the Fort Wayne Treaty. It was assigned and ratified under the same signature date as the Fort Wayne Treaty, although it was not signed till October 5, the morning after a "drunken frolick," in which one man was killed and everyone was drunk or badly hungover.[295] It was signed on the promise of additional annuity goods, with permanent, extra annuity money, should the Kilatika and, vaguely, the "Miami" pressure the Kickapoo into confirming the Fort Wayne Treaty, ceding Kickapoo land, although the Kickapoo had not been at the treaty council.[296]

At the same Kilatika town, Harrison ordered the Wea to a separate council in Vincennes, for their agreement to the Fort Wayne Treaty. By October 22, 1809, sixty-one representatives of the Wea and Shawnee arrived, having acquired liquor from "some bad white men." Harrison declared the delegates sober and opened the council, anyway. Essentially, the Wea agreed to move north of Vincennes and, although not in the treaty minutes, the Wea were bribed to push the Kickapoo into ceding land and agreeing to the Grouseland treaty.[297] Nearly the same crowd attended as had been at Mississinewa, with *Quewa* ("Negro Legs"), *Chequia* ("Little Eyes"), and "Shawnee" signing again, for different set of bribes. This "supplemental" treaty was signed on October 26 and ratified by the Senate.[298] The Wea chief *Papahonga* ("Lapoussier") said that ratification was obtained through threats: the treaty was forced "with the tomahawk over their heads."[299]

Harrison was desperate now to acquire Kickapoo signatures, for his continued tenure as governor was on the line. The shenanigans he had pulled under Jefferson were not going to fly with the Madison administration, which required actual minutes of treaty talks, tracking such details as who had shown up—and who had not.[300] This was unfortunate for Harrison, as including the Kickapoo in this Fort Wayne Treaty had always been his plan for this treaty. It is not incidental that he had received the go-ahead to do so on December 31, 1808, from the outgoing Jefferson, making it look as though the two had planned to slide a Kickapoo treaty in under the wire, before Jefferson left office.[301]

Madison and Eustis conferred as soon as they learned of this plan in April 1809 and quickly messaged Harrison not to go forward with a Kickapoo treaty touching the south side of the Illinois River. (Illinois was a separate territory.[302]) Why Harrison would include the Kickapoo in the Fort Wayne Treaty is a little puzzling, then, but perhaps bad habits die hard.[303] The majority of the Kickapoo stood with *Tenskwatawa*, so Harrison's standing trick of dealing only with his handpicked ringers would not work here.

The Kickapoo refusal to cede land had been sticking in Harrison's craw since his preliminary talks in 1802, but he had seeded the problem, himself, with his glad-handed method of dealing only with pliant "chiefs."[304] Then, he made matters worse by sending a two-man delegation to deliver his reprimand condemning traditional Kickapoo swidden practices. Kickapoo chief *Pawatamo* returned a message blistering Harrison for interference.[305] Kickapoo began sending war belts around against the United States. Stewing till July 1806, Harrison menaced them, threatening war and announcing that they "must take the penalty of their own rashness."[306] By August 1806, Harrison was griping to Dearborn that the Kickapoo "ought to be called to a conference," where all prior "deceptions" practiced on them could be "explained away."[307]

The Kickapoo were not interested in being lied to anymore; however, the majority of them now eagerly listened to the Holy Man, *Tenskwatawa*. Considering the Kaskaskia as U.S. allies, in May 1807, the Kickapoo killed the brother-in-law of *Panisciowa*, who had helped Harrison create the Kaskaskia treaty. A flap followed, as Harrison sent belligerently inflammatory "message" to his "Children," demanding that the Kickapoo killers be turned in and authorized commandos to chase the Kickapoo west. The affair died down, but the feather in Harrison's cap was seriously ruffled by the Kickapoo defiance.[308]

Now under direct orders from Eustis actually to meet present representatives of the people whose lands were at stake in treaties, Harrison returned to his old tactic of selecting the negotiating team for the other side. Calling up his Kickapoo ringers, *Nemahson* ("Joe Renard"), *Knoshania*, *Wakoah*, *Nonoah*, and *Moquiah*, he declared that the treaty council was on. Although Harrison expected these "chiefs" on November 10, 1809, no one arrived until almost one month later around December 8, no doubt because those coming realized that their lives could be forfeit at home.[309] The closest thing to a real chief in the bunch, *Nemahson* was not even considered important enough to kill in 1806. Instead, *Tenskwatawa* had *Nemahson* kicked out of office.[310]

Forestalled at Fort Wayne from having taken the Kickapoo tract he desired—"one of the most beautiful that can be conceived," especially as it came with the bonus of a probable copper mine—Harrison now treated for, and acquired, that very land. Despite Eustis's order to keep treaty minutes, the extent of Harrison's minutes came in the letter of transmittal of the treaty, extolling the worth of the land, with a wistful nod to the good old days of the Jefferson presidency.[311] The treaty was signed by the bogus negotiators one day after they arrived, on December 9, 1809, strongly suggesting that the treaty's text had been composed prior to their arrival.[312] Notwithstanding, Madison reappointed Harrison as governor, for Harrison was achieving the unspoken goal of the government: land usurpation with quick yeoman occupation to hold it.[313]

By 1809, the missionaries were in, the roads were appropriated from the Indians, Miami land was stuffed with settlers, and forts surrounded the Miami peoples. All that remained was to secure the land by killing Indigenous dissenters.

NOTES

1. Carter, 1934–1975, Harrison appointment, vol. 7, 5/13/1800, 13–15; USS, 1828, Harrison appointment, vol. 1, 2/4/1802, 441; Harrison appointment, vol. 2, 12/15/1806, 44; Harrison appointment, vol. 2, 12/19/1809, 130–32; and Esarey, 1922, Johnson and Downs, vol. 1, letter 11/4/1809, 391–92.

2. Carter, 1934–1975, Jefferson to Madison, vol. 7, Proclamation 2/8/1802, 84–85; Dearborn to William Harrison, vol. 7, letter 2/21/1803, 86–87.

3. USS, 1828, Harrison, Brigadier General, vol. 2, 300, 303, 304, 308; Carter, 1934–1975, Dearborn to Howard, vol. 14, letter 8/22/1812, 592; for Harrison's February 27, 1813, appointment as major general, see USS, 1828, 2/27/1813, and vol. 2, 3/1/1813, 329–30; and Esarey, 1922, Armstrong to Harrison, letter 3/3/1813, vol. 3, 377.

4. Esarey, 1922, Harrison to Eustis, vol. 2, letter 8/28/1812, 98–101.

5. For Indian policy, Owens, 2007; for "Indian fighter," see Collins, 2012, 70; Loveman, 2010, 82, 104; for "Red Muslimism," Hess, 2016, 230.

6. Thwaites, 1899; Dreuillettes, vol. 44, 247; Alloues, vol. 58, 41–43; Trowbridge, 1938, 6–7; for "Kakachiouek," or Kaskaskia; "poueteouatami," or Potawatomi; and "Kikaboua," of Kickapoo, see Krzywicki, 1934, 379, 425, 444.

7. Trowbridge, 1938, 2.

8. Krzywicki, 1934, 444; Heath, 2015, Eel River/Kilatika 95, 423, note 69.

9. Mann, 2004, Wayne, Kaskaskia, and Kickapoo, 195; Stout, 1974, 345–63.

10. Krzywicki, 1934, 405–7, 415, 531–32.

11. Jablow, 1974, 4.

12. Ibid., 6.

13. Bellfy, 2011, 139; *makwa ogimaa*, 2013, 113–15; Potawatami population, *ASPIA*, 1832, vol. 1, 572.

14. McCafferty, 2008, notes 34 and 35, 184–85; Trowbridge, 1938, *Keekaukaumeeoangee*, 3, *Kekionga* ("Fort Wayne"), 7.

15. *ASPIA*, 1832, vol. 1, 572, 575; Clifton, 1998, 154. *Mtamins* was also "*le Petit Bled*," "Little Corn."

16. Esarey, 1922, note 2, 240–41.

17. Claiborne, 1860, 60.

18. Heath, 2015, for 1784, 36; warfare, 77–91; Wayne, 226.

19. Noyelle, 1906, vol. 17, 222.

20. McCafferty, 2008, 80.

21. Greene, 1911, Vincennes-*Chippecoke*, 26.

22. Mann, 2016, 41–77.

23. Callendar, 1994, 108; Trownbridge, 1938, 18.

24. Callendar, 1994, 113–14.

25. Trowbridge, 1938, 13.

26. Quimby, 1960, 136.

27. Willig, 2008, 24.

28. Trowbridge, 1938, 14.

29. *ASPIA*, vol. 1, 571–72; Wayne, 573.

30. Hewitt, 1915, 322; Hewitt, 1927, 240–41.

31. Trowbridge, 1938, 12.

32. Ibid., 3–4, 8.

33. Johansen and Mann, 2000, 7–10.

34. Trowbridge, 1938, settlement, 11, for "Senecas" as Six Nations, 8; McCafferty, 2008, 83.

35. Heckewelder, 1958, 98; Mann, 2003, 147.

36. For Miami vacating in favor of the Lenape and Mahicans, Brinton, 1999, 144; for tradition recited to Miami, Heckewelder, 1971, 47–53.

37. Halsey, 1983/1992, 33–34, 37.

38. Booker, 2011, vol. 1, 458.

39. Carter, 1934–1975, Dearborn to Harrison, vol. 7, letter 7/3/1802, 55–56.

40. Mann, 2000, 223–26.

41. *ASPIA*, 1832, Wilkinson to St. Clair, vol. 1, Report 8/24/1791, 135.

42. Berthrong, 1974, 184.

43. Washington, 1931–1944, Washington to Duane, vol. 27, letter 9/7/1783, 132.

44. McKee, 1792, 13–14.

45. Rochefoucauld-Liancourt, 1798, vol. 8, 91–93.

46. Thornbrough, 1957, vol. 19, 29.

47. Rochefoucauld-Liancourt, 1798, vol. 8, 93–94.

48. Esarey, 1922, Harrison to Dearborn, vol. 1, letter 7/15/1801, 25.

49. Carter, 1934–1975, Dearborn to Harrison, vol. 7, letter 7/3/1802, 55–56, note 29, 55; Jefferson to Dearborn, vol. 7, letter 11/6/1802, 75–76; Dearborn to Harrison, vol. 7, letter 11/11/1802, 76; for rationales taken at face value, Owens, 2002, 413–14.

50. Esarey, 1922, vol. 1, note 1, 49; Dawson, 1824, 7–8.

51. Carter, 1934–1975, Dearborn to Harrison, vol. 7, letter 7/3/1802, 55–56, note 29, 55; Esarey, 1922, vol. 1, Proclamation 5/5/1802, 48–49; Dawson, 1824, 31.

52. Dawson, 1824, 45.

53. Carter, 1934–1975, Dearborn to William, vol. 7, letter 7/14/1801, 26–27.

54. Thornbrough, 1961, 11.

55. Woehrmann, 1971, vol. 24, 144–45, note 2, 145; Smith, 1882, St. Clair to Wells, vol. 2, letter 8/10/1799, 445–46; Thornbrough, 1961, 1802 appointment, 10–11, orders, 12; 1804 appointment, Carter, 1934–1975, Dearborn to Wells, vol. 7, letter 1/19/1804, 168.

56. Esarey, 1922, Wells to Harrison, vol. 1, letter 6/1807, 288, note 1, 288.

57. Carter, 1934–1975, Wells to the Dearborn, vol. 7, letter 4/20/1808–4/22/1808, 558–59.

58. Ibid., Smith and Wells, vol. 7, letter and response 7/9/1807, 464; Wells to Dearborn, vol. 7, letter 7/14/1807, 465–66.

59. Carter, 1934–1975, Wells to Dearborn, vol. 7, letter 8/20/1807, 470.

60. Thornbrough, 1961, accepted without testing the narrative, 18–19.

61. Ibid., 12; Esarey, 1922, Harrison to Dearborn, vol. 1, letter 3/3/1803, 76, 80, 81, 83.

62. Esarey, 1922, Harrison to Dearborn, vol. 1, letter 3/3/1803, 76; Carter, 1934–1975, Harrison to Jefferson, vol. 7, letter 6/18/1805, 294.

63. *ASPIA*, 1832, Greenville Speaker, vol. 1, 564, 567, 570–71, 574–77, 583; Esarey, 1922, Fort Wayne Speaker, vol. 1, 137.

64. Esarey, 1922, McKee to Indiana Territory Indians, vol. 1, letter 1/11/1804, 112; "Great White Elk," *Wampomshuwah,* also transcribed as *Wappemassawa,* referenced as McKee among the Old Northwest Indians, Aupaumut, 1827, 105.

65. Heath, 2015, 386.

66. Thornbrough, 1961, 13.

67. Carter, 1934–1975, Wells to the Dearborn, vol. 7, letters 4/(20)22/1808, 558–59.

68. Brackets mine. Jefferson, Bergh, ed., 1903–1907, vol. 10, 369–70; Miller, 2012, 34–35.

69. *ASPPL*, 1834, vol. 1, 2/18/1802, 111–12.

70. Hulbert, 1902–1905, "War Trail of Nations," vol. 2, 92, 149; 600 miles and usage, vol. 6, 81.

71. Ibid., vol. 8, 11.

72. Hulbert, 1902–1905, vol. 8, 37; Trowbridge, 1938, *Tshipkoheēoāngee,* 11.

73. Ibid., vol. 8, 28.

74. Ibid., vol. 7, 65.

75. Ibid., vol. 2, 146; *ASPIA*, 1832, Wilkinson and "Miami trace," Wilkinson to St. Clair, vol. 1, Report 8/24/1791, 134.

76. Esarey, 1922, vol. 1, note 1, 227.

77. Allison, 1986, 321–22. Allison presents these as "Indian Trails and Pioneer Traces," but all so-called pioneer traces used prior Indian roads; see Esarey, 1922, vol. 1, Proclamation 2/3/1801, 21.

78. Esarey, 1922, Harrison to Dearborn, vol. 1, letter 2/26/1802, 43.

79. Carter, 1934–1975, Report, vol. 7, 11/1803, 159.

80. Ibid., Memorandum, vol. 7, 11/21/1803, 156, note 96, 156.

81. Ibid., Habersham to Harrison, vol. 7, letter 8/24/1801, 32.

82. Ibid., Granger to Jefferson, vol. 7, letter 2/6/1805, 259–61.

83. Ibid., Gallatin to Badollet, vol. 7, letter 5/14/1806, 360.

84. Ibid., Gallatin to Badollet, vol. 7, letter 7/4/1806, 378–80.

85. Ibid., Petition, vol. 7, 12/6/1804, 241–42; Petition, vol. 7, 2/13/1806, 340–42; Petition, vol. 7, 10/1/1807, 477–78.

86. Esarey, 1922, Harrison to Dearborn, vol. 1, letter 2/26/1802, 44; Harrison to Dearborn, vol. 1, letter 3/3/1803, 83–84.

87. *ASPPL*, 1834–1861, vol. 1, no. 76, 146; Esarey, 1922, vol. 1, 75; Harrison to Dearborn, vol. 1, letter 2/26/1802, 43–45 passim.

88. Esarey, 1922, vol. 1, tavern as meetinghouse, 9/20/1807, "Resolutions," vol. 1, 256; Harrison to Jefferson, vol. 1, letter 10/10/1807, 262; taverns as headquarters, Scovell *et al.,* 1912, 28.

89. State of Indiana, 1807, militia, 61–63; State of Indiana, 1934, Supplemental Act, Sec. 15, vol. 20, 12/10/1810, 182–83.

90. Esarey, 1922, for officer, "General Orders," vol. 1, 9/20/1811, 585; for tavern, sheriff, and FOB, see vol. 1, note 1, 585.

91. Ibid., Harrison to Dearborn, vol. 1, letter 2/19/1802, 38.

92. Ibid., Harrison to Dearborn, vol. 1, letter 2/19/1802, 37–38; Dearborn to Harrison, vol. 1, letter 2/23/1802, 38–41.

93. *ASPPL*, 1834–1861, vol. 1, no. 66, 2/18/1802, 111–12.

94. Esarey, 1922, Harrison to Dearborn, vol. 1, letter 2/23/1803, 37–38; Carter, 1934–1975, Dearborn to Jefferson, vol. 7, letter 7/29/1802, 61–62.

95. Carter, 1934–1975, Dearborn to Harrison, vol. 7, letter 2/23/1802, 49.

96. Esarey, 1922, vol. 1, Harrison to Hargrove, vol. 1, letters 4/16/1807, 4/21/1807, 4/29/1807, 5/10/1807, 208–11, 213; Cockrum, 1907, 201.

97. Esarey, 1922, Harrison to Dearborn, vol. 1, letter 2/19/1802, 37.

98. Ross, 1938, "Fort Knox," 418.

99. Nunnally, 2007, 45; Watts, 1966, renamed Fort Sackville, 51; Fort Knox relocated in 1812, 53; as staging ground, Mann, 2013, 170–82; Tucker, 2014, 229.

100. Ross, 1938, 418.

101. In 1681, La Salle rendered it, *Checago*, while it appeared as *R. Chekagou* on the 1684 Franquelin map, alternately indicating the river and the region; Kelton, 1884, 119–20; Franquelin, 1896. The original 1684 map is now lost, but a facsimile made in Paris for historian Francis Parkman still exists and is the cited Smithsonian image.

102. *ASPMA*, 1832–1861, vol. 1, no. 46, 156.

103. Ibid., vol. 1, no. 55, 2/13/1805, 174–84; Northwest forts, vol. 1, 175.

104. Carter, 1934–1975, sent up the Mississippi, "two Brass field pieces" with ammunition, War Department to Stoddard, vol. 7, letter 2/19/1803, 85–86. Preparations getting supplies along the Ohio River and at Chicago, Dearborn to Cushing, vol. 7, letter 3/9/1803, 94–95; a suitable "scite" for "one or two posts" between Kaskaskia and mouth of Illinois River, or Missouri, and supplies including "powder" sent, Dearborn to Cushing, vol. 7, letter 3/10/1803, 95–96; post established at "Chikago," Dearborn to Wells, vol. 7, letter 5/26/1803, 115; new post at Vincennes, Dearborn to Lyman, vol. 7, letter 8/4/1803, 117.

105. Allison, 1986, additional small, militia forts, 318–20.

106. Owens, 2007, 27–32.

107. Mann, 2004, 197; Rafert, 1996, 60; 1904, vol. 2, 39–45; for acreage ceded, Bateman and Selby, 1916, vol. 1, 294.

108. USS, 1900, entry 2/18/1800, 270.

109. USC, 1845–1875, "An Act," vol. 2, 73–78, for 320 acres, see Sec. 3, 73; for $2 per acre, see Sec. 5, 74.

110. Ibid., "An Act," sale by "quarter sections" (160 acres), Sec. 10, vol. 2, 281.

111. Ibid., "An Act," Sec. 5, vol. 2, no. 2, 74.

112. Carter, 1934–1975, McNamee to Senate, vol. 7, letter 12/12/1809, 682–86.

113. Ibid., Ewing to Gallatin, vol. 8, letter 6/26/1810, 25–28, *et seq.*, massive correspondence, including back and forth charges of wrongdoing.

114. Jennings, 1932, Jennings to Duane, letter 12/1809, 170–72.

115. Stout, 1974, 345; Esarey, 1922, Harrison to Dearborn, vol. 1, letter 2/6/1802, 41; Harrison to Dearborn, vol. 1, letter 3/3/1803, 79.

116. *ASPIA*, 1832, Minutes, vol. 1, 564–82; Stout, 1974, 346, 351–56.

117. Stout, 1974, note 10, 362.

118. Ibid., 360.

119. Owens, 2007, 28.

120. "General Wayne's Orderly Book," 1905, orders, 6/16/1794, 520–21; orders, 7/4/1794, 526; orders, 7/6/1794, 527.

121. *ASPIA*, 1832, vol. 1, 573.

122. Sankey, 2003, vol. 1, 163.

123. Mann, 2004, 135; Fort Stanwix Treaty, 151–53; Fort McIntosh Treaty, 154–56; Mouth of the Great Miami Treaty, 156–58; Fort Harmar Treaty, 161–62.

124. Esarey, 1922, Jefferson to Harrison, vol. 1, letter 2/27/1803, 72.

125. Miller, 2017, 109–10; Lakomäki, 2014, 140; Dawson, 1824, 48.

126. Bergh, 1903–1907, Jefferson to Harrison, vol. 9, letter 2/27/1803, 368–71; same letter, Esarey, 1922, 1, 69–73; and Carter, 1934–1975, vol. 7, 88–92.

127. Treating separately with Kaskaskia, Potawatomi, and Kickapoo, Esarey, 1922, Jefferson to Harrison, vol. 1, letter 2/27/1803, 71–72.

128. Carter, 1934–1975, Jefferson to James Madison, vol. 7, Proclamation 2/8/1802, 84–85; Dearborn to Harrison, vol. 7, letter 2/21/1803, 86–87.

129. Esarey, 1922, Harrison to Dearborn, vol. 1, letter 3/25/1801, 47.

130. Ibid., Harrison to Dearborn, vol. 1, letter 3/25/1802, 47; plans, vol. 1, letter 6/24/1804, 99–100.

131. Ibid., Harrison to Dearborn, vol. 1, letter 2/26/1802, 42; Harrison to Dearborn, vol. 1, letter 3/3/1803, 80, 82. Esarey had "1803" but given the context, this is an error. The correct year was 1802.

132. Esarey, 1922, note 1, vol. 1, 47.

133. Carter, 1934–1975, Dearborn to Harrison, vol. 7, letter 2/23/1802, 49.

134. *ASPIA*, 1832, vol. 2, no. 101, 683.

135. Esarey, 1922, Harrison to Dearborn, vol. 1, letter 7/15/1801, 29–30; Carter, 1934–1975, Dearborn to Harrison, vol. 7, letter 2/23/1802, 49.

136. Thornbrough, 1961, Jefferson, Deposition 12/21/1808, 53–54; Esarey, 1922, Harrison to Dearborn, vol. 1, letter 3/3/1803, 82; Jefferson to "Delawares," vol. 1, letter 12/1808, 334. A Mahican Moravian convert, Hendrick Aupaumut considered a traitor by the nonconverts for marching with the Sullivan Expedition (Ronda, 1993, 104); working for the U.S. government to seize Ohio (Aupaumut, 1827, 9–131; Mann, 2004, 166, 171–74); and working point for land seizure at Fort Wayne. In 1816, Aupaumut resigned as chief, and the U.S. government promptly double-crossed his "Stockbridge Indians," fraudulently moving them in 1818 from Oneida, New York, where they had refuge, first to "New Stockbridge," Indiana, and second to Green Bay, Wisconsin (Pilling, 1891, 416–17; Brasser, 1978, 208–9). Aupaumut died of drink and despair (Rubin, 2013, 278).

137. Clanin, 1993, Harrison to Dearborn, vol. R1, letter 3/25/1802, 285–86.

138. Carter, 1934–1975, Dearborn to Harrison, vol. 7, letter 4/23/1802, 51; Esarey, 1922, Harrison to constituents, vol. 1, letter 5/14/1800, 17.

139. Carter, 1934–1975, Dearborn to Harrison, vol. 7, letter 6/17/1802, 53.

140. Ibid., Jefferson to Dearborn, vol. 7, letter 8/12/1802, 68.

141. Clanin, 1993, vol. R1, Speech 9/15/1802, 388–90.

142. Esarey, 1922, Harrison, Address, vol. 1, letter 8/12/1802, 52–55, "Minutes," vol. 1, 9/17/1802, 56; Clanin, 1993, vol. R1, Speech 9/12/1802, 373.

143. Dawson, 1824, 25, 49; Clanin, 1993, Reel 1, "Notes of Speech at an Indian Council," 9/15/1802, 388–90; Libby, 1974, 118.

144. Esarey, 1922, 1, Minutes, vol. 1, 9/17/1802, 56–57.

145. Dawson, 1824, 25–27; Clanin, 1993, "Negotiations," whole, vol. R1, 9/12–17/1802, 380–85.

146. Carter, 1934–1975, vol. 1, letter 11/2/1802, 75; *ASPIA*, 1832, Dearborn to Jefferson, vol. 1, letter 1/17/1803, 683.

147. Esarey, 1922, Harrison to Dearborn, vol. 1, letter 3/3/1803, 76.

148. Carter, 1934–1975, Dearborn to Jefferson, vol. 7, letter 7/29/1802, 61–62.

149. Ibid., Dearborn to Harrison, vol. 7, letter 2/21/1803, 86–87.

150. Clanin, 1993, for instance, letter 1/24/1803, Harrison to Dearborn "In relation to the remov [sic]," letter 1/24/1803, received by Dearborn 2/18/1803, vol. R1, 495; replied to 2/21/1802, Carter, 1934–1975, Dearborn to Harrison, vol. 7, letter 2/18/1803, 88.

151. Esarey, 1922, vol. 1, Harrison to Dearborn, vol. 1, letter 3/3/1803, 76–84.

152. Ibid., vol. 1, letter 2/27/1803, 72.

153. USS, 1804, 441, 442; Carter, 1934–1975, Dearborn to Harrison, vol. 7, letter 2/21/1803, 86–87.

154. Dawson, 1824, 48.

155. Clanin, 1993, Journal, vol. R1, 6/5/1803, 575–80.

156. Esarey, 1922, Minutes, vol. 1, 9/17/1802, 56–57; Kappler, 1904, vol. 2, 64–65; Bateman *et al.*, 1916, vol. 1, 294.

157. Kappler, 1904, *Buckongehelas*'s signature, vol. 2, 65.

158. Carter, 1934–1975, Act, Sec. 2, vol. 7, 3/26/1804, 174–75; note 50, 175, note 51, 175–76.

159. Ibid., Dearborn to Wells, vol. 7, letter 1/19/1804, 168.

160. Ibid., Harrison to Jefferson, vol. 7, letter 10/29/1803, 145–47.

161. Ibid., Harrison to Jefferson, vol. 7, letter 10/29/1803, 146.

162. Ibid., Gallatin to Jefferson, vol. 7, letter 2/16/1805, 261–62; Jefferson to Gallatin, vol. 7, letter 2/17/1805, 262; Gallatin to Jefferson, vol. 7, letter 4/27/1805, 285.

163. Ibid., Gallatin to Badollet and Ewing, vol. 7, letter 10/11/1806, 396; Gallatin to Harrison, vol. 7, letter 5/1/1809, 650.

164. Esarey, 1922, Petition, vol. 1, 12/28/1802, 63.

165. Kappler, 1904, "Eel River," vol. 2, 66.

166. *ASPIA*, 1832, Jefferson's transmittal, vol. 1, no. 104, 687; Treaty, vol. 1, 688.

167. Kappler, 1904, "Eel River," vol. 2, 66.

168. Ibid., Delawares, Article 4, vol. 2, 65.

169. Ibid., Piankeshaw, 1804, vol. 2, 72; Piankeshaw, 1805, vol. 2, 89.

170. Esarey, 1922, vol. 1, note 5, 241–42.

171. Clanin, 1993, vol. R1, Speech 9/9/1802, 387; Esarey, 1922, vol. 1, note 5, 167.

172. Esarey, 1922, vol. 1, note 1, 114; Jefferson to Harrison, as "Decaigne," letter 2/27/1803, 72; Carter, 1934–1975, vol. 7, as "Ducoigne," vol. 7, 92; "half-breed," vol. 7, note 6, 92.

173. Ekberg and Person, 2015, 42.

174. Esarey, 1922, Journal, vol. 1, 10/7/1803, 377; Snelling to Harrison, vol. 1, letter 11/20/1811, 643–46; vol. 1, note 2, 645.

175. Carter, 1934–1975, Dearborn to Harrison, vol. 7, letter 2/21/1803, 86.

176. Ibid., Dearborn to Harrison, vol. 7, letter 8/5/1802, 63–64.

177. Ibid., Jefferson to Dearborn, vol. 7, letter 8/12/1802, 67–70.

178. Ibid., Jefferson to Harrison, vol. 7, letter 2/27/1803, 92. The same letter appears in Esarey, 1922, vol. 1, 72, but Esarey transliterated Jefferson's "Caskia" as Kaskaskia, not Cahokia. Because in the second sentence after "Caskia," Jefferson referred separately to the "few families" of Kaskaskia remaining, I agree with Carter's reading.

179. Kappler, 1904, Kaskaskia, vol. 2, 67–68.

180. Carter, 1934–1975, Dearborn to Cushing, vol. 7, letter 3/9/1803, 94–95; Dearborn to Cushing, vol. 7, letter 3/10/1803, 95–96.

181. Ibid., Harrison to Dearborn, vol. 7, letter 9/23/1803, 123; Harrison to Jefferson, vol. 7, letter 10/29/1803, 145; for acreage, Bateman *et al.*, 1916, vol. 1, 295; for bribe, Kappler, 1904, Kaskaskia, Article 3, 67, and Article 4 and "Ducoigne," as first "mark x," vol. 2, 68.

182. *ASPIA*, 1832, "great chief," vol. 1, no. 104, 687; Kappler, 1904, vol. 2, 67–68.

183. Carter, 1934–1975, Dearborn to Harrison, vol. 7, letter 2/21/1803, 86.

184. Clanin, 1993, Harrison to Jefferson, vol. R1, letter 5/12/1804, 797–800; Carter, 1934–1975, Dearborn to Harrison, vol. 7, letter 6/21/1804, 203–4.

185. Heckewelder, 1976, 48–70; Schweinitz, 1870, 32–35; Beatty, 1768, 27–28; McCafferty, 2008, 42.

186. Carter, 1934–1975, Harrison to Dearborn, vol. 7, letter 6/18/1805, 294.

187. Schweinitz, 1870, 404–5; White, 2011, 382.

188. Kappler, 1904, Delawares, vol. 2, 70–72.

189. Monette, 1846, acreage, vol. 2, note 4, 521–22; "Treaty with the Delawares" given as "Treaty of Vincennes."

190. Esarey, 1922, Dearborn to Harrison, vol. 1, letter 6/24/1804, 101.

191. Kappler, 1904, Delawares, vol. 2, 71.

192. Carter, 1934–1975, Gibson to Madison, vol. 7, letter 1/17/1805, 258.

193. Kappler, 1904, Piankeshaw, vol. 2, 72–73.

194. Carter, 1934–1975, Petitions, vol. 7, 1/1/1800, 3–4; vol. 7, 11/13/1802, 76–77; post office and road, Habersham to Harrison, vol. 7, letter 8/24/1801, 32; courts, "Note on the Government of Indiana Territory," vol. 7, 1/1/1803, 137.

195. Ibid., Dearborn to Stoddard, vol. 7, letter 2/19/1803, 85–86; Dearborn to Harrison, vol. 7, letter 2/21/1803, 86–87.

196. Esarey, 1922, Harrison to Dearborn, mine, vol. 1, letter 2/26/1802, 44; annuity, vol. 1, 45.

197. Carter, 1934–1975, Bruff to Wilkinson, vol. 13, letter 11/5/1804, 80.

198. *Makataimeshekiakiak* and Patterson, 1839, 58.

199. Carter, 1934–1975, Dearborn to Chouteau, vol. 13, letter 7/17/1804, 31; commission, vol. 13, letter 7/17/1804, 33.

200. Nasatir, 2002, Part II, Item XV, Chouteau to Gallatin, letter 11/7/1804, 759. Wallace, 1970, 17, mentions *Sauk and Meskwaki v. Grand Osage* but included only the Grand Osage emoluments, whereas I include both the Grand and the Petit Osage amounts. Chouteau broke the Osage numbers down as "Grand Osages" at $35,000 and "Petit Osages" at $8,000 and gave the Lakota as "Sioux."

201. Carter, 1934–1975, Wherry to Stoddard, vol. 13, letter 9/15/1804, 64.

202. Ibid., Bruff to Wilkinson, vol. 13, letter 9/29/1804, 57.

203. Esarey, 1922, Harrison to Dearborn, vol. 1, letter 2/26/1802, 46.

204. Ibid., Harrison to Dearborn, the $500, vol. 1, letter 2/26/1802, 45; copper, 46.

205. *ASPIA*, 1832, Jefferson to Congress, vol. 1, no. 107, letter 12/31/1804, 693.

206. Carter, 1934–1975, Bruff to Wilkinson, vol. 13, letter 9/29/1804, 57.

207. Armstrong, 1887, 59–60; Kinzie, 1875, Appendix, 381. Forsyth was a long-time, St. Louis trader and eventual Indian agent to the Sauk and Meskwaki who wrote down his knowledge of the Black Hawk War in 1832.

208. Carter, 1934–1975, Cattle to Bruff, vol. 13, letter 9/9/1804, 62–63; Bruff to Wilkinson, vol. 13, letter 9/29/1804, 56–57.

209. Owens, 2007, 87.

210. Italics in the original. Gue, 1903, vol. 1, 77.

211. *Makataimeshekiakiak* and Patterson, 1839, 58.

212. Armstrong, 1887, 60; Carter, 1934–1975, Wherry to Stoddard, vol. 13, letter 9/15/1804, 63–64; Bruff to Wilkinson, vol. 13, letter 11/5/1804, 76.

213. Carter, 1934–1975, Bruff to Wilkinson, vol. 13, letter 9/29/1804, 58, 60.

214. Kinzie, 1875, 382.

215. Gue, 1903, vol. 1, 77.

216. Kinzie, 1875, 383; Kappler, 1904; Sauk and Meskwaki, vol. 2, 76.

217. Gue, 1903, vol. 1, 77.

218. Kinzie, 1875, 383.

219. Clanin, 1993, Harrison to Dearborn, vol. R2, letter 5/27/1805, 200; as copyedited, Esarey, 1922, vol. 1, 134.

220. Esarey, 1922, Harrison to William Prince, vol. 1, letter 7/1806, 193.

221. Ibid., Harrison to Dearborn, vol. 1, letter 5/27/1805, 134.

222. Ibid., Chouteau to Harrison, vol. 1, letter 5/22/1805, 128–30; Harrison to Dearborn, vol. 1, letter 5/27/1805, 132.

223. Clanin identified that friend as Benjamin Parke, Clanin, 1993, Harrison to Dearborn, vol. R2, note 3, letter 5/27/1805, 201–2; Esarey omitted the enclosure list, Esarey, 1922, Harrison to Dearborn, vol. 1, letter 5/27/1805, 134.

224. In past research, I have before found other documents to have gone mysteriously missing from the record, in circumstances that smelled fishy, for example, Mann, 2009, 8–17; Mann, 2005, 167–69.

225. Clanin, 1993, Chouteau to Harrison, vol. R2, letter 5/31/1805, 203–4.

226. Esarey, 1922, Parke to Harrison, vol. 1, letter 5/25/1805, 131–32.

227. Ibid., Parke to Harrison, vol. 1, letter 5/25/1804, 131.

228. Ibid., Harrison to Dearborn, vol. 1, letter 5/27/1805, 134.

229. Ibid., Harrison to Chouteau, vol. 1, letter 5/27/1805, 134.

230. Carter, 1934–1975, Wilkinson to Dearborn, vol. 13, letter 6/27/1805, 144–45.

231. Ibid., Wilkinson to Dearborn, vol. 13, letter 7/27/1805, 165.

232. Cole, 1921, 61.

233. Esarey, 1922, note 2, vol. 1, 132.

234. *Makataimeshekiakiak* and Patterson, 1839, 59.

235. Esarey, 1922, Harrison to Dearborn, vol. 1, letter 5/27/1805, 134.

236. Kappler, 1904; Sauk and Meskwaki, vol. 2, 74–77.

237. Bateman *et al.*, 1916, vol. 1, 295; Kinzie, 1875, 383.

238. *Makataimeshekiakiak* and Patterson, 1839, 59; blaming Chouteau, Cole, 1921, 61.

239. Kinzie, 1875, 382; *Makataimeshekiakiak* and Patterson, 1839, 58–59.

240. Whitney, 1973–1975, note 2, vol. 2, 22.

241. Carter, 1934–1975, Gallatin to Mansfield, vol. 7, letter 3/13/1805, 269.

242. Ibid., *Territorial Papers*, Wilkinson to Jefferson, vol. 13, letter 11/6/1805, 265.

243. Esarey, *Messages*, Dearborn to Harrison, vol. 1, letter 5/24/1805, 130.

244. Carter, 1934–1975, Dearborn to Harrison, vol. 7, letter 5/24/1805, 287–88. Esarey omitted the two paragraphs suggesting the payoff, Esarey, 1922, Dearborn to Harrison, vol. 1, letter 5/24/1805, 130.

245. Carter, 1934–1975, Dearborn to Harrison, vol. 7, letter 6/11/1805, 292–93. The letter merely indicated "mouth of," but the Maumee River ("Miami of the Lake") was the river in question.

246. Ibid., Mansfield to Gallatin, vol. 7, letter 6/29/1805, 297.

247. Ibid., Harrison to Jefferson, vol. 7, letter 6/18/1805, 294.

248. Esarey, 1922, Harrison to James Findlay, vol. 1, letter 10/15/1801, 34–35; Harrison to Findlay, vol. 1, letter 9/22/1804, 108.

249. Carter, 1934–1975, Harrison to Jefferson, vol. 7, letter 6/18/1805, 295.

250. USWPA, 2014, Item 22, 282; for Johnson House, see Owens, 2007, 57.

251. Esarey, 1922, Indian Council, vol. 1, 6/21/1805, 138.

252. See explanation in Aupaumut, 1827, 76–77.

253. Quoted in Richter, 1992, 184.

254. Heckewelder, 1958, 140; Heckewelder, 1976, 134.

255. Esarey, 1922, Indian Council, vol. 1, 6/21/1805, 139.

256. Robertson, 1890, 45–51.

257. Esarey, 1922, Harrison to Dearborn, vol. 1, letter 3/3/1803, note 3, 76.

258. Ibid., Indian Council, vol. 1, 6/21/1805, 139.

259. Ibid., Wells to Francis Vigo, vol. 1, letter 6/22/1805, 139–40.

260. Ibid., Patterson to Wells, vol. 1, letter 4/5/1805, 121–23; Harrison to Dearborn, vol. 1, letter 5/27/1805, 133; Gibson and Vigo to Harrison, vol. 1, letter 7/6/1805, 141–46; quotation, vol. 1, 142.

261. Harrison ordered Gibson and Vigo to visit all the Miami nations, Esarey, 1922, Harrison to Dearborn, vol. 1, letter 5/27/1805, 133.

262. Esarey, 1922, Gibson and Vigo to Harrison, vol. 1, letter 7/6/1805, 141–46.

263. Ibid., British "talk," vol. 1, 7/6/1805, 146–47; Harrison to Dearborn, vol. 1, letter 7/10/1805, 147, 150–51.

264. Ibid., Harrison to Dearborn, vol. 1, letter 8/10/1805, 161, 164.

265. Ibid., Harrison to Dearborn, vol. 1, letter 8/26/1805, 161–62; Harrison to Dearborn, letter 9/16/1805, 165; Harrison to Dearborn, vol. 1, letter 12/24/1805, 181; Osage war, Carter, 1934–1975, Harrison to Jefferson, vol. 7, letter 6/18/1805, 294.

266. Carter, 1934–1975, Wells to Dearborn, vol. 7, letter 4/20/1807, note 25a, 557.

267. Esarey, 1922, Harrison to Dearborn, vol. 1, letter 8/26/1805, 163; Carter, 1934–1975, Harrison to Jefferson, vol. 7, letter 8/29/1805, 302.

268. Ibid., Harrison to Dearborn, vol. 1, letter 8/26/1805, 163; Carter, 1934–1975, Harrison to Jefferson, vol. 7, letter 8/29/1805, 302.

269. Kappler, 1904, Delawares, vol. 2, 80–82.

270. Esarey, 1922, Dearborn to Harrison, vol. 1, letter 10/11/1805, 169.

271. Carter, 1934–1975, Harrison to Jefferson, vol. 7, letter 11/12/1805, 313.

272. Esarey, 1922, Harrison to Dearborn, vol. 1, letters 11/29/1805, 176; Perry and Bond to Harrison, vol. 1, letter 12/10/1805, 176–77; Carter, 1934–1975, Mansfield to Gallatin, vol. 7, letter 12/8/1805, 324.

273. Carter, 1934–1975, Harrison to Jefferson, vol. 7, letter 8/29/1805, 302; Harrison to Jefferson, vol. 7, letter 11/12/1805, 313.

274. Esarey, 1922, Harrison to Dearborn, vol. 1, letter 11/29/1805, 175–76.

275. Ibid., Harrison to Dearborn, vol. 1, Postscript 11/28/1805, 181.

276. *ASPIA*, 1832, vol. 1, no. 112, 704–5; Kappler, 1904, Piankeshaw, vol. 2, 89–90; Esarey, 1922, vol. 1, 57.

277. Carter, 1934–1975, Wells to the Dearborn, vol. 7, letter 4/(20)22/1808, 558–59.

278. Thornbrough, 1961, Johnston to Eustis, letter 4/15/1809, notes 1 and 2, 33, 33; Carter, 1934–1975, Eustis to Harrison, vol. 8, letter 2/12/1811, 107; Johnston to Eustis, vol. 7, letter 4/15/1809, 647–48.

279. Thornbrough, 1961, Johnston to Smith, letter 4/15/1809, 43.

280. For *Tenskwatawa* and *Tecumseh*, Thornbrough, 1961, Letter Book, entries 5/18/1809 and 5/26/1809, 51–52; Carter, 1934–1975, Parke to Eppes, vol. 7, letter 5/2/1809, 650; Esarey, 1922, Harrison to Eustis, vol. 1, letter 7/5/1809, 349–55. Harrison linked his worth to Madison to the new treaty being pushed, Esarey, 1922, Harrison to Eustis, vol. 1, letter 7/5/1809, 349.

281. Kappler, 1904, vol. 2, 81.

282. Thornbrough, 1961, entries 6/20/1809–6/23/1809, 6/26/1809, 56.

283. Esarey, 1922, Harrison to Eustis, vol. 1, letter 7/5/1809, 353.

284. Ibid., Harrison to Eustis, British, vol. 1, letter 7/5/1809, 349; French, vol. 1, 353.

285. Ibid., Eustis to Harrison, vol. 1, letter 7/14/1809, 356–57; Journal, vol. 1, 362.

286. Adams, 1894, 297.

287. Esarey, 1922, Journal, vol. 1, 363.

288. Ibid., Journal, vol. 1, 366; Thornbrough, 1961, 56–57.

289. Ibid., Proclamation, vol. 1, 357.

290. Owens, 2007, 201.

291. Esarey, 1922, Journal, vol. 1, 368–70.

292. Ibid., Harrison to Dearborn, vol. 1, letter 8/26/1805, 163.

293. Kappler, 1904, vol. 2, 101–2; U.S. Senate, 1828, vol. 2, 134–35.

294. Esarey, 1922, Journal, vol. 1, 373–76.

295. Kappler, 1904, vol. 2, 102; Esarey, 1922, Journal, vol. 1, 376. Brackets are Esarey's. The journal gives this as the "Raviere" with Esarey adding ["Petit"], with a reference immediately following to the "Mississinway" River, vol. 1, 376. The "Riviere Petit" of the French was the Tippecanoe River, which was not Kilatika land, so that Esarey's cross-identification seems unlikely. For Riviere Petite, see Baldwin, 1875, 7–8.

296. Kappler, 1904, vol. 2, 103; USS, 1828, vol. 2, 135.

297. Esarey, 1922, Journal, vol. 1, 376–78.

298. Kappler, 1904, vol. 2, 103–4; USS, 1828, vol. 2, 12/26/1809–1/2/1810, 133–35.

299. Badollet and Gallatin, 1963, Badollet to Gallatin, letter 8/6/1811, 188–89.

300. Esarey, 1922, Eustis to Harrison, vol. 1, letter 7/5/1809, 357.

301. Ibid., Harrison to Eustis, vol. 1, letter 4/5/1809, 336.

302. Ibid., Eustis to Harrison, vol. 1, letter 4/29/1809, 343.

303. Ibid., Harrison to Eustis, vol. 1, letter 10/1/1809, 359.

304. Ibid., Minutes, vol. 1, 9/17/1802, 57.

305. Ibid., vol. 1, Perry to Harrison, vol. 1, letter 12/10/1805, 176–77; Bond to Harrison, vol. 1, letter 12/16/1805, 177–78; Message, Answer, vol. 1, 12/16/1805, 178–79.

306. Esarey, 1922, Harrison to William Prince, vol. 1, letter 7/1806, 192.

307. Carter, 1934–1975, Harrison to Dearborn, vol. 7, letter 8/11/1806, 377.

308. Esarey, 1922, Harrison to Hargrove, vol. 1, letter 11/23/1807, 276–77; Harrison to Hargrove, vol. 1, letter 11/27/1807, 278.

309. Ibid., Harrison to Eustis, instructions, vol. 1, letter 11/3/1809, 388; arrival date, vol. 1, 390; Harrison to Eustis, vol. 1, letter 12/10/1809, 396.

310. Dawson, 1824, 85.

311. Esarey, 1922, Harrison to Eustis, vol. 1, letter 12/10/1809, 396.

312. Kappler, 1904, Kickapoo, vol. 2, 104–5; U.S. Senate, 1828, 1/10/1810–2/23/1810, 137–39.

313. USS, 1828, vol. 2, 12/19/1809, 130; vol. 2, 12/21/1809, 132; Esarey, 1922, Washington Johnson, and Downs, vol. 2, letter 11/4/1809, 391–92; Carter, 1934–1975, commission, vol. 8, 12/21/1809, note 2, 3.

CHAPTER 3

❦

"The Sun Is My Father, and the Earth Is My Mother": Harrison's War on Tecumseh

Harrison had done tremendous damage to the Miami Confederacy with his twelve treaties between 1803 and 1809, but it was not the Miami peoples who raised the banner against the settlers. Under *Mihšihkinaahkwa* ("Little Turtle"), the Miami had signed the Greenville Treaty, and they had intended to keep the peace. It was not until they had been surrounded by forts, crisscrossed by roads, inundated with missionaries, and bullied for land that they began inclining toward the Shawnee resistance.

Although looming large in settler records as Woodlanders, the Shawnee were actually the new kids on the block, relatively speaking, arriving in North America only shortly before the Europeans and, then, only after a frightening voyage across the open sea. (Yes, Indians had seaworthy vessels.[1]) In 1825, *Catahecassa* ("Black Hoof") mentioned the voyage, while speaking in 1829, *Nawahtahtha* ("George Bluejacket") described the original Shawnee homeland as "swallowed up in the great salt water," by the sea spirit, *Watchemenetoo* (probably flooding).[2] Before sailing north, twelve Shawnee questors on a Sky journey saw Turtle Island from a great height.[3] In other words, they knew that the North American continent was there before they sailed. Hearing this tradition, Moravian missionary John Heckewelder repeated it in 1798, identifying their point of origin as northern Mexico and their point of arrival, the southern tip of Florida.[4] John Law of Indiana also recorded the tradition in 1839, putting the Shawnee voyage vaguely through the Gulf of Mexico.[5] Clearly, the Shawnee had traveled north, across the Caribbean Sea.

Watchemenetoo was a spirit not a human force, but Western speculation has the emergency driving the Shawnee from Mexico as the arrival of the Spaniards, who stepped foot on Vera Cruz, Mexico, in 1519.[6] The antiquity of Shawnee sites in

North America makes this unlikely, however. North of Cincinnati, Ohio, sits "Fort Ancient," recent Shawnee stone works, which archaeologists date from 1450 to 1650 CE.[7] Not only does 1450 predate the Spanish arrival but even if the Shawnee ran the whole way from Florida to Ohio, it strains credulity that they arrived out of breath one day and built impressive complexes the next. Assuming that they were escaping human enemies, those would have been Indigenous enemies, perhaps the Aztec, who arrived in Central Mexico around 1200 CE, becoming dominate around 1325.[8] If so, between repeated flooding and the Aztec conquest, the old homeland became insufferable. Under this scenario, the Shawnee could make it across the continent to the Ohio Valley to start building by 1450, but again, tradition has the sea, not humans, as the problem.

In 1824, *Tenskawatawa* ("Open Door") described the post-arrival period as complicated by the unwelcome mat they found, forcing them to erect *Kaāhta linee Waukauhoowāā* ("Old Men's Forts"), to repulse furious attacks by Floridians, whose lands they were invading.[9] Now, they met the Spaniards. In 1662 and 1674, Jesuits recorded that the Shawnee were long-time trading partners with the Spanish of *La Florida* (extending from Florida to South Carolina).[10] The Shawnee also spread throughout the south and north to the Ohio valley, the reason that the English word "Shawnee" is thought to come from the Algonkin term, *shawunogi* ("Southerner").[11] James Mooney also proposed another origin of Shawnee, as from *sewan*, Algonkin for "salt," because of the large measures of salt that the Shawnee used, unlike any other North American people.[12] Mooney is alone in this contention, however, while salt usage was not a traditional, but a Euro-imposed, development, later on.

The Shawnee's six original "families" (primary clan lineages) are *Thawegila*, *Chalakawtha* ("Chillicothe"), *Peckowe* ("Piqua"), *Kispogo*, *Makojay*, and *Shawano*.[13] According to *Catahecassa*, the entire Shawnee Confederacy of six "families" adopted the overall name of its most powerful nation, the Shawano (*Shāūwonoa*).[14] The Kickapoo were closely related to the Shawnee, as were the western Lenape, granting the Shawnee easy access to both nations and their territories.[15] Importantly, Shawnee clans migrated separately, dispersing widely across the eastern Woodlands, accounting for the earliest settler chronicles recording them as far Midwest as the Wabash River and as far southeast as Alabama. In 1681, advised by two Shawnee, the Franquelin map placed clans of the Shawnee at the "*Skipakicipi ou la rivière bleue*" (*Skipakicipi* or the Blue River, that is, the Cumberland). The 1718 De Lisle Map also recorded Shawnee on the Cumberland River, calling it "*des anciens Chauanons*" (the old Shawnee's). English settlers later bifurcated the original river into the Cumberland and Shawnee Rivers.[16] The 1710 Senex Map located other Shawnee clans at the headwaters of the Savannah River, and in 1823, Tennesseean John Haywood combined the Savannah and Cumberland Rivers, assigning the Shawnee to his mash-up.[17] The earliest map (Franquelin) also placed the Shawnee smack on the Wabash and Ohio Rivers.

Although formally categorized as an Algonkin language, Shawnee is a language isolate gradually absorbed by and reframing itself as Algonkin. Originally, all six Shawnee nations spoke the original language, making communication convenient for them, despite their wide dispersal. This language continued into the nine-teenth century, but as a holy language, used only by spiritual leaders who worked with children under four years of age. It became extinct when its last speaker died in 1877–1878. The few words of classical Shawnee remaining are untranslatable, being personal names relating to a matriarchal heritage around *Kokomthena* ("Star Woman"). Although the old language was lost, the Makojay nation continued to have the obligation of producing holy leaders, until its bundle ("medicine bag") was lost. Some Makojay remnants intermarried with the Seneca of Oklahoma, with Western scholars claiming that they were absorbed by them, but I have met modern Ohio Makojay.[18]

Shawnee families freely intermarried with other nations that they encountered, explaining why the *Kispogo* triplets, a girl who died in childhood and her broth-ers, *Tenskwatawa* and *Tecumseh* ("Sky Panther," "Shooting Star"), had a Muskogee mother and aunt.[19] For Indigenous America, comets, or Sky-Walking Panthers, portended a major event, often a war, for Sky Panthers were, as the Iroquois put it, *Oshondowekgona*, "Fire Dragons of Discord."[20] Thus, as the Crouching Sky Panther, *Tecumseh* was the very embodiment of trouble for the set-tlers, even though *Tecumseh* is actually the name of the clan lineage holding Shawnee war chief titles and not a personal name.[21]

Following their arrival on Turtle Island, the Shawnee came to have been con-sidered very spiritual by the locals. They shared the concept of the Twinned Cosmos, whose Blood and Breath powers had to have been balanced, for har-mony to reign. The balancing is common in matriarchal cultures, so it is not acci-dental that the Shawnee had female chiefs.[22] If *Tecumseh* was charged with war, then *Tenskwatawa*'s job was to create the spiritual basis of the Shawnee resistance, and by July 1807, Indiana governor William Henry Harrison was alarmed that "several tribes" were now enthralled by his message. He shuddered at the thought that *Tenskwatawa* might "remove," that is, kill, his handpicked chiefs. With his yes-men gone, the "fidelity" of the bulk of the people would be thrown into ques-tion.[23] Thus, when in December 1807, one thousand Anishinabe were on their way down from Green Bay, Lake Michigan, to Greenville, Ohio, to hear *Tenskwatawa* speak, it set off Harrison's alarm bells.[24]

On December 5, 1807, Indian agent William Wells ginned the panic up by assuring Secretary of War Henry Dearborn that the "Shawnee impostor," *Tenskwatawa*, was being reinforced by "seven Large vessels" sent by King George III to "america Loaded with Soldiers" to "releave his red children" by wrenching their land from the United States. Fingering the British as siccing Indians on set-tlers was a commonplace, but it worked. In reply, Dearborn ordered Wells to keep his "eye on the Propet" and "foreign agents," thus nipping trouble in the bud.[25] Unnipped, however, in the spring of 1808, *Tenskwatawa* upped the ante by moving permanently from Greenville to Tippecanoe on the Wabash in Indiana, among the Potawatomi. The kernel of Shawnee resistance at this point consisted of the Three Fires: the Anishinabe, Ottawa, and Potawatomi.[26]

From 1807 to 1809, Indiana settlers were itching for war, as their primary method of seizing land. It carried the perquisite of killing Indians, at will. For all the fiction that fear motivated the settlers, land and scalp bounties with which to buy it were always the incentive. As much was obvious in 1807, when Vincennes land registrar John Badollet condemned the 1807 war-mongering as a put-up job of Harrison's land fraud and greed.[27] Fort Wayne trading-post factor John Johnston was also gleeful, stocking up on inventory, because even if war were forestalled, the war drive would force the Indians to trade with him, not the British, putting them in debt payable in land.[28]

Understanding the debt game, *Tenskwatawa* restrained his followers from dealing with the Americans, leaving Tippecanoe "in a state of starvation" by April 1808.[29] Under *Tenskwatawa*'s old ways, head men and women ensured food and shelter for all the people through proper management of farmland (Blood, woman's purview) and free-range animal preserves (Breath, men's purview). In assuming leadership, *Tenskwatawa* had taken on the responsibility of ensuring provisions for all. However, as the land base of Indiana was stripped from the Indians, this approach became untenable, especially as more and more people flocked to Tippecanoe, their numbers overwhelming his ability to provide.[30] Not without calculation, then, Harrison gave the 1808 Shawnee annuity, on which *Tenskwatawa* was counting, to *Catahecassa* at Wapakoneta, Ohio, and *Catahecassa* did not share it. (Those at Tippecanoe were Potawatomi not Shawnee.) By November 1808, *Tenskwatawa* was desperate enough to request humanitarian aid from Harrison. Accordingly, Harrison fronted *Tenskwatawa* $102, to be subtracted from the 1809 Shawnee annuity.[31]

Tenskwatawa next connected with the Miami on the Wabash, with Wells inevitably attributing that effort to British prodding. Meantime, the Wyandot and the Three Fires were meeting "in secret council" to organize opposition to the November 17, 1807, land-concession Treaty of Detroit (Treaty with the Ottawa), starting with killing those chiefs who had signed it.[32] Intent on undermining *Tenskwatawa*, Harrison listened to his Potawatomi informant, *Wonongasea* ("Five Medals"), who reported that his people at the St. Joseph River in Michigan were backing *Tenskwatawa*. The only way to deflect them, said *Wonongasea*, was to pay them off or hit them militarily.[33] Wells attempted the first on April 20, bribing their chief *Main Poc* to take his 120 people home for $800 and three U.S. medals, but *Main Poc* turned around and supplied *Tenskwatawa* with one hundred horses with which to buy necessities from the settlers—that is, Wells had just expensively supplied the resistance.[34]

By 1808, settler records had *Tenskwatawa* openly calling for all Indians to disrupt U.S.-aligned chiefs by making war on those chiefs who refused his message. If collaborators were "subdued," then the resisters could attack the "white people," Wells warned.[35] *Tenskwatawa* framed the situation differently. U.S. messages "plainly showed" that collaborating Miami chiefs had "abandoned" their people to sell land to the United States, with the United States making the Indian men into women, but *Tenskwatawa* would remake them into men.[36] In the eastern Woodlands, jobs are gendered, not people. Peacemaking is a female-gendered job. If men perform it, they are "made women" for the duration of the task.[37] *Tenskwatawa* meant that there would be no more land-selling "peace" councils.

Wells's repeated accusations of *Tenskwatawa*'s plan to make war contradicted every message coming directly from *Tenskwatawa*, who continually told Harrison that he was for peace, specifically warning Harrison that "bad birds" were carrying false messages about him.[38] Significantly, *Tenskwatawa* had women and children at Tippecanoe, and Indians never intentionally put women and children in a war zone, as the settlers well knew.[39] The war talk was settler projection, their propaganda stating that Indians wanted to "exterminate the [settler] race" while settlers were still "sparse in population."[40] Extermination, extirpation, annihilation—these were settler, not Indian, mindsets.

Nevertheless, Wells continued to beat the war drums, as fifty Ho-Chunk ("Winnebago") came to join *Tenskwatawa* in the spring of 1809, while the traders eagerly anticipated a war that could only feed their bottom line.[41] Alarmed, *Tenskwatawa* personally visited Harrison at Vincennes in the last week of June 1809 to deny "most strenuously" that he planned any attack.[42] Harrison's reaction was to write, at length, to Dearborn on fortifications to "keep the Indians in check."[43] Although there were but one hundred people, tops, at Tippecanoe, Illinois Territory chimed in with its own tales of "British interference with our Indian Affairs."[44] The war hawks were out in force, driving their narrative as hard as they could when, in a move that could only inflame the situation, Harrison proceeded to the 1809 Treaty of Fort Wayne. His war bubble burst on May 16, 1809, when he failed to provoke the Indians into war, leaving him to confess that the war hysteria had just been one, terrible mistake.[45]

The mistake continued, however. Going into 1812, the War Department received overwrought letters from territorial officials and citizens, alike, frantically proclaiming that the British had "the Prophet" set to attack, at any moment.[46] Harrison tended his end of the flow throughout 1810, announcing that the "Prophet" was "exciting" hostility with his 1,000 men, women, and children at Tippecanoe.[47] By June, Harrison was in such high dungeon as to assure Dearborn, quite ridiculously, that *Tenskwatawa* was planning a surprise attack on Vincennes.[48] When *Tenskwatawa* returned his undesired, 1810 annuity of salt, Harrison flew into manufactured rage, railing against Indian insolence and reporting that the Sauk, Meskwaki, and Kickapoo, as well as the Potawatomi under *Main Poc,* were adding their men to *Tenskwatawa*'s.[49] Still just "the Prophet's brother," *Tecumseh* was accused of stirring up people on the Auglaize River, Ohio.[50] At the same time as he pushed this narrative, Harrison was organizing his hip-pocket chiefs to block the traditionalists' moves.[51] The old European game of *divide et impera* was on.

The Indians were upset, not because it was their "nature," but because the United States was industriously surveying their lands for takeover. By mid-November 1810, the land office was so busy, that it needed to hire "Many surveyors" to finish (prompting a patronage request from Harrison to hire two friends of his).[52] On October 13, 1811, even as Harrison was about to engage the Indians militarily, he blithely sent men "to survey" a disputed "tract of country," because "the whole affair with the Indians" would be "settled" before they could arrive.[53] The lead surveyor termed these "Western Lands" the "most precious portion" of the U.S. "patrimony."[54] The Miami and Illiniwek Confederacies had every reason for concern about what was going on.

July 1810 yielded diametrically opposed Indian and settler messages. *Tenskwatawa* sent Harrison multiple communications stating that he had no intention of attacking the settlers, but Harrison promoted hearsay accounts claiming inside information that war was absolutely intended.[55] On the same day that Secretary of War William Eustis expressed gratification that *Tenskwatawa* was unable to raise a war, Harrison wrote that war was imminent. Reluctantly acknowledging President Madison's peace policy, Harrison promised heroic work toward peace, yet one week later, returned to ominous tones on the matter.[56]

Harrison's idea of peacemaking was to send *Tenskwatawa* a threatening message, assuring him that Indians would not join him, warning that no help would be forthcoming from the British, and menacing him with the "innumerable Warriors" of the United States.[57] Next, Harrison organized his chiefs to "disperse the banditti" at Tippecanoe, crowing that his bullying had worked, for *Tenskwatawa* was fading while his chiefs were moving against *Tenskwatawa* to prevent a U.S. attack on themselves.[58] It is possible that Harrison was living in such a bubble of Miami, Lenape, and Potawatomi yes-men, that he actually believed that *Tenskwatawa* was "hated and feared" by everyone but the Kickapoo. Still, no one drove anyone from Tippecanoe.[59]

Still pushing war, Harrison cajoled fellow territorial leaders into reporting that the Indians were massing, with settlers at Jeffersonville put to flight.[60] The Sauk, Meskwaki, and Kickapoo had become active in the west, he averred, while the Muskogee of the south were sending messages to the Miami. Harrison all but demanded that Eustis set up military posts along the Wabash.[61] He also instigated a transparent petition-and-resolution drive to paper Washington, D.C. with overwrought accusations of Indian treachery, writing the documents himself and rendering his followers so gloriously drunk that they signed his documents.[62] Notwithstanding, the Indians continued as stubbornly at peace in Indiana as did Madison in Washington, D.C.

Had Harrison understood Woodlands culture, he might have been cheered by the fact that *Tecumseh* now rose to prominence in his parleys, to the point that Harrison began identifying him by name.[63] This change in interlocutors signified a crucial shift in policy: *Tenskwatawa* was the holy man; *Tecumseh* was the war chief. The United States had finally pushed the traditionals into a ready stance. Looking to their own culture for story frames, settlers decided that *Tecumseh*'s authority had to have derived from his "skill and bravery," which gave him "power and influence such as no other chieftain ever possessed over the children of the forest."[64] Actually, it was grown-up women who gave *Tecumseh* his position, for under Woodlands law, only the Grandmothers could appoint "warriors."[65]

In 1810, the Wyandot female officials of the Ohio Union conferred its "war belt" (alliance wampum) on *Tecumseh*.[66] Before they gave him the wampum, *Tecumseh* was demur. It was only after the Grandmothers had announced *Tecumseh*'s appointment that he could maneuver.[67] First, women gave three warnings, which settlers seldom recorded.[68] If unsuccessful, they handed the matter to the men. Contrary to settler stereotype, this did not mean war. Instead, more sternly than the women, the men would issue their own three-set warnings to offenders. Thus, the holy man *Tenskwatawa* gave the settlers his three warnings. Although more warnings were not required, *Tecumseh* looked to give another three warnings.[69] It was not until 1813 that *Tecumseh* was League-authorized to tell the British that he was ready to "take up the hatchet" against the United States.[70] This dramatic development indicated that the traditionals were thoroughly fed up, yet Harrison insisted that the British, not the Wyandot—let alone, the women—had conferred power on *Tecumseh*.[71]

Beginning his three sets of warnings early in June 1810, *Tecumseh* proposed bringing upward of one hundred men, or "a great many more," to Vincennes to clear matters up.[72] Harrison immediately touted this as the "attack" on Vincennes that he had been falsely assuring Washington, D.C. was imminent. He whipped up fear in Vincennes, so that it "flew like wild fire." Some inhabitants laughed at its absurdity, but "for most" the "terror" was "great and distress inexpressible," said Badollet.[73] Harrison called up the "light horse and several companies of militia," ordering the regulars from Fort Knox to be on hand. When *Tecumseh* arrived, he had to walk through "a passage formed by the military drawn up with bayonets fixed and glistening in every direction." To *Tecumseh*, this would have looked like the gauntlet that male prisoners were forced to run after capture. To its credit, his entourage was "surprised but not appalled by such a formidable reception."[74]

Per Harrison's request, nothing like hundreds showed up, just *Tecumseh* and thirty to forty men, women, and children.[75] Oblivious of this concession, Harrison consistently characterized *Tecumseh*'s speeches in council as "insolent."[76] Apparently, his first insolence was addressing Harrison as "brother" not "father." Then, on August 20, 1810, *Tecumseh* rehearsed the history of local troubles, starting with the French, segueing into the British takeover, and finally, the U.S. usurpation, detailing how deceptively each had killed Indians by using them as proxy soldiers in European disputes. He noted that, during the Revolution, people in the U.S.-allied Shawnee and Lenape towns had all been murdered, despite their loyalty to the United States.[77] This history lesson riled Harrison, along with what Harrison called *Tecumseh*'s "strange inconsistency" in asserting that "it was not his intention to go to war." *Tecumseh* cut Harrison off midstream, contradicting Harrison's version of events in an "indecent manner" using "violent jesticulations," insisting that whoever told Harrison that were "liars."[78]

Tecumseh next accused the United States of fraudulently acquiring lands via treaties agreed to by "only a few." The traditionals had called a council of the whole, he continued, requiring that Harrison come justify his treaties. Should Harrison refuse, then it was his fault should wheeling, dealing chiefs be killed. Meantime, the people would accept presents from neither the United States nor the British, so that neither could claim that they had sold anything, but they would take powder, should the British offer it. At this point, Harrison interrupted *Tecumseh*, a grave breach of Woodlands protocol.[79]

John Law's account of exchange, taken from people who actually understood Shawnee, showed Harrison attempting to weasel around an explanation of, especially, the 1809 Treaty of Fort Wayne. Insisting that the United States abided by "the strictest rules of right and justice," Harrison proclaimed that he always acted with "honor, integrity, and fair dealing," even when treating with the "most insignificant tribe." Proceeding long-windedly in this vein, he pushed the Indians to leap up, gripping their tomahawks, with *Tecumseh* crying in Shawnee to interpreter Joseph Barron, "He lies!" When Barron deliberately mistranslated these words to Harrison, *Tecumseh* spoke enough English to realize it. "No, no," he shouted at Barron in Shawnee. "Tell him he lies!" Harrison did not comprehend, but territorial secretary John Gibson, who was also present, did understand. Out of caution, he called up Harrison's armed guard.[80] Not grasping that he was the one who had offered the insult, Harrison angrily called off the conference. The next day, *Tecumseh* petitioned him to continue the discussions, as his purpose was to settle the issues "amicably."[81]

The conference resuming on August 21, *Tecumseh* said a settler had come to him and *Tenskwatawa*, saying that he represented a large number of settlers. The man told them that Harrison had conducted the second Fort Wayne Treaty negotiations in "the greatest secrecy," pulling it off using a small cadre. Afterward, he planned to "confine" the Indians to a "small piece" of land and intended to sell items to the Indians so expensively that they could not afford them (per Jefferson's lopping plan). Harrison gave gifts for the sole purpose of cheating the Indians of their lands. A second "American" then told the traditionals that Harrison was planning yet another treaty council to take even more land. The only way to forestall the theft, this man said, was to go to Vincennes and speak "very loud" to Harrison.[82] Badollet claimed that some of this account was concocted by Harrison, so he could pass a law making it "highly penal to hold conferences with the Indians."[83] To be sure, paragraph 5 of an Act Regulating Trade with the Indians, signed by Harrison on December 15, 1810, held exactly that provision.[84]

Tecumseh also knew that, by 1812, Indiana settlers looked forward to having a better man than Harrison take over as governor and had been told that the United States had not countenanced his treaties. Although Harrison resented *Tecumseh's* imputations, formal inquiries into Harrison's dealings had begun as early as 1808, in an attempt to curb his gubernatorial powers.[85] Badollet certainly loathed "our immaculate Governor." Originally angered by Harrison's illegal introduction of slavery to Indiana, Badollet soon came to hate him for shifting blame away from himself onto others while leveraging "people to praise him and extol his talents." Badollet sneered that Harrison then used the orchestrated praise to justify actions he had already decided on.[86] The principle onslaught against Harrison was led by Jonathan Jennings, then Indiana territorial representative to Congress and eventual first governor of the State of Indiana. From December 1810 through January 1812, Jennings raised impeachment articles against Harrison in the U.S. House of Representatives, charging corruption in office.[87]

Jennings was onto something, and Harrison was running scared, constituting an inexplicably ignored reason for Harrison's all-out effort to engineer an Indian war: distraction. As a commander-in-chief in the field during a war, he could not be impeached. It was not incidental that, of *Tecumseh's* lengthy presentation, all Harrison heard was that *Tecumseh* knew half of Indiana opposed him as governor. War was Harrison's salvation. Thus, when *Tecumseh* offered that, pitying the suffering of the women and children, he "alone" was now the "head of all the Indians," Harrison's reaction was to countenance (or, perhaps, to instigate) the formation of a militia dragoon, seventy-five strong, for which he implored Eustis to supply arms.[88]

Awaiting instructions from Eustis, Harrison intensified his mobilization, readying the militias, although already midway through October, it was too nearly winter for settlers to build forts or move troops.[89] In his November 1810 annual governor's message, he hawkishly denigrated the "numerous and warlike" Indians, slammed *Tenskwatawa*, insisted hardly any Indians repudiated the treaties, used *Tecumseh's* August 21 speech to whip up paranoia about settler treason, and attributed all the displeasure with himself to the "blackest treachery and hatred" of fellow settlers toward the government.[90] His war drive had shifted into fourth gear.

At the same time, Harrison offered self-contradictory assessments of the situation to his superiors. He rejoiced that Indians were gobbling up their annuities (accepting annuities legally accepted the treaties). Peace was at hand! Within the same paragraph, however, he admitted that half of the people had refused their annuities, adding that all the peoples west of the Wabash claimed land ownership in common, a de facto repudiation of all the Harrison's treaties. The Miami were all frightened of *Tenskwatawa*, he asserted, while the very valuable land of the traditionals was surrounded "upon three sides" by lower-class settlers rushing in from Ohio and Pennsylvania.[91] Holding that those settlers would not accept lesser lands, when they saw Indians on the "finest country as to soil"— his actual argument—Harrison offloaded his cupidity onto the squatters, whom he knew were easily removed.[92] The fact was, Harrison's land speculation business was just then deeply in debt, so he needed that "finest" soil to sell in 160-acre plots for $2–$6 per acre.[93] Thus, he assured Eustis that it was imperative to strike while the peace was hot, before the traditionals occupied the land with new Wyandot towns.[94]

Claiming no receipt of instructions from the Madison administration by February 6, 1811—despite having acknowledged Madison's peace policy on December 24, 1810[95]—Harrison threatened to use his old instructions from Jefferson to continue securing land, while insinuating Canadian plots against the United States. On April 23, he whined that he had done his best to follow Madison's instructions to keep the peace.[96] Then, he devoted pages to Potawatomi murders and horse theft (*Tecumseh* and *Tenskwatawa* returned the horses), glowering that the only reason the brothers had not yet started the war was because they could not raise the army.[97] Area war hawks also upped their quota of "bad Indian" letters to officials, to the point that the House of Representatives began to take the complaints seriously, albeit as fixated on British interference, for in the east, the war drive focused on the British, not the Indians.[98]

In June 1811, Harrison treated Indigenous overtures to the various Indian nations as definitive intentions of war, even though he surely knew that duly constituted speakers carried belts as their authorization, just as U.S. ambassadors carried their authorizing documents. Disregarding that, Harrison replayed rumors of a surveyor supposedly having been chased off Wea land, even though the surveyor had gone to St. Louis rather than work over the winter. Harrison alleged murders of settlers and accused the Lenape of theft when they claimed the annuities due them. A surefire method of riling the troops was to talk of a "white" woman being captured by the "savages." Harrison really had one such incident, but alas, the woman was recovered.[99] Attempting to force a confrontation and knowing full well that *Tenskwatawa* wanted no annuity salt (traditionally, salt interferes with spiritual vision), Harrison rubbed salt in the wounds by sending salt to him. In response, *Tenskwatawa* seized the entire annuity salt shipment, so that it could not be distributed to other Indians, providing another complaint against "the Prophet."[100]

Harrison's not-so-hidden agenda was to drum up pretexts for his "just war," and he did not await Madison's go-ahead to prepare for it, writing and signing a law on December 19, 1810, empowering him to call up the militia at will.[101] By June 6, 1811, he had acquired seventy pairs of pistols and seventy iron swords, good enough, he said, to crack the "naked skull of a savage," but his little militia was hopeless with its old musketry and resistant to training. When settlers in Illinois skedaddled to their forts, Harrison made no effort to hie Indiana settlers to theirs, despite predicting that, in the event of war, settler families would be "butchered," and Vincennes, "sacked." Any injuries to person and property, he hinted darkly, would flow from a "want of resolution" on Madison's part.[102] In an era when the evil-eyed British siccing "savages" on helpless settlers was the hottest of conspiracy buttons, this was a calculated stab at the heart of Madison's policy of peace with the Indians.

New rumors of war flowed from Harrison's pen on June 19, 1811, with Harrison charging that the "scoundrel" *Tecumseh* was about to invade Vincennes.[103] (No attack materialized.) Impatient with the lack of alarm in Washington, D.C., Harrison began coordinating directly, orders or no, with General William Clark in Illinois Territory, where the chief concern was *Main Poc*, not *Tecumseh*.[104] Nevertheless, Harrison sent a threatening message to *Tecumseh*, saying that he knew all about *Tecumseh*'s (nonexistent) plot to kill him and would send "swarms of hunting-shirt men"—militiamen—after him. He simultaneously offered to reopen the 1809 Fort Wayne Treaty should *Tecumseh* agree to a parley, as *Tecumseh* did in a very conciliatory reply.[105] Despite this, on July 2, Harrison pressed Eustis as hard as he could for war, with Clark chiming in on July 3 with exaggerated claims.[106] The Madison administration remained skeptical of the synthetic hysteria, however.[107]

Meantime, Harrison's messengers, translator Joseph Barron and Captain Walter Wilson, had arrived at Tippecanoe, to a warm greeting by *Tenskwatawa*, but not by the women, who held a council proposing to seize and hold—perhaps even kill—them both. (Legally, the women welcomed, declared war, and took charge of prisoners.) *Tecumseh* nixed the plan, for legally, he had as yet delivered but one warning, and Harrison's men had come under a white flag.[108] Long before the Europeans had arrived, Indigenous law recognized "emissaries of peace," who had free and secure passage, even in time of war.[109] Thus, the European custom of safe passage under white flags was respected because *Tecumseh* was observing the old ways, which was, after all, the whole point of Tippecanoe.

Despite his direct orders from Madison to maintain the peace, Harrison announced an "absolute necessity" to deliver an "early blow, heavy enough to crush" the Indiana Union.[110] At last, the war-hawk letters, petitions, and resolutions "had the desired effect," as Robert McAfee put it, for Eustis ordered 500 men from Pittsburg to Vincennes, as a precaution.[111] Madison and Eustis seemed to have authorized Harrison's troops more to shut him up than to put anyone into the field, however, for Madison reemphasized that Harrison should not start anything.[112] Harrison immediately replied that *Tecumseh* was approaching Vincennes with up to 130 men, implying that he came to attack. This spin completely ignored the fact that Harrison had, himself, invited *Tecumseh* to meet with him and that *Tecumseh* had accepted.[113] No matter: Harrison's letter was followed immediately by a petition to the president and a resolution from citizens of Knox County calling for war, both orchestrated by Harrison, who seemed palpably angry at not being taken seriously by Washington, D.C.[114]

Tecumseh arrived to deliver his second warning on July 27, with 10 percent of his retinue of 300 being women and children, yet Harrison snarled that *Tecumseh* had reneged on attacking Vincennes only upon seeing Harrison's troops. Demanding an explanation for the seizure of a salt shipment, along with the killers of settlers in Illinois, he refused to reopen the 1809 Fort Wayne Treaty, ultimately sending *Tecumseh* away, his tail tucked between his legs, as he characterized it.[115] Humphrey Marshall's contrary portrait presented *Tecumseh* as self-possessed and dignified throughout, with Harrison taunting him, offering to pay him for the Fort Wayne Treaty land, if he could prove that it was his. *Tecumseh* refused.[116] (Taking the money would have confirmed the treaty.) Badollet stated that, when confronted about the salt, *Tecumseh* replied that there was just "no pleasing" Harrison: when *Tenskwatawa* refused the salt, he was angry, yet when he took the salt, Harrison was equally angry.[117] According to Henry Rowe Schoolcraft, concluding his speech, *Tecumseh* made as if to sit on the ground. Seeing this, Harrison sent a chair to him, with the message that his "Father" had provided it. "My Father!" cried *Tecumseh*, indignantly. "The *Sun* is my father, and the *Earth* is my mother, and on *her* bosom, I will repose!" With that, he plopped to the ground with his Young Men.[118]

Western historians privilege Harrison's account over the others and then take Harrison's at face value, attributing the conference's supposed failure to *Tecumseh*, but we should ask, why?[119] First, women and children attended peace councils, only. Second, this was but the second of the three warnings requisite before war ensued, while a direct witness to events, Badollet, insisted that the Indians had no intention of starting a war in 1811.[120] Third, *Tecumseh*'s avowed purpose at the meeting was "setting limits to the encroachments" of the settlers.[121] This did not mean killing them but simply holding the current line.[122] Fourth, *Tecumseh* offered wampum for the dead settlers, even though his men had not killed them.[123] Finally, Badollet was on the spot, while the 1824 Marshall and 1825 Schoolcraft accounts were penned from the living memory of informants, making their versions of events worth consulting. Not only do the Badollet, Marshall, and Schoolcraft accounts square with traditional motives, but they also support one another over Harrison's version.

The third player in this drama, the British were watching the developments of 1810–1811. On November 16, 1810, Matthew Elliott, superintendent of Canada's Indian Department, reported that the United States was on the verge of starting a war with the Indians and claimed to have it from *Tecumseh* that Harrison had forced him to disclose secret plans.[124] Westerners eagerly but dubiously seize on this to mean that *Tecumseh* was planning war, but Harrison's minutes would certainly have recorded a slip-up like that, whereas *Tecumseh* was not finished delivering legally mandated warnings. Elliott could spin as well as Harrison.

On January 1, 1811, lieutenant governor of Lower Canada James Henry Craig gave war another push, ordering the British *Chargé d'Affaires* in Washington, D.C. to notify his U.S. counterpart of *Tecumseh*'s imputed plans.[125] On February 26, 1811, Upper Canada lieutenant governor Francis Gore ordered Elliott not to leave the Indiana Union with the impression that the British encouraged hostilities against the United States, but this message was somehow not delivered till 1812.[126] The British were covering their tracks while orchestrating war on their end, with the Indians as sacrifice. The more the United States focused on the Indians, the fewer the U.S. troops available to engage British regulars.

While this British flurry of messages rained down, Badollet notified Treasury Secretary Gallatin that Harrison had needlessly trumped up an Indian war through a series of dirty tricks, extorting treaties while knowingly misinforming Washington, D.C. about *Tecumseh* and *Tenskwatawa*.[127] Meantime, Eustis approached Madison on August 21, telling him that the Indians did not seem likely to start hostilities, although he allowed Harrison to mobilize on August 22.[128] On August 29, the U.S. war machine clanked into slow motion, preparing to face the British by dispatching Colonel John P. Boyd down the Wabash River.[129] Waiting at Jeffersonville, it did not occur to Harrison until September 3 that perhaps Boyd had actually been ordered to the Canadian border, and not to his command.[130]

Meantime, Harrison claimed that he had been given the go-ahead by Madison. On August 29, a recruitment was posted in Lexington, Kentucky, stating that Harrison planned to take the field by September 20.[131] This was ridiculous. Madison had not authorized Harrison to attack, so in something of a panic on September 18, Eustis clarified that any further U.S. action should depend solely upon what *Tenskwatawa* actually did in response to Harrison's approach.[132] Notwithstanding, the Kentucky recruiting advertisement was posted on October 2.[133] Hearing only what he wanted to hear, Harrison went on a shopping spree. Frantically now, Eustis wrote on October 3, to reiterate that no order for attack had been issued. He urged that precautionary preparations stay within reason, confined to the 500 men already authorized plus two companies of cavalry or mounted riflemen, which Eustis figured would be sufficient to disperse the Indians.[134] Harrison ignored Eustis. If his forces did not scare "the Prophet" (not *Tecumseh*) into disbanding his men, then Harrison would attack.[135]

Noting Harrison's forces gathering, a delegation from Tippecanoe informed Harrison that the women and children at Tippecanoe were "all in tears" over it, while the Kickapoo civil chief "expressed his astonishment" at Harrison's war preparations. At that, Harrison played the victim, reciting his litany of injuries, for which the Indians' "Father" required immediate "retribution."[136] He set out for Tippecanoe, well knowing that *Tecumseh* was not there, for *Tecumseh* had told him in August that he would leave directly from Vincennes on an embassy to the south.[137] Harrison did not respect that *Tenskwatawa* was the holy man, not the war chief.

In his headlong rush to war, Harrison had not thought through his forces, which except for two regular regiments, consisted entirely of untrained and obstreperous militiamen who resented commanders telling them what to do. Despite requirements to bring tents, blankets, coats, and saddles, militiamen arrived at their rendezvous without rifles, powder, and bullets, and often enough, shoes or shirts, because they figured that if the government wanted them to fight, then it should supply them with everything.[138] They would, however, arrive with liquor, and quickly dispatch any "whisky" acquired at the rendezvous.[139] Seeing what he had to work with, Harrison had reason to backtrack on his earlier, politically motivated exultations of militias over standing armies. Once in the field, witnessing daily militia incompetence, he spouted an entirely different estimate of the matter.[140]

Harrison's "Indian-fighting" credentials for his 1836 and 1840 presidential runs rested on the three actions that followed—Tippecanoe, Fort Meigs, and Thames—yet it is highly questionable whether Tippecanoe or Fort Meigs had even been U.S. "victories." It mattered not, though, for however hazily, settlers grasped that Indian-fighting was what the Doctrine of Discovery looked like in action. For the Doctrine to allow a "legal" land seizure, the war had to be "just," that is, it had to look as though the "heathen" (non-Christian) "savages" had brought it on themselves. For this, an Indian attack was required, explaining why Harrison had been trying to provoke just that.[141]

Given Madison's direct orders that he start nothing, it was important for Harrison to send a Lenape delegation to *Tenskwatawa* as he neared the town, ordering him to lay down his arms.[142] It was probably also as a nod to Madison that Harrison had brought no cannons with him, a fact revealed to the Indiana Union by Harrison's free, "Negro" driver, Ben, who also told the Indians that Harrison intended to "deceive them." Harrison erupted in rage upon discovering this, court-martialing Ben (who was not in the army) and sentencing him to death, should the Indians attack.[143]

Harrison's militia was "entirely without tents" as he started out from Vincennes on September 26, 1811, with around 1,000 men counting 140 dragoons and sixty mounted riflemen. By October 2, Harrison had traveled sixty-five miles up the Wabash, where he decided to set up a winter post, Fort Harrison, which he left under the command of then captain Zachary Taylor.[144] By the time that Harrison was within two miles of the Wea towns on the Wabash, he had issued scattergun threats and insults to the Miami, Kilatika, and Wea, who had worked with him in the past. Shocked, the Wea replied that they were holding the hands of both Harrison and *Tenskwatawa* (meaning that they were standing neutral), waiting to see which of the two was telling them the truth about what was going on. Seeing his approach now, however, they feared the worst, so the Wea men quickly evacuated all the women and children.[145] Not provoking an attack at Wea, Harrison continued on to Tippecanoe.

Eustis ordered Harrison's militia to Pittsburgh, without making the slightest dent in Harrison's plans. On the excuse that the soldiers were ill, with the Pittsburgh militia "in great want of clothing," besides, Harrison countermanded Eustis. Still, Madison had ordered him to peace, not war, so Harrison stressed that all he intended was to meet with *Tenskwatawa*, honest.[146] His plans might actually have changed. Harrison had expected up to 1,500 to turn out for his rendezvous, but only 880 effective men accompanied him—and then his militia contingent dwindled to about 550.[147] By way of contrast, Tippecanoe's being under threat had attracted Indian men apace. The unwelcome reality dawned on Harrison of what it meant to meet armed men determined to defend their land and their families.[148]

On October 13, 1811, Harrison estimated that there were 600 Indian men at Tippecanoe, while Captain Josiah R. Snelling ballparked from 559 to 700. Two Lenape marching with Harrison's command cheerfully opined that Harrison's complement was "too small" to win, a sentiment glumly shared around camp.[149] Thus, it must have comforted Harrison to learn by October 29 that some Potawatomi had departed Tippecanoe (perhaps to defuse matters), leaving the Indian forces as low as 450 men.[150] U.S. forces liked to field double the number of anticipated "warriors," for it was well known that "no victory had ever been won" when the armies' "numbers were any thing like equal."[151]

What happened once Harrison arrived at Tippecanoe remains eminently unclear from his self-serving accounts. On November 8, he announced his "complete and decisive victory." Not yet knowing what a fib this was, Eustis congratulated Harrison on an "important issue of a conflict unparalleled" in U.S. history.[152] After that, Harrison realized that he was in trouble for starting a war that he had been ordered to avoid, so he followed up with a long report to Eustis on November 18, shooting another to Kentucky governor Charles Scott on November 27. Neither report clarified much, as their intention was to muddy politically dangerous waters.

In addition to Harrison's accounts, there is the expedition's journal, along with stray statements by Harrison's officers defending his orders, once they came under scrutiny. Ensign Isaac Naylor penned the best primary account, although it was not published until 1909. William Brigham's account, collected at the time, was wildly unreliable. Major Walter Taylor and Lieutenant Charles Larrabee wrote useful accounts in 1823, with that of Captain Peter Funk not published till 1939. The Indians' eyewitness accounts came from *Tenskwatawa*, as recorded by Michigan governor Lewis Cass in 1816, and from the Tippecanoe Kickapoo, written down soon after the attack by Matthew Elliott. The purportedly primary account of Potawatomi chief *Zhabné*, styled "Shabonier," was written down in 1859, five years after *Zhabné* had died. This secondhand account was revived by J. Wesley Wickar in 1917.[153] The rest of the accounts were secondary, tertiary, and in some instances, purely confabulatory but nevertheless seeded into the Permanent Record.

What is certainly known is that on November 6, Harrison marched his 880 men, a large number of them sick, on Tippecanoe. He was tracked the whole way by Indiana Union men, insulting the militia with unspecified "gestures."[154] According to the daily journal of the expedition, the army was about to attack Tippecanoe peremptorily, leaving the Indians very "surprised and terrified" to see them on its outskirts.[155] At that point, Naylor saw an Indian delegation approach with a white flag to proclaim their intentions of peace, an event also recorded by Harrison, albeit without mentioning the flag.[156] Seeing the women and children in Tippecanoe, the army, itself, realized that there was no plan to fight.[157] *Tenskwatawa* asked why Harrison was marching on the town.[158] Both men disclaimed any hostile intent, settling on a truce.[159] According to the Kickapoo, Harrison asked where he might set up camp. Seeing Harrison's intent to surround Tippecanoe, *Tenskwatawa* replied, "wherever he pleased except round their Village."[160]

Here, Harrison's account departs from those of the Kickapoo, Naylor, Taylor, and "Shabonier." Harrison said that one of the Indian negotiators (who magically transmuted into *Tenskwatawa* in subsequent settler histories) pointed out a secure place for him to pitch camp, a spot that two of his officers examined and pronounced "excellent."[161] In 1817, however, Taylor insisted that he and Colonel Marsten Clarke had chosen the campsite, all by themselves, with no Indian input, an account supported by Naylor, the Kickapoo, and Shabonier but flatly contradicted by Harrison and Larrabee.[162] Disagreeing that it was a good site once he saw it, because it was easily invaded from one side (probably the "cluster of trees" of Larrabee's account), Harrison nevertheless camped there, putting up no fortifications. These lapses look as though Harrison were inviting attack, probably explaining why Harrison later went into excruciating detail over how he had disposed his men in the camp.[163]

Harrison next omitted the militia's actions immediately precipitating the Indiana Union sally into his camp on November 7.[164] According to the Kickapoo, Harrison promised that his spies would not approach Tippecanoe during the night, advising the Unionists not to approach his camp, lest his sentinels shoot them on sight. Notwithstanding, Harrison's spies did sneak up on Tippecanoe and were turned back unharmed by the Tippecanoe pickets, yet when two Ho-Chunk youths on an adolescent lark approached Harrison's camp, they were immediately shot at by a sentinel. Dropping down to play dead till they were approached by militiamen to finish them off, the Ho-Chunk youths leapt up, tomahawked the sentinels, and fled.[165] Once the boys returned to Tippecanoe, telling of the sentinels' actions, some impetuous Young Men ran off without authorization, leaving the Tippecanoe women and children to escape alone and suddenly across the river, when the firefight began.[166] In 1816, *Tenskwatawa* agreed with the Kickapoo report, that those Ho-Chunk Young Men had started the fracas.[167] Five months later, *Tecumseh* stated that, had he been at Tippecanoe, "there would have been no bloodshed," indicating that no vetted war chief had been present in the town.[168]

"Shabonier" also included a militia sentinel as firing first, the ghostwriter excusing this violation of the truce as justified by an impending, all-out Indian attack, including a supposed plot to assassinate Harrison, a story that had been gristing the settler rumor mill since June 1811. Harrison did acknowledge that "a single shot" from one of his sentinels touched off the fracas, with Naylor identifying the sentinel as Kentucky militiaman Stephen Mars, killed in the battle. Although alluding to a purported assassination plot in his hostile message to *Tecumseh* of June 24, Harrison never mentioned it in connection with Tippecanoe, reporting only a vague mention of his luck in surviving the battle, when every Indian knew him on sight. "Shabonier" insinuated that *Tenskwatawa* had led the attack, having taught the Young Men how to "crawl like snakes through the grass." Settler accounts often featured *Tenskwatawa* as instigating and even leading the attack, but Naylor claimed that the Wea chief *Wawpawwawqua* ("White Loon") led the attack, while *Tenskwatawa* sat on a hill at some remove, in deep prayer for the militia's powder to turn to sand.[169] (It was misting, and water rendered gunpowder unusable.)

Naylor's account as well as the expedition journal supported the Kickapoo version, recording shots fired around 4:00 A.M. Awakened but noticing that "all things were still and quiet" otherwise, Naylor drifted off again till he heard a second shot. Still thinking it was panic fire from a sentinel, he disregarded it, until he heard an "awful yell," signaling attack. Naylor's lapse of time accords with Harrison's report putting the all-out attack as beginning shortly before 4:30 A.M., the half-hour giving the Ho-Chunk boys time to run home and incite the Young Men to retaliate, running right through Harrison's wide, unfortified opening. Naylor stated that all the Indians who made it into camp were killed. Meantime, jerked from sleep, Harrison's army ran about ineffectually. The Indians retreated just after sunrise, carrying off their dead and wounded.[170]

Other than these, there are unreliable to wildly unreliable, if heavily popularized, accounts. Brigham falsely alleged that Harrison's hip-pocket Potawatomi chief *Winemac* led the attack, while in 1832—without any citations—Samuel Drake listed *Winemac*, *Sanamahhonga*, and a Kilatika, *Wapamangua* ("White-Lion"), as leading the attack, a Kentucky militia contention, repeated in 1853. Historian Alfred Pirtle perpetuated this false story in 1900, although according to the Kilatika chief *Hibou* ("Owl") in 1811, not only was *Winemac* the only noted Potawatomi *not* in the action at Tippecanoe, but also British documents show *Winemac* deliberately spreading disinformation about the Tippecanoe battle to the British.[171] Indeed, Harrison's November 18 report was fairly clear that *Winemac* was Harrison's spy in *Tecumseh's* camp before the action, so if *Winemac* fomented the attack, then it was as an *agent provocateur* and on Harrison's orders—perhaps the "trick" that Ben had warned the Indians about.[172]

From there, the settler narratives diverge into such spurious propositions as treacherous Indians egged on by British cunning, against valorous marksmanship on the U.S. side.[173] Thus, did "Shabonier" end with brave militiamen gloriously charging the fleeing Indians, cutting them down with their swords "by hundreds," whereas Naylor claimed that at least one American died of friendly fire, suggesting a militia firing in circular disorganization. Naylor also described rain-soaked ground too marshy to allow horsemen to charge, saying that Harrison was begged three times to allow a pursuit before he agreed. Harrison's account just had his dragoons killing an unspecified "number" of Indians but unable to pursue them.[174] Kentucky militia colonel Joseph H. Davies foolishly gave chase of his own accord but by charging off in the wrong direction with too few men, getting himself killed for his pains.[175]

There is considerable confusion as to the numbers wounded and killed on each side. On November 8, 1811, Harrison recorded 133 U.S. casualties, a count he refined on November 18 to 62 dead and 126 wounded, for a total U.S. casualty count of 188. He also alleged that the sinister Indians had poisoned their lead balls to enhance the kill, but Indian reports made no such claim.[176] On January 12, 1812, the Kickapoo report carefully tallied up, by nation, twenty-five Indians dead, but Naylor said that he and his cohorts found thirty-six Indians dead near U.S. lines, with more carried off by their comrades. Harrison at first guessed that the Indian losses were "considerable" and "perhaps" comparable to his own losses, suggesting up to forty Indians dead. Then, a fifth-hand report, from an anonymous Ho-Chunk through the Miami chief *Ohequanah* ("Little Eyes") to a surveyor who told Captain Snelling who reported it to Harrison, said that fifty Indians had died, a number that Harrison amended a month later to fifty-one.[177] Astoundingly, Brigham claimed that Indian casualties amounted to 400 "killed and wounded," but then, he also fantasized that Harrison had been attacked by 1,000–1,200 "warriors."[178]

The numbers proposed for the Indian dead (twenty-five to fifty-one) present a large discrepancy. Even allowing Naylor's count of thirty-six leaves an overage of fifteen, a discrepancy that might be accounted for by a common, if disgusting, militia tactic following battles. When militiamen did not feel that they had a sufficient kill count for pride—or, more precisely, for scalps to turn in for the lucrative bounties—they found the local Indian cemetery to disinter and scalp the deceased.[179] Snelling recorded that, while Harrison's men were burning Tippecanoe, they located its cemetery and dug up the Indian graves, leaving the disturbed corpses above ground.[180] Naylor also recorded that following the battle, as a wounded Indian ran for the tree line, he was shot down and scalped by the militia, his scalp promptly divided into four pieces that were hung as trophies on militiamen's rifles. The same fetishizing of scalps was then done with all the Indians found dead on the battleground.[181] The slicing and dicing might have inflated the count of Indian dead.

Next, after looting household goods, Harrison's troops set fire to Tippecanoe. The army's herd of forty cattle having run off during the skirmish, most of the militiamen were reduced to eating their horses. Before Tippecanoe's complete store of winter food, 3,000–5,000 bushels of harvest could be burned, Naylor and five friends perspicaciously crammed their knapsacks with as much as they could carry of corn, beans, and peas.[182] The destruction of the entire Tippecanoe harvest had further implications than temporarily hungry militiamen, however. It deliberately left the entirety of the Tippecanoe cohort, including the women, children, and noncombatants, starving that winter.

Angered by the high U.S. casualty count, as soon as they returned home, Kentucky militiamen began disparaging Harrison, with newspapers uniformly pouncing on him and the Kentucky legislature refusing to honor him with accolades. Although Andrew Jackson (gearing up for his own attack on the Muskogee) sent Harrison a letter of support, the withering reports of Harrison as an incompetent commander reached Kentucky governor Scott. Harrison fired off a self-exculpatory report to him, on December 13, saying that it would "bitter the rest of his life" to think that his fumbling had killed so many.[183]

The example of Josiah Harmar was clearly on Harrison's mind, at this point.[184] Harmar faced court-martial following his similarly high casualty count in 1790. In his defense, Harmar had claimed that his losses were "not more than man for man," adding that the United States could "afford them two for one."[185] Harrison was attempting the same excuse, but it was true on the crudest of scales, only. The total number of Indian combatants at Tippecanoe was around 600, so Harrison's kill claim of fifty-one of them represented an 8.5 percent drop, in one day. Yes, 8.5 percent of 880 is seventy-five men, thirteen more than Harrison's sixty-two dead, so Harrison could echo Harmar to claim a raw equivalency, but that is bogus accounting. For Tippecanoe to have lost Naylor's thirty-six of its 600 men meant a 6 percent drop in the male population. If we credit Harrison's count of fifty-one dead, then it yields an 8.5 percent drop. The U.S. Census enumerated 6,048,519 "free whites" in 1810, about one-fourth male. An equivalent drop in the U.S. male population would have been 90,728 (at 6 percent) or 128,531 (at 8.5 percent) male deaths. There is no equivalency here.[186]

Harrison's Harmar argument notwithstanding, under angry pressure from the Madison administration, Harrison "dissolved" his brigade, relinquishing command on November 18, 1811.[187] Moreover, regardless of U.S. propaganda that the Indians had abandoned "the Prophet" post-battle, even wanting him dead, by January 21, 1812, *Tenskwatawa* quickly re-established Tippecanoe, with a nucleus of 150 Shawnee, 200 Sauk, 200 Muskogee, and an undisclosed number of Ho-Chunk, information confirmed by February 18.[188] In a brash move, *Tenskwatawa* announced plans to make a peace call on Harrison at Vincennes. On July 7, 1812, the Kickapoo, Ho-Chunk, and Shawnee asked Harrison for food for the starving (a traditional means of opening peace talks), but Harrison told them that they deserved no such consideration.[189] By July 8, a Wea had told Zachary Taylor that the Indians knew that Harrison would soon no longer hold any office, while *Tecumseh* was acquiring twelve "horse loads" of ammunition from the British to supply the resurrected Tippecanoe.[190] To restock their families, Tippecanoe men had begun raiding the settlers, now huddled fearfully in their cabins.[191] Although Harrison wriggled out the political brouhaha that followed his failures at Tippecanoe, it was but the first of many tempests deriding his martial abilities, which would come back to haunt his presidential campaigns.[192]

However deviously it had come about, Harrison's Indian war was on now, in concert with war hawks pushing to attack the British. On January 2, 1812, under U.S. 2 *Stat.* 671–74, Congress authorized an increase in the army, including pay of 160 acres of land and $16 per soldier, while on January 14, U.S. 2 *Stat.* 674–75, it authorized $1.5 million toward the war effort. Even though Great Britain was still an unofficial enemy (war on it was not declared until June 12), the land to be handed out as soldiers' pay was Indian land to be seized in Harrison's "just war." Harrison now pressed for command of the U.S. Army of the Northwest, but the Madison administration's faith in his abilities had been shaken. It was solely because of his geographical location that one company of rangers was put under Harrison's command.[193] Looking past Harrison, in April 1812, the Madison administration tapped Michigan governor William Hull, elevating him to brigadier general, after he successfully lobbied for appointment as the commander of the Northwest Army.[194] It was the selfsame appointment that Harrison had coveted.

Hull's appointment might have been a punishment of Harrison, but it simply moved the Madison administration from the frying pan into the fire. Like Indiana Territory, Michigan Territory was a hotbed of oligarchic sleaze, with Governor Hull absent from Michigan as often he was as present, appointing his cousin Reuben Attwater (also Atwater) as acting governor in his stead whenever he left. With his cronies, Hull skimmed from Indian annuities, remade laws to benefit himself and his coterie, and even attempted to seize title to already sold territorial lands. His weakness of character had been known to the federal government since at least 1807, but as with Harrison, nothing was done to correct the situation, probably because, also like Harrison, Hull was engineering massive, land-grabbing treaties.[195]

Adding insult to the injury of choosing Hull, in May, Eustis transferred Harrison's Fourth Regiment to Detroit, saying no further Indian attacks were expected in Harrison's neck of the woods.[196] Harrison was irate upon realizing that he was cut out of the loop of Indian affairs in July.[197] Worse, in August, Tennessee militia general James Winchester came to Indiana, recruiting volunteers for a year-long stint in the Tennessee army, which was on its way north, to where the British were.[198] Leaving Vincennes, where he belonged as governor, Harrison camped out in Cincinnati, a launching point of military action, lobbying for a general's commission. Fingering Eustis as the roadblock, Harrison begged Kentucky governor Scott to plead his case directly to Madison, while he orchestrated pressure through officers of the Kentucky militia.[199] Harrison did receive his general's commission in the Kentucky militia this way, but he had to wait for Hull to crash and burn, before he ascended to the federal commission.[200]

Hull obliged Harrison on August 16, 1812, as war with the British moved into the spotlight, particularly at the siege of Detroit, although Eustis wrongly doubted that any action would occur there.[201] Once the British attacked, Hull mounted a feint-hearted defense before handing Detroit to the British, essentially for the asking, calling forth thunderous U.S. condemnations of Hull's villainy.[202] Charged with treason, court-martialed, and sentenced to death, Hull proved as slippery as Harrison, managing to die naturally in 1825.[203] With Hull now gone, on September 17, 1812, Madison appointed Harrison as commander of the Army of the Northwest, as backdated to August 22, 1812.[204] In light of Eustis's complete failure to control Harrison, and his poor choice of Hull, as well as his obvious inability to grasp military realities, Madison replaced Eustis as secretary of war with John Armstrong in January 1813.

Harrison was not Armstrong's only problem child, for piqued by Harrison's command despite his lower rank, in January 1813, Brigadier General James Winchester had taken it upon himself to march his 1,300 men north, to the River Raisin in the Michigan Territory, about thirty miles from Detroit, despite Armstrong's clear orders not to make any unsustainable invasions of British Michigan.[205] After some tit-for-tat skirmishing in which he took Frenchtown (modern-day Monroe, Michigan), Winchester made camp at River Raisin in a layout as foolish as Harrison's at Tippecanoe, leaving one flank wide open, with no fortifications or even sentinels on guard at the road to the opening, while he slept about a mile away.[206] Unable to pass up such an opportunity for fear that Harrison (who was not far away) might reinforce Winchester, British general Henry Proctor attacked early on January 22. Along with 522 men, Winchester was taken prisoner, with his eighty or so wounded left behind for transport, killed. Harrison reported Winchester's entire army as lost, whereas Proctor reported that his army had killed 400 of Winchester's men.[207] Armstrong must have had a couple of stiff brandies, once he got word of all this. More galled than ever that others including Winchester outranked him, even though he was their commander, Harrison pushed Armstrong on the matter, resulting on March 2 in Harrison's elevation to the rank of major general.[208]

The British now in Detroit, Harrison looked to prevent their southern reach, moving up to Lake Erie. Captains Oliver Hazard Perry and Jesse Elliott would not win the Battle of Lake Erie until September 10, 1813, but in mid-winter of 1812, Harrison set up a headquarters near the mouth of the Maumee River (Miami of the Lake) near the lake. [209] Looking like a hill to Europeans, the locale had been repeatedly chosen by European military leaders since 1680, with Anthony Wayne there in 1794, but the hill was a 1,400-year-old Erie ("Panther People") burial mound, accounting for all the human remains unearthed in erecting a blockhouse.[210] On February 24, 1813, Harrison was "fortifying" the reincarnated camp. Expecting it to accommodate up to 1,500 men within days, with work completed by March 12, he left militia colonel John Miller in charge on March 17.[211] In April 1813, Harrison elevated Camp Meigs to Fort Meigs, and it was to play a major role in the northern war and in his presidential runs.[212]

Although Harrison's purported aim was to invade Canada, by March 1813, the one-year term of his recruits was up, leaving him scrounging for men for Fort Wayne and fretting how to maintain his polka-dot pattern of forts around Lake

Erie.[213] On April 4, 1813, even though Armstrong had annulled his authorization to raise militias outside of Indiana, Harrison implored Kentucky governor Isaac Shelby for 1,500 men.[214] *Tecumseh* was likewise recruiting, headed to Fort Meigs with 1,500 men, while Proctor was leading south with 1,300 of his own men.[215] By April 19, Proctor knew exactly where Harrison was and that he possessed artillery including Howitzers and "some 18[prs]."[216] (Eighteen-pounders were long cannons, typically mounted on frigates, suggesting that a U.S. lake campaign was in the works.) Arriving at the rapids where Maumee, Ohio, now stands on April 25, Proctor camped at the deserted British Fort Miamis site, across the river from Fort Meigs.[217] By April 28, Proctor's gun boats were plying the river so that Harrison could see his troops, positioning. *Tecumseh*'s men had also arrived.[218] Meantime, Harrison's commander at Fort Meigs had not even attempted to complete the ordered fortifications, so Harrison was left scrambling to meet Proctor. Despite his unreadiness for battle, Harrison opened fire on Proctor's troops on April 30. Fearing to wait till Harrison's anticipated reinforcements arrived, Proctor replied on May 1, 1813.[219] The siege of Fort Meigs was on.

Exchanging fire for the next two days, on May 3, Proctor's men were prevented by Harrison's howitzers from breaching Fort Meigs. Around midnight on the fourth, an advance messenger from General Green Clay of the Kentucky militia arrived at Fort Meigs, with news that Harrison's reinforcements were nearby.[220] Immediately, Harrison dispatched 800 of Clay's men to destroy the British artillery. Around 9:00 A.M., Clay's men took four of the batteries, as ordered.[221] So far, so good, but then success was soured by militia lieutenant colonel William E. Dudley. Three years after the event, Captain Leslie Combs assured Clay that Dudley had dashed into the woods to save his regiment of "spies," but on-the-spot accounts claim otherwise.[222]

Described as "ignorant and rash," Dudley "had never heard a hostile gun" in his life. Instead of rolling the British artillery into the river, as ordered, Dudley was lured by a ruse into an impulsive pursuit of the British fleeing into the woods—directly into the waiting arms of *Tecumseh*'s men. Sixty to seventy militiamen were killed immediately in the firefight, while eighty to ninety escaped the fracas, making it to Fort Meigs, with ten or twenty skedaddling all the way to Fort Wayne. At some point in the skirmish, Dudley was killed and scalped, "his breast cut open and his heart taken out." The other 600 were taken prisoner to Fort Miamis. Arriving after this skirmish, 400 to 500 of Clay's men were originally to attack the British batteries on the side opposite Dudley in a pincer move, but with no Dudley, those men instead required a hasty rescue by the 100 men Harrison could spare.[223]

After surrendering to the Indians in the woods, a few of Dudley's militiamen were killed and scalped, while the British soldiers hurried the survivors through a traditional gauntlet upon entering "Fort Maumee" (Miamis). A massacre threatened, but *Tecumseh* halted the gauntlet, with 530 prisoners marched to the Huron River near Sandusky, Ohio, where they were "turned loose" to make their way home. On May 6, Harrison accepted Proctor's offer of a prisoner exchange.[224] On May 9, Proctor broke off his assault and retreated, so all U.S. histories treat

Fort Meigs as a Harrison victory. By contrast, Proctor claimed that the victory was his, not a little based on Dudley's pitiful failure, while British adjutant general Edward Baynes described Proctor's siege as "a complete defeat of the enemy."[225] In fact, the only reason that Harrison remained standing after Dudley's rout was that *Tecumseh*'s men went home. One of the many, built-in peace structures of Woodlands law authorized Young Men to fight one action, only, after which they were to return home. Accordingly, *Tecumseh*'s army dissolved, taking home their wounded, "their Prisoners," and their "considerable Quantity" of "Plunder."[226]

Casualty-wise, Proctor certainly won the siege of Fort Meigs, with fifteen British killed.[227] Only nineteen Indians were killed or wounded, so it also was a good day for *Tecumseh*.[228] Harrison's rambling and imprecise account of the disaster at Fort Meigs never got around to listing the numbers of his dead and wounded, so historians have been left to guesstimate. Proctor theorized that, including killed, wounded, and captured, U.S. losses ran 1,000–1,200, but that rather overstated the case.[229] The two earliest U.S. accounts, both written in 1816, gave slightly divergent tallies. Adam Walker claimed seventy-two killed and 196 wounded, whereas Robert McAfee said that, on the battleground and at Fort Miamis, there were eighty-one U.S. dead and 189 wounded.[230] However, including Dudley's militia losses, U.S. casualties came to 148 killed and 170 wounded, with another 100 wounded among the 530 paroled at the Huron River.[231] Worse, throughout the winter, Harrison's men had been sick and dying of "camp fever," most likely typhoid, and between June and July, 200 more U.S. soldiers died of that "most fatal epidemic." Many troops at Fort Meigs remained very sick through August, the number ill mounting in September till half of the men at Fort Meigs were down with a "billious" fever.[232] Some victory.

Chasing Proctor and *Tecumseh*, on October 5, 1813, Harrison overtook them at the Thames River near Moraviantown, Ontario. Harrison attacked, devastating the British forces. Proctor escaped with a few of his cavalry, whom Harrison ordered pursued.[233] This much was clear in his excited and uncharacteristically brief letter of October 5. Between October 9 and 11, he filled in some gaps, but as usual with Harrison, the details changed with every account. At the same time that he revised his own troop count downward, he inflated Indian forces upward, then a common militia and army practice. The same obtained on the Canadian side, whose sources put Harrison's forces at 3,500, while Bullock fantasized that the U.S. forces "could not have been less than 6,000."[234] Harrison claimed "something above" 3,000 men but later yielded to an estimate "short of" 2,500, with 2,100 of them being Kentucky militia.[235] The British fielded around 944 regular soldiers, while McAfee estimated the combined British and Indian forces at around 2,350.[236]

Reported Indian numbers are all over the map. Harrison said that *Tecumseh* had 3,000 men, but that 1,500 left before the battle.[237] One captured British rations report tallied 2,000 Indians, but this included the women, children, elderly, sick, and wounded at Moraviantown, whom Proctor was feeding to prove that the British were not abandoning them.[238] Proctor claimed 1,200–1,500 Indians were present, whereas his boss George Prévost later claimed that *Tecumseh*'s Thames complement was 1,200, a number that he almost certainly had from Proctor. Lt. Richard Bullock of the British Second Battalion was in the action. His report of December 6, 1813, claimed that there were only 800 Indians in the fight, while historian John Sugden put the total forces under *Tecumseh* at 500.[239] Another 300 were under Wyandot war chief *Stayeghtha* ("Round Head"), however, so Bullock's 800 looks correct.[240]

Harrison's casualties are likewise hard to pin down. On October 9, 1813, he put U.S. losses at twelve killed and seventeen wounded, but McAfee recorded losses of the "mounted unit," alone, as seventeen killed and thirty wounded, with the twentieth-century count putting the summary total at twenty-five killed with fifty wounded.[241] Harrison eagerly reported the 601 British soldiers captured, with the final British casualties at eighteen killed and twenty-six wounded.[242] The Indians "suffered the most," said Harrison, leaving thirty-three on the battle-field, with "ten or twelve" more killed in pursuit, said McAfee, claiming that "the principle slaughter took place in the woods."[243] The Kentucky militia proudly took scalps, of course.[244] All in all, Harrison thought that "upwards of" 1,000 Indians were killed.[245] Proctor added that Harrison's cavalry was "marked by peculiar cruelty to the Families of the Indians who had not Time to escape, or conceal Themselves."[246] Presumably, those unspecified "cruelties" to civilians, including women, children, and old folks, is what helped escalate the Indian death count to 1,000.

There is a Canadian tale of *Tecumseh* foreseeing his death at the Battle of Thames. Knowing of Harrison's approach against the weakness of Proctor, *Tecumseh* was said to have smoked glumly with his men, stating that they would be in "smoke before sunset" and predicting that he would not survive the clash.[247] Another account records that, sitting on a log awaiting battle, *Tecumseh* flinched and jumped, as if shot. When asked what had startled him, he replied that a spirit presaging "no good" had overcome him.[248] However apocryphal those accounts might (or might not) be, *Tecumseh* was killed in action.

Militiamen rumored heavily that, once dead, *Tecumseh* had been abandoned on the battlefield by his men, but Ohio and Michigan Indian oral tradition says that, after *Tecumseh* was killed, his body was carried off the field by his men, so that U.S. soldiers could not mutilate him. Importantly, Harrison, who knew *Tecumseh* well by sight, could not identify the body he was shown as *Tecumseh*'s, commenting that it might have been *Zhabné* ("Shabonier"), the Potowatomi chief often with *Tecumseh*. *Zhabné* survived the battle, but *Stayeghtha*, another chief often with *Tecumseh*, did die there, so the body might have been his. In 1834, Harrison, himself, impatiently waved off the story of *Tecumseh* as abandoned on the battlefield, noting that none of the British with *Tecumseh* said the body was his, while the U.S. troops did not even hear that *Tecumseh* was dead, till they returned to Detroit.[249]

Five days after the battle, with *Tecumseh* smoke in the wind, the Three Fires sent a peace delegation of Ottawa and Anishinabe to Harrison at Fort Meigs. When they came to the peace conference with some Miami and Potawatomi, Harrison spitefully held that the latter "deserve[d] no mercy," having been the "tribes most favored" by the United States before the war. By October 14, however, Harrison signed an "armistice" with all the Northwest Indians, formally proclaiming it in force two days later.[250] Even so, on November 11, the president halted the shipment of annuity goods that Harrison had promised the "friendly Indians," until it was "known what tribes deserve[d] the consideration of the government."[251]

Harrison formally ended his Indian war with the 1814 Treaty of Greenville and the 1815 Treaty of Spring Wells. The third Greenville Treaty forbade the Indiana Union nations, as well as those Wyandot, Lenape, and Shawnee clans that had remained allies of the United States throughout, to make peace without U.S. permission either with the British or with still-"hostile" nations. The Union also had to supply whatever Indian troops the United States might require. The United States would, to its liking, lay out boundaries between the Indians and the United States.[252] The Spring Wells Treaty established peace with the Three Fires (Potawatomi, Ottawa, and Anishinabe), pardoning chiefs of the Wyandot, Lenape, Seneca, and Shawnee who might have taken part in the war. It also restored the Miami to the good graces of the Unites States. The kicker was that all the nations had to agree to all the terms of all prior treaties, that is, the land-grabbing causes of the war, in the first place.[253] Armstrong wanted removal west as the price the Indians paid for the war that Harrison had started, although Harrison did not manage that much.[254]

With this, Harrison's military and territorial career essentially closed. Although he remained in his generalship for another half year, he sat tight, not engaging the British, for war hawk expansionism, originally eyeing British Canada equally with Spanish Florida and Texas, suddenly realized that Canada was free soil. Anti-expansionist Massachusetts representative Artemis Ward Jr. goaded his southern colleagues to consider what it would mean to their "constituents" for the United States to admit "half a dozen" free Canadian states, as though giving slavers pause.[255]

Following the war, Harrison was deeply in debt, the Indian war he brought on having interfered with his normal business in land speculation.[256] Probably not unconnected to this, in 1813 and 1814, Harrison was accused of hanky-panky in his army contracts.[257] He allegedly used much-needed army officers as servants to truck his personal property from Vincennes to Cincinnati, where he set up for civilian life.[258] As a final straw, missionaries of the Christian Indians at Moraviantown, savaged after the Battle of the Thames, were suing the United States for reparations on behalf of the Indians.[259] Armstrong's opinion of Harrison steadily deteriorated with each revelation, until he lost all patience. Feeling the walls closing in, on May 11, 1814, Harrison sent Madison a decorous, even obsequious, letter of resignation from the army.[260] Simultaneously, he sent Armstrong a letter that must have singed at least three of the war secretary's fingers. Harrison intimated Armstrong's involvement in the "most Malicious insinuations" laid against him in Washington, D.C. and demanded not an inquiry but a court-martial, wherein he might defend his good name.[261] It was, however, an inquiry that was called for on April 30, 1814, which was duly concluded, with no penalties to Harrison, on December 31, 1816.[262]

High and dry, for the next fifteen years, through intensive lobbying and political favors, Harrison cobbled together a series of public offices, but after 1830, no one would nominate him for dog catcher. For the next four years, with his farmland in Ohio hit by floods and crop-destroying droughts, he scrambled up what money he could by selling his properties.[263] In dire straits by 1834, the best he could land was an appointment as the clerk of the Court of Common Pleas in Hamilton County, Indiana.[264] Fiscal survival looked grim for him until, on December 14, 1834, out of the blue, the *Pennsylvania Intelligencer* put him forward as its candidate for the 1836 presidential run.[265]

The *Pennsylvania Intelligencer* was a Whig rag pumping out anti-Masonic conspiracy theories. The Anti-Masons wanted legitimacy, and the dying Whig Party wanted continued existence, so the Whigs busily sopped up as many Anti-Masons as they could.[266] Such a daffy coalition could not long stand, but it staggered forward long enough to put Harrison up for president, twice. The only problem Harrison had, was being on record as stating that outlawing Masonry would be unconstitutional, but he managed to reverse himself in time for the 1836 campaign.[267]

Despite his newfound Anti-Masonry, Harrison's 1836 presidential bid did not go well for him, as his critics took direct aim at his denigration of the militias. The tension between "regulars" (U.S. Army soldiers) and militias was one of long-standing, based on mutual class prejudice. Dating back to colonial times, the militia was denigrated as consisting of "Blacksmiths, Taylors and all the Banditti the country affords."[268] For their part, those blacksmiths and tailors (the attitudes of the banditti are unrecorded) resented paying high taxes to fund standing armies and their fancy-pants officers.[269] By 1813, seeing themselves as the "patriots" of the military drama, militiamen resented that they might "perform duty in common" with regular army soldiers who were "paid three dollars per month more."[270] In return, U.S. Army officers scorned militiamen as convicts or "wheelbarrows" (period slang for hopeless alcoholics), scrounged up from "brothels." They deeply resented the ridiculously lofty ranks that incompetent militia commanders like "Lt. Colonel" Dudley claimed.[271]

Oblivious of the class friction, writing from Chillicothe, Ohio, on March 17, 1813, Harrison was "sorry to mention" to Armstrong the "dismay and disinclination to the service which appear[ed] to prevail in the Western country," that is, among militiamen of the Old Northwest. Whereas those militiamen who had wintered with Harrison were worthwhile, his new recruits displayed an entirely different "character" that was "not to be depended upon." Militias needed the advantage of overwhelming numbers of regulars to buoy up their nerve for action.[272] Again on March 28, Harrison assured Armstrong of "the impolicy of relying upon the Militia" in a war, preferring 2,000 "regular troops" to 4,000 costly "Militia."[273] After the Battle of Fort Meigs, Harrison had characterized Dudley as "weak and obstinate" (if "brave").[274] No doubt, Harrison further outraged the militias by issuing an order that the first militiaman to break ranks in a Dudley-style, yahooing pursuit was to be shot down on the spot.[275]

These declarations came back to haunt Harrison after U.S. representative Benjamin Hardin, Jr., a Kentucky Whig, praised Harrison for having "spent his youth, his manhood, and the prime of his life in camps and battles, in fire and smoke" for the United States.[276] These spins did not confuse Harrison's political opponents, who knew full well that he was a poor to dangerous general. In reply, Kentucky Democratic representative Albert Gallatin Hawes scoffed at Harrison's shaky performance as an elite, regular officer, presenting it as less than illustrious. In a slap back at Harrison's slap at Dudley's judgment, Hawes questioned Harrison's judgment at Tippecanoe in camping on grounds offered him by the Shawnee, thereby implying that Harrison was the sucker for a ruse, losing "many brave sons" of the Kentucky militia thereby. Next, Hawes intimated that it was Harrison (not the militia) who was cowardly for likewise having failed to help Winchester at the Battle of River Raisin, even though it was within his easy reach. For his grand finale, Hawes suggested that Harrison had fumbled his greatest claim to fame, the Battle of Thames at Moraviantown, Ontario, Canada. In a sly political jab, Hawes stated that Martin D. Hardin (cousin of Benjamin Hardin), and not Harrison, had been "the hero of that day." All told, Harrison might have killed about 1,100 Indians, but he also killed about 500 militiamen.[277]

Harrison lost the election of 1836, but in 1838, the Anti-Masonic Party again nominated him, an "honour" that Harrison accepted with "deepest gratitude" (and alacrity), ironically pledging not to seek two terms, anticipating criticism for running at the age of sixty-seven.[278] To be sure, he was disdained by his enemies as "nothing but a mummy," a resuscitated Federalist.[279] The Whigs were on their way to mummification, too, trolling for candidates from a list of but two names: John Tyler and William Henry Harrison. To obviate elite-hating, it was gingerly left unmentioned that John Tyler was Harrison's cousin, both of them connected to the upscale Armistead line.[280] Clearly, the Whig strategy was to play to slaveholders. Tyler was openly pro-slavery, while those paying any attention already had Harrison's number concerning slavery, despite his attempts to muddy the waters of his position.

Playing the slavery card with an anti-elitist twist, the Democrats published a pamphlet, "White Slavery! or Selling White Men for Debt!" to make public Harrison's 1807 Indiana Territorial law that allowed the virtual enslavement of "whites."[281] One did not have to be a slaveholder to have been shocked by Harrison's draconian debtors' law of 1807. Debt slavery resonated with the generality of voters, because of the Panics (major depressions) of 1819 and 1837, which had ruined many a worker, as well as many a middle-class businessman.[282]

To dispel the image of elitism, not a little incredibly, Harrison presented himself as just another good ol' boy. His presidential campaign projected him as a cider-swillin', log cabin-dwellin' "pioneer," producing by way of proof *Harrison's Log Cabin Song Book* (1840), whose second song, "Log Cabin and Hard Cider" (sung to the tune of "Auld Lange Syne"), ran:[283]

> Should good old cider be despised
> And ne'er regarded more
> Should plain log cabins be despised
> Our fathers built of yore?

Of course, the answer was a resounding, "No!" with the hard-drinking values of yore to be safeguarded by a vote for Harrison.

Despite the ludicrous inaccuracy of its claims, the log-cabin campaign and its slogan, "Tippecanoe and Tyler Too," proved wildly successful. It tapped into all the right settler memes: Indian-killing, slavery, log cabins, and hard cider. Harrison won in an electoral landslide, 234–60, carrying nineteen of the twenty-six states.[284] He died exactly one month into his term.

NOTES

1. Reid, 2009, 100–10; Forbes, 2007, 2–4, 136–39, 178.

2. Trowbridge, 1939, 62; *Nawahtahtha*, 1886.

3. Trowbridge, 1939, 2–4. The "Great Spirit" lingo was inserted by Trowbridge. The guide was simply one of many Breath spirits, Mann, 2016, 126.

4. Barton, 1976, Heckewelder to Barton, letter 3/27/1798, 3.

5. Law, 1858, vol. III, 75.

6. Downes, 1968, 9.

7. Griffin, 2008, 54; Griffin, 1943, 11–35; Griffin, 1952, 364; Mann, 2003, 58–89; stone structures, 90–91; Fowke, 1902, stone works, 239–42.

8. Mayor, 2005, 88.

9. Trowbridge, 1939, 57–58.

10. Clark, 1977, Jesuit claims, 12; Alabama, 14.

11. Mooney, 1912, vol. 2, 531.

12. Mooney, 1900, 494.

13. *Gaynwawpiahsika*, 1935, 8; Voegelin, 1980, 243; see Trowbridge, 1939, sixth nation, 62.

14. Trowbridge, 1939, 62.

15. Spencer, 1908, 385; as western Lenape, 386.

16. Franquelin, 1681; Trowbridge, 1939, 5; Paullin, 1932, Plate 24.

17. Thomas, 1891, 40; Haywood, 1832, 220.

18. Trowbridge, 1939, 62; Voegelin, 1936, 4; Mann, 2006, 125; *Gaynwawpiahsika*, 1935, 8.

19. Claiborne, 1860, 59–60; Johansen and Pritzker, 2008, vol. 1, 684; Trowbridge, 1939, note 18, xiii, xi–xii; Schoolcraft, 1825, 138–39.

20. Parker, 1916, note 3, 103.

21. Sugden, 1997, 23.

22. Jones, 1774, 65–66.

23. Esarey, 1922, Harrison to Dearborn, vol. 1, 223–24.

24. Carter, 1934–1975, Jouett to Dearborn, vol. 7, letter 12/1/1807, 497.

25. Ibid., Wells to Dearborn, vol. 7, letter 12/5/1807, 498–99.

26. Esarey, 1922, Harrison to Dearborn, vol. 1, letter 5/19/1808, 291.

27. Badollet and Gallatin, 1963, 8/6/1811, 184, 186–87, 189–90.

28. Carter, 1934–1975, Johnston to Mason, vol. 7, letter 2/4/1808, 521.

29. Ibid., Wells to Dearborn, vol. 7, letter 4/2/1808, 540.

30. Esarey, 1922, Harrison to Dearborn, vol. 1, letter 5/19/1808, 190–91.

31. Ibid., Harrison to Dearborn, vol. 1, letter 11/9/1808, 321–22.

32. Carter, 1934–1975, Wells to Dearborn, vol. 7, letter 4/2/1808, 540–41; Wells to Dearborn, vol. 7, letter 4/20/1808, 556; Kappler, 1904, vol. 2, 92–95.

33. Carter, 1934–1975, Wells to Dearborn, vol. 7, letter 4/20/1808, 559.

34. Ibid., Wells to Dearborn, vol. 7, letter 4/20/1808, 556, 559; Indian Claims *et al.*, 1973, 343.

35. Carter, 1934–1975, Wells to Dearborn, vol. 7, letter 4/20/1808, 557–59.

36. Ibid., Wells to Dearborn, vol. 7, letter 4/20/1808, 560.

37. Mann, 2000, 123, 172–73.

38. MacLean, 1903, 226; Esarey, 1922, *Tenskwatawa* to Harrison, vol. 1, letter 8/1807, 251; *Tenskwatawa* to Harrison, vol. 1, letter 6/24/1808, 291–92; Harrison to Dearborn, vol. 1, letter 7/12/1808, 295; *Tenskwatawa* to Harrison, vol. 1, letter 8/1/1808, 299; Harrison to Dearborn, vol. 1, letter 9/1/1808, 302.

39. Esarey, 1922, *Tenskwatawa* to Harrison, vol. 1, letter 6/24/1808, 292; women and children were evacuated from war zones, Mann, 2005, 74, 78–79, 88.

40. Law, 1858, 79–80.

41. Esarey, 1922, Wells to Harrison, vol. 1, letter 4/8/1809, 337–39.

42. Ibid., Harrison to Eustis, vol. 1, letter 7/5/1809, 349.

43. Ibid., Harrison to Eustis, vol. 1, letter 7/5/1809, 350.

44. Ibid., Harrison to Eustis, vol. 1, letter 4/18/1809, 340–42; Clark to Dearborn, vol. 1, letter 4/30/1809, 344; Harrison to Eustis, vol. 1, letter 5/3/1809, 344–45.

45. Esarey, 1922, Harrison to Eustis, vol. 1, letter 5/16/1809, 346–47.

46. *ASPIA*, 1832, "Northwestern Frontiers," vol. 1, no. 135, 798–804.

47. Esarey, 1922, Harrison to Eustis, vol. 1, letter 4/25/1810, 417–18; Harrison to Eustis, vol. 1, letter 5/10/1810, 420–22.

48. Ibid., Harrison to Eustis, vol. 1, letter 6/14/1810, 425.

49. Ibid., Addendum, vol. 1, 6/15/1810, 426–27.

50. Ibid., Harrison to Eustis, vol. 1, letter 6/24/1810, 430–31.

51. Ibid., Harrison to Eustis, vol. 1, letter 6/26/1810, 433–36.

52. Carter, 1934–1975, Harrison to Mansfield, vol. 8, letter 11/18/1810, 57–58.

53. Ibid., Harrison to Mansfield, vol. 8, letter 10/13/1811, 137.

54. Ibid., Mansfield to Gallatin, vol. 8, letter 11/3/1810, 59.

55. Esarey, 1922, Harrison to Eustis, vol. 1, letter 7/4/1810, 438–40.

56. Ibid., Eustis to Harrison, vol. 1, letter 7/11/1810, 443; Harrison to Eustis, vol. 1, letter 7/11/1810, 444–45; Harrison to Eustis, vol. 1, letter 7/18/1810, 446–47.

57. Ibid., Harrison to *Tenskwatawa*, vol. 1, letter 7/19/1810, 447–48.

58. Ibid., Harrison to Eustis, vol. 1, letter 7/25/1810, 449–53.

59. Ibid., Harrison to Eustis, vol. 1, letter 4/26/1809, 342.

60. Ibid., Hull to Eustis, vol. 1, letter 7/27/1810, 453; Harrison to Eustis, vol. 1, letter 8/1/1810, 453–54.

61. Ibid., Petition to Eustis, vol. 1, letter 8/6/1810, 455; Harrison to Eustis, vol. 1, letter 8/6/1810, 456–59; Harrison to Eustis, vol. 1, letter 8/7/1810, 455–56.

62. Badollet and Gallatin, 1963, 8/6/1811, 189–90.

63. Esarey, 1922, Harrison to Eustis, vol. 1, letter 8/22/1810, 460.

64. Law, 1858, 76.

65. Mann, 2000, 180–82.

66. Esarey, 1922, Harrison to Eustis, vol. 1, letter 6/14/1810, 423; Edmunds, 1983, 84–85; Dowd, 1992, 143–44.

67. Edmunds, 1983, 143–44.

68. Law, 1858, female actions as dismissed, 100–1.

69. Mann, 2016, 44–45.

70. Esarey, 1922, Speech, vol. 2, 9/18/1813, 542.

71. Ibid., Harrison to Eustis, vol. 1, letter 8/28/1810, 470–71.

72. Ibid., Harrison to Eustis, letter 8/6/1810, 457–58.

73. Badollet and Gallatin, 1963, 6/24/1810, 153–54.

74. Ibid., 8/6/1811, 188.

75. Ibid., 8/6/1811, 187; Esarey, 1922, Harrison to Eustis, vol. 1, letter 8/6/1810, 458.

76. Esarey, 1922, Harrison to Eustis, vol. 1, letter 8/6/1810, 458; Harrison to Eustis, vol. 1, letter 8/22/1810, 460.

77. *Tecumseh* was referring to the 1782 Goschochking genocide, Mann, 2005, 1782 Leanape, Goschochking, 150–69; and 1786 destruction of Shawnee, Mann, 2004, 158.

78. Esarey, 1922, Harrison to Eustis, vol. 1, letter 8/22/1810, 460.

79. Ibid., Speech, vol. 1, 8/20/1810, 463–68.

80. Law, 1858, 88–89.

81. Esarey, 1922, Harrison to Eustis, vol. 1, letter 8/22/1810, 461.

82. Ibid., Speech, vol. 1, 8/21/1810, 468–69.

83. Badollet and Gallatin, 1963, 8/6/1811, 190–91.

84. Ewbank and Riker, 1934, 150–51.

85. Esarey, 1922, Speech, vol. 1, 8/21/1810, 468; Webster, 1907, 243–44.

86. Badollet and Gallatin, 1963, 11/13/1809, 121–22; 8/6/1811, 189–90.

87. USC, 1853, 12th Congress, 11/8/1811, 332; 11/28/1811, 372; 12/7/1811, 420; 12/11/1811, 455–56; 12/24/1811, 581–83; 1/1/1812, 607; 1/3/1812, 618–19; 1/13/1812, 749–50; 1/20/1812, 846; 1/25/1812, 939–40; Esarey, 1922, Harrison to Eustis, vol. 1, letter 8/22/1810, 460–63; Johnston to Harrison, vol. 1, letter 10/14/1810, 477; Jennings to Manwaring, vol. 1, letter 1/22/1811, 501–2; Paul to Manwaring, vol. 1, letter 1/9/1811, 501; Jennings to Manwaring, vol. 1, letter 1/22/1811, 501–3 and note 1, vol. 1, 502; Carter, 1934–1975, Ewing to Gallatin, vol. 8, letter 6/26/1810, 25–28 *et seq*; Harrison to R. Smith, vol. 8, letter 1/10/1811, 72–75; Harrison to John Eppes, vol. 8, letter 1/22/1811, 87–102.

88. Esarey, 1922, Harrison to Eustis, vol. 1, letter 8/22/1810, 461–62, 463, 469; Harrison to Eustis, vol. 1, letter 2/6/1811, 503.

89. Ibid., Harrison to Eustis, vol. 1, letter 10/10/1810, 475; Eustis to Harrison, vol. 1, letter 11/17/1810, 482.

90. Ibid., Annual Message, 11/12/1810, 487–96.

91. Ibid., Harrison to Eustis, vol. 1, letter 12/24/1810, 497–98.

92. Ibid., Harrison to Eustis, vol. 1, letter 12/24/1810, 498; Carter, 1934–1975, Badollet to Tiffin, vol. 8, letter 4/25/1814, 426–27; Badollet to Tiffin, letter 4/27/1814, 298–301; Badollet to Tiffin, vol. 8, letter 5/4/1814, 301–2; Badollet to Posey, letter 5/4/1814, 302; Tiffin to Badollet, vol. 8, letter 5/20/1814, 304–5.

93. Carter, 1934–1975, Ewing to Gallatin, vol. 8, letter 6/26/1810, 25–28.

94. Esarey, 1922, Harrison to Eustis, vol. 1, letter 12/24/1810, 498–99.

95. Ibid., Harrison to Eustis, vol. 1, letter 2/6/1811, 504–5.

96. Ibid., Harrison to Eustis, vol. 1, letter 12/24/1810, 497.

97. Ibid., Harrison to Eustis, vol. 1, letter 4/23/1811, 506–8.

98. *ASPIA*, 1832, vol. 1, no. 135, 797.

99. Esarey, 1922, Harrison to Eustis, vol. 1, letter 6/6/1811, 513–15, 517.

100. Ibid., Harrison to Eustis, vol. 1, salt shipment, letter 6/19/1811, 518; and Harrison to Clark, vol. 1, letter 6/19/1811, 520–21.

101. Badollet and Gallatin, 1963, 8/6/1811, 191; Ewbank and Riker, 1934, paragraph 13, 182.

102. Esarey, 1922, Harrison to Eustis, vol. 1, letter 6/6/1811, 517–18.

103. Ibid., Harrison to Eustis, vol. 1, letter 6/19/1811, 518.

104. Ibid., Harrison to Clark, vol. 1, letter 6/19/1811, 519–21.

105. Ibid., Harrison to *Tecumseh*, vol. 1, letter 6/24/1811, 522–24; *Tecumseh* to Harrison, vol. 1, letter 7/4/1811, 529.

106. Ibid., Harrison to Eustis, vol. 1, letter 7/2/1811, 526–28; Clark to Eustis, vol. 1, letter 7/3/1811, 528–29; Harrison to Eustis, vol. 1, exaggeration, letter 7/10/1811, 531.

107. Esarey, 1922, Harrison to Eustis, vol. 1, letter 7/10/1811, 533–34.

108. Law, 1858, 99–105; for Law's "Captain W." as Captain Walter Wilson, Esarey, 1922, vol. 1, note 1, 529.

109. Mann, 2001, 42–44; Parker, 1916, Article 89, 54.

110. Robinson, 1867, 32.

111. McAfee, 1816/1919, 27; Esarey, Eustis to Harrison, vol. 1, letter 7/17/1811, 535–36.

112. Esarey, 1922, Madison through Eustis to Harrison, vol. 1, letter 7/20/1811, 536–37.

113. Ibid., Harrison to Eustis, vol. 1, letter 7/24/1811, 537–38.

114. Ibid., Petition, vol. 1, 7/31/1811, 538–40; Resolutions, vol. 1, 7/31/1811, 540–42.

115. Ibid., Harrison to Eustis, vol. 1, letter 8/6/1811, 542–46.

116. Marshall, 1824, vol. 2, 482–83.

117. Badollet and Gallatin, 1963, 8/6/1811, 188.

118. Schoolcraft, 1825, 145.

119. Sugden, *Tecumseh*, Harrison's account taken at face value, 220–24; for Owens, *Jefferson's Hammer*, failure as Tecumseh's, 213.

120. Parker, 1916, 54. Although only the Iroquois Constitution was recorded, the law remained the same throughout the Woodlands; Badollet and Gallatin, 1963, 8/6/1811, 184.

121. Schoolcraft, 1825, 144. Schoolcraft's documentation was very sloppy, but he was probably working from what he called "the Detroit MSS."

122. Esarey, 1922, Harrison to Eustis, vol. 1, letter 8/6/1811, 545; Marshall, 1824, vol. 2, 482.

123. Esarey, 1922, Harrison to Eustis, vol. 1, letter 8/6/1811, 545.

124. Brymner, 1894, Elliot to Claus, Q. 114, letter 11/16/1810, 45.

125. Ibid., Craig to Liverpool, Q. 114, letter 3/29/1811, 46; Wood, 1920, vol. 1, 164–65; *ASPFR*, 1833, Foster to Monroe, vol. 3, no. 239, Part I, letter 6/7/1812, 462–63.

126. Brymner, 1894, Gore to Claus, Q. 114, letter 2/26/1811, 46.

127. Badollet and Gallatin, 1963, 8/6/18111, 82–94.

128. Carter, 1934–1975, Eustis to Madison, vol. 8, letter 8/21/1811, 130–31; Eustis to Harrison, vol. 8, letter 8/22/1811, 131–32.

129. Esarey, 1922, Eustis to Harrison, vol. 1, letter 8/29/1811, 560–61.

130. Ibid., Harrison to Eustis, vol. 1, letter 9/3/1811, 563.

131. Ibid., "Volunteers," 8/29/1811, 562–63.

132. Carter, 1934–1975, Eustis to Harrison, vol. 8, letter 9/18/1811, 133–34.

133. Esarey, 1922, "Volunteers," vol. 1, 8/29/1811, 561.

134. Carter, 1934–1975, Eustis to Harrison, vol. 8, letter 10/3/1811, 135–36.

135. Esarey, 1922, Eustis to Harrison, vol. 1, letter 9/3/1811, 563.

136. Ibid., Harrison to Eustis, vol. 1, letter 9/25/1811, 589–92.

137. Ibid., Harrison to Eustis, vol. 1, letter 8/6/1811, 544.

138. Ibid., "Volunteers," vol. 1, 8/29/1811, 561.

139. Badollet and Gallatin, 1963, 8/6/1811, 189.

140. Esarey, 1922, Harrison to Eustis, vol. 1, letter 10/13/1811, 601.

141. Ibid., Harrison to Eustis, vol. 1, letter 9/25/1811, 590; Harrison to Eustis, vol. 1, letter 10/6/1811, 595; Harrison to Eustis, vol. 1, letter 10/13/1811, 600.

142. Ibid., Harrison to Eustis, vol. 1, letter 11/18/1811, 620.

143. Ibid., Harrison to Eustis, vol. 1, letter 9/25/1811, 590; Elliott to Brock, vol. 1, letter 1/12/1812, 616; *Western Sun*, vol. 1, 12/21/1811, 677; Harrison to Scott, vol. 1, letter 12/1811, 690–91; Funk's Narrative, vol. 1, 1811, 720.

144. Naylor, 1909, Taylor's command, 146.

145. Esarey, 1922, Harrison to Eustis, vol. 1, letter 10/13/1811, 602; Council of 1811, Harrison's message, vol. 1, 1811, 576–77.

146. Ibid., vol. 1, 10/6/1811, 595; Harrison to Eustis, vol. 1, letter 11/2/1811, 607.

147. Ibid., Harrison to Eustis, vol. 1, letter 9/17/1811, 571; Harrison to Scott, vol. 1, letter 12/13/1811, 667.

148. Ibid., Parke to Harrison, vol. 1, letter 9/13/1811, 565–67.

149. Ibid., Harrison to Eustis, vol. 1, letter 10/13/1811, 601; Snelling, vol. 1, 12/21/1811, 680.

150. Ibid., vol. 1, October 29, 1811, Harrison to Eustis, 605.

151. Pirtle, 1900, 42.

152. Esarey, 1922, Harrison to Eustis, vol. 1, letter 11/8/1811, 614; Carter, 1934–1975, Eustis to Harrison, vol. 8, letter 12/11/1811, 141.

153. Wickar, 1921, note 1, 353, 354; Robinson, 1867, 30–32.

154. Dawson, 1824, 204; McAfee, 1816/1919, 33.

155. Esarey, 1922, Journal, vol. 1, 700.

156. Naylor, 1909, 149; Esarey, 1922, Harrison to Eustis, vol. 1, letter 11/18/1811, 620.

157. Naylor, 1909, 147; Esarey, 1922, Funk's Narrative, vol. 1, 720.

158. McAfee, 1816/1919, 35; Esarey, 1922, Harrison to Eustis, vol. 1, letter 11/18/1811, 620; Elliott to Brock, vol. 1, letter 1/12/1812, 616.

159. Dawson, 1824, 207; McAfee, 1816/1919, 26, 35; *ASPIA*, 1832, Harrison to Eustis, vol. 1, no. 131, letter 11/18/1811, 776; Esarey, 1922, Harrison to Eustis, vol. 1, Messages, letter 11/8/1811, 614–15; Harrison to Eustis, vol. 1, letter 11/18/1811, 620–21; Elliott to Brock, letter 1/12/1812 (11/8/1811), 616–17.

160. Esarey, 1922, Elliott to Brock, vol. 1, letter 1/12/1812 (11/8/1811), 616.

161. McAfee, 1816/1919, 36–37; Esarey, 1922, Harrison to Eustis, vol. 1, Messages, letter 11/8/1811, 621; Elliot to Brock, vol. 1, letter 1/12/1812, 616; Larrabee to Dawson, vol. 1, letter 10/13/1823, 713; Pirtle, 1900, 43.

162. Esarey, 1922, Taylor to *National Intelligencer*, vol. 1, letter 2/22/1817, 614; Naylor, 1909, 146; Robinson, 1867, 31–32.

163. Pirtle, 1900, 47; Esarey, 1922, Harrison to Eustis, vol. 1, letter 11/18/1811, 621–22; Wayne's example, vol. 1, 618; Larrabee to Dawson, vol. 1, letter 10/13/1823, 713.

164. Esarey, 1922, Harrison to Eustis, vol. 1, letter 11/8/1811, 615.

165. Ibid., Elliot to Brock, vol. 1, letter 1/12/1812, 616. For scalp bounties, Whittlesey, 1874, 5–6; Tucker, 2014, vol. 1, 640–41.

166. Esarey, 1922, Elliott to Brock, vol. 1, letter 1/12/1812, 616; Pirtle, 1900, 56; Drake, 1832, 337.

167. Cave, 2002, 655.

168. Esarey, 1922, Speech, vol. 2, 5/15/1812, 51.

169. Lossing, 1869, Mars, note 2, 204; Esarey, 1922, Harrison to *Tecumseh*, vol. 1, letter 6/24/1811, 522–23; Harrison to Eustis, vol. 1, letter 11/18/1811, 622; Harrison to Scott,

vol. 1, letter 12/1811, 689–90; *Western Sun*, vol. 1, 12/21/1811, 676–77; Mars, Toasts, 12/27/1811, 682; Naylor, 1909, 150; early insinuation that *Tenskwatawa* led, Robinson, 1867, 31.

170. Naylor, 1909, 147–48; Esarey, 1922, Harrison to Eustis, vol. 1, Messages, letter 11/8/1811, 615; Harrison to Eustis, vol. 1, letter 11/18/1811, 622, 626–28; Journal, vol. 1, 701.

171. Drake, 1832, 337; Esarey, 1922, Harrison to Eustis, vol. 1, letter 11/18/1811, 620; Elliott to Claus, vol. 1, disinformation, letter 12/9/1811, 660; Harrison to Eustis, vol. 1, *Hibou*, letter 12/24/1811, 684; Statement of Brigham, 705; *Book of American Indians*, 1854, 219; Robinson, 1867, 31–32.

172. Esarey, 1922, Harrison to Eustis, vol. 1, letter 11/18/1811, 620.

173. Robinson, 1967, 31–32.

174. Ibid., 32; Lossing, 1869, too soft, 206; friendly fire, note 2, 205; Esarey, 1922, Harrison to Eustis, vol. 1, letter 11/18/1811, 625; Naylor, 1909, three requests, 713.

175. Esarey, 1922, Harrison to Congress, vol. 1, letter 12/9/1811, 663–64.

176. Ibid., Harrison to Eustis, vol. 1, letter 11/8/1811, 615; Harrison to Eustis, vol. 1, letter 11/18/1811, 630. For 108 U.S. dead and wounded, Naylor, 1909, 149. Brigham claimed 41 dead and 147 wounded, Esarey, 1922, Brigham's Statement, vol. 1, 705; Harrison to Eustis, vol. 1, poison bullets, letter 12/4/1811, 657.

177. Esarey, 1922, Harrison to Eustis, vol. 1, letter 11/18/1811, 630; Harrison to Eustis, vol. 1, letter 12/4/1811, 657.

178. Naylor, 1909, 149; Esarey, 1922, Elliot to Brock, vol. 1, letter 1/12/1812, 617; Harrison to Eustis, vol. 1, letter 11/18/1811, 628; Snelling to Harrison, vol. 1, letter 11/20/1811, 645; Brigham, vol. 1, 705. Snelling was given in Esarey as "R. I. Snelling," but this was a reversal mistake. "J" was often rendered as "I" at the time. He later became Colonel Snelling.

179. Seineke, 1981, Homan to Bird, letter 8/15/1780, 453.

180. Esarey, 1922, Snelling to Harrison, vol. 1, letter 11/20/1811, 644–45.

181. Naylor, 1909, 150.

182. Ibid., 3,000 bushels, 151; Esarey, 1922, Journal, vol. 1, 705; for 5,000 bushels, Edmunds, 1983, 114.

183. Carter, 1934–1975, Harrison to Eustis, vol. 8, letter 1/14/1812, 159–61; Hopkins to Harrison, vol. 8, letter 1/15/1812, 161–62; Esarey, 1922, Andrew Jackson to Harrison, vol. 1, letter 11/28/1811, 665–66; Harrison to Scott, vol. 1, letter 12/13/1811, 671–72.

184. For Harmar, Esarey, 1922, Harrison to Eustis, vol. 1, letter 12/24/1811, 683.

185. *ASPIA*, 1832, Harmar, vol. 1, no. 15, 10/22/1790, 106.

186. Krzywicki, 1934, "Shawnee," 474; Sauk, Meskwaki, and Kickapoo, 406; combined total, Sugden, 1997, 189.

187. Esarey, 1922, Orders, vol. 1, 11/18/1811, 632.

188. Esarey, 1922, Harrison to Eustis, vol. 1, Indians as anti-*Tenskwatawa*, letter 11/18/1811, 629; Harrison to Eustis, vol. 1, letter 12/4/1811, 656–57; Brigham, 707; returning, Carter, 1934–1975, Attwater to Eustis, vol. 10, letter 1/21/1812, 377; Forsyth to Howard, vol. 14, letter 2/18/1812, 535.

189. Esarey, 1922, Harrison to Eustis, vol. 2, letter 7/7/1812, 66.

190. Ibid., Harrison to Eustis, vol. 2, letter 7/8/1812, 69–70; Harrison to Eustis, vol. 2, letter 7/12/1812, 76.

191. Edmunds, 1983, 115.

192. For the wiggling, see Esarey, 1922, Jackson to Harrison, vol. 1, Messages, letter 11/28/1811, 665–66; Harrison to Scott, vol. 1, letter 12/13/1811, 667–68; Harrison to

Eustis, vol. 1, letter 12/24/1811, 683–85; Harrison to Eustis, vol. 1, letter 12/28/1811, 686–87; Harrison to Legislature, vol. 1, letter 12/9/1811, 663; Orr Statement, vol. 1, 704; *ASPIA*, 1832, Madison to Congress, vol. 1, no. 131, letter 12/18/1811, 776; investigation, vol. 1, no. 132, 780–82; vol. 1, no. 135, 797–804.

193. Carter, 1934–1975, Eustis to Harrison, vol. 8, letter 2/28/1812, 168.

194. U.S. Senate, 1828, Madison nominated Hull, vol. 2, 4/3/1812, 243; referred to committee, vol. 2, 4/4/1812, 244; Hull confirmed, Yea, 4/8/1812, 19; Nay, vol. 10, no. 2, 244–45.

195. Carter, 1934–1975, Detroit to Jefferson, vol. 10, litany of corruption, letter 7/25/1807, 115–22; Bradley to Jefferson, vol. 10, cousin and corruption, letter 12/26/1807, 166–67. Jefferson forwarded these complaints to the Senate, where they died, U.S. Senate, 1828, vol. 2, 3/1/1808, 71; vol. 2, 3/21/1808, 74; vol. 2, 3/25/1808, 75–76.

196. Carter, 1934–1975, Eustis to Harrison, vol. 8, letter 5/14/1812, 181.

197. Esarey, 1922, Harrison to Eustis, vol. 2, letter 7/8/1812, 68–69.

198. Esarey, Harrison to Eustis, vol. 2, Messages, letter 8/18/1812, 90.

199. Esarey, 1922, Harrison to Charles Scott, vol. 2, letter 7/14/1812, 74. Esarey gave Allen in brackets as "William," but William Allen was a corporal. John Allen was the lieutenant colonel.

200. Ibid., Harrison to Eustis, vol. 2, letter 8/28/1812, 98.

201. Carter, 1934–1975, Hull to Madison, vol. 10, acting governor, letter 12/12/1811, 372; Eustis to Attwater, vol. 10, war, letter 3/6/1812, 379.

202. Burton, 1922, vol. 2, 1013.

203. Carter, 1934–1975, Eustis to Hull, vol. 10, letter 10/26/1812, 415; Jesup to Cushing, vol. 10, letter 1/6/1813, 419–22; Watson Affidavit, vol. 10, 1/11/1813, 424–25; Hull's court-martial, Burton, 1922, vol. 2, 1027–33; Hull's after-career, vol. 2, 1033; "Trial of Hull," vol. 2, 5/7/1814, 101–21; Van Deusen, 1933, 1–9.

204. Esarey, 1922, Eustis to Harrison, vol. 2, letter 9/17/1812, 136–37; U.S. Senate, 1828, nominated, vol. 2, 11/9/1812, 300; confirmed, vol. 2, 11/10/1812, 303.

205. Ibid., Armstrong to Harrison, vol. 2, letter 1/17/1813, 312–14; for 1,300, Harrison to Armstrong, vol. 2, letter 1/20/1813, 316; Carter, 1934–1975, Woodward to Armstrong, vol. 10, letter 3/22/1813, note 67, 434.

206. Ibid., Winchester to Harrison, vol. 2, letter 1/19/1813, 315–16; McAfee, 1816/1919, 228, 232.

207. Ibid., Winchester to Armstrong, vol. 2, letter 1/23/1813, 327–28; Harrison to Armstrong, vol. 2, letter 1/24/1813, 331–34; *ASPMA*, 1832–1861,Labbardie Affidavit, vol. 1, 2/11/1813, 371; Wood, 1920–1926, Proctor to Baby, vol. 2, letter 1/19/1813, 5–6; Proctor to Shaeffe, vol. 2, letter 1/24/1813, 6–7; Proctor to Shaeffe, vol. 2, letter 1/25/1813, 7–9; "Events of the War," *Niles'*, vol. 4, 3/6/1813, 10–13; nightshirt, Cleaves, 1990, 143.

208. Carter, 1934–1975, Worthington to Harrison, vol. 8, letter 11/28/1812, 218; Harrison to Armstrong, vol. 8, letter 2/16/1813, 237; Esarey, 1922, Armstrong to Harrison, vol. 2, letter 3/3/1812, 377.

209. Cooper, 1846, vol. 2, 186–99; Skaggs, 2014.

210. Cushing, 1975, 6/26/1813, diary, 129; Scott, 2002, A1/A9; Averill, 1886, 3, 5; Europeans translated lynx and panther as "cat;" for Erie as cat (typo of "cap" for "cat"), Cusick, 1827, 12–13; Thwaites, 1899, vol. 33, 63.

211. Esarey, 1922, Harrison to Armstrong, vol. 2, letter 2/24/1813, 368; Harrison to Armstrong, vol. 2, letter 3/13/1813, 383; Harrison to Armstrong, vol. 2, letter 3/17/1813, 390.

212. Ibid., Harrison to Armstrong, vol. 2, letter 4/18/1813, 421.

213. Ibid., Shelby to Harrison, vol. 2, letter 3/27/1813, 398–400; Harrison to Armstrong, vol. 2, letter 3/27/1813, 400–1; Harrison to Armstrong, vol. 2, letter 3/28/1813, 404–6; Harrison to Armstrong, vol. 2, letter 3/30/1813, 408–9.

214. Ibid., Harrison to Shelby, vol. 2, letter 4/4/1813, 416; Shelby to Harrison, vol. 2, letter 4/18/1813, 420–21.

215. Wood, 1920–1926, vol. 2, 28; Wood, 1879, 385.

216. Wood, 1920–1926, Proctor to Shaeffe, vol. 2, letter 4/19/1813, 31; Proctor, vol. 2, 4/9/1813, 32. "April 9," cannot be correct, as Harrison did not arrive at Meigs till April 12 (Esarey, 1922, Harrison to Armstrong, vol. 2, letter 4/14/1813, 417), so I am assuming that the date should have been April 19.

217. Esarey, 1922, Harrison to Armstrong, vol. 2, letter 4/21/1813, 422; Wood, 1879, 385.

218. Esarey, 1922, Harrison to Meigs, vol. 2, letter 4/28/1813, 429; Harrison to Armstrong, vol. 2, letter 4/28/1813, 430.

219. Wood, 1920–1926, Proctor to Prévost, vol. 2, letter 5/14/1813, 33; Esarey, 1922, Harrison to Armstrong, vol. 2, ca. 4/15/1813, 417–18; Harrison to Armstrong, vol. 2, letter 5/5/1813, 431; Wood, 1879, 389.

220. Wood, 1879, 392–94; Esarey, 1922, Harrison to Armstrong, vol. 2, Messages, letter 5/5/1813, 431–32.

221. Esarey, 1922, Harrison to Armstrong, vol. 2, letter 5/5/1813, 432.

222. Combs, 1869, Combs to Clay, letter 5/6/1815, 6.

223. Wood, 1920–1926, Proctor to Prévost, vol. 2, letter 5/14/1813, 33–34; Esarey, 1922, Harrison to Armstrong, vol. 2, letter 5/5/1813, 432; Wood, 1879, 394–97; for Dudley eviscerated, 397; Christian, 1874, 5; Rainwater, 1932, Cushing to Brothers and Sisters, letter 6/8/1813, 262–63.

224. Christian, 1874, 6–7; Combs, 1869, 8; Wood, 1920–1926, Proctor to Prévost, vol. 2, letter 5/14/1813, 34–35; Esarey, 1922, Agreement, vol. 2, 5/7/1813, 433–34; Eaton, 1850–1851/2000, 9.

225. Wood, 1920–1926, Proctor to Prévost, vol. 2, letter 5/14/1813, 35; Baynes to Prévost, vol. 2, letter 5/21/1813, 37.

226. Ibid., Proctor to Prévost, vol. 2, letter 5/14/1813, 34–35.

227. Ibid., Baynes to Prévost, vol. 2, letter 5/21/1813, 40.

228. Cruikshank, 1902, Askin to Cameron, vol. 1, letter 6/3/1813, 297. Documents did not distinguish numbers of killed as opposed to wounded Indians.

229. Wood, 1920–1926, Proctor to Prévost, vol. 2, letter 5/14/1813, 35.

230. McAfee, 1816/1919, 296; Walker, 1816, 111.

231. Eaton, 1850–1851/2000, 9.

232. McAfee, 1816/1919, 326; Esarey, 1922, Harrison to Armstrong, vol. 2, letter 8/29/1813, 532; Harrison to Armstrong, vol. 2, letter 9/8/1813, 538.

233. Esarey, 1922, Harrison to Armstrong, vol. 2, letter 10/5/1813, 557.

234. Richardson, 1842, 140; Wood, 1920–1926, vol. 1, 73.

235. Esarey, 1922, Harrison to Armstrong, vol. 2, letter 10/9/1813, 561; Harrison to Meigs, vol. 2, letter 10/11/1813, 576; Harrison to Armstrong, vol. 2, letter 10/11/1813, 576. McAfee claimed that illness and detachments left as guards had reduced Harrison's over 3,000 to 2,500, McAfee, 1816/1919, 426–27.

236. McAfee, 1816/1919, 427.

237. Esarey, 1922, Harrison to Armstrong, vol. 2, Messages, letter 10/9/1813, 563.

238. McAfee, 1816/1919, 427; Wood, 1920–1926, Proctor to [Prévost], vol. 2, letter 10/23/1813, 323–24.

239. Richardson, 1842, 140; Sugden, 1997, 370; Wood, 1920–1926, Prévost to Bathhurst, vol. 2, letter 10/30/1813, 326; Proctor to [Prévost], vol. 2, letter 10/5/1813, 319.

240. *Teyoninhokarawen*, 2011, 289.

241. Esarey, 1922, Harrison to Armstrong, vol. 2, letter 10/9/1813, 565; McAfee, 1816/1919, 225; Richardson, 1842, 140; Cleaves, 1939/1990, 204.

242. Esarey, 1922, Harrison to Armstrong, vol. 2, letter 10/9/1813, 565; McAfee, 1816/1919, 425–26.

243. Esarey, 1922, Harrison to Armstrong, vol. 2, letter 10/9/1813, 565; McAfee, 1816/1919, for ten or twelve, 425.

244. Cleaves, 1990, 203.

245. Esarey, 1922, Harrison to Armstrong, vol. 2, letter 10/9/1813, 563.

246. Wood, 1920–1926, Proctor to Rottenburg, vol. 2, letter 10/23/1813, 327.

247. Raymond, 1922, 145–46.

248. Sugden, 1997, 370.

249. Esarey, 1922, Harrison to John Tipton, vol. 2, letter 5/2/1834, 751. For the best rundown on and analysis of the various stories afloat about *Tecumseh*'s death, see Sugden, 1997, 372–80.

250. Esarey, 1922, Harrison to Armstrong, vol. 2, letter 10/10/1813, 573–74; Armistice, vol. 2, 10/14/1813, 577–79; Proclamation, vol. 2, 10/16/1813, 579.

251. Carter, 1934–1975, Parker to Cass, vol. 10, letter 11/11/1813, 453–54.

252. Kappler, 1904, vol. 2, 105–6.

253. Ibid., vol. 2, 117–19.

254. Esarey, 1922, Armstrong to Harrison, vol. 2, letter 3/3/1814, 631.

255. Pratt, 1957, 133–41; U.S. Congress, 1854, Ward, Speech, 2/1814, 1569.

256. *ASPMA*, 1832–1861, vol. 8, no. 150, 1/20/1816, 658.

257. Esarey, 1922, Harrison to Armstrong, vol. 2, letter 5/19/1813, 456–57; Armstrong to Harrison, vol. 2, letter 5/31/1813, 464–65; Harrison to Orr, vol. 2, letter 6/22/1813, 476; Orr to Harrison, vol. 2, letter 9/7/1813, 535–37; Harrison to Armstrong, vol. 2, letter 9/8/1813, 538; Armstrong to Harrison, vol. 2, letter 4/22/1814, 644–45; Harrison to Congress, vol. 2, letter 12/30/1815, 700–10; U.S. Congress, 1814, Report 96, 3–6.

258. Jennings, 1932, Jennings to Armstrong, letter 6/15/1813, 201.

259. *ASPMA*, 1834, vol. 2, no. 364, 2/10/1814, 236–37; U.S. Congress, 1900, reparations request, 2/18/1814, 676.

260. Esarey, 1922, Harrison to Madison, vol. 2, letter 5/11/1814, 648.

261. Clanin, 1993, Reel 10, 150–51.

262. *ASPMA*, 1832–1861, vol. 1, no. 150, 12/31/1816, 644–61.

263. Cleaves, 1990, 276–87; Goebel, 1926, 294–307.

264. Cox, 1908, vol. 3, no. 3, note 39, 82.

265. Vaughn, 2009, 174–75.

266. Richardson, 2004, 66.

267. Vaughn, 2009, 175.

268. Gilbert and Gilbert, 2016, 29.

269. Swiney, 2011, vol. 1, 244.

270. Esarey, 1922, Harrison to Armstrong, vol. 2, letter 3/27/1813, 404.

271. Symmes, 1910, Symmes to Budinot, letter 1/12/1792, 95–97; for "wheelbarrow" slang, Farmer and Henley, 1889–1905, vol. 7, 521; Thornbrough, 1957, 116–17.

272. Esarey, 1922, Harrison to Armstrong, vol. 2, letter 3/17/1813, 389–90.

273. Ibid., Harrison to Armstrong, vol. 2, letter 3/28/1813, 405.

274. Ibid., Harrison to Armstrong, vol. 2, letter 5/13/1813, 443.

275. Ibid., Harrison to Johnson, vol. 2, letter 6/11/1813, 470.

276. Hardin, 1836, 25.

277. USC, 1836b, 2992–95; Martin D. Hardin as Benjamin Hardin's cousin, Little, 1887, 27.

278. "Letter of Harrison to Denny," 1918, 145–46.

279. Sheppard, 2008, 110.

280. Gordon, 1916, 10.

281. Italics in the original. "White Slavery!" 1840, 1, 3–4; Philbrick, 1930, 250.

282. "Banks and Banking," *Niles*, vol. 17, 10/30/1819, 139; Ohio, 1820, tax relief, vol. 18, 12/14/1819, 84; bank tax, vol. 18, 12/27/1819, 113–14; vol. 18, 12/28/1819, 115–16.

283. *Harrison Log Cabin Song Book*, 1888, 5–8.

284. Cleves, 1990, 328.

PART II

$\sim$

Andrew Jackson, 1767–1845, Admin., 1829–1837

CHAPTER 4

※

Mammoths of Iniquity: The Rise of the Braggadocio General

When the "Founding Fathers" of the United States wrote their Constitution, they melded the democratic and matriarchal political structure of the Iroquois Constitution with the elite, landed, and male-dominated structure of old Europe, resulting in a pretense of popular, but a fact of moneyed, control of the country.[1] At the time of the Creek War, 1813–1814, social inequality in America was extreme, ranging from the lowliest hunter, his rifle his only possession, up to the privileged owners of the antebellum mansions in the Slave South, who presumed to run the show. George Washington, Thomas Jefferson, James Madison, James Monroe, Martin Van Buren, William Henry Harrison, John Tyler, James Polk, Zachary Taylor, Andrew Jackson, and Ulysses S. Grant—all presidents of the United States—were slaveholders, with Grant the "free" North's top general during the Civil War. Not unimportantly, Madison, Monroe, and especially, Jackson all figured heavily in the seizure of Muskogee ("Creek") lands during the Creek War, with Jackson, like Harrison after him, carefully puffing his Man-of-the-People credentials for his presidential runs.

Jackson rose to power and fame in the corner of the Northwest Territory that came to be Tennessee. Originally a lawyer in private practice, by 1789, he was elected local attorney general and remained in that capacity until 1799, although by the late 1790s, he was segueing into land speculation.[2] When Tennessee became a state in 1796, he was sent as its first U.S. representative, next quickly succeeding his crony, William Blount, as senator, 1797–1798.[3] Finding "publick life" in Philadelphia not to his taste, in 1798, when William Blount, then governor of Tennessee, proposed to elevate him to a judicial position, Jackson tried to beg off.[4] Notwithstanding, Blount appointed him to the superior court, to which Jackson was subsequently elected and which he held through to his resignation from the Court on July 24, 1804.[5]

Although Jackson served again, briefly, as a senator, from March 4, 1823 to October 14, 1825, seeing this as the route to the U.S. presidency, his primary public positions thereafter were in the military.[6] After a contentious struggle to take the generalship of the Tennessee militia from John Sevier, Jackson was elected major general of the Tennessee militia in 1802 but was drawn back when Sevier, his rival for the generalship, became governor. With a Tennessee act of November 5, 1803, splitting the militia in two, Sevier essentially demoted Jackson to major general of the western Second Division, only.[7] After the Creek War, on May 28, 1814, Jackson was offered and accepted the commission of major general in the U.S. Army, over the Seventh Military District, encompassing Mississippi and Louisiana Territories.[8] In 1815, he was handed command of the U.S. Army, Southern Division.[9] He remained in this position till his unsuccessful 1824 presidential run, followed by his successful bid for presidential office in 1828.

Andrew Jackson is purveyed as the champion of the "little guy," on the plea that he was one. What is typically cited as evidence of his little-guydom are his early years, his loss of family as a teenager, his supposed lack of education, and his asserted lack of family position, leading to poverty of opportunity. Yes, Jackson's father died in 1767, while he was still in the womb, and his brothers and mother perished as a result of illness during the Revolution, with Jackson imprisoned and mistreated by the British, to boot. By fifteen, he was living with relatives. These events are certainly unfortunate, but Jackson's early life was not the lonely, abandoned, three-hanky tragedy of Jacksonian myth.

The Scots-Irish Jackson family migrated from Carrickfergus, Ireland (near Belfast) in 1765, but in coming to America, the family was neither poor nor taking a leap of faith into the unknown. Instead, Jackson *père* was the son of a "well to-do linen weaver" and a linen weaver, himself, who went straight to Waxhaw Creek on the border of North and South Carolina, because his wife's family was already an established and noted presence there. The Jacksons immediately acquired 200 acres and set to farming.[10] Fifty choice acres in North Carolina were going for £25 in 1765, so 200 acres would have cost the family £100, or in 2019, worth almost £20,000, or about $26,000.[11] Thus, even were the Jackson land less than choice, the ability to purchase 200 acres of it did not bespeak poverty. When the family fell on hard times, it was primarily due to the death of Jackson *père* right as the Revolution hit, but it was also because linen weavers did not know how to farm, especially the reluctant soil that the Jacksons had acquired. Furthermore, Jackson was not completely alone after his brothers and mother died. He had considerable family left in Waxhaw, enough to shift teenage residences among them, when he fell out with this or that relative.[12]

Neither did Jackson live in poverty. His meticulous first biographer, James Parton, concluded that his widowed mother received support from his grandfather in Ireland, and Jackson recalled later that she received regular gifts of linen from him. When Jackson's Carrickfergus grandfather died, he left young Jackson £300–£400, a sum that Jackson collected in 1781. In 2019 money, that is worth between £60,000–£80,000, or $78,000–$104,000, but Jackson managed to blow through this entire inheritance in what biographer Robert Remini termed "one glorious spree."[13] This may demonstrate the acute irresponsibility of a gambling addiction, but not poverty.

By the same token, the fable that Jackson had no schooling is untrue, especially in comparison with his peers of the era. He had at least three bouts of schooling, including law training. Destining her son for the Presbyterian clergy (more on hope than on observation), Elizabeth Jackson first sent her son to "some of the better schools of the country" (meaning North Carolina), first in Waxhaw under Dr. William Humphries and then under James Stephenson. Purportedly Jackson, himself, as well as many residents of Charlotte interviewed by Parton, said that Jackson then went to Queens College in Charlotte, studying under Dr. Waddell, although this claim has been questioned since 1929 for its lack of documentation.[14] Jackson had tucked a tidbit of Latin under his belt, but one might expect a Queens College man to have had a better handle on grammar, spelling, and punctuation than had Jackson. He did, however, have enough education to teach elementary school in Waxhaw from 1782 to 1783.[15] Given his famous temper, one can only imagine what his classroom was like.

Jackson's literacy level by 1784 was sufficient to allow him to read for the law under Spruce McCay of Salisbury, North Carolina, and thereafter continue his legal studies under Judge John Stokes. In 1787, he was examined and found competent to obtain his license to practice law in North Carolina, even though Robert Remini characterized his actual knowledge of the law as "shaky."[16] As North Carolina already had enough half-baked lawyers, Jackson moved to the "western" territory (Tennessee), apparently having heard of opportunities there from his old mentor, McCay, who had been present at the "first court ever held" in Tennessee.[17] Jackson was admitted to the Tennessee bar on January 12, 1789.[18] By the 1790s, as a district attorney, he had become a "prodigious litigant" for actions in which he was "[u]sually the plaintiff," thus building his personal fortune.[19] So far, what is being described constituted considerable advantages for any young man in the 1780s–1790s.

Once in Tennessee, Jackson immediately came to the notice of the powerful Donelson clan, who first arrived in Jonesboro in 1784–1785, under a 1784 Georgia state law to take over land at the "bend of the Tennessee" River. Land grants in the amount of 1,000 acres each were at stake, with John Donelson, a wealthy Virginian surveyor, in the lead and John Sevier his second.[20] Both became movers and shakers in Tennessee, because surveyors had the best lands under their control. Surveying was thus the fast track to riches and power, with Donelson having his pick of "negroes, cattle, horses," and land, thus accumulating "wealth in abundance."[21] Perhaps, unsurprisingly, the flashy Donelson was soon found dead, his wallet missing, in an apparently fatal robbery, although locals liked to throw the blame onto the Indians.[22] (It cut down on the efforts of authorities to investigate.) By the time Jackson arrived in 1788, John Donelson's widow, Rachel Stockly Donelson, was letting out rooms in her house, the best in the area, albeit an expanded blockhouse. No common boarding-room matron, Mrs. Donelson had her choice of boarders. The up-and-coming young lawyer caught her eye.[23]

Donelson's daughter, Rachel Donelson Robards, likewise had her choice of men. A reputed beauty and, given events, a flirt of some magnitude, Rachel Robards had somehow married one of the most paranoid men in the South, Lewis Robards. Unbalanced and possessive, Robards was constantly kicking Rachel out, repenting, begging her to return, and then repeating the cycle, all the while ferociously accusing her of infidelity, first with Peyton Short, another Donelson boarder, and then with Andrew Jackson.[24] Today, she could acquire a restraining order against Robards, but then, she was expected to exhibit wifely Christian patience. However, in 1791, hearing that Robards was coming to collect her yet again, she fled to Natchez, then Spanish-governed territory, as escorted by Jackson and another friend. His mission accomplished, Jackson primly returned to Nashville, but hearing shortly after his return that Robards had filed for divorce in Virginia, Jackson immediately returned to Natchez to claim Rachel for himself. Purportedly, the couple married in Natchez in August 1791, although there is no record of the marriage in Spanish Catholic or Protestant Church records.[25]

Jackson later claimed to have believed that Robards had divorced Rachel in 1791.[26] As a lawyer, Jackson could not possibly have believed that. He had to have known that under the law at the time, an accusation of adultery was first laid before a legislature for investigation, with the wife summoned for interrogation. What Lewis Robards had done was to sue for a writ in the Virginia legislature on December 20, 1790. Rachel Robards did not respond to her summons, other than to flee the United States in January 1791, so no investigation could follow.[27] The sheriff of Mercer County, Virginia, was again ordered to summon Rachel to proceedings on January 24, 1792, to no avail. Finally, on September 27, 1793, after Jackson and Rachel Robards had returned to Nashville, there to live openly as a couple, Lewis Robards received his divorce on indubitable evidence of his wife's adultery. On January 17, 1794, a bond of marriage was then posted for Jackson and Rachel Robards, with the couple receiving their marriage license on January 18, 1794.[28] Jackson's novel route to marriage was used against him for the rest of his career.

The Rachel Robards affair is usually downplayed using nineteenth-to-twentieth-century memes of heterosexual romantic love, which script reduces the distressed "lady" to the hero's "prize." It is, however, important to remember that oppressive Victorian mores had not yet descended upon the Western world in the 1790s. Instead, the permissive values of the eighteenth century were abroad, winking at sexual escapades as just part of life, leaving couples, especially in the hinterlands, free to appraise the social value of one another frankly. No doubt, hormonal attraction worked on the impetuous personalities of both Andrew and Rachel, yet calculation on the part of each also cannot have been absent, given the resulting symbiosis. Rachel would have seen a successfully rising lawyer, who looked to become politically and socially prominent (as Lewis Robards was originally to have done), thus securing her position in her patriarchal world. For his part, Andrew would have known that the Donelsons were the high-account people of their milieu, his social-climbing portal to distinction. It is hardly accidental that his sociopolitical prominence began immediately following his Donelson union. After his purported Spanish wedding of 1791, Jackson was "elected a trustee of the Davidson Academy," which was akin to an invited membership in the most exclusive golf club in the territory.[29] His real social ascent began with his Donelson connection.

If Jackson chose his wife carefully, then he chose his state of residence prudently, too. The place for ambitious youths to start their careers as oligarchs-in-training was the so-called frontier, places like Tennessee, carved from the "Territory South of Ohio" (Mississippi Territory), where the laws were loose, and their enforcement, looser. Consequently, contemporary evaluations of the settlers in the Mississippi Territory were uniformly unkind to their reputations. Louis Le Clerc Milfort, who lived with the Muskogee from 1776 to 1795, left horrifyingly amusing stories of the quality of culture among southern settlers in this period. Called "Crackers" or "Gougers," Milfort said, the settlers were "very fond" of "tafia," or taffy (later called White Lightning), a nearly lethal liquor, existing just this side of rubbing alcohol. Cracker men went "around almost naked," having been "addicted to idleness and drunkenness to such an extent," that it was "the women" who were "obliged to do everything."[30] By "nature quarrelsome and mean," Crackers were "nearly all one-eyed," as well, having earned the name of Gougers, because in their violent yet frequent boxing matches, the man gaining the upper hand would "inhumanly" tear his opponent "to pieces." This included "easily" ripping out "one of his eyes."[31] When pursued by the "upper" class of western settlers, this same, senseless aggressiveness was cast as dueling.

Dining was also an ordeal, with the settlers apparently not up on that new-fangled drink called "tea." Milfort was invited to sup with a settler family, the wife of which knew "it was proper to serve tea," while having had no idea of what tea was or how to prepare it. Consequently, she took a bushel of tea leaves, put them in her grand cooking pot, and proceeded to boil a "large ham" in the entire bushelful. Throwing away the tea-and-ham broth, she then served the boiled tea leaves to the eager guests who had come to experience the gala event. Her guests tried gamely but unsuccessfully to masticate the leaves, causing the wife to fly "into a great rage against her husband," at whose head she heaved her plate, "reproaching him" for having bought her "inferior tea." Meanwhile, famished from his travels, Milfort ate the ham, tea-boil notwithstanding, and even found it "rather good."[32]

Another contemporary assessment of the Southern settlers came on May 1, 1804, from the pen of Jeffersonian judicial appointee, Mississippi territorial justice, Ephraim Kirby, a well-connected, Connecticut Revolutionary War veteran, with a classical education and an MA from Yale.[33] Written in response to specific queries from Jefferson, Kirby's lengthy, on-the-spot assessment went into some detail, none of it flattering to the settlers. He described the Mississippi Territory as having "long afforded asylum" to "miscreants" otherwise facing "punishments ordained by law for heinous offences." With "few exceptions," Kirby said, the settlers were "illiterate, wild and savage, of depraved morals, unworthy of public confidence or private esteem; litigious, disunited, and knowing each other, universally distrustful of each other." Worse, there was no hope at law, for the "magistrates" were "without dignity, respect, probity, influence or authority." This deplorable situation left the "administration of justice, imbecile and corrupt," while the militia lacked all "discipline," not to mention, "competent officers."[34]

Kirby noted that the "emigrants" from Georgia and the Carolinas were those "proscribed for treasonable practices" during the American Revolution. Far from repenting, they now hated the U.S. government and, "having lived long without any restraint, committing many enormities against society," had become "hostile to all law" and to "every government." Those arriving after this group were "almost universally fugitives from justice," with "many of them" being "felons of the first magnitude." The remainder were "poor people" who had come to escape "the demands of creditors" or in search of a "precarious existence" eked out in the woods. As a result, the number "worthy" of appointment to U.S. offices in the territory was "necessarily ... small." Worse, because no one trusted anyone else, they preferred the appointment of "strangers" to anyone "among themselves." Jefferson could therefore make "very few selections" from the territorial population that would carry "any appearance of propriety."[35] One might think Kirby overly hard on the settlers, if this were not the standing assessment of nearly all qualified observers of the period. During the federal and antebellum periods, the invaders were frankly dubbed "squatters" and "banditti" by their counterparts in the dainty east (who had conveniently forgotten how they had acquired their own land).[36]

Modern historians paint portraits of the settlements similar to those of Milfort and Kirby. In a long look at those invading Muskogee land, Sean Michael O'Brien particularly cited one "little frontier community" in Alabama, which somehow found that it needed "a dozen or so saloons," with one "displaying a prominent sign boasting the slogan 'Dum Vivimus, Vivimus,'" which O'Brien translated accurately as to sentiment, as "while we live, let us live it up."[37] Similarly, Gregory Waselkov showed at great length that, leading into the Creek War, the most honorable and refined people in the heavily desired Tensaw region were the Muskogee and their mixed-heritage families. Reviled even by their own as horse thieves and hooligans, the Euro-squatters transmuted lexically into those respectable ancestors, the "pioneers," only in the latter nineteenth century, as a proper Victorian drapery was arranged becomingly over the one-eyed ugliness of American history in the buff.[38]

Among those high-placed miscreants described by Kirby was U.S. senator William Blount, a major land speculator from a family of rich land speculators in North Carolina and Tennessee. Initiating in 1797 an early, Burr-style attempt at empire, Blount's "filibuster" (private war against a foreign country) centered on then-Spanish territory including Natchez, Mobile, Pensacola, and the Tombigbee settlements near the Alabama border. For his pains, Blount was impeached and kicked out of the Senate once his involvement was discovered in the scheme to create a private country out of Spanish-held Florida and Louisiana. This did not keep him from being elected to the Tennessee State Senate.[39] Blount's half-brother Willie (also called "Wylie") Blount served as governor of Tennessee, 1809–1815, from which position he precipitately ordered Jackson into the Creek War in early October 1813.[40] As Kirby noted, being felonious did not matter on the so-called frontiers.

Meantime, the Claiborne brothers of Louisiana were involved in their own Donelson-allied schemes, in which patronage was open and unabashed. For instance, Louisiana territorial governor William Charles Cole Claiborne sent his brother, Ferdinand L. Claiborne, general of Mississippi Territory, into Muskogee County to reinforce Jackson once the Creek War began.[41] Governor Claiborne pleaded also with Paul Hamilton, secretary of the navy, to find a suitable commission for another brother, Dr. Thomas A. Claiborne.[42] On March 15, 1813, in the mistaken belief that Jackson would immediately reinforce New Orleans against the British (as actually ordered), Governor Claiborne wrote to him that the "friendship" that he had "formed" for Jackson "in early life" was "still ardent & sincere, & my best wishes, have & will always, attend you," adding, "Can you not obtain a Command in the Northern Army?" that is, a free hand in directing the Creek War.[43] Because Jackson was still an untried military commander, this enthusiasm was not about skill but about grabbing the valuable Muskogee lands in Alabama before anyone else could.

Then, there was what passed for justice, in the hands of such territorial officers of the court as the fractious, dueling Jackson and Judge Harry Toulmin, the presiding judge of St. Tammany Parish in the Tombigbee settlement of today's Louisiana state, which loomed so large in the Creek War.[44] Father-in-law of the utterly corrupt James Wilkinson, major general of the Seventh U.S. Military District (over the Mississippi and Louisiana Territories), the loquacious and self-important Toulmin was up to his elbows in shady land speculations.[45] His personal unsavoriness, as well as that of Wilkinson, aside, during the Creek War and the War of 1812, Toulmin remained on free letter-writing terms with Secretary of State James Monroe and Secretary of War William Eustis, as well as with President James Madison.[46] It was only by comparison with the outright murderers and felons who comprised his five fellow justices in the territory that Toulmin attained his reputation as an honorable man.[47]

The borderlands, then, were not inhabited by the sweets of Western culture but by its dregs. In such company, it was not hard to rise, simply by showing up. For those like John Donelson, with a position such as surveyor, or those like Sevier, with a reputation as a Revolutionary War veteran, success was a forgone conclusion. Within half-a-generation, one could become a major landowner, like Donelson, or governor of a state or a territory, like John Sevier. In 1975, Michael Paul Rogin analyzed such activity in Marxist terms of "primitive accumulation" and "paternal authority," but whereas the patriarchy might have been raw, the economics at play were not primitive.[48] They were mature and working entirely from the hoary European model of landed nobility. The Marxist step theory of history's inexorable progression through set stages does not describe what happened in America. The Donelsons and their coterie of Coffees, Jacksons, Blounts, and Claibornes were not interested in replacing, but in replicating, European structures, just with themselves at the top, as an oligarchic, landed elite was conceived along the "frontiers." In the territories, they comprised family relations more resembling gangs than an actual social order. Their claim to fame was getting there first and stealing the most.

Thus, it is not unimportant that when Jackson came, he saw and conquered his way into the Donelson clan via Rachel Donelson, running over the less valuable Robards to do it. He carefully connected with the Blounts and the Claibornes, for as in Europe, the patronage of the already powerful was the only way up for those second or third into the area. Jackson might have foolishly sacrificed relations with Sevier early on, but he thereafter minded his P's and Q's with the Donelson crew, including the first governor of the Territory South of Ohio and U.S. senator William Blount; his half-brother and governor of the Mississippi Territory, Willie Blount; and the governor of the Louisiana Territory, William Charles Cole Claiborne, just to name the most prominent.[49] If Jackson were secondary to this cadre, then a tertiary coterie sprang up around Jackson.

Among the most significant of those connections was that between Andrew Jackson and eventual brigadier general John Coffee, who served under Jackson during the Creek War. Coffee and Jackson were relations through marriage, Coffee's wife Mary having been Rachel Donelson Jackson's niece, a granddaughter of John Donelson.[50] Starting in 1804, Jackson and Coffee occasionally partnered in business enterprises, including a store, a tavern, a boatyard, and a racetrack, thus trying to corner all the markets in the area.[51] A surveyor, Coffee's businesses depended largely on land.[52] Despite Jackson's habit of falling out with acquaintances over trifles, he and Coffee remained close, with both prospering from their Donelson family connections.

In 1795–1796, Jackson looked to make a fortune in the business of land speculation, but with a poor grasp of business, he embroiled himself in profound debt in trying to unload 68,750 acres of land.[53] Philadelphia sharpie David Allison looked like a buyer to Jackson, but Allison paid only 20¢ on the dollar of value and then compounded matters by paying in notes for debts. A lamb to the financial slaughter, Jackson promptly endorsed all the notes in payment for goods he planned to sell as a merchant in Tennessee, thus acquiring the bad debts that came due following Allison's bankruptcy in 1797.[54] Jackson consequently took an enormous financial hit, which lingered for years.

By July 1804, clearing the debt had forced Jackson to sell his 640-acre plantation, Hunter's Hill, acquired in 1796 (after once belonging to Lewis Robards) to move to a kind of cabin, the Hermitage. In 1804, it was still a three-room, two-story log cabin, with three associated out-cabins for family and guests.[55] Thanks, it would seem, to Rachel Jackson's management, it became a two-story brick building on 640 acres by 1809.[56] Jackson's slaves increased from nine in 1804 to forty-four in 1820 and eighty-five by 1825.[57] Meantime, the Hermitage was built and rebuilt till it became the 1,000-acre slave plantation known today, with its fifty associated acres of cedar growth, and 161 slaves, counting the fifty-one slaves stashed on Jackson's 2,700-acre plantation in Mississippi.[58] Thus, Jackson did live in a cabin at one time, but aside from the North Carolina cabin of his birth, a cabin was really not where he started. Instead, the 1804

Hermitage was where his overreach and fiscal naivete had landed him after a solid start. Forced to return to the law to start rebuilding, Jackson resigned conclusively from the law only on July 24, 1804, after he got out from under his Allison mess.[59]

Although Jackson had sworn off paper notes, he had not sworn off land deals but continued trading in land, adding to his wealth by trading in slaves, besides. It is strange that so many biographies of Andrew Jackson exist, yet so little treatment has been given either to his slave trafficking or to his land-dealing. Although John Meacham did not duck the issue of slavery in *American Lion*, he positioned Jackson's slaveholding in the larger context of Nullification.[60] All mentions of Jackson's slave-trading wind up like this, posited in another context, if not of Nullification, then of the Missouri Compromise, the South Carolina planter-hysteria over potential slave rebellions, or "Indian-fighting" in Florida, to which slaves were escaping to make common cause with the Seminole resistance. Otherwise, there seems to be an embargo on discussion of the acute misery that Jackson's slave-trading caused Africans, other than to downplay it even while admitting it, as did Robert Remini in 1966, in saying that Jackson "merits censure for the few times he stooped to this filthy business."[61] Not only was his slave trading more frequent than this suggests, but also it was highly lucrative, contributing not a little to Jackson's wealth and ultimate social standing.

Other than those brief mentions, we are regularly assured that Jackson was not a cruel master but "treated his slaves decently"—unless he was having them whipped.[62] The screaming contradiction of this juxtaposition apparently has little fazed discussion, but it should, for as Meacham pointed out, "Jackson could be a harsh master."[63] Indeed, his advertisement of September 26, 1804, for an unnamed, "eloped" (escaped) slave of thirty, over six feet tall, "stout made and active," who talked "sensible" and would "pass for a free man" promised a reward of $50 plus expenses for his return. Moreover, Jackson pledged "ten dollars extra" for any "hundred lashes" up to $300.[64] This necessarily encompassed a death sentence for the runaway, so that Jackson cannot be excused here, on the common pleading, on the one hand, that he was being employed to find the escaped slave or, on the other hand, that this was as an example of his famous vindictiveness. Yes, and yes, but Jackson drew up and placed the ad, knowing exactly what it could mean for the unnamed fugitive.

Neither is Jackson quite as kind a master as common report would have it. Yes, he did supply medical treatment for one sick slave in 1798; in 1806, he sarcastically styled as "humane" buying slaves in Maryland for resale in Natchez and Louisiana, and as a lawyer and a judge, he dealt with cases concerning the murder of slaves.[65] To mention these instances to the exclusion of his slave-trading business is, however, pure cherry-picking, while ignoring the context of these three examples is intellectually dishonest. Medical treatment came under the economic heading of "property conservation," while his 1806 excoriation of Dickinson as a slave trader came in the larger context of his self-defense in the *Impartial Review* for having killed Dickinson. Moreover, as his letters show, Jackson was no mere dabbler, jumping in and out of the slave-trading business. Multiple and ongoing transactions are given, starting in 1795, and these instances represent only the surviving records of his trade.[66] The great wealth he amassed testifies to the size of his business.

Meanwhile, Jackson's legal papers show that the slave actions for which he was the attorney or the judge were not about "human rights," the false impression left today by brief mentions of them, but about the value of the "chattel" involved. For instance, in the case of *Hampton v. Boyd and Foster* (1790), Jackson was attorney for two defendants who had assaulted a slave, Caesar, breaking his leg in such a way that he later died. As Caesar's "owner," Hampton sued the pair for £1,000, as the "Damages" sustained by Hampton (not Caesar). On appeal, which might or might not have been filed and argued by Jackson, the damages were reduced to £200.[67] This was clearly about property values, not the life of Caesar. Similarly, when Garrett Fitzgerald simply appropriated the slave Neptune from Samuel Smith Sr., the "Trespass" was let go, because Smith died in 1800, while the case was going on, and the law dropped a case upon the death of the person who filed it. Once more, this was not about the human rights of Neptune but about which "white man" owned whom, when. Furthermore, Jackson was a judge in this instance, as was Garrett Fitzgerald, so that the verdict in Fitzgerald's favor, with the plaintiffs ordered to pay his legal costs in the case, was a foregone conclusion.[68]

When Jackson defended John Williams in *Gilmore v. Williams* (1791), Williams was claimed as a slave by William Gilmore. The win for Williams as "free" was based entirely on the testimony of highly place Euro-settlers: a Virginia militia commander against the Kaskaskia, a Cumberland district sheriff, and a man who was to become a justice of the Tennessee Davison district court. This case was about the social credentials of these men, as opposed to those of a lesser-status man, Gilmore. Furthermore, the credibility of the slave laws of other states, in this case, North Carolina, the parent state of Tennessee, was on the line. Again, the concern was not for Williams but for procedure and what passed for high connections in backwoods settler society. Jackson was aware of the relative social positions of the players.[69]

In *Greer v. Emerson* (1801), Jackson was again the judge. Andrew Greer Jr. filed suit against his plantation overseer, Pleasant Emerson, for forcing the Greer plantation slave Cato to ride a wild, unbroken horse around a racetrack at breakneck speed. The speed did indeed kill Cato, when the completely untrained horse threw him in a panic. Jackson's friend John Overton was Greer's lawyer, while another Jackson friend, George Washington Campbell, was Emerson's lawyer. As one of the presiding justices, Jackson *et al.* split the difference between the lawyers in finding for Greer but by awarding him only $350 for "damages," knocked down from the $500 that he had demanded. Cato's life was certainly not the concern here, and it is not even clear how much of the $350 was awarded for the death of Cato, and how much, for the "strain" to the horse.[70]

The 1802 case of *Vaughn v. Barnes* was filed after Joseph Barnes was found to have been harboring runaway slaves. Only does a later reference in finding for David and Susanah Vaughn mention "the Negro," so that it is not clear who she or he was, or even why Barnes was found guilty of "enticing" said "Negro." Barnes could either have been an early abolitionist or a speculator of the sort who kidnapped slaves for resale elsewhere. In either case, Barnes was originally ordered to pay the Vaughns $250, but on appeal, that was reduced to $25 (for "depreciation," puzzlingly calculated). Andrew Jackson was one of the judges in both the trial and the appeal. Clearly, the fight was, once more, over property values rather than the human rights of the slave.[71] None of these cases count as "kindness" to slaves.

The next dodge around Jackson's slave trading insists that it was simply an accepted practice in Jackson's day, but this is a highly circumscribed description of "Jackson's day." Africans certainly did not accept their enslavement, while Article 1, Section 9, of the U.S. Constitution countenanced the free importation of new slaves only until 1808, thereafter prohibitively taxing each "Importation" by up to $10 (around $220 today).[72] This constitutional provision was tantamount to cutting off the Atlantic slave trade. Moreover, the abolition movement was swinging into gear in "Jackson's day," with the British heavily patrolling the oceans partly to prevent the Atlantic slave trade (an unsung reason for the War of 1812).[73] John Quincy Adam's famous lawyering for the Africans of the *Amistad* in 1825 absolutely occurred during "Jackson's day." Thus, the "back then, everybody did it" argument fails, regarding the Euro-American values of the era.

Jackson's land ventures are always presented as a topic separate from his slave trading, yet his slave-trading ventures were heavily linked to his land ventures. The oblivion of the confluence here is not for lack of letters referencing Jackson's land usurpation in connection with slave trading. The same 1795 letter from Jackson's frequent business partner, John Overton, instanced above, discussed the acquisition of not only slaves for trafficking but also of Indian land that Overton and Jackson were looking to sell in speculation.[74] The slaves were brought in to work the land being seized.

If Western historians have missed these connections, then the Indians and the Africans on the ground did not. There was more to Jackson's 1816 obsession with rooting out the "Negro Fort" of Seminole Florida than simply ending a place of refuge for runaways or the U.S. rivalry with Spain.[75] One of the fears of the settlers, so terrifying to settlers that it had to be circumlocuted with energy, was that the Indians and the Africans might make common cause, as seemed to be happening in Florida. Interestingly, Africans in America were not afraid of openly positing the possibility, as Martin Delaney showed in his literary take-off on Denmark Vesey's 1822 slave revolt in *Blake, or the Huts of America*. His Vesey-Blake talked openly with the Chickasaw about their natural common cause.[76] One can only assume that the dearth of either Native American or African American historians is responsible for the insensibility of these vital linkages.

If Jackson's businesses were unsavory, then his penchant for brawling was murderous. He would duel at the drop of a hat, and being badly wounded, twice, did not dissuade him from dueling again, nor did killing his opponent Charles Dickinson in 1806.[77] Jackson acquired a reputation for dueling not a little because of the Rachel Robards affair. Despite the persistent myth that Jackson dueled Lewis Robards over Rachel, the recorded duel involving the Andrew-Rachel adultery was with John Sevier in 1803, and Rachel Jackson was more prop than focus for Sevier. He and Jackson were already trading insults in a spat over which one of them, the Revolutionary War hero John Sevier or the untrained and untried Andrew Jackson, should be elected major general of the Tennessee Militia. Publicly scoffing at Jackson's complete lack of military credentials in late July 1803, Sevier sneered that the only service that Jackson had ever rendered the United States was in "taking a trip to Natchez with another man's wife." Jackson was beside himself. "Great God!" he shouted, "do you mention *her* sacred name!"[78] No, actually, Sevier did not, but the hint was close enough for anyone paying attention to have grasped. In 1803, Sevier's quip was tantamount to scrawling, "For a good time, call Rachel Jackson" on the stall door of a public restroom.

Not willing to let that pass, on July 27, 1803, Jackson placed a notice in the *Tennessee Gazette* announcing, "To all" who should see it, Jackson's declaration that "his excellency John Sevier" was nothing but a "base coward and poltroon," who would issue insults but had "not courage to repair" them through dueling. While one can only speculate as to what Jackson might have accomplished with a Twitter account, this advertisement failed to prompt a challenge from the old general. Upping the ante, on October 2, Jackson sent a frothy missive directly to Sevier, which Sevier answered on the same day, making a point of refusing to "meet"—period code for "duel"—in Tennessee, slyly calling instead for a face-off in Kentucky (Robards's home state). At this, Jackson accused Sevier of "subterfuge" and demanded satisfaction in Knoxville, where the insult had passed Sevier's "poluted lips," or Jackson would again "Publish" him "a coward and a poltroon." On October 3, Sevier was forced to meet Jackson in a duel.[79]

In 1966, Remini described the ensuing duel as a farce, with Sevier arriving late and Jackson angrily charging him on horseback and leveling his "sword cane" at Sevier like "a medieval knight," thus frightening the seconds' horses into running off with the dueling pistols. Sevier hid behind a tree, as the seconds now drew down on one another. The principals lacking their pistols, everyone eventually cooled off enough to trudge back to Knoxville in company, where Sevier won his second and then third term as governor and Jackson lost his bid for the militia generalship.[80] Despite its comical aspects, the Sevier duel was about Jackson's future, for Rachel Donelson was inextricably bound up with his prospects. A founding father of Tennessee, second only to John Donelson, John Sevier held considerable power. Thus, to have been opposed by Sevier, based on his Donelson connection, no less, was potentially fatal to Jackson's prospects.

Another of Jackson's famous duels resulted in manslaughter, although some called it outright murder when Jackson killed fellow lawyer Charles Henry Dickinson over a November 1805 bet on a horserace.[81] The race never occurred, which triggered a forfeit to the Jackson coterie of $800 (today, worth around $17,000). The Dickinson cadre paid up in promissory notes, but in Winn's

Tavern, Jackson subsequently spoke publicly and disparagingly of Dickinson's party, claiming that it had attempted to pay up in cut-rate notes. Because in 1805, Tennessee "society" worked on roughly the same rules as those of rival inner-city gangs today, Jackson's idle talk called up questions of who had "disrespected" whom, necessitating lethal force. Thomas Swann of the Dickinson cadre wrote Jackson on January 3, 1806, essentially demanding an apology, eliciting an irate and ill-written response from Jackson, which eventually escalated to a challenge from Thomas Swann to a duel. Jackson declined (an affront publicly suggesting that Swann was no gentleman), opting instead to meet Swann at Winn's Tavern on January 13, where Jackson proceeded to whack Swann about with his cane, till guns entered the fracas. At that point, friends separated Jackson and Swann.[82]

That should have ended the matter, but publishing numerous testaments to his gentlemanly character, Swann demanded an inquiry, which inflamed tempers, resulting in an unseemly gunfight between John Coffee of the Jackson faction and Nathaniel A. McNairy of the Swann faction, in which Coffee received a "slight wound." Although (or perhaps because) McNairy's brother John had long worked closely with Jackson in the Tennessee legal community, Nathaniel McNairy knew Jackson's tender spots, explaining why he challenged the "*braggadocio General*" (Jackson) to a duel, ladling on the insults in an incendiary article printed in the *Impartial Review*, which had a field day, publishing all the nasty accusations and counteraccusations.[83] Dickinson wisely left town, not to return till May, but this did not help, for upon his return on May 21, Dickinson imprudently wrote to Thomas Eastin's *Impartial Review*. Dickinson's May letter called forth a predictable challenge from Jackson on May 23, with the duel arrangements made on May 24.[84]

Dickinson had allegedly bet $500 that he would kill Jackson, but the May 30 duel turned out otherwise.[85] At the command, "Fire," Jackson's pistol jammed, leaving Dickinson a free shot. Although Dickinson hit Jackson, it was not in the heart, at which Dickinson had carefully aimed. Instead, deflected by Jackson's coat, Dickinson's bullet grazed his ribcage, in a wound that John Overton likened to "the stumping of a toe."[86] Per dueling rules, the fight should have ended there, for Dickinson had his so-called satisfaction, but Jackson took a second shot, his pistol again jamming. The third time Jackson pulled the trigger, however, his pistol fired, killing Dickinson.[87] Because most counted "a snap" (a jamming) as "a fire," Jackson was heavily pilloried for "snapping" a second time and then firing the kill shot in a third trigger pull, because that gave him three shots to Dickinson's one.[88]

Given Jackson's gratuitous snap and shot, Dickinson's death became a *cause célèbre*, published well beyond Tennessee, partly thanks to the *Impartial Review*'s having draped the page edges of its next issue in black mourning for Dickinson.[89] The affair thereafter morphed into the duel that just would not die, for Jackson now took the *Review*'s editor Eastin to task, angrily demanding that he reveal just who had urged him to dress his pages in mourning. Somehow discovering that Thomas Gassaway Watkins had primarily instigated the mourning border, Jackson next challenged him to a duel, using his usual combustible language. Instead of mailing his challenge, Jackson charged

Thomas A. Claiborne with delivering the letter, thus further and unnecessarily widening the feud, for when Claiborne attempted delivery at Winn's Tavern, Watkins whacked Claiborne over the head with his cane.[90]

Meantime, Thomas Overton bullied Dickinson's second, Hanson Catlet, into writing a statement favoring Jackson's version of the Dickinson duel, although five days later, absent Overton, Catlet made another statement supporting Dickinson, instead.[91] From there, territorial governor William Henry Harrison got into the act, as Dickinson had managed to die in his home near North Bend, Ohio, just across the river from Kentucky. In a friendly missive quieting Jackson's apparent fears, as expressed in a letter no longer extant, Harrison assured him that "Dickerson" had not named him as his killer and that, although called by the Logan County, Kentucky, grand jury to testify, he had refused to help indict Jackson for murder.[92] Unable to let sleeping dogs lie, Jackson then drafted but perhaps did not send another letter to Eastin. Matters simmered until September 1806, when John Overton urged Jackson to call it quits, as lowering himself to feuding with "an inferiour gang" eroded his honor, not theirs.[93] Apparently, this—and the refusal of anyone else to duel Jackson—dissolved the matter, although its notoriety resurged during his 1828 presidential bid. The Dickinson duel was the sort of wild and, given the continuing mention of Winn's Tavern, woozy behavior that Kirby said characterized all the backwater territorial "elites."

Following the Louisiana Purchase in 1803, Jackson hoped to be appointed its first territorial governor. Perhaps with Kirby's caution in mind, especially after the Dickinson debacle, President Thomas Jefferson shied away from handing Jackson the appointment. It went, instead, to the better connected and less duel-prone William Charles Cole Claiborne.[94] Jackson consoled himself for the disappointment by continuing in partnership with his brother-in-law, Coffee.[95] Jefferson's snub might have been in the back of Jackson's mind, however, when another tasty pickle arose to tempt his vanity: the Burr Conspiracy. By 1804, as a Tennessee planter, judge, militia general, land speculator, slaveholder, and slave dealer, Jackson was up to his teeth in the establishment of the Tennessee oligarchy.[96] His name was well known. It was not incidental, then, that in aiming to achieve high national office, Jackson cultivated his connection with that "trusty friend" of Tennessee statehood, Vice President Aaron Burr.[97]

Burr played upon contemporary events. Napoleon had forced Spain to sign the secret Treaty of San Ildefonso in 1800, ceding "Louisiana" to France. Jefferson then acquired Louisiana from Napoleon in 1803, partly to settle difficulties over shipping along the Mississippi River, for the purchase meant that the 1795 U.S. agreement with Spain allowing free transport no longer held. Worse, the Louisiana Purchase was hazy as to whose borders fell where. By 1806, sitting in Mobile and Pensacola, the Spanish were attempting to contain American expansion.[98] Spain was, however, failing as a power, worldwide. Both Napoleonic France and the United States saw as much, with Napoleon invading Spain to set his brother up as its king in 1808 and the United States licking its chops over "Spanish" Florida and Texas. Even in the east, the incipient U.S. war drive against Spain had been building steam since 1800, so that Spain was heavily castigated in

American propaganda. Thus, Burr's excited chatter to Jackson about the "Floridas" worked because it was part of an extant, generalized war drive.

Perhaps Burr's major story in selling his breakaway scheme was that the U.S. government was entirely aware of his mission to mount a resistance to the machinations of Spain.[99] Thus, it is not surprising that after the collapse of Burr's plot, Jackson claimed that Burr had assured him that he carried orders from the "Secratary of wars" and would produce them "when necessary."[100] The staggering unlikelihood that the administration would entrust the killer of Alexander Hamilton with a secret mission against a foreign power, or if it had, the impropriety of Burr's then freely flapping his jaws about it, apparently did not occur to Jackson, perhaps because the Dickinson affair was then consuming him.

The path by which Burr secured Jackson's faith in him is unclear, but an opening that both Dickinson's associates and Burr crawled through to stage-manage his moods was Jackson's somewhat pathetic insistence that he was a "gentleman."[101] At that time, far from the courtesy title of today, "gentleman" indicated a specific class status in the gentry. It sat the lowest rung of the British landed aristocracy, as a socioeconomic birth status that excluded the spawn of Irish linen weavers. American levelers were busily pretending that just having acreage made them gentlemen, but the false claim was regarded as a paltry trick by actual gentry, one easily dashed. Consequently, Jackson's pretensions motivated Dickinson associate Nathaniel McNairy to sneer at Jackson's posturing as a "*gentleman General*."[102] If McNairy could see this Jackson trigger, then Burr certainly could. Having a genuine, east-coast gentleman by birth—that is, Burr—appeal to Jackson confidentially as a social equal would have stroked Jackson in his biggest insecurity, and right when the Dickinson crowd was kicking it in.

The initial meeting of Burr and Jackson appears to have occurred on May 30, 1805, in Logan County, Kentucky, when Burr was setting out on his 1805 trip to New Orleans.[103] The pretext on which Burr first approached Jackson is unclear, but the pair had infamous dueling in common, and Burr's duel with Alexander Hamilton rather raised than lowered him in the esteem of the Federalist-hating, rough-hewn western settlers.[104] However it came about, when Burr later crossed into Tennessee at Nashville, he asked Jackson to quarter his coachman and stable his horses while he was gone.[105] Returning on August 6, Burr spent at least till August 13 with Jackson at the Hermitage, as he recorded in his diary.[106] Jackson clearly kept in touch thereafter, for a Burr letter of March 24, 1806, from "Washington City" mentioned a now-missing letter from Jackson dated January 1. Burr hinted ominously at an impending war over "the purchase of the Floridas," seemingly to have been mounted by the Spanish, disgruntled over the Louisiana Purchase.[107] Documents are scarce, but it appears that Burr enlisted Jackson to keep his militia in readiness, should it be called upon (by Burr, of course). The next extant Burr letter to Jackson, dated April 5, 1806, enclosed congressional speeches regarding a possible war, making this supposition probable.[108]

Throughout the spring and into the summer, it does not appear that Jackson realized the skullduggery in which Burr was engaged, but by fall, the level of

Jackson's oblivion is questionable. On September 24, 1806, Burr arrived at the Hermitage, with Jackson giddily writing to local notables, including militia generals John Overton and James Robertson, inviting them to join the august company. On September 27, Overton and Robertson followed up by throwing a gala ball in Burr's honor, officially promoted as thanks for Burr's earlier support of Tennessee's bid for statehood.[109] If Jackson and Overton were starstruck, then Robertson was hesitant about Burr. He attempted to ferret out of him "how the Executive of our government was held with," but Burr was "so guarded" on the point that his effort proved fruitless.[110] Unfazed, on October 4, Jackson expressed regret at having been unable to pull militia general James Winchester into the group, as well. He hoped, however, to have 2,000 men in the field "on short notice," including "firm officers" and "men of enterprise" for a venture in "Santafe and Maxico." The result would provide a "handsome theatre" for Tennessee's "enterprising young men," Jackson assured Winchester.[111] On November 7, the major Burr co-conspirator Harman Blennerhassett told Virginia militia colonel Hugh Phelps that Jackson and "other characters of distinction" were planning to join Burr's southwestern settlement, "with many associates."[112]

Jackson's awareness of specifics accords with Blennerhassett's assertion to make Jackson sound no longer quite so ignorant of Burr's plan as before, especially in light of Jackson's orders, also of October 4, to "Brigadier Generals of the 2nd Division" to be "in readyness." This was because of the "late conduct of the Spanish Government," Jackson explained in the order, instancing such trumped-up offenses as Spain's cutting down and carting off the "flag of the U. States" and taking an "unjustifiable & insulting," if vaguely specified, "position" all the way south to New Orleans.[113] Accounts for supplies, including among other things, a "Spanish Horse," a "Keel Boat," and "3 Boats" were drawn on Jackson and Coffee's business by Burr.[114] In 1812, Blennerhassett still had the bill for "$1,726 $\frac{26}{100}$" in Jackson's "own hand-writing."[115] These preparations show that Jackson was fairly aware of at least parts of Burr's plan to send his flotilla down the riverways to seize the Bank of the United States at New Orleans.

Burr's plans were temporarily interrupted in Frankfort, Kentucky. The federal district attorney there, Joseph Hamilton Daveiss, had long smelled a rat, trying rather urgently to alert Jefferson to the problem since February but to no avail. On November 5, 1806, Daveiss acted on his own to have Burr arrested in Frankfort but withdrew the case on November 12, for lack of evidence. Undaunted, Daveiss continued probing, next dragging Burr up before a grand jury on December 6, 1806, but again having to withdraw the charges for lack of evidence, when a chief witness, Davis Floyd, proved elusive.[116] Throughout the Frankfort grand jury proceedings, Burr's lawyer, the young Henry Clay, had been an open and ardent Burr believer, his opinion shifting only gradually from admiration to anger and, finally, contempt as he discovered the depth of Burr's deception.[117] Because Clay was neither a stupid nor an unsophisticated man, his initial support demonstrates Burr's ability to bamboozle people both by flattering their bubbled perceptions and by zeroing in precisely on the vulnerabilities of the individual before him. The difference between Clay and Jackson was, however, Clay's humility, which allowed him to admit that he had been horribly wrong, as opposed to Jackson's lack of self-critical faculties. Rather than to acknowledge that he had been fooled, Jackson simply dug in his heels, even to his own detriment.

Burr's acquittal in Frankfort freed him to proceed directly to Ohio to launch his filibuster, his boats leaving Blennerhassett Island in the dead of night on December 11, 1806, with Burr himself following on December 22.[118] By this point, Jackson's perceptions and allegiances are too slippery to pin down, but the context of dates is suggestive. Jackson's letter of November 5, 1806, to President Jefferson reads strangely, "tendering" as it does, the "services" of his militia in the "event of insult or aggression" against the United States.[119] It is unclear whether he is warning of Burr's plot or announcing his readiness to attack Spanish territories. On November 10, "Capt." John A. Fort visited Jackson and filled him in on just what Burr was up to.[120] Jackson obviously took two days to consider what Fort had told him. After that, the plot thickened.

On November 12, Jackson contacted a U.S. senator from Tennessee, Daniel Smith. In a convoluted text, he intimated that untoward plans were afoot. Dancing around Burr without mentioning him by name, Jackson offloaded the contumely of "separating the Union" onto Spanish "dons," indicating how Burr had probably framed the issue to him.[121] The text of the letter suggests that Smith had prior context to aid his reading of the tortuous composition. On November 17, having heard nothing in response to his lengthy letter to Smith, Jackson wrote briefly again mentioning that Burr had been arrested in Frankfort.[122] On the same day as his first Smith letter, Jackson shot off a much shorter and less blemished letter, which he had slyly hand-delivered to Governor Claiborne of Louisiana Territory, warning him of "something rotten in the state of Denmark," to wit, an "attack" from "quarters" that Claiborne would not "expect."[123] It is unclear whether Jackson meant Burr's plot or Wilkinson's flip, but Claiborne certainly scrambled to cover his posterior once everything fell apart, not scrupling later to use this letter, as expedient to his purposes.

In either case, Denmark was even more rotten than advertised because of three draws Burr made on Jackson and Coffee's Clover Bottom Store, the first, undated other than 1806, including five boats and two keel boats; the second, on December 9, 1806, two days before Blennerhassett's flotilla departed; and the third, on December 17, 1807, five days before Burr, himself, left with two boats.[124] Then, on December 31, Jackson's aide-de-camp and messenger to Joseph Alston (Burr's son-in-law), William Preston Anderson wrote Jackson his own word soup of a letter, filled with italics that looked a lot like in-crowd argot while referencing now-missing letters. Anderson stated that he had "changed his sentiments" and begged Jackson, given a "safe oppty." to give him "news of *Nashville*" (italics in the original).[125]

As one Jackson version of events has it, when Burr stopped by the Hermitage on December 14, following his acquittal in Frankfort, he discovered Jackson out, with Rachel Jackson cold-shouldering him. Thus, instead of lodging at the

Hermitage as he had expected, he had to put up at the village of Clover Bottom, where Jackson and Coffee's businesses were. John Coffee's later affidavit stated that Jackson confronted Burr there concerning the possible illegality of his schemes, but Burr talked him down. Supposedly, Burr used his acquittal in Frankfort as conclusive proof of his purity. Coffee also asserted that, leaving on December 29, Burr did not take all the items he had requisitioned from their store, receiving a refund of $1,725.62, the same amount that Blennerhassett later published.[126] Coffee was securely in Jackson's entourage and largely dependent on him for his status, so it is unclear whether this testimony was the truth or a helpful prevarication to clear up the little problem of the merchandise statement in Jackson's handwriting. In any case, the last order was drawn up on December 17, and Burr left on December 22.

Just what Jackson had been doing from October through December 1806 is opaque. General Wilkinson had written his explosive letter exposing the plot to Jefferson on October 21, 1806, although Jefferson did not receive it till November 21.[127] Finally grasping that what Daveiss had been telling him for ten months was more than partisan bickering, on November 27, Jefferson issued his proclamation denouncing the Burr plot. The proclamation arrived in Nashville on December 23, although Jackson supposedly did not see it till January 1, 1807 (that is, after he had supplied Burr).[128] Given the goods order by Burr two days before Blennerhassett's flotilla launched and five days before Burr launched, Jackson's baffling Jefferson letter, intricate Smith letter, and Claiborne warning letter start to look a lot as if Jackson was still in the plot but engineering plausible deniability. This was certainly the spin that his enemies took from the facts.

Wilkinson wrote directly to Jackson on December 19, 1806, that he hated "a Don" yet maintained pristine loyalty to the United States.[129] Also on December 19, having seen the Smith letters, Secretary of War Henry Dearborn wrote Jackson orders that tacitly assumed his loyalty and enlisted his help in putting a lid on the conspiracy.[130] Then, from December 19 to February 6, 1807, Dearborn sat back, quietly watching Jackson's moves to judge his loyalty, as Jackson later discovered to his incandescent ire.[131] Jackson did not hear back from Senator Smith until after Dearborn had written, and then Smith's apparent purpose in his December 29 letter was to tell Jackson that Jefferson "confide[d]" in the "fidelity" of Wilkinson.[132] The Anderson, Wilkinson, and Smith letters read as furious winking and nodding, signaling each other as to the preferred party line.

On January 1, 1807, claiming just that moment to have received Dearborn's December 19 orders, Jackson contacted James Winchester, enclosing a copy of Dearborn's letter and ordering Winchester's readiness to act against Burr's army. Jackson also mentioned his correspondence with Jefferson and otherwise put Winchester on notice of the energetic "check" that the Tennessee militia was to "put to the illegal project."[133] On January 2, Jackson notified Captain Daniel Bissell of an outlaw enterprise afoot involving boatloads of armed men, ordering Bissell to be on the lookout for the flotilla but without ever mentioning Burr by name. Comically enough, Bissell replied on January 5 that he had seen nothing other than Burr passing along the river on December 31, with around ten boats.[134] Otherwise, Jackson gave every indication of vigorous action to root out the Burr business, on January 4, filling Dearborn in on his warning to Claiborne, along with his tender of services to Jefferson, apparently now depending on these documents as the bona fides of his loyalty as a U.S. citizen.[135] Noticing the energy, by January 17, the peripatetic *Impartial Review* began praising Jackson's patriotic alacrity.[136]

Backpedaling and obfuscation did not save Jackson from being heavily suspected of taking part in the conspiracy. On January 15, 1807, after Burr's conspiracy had conclusively imploded, Jackson wrote a long, self-exculpatory letter to his friend, U.S. representative George Washington Campbell. On February 6, Campbell replied to what was probably Jackson's primary concern, to wit, how he was viewed in Washington, D.C. given his prior and very public fawning over Burr. The "suspicions" Jackson had feared of his "joining Burr &c. being in circulation" in Washington, were short-lived and confined exclusively to those who did not know Jackson, Campbell assured him.[137] However soothing to Jackson, Campbell's reassurances were not entirely true. The *Richmond Inquirer* had been as industrious as ever the *Impartial Review* could have been, its editorial "we" having "entertained involuntary suspicions" of a rabble-rousing "militia General in Tennessee," who had been loud enough in his "thundering proclamation" against Spain to have been audible on the east coast.[138]

Under this pressure on March 17, 1807, Jackson had one of his legendary meltdowns upon discovering through Campbell that in his orders of December 19, 1806, Dearborn had been deliberately testing Jackson's loyalty to the United States by giving him just enough rope to hang himself, were he in the conspiracy.[139] Interestingly in this same context, Jefferson had been in private conversation with Dearborn over Wilkinson's news, which certainly backed up what Daveiss had been telling him for ten months. Jefferson waited to respond to Jackson until December 3, almost a month after Jackson wrote him and on the thirteenth day after he had received Wilkinson's letter. Jefferson's answer took Jackson's letter at face value, thanking him for his military "readiness" and his "honorable tender" of aid.[140] In the administration's good graces, Wilkinson had written Jackson defensively. It was pretty clear that Jefferson and Wilkinson were in on Dearborn's "test," so that Jackson's subsequent loathing of Dearborn and Wilkinson, not to mention his histrionic attack on Jefferson in Richmond, probably stemmed from his resentment of Dearborn's test.

Seething at his discovery, Jackson ripped off a breathtakingly sulfurous letter to Dearborn, reproaching him for supporting Wilkinson while suspecting himself. For this, Jackson accused Dearborn of such "notorious & criminal acts, of dishonor, dishonesty, want of Candour & justice" that he was "more unprincipled and worthy of punishment" than "nine-tenths" of those killed by "Robespierre, Marat & Wilkinsons despotism."[141] Although his convoluted diction actually cast Dearborn as a tyrant's victim, it is pretty obvious that Jackson had meant to indict Dearborn as a ruthless "tyrant." Granted, Wilkinson was, as Virginia U.S.

representative John Randolph styled him, a "mammoth of iniquity," but he was not in Robespierre's league, while Dearborn was not even driving past the ballpark.[142]

Jackson then dredged up an old court-martial to throw in Dearborn's face. From November 21 to December 6, 1803, Colonel Thomas Butler was called up on charges, first, for an infraction against 1801 army grooming regulations and, second, for neglect of duty. On the first count, Butler continued to wear an old-fashioned queue instead of cutting his hair according to the 1801 regulations. On the second count, instead of proceeding directly to Fort Adams at Rockville, Ohio, as ordered, he went first to Pittsburgh to take care of personal business. Butler was found guilty of not cutting his hair but acquitted on the neglect-of-duty charges. Wilkinson interfered at that point, apparently for purely political reasons, demanding harsh punishment of Butler. The matter became a rallying cry against the Federalists, with Democrats blaming them for Butler's death in 1805, even though he died from smallpox, not from the stress of the court-martial.[143] None of the Butler business had the slightest connection with the Burr Conspiracy, but apparently, on a tear, Jackson pulled it up as a Butler supporter in the political food fight against Wilkinson's supporters. Jackson's point seems to have been that, as "uniformly the intimate friend of Wilkinson," Dearborn's "hatred" of Jackson had become "fixed" in that very moment.[144] Another page's worth of spleen argued that Dearborn therefore was the one spreading the gossip about Jackson in Washington.

Exaggerated to the point of absurdity, the claims and charges in the March 17 letter are more than just posturing for position. They are genuinely unhinged. Although some historians have questioned whether Jackson ever sent this letter, it nevertheless shows the sort of hysterical overreaction to which he was prone.[145] Moreover, other letters equally vicious toward Dearborn flew from Jackson's pen and were indisputably sent. To Patten Anderson, Jackson styled Dearborn "not fit for a granny"; to Governor Claiborne, he characterized Dearborn's "nerves" as so "weak" that among other things, he wished "to throw the responsibility off his shoulders"; to Daniel Smith, he lunged at Dearborn for believing his "virtuous, immaculate, unspotted, and patriotic Genl Wilkinson" to suspect Jackson of being a Burr conspirator.[146]

Much of the brouhaha was because, when Burr's plot came to light, former co-conspirators judiciously scurried for the shadows, leaving the slower Jackson stunned under the swinging spotlight. Evidence with Jackson's name on it kept popping up. During his trial for the conspiracy, one jackrabbit that Wilkinson pulled out of his hat was Jackson's November 12, 1806, letter to Claiborne, apparently having received a copy of it from Claiborne. Wilkinson claimed that the letter showed his innocence by warning Claiborne not to trust him. Of course, this defense worked only if Jackson and Claiborne were both in on Burr's plot.[147] Claiborne served up the same letter to the congressional investigation of the Burr matter, with Burr now using Jackson's stated suspicions of Wilkinson to divert blame from himself to Wilkinson.[148] Neither of these usages boded well for Jackson (or Claiborne). Claiborne contacted Jackson on March 27, 1807, trying to explain away his weaseling.[149] Jackson seems to have bought it, not a little because in February 1807, during the Burr trial, Claiborne was rumored to have "slapt" Wilkinson "in the face" at the courthouse as part of "a violent dispute." Jackson eagerly passed on this gossip without naming his source, although the *Impartial Review* had carried the story.[150] How this otherwise unsupported tale got abroad in the first place is unknown, but it is not unlikely to have been part of Claiborne's effort to tamp down Jackson's predictable responses to his freewheeling use of the November 12 letter.

On May 22, a grand jury inquiry into the Burr Conspiracy began in Richmond, Virginia. Jackson was a named witness, along with William Preston Anderson, Jackson's aide-de-camp. Jackson acted out with fervor, again sabotaging himself. Most notably in mid-June, he "harangued the crowd in Capitol Square" against Jefferson as a vile persecutor of Burr, in a speech published in 1824 (during Jackson's first presidential run).[151] More immediately, Jackson's loud and unsettling rant was so outrageous as to have left a permanently sour taste in James Madison's mouth. Then Jefferson's secretary of state Madison was soon to become the president. Recalling Jackson's erratic behavior in 1807, he understandably hesitated to call him up during the War of 1812.[152]

On September 25, 1807, during his sworn testimony, witness Edmund P. Dana of Belpre, Ohio, directly named Andrew Jackson as a Burr co-conspirator. In November 1806, said Dana, Burr had assured him (as a gentleman) that Generals James Wilkinson and Andrew Jackson were both tight with the plan, with Jackson then "preparing a body of militia" 200 to 300 strong.[153] However, counteracting the ill impression made by Dana was Jefferson's letter of January 3, 1807, with its direct affirmation: "Be assured that Tennessee, and particularly General Jackson, are faithful."[154] Jackson's own, panicked letter to Jefferson of November 5, 1806, prompting this faith, did not make the exhibits. In the end, Burr's trial proved to have been an exercise in futility, as Burr walked away with a second acquittal, ruined but free, as a perquisite of his elite social status.

After the shouting died down, a cloud remained over Jackson's reputation, for enough documentation existed to incriminate him. Whispers were constant, with the danger of his Burr association resurfacing in blackmail letters sent to Jackson in 1812, threatening to release untoward documents to the public if Jackson did not ante up, naming the statement in the amount of $1,726.62½ for the supply order that Jackson and Overton had taken from Burr in 1806.[155] There is no indication that Jackson replied to (or even received) the blackmail letters, as they were sent from Spanish Natchez during the War of 1812, but Blennerhassett did publish the supply statement in 1812, suggesting that Jackson did not pay. Notwithstanding, Jackson knew how far he had been drawn in by a con man and obviously did not relish the thought of being ruined like Burr. (Landing on his feet, Wilkinson had incredibly remained the commander of the U.S. Army.)

To distract attention from his likely collaboration in the Burr plot, Jackson began to bellow out anti-Indian rhetoric against the Muskogee. Heavily laden with Christian jargon, his lurid excoriations of the HEATHEN SAVAGE worked wonderfully, at least in the hinterlands, to drown out the Burr noise. It carefully turned the public panic over events in the southeast away from treason and onto the ever-popular narrative of incipient "savage" attack on innocent settlers. The additional menace of the hated Spanish Don, in league with the imperious treachery of the British in egging on the Indians, was simply political gravy. For all the failure of the filibusters under William Blount and Aaron Burr, the allure of "Spanish" territory continued to be high, not the least because slavers were pushing inexorably west, in search of fresh plantation lands. Not unimportantly, the south was where Jackson's land speculations were robust, so that his end game of collateralizing himself using Indian lands remained the same, whether Burr or the United States seized them.

The beauty of this tack was that seizing land was an easy sell to the public, so that Jackson could tap into land greed as a non-divisive issue, shared settler-wide. Thus, even as the Burr Conspiracy was blowing up in his face on December 29, 1806, Jackson (and Daniel Smith) saw a glimmer of an out in scheming to appropriate federal funds to "pay the indians for their land."[156] In December 1809, just two months into his term as Tennessee governor, Willie Blount hit on an even better scheme, suggesting to Jackson the possibility of simply removing the Cherokee and Chickasaw west of the Mississippi River.[157] Jackson had found his métier.

The initial moves in the play were not, however, directly against the Muskogee but against the hated "Dons." As part of the Napoleonic Wars, after Bonaparte took over Spain in 1808, Spanish nationals were supported by Britain, Napoleon's arch enemy. Building up to the War of 1812 against England, it was popular to finger the Spanish as active British allies in North America, who had to be neutralized by displacing them from the continent, as a dreaded fifth column. Under this rationale in the fall of 1810, U.S. settlers in Baton Rouge took that town from the Spanish, in what is usually presented as a grassroots effort of their militias but in what the Spanish accurately fingered as an outgrowth of an *"ambición constante del gobierno americano"* (a constant ambition of the American government) to acquire all the land in the continental South.[158] On October 27, 1810, by unilateral proclamation, President Madison sanctioned the Baton Rouge seizure legally, on the theory that it had been part of the Louisiana Purchase, anyway.[159]

Baton Rouge was just the first step in a manifestly destined feint at all Spanish-held lands in the south. In train with such ambitions, Mobile and Pensacola were the next Spanish dominos to fall. Consequently, in the summer of 1810, settlers in the American Tombigbee settlements mounted an assault on Mobile but were driven back by the Spanish garrison.[160] In December 1811, U.S. regulars along with the inevitable militia again demanded "the Town of Mobile from the Spanish Commandant," a claim haughtily refused by the Spanish.[161] Nevertheless, Congress summarily and unilaterally annexed Mobile to the United States on May 14, 1812 (2 *Stat.* 734).[162]

Then, in July 1812, Governor Claiborne pushed William Eustis, the new secretary of war, to take "immediate possession of Pensacola & Mobile," as indispensable to both the settlers and the U.S. government.[163] When the Spanish arrived in Pensacola that fall with 150 fresh soldiers to defend their territory, General Wilkinson still lacked orders to secure the towns.[164] This situation was cried up as dangerous but for a new and promising reason: the ability of the Spanish in Pensacola to arm the Muskogee of Alabama, then engaged in the Muskogee civil war. Obviously, the Spanish had just shifted from a dangerous British to a dangerous Muskogee ally, a morphing that was to continue throughout the Creek War, depending on the expediencies of the moment.

Attempting in July 1812 to shake loose federal action against the Indian proprietors of the southeastern lands, Claiborne went through Mississippi territorial governor David Holmes to declare that the British were skulking behind the "menacing tone" he read in the Spanish resistance to U.S. demands. Claiborne helpfully added that Wilkinson was willing to act, should the militia be called up.[165] Still muttering darkly about British intentions on August 10, 1812, Claiborne insistently pressed Secretary of State James Monroe to authorize Wilkinson "to take Mobile & Pensacola!"[166] By September 1812, Holmes informed Wilkinson that he had helpfully formed the lands in question into Mobile County.[167] In April 1813, although *still* lacking presidential orders, Wilkinson simply entered Mobile and took Fort Charlotte.[168] The Spanish retaliated by burning their blockhouses in Mobile in June 1813, but the Americans remained in retention of the town.[169]

These actions were part of the larger goal of isolating the Muskogee nation from "friends" while encircling it with settlers prior to seizing what is now primarily the State of Alabama but which was then the part of the Muskogee homeland still in Muskogee hands. (Their Georgia lands had already been seized.) As in Indiana, construction of settler roads and forts fortuitously preceded, thus to enable, the Creek War. Roads came first, disguised as innocent postal routes, again laid over preexisting Indian roads—and the Muskogee nation had "quite a system of roads" to follow. The settler-named Etowah Path started at a branch of the Oconee River, called High Shoals, and ran across the Chattahoochee River, near modern-day Atlanta. From there, it proceeded to the Cherokee city of *Etowah* and through several other Cherokee towns to Chickasaw, in what is now northern Mississippi and western Tennessee.[170]

Also crossing the Chattahoochee River, but starting farther south, the second branch of the Etowah Road led through middle to southern Muskogee towns. The third major road ran farthest south. It started near modern-day Milledgeville, Georgia, on the Oconee River and ran fairly due west to Cosseta and Coweta, near modern-day Columbus, Alabama, today on the border of Georgia and Alabama, very near to where Fort Hawkins was set up. From there, the third route ran to old Okfuskee near present-day Midland City, Alabama, and on to the old French Fort Toulouse (later Fort Jackson), near modern-day Wetumpka, Alabama. When the Europeans first invaded what is now Georgia, they simply overran the fourth route, which lay almost entirely within Georgia, with the settlers then destroying its old traces.[171] The second southern route was first renamed the "Dixie Overland Highway" but later became U.S. Route 80.

Settler-reported difficulties of crossing rivers or scaling heights in traversing Muskogee lands must be evaluated, not swallowed whole.[172] As anyone who has walked the old roads knows, the ancestors did not lay them directly up the face of a cliff or across deep, impassable rapids, so such tales came from honest travelers who were simply lost or from squatters hiding their illegal trespass by sidestepping the roads. It was also commonplace for settlers to exaggerate their difficulties to fit the preferred settler narrative of the so-called "howling wilderness," the cant phrase of the time, which made Indian territory sound so much more like uninhabited, virgin land for the taking than anciently settled and claimed land being stolen.[173]

The Federal Road and its branches were to follow the Muskogee roads, but first, in 1801, another road was gotten up to from Nashville to Natchez, across what settlers called "the Natchez trace," the same route by which Jackson had returned to Nashville after depositing Rachel Robards in Natchez.[174] Immediately, the Natchez Road began expanding south, with the ultimate goal of reaching New Orleans, at which point Dearborn began nosing about for Muskogee land across which to build the project officially named the Federal Road on February 11, 1804.[175] One year later, possible routes were being reviewed, and on March 3, 1805, Congress gave official color to the road, appropriating $6,000 to build it (2 *Stat.* 338).[176] Only at this point was the Treaty with the Creeks (the so-called first Washington Treaty) pushed through the Muskogee Council on November 14, 1805.[177]

Like all other treaties, the Washington Treaty was arranged with ringers selected, in this instance, by the Indian agent of the south, Benjamin Hawkins, and sent forward as purportedly authorized by representatives of the people. Handled in Washington, D.C. by Dearborn, the resultant treaty "forever quit" the Muskogee title to the swath of land between the Ocmulgee and Oconee Rivers, cutting through the heart of Red Stick (traditionalist) Muskogee land, ceding to the United States all "right, title, and interest" in it. The United States was empowered to maintain a military fort and a "factory" or trading post, as well as anything else it later decided on. U.S. citizens had free passage on the road, any time they liked, while the Muskogee had to provide ferry service to the settlers.[178] In return, the Muskogee nation, vaguely identified, would receive $12,000 annually for eight years, followed by $11,000 for another ten years, all without interest on the mortgage. In addition, the United States would "furnish" one blacksmith and one striker for eight years. The treaty was X'ed by:[179]

- *Oche Haujo* ("Alexander Cornells"), who was an entirely Europeanized, mixed-lineage Muskogee.[180]
- "William McIntosh," or *Taskanugi Hatke* (White Warrior), another well known, mixed-lineage assimilant who supported Jackson's invasion during the Creek War and was executed by the Muskogee in 1825 for selling their land.[181]
- *Tuskenehau Chapco*, the assimilant Coweta chief, involved in the 1802 Treaty of Fort Wilkinson.[182]

- *Tuskenehau*, a chief who is poorly recorded, probably because, as *Tuskenehau Chapoco* (as opposed to *Tuskenehau Chapco*), he was listed as "one of the leaders of the opposition."[183]
- *Enehau Thlucco*, a counselor who had been collecting "stipends" from the United States since 1797.[184]
- *Chekopeheke Emanthau*, who apparently signed this one treaty and then disappeared from written history.

Congress had authorized the Federal Road on March 3, 1805, as a straight route connecting Athens, Georgia, and New Orleans.[185] Surveys and land acquisitions followed, starting in April 1806, and by February 1807, matters had progressed past simple military or postal uses, with orders promulgated for the "establishment of Stages for the convenient accommodation of Travellers."[186] These were terrible developments for the Muskogee, Cherokee, and Chickasaw peoples. In a mere six years, Muskogee territorial sovereignty had been completely usurped without so much as a howdy-do. Trouble necessarily followed.

Never having believed that the Federal Road could really have been intended, as advertised, for peaceful uses, both assimilationist and traditionalist Muskogee mightily resisted it, only to see it imposed on them by fiat.[187] They knew full well that a main, if quiet, reason for the road was that in case of hostilities, it neatly bisected Muskogee territory. Unsurprisingly, by 1811, the Federal Road was widened into a heavy wagon highway, trucking in military troops, gear, and supplies, not to mention, settlers.[188] Between October 1811 and March 1812, alone, 3,276 settlers crossed Muskogee Country to the Tombigbee and Tensaw region.[189] All too predictably, once the Creek War began a year later, the road was used by the federal, territorial, and state militaries to invade and destroy Red Stick towns.

The civil war between the Red Sticks, or traditionalists of the northern part of Muskogee lands, and the lower, southwestern-quarter assimilants, most of them of mixed European-Muskogee lineage, had long been brewing, but the Washington Treaty of 1805 put energy into the split, the factions soon tussling over Muskogee policy toward the United States. It was not unpolitical or unwitting that, signed off on by the assimilants, the Federal Road cut straight through traditionalist territory. Furthermore, the Federal Road was not a single route but like the original Muskogee roads, had branches here and there, wandering off into Muskogee land.[190] In addition, the "Cherokee Road" was cut from Savannah, Georgia, to Knoxville, Tennessee. As such, this road and its branches trucked in tens of thousands of settlers, dragging along their many slaves, all headed "west" to the new Promised Lands in the Mississippi and Louisiana Territories, with populations as tracked in Table 4.1.[191]

Settler forts inexorably accompanied the roadbuilding, with settlers seeing the establishment of militia forts as a prime order of business. Fort planning began as soon as the "Mississippi Territory" was declared. On December 10, 1798, Secretary of State Timothy Pickering instructed Winthrop Sargeant, then at Natchez, to take U.S. control of all "public buildings" except forts. Should war

Table 4.1 Population of Georgia, Tennessee, Mississippi Territory, and Muskogee (1708–1814)

Years	Euro-Settlers			Africans	Muskogee	Total by Years	
	Georgia (GA)	Tennessee (TN)	Muskogee (MS)	GA, TN, MS	AL	Settlers and Africans	Muskogee
1708					7,600[a]		7,600
1725–1726					8,800		8,800
1780–1794	52,886	31,719		34,330	26,000	118,935	26,000
1796[b]		66,649[b]		10,613[c,d]		77,262[b]	
1800	102,261	91,709	5,179	77,899		277,048	
1810–1814	145,414	215,875	23,024	170,199	17,750[e]	554,512	17,750

[a] Settler statistics give only "warrior" counts, which were calculated as one-fourth of the whole population. Thus, "warrior" head counts are multiplied by four to recover the total population counts. All of these counts were settler estimates, not actual enumerations. Especially from 1708 to 1726, they are almost certainly too low.

[b] Probable overestimate.

[c] The 1796 Tennessee census was performed in preparation for application to Congress for statehood.

[d] These slaves were in Tennessee, only.

[e] Includes Seminole.

Table 4.1 shows the relative increase of settler and African populations against the concurrent decrease of the Muskogee population.

Sources: Krzywicki, 1934, 526–28; U.S. Census, Cummings and Hill, 1918, 45; for 1796 Tennessee census, Remini, 1966, 34; Swanton, 1922, 434–36, 443.

erupt, the U.S. Army would take control of the forts through application to the territorial governor. Secretary of War James McHenry "entirely" concurred with Pickering in this decision.[192] Thus, militias were allowed to act for and as the U.S. military, despite the deplorable reputation of militias when it came to self-restraint, sobriety, or coherent strategy. The government was not unaware of these problems, so only some of this decision can be laid to cost control. The rest must be laid to plausible deniability in the probable event of settler wrongdoing (that is, it could be blamed on those doggoned militias). By the outbreak of the Creek War, Muskogee lands were completely surrounded by forts, as listed in Table 4.2. As Peter Hamilton noted in 1900, one had but to "take up a good map" of Alabama to run one's finger along what became the Federal Road to encounter Forts Bainbridge, Deposit, Hull, Mitchell, and Montgomery, along with Burnt Corn, where the Muskogee Civil War was turned into the settler Creek War.[193]

Shifting focus from "Dons" to "Creeks" was no giant leap for Jackson. Always an "inveterate" Indian-hater, Jackson knew the right buttons to push to rouse the dander of his fellow "frontier" settlers against the Muskogee.[194] Exaggerating occasional crimes by individual Indians against individual settlers into hideous atrocities by all the Indians against all Europeans was a settler commonplace, which usually worked to stir martial sentiment. The catch was that an instance of sufficient gore had to have existed to pull off the puff. A successful instance included harm to Euro-American women and children, or at least a feint at a settler village.

By March 1808, with Burr in the rearview mirror and Britain having heated up its runs at the United States, especially in the Chesapeake "insult" of June 1807, Congress authorized, and President Madison enabled, Tennessee to call up its militia, essentially at will, should a perceived threat arise.[195] By April 20, 1808, Jackson was calling up his second division of state militia, alleging that "25 of our inocent Citizens have fell victims, to the ruthless hands of Savage barbarity" of the "Creeks." Although the report empowering this alert was soon found to have been a fraud, a glowering Jackson remained "apprehensive" that "part of the Creeks" were hostile to the settlers.[196]

A few more promising candidates popped up, including the murder in April 1812 of Thomas Meredith, a settler traveling the hotly disputed Federal Road where it cut through Muskogee territory.[197] With the road on which Meredith died construed as federal land, this potentially called for an armed response. A debate erupted over whether the Meredith killing was accidental or intentional, but the Muskogee National Council muted the issue by punishing the culprits itself, exercising a sovereign power reserved to the Muskogee in the 1790 Treaty of New York.[198] Although the Meredith brouhaha was defused, opportunity for a war soon resurfaced with the death of another traveling settler, William Lott, but once more, the Muskogee cited the 1790 treaty, allowing them authority over their own criminals.[199] Consequently, the Federal Road notwithstanding, the war pretexts of Meredith and Lott fizzled as nonstarters.

Table 4.2 Forts Heading into the Creek War of 1813–1814

Dates	Fort Names	Locations	Usage	Notes
1814	Camp Defiance	Calebee Creek Mason Co., Alabama	Georgia state militia	Subpost of Fort Hull
1813	Fort Armstrong	Coosa and Chattooga Rivers, Alabama	Tennessee state militia	Supply depot
1814	Fort Bainbridge	Near Hurtsboro, Alabama	Georgia state militia	Fort and supply depot
1814	Fort Bowyer	Tip of Mobile Point	Militia fort	Replaced by Fort Morgan, in Civil War
1813	Fort Carney	Tombigbee River, Alabama; north of Fort Powell	Settler fortification	North of U.S. Fort Powell; also called Fort Hawn
1813	Fort Cato	Coffeeville near Frankville, Alabama, Washington Co.	Settler fortification	Tombigbee River, west side; abandoned as war heated up
1813	Fort Charlotte	Mobile, Alabama	U.S. Army	Seized from Spanish, 1813; Former Fort Condé de la Mobille (French) and then Fuerte Carlota de Mobila
1813–1814	Fort Claiborne	Weatherford's Bluff, Alabama River, Highway 84	U.S. Army Fort	Supply depot; three blockhouses, crescent battery
1813	Fort Curry	Near Jackson, Alabama	Settler fortification	Small fort
1814–1815	Fort Decatur	Near Milstead, Alabama	North Carolina state militia	Militia fort
1813–1814	Fort Deposit #1	Lowndes Co., Alabama	U.S. Army fort	Supply depot and army hospital abandoned after 1814
1813	Fort Deposit #2	Tennessee River at Thompson's Creek	Tennessee state militia	Supply depot
1813	Fort Easley	Wood's Bluff Clarke Co., Alabama	Settler fortification	Also called Easley's Station
1813	Fort Glass	Next to Fort Madison	Settler fortification	State troops and 1,000 settlers
1813	Fort Gullet	Gullet's Bluff, Alabama	Settler fortification	
1813–1820	Fort Hawkins	Near Coweta, Alabama	Georgia militia fort	Set up by militia general Floyd
1809–1817	Fort Hampton	Near Athens, Alabama	U.S. Army fort	Also as Fort at Muscle Shoals

Date	Fort	Location	Type	Notes
1813–1814	Fort Hull	Near Tuskegee	Georgia state militia	On the Federal Road to Alabama
1814	Fort Jackson	Near Wetumpka, Alabama	Tennessee state militia	Log blockhouse; also called Jackson's Blockhouse; formerly Fort Toulouse
1813	Fort Landrum	Clarke County, Alabama	Settler fortification	Eleven miles west of Fort Sinquefield near Fort Mott
1813	Fort Lavier	Bassett Creek, Clarke Co., Alabama	Settler fortification	Abandoned September, 1813
1813	Fort Madison	4½ miles south of Suggesville, Alabama	Major U.S. Army Fort	602 yd log stockade plus trenches
1813	Fort McGrew	Three miles north of St. Stephens, Alabama	Settler fortification	Two acres, large stockade with palisades
1813	Fort Mims	Co. Rd. 80, Baldwin Co., Alabama	Settler fortification	One acre, stockade enclosure plus associated cabins
1814–1818	Fort Montgomery	Near Tensaw	U.S. Army	Built two miles from Fort Mims
1813	Fort Mott	Salitpa Creek, Clarke Co., Alabama	Settler fortification	Small stockade
1813–1837	Fort Mitchell	Russell Co., Alabama	Georgia state militia	On border of Alabama and Georgia
1813–1837	Fort Mitchell	Russell Co., Alabama	Georgia state militia	On border of Alabama and Georgia
1813	Fort Patton	Wayne Co., Mississippi Territory	Settler fortification	Stockade
1813	Fort Perry	Buena Vista, Georgia	Georgia state militia	Created by General Floyd
1813	Fort Pierce	Northern Baldwin Co., Alabama	Settler fortification	U.S. Army garrisoned, 1813
1813	Fort Pitchlynn	Plymouth Bluff on Black Warrior River, Alabama	U.S. fort	Also called Fort Smith
1813	Fort Powell	Oven Bluff, near Carleton, Alabama	Setter fortification	Small stockade
1813	Fort Rankin	near St. Stephen's, Alabama	Settler fortification	Large stockade
1813–1815	Fort Republic	St. Stephens, Alabama	Settler militia fort	At site of old fort
1813	Fort Roger	Wayne Co., Winchester, Alabama	Settler fortification	Minimal usage, soon abandoned
1813	Fort Shackleford	Escambia Co., Florida	Settler fortification	Oral tradition
1813	Fort Sinquefield	Fort Sinquefield Rd., US 84, Alabama	Settler fortification	

(continued)

145

Table 4.2 (Continued)

Dates	Fort Names	Locations	Usage	Notes
1799–1814	Fort Stoddert	Mt. Vernon Landing, Florida	U.S. Army	Major installation, also as "Stodderd"
1813–1814	Fort Strother	St. Clair Co., Alabama	Tennessee state militia	Jackson's HQ, Creek War
1813	Fort Turner	West Bend, Alabama	Settler fortification	2–3 blockhouses
1813	Fort White	Near Grove Hill, Alabama	Settler fortification	Stockade
1813	Fort Williams	Joining Cedar Creek, and Coosa River, Alabama	Tennessee state militia	Supply depot
1813–1894	Mount Vernon Cantonment	Mt. Vernon, Florida	U.S. Army	Associated with Fort Stoddert
1814	Sand Fort	Near Seale, Georgia	Georgia militia fort	On the Federal Road to Alabama

Table 4.2 shows the primary forts extant in the United States at the opening of the Creek War and their locations.

Sources: Generally, Hannings, 2006, *Alabama*, 5–14; **Camp Defiance**, Payette, 2010 "American Forts, East: Alabama"; **Armstrong**, Bunn and Williams, 2008, 90; Hannings, 2012, 86; **Bainbridge**, Payette, *op. cit.*; Southerland and Brown, 1989, 43, 47, 54, 55, 65, 83, 85, 98, 141; **Bowyer**, Bunn and Williams, 2008, 119; **Carney**, Bunn and Williams, 2008, 47; Payette, *op. cit.*; **Cato**, Bunn and Williams, 2008, 47; Payette, *op. cit.*; **Claiborne**, Southerland and Brown, 1989, 41, 42, 55; Bunn and Williams, 2008, 47; Payette, *op. cit.*; **Charlotte**, Monette, 1846, vol. 2, 389; Carter, 1934–1975, vol. 6, 360, 364; **Curry**, Payette, *op. cit.*; **Decatur**, Southerland and Brown, 1989, 47; Payette, *op. cit.*; **Deposit (1)**, Southerland and Brown, 1989, 41, 42, 95, 141; Bunn and Williams, 2008, 48; Payette, *op. cit.*; **Deposit (2)**, Bunn and Williams, 2008, 90; **Easley**, Bunn and Williams, 2008, 48–49; Payette, *op. cit.*; **Glass**, Bunn and Williams, 2008, 50; Payette, *op. cit.*; **Gullett**, Payette, *op. cit.*; **Hampton**, Meynard, 1981, 103; Payette, *op. cit.*; **Hawkins**, Southerland and Brown, 1989, 42, 52, 54, 56, 60, 71, 72, 76; **Hull**, Southerland and Brown, 1989, 44, 47, 65, 85, 87, 98; Payette, *op. cit.*; **Jackson**, Southerland and Brown, 1989, 117; Payette, *op. cit.*; **Landrum**, Bunn and Williams, 2008, 50; Payette, *op. cit.*; **Lavier**, Bunn and Williams, 2008, 50; Payette, *op. cit.*; **Lawrence**, Southerland and Brown, 1989, 29, 26, 40–41, 68, 98, 103, 142; Bunn and Williams, 2008, 51; Payette, **McGrew**, Bunn and Williams, 2008, 51; **Mims**, Southerland and Brown, 1989, 29, 26, 40–41, 68, 98, 103, 142; Bunn and Williams, 2008, 51; Payette, *op. cit.*; **Montgomery**, Bunn and Williams, 2008, 119–20; Payette, *op. cit.*; **Mott**, Bunn and Williams, 2008, 52; Payette, *op. cit.*; **Mitchell**, Southerland and Brown, 1989, 44, 60, 64, 67, 68, 76–78, 80–82, 89, 124, 129–30, 141; Payette, *op. cit.*; **Patton**, Bunn and Williams, 2008, 52; **Perry**, Hannings, 2012, 86; Southerland and Brown, 1989, 4, 81; **Pierce**, Bunn and Williams, 2008, 52; **Pitchlynn**, Bunn and Williams, 2008, 53; Payette, *op. cit.*; **Rankin**, Bunn and Williams, 2008, 53; Payette, *op. cit.*; **Republic**, Payette, *op. cit.*; **Roger**, Bunn and Williams, 2008, 54; Southerland and Brown, 1989, 18–19, 29–36; Payette, *op. cit.*; **Sinquefield**, Bunn and Williams, 2008, 54; Payette, *op. cit.*; **Stoddert**, Hannings, 2012, 141; Bunn and Williams, 2008, 92; Southerland and Brown, 1989, 49; **Turner**, Bunn, and Williams, 2008, 56; **Strother**, Hannings, 2012, 170, 177, 187, 190, 195; Bunn and Williams, 2008, 56; Payette, *op. cit.*; **Williams**, Hannings, 2012, 205; Bunn and Williams, 2008, 93; Southerland and Brown, 1989, Payette, *op. cit.*; **White**, Bunn and Williams, 2008, 56; Payette, *op. cit.*; **Sand Fort**, Southerland and Brown, 1989, 52, 82–83, 141; Payette, *op. cit.* 111; **Mount Vernon**, Hannings, 2012, 141; Bunn and Williams, 2008, 57; **Sand Fort**, Southerland and Brown, 1989, 52, 82–83, 141; Payette, *op. cit.*

The next likely opportunity hit on March 25, 1812, when Jackson spotted a flyer recounting "a horrid Carnage on Bradshaw Muskogee," a spot fifteen miles south of Fayetteville, Tennessee. Fortunately, twenty-five families were rumored to have been murdered and by none other than the Muskogee, so that Jackson lost no time in ordering Tennessee militiamen and federal soldiers to the place. The next day, chagrinned, he had to pull back, when it was disclosed that instead of the Muskogee, the perpetrators were "some villians who was encamped on the Indian land who had a wish to get possession of some houses possessed by others, who painted themselves, raised the indian yell and fired."[200] (Disguising themselves as Indians while committing crimes was a settler tactic with a well worn history.[201]) Although this sad tale was amplified into a genuine Indian threat by those fleeing the onslaught, the attack was soon enough discovered to have been settler-conceived and perpetrated.

Thwarted, Jackson was forced to cool his heels until three months later, when luckily for him, Martha Crawley happened along.[202] Because her story had the advantage of being mostly true and involved, moreover, the deaths of children as well as the abduction of a woman, it seemed ready-made to Jackson's purpose. The excited letter on the Crawley case coming from his militia general, so close on the heels of the disappointing Bradshaw Muskogee incident, strongly suggests that Jackson had issued a standing order for his officers to have been on the look-out for just such a worthy cause.

It was in late May 1812 that Jackson was informed by a militia general under him of "intelligence"—this time, "certain"—of the "Murder of Six Persons" on the Duck River by Muskogee "Indians."[203] Better and better, Martha Crawley had been carted off bodily by the perpetrators when they departed the scene, allowing Jackson to bawl to Tennessee governor Willie Blount that his heart bled at "the wanton massacre of our women and children by a party" of Muskogee, and the only remedy for it was that the "assassins of Women and Children" be "punished."[204] It also did not hurt that the lands on Duck River were so "valuable" that Jackson had been lusting after them since 1798, advising his brother-in-law, Robert Hays, to "keep all" of them he had and to "get" whatever of them he could.[205] Lost in the shuffle was that Duck River was Muskogee land, with the Crawleys, complete squatters.

Of course, the propaganda mills improved on Mrs. Crawley's plight by adding that the Muskogee men who had abducted her had exhibited her naked—a little sexual titillation never hurt a war drive—whereas, in fact, she had simply been pressed into service as the chef of the retreating war party.[206] The misrepresentation of Mrs. Crawley's condition had obviously sprung from the official notice to the United States from Governor Blount. He had described Mrs. Crawley as having escaped from the Muskogee, only to have been recaptured a couple of days later by a scouting party, which found her "half starved and half naked."[207] The Tennessee Legislature called on the federal government to declare an all-out war on the Muskogee, while the *Nashville Clarion* gloated that the Muskogee had just "supplied us with a pretext for the dismemberment of their country."[208] What Jackson and Blount were engineering could not have been more obvious.

For his part, in an unsigned article in the July 8, 1812, *Clarion* section of the *Democratic Clarion & Tennessee Gazette*, Jackson announced that a "thousand stand of arms" was coming to Tennessee from the federal government. These arms were, however, not for use against the Muskogee but against the British, for on June 18, 1812, Congress had declared war on Great Britain. This is probably why Jackson announced his fear of relying "with an implicit confidence" on that same U.S. government: it was fighting the wrong enemy. Instead, Jackson obliquely reminded his readers that, in the "settlement of Kentucky" and its environs, "every expedition" against Indians undertaken by the settlers had been "made without the consent of the general government, but in defiance of its prohibition."[209]

From these obliquely treasonous hints, Jackson moved to chill and thrill the reader with the ill-omened report that "the blood hounds of the prophet" (*Tenskwatawa*) were out gathering steam.[210] One day later, in his official July 9, 1812, message to his military division, Jackson ranted not about the official enemy, the British, but about the need "to appease the manes of so many women and children inhumanly massacred," citing the "distracted mother crying in vain for pity"—and oblique reference to Martha Crawley—"and receiving from the hands of savage monsters"—that is, the Muskogee—"stab after stab." Jackson declared that these situations could only kindle a "kindred spirit" with the victims that would "burn for revenge."[211]

Matters seemed to be progressing well, until U.S. secretary of war Eustis canceled the party by ordering Muskogee Indian agent Benjamin Hawkins to handle the Crawley matter through negotiations with his handpicked Muskogee Council, not through a military expedition against the Muskogee.[212] Jackson's frustration at Madison's peace policy with the Indians was undoubtedly increased by the fact that the Duck River lands that the Crawleys had squatted on were ripe for the plucking, having just been effectively cleared of both trees and interlopers and still better, at no expense to himself, yet Madison and Eustis stubbornly persisted in thinking that the British, not the Muskogee, were the enemy.

While disenchantment with the Madison administration brewed in Tennessee, Governor Claiborne of Louisiana hit upon the happy alternative of targeting the Choctaw, who lay just west of the Muskogee along the Mississippi River on land also coveted by the settlers. Always churlish about the "Chactaws," Claiborne unleashed a positive barrage of agitation against them, papering every official he could think of with his suspicions, beginning the month after Eustis belayed Jackson's military action.[213] On August 9, in pursuit of war on the Choctaw, Claiborne even lowered himself into hot water with the federal government by presuming to send a "talk" warning off the "Chief Head Men & Warriors of the Chactaw Nation," a violation of the Intercourse Acts, under which only the federal government was legally empowered to communicate with the Indians.[214]

Notwithstanding, Claiborne gravely counseled the Choctaw not to listen to the Shawnee "proffet" (*Tenskwatawa*) or "his Brother Ticumsey" (*Tecumseh*), both of them then out and about, collecting an international cadre of Indigenous followers, allegedly "to drive the Americans into the Sea."[215] Despite having his speaker to the Choctaw promptly arrested by the U.S. agent to the Choctaw, Claiborne continued his smear campaign until late in the Creek War, when the Choctaw were treacherous enough actually to ally with Andrew Jackson against their traditional enemy, the Muskogee.[216] This unwelcome development effectively ended the Bad Choctaw stories flowing from Claiborne's pen, but he could still be heard in the background, chewing nails.

Happily for the war hawks, the Muskogee Red Sticks acquired arms for their side of the Muskogee civil war from the Spanish at Pensacola. This fact provided the desired pretext for officially opening aggression against both the Spanish and the Muskogee.[217] Not skipping a beat, Claiborne solemnly turned to the safe condemnation of the "conduct of the Spanish Governor at Pensacola" in supplying the Muskogee with arms, asking pointedly "whether this is not such an act of hostility, as to justify the American Government in directing Pensacola, to be immediately taken possession of."[218] Although on August 25, 1813, Claiborne breathlessly forwarded this news of the Red Sticks' arming as unexpected and alarming intelligence, in fact, he had been trolling for the information all month. Twenty-four days earlier, on August 1, 1813, he knew enough to tell Secretary of State Monroe that 700 Muskogee had crossed the Perdido River, sending the local settlers to the fort of Mobile for "asylum."[219] The jockeying for position could not have been more obvious, but this was still not quite enough on which to declare war against the Muskogee.

Nevertheless, militia colonel James Caller took it upon himself to get up an unauthorized military expedition 180–strong, including both assimilationist Muskogee and U.S. settlers from Tombigbee settlement, to attack the Red Sticks.[220] A close colleague of the area's felonious judges upbraided by Ephraim Kirby, Caller was one of those incompetently criminal officers whom Kirby had also skewered: Caller had a long history of plundering his settler neighbors.[221] Caller's premature martial action was probably not unconnected with the fact that he was a dedicated land speculator, who had once beaten out judge Toulmin on a juicy land deal.[222]

On July 27, 1813, as the Red Sticks were coming back from Pensacola with their arms, they stopped along Wolf Path for lunch at a place called Burnt Corn. There Caller's regiment of 180 men launched their attack, taking the sixty Red Sticks entirely by surprise.[223] Caller's apparent victory was soon sacrificed to greed, however, when instead of pursuing their advantage against the Red Sticks, the militiamen promptly busied themselves with looting the Red Sticks' booty. This allowed forty of the Red Sticks of the supply train to regroup and fire on the militia, which promptly broke and fled, leaving Caller to rally but eighty of his original 180 men.[224]

During Caller's counterattack, the Red Sticks were not just outnumbered by eighty to forty but also greatly outgunned: only thirteen of their forty men had rifles.[225] Notwithstanding, as reported officially by Governor Claiborne, Caller's remaining militiamen again panicked and ran at the Red Sticks' resurgence, so that "in a short time all Col° Caller's party except twenty or thirty" had "sought safety by flight."[226] It was only the quick thinking of "a half breed Indian" with

Caller, said Claiborne, that some of "the ammunition, and some clothing which the party had procured at Pensacola" was plundered from the Red Sticks for the second time, although the Red Sticks managed to hang onto most of their goods.[227] Accounts of casualties in the Burnt Corn blunder vary widely. According to the Muskogee memoirist, George Stiggins, writing in 1830, the Americans lost five men killed with another five wounded against two Muskogee dead and five wounded.[228] Reports from the American side give the militia as having suffered two dead and between fifteen to twenty wounded.[229] Militias never counted dead Indian allies, so Caller's remaining three dead were probably assimilant Muskogee.

Although still billed in Western accounts as a respectable military action, the Burnt Corn action was less a glorious victory than an embarrassing fiasco, which had "disgraced and humiliated the Tensaw and Tombigbee settlements."[230] A month later, Burnt Corn nevertheless resulted in a cause around which the settlers could finally rally. Post-fiasco, running for their skins, Caller's panicked militiamen recklessly sought refuge at the nearby settler "Fort" Mims, in actuality a small Muskogee-and-settler community with some fortification. In so doing, Caller's fleeing militia remnants brought on the tragedy that finally sparked Jackson's "just war," for the Red Sticks pursued Caller's militia fragments to Fort Mims, probably trying to reclaim their stolen goods.[231]

Now effectively cut off from Spanish or British aid, the Red Sticks were surrounded by Tennessee, Georgia, and Louisiana, all eager to conquer Muskogee Country. Via the wide Federal Road, supported by at least forty-one forts, the Muskogee were about to be picked clean of 23,000,000 acres of the prime land so long sought after by the frontier oligarchy.

NOTES

1. For Iroquois influence on U.S. Constitution, Johansen, 1982; and Grinde and Johansen, 1990; for matriarchal Iroquois and Woodlands gift economy, Mann, 2000, 161–82, 216–37.

2. Ely and Brown, 1987, xxxvii–xxxviii.

3. Parton, 1860/1870, Jackson, vol. 1, 174, 217; Blount, vol. 1, 201.

4. Moser *et al.*, 1980–2013, Rejection of Judicial Appointment, Jackson to Blount, vol. 1, letter 6/24/1798, 198; dislike of "publick life," Jackson to Jackson, vol. 1, letter 5/9/1796, 1.

5. Ely and Brown, 1987, xlvii–xlviii.

6. Remini, 1988, 46–50.

7. Moser *et al.*, 1980–2013, vol. 1, note 1, 162; Campbell to Jackson, vol. 1, letter 1/24/1802, 274; Election Returns, vol. 1, 2/5/1802, 277; Dispute with Sevier, vol. 1, 3/27/1802, 290–91; Roane, commission, vol. 1, 4/1/1802, 291–92; Reduction, vol. 2, note 5, 98; Bassett, 1911, vol. 1, 76.

8. Bassett, 1911, vol. 1, 122–23.

9. Remini, 1988, 111.

10. Remini, 1966, 15; Brady, 1906, 29.

11. North Carolina land costs in 1765, Gregory, 1986, 11.

12. Remini, 1966, 20.

13. Parton, 1860/1870, vol. 1, mother, 61; Remini, 1966, inheritance, 20.

14. Ibid., vol. 1, 62; Karsner, 1929, 25–26; Remini, *Andrew Jackson*, 15–16.

15. Remini, 1966, 21; Brady, 1906, 32.

16. Parton, 1860/1870, vol. 1, 101, 109–10; Remini, 2008, 21–22; Brady, 1906, 32–33; Brady spelled McCay as "McKay."

17. Parton, 1860/1870, vol. 1, 116.

18. Parton, 1860/1870, vol. 1, 136.

19. Ely and Brown, 1987, xlvii.

20. *ASPPL*, 1834–1861, vol. 4, no. 549, 1/20/1826, Cox, 868–69; Georgia to Donelson, head surveyor, letter 12/21/1785, 869; Parton, 1860/1870, vol. 1, 126.

21. Parton, 1860/1870, vol. 1, 132.

22. Remini, 1966, 28.

23. Parton, 1860/1870, vol. 1, 133; Clayton, 1880, 136–37.

24. Brands, 2006, 57; Parton, 1860/1870, vol. 1, 148–50.

25. Remini found no record, whatsoever, of a Natchez wedding. Remini, 1966, 31–32; Remini, 1988, 23–26.

26. Parton, 1860/1870, vol. 1, 152.

27. For 1791 date of flight, see Remini, 1988, 23.

28. Moser *et al.*, 1980–2013, Robards's Permission to Sue for Divorce, vol. 1, 12/20/1790, 424; Public Writ of Proceedings, vol. 1, 1/24/1792, 427; Divorce Decree, vol. 1, 9/27/1793, 427–28; Marriage Bond, Jackson and Donelson-Robards, vol. 1, 1/17/1794, 428; Marriage License, vol. 1, 1/18/1794, 44.

29. Remini, 1966, 33.

30. Milfort, 1802/1959, 120.

31. Ibid., 116, 117.

32. Ibid., 119–20.

33. Lanman, 1876, 244.

34. Carter, 1934–1975, Kirby to Jefferson, vol. 5, letter-cum-report, 5/1/1804, 323–24.

35. Ibid., Kirby to Jefferson, vol. 5, letter 5/1/1804, 324.

36. Ibid., Kirby to Jefferson, "banditti," vol. 5, letter 5/1/1804, 318.

37. Ibid., Kirby to Jefferson, "banditti," vol. 5, letter 4/20/1804, 318; see O'Brien, 2003, quotation, 9; settlers, 8–14.

38. Buss, 2011, 4–6, 42–70.

39. Melton, 1999; Masterson, 1955, 8.

40. Peeler, 1942, 309–27.

41. Carter, 1934–1975, Holmes to Wilkinson, vol. 6, letter 8/23/1812, 317; as brothers, Claiborne, 1917, Claiborne to Jefferson, vol. 6, letter 8/14/1813, 259.

42. Claiborne, 1917, Claiborne to Hamilton, vol. 6, letter 2/17/1812, 58.

43. Ibid., Claiborne to Jackson, vol. 6, letter 3/15/1813, 214.

44. For jurisdiction, see Claiborne, 1917, Claiborne to Toulmin, vol. 6, letter 9/16/1813, 267; for area, see Doster, 1959, 89.

45. Carter, 1934–1975, as father-in-law, Wilkinson to Benjamin Hawkins, vol. 6, letter 9/16/1812, 322; for speculation, Toulmin to Edward Tiffin, vol. 6, letter 6/7/1814, 432; Deposition of Dodge, vol. 6, 2/17/1814, 438.

46. Carter, 1934–1975, Toulmin to Madison, vol. 6, letter 11/22/1810, 135–39; Toulmin to Madison, vol. 6, letter 11/28/1810, 140; Toulmin to Madison, vol. 6, letter 12/6/1810, 149–51; Toulmin to Madison, vol. 6, letter 12/12/1810, 152–55; Toulmin to Madison, vol. 6, letter 2/6/1811, 175–77; Toulmin to Madison, vol. 6, letter 2/27/1811,

179–80; Toulmin to James Monroe, vol. 6, letter 6/23/1813, 377, 379; Holmes to John Armstrong, vol. 6, letter 8/3/1813, 390–91.

47. Doster, 1959, 92; I disagree with Doster's puff of Toulmin's character, 89.

48. Rogin, 1975, 167; see also, all of Chapter 6, 165–205.

49. Peeler, 1942, 309–10; Rogin, 1975, 55.

50. There is some confusion as to whether Coffee's wife was the niece of Rachel Donelson or her sister. Moser *et al.* gave her as a niece, Moser *et al.*, 1980–2013, vol. 1, note 1, 331–32, as does Ratner, 1997, 41. Mary Coffee was long, wrongly given as a daughter of John Donelson, Owen and Owen, 1921, vol. 3, 368.

51. Moser *et al.*, 1980–2013, vol. 1, note 1, 331–32.

52. Ratner, 1997, 42–43.

53. Remini, 1988, 33.

54. Moser *et al.*, 1980–2013, Agreement with Allison, vol. 1, 5/14/1795, 56–57; Overton to Jackson, vol. 1, letter 12/18/1796, 104–5; Jackson to Smith, vol. 1, letter 12/18/1796, 105–6; Jackson to Hays, vol. 1, letter 1/8/1797, 112; Jackson to Overton, vol. 1, letter 2/3/1798, 175.

55. Moser *et al.*, 1980–2013, Deed for Hunter's Hill, vol. 1, 3/10/1796, 84; sale of Hunter's Hill and Hermitage, vol. 2, 27.

56. Remini, 1988, 193.

57. Galle, 2004, 41.

58. Remini, 1988, 359; Remini, 1984, note 63, 602.

59. Parton, 1860/1870, vol. 1, 238.

60. Meacham, 2008, 302–4.

61. Remini, 1966, 46.

62. Ibid., 45; Remini, 1988, 51.

63. Meacham, 2008, 302.

64. Moser *et al.*, 1980–2013, Advertisement, vol. 2, 9/26/1804, 40–41.

65. Ibid., sickness, *ca.* 1798, Jackson to Rawlings, vol. 1, 160; murder, Roane to Superior Court, vol. 1, letter 7/13/1803, 336–37 and vol. 31, notes 1 and 2, 37; Jackson to Eastin, vol. 2, ca. 06/1806, 106.

66. Moser *et al.*, 1980–2013, Overton to Jackson, vol. 1, letter 3/8/1795, 54.

67. Ely and Brown, 1987, 30–31.

68. Ibid., 142–45.

69. Ibid., 32–33.

70. Ibid., 207–11.

71. Ibid., 238–41.

72. I have only seen John Meacham mentioning the African perspective in Meacham, 2008, 303.

73. Gilje, 2013, 293.

74. Moser *et al.*, 1980–2013, Overton to Jackson, vol. 1, letter 3/8/1795, 54.

75. Remini, 1988, 116–17; for "Negro Fort," Moser *et al.*, 1980–2013, Gaines to Jackson, vol. 4, letter 5/14/1816, 31.

76. Delaney, 1852–1853/1970, 85–87.

77. Remini, 1966, 43, 55–56; For Dickinson, Cave, 2017, 15–17. Counts claim that Jackson was involved in up to 103 duels Tasler, 2008, 55.

78. Parton, 1860/1870, vol. 1, 164.

79. Moser *et al.*, 1980–2013, Jackson to Sevier, vol. 1, letters 10/2/1803, 367–68; Sevier to Jackson, vol. 1, letter 10/2/1803, 378; Jackson to Sevier, vol. 1, letter 10/3/1803, 368–69; Sevier to Jackson, vol. 1, letter 10/3/1803, 369.

80. Remini, 1966, 41–42.

81. Moser *et al.*, 1980–2013, vol. 2, 77.

82. Ibid., Swann to Jackson, vol. 2, letter 1/3/1806, 78; Jackson to Swann, vol. 2, letter 1/7/1806, 79–80; Dickinson to Jackson, vol. 2, letter 1/10/1806, 81–82; Swann to Jackson, vol. 2, letter 1/12/1806, 82 and note 2, 82–83.

83. Parton, 1860/1870, vol. 1, 286–87; Moser *et al.*, 1980–2013, Jackson to Eastin (*Impartial Review*), vol. 2, letter 2/10/1806, notes 1–19, 84–85, 89; Brahan to Overton, vol. 2, letter 3/8/1806, 90–91; for close relationship, vol. 2, xxxvi.

84. Moser *et al.*, 1980–2013, Dickinson to Eastin (*Impartial Review*), vol. 2, letter 5/21/1806, 97–98; Jackson to Dickinson, vol. 2, letter 5/23/1806, 98; Dickinson to Jackson, vol. 2, letter 5/23/1806, 99; between Dickinson second Catlet and Jackson second, Overton, vol. 2, various arrangements 5/23/1806–5/24/1806, 99–100.

85. Parton, 1860/1870, bet, vol. 1, 294; date of duel arrangements, vol. 1, 295.

86. Moser *et al.*, 1980–2013, Overton to Jackson, vol. 2, letter 6/1/1806, 100.

87. Parton, 1860/1870, vol. 1, 299.

88. Ibid., vol. 2, 104.

89. Ibid., vol. 2, 101.

90. Ibid., vol. 2, 102; Jackson to Watkins, vol. 2, letter 6/15/1806, 102–3.

91. Ibid., vol. 2, 14; Catlet Statements, vol. 2, 6/20/1806 and 6/25/1806, 104.

92. Ibid., Harrison to Jackson, vol. 2, letter 6/30/1806, 105; for Harrison's Ohio home, Esarey, 1922, vol. 1, 8.

93. Moser *et al.*, 1980–2013, Jackson to Eastin, vol. 2, letter 06/1806, 106–7; Overton to Jackson, vol. 2, letter 9/12/1806, 108–9.

94. Ibid., Jackson to Campbell, vol. 2, letter 4/28/1804, 18–19; Jackson to Coffee, vol. 2, letter 4/28/1804, 19–20; appointment to Claiborne, vol. 2, note 2, 19.

95. Moser *et al.*, 1980–2013, Jackson to Coffee, vol. 2, letter 5/3/1804, 21–22, *et seq.*

96. For instances of Jackson as plantation owner, slaver, and slave dealer, Moser *et al.*, 1980–2013, Jackson to Ward, vol. 2, letters 6/10/1805, 59–60; Hutchings to Jackson, vol. 2, letter 4/24/1806, 96; Jackson to Eastin, vol. 2, letter 6/1806, 106–107; Jackson to Jackson, vol. 2, letter 12/20/1809, 225–26; Memorandum, vol. 2, 3/18/1811, 262–63; vol. 2, note 4, 271; Jackson to Jackson, vol. 2, letter 12/17/1811, 273; Jackson to Caffery, vol. 2, letter 2/8/1812, 281; Jackson to Arbitrator, vol. 2, letter 2/29/1812, 286–90; Jackson to Unk., vol. 2, letter 3/20/1812, 293. For renown land speculator, Adams, 1882/1894, Randolph to Nicholson, letter 4/30/1805, 156.

97. Moser *et al.*, 1980–2013, Jackson to Anderson, vol. 2, letter 9/25/1806, 110.

98. McMichael, 2008, 54–60.

99. Parton, 1860/1870, vol. 1, 318.

100. Moser *et al.*, 1980–2013, Jackson to Campbell, vol. 2, letter 1/15/1807, 149.

101. Remini, 1988, 14.

102. Italics in the original. Parton, 1860/1870, vol. 1, 286.

103. Cheathem, 2015, 50.

104. Ranck, 1930, 17–18.

105. Moser *et al.*, 1980–2013, Burr to Jackson, vol. 2, letter 6/2/1805, 59.

106. Parton, 1860/1870, vol. 1, 311–12.

107. Moser *et al.*, 1980–2013, Burr to Jackson, vol. 2, letter 3/24/1806, 91–92.

108. Ibid., Burr to Jackson, vol. 2, letter 4/5/1806, 93; the most probable speeches enclosed were, USC, 1852a, Randolph, 3/5/1806, 555 *et seq.*; Sloan, 3/7/1806, 605 *et seq.*

109. Moser *et al.*, 1980–2013, Jackson to Anderson, vol. 2, letter 2/25/1806, 110 and, vol. 2, note 1, 110.

110. Parton, 1860/1870, vol. 1, 316.

111. Moser *et al.*, 1980–2013, Jackson to Winchester, vol. 2, letter 10/4/1806, 110–11.

112. Blennerhassett and Safford, 1864, 150–51.

113. Moser *et al.*, 1980–2013, order, vol. 2, 10/4/1806, 111–12.

114. Ibid., Account with Burr, vol. 2, 10/4/1806, 113.

115. Blennerhassett and Safford, 1864, Blennerhassett to Unk., letter 2/22/1812, 552.

116. Cox, 1928, 84; Lewis, 2017, 48–49; Moser *et al.*, 1980–2013, vol. 2, note 14, 114, and vol. 2, note 2, 120.

117. Clay, 1959, Clay's movement from belief to disgust as traceable, Burr to Clay, vol. 1, letter 11/7/1806, 253; Burr to Clay, vol. 1, letter 11/27/1807, 256; Burr to Clay, vol. 1, letter 12/1/1806, 256–57; Defense of Burr, vol. 1, letter 12/3/1806, 258–59; Clay to Innes, vol. 1, letter 1/16/1807, 269–70; Clay to Todd, vol. 1, letter 1/24/1807, 271–72; Clay to Hart, vol. 1, letter 2/1/1807, 273–74; Clay to Plummer, vol. 1, 1807, note 3, 274–75.

118. Burton, 1951, 737–38; Burr's departure date, Moser *et al.*, 1980–2013, vol. 2, 124.

119. Moser *et al.*, 1980–2013, Jackson to Jefferson, vol. 2, letter 11/5/1806, 114–15.

120. Ibid., vol. 2, note 115; Jackson to Campbell, vol. 2, letter 1/15/1807, 148.

121. Ibid., Jackson to Smith, vol. 2, letter 11/12/1806, 117–19.

122. Ibid., Jackson to Smith, vol. 2, letter 11/17/1806, 120.

123. Ibid., Jackson to Claiborne, vol. 2, letter 11/12/1806, 116–17.

124. Ibid., 1806, Burr account, vol. 2, 113; Clover Bottom Store account, vol. 2, 12/9/1806, 122; Jackson and Hutchings-James and Washington Jackson Account, vol. 2, 12/17/1806, 123–24.

125. Ibid., Anderson to Jackson, vol. 2, letter 12/31/1806, 128–29.

126. Parton, 1860/1870, vol. 1, 320–22; Ranck, 1930, 20; acquittal as innocence, Moser *et al.*, 1980–2013, *The Papers of Andrew Jackson*, vol. 2, 116.

127. *ASPMISC*, 1834, communication, Jefferson to Senate, vol. 1, no. 217, letter 1/22/1807, 468.

128. Moser *et al.*, 1980–2013, vol. 2, note 1, 132.

129. Ibid., Wilkinson to Jackson, vol. 2, letter 12/19/1806, 126.

130. Ibid., Dearborn to Jackson, vol. 2, letter 12/19/1806, 125.

131. Ranck, 1930, 21; Dearborn's test, Moser *et al.*, 1980–2013, Campbell to Jackson, vol. 2, letter 2/6/1807, 152.

132. Moser *et al.*, 1980–2013, Smith to Jackson, vol. 2, letter 12/29/1806, 127.

133. Ibid., Jackson to James Winchester, vol. 2, letter 1/1/1807, 130.

134. Ibid., Jackson to Bissell, vol. 2, letter 1/2/1807, 133–34; Bissell to Jackson, vol. 2, letter 1/5/1807, 137–38.

135. Ibid., Jackson to Winchester, vol. 2, letter 1/1/1807, 130–31, *et seq.*; Dearborn to Jackson, letter 1/4/1807, 136–37.

136. Parton, 1860/1870, vol. 1, 325–26.

137. Moser *et al.*, 1980–2013, Campbell to Jackson, vol. 2, letter 2/6/1807, 151.

138. Parton, 1860/1870, vol. 1, 330.

139. Moser *et al.*, 1980–2013, Campbell to Jackson, vol. 2, letter 2/6/1807, 152.

140. Ibid., Thomas Jefferson to Jackson, vol. 2, letter 12/3/1806, 121.

141. Ibid., Jackson to Dearborn, vol. 2, letter 3/17/1806, 156.

142. Adams, 1882/1894, Randolph to Nicholson, letter 6/25/1807, 221.

143. Williams and McKinsey, 1910/1997, vol. 1, 142.

144. Moser *et al.*, 1980–2013, Jackson to Dearborn, vol. 2, letter 3/17/1807, 156–57.

145. Ranck, 1930, 24; Moser *et al.*, 1980–2013, vol. 2, unnumbered note, 158.

146. Moser *et al.*, 1980–2013, Jackson to Claiborne, vol. 2, letter 1/8/1807, 141; Jackson to Smith, vol. 2, letter 11/28/1807, 174–75; Parton, 1860/1870, Jackson to Anderson, vol. 1, letter 1/4/1807, 329.

147. Shreve, 1933, 180.

148. *ASPMISC*, Jackson to Claiborne, vol. 1, no. 230, letter 11/12/1806, 563; USFC, 1808, vol. 3, 284–85, 302, Exhibit U, xxxviii–xxxix.

149. Moser *et al.*, 1980–2013, Claiborne to Jackson, vol. 2, letter 3/27/1807, 139–40.

150. Ibid., Jackson to Smith, vol. 2, letter 2/11/1807, 154; vol. 2, note 3, 155.

151. Buell, 1904, vol. 1, 204–5; for harangue, Parton, 1860/1870, vol. 1, 383.

152. Parton, 1860/1870, vol. 1, 333–34; Ranck, 1930, 21.

153. USFC, 1808, vol. 3, 228.

154. USC, 1852b, Jefferson to Wilkinson, letter 1/3/1807, Appendix, Exhibit Z, 580.

155. Moser *et al.*, 1980–2013, Jonathan Thompson to Jackson, vol. 2, extortion attempts, letter 7/3/1812, 309; Thompson to Jackson, letter 9/30/1812, 322.

156. Punctuation as in original. Moser *et al.*, 1980–2013, Smith to Jackson, vol. 2, letter 12/29/1806, 127.

157. Moser *et al.*, 1980–2013, Willie Blount to Jackson, vol. 2, letter 12/28/1809, 226.

158. Translation mine. Tello, 1980, vol. 4, 466.

159. US, 1817, vol. 7, 480–82.

160. Carter, 1934–1975, Holmes to Madison, vol. 6, letter 2/2/1811, 173–74.

161. Ibid., Cushing to Claiborne, vol. 6, letter 1/8/1811, 167.

162. Ibid., Proclamation, vol. 6, 8/1/1812, 305.

163. Claiborne, 1917, Claiborne to Eustis, vol. 6, letter 7/20/1812, 130.

164. Ibid., Claiborne to Madison, vol. 6, letter 7/20/1812, 132; for lack of orders, Carter, 1934–1975, Holmes to Wilkinson, vol. 6, letter 10/19/1812, 328.

165. Claiborne, 1917, Claiborne to Holmes, vol. 6, letter 7/27/1812, 135.

166. Claiborne, 1917, Claiborne to James Monroe, vol. 6, letter 8/10/1812, 159.

167. Carter, 1934–1975, Holmes to Wilkinson, vol. 6, letter 9/7/1812, 321.

168. Ibid., Holmes to Monroe, vol. 6, letter 4/14/1813, 360; Holmes to Zuniga, vol. 6, letter 4/30/1813, 362.

169. Ibid., Flournoy to Armstrong, vol. 6, letter 6/27/1813, 381; Holmes to Armstrong, vol. 6, letter 8/10/1813, 394.

170. Hamilton, 1901, 422.

171. Ibid., 422.

172. Hudson, 2010, 68.

173. Example, "howling wilderness," Filson, 1784, 53; difficulties exaggerated, Moser *et al.*, 1980–2013, Jackson to Call, vol. 5, letter 11/15/1821, 114; Parton, 1860/1870, "wild road," vol. 1, 175.

174. Carter, 1934–1975, Habersham to Dearborn, vol. 5, letter 3/12/1801, 118–19; Natchez Trace, see Remini, 1966, 32.

175. Carter, 1934–1975, Habersham to Steele, vol. 5, letter 3/26/1801, 120; Dearborn to Hawkins, vol. 5, letter 2/11/1804, 306–307.

176. Carter, 1934–1975, Gideon Granger to Jefferson, vol. 5, letter 2/6/1805, note 3, 396–97; vol. 5, note 5, 443; Jefferson to Granger, vol. 5, letter 7/8/1806, 471.

177. Kappler, 1904, "Treaty with the Creeks," vol. 2, 85–86.

178. Ibid., vol. 2, 85.

179. Ibid., vol. 2, 86.

180. "Descendants of Joseph Cornhill,".

181. Fredriksen, 1999, vol. 2, 503–504.

182. Davidson, 1930, 126; Kappler, 1904, vol. 2, 58–59.

183. Davidson, 1930, 285.

184. Hawkins, 1916, Hawkins to Burges, vol. 9, letter 5/30/1798, 324.

185. Southerland and Brown, 1989, 1–2; authorization, 17.

186. Carter, 1934–1975, Gallatin to Perkins, vol. 5, letter 4/24/1806, 459; Granger to Jefferson, vol. 5, letter 8/4/1806, 472–76; Jefferson to Granger, vol. 5, letter 8/9/1806, 476–77; Granger to Meriwether, vol. 5, letter 2/25/1805, 518.

187. Henri, 1986, 272.

188. Carter, 1934–1975, Eustis to Hampton, vol. 6, letter 7/11/1811, 213.

189. Doster, 1959, note 14, 91.

190. Waselkov and Christopher, 2012.

191. Harrell, 2010.

192. Carter, 1934–1975, Pickering to Sargeant, vol. 5, letter 12/10/1798, 55.

193. Hamilton, 1901, 425–26.

194. Remini, 2001, 14.

195. USC, 1850, vol. 2, 490–91; Moser *et al.*, 1980–2013, Sevier to Jackson, vol. 2, letter 1/9/1809, 205; for Chesapeake "insult," Madison, 1908, Madison to Monroe, vol. 7, letter 7/6/1807, 454–60.

196. As in original, Moser *et al.*, 1980–2013, Jackson to Second Division, vol. 2, letter 4/20/1808, 190; Jackson to Jefferson, vol. 2, letter 5/14/1808, 196.

197. *ASPIA*, 1832, Hawkins to Eustis, vol. 1, no. 137, letter 4/6/1812, 811; Hawkins to Eustis, vol. 1, letter 7/28/1812, 812.

198. Henri, 1986, 272.

199. *ASPIA*, 1832, Hawkins to Eustis, vol. 1, no. 137, letter 5/25/1812, 811; Hawkins to Eustis, vol. 1, letter 6/9/1812, 812; Hawkins to Eustis, vol. 1, letter 7/13/1812, 812; O'Brien, 2003, 26. The Moravians gave the victim's name as *Arthur* Lott, in Mauelshagen and Davis, 1969, 72, and note 52, 72.

200. Quoted text as in the original, Moser *et al.*, 1980–2013, Jackson to Coffee, vol. 2, letter 3/25/1812, 294; Jackson to Coffee, vol. 2, letter 3/26/1812, 295.

201. Examples of disguising as Indians to commit crimes, Mann, 2005, 21, 25, 40.

202. *ASPIA*, 1832, Hawkins to Eustis. vol. 1, no. 137, letter 6/22/1812, 812.

203. Moser *et al.*, 1980–2013, Johnson to Jackson, vol. 2, letter 5/27/1812, 298.

204. Ibid., Jackson to Blount, vol. 2, letter 6/5/1812, 301.

205. Henri, 1986, 273.

206. Ibid., 272.

207. *ASPIA*, 1832, Blount (Henry to Henry), vol. 1, no. 137, letter 6/26/1812, 814.

208. Waselkov *et al.*, 1982, 211.

209. Jackson, 1812, 7/7/1812.

210. Ibid., 7/7/1812.

211. Moser *et al.*, 1980–2013, Jackson to Second Division, vol. 2, letter 7/9/1812, 314.

212. *ASPIA*, 1832, Hawkins to Eustis, vol. 1, no. 137, letter 8/24/1812, 812; Hawkins to Eustis, vol. 1, letter 9/7/1812, 812–13; Eustis to Blount, vol. 1, letter 6/22/1812, 813; Blount to Eustis, vol. 1, letter 6/25/1812, 813; Blount to Eustis, vol. 1, letter 7/25/1812, 813; Blount to Eustis, vol. 1, letter 10/14/1812, 814; Moser *et al.*, 1980–2013, Announcement, vol. 2, 7/9/1812, 314.

213. Carter, 1934–1975, Homes to Wilkinson, vol. 6, letter 7/22/1812, 299; Holmes to Wilkinson, vol. 6, letter 9/7/1812, 321; Claiborne, 1917, vol. 6, 8/[9]/1812, 153; Claiborne to Holmes, vol. 6, letter 9/29/1812, 182; Claiborne to Armstrong, vol. 6, letter

4/14/1813, 233–34; Claiborne to James Madison, vol. 6, letter 7/9/1813, 236; Claiborne to James Brown, vol. 6, letter 8/25/1813, 263–64; Claiborne Circular, vol. 6, 9/8/1813, 265; Claiborne to Flournoy, vol. 6, letter 9/17/1813, 269–70.

214. Claiborne, 1917, Claiborne to Choctaw, vol. 6, letter 8/9/1812, 153.

215. Ibid., Claiborne to Choctaw, vol. 6, letter 8/9/1812, 154.

216. Claiborne, joining Jackson, Claiborne to Perkins, vol. 6, letter 10/21/1814, 283; arrest of Favre, Claiborne to Armstrong, vol. 6, letter 4/14/1813, 234.

217. *ASPIA*, 1832, Blount to Flournoy, vol. 1, no. 139, letter 10/15/1813, 855.

218. Claiborne, 1917, Claiborne to Claiborne, vol. 6, letter 8/25/1813, 263.

219. Ibid., Claiborne to Monroe, vol. 6, letter 8/1/1813, 250; Waselkov, 2006, 98. For Wolf Path, see Carter, 1934–1975, Holmes to Eustis, vol. 6, letter 8/30/1813, 396.

220. For lack of authorization, see Carter, 1934–1975, Holmes to Armstrong, vol. 6, letter 8/30/1813, 397.

221. Doster, 1959, 92.

222. Carter, 1934–1975, Toulmin to Tiffin, vol. 6, letter 6/7/1814, 432–33.

223. Stiggins, 1989, 100; Waselkov, 2006, 100.

224. Stiggins, 1989, 100; O'Brien, 2003, 41.

225. Stiggins, 1989, 13.

226. Carter, 1934–1975, Holmes to Armstrong, vol. 6, letter 8/30/1813, 396.

227. Ibid., Holmes to Armstrong, vol. 6, letter 8/30/1813, 396–97; Red Sticks keeping goods, Waselkov, 2006, 100.

228. Stiggins, 1989, 101.

229. Waselkov, 2006, note 12, 100, and 304.

230. Ibid., 101.

231. Ibid., 102.

CHAPTER 5

❧

Sky Panthers and Ground Snakes

*L*ong ago, the "Earth opened" in the west, where her "mouth" is, so that the Muskogee people could emerge. They settled near Earth's mouth, but as it turned out, that Nearby Land had a nasty tendency to become "angry" and "eat up" Earth's children. They moved yet further west to settle down, again.[1]

As told by *Chekilli*, a primary chief of the confederated Muskogee in 1735, this is a standard emergence tale of the sort kept by the women. It is probably not unconnected with the traditions of many North American Indians about having lived underground in crisscrossing tunnels during a time of general geological havoc, before coming back to the surface of the earth.[2] The landscape that *Chekilli* was describing was earthquake-prone, putting the Muskogee ancestors originally around the Rocky Mountains. Vine Deloria Jr. linked the many traditions of earthquakes and volcanoes, like that of *Chekilli*'s opening, to the Pacific Northwest, which seems a very likely candidate as a starting point of the Muskogee people.[3] The tradition likewise indicates considerable antiquity, for the last heavily geological period, filled with earthquakes and volcanoes as witnessed by humans was what geologists are now calling the "Anthropocene," dating from 50,000 to 10,000 BP.[4]

Chekilli continued that the group eventually split into two, as some hankered to return to their Nearby Land, while the rest wanted to stay put in their new land. Unfortunately, the returnees once more met with geological disaster, so that they pushed east, "toward the sunrise." They lingered for a couple of years at a "red, bloody river," but the area was simply too untenable to remain, so they continued east to the "end of the bloody river," where they heard a "noise as of thunder." Curious, they investigated the mountain making this noise, saw "red smoke," and realized that it was the mountain that had thundered out a "singing noise." Scouts sent to check out the situation found that the top of the mountain was "a great fire which blazed upward" and sang. The people were properly afraid of this mountain but meeting others who lived around it, they acquired a starter kit of fire for themselves, along with a "knowledge of herbs," among other useful things. Continuing their travels, they encountered more fire, a white fire from the east, a blue fire from the south, a black fire from the west, and a red-yellow fire from the north. The last, they combined with the volcanic fire they already carried and continued east with their singing fire.[5] This portion of the tradition is heavily mixed with the ceremonial import of cultural color-codes, linking colors to directions, as all Indigenous American traditions do (although not necessarily in identical combinations of color and direction).

The mountain from which the Muskogee obtained the second fire was restless, so the people sacrificed a "motherless child" (a community burden) to it, on a pole that already existed at its summit, apparently for this purpose. This is a probable reference to a national staff. They also found four singing herbs or roots (another ceremonial reference, here to directions in their sweating and Busk purification usages). Both men and women learned to sweat, with the women separating their own "fire" for "five, six, seven days" (that is, synchronized menses in a habitation lodge, considered powerful medicine).[6] Taking the pole, herbs, roots, and fire, the people continued their eastward walk, but along the way, the four phratries locked in debate over which was the "oldest," meaning the elder group, to which the rest should listen. Setting up four poles now, as opposed to one, they agreed to war against one another, till one had covered its pole with scalps from the others. Then, that one was named the Elder phratry.[7] There is considerable debate over scalping, whether it actually a Native American custom before the European arrival thrust it upon them or homegrown. By 1735, however, when *Chekilli* spoke, scalping was practiced, and it is not uncommon for traditions to be "updated" to include contemporary uses, for the point is the sweep of the story. Whereas the details may vary, the point never varies.

The point of this last passage is the governance structure of elderhood. Typically, the designation of Elder or Grandparent refers to who arrived where, first, geographically speaking. For instance, in the northeast, the Lenape were "the Grandfather nation," because they were the first to settle in "Dawnland" or the mid-Atlantic coastal region.[8] This rationale is why the Europeans were uniformly designated "Younger" siblings, because they were the dead last to arrive on the continent.[9] In the Muskogee instance, however, the four phratries were all of the same inception and arrival date, so they adopted the war as their method of settling conflicting claims to leadership. Covering their pole first, the Cussetaw were named the Elders.[10] Later known to the English as the "Cussatoes" or "Westos," they occupied European attention in the 1670s and, in 1680–1681, were the first decimated by the European invaders of modern-day Georgia, where the Muskogee met the Europeans, clambering ashore.[11]

Elderhood is socially organized as a governing institution, rather than being a case of biological old age in this or that individual Indian, as too many Westerners still think. Elders are those elevated by their clans to recognized leadership positions, and they have specific duties. On the confederated level, it might still be impenetrable to Western scholars why the Wind Clan of the Muskogee should have enjoyed the high organizational status to which the rest bowed, but the simple reason was that they became the Grandparents, the Elders of the Muskogee in the Southeast, following the demise of the Cussetaw. Their "other half" were the *Tchilokogalgi*, "speakers of a different language," who, having arrived thereafter, "listened to" the Wind.[12]

Next in the travels east, the Muskogee ran into a blue "bird of large size," which continually carried off people as its dinner. This is a standard reference to what is commonly styled a "Thunderbird."[13] Refusing to be raided to death, the people set up a female scarecrow, which the Blue Bird carried off and kept for some time. When the Thunderbird returned the scarecrow, it was pregnant, bringing forth a red rat, which helped the people find the medicine to kill the troublesome Thunderbird.[14] Most probably, what has been translated as "rat" was a prairie dog or a squirrel, for rats, as such, did not appear in North America until they were brought by European ships, early on.[15] The color-coding here goes back to the fire-color-direction passage, so that this story is about coordinating what comes from the north and the south. In the middle of the country, from the high plains to the desert Southwest, the change of seasons is linked to north and south, with towns moving by season, so that this tradition is probably also about seasonal and/or habitation shifts, because the peoples of Plains, where the Muskogee probably were at this point, move on a north-south axis with the seasons. There is also probably reference to life-death cycles, as the directions and the colors are again closely allied with traditions of death and reincarnation.[16]

Continuing east with their four poles, singing fire, herbs, and roots, the Muskogee came to a "white footpath," showing signs that people had made it and lived in the area. White is the color of peace, and following white roads is a traditional reference to a policy of peace. Following the white road, the Muskogee arrived at the town of Coosaw, where they lingered four years, saving the people of the town from a "wild beast, which they called man-eater," a "lion," probably a panther although possibly a mountain lion. It pounced on a victim every seven days. The Cussetaw dispatched the lion for the Coosaw people by lying in wait for six days and trapping it on the seventh, using as bait another "motherless child." Following their success in killing the lion, the Muskogee adopted the remembrance ceremony of fasting in prayer for six days before engaging in a battle on the seventh day. Now, for the good fortune they conferred, the people also carried with them bones of the lion, all colored red on one side and blue on the other.[17] The color-coding is again important, for the blue and the red are ceremonial signals of death and rebirth.

Moving east again, they crossed the "Callasihutche" River, where they tried to live, but unsuccessful in growing corn or fishing, they continued east, past the "*Wattoolahawka hutche*" or Whooping Crane Creek, the "*Owatuaka-river*," and the "*Aphoosa pheeskaw*" River, passing another mountain. Apparently, they had just entered the Appalachian region. Believing that the people here were the same as the White-Path People they had recently left, they announced their return by shooting white arrows into the town, a sign of peace. Alas, these were different people who took their white arrows of peace, painted them red, and shot them back. Red is associated with war.

Planning therefore to circumvent the town, the Muskogee plowed on, but a few of their number scouted the red-arrow town, anyway, "to see what sort of people they were." They were the sort of people to evacuate town at the sight of the Muskogee, in anticipation of attack. The scouts tracked the townsfolk to a river, but the path did not continue on the opposite bank of the river, so scouts decided that they must have fled down the river. Following the river to the mountain "*Moterell*," the scouts heard the noise of war drums and found bows lying across great rocks below a waterfall. Ever hopeful that these belonged to the White Path People they sought, the scouts again attempted shooting white arrows into their midst but once more received only red arrows in return.[18]

Hearing of the scouts' reception, the Cussetaw decided that these "flat heads," the Red- Arrow People with the beating drums, simply wanted war.[19] Who the head-flattening people were is unknown, but head binding and flattening was a known Woodlands Mound-Builder practice.[20] The Choctaw were known for head flattening in infancy. Muskogee-related, the Choctaw might have picked up the head-flattening custom, here, although the Salish and Kootenai of the High Plains, whose lands the Muskogee might have passed through, also practiced head flattening.[21]

Be that as it may, the Muskogee obliged the flat-headed drumbeaters, attacking the red-arrow town, with the intent of taking it over, killing all but two of its inhabitants. Following those two fugitives, they stumbled across the white road again. Descending into the town, they met the "Palachucolas" or the ancestral Tomochichi of what is now Savannah, Georgia. Figuring that the Tomochichi must be the people with whom they were at war, they proceeded "bloody-minded," but the Tomochichi sent them their Black Drink (without which they could not make war), as their quelling sign of peaceful intentions. Although the Muskogee planned to continue the war, the "hearts" of the Tomochichi were "white." Acquiring the "bloody tomahawk" from the Cussetaw, the Tomochichi hid it under a bed, a ceremonial reference. "Burying the hatchet" was a widespread signal of peace across the Woodlands, from Wisconsin east to the Atlantic coast.[22] The Tomochichi then sealed the peace with the gift of white feathers and a request that they both live together with one chief. It was made so.[23]

Throughout this tradition, the white and the red of matters are symbolic, for the Muskogee were thereafter organized into dual structures of white/"peace" and red/"war" towns. It is possible, given the "bloody minds" of the Muskogee, as opposed to the "white hearts" of the Tomochichi, that the designation of the two groups as red or white began here, and certainly the twinned structure accommodated the newcomers. Some question has come up, however, about whether "red" was original to the Muskogee tellings or later imposed. Although appearing in *Chekilli*'s 1735 recital of Muskogee tradition, "red" as connected with warfare might have been instigated later on by early European traders, so that "red" might not have been the original designation of the clan-half contrapuntal to the white.[24] Elsewhere in the Woodlands, blue-purple balances white, with bright red the color of success. Between white and red, then, the cultural consistency of color belonged to whiteness, as age-associated, an Indigenous commonplace.

Terminology aside, what the Tomochichi and Muskogee set up—or perhaps, the Muskogee segued into—was the eastern system of complementary town governments. Although the impression often left of the Muskogee *talwa*, or town governments, is that they existed in the one-off, Greek city-state mode, they were nothing of the sort but existed covalently by twos, in the mode of the Twinned Cosmos familiar to all North American Indians.[25] This philosophical framework sees reality as infinitely replicating fractals, continually repeating the Twinship of Blood/Water and Breath/Air (or the ethnographical "earth" and "sky," respectively). Far from a Manichean polarity, as Western scholars typically interpret it as being, the Twinship is really seen as cooperative, cosmic halves, which it is the responsibility of all spirits (not just human spirits) to maintain, continuously.[26] Thus, Muskogee society was deliberately set up to replicate the cosmic balance, so that, just as with the dual *talwa*, the clans existed by mirrored halves to balance the first halves of Blood and Breath.[27]

The *talwa* included the *Italwalgi*, or "his own towns," complemented by the *Kipayalgi* or "his opposites."[28] (Indigenous American consensus philosophy requires singular pronouns to refer to entire groups.[29]) In the short-hand communications of the color codes, white denoted wisdom (Elderhood/Breath) and smooth things, whereas red denoted haste (Youth/Blood) and wrinkled things, which might turn outwardly hostile.[30] As seen in this tradition, white was always linked with peace and later with the *Italwalgi*, whose functionaries handled domestic and civil matters including agriculture. Conversely, red was connected with the *Italwalgi*'s twin, the *Kipayalgi*, whose officials handled external things like hunting and foreign relations.[31] The fact that the later, very traditional Red Sticks founded *two* "holy ground" towns should, therefore, cease to baffle, annoy, or surprise Western historians.[32] The Red Sticks needed both their *Italwalgi* and the *Kipayalgi* halves.

The Muskogee migration tradition concludes with the transformation of the Muskogee into "one people," broken into the expected two and living on opposite sides of the river, as the Cussetaw and Coweta, the Upper and Lower "Creeks" of European acquaintance. This confederacy eventually consisted of multiple groups of southeastern peoples, collectively dubbed "Creeks" by the British, due to the fact that one of the early-contact Muskogee groups had lived along a creek.[33] Those groups situated on the northwestern-most lands, primarily along the Tallapoosa and Coosa Rivers and their tributaries, came to have been called "Upper Creeks," while those farther south, along the Chattahoochee River and its feeders, became the "Lower Creeks."[34] Both were comprised of several distinct yet still Muskogee ethnicities.[35] If the original Cussetaw remained bloody in their hearts, because they "first saw the red smoke and the red fire," their hearts were nevertheless "white on one side and red on the other," that is, they replicated the Twinship in all their towns, until 1781, when they were completely demolished by the English, as we have seen.[36] The remaining Coweta continued into Jackson's Creek War of 1813–1814.

The Muskogee terminology of white and red in this instance should *not* be confused with racist assumptions about the connotations that Europeans associated with them, although this conflation certainly happened in Jackson's time, with the "red" of Red Sticks thoughtlessly abused for the sake of settler propaganda. The term "Red Sticks" (also rendered "Red Clubs") certainly had a more ominous feeling to it for the Europeans than it had for the Muskogee. For Indians, bright red and blood involve innocent joy and are associated with success in undertakings like childbirth, but these are not typically the first associations elicited by blood or the color of red for Europeans.[37] Instead, for them, "red" inevitably carries a sense of sex, usually illicit (as in "red-light districts"), and death, usually violent (as in the Christian crucifixion story). Across the board, Europeans from Germany, Mexico, Poland, Russia, and the United States, conflated the color red with anger and jealousy in a 1997 psychological experiment.[38] The European apprehension of danger as signaled by red might well have shaped the persistent settler naming of the traditionalists as Red Sticks in the early settler chronicles, until the fearsome "warrior" Red Sticks of the 1813–1814 tellings emerged.

Although the Muskogee were farmers, and apparently had long been so, as their unsuccessful attempt at raising corn along the "Callasihutche" River demonstrates, until embarrassingly recent days, Western texts derogated all Indians, not just the Muskogee, as "hunters and gatherers." This characterization rested not on actual evidence but solely on the Euro-racist step-theory of history, based on a supposed "human progress" through set stages of history, from the savage to the barbarian and, finally, to the civilized. Of course, only western (not eastern) Europeans qualified as "civilized," and the hallmark of their "civilization" was "cultivation," that is, farming. Hence, the Indians whom the Europeans had, a priori, seated in base "savagery" could not be farmers, so that facts were chucked.[39] Unfortunately for all the sage theorizing of the eighteenth through the twentieth centuries, Muskogee women were expert farmers and had been since at least 1,000 BCE.[40]

Like all Native American female farmers, they "made dirt," which was more than just composting, as it involves mixing in right balances of chemical agents and carbon in a wet burn to fertilize the soil. This was necessary in the Southeast, as well as in the Amazon, because the base of the land was not fertile, otherwise. Although women's traditions are full of stories about creating fertile soil, archaeologists have only begun to take them seriously, with the "discovery" of what Brazilian scientists are called *Terra Preta* or Dark Earth.[41] Indian Dark Earth was why the Muskogee women's Dark Earth was at least a "foot deep" when the settlers arrived.[42] Indeed, the naturalist William Bartram, who toured the Southeast from 1773 to 1778, was especially intrigued by the "perfectly black, soapy, rich earth, or stiff mud," which he saw at "two or three feet deep" around the area's swamps—precisely the land described today as Dark Earth, and in the same sort of landscape. Bartram claimed that this land would "never wear out or become poor, but on the contrary," it was made "more fertile by tillage."[43] He attributed this startling fertility to nature, but it was the human activity of the female farmers causing it, which was why the land did, indeed, wear out, and quickly, as shown by the rapidity with which the Europeans tore through the land. The depletion of the soil is laid to cotton cropping's "carless practices," but we should also note that the displaced Muskogee women were no longer available to replenish it.[44]

The women's farming was contemporary with the mound culture of the Southeast. The Muskogee called their mounds *ecunligee*, meaning "earth placed," and said that they formed refuges during flooding, which occurred regularly in the Southeast before the U.S. Army corps of engineers got busy.[45] Of course, mounds had many more usages than just refuge, with various types reflecting various purposes: habitation mounds, where the chiefs primarily lived; burial mounds; ceremonial mounds; effigy mounds; and loaf mounds, which, for the most part, marked roadways. When resting on high grounds, mounds allowed the chiefs to look out across the landscape. The Apalachicola, Floridian relatives of the Muskogee, showed Bartram the remains of a once-bustling capital city of the Mound Builders, with its high mound of terraces, on which sat both a "rotunda" and a "square," in the familiar circle-square motif of ceremonial mounds.[46] The complex was still quite visible when Bartram stopped by, with the Muskogee tradition holding that the "ancients" had built it all, before the Muskogee arrived.[47] It was not unusual for newcomers to the mound-building east to become Mound Builders, themselves.

Misrepresentation of Muskogee culture began the moment that the first Europeans began to write about it. Because the Doctrine of Discovery empowered invasion and land seizure based on Christian precepts, the first inquiry made by Europeans was as to the "gods" of the invadee at hand, and the automatic Euro-assumption was that monotheism would be somehow in the answer's mix. Traditional Muskogee spiritual philosophy focuses, however, on a recognition of the interdependent halves of the cosmos, the half of Breath, connected to the sky, and the half of Blood, connected to the earth. As with the red and white towns, the Indigenous point is to balance the Cosmic Twins in eternal equilibrium, not for the one to seize, dominate, and dictate to the other in monopolar sequence, as in the Christian Manichean Dichotomy. The Muskogee sun is in the Breath realm, which is typically favored by men, so that the sun was a generally popular spirit among Muskogee men, yielding *Hisagita misi*, which is just one of the many stylized references to the sky half but which is relentlessly translated into English to this day as "Master of Breath" and conflated with the Christian god.[48]

The early French explorers among the Muskogee in the mid-eighteenth century, notably Jean-Bernard Bossu, thoughtlessly applied the Great-Spirit terminology of the sixteenth- and seventeenth-century French missionaries. Thus, Bossu referred to *Hisagita misi* as the "*maître de la vie*" (master of life) which he facilely if falsely equated with the "*Grand Esprit*" of the missionaries, presenting it as THE Muskogee "Master of Life."[49] Interestingly, Bossu occasionally broke stride to hint at the subtleties of Muskogee thought in naming other spirits, including the "*maître du serpent*" meaning the "Master of the Serpent"—a direct reference to *Estakwvnayv*, "Tie Snake," a water connection with the Horned Serpent of the

Blood half of the Muskogee cosmos.[50] Not incidental to this Blood reference was that Bossu actually spoke with women from time to time, for they are associated with the earth half of the cosmos, to which the Horned Serpent and his minions belongs.[51]

It was traditional across the Woodlands to replicate the Twinship in all endeavors, so it is not surprising that the early French found the close relatives of the Muskogee, the Natchez, with a twinned governmental system, although they recorded only the male half of the twinned functionaries, as *le Grand Soleil* (the Great Sun) and *le Serpent Piqué* (the Horned Serpent). When the Horned Serpent chief fell gravely ill, the French were deeply puzzled by the insistence of the Sun chief that *"le Grand Soleil frere du Malade se donneroit la mort que s'aimant beaucoup, ils s'étoient promit et de ne point se survivre"* (the Great Sun, brother of the Sick man, would kill himself for love of his brother, for they had a pact to go out together).[52] The brother terminology here was ceremonial, for in the clan moiety system, they would have been cousins, yet this should not distract us from the sentiment. The Great Sun chief and the Horned Serpent chief lived and died together, in an arrangement very consciously reflective of the Cosmic Twinship in action. The cosmic halves of the Indigenous Twinship "loved" each other as siblings. Moreover, this was not personal love, in the way that Westerners would interpret it. It was collective love. Others of the nation from both the Sun and the Serpent halves would die with the two chiefs. Thus, it is hardly incidental that it was *"une femme noble,"* that is, a "noble" woman, not man, connected with the Horned Serpent (*Serpent Piqué*), who volunteered *"à l'aller joindre dans les pays des Esprits"* (to go join him in the land of the Spirits).[53]

If conflicts emerged, the "red" half of the Muskogee Confederacy took over, as *Chekilli* made clear. Always incorrectly rendered as "warriors" in the European chronicles, the Young Men, as led by older, female-appointed War Chiefs, were the only ones who prosecuted war or who could be honorably touched by it.[54] Before any hostilities, it was standard to move the aged, the women, and the children out of harm's way, as were the people the Muskogee found at the *"Aphoosa pheeskaw"* River.[55] Neither did Young Men rush off to hostilities, but they first went through the ceremonial round of spiritual preparation around the lion bones, while the level of any honor subsequently earned in action was entirely dependent upon the intensity of the personal risks the Young Men had run.[56] Muskogee as mindlessly bloodthirsty warmongers, and even as cannibals, was settler propaganda, not Muskogee reality.[57] It was the settlers who killed thousands at a crack, as did the French against the Natchez in 1731 and later, Andrew Jackson in the Creek War, 1813–1814.

Besides corrupting the Indigenous meaning of red, the name "Red Sticks" applied to the traditionalist faction confused and conflated two distinct cultural objects: sticks and clubs. Count Sticks, or "broken days," were very common devices in Indigenous America, used to keep track of time by people on the road. If moccasins (messengers) were sent about to call any gathering, from a festival to a council, they set off with a certain number of sticks in hand. Moccasins then discarded one each day to keep track of how soon the event would occur, enabling them correctly to inform their listeners, who then created their own count sticks, to mark the time remaining.[58] Thus, count sticks were count downs, with no dire meaning necessarily attached.

If potential danger were involved, then a war club came with the sticks. A French explorer of the mid-eighteenth century who lived with the Muskogee, Jean-Antoine Le Clerc, Louis Milfort claimed that the club would have been "painted red" (success) and "immediately exhibited in public," as a sort of early notification system.[59] The chief responsible for security in his region was then to send moccasins with red-painted clubs to all towns in his purview, with count sticks also in hand, to keep track of the time elapsed since the situation was first heard of.[60] In the European mind, the count sticks, the red paint of success, and the war clubs were all confused, yielding the modern "Red Sticks" terminology, with French traders importing the "red" into the business.[61]

As European invasion intensified, the political structure of the *Italwalgi* and *Kipayalgi talwa* was disrupted, with the red towns beginning to gain unwarranted political ascendancy due to continual settler aggression against which the red defended the whole. This disastrous development started to shift political control from the wise and thoughtful white Elders to deliver it into the hands of the hasty and reckless red Youngers. The shift was only exacerbated by the American Revolution, which for the settlers occurred partly out of resistance to the British policy of restricting land seizure from the Indians. Invasions of Indian land constituted a large, if largely ignored, aspect of the American Revolution, requiring red attention, so that, by 1776, the red towns had taken de facto control of the Muskogee Confederacy.[62]

Traditionally, all matters were discussed and decided in gendered councils. Although Western histories focus almost exclusively on the male functionaries, the culture was fairly parallel, in terms of the male-female power balance.[63] The earliest Spanish records freely described the "*cacicas*," the Spanish term for female chiefs, but discussions of them thereafter became scarce.[64] This was not because the women were scarce but because early English chroniclers like James Adair deeply resented their "petticoat-government."[65] Culturally ill-equipped to understand matriarchy, European chroniclers and missionaries privileged men—and military men at that—to the exclusion of all women, so that the Grandmothers' and Clan Mothers' councils are, today, all but invisible in Western histories, distorting understanding of traditional Muskogee culture. Consequently, it still typically eludes historians that authorization of war rested in the hands of the Muskogee Grandmothers, who retained control of the implements of war. Once a decision for war had been reached, the Grandmothers made it public by having the Clan Mothers "bring their weapons and the things needed" to prosecute the war and "lay all of it down one hundred paces" from the town "square," where the men met.[66] The men were then free to pick up the weapons—or not—at their discretion. Importantly, just because the Grandmothers had authorized an action and the Clan Mother had promoted it did not mean that the Grandfathers and the Young Men had to take them up on it. This approach was consistent throughout the Woodlands.

The emergence and migration tradition of the Muskogee as told by *Chekilli* in 1735 came at a "talk" in Savannah, Georgia, delivered to the English settlers. His address connected with James Edward Oglethorpe's founding of his penal colony in modern-day Georgia, a project that had been in agitation since 1733.[67] In company with all area Muskogee leaders, *Chekilli* presented the ancient history of the Muskogee, from their origin and long trek across the continent to their coming to the Southeast. This was for a reason. Under Indigenous protocol, when the arrival traditions of an original group were told to a newcomer group, it was for the express purpose of alerting the newcomers to the fact that they were squatting on someone else's land. The newcomers were supposed to acknowledge the prior claim and move on to unclaimed land.[68] If Oglethorpe understood this, then he ignored it.

Oglethorpe's bunch was only the most recent of the European trespassers. The American southeast had suffered European intrusion long before the northeast, as Ferdinand de Soto had rampaged through the southeastern Woodlands, especially Muskogee lands, from 1539 to 1542, with his armies continuing their slaughter after his death in 1542, until splintered and driven off the mainland.[69] By 1565, the Spaniards had set themselves up as overlords of "La Florida" or the entirety of the North American southeast, primarily Muskogee land, although the subsequent French and English invasions drove the Spaniards to the Floridian peninsula.[70] When the Creek-related Natchez people resisted French invasion in 1731, the French responded ferociously by killing 1,000 of the Natchez people in one fell swoop, selling 400 survivors into slavery.[71] The haggard remnants of the Natchez fled to the Muskogee, their close cousins, for sanctuary, thereafter for all intents and purposes being incorporated as Muskogee in the Muskogee ("Creek") Confederacy.[72]

Spanish and French crimes remained common topics of Muskogee discourse, even among assimilated Muskogee, into the late nineteenth century, so that, for instance, when handwriting his people's history in the 1830s, historian George Stiggins, himself Muskogee, highlighted de Soto's sweep and the French destruction of the Natchez.[73] Similarly, in writing about his people in 1857, the Muskogee historian *Chula Tarla Emathla* ("Thomas Simpson Woodward") not only began with the brutal scattering of the Natchez by the French but also talked much of de Soto and, even, of Hernando Cortez.[74] The Muskogee found these instances of wanton aggression remarkable largely because carnage was not a recognized tool of Muskogee leadership. War was not traditionally sought out but something that the Muskogee were forced into by the actions of others.[75]

The United States severely dented Muskogee cultural and territorial sovereignty, preparatory to seizing Alabama. Under the Articles of Confederation, the United States first sought to control Muskogee culture, as justified by the philosophical alchemy of the Euro-Christian Doctrine of Discovery.[76] The attempt at forcing a transition of cultural patterns from the twinned *talwa* to the monopolar, centralized form of the United States began in 1783, with the imposition of a "national" council in connection with *Hoboi-Hilr-Miko*, better known to Western history as "Alexander McGillivray." A wealthy plantation owner of mixed

European and Muskogee ancestry who was raised as a European, McGillivray has long been falsely privileged in Western history as the "leader" of the Muskogee, whereas he was entirely self-appointed and deeply resented by the Muskogee for claiming to speak for them in treaty negotiations with Spain and the United States.[77]

Once the new United States had consolidated federal power in its new Constitution of 1789, Congress passed The Intercourse Act, 1 Stat. 137 (1790). Under Section 1 of the act, a system of Indian agents, officially called "superintendents," was established. Superintendents were granted complete political, social, religious, and economic power over the Indian groups to which they were assigned, without regard to Indigenous governance structures but, instead, with the direct goal of subverting them. However legal sophisticates might have dissembled, dressing up their greed in mystifying mumbo jumbo, the ordinary folks on the ground knew and named what was afoot. "The doctrine" of the Muskogee Country settlers, as officially reported by the Benjamin Hawkins in 1797, was this: "let us kill the Indians, bring on a war, and we shall get land."[78] That is the Doctrine of Discovery, in a nutshell.

Benjamin Hawkins was America's first Indian agent. A well-heeled southern plantation owner, one-time delegate to the Revolutionary Continental Congress, and senator from North Carolina, Hawkins was appointed in 1796 as the general superintendent of all Indians, south of the Ohio River.[79] Because the Muskogee Confederacy occupied many of the southeastern lands, Hawkins became, in effect, the Muskogee Indian agent, the capacity with which he is usually identified today. Southern planters, including Hawkins, were continually in quest of fresh lands to replace those that their slave plantations had already exhausted with tobacco and cotton crops, so Hawkins took his charge quite to heart, profiting handsomely from his position.

One of the first things Hawkins did by way of tinkering was to dust off the McGillivray model of concentrated power. If McGillivray never quite succeeded, then Hawkins determined conclusively to dash the clan-based, dual structure of traditional Muskogee culture, replacing it with his U.S.-friendly, male-only "National Council," whose members arose not from the internal Muskogee system of recognizing leaders through the matrilineal clans but from Hawkins' own sensings of whom he could count on to be the most cooperative with invasion and acculturation.[80] One of Hawkins's initial attacks on traditional sovereignty obviated clan-based justice, under which clans sought satisfaction from any member of the clan of the offender, a system that had concentrated power in the hands of female clan elders.[81]

Group retribution makes sense to communal peoples but not to individualistic peoples. Truly baffled, the United States decided that part of "civilizing" the Muskogee meant atomizing punishment, as imposed in the detached Western style, by an entity far removed from the impact of the offense and unconcerned in its events. By 1798, Hawkins had, therefore, set up a European-style mechanism of hierarchical social coercion, forcing his so-called friendly Muskogee chiefs, to mete out individualized whippings and executions against fellow

Muskogee.[82] Not only did this disempower the clan mothers but it also made Hawkins's hip-pocket chiefs complicit in their own conquest. Hawkins worked closely with especially those assimilated Muskogee of the Tensaw settlements, the tiny minority who, like McGillivray, were willing to emulate European life-styles, including plantation slavery.[83] Although prized by the United States, these elite assimilants were hated by ordinary Muskogee.[84] Thus, Hawkins not only established a disruptive new governance pattern, but he also helped to secure the wealthy Muskogee elite in the Tensaw district, after the model of the patri-archal southern plantation gentry.[85]

Perhaps the most frustrating of all to traditional Muskogee was Hawkins's effort to kill their spiritual system by imposing Christianity. Since this was governmen-tal policy, Hawkins forwarded it, although he was, himself, but an imperfect example of Christianity, never bothering to marry the mother of his seven chil-dren until fifteen years into their cohabitation, when he fell seriously ill.[86] There has been much Western scholarship on the inclusion of Christian ideas in "traditional" spirituality from this period, and it is true that some overlays of Christianity were adopted by the assimilant faction, but the foreign trappings should not fool us. Gregory Waselkov is correct that even the most assimilated of the Muskogee remained "faithful to their core traditions and values."[87]

Although the skew of Hawkins's "national" council led him to assert, quite falsely, that all Muskogee were satisfied with the U.S.-Muskogee interface, overall Muskogee displeasure with U.S. moves was obvious well before the Creek War.[88] It can be ascertained from such actions as the assassination attempt on Hawkins in June 1798, barely two years into his tenure as the lead U.S.-Indian agent.[89] The Grandmothers had to have authorized this action, for the Grandfathers knew of it but could not stop it, although they warned Hawkins that his life was in dan-ger.[90] Undeterred, Hawkins forwarded U.S. aims in forcing on the Muskogee fed-erally monopolized trading posts, or "factories," another disruptive artifact of the Intercourse Act of 1790.

Europeans simply have had no terms to describe the Indigenous gift economy, other than the weak-kneed descriptions of "hospitality" and "charity," both of which Euro-concepts miss the Indigenous point.[91] The gift is not a capricious, individual impulse but a cultural duty. The idea that people must—and collec-tively—give as a matter of course utterly eluded Europeans, so that Milfort expressed astonishment at being immediately fed and housed by the Grandfather who found him desperate and starving in Muskogee country in 1776.[92] Milfort took this as a personal kindness, not understanding that it was an expression of the gift economy, under which anyone "so churlish of his eata-bles as to be inhospitable to one of their own people, especially to a traveling stranger" was "termed a nobody."[93] Whoever had anything, especially the much prized "tafia" (taffy, or the vile liquor used in Indian trade) was "obliged to share it with all, or to hide it."[94] This requirement to share whatever one possessed was inviolable before the Europeans arrived, and any who were later infected with the possessive spirit were subject to what Europeans misconstrued as "theft."[95] Indigenously understood, it was not theft but an attempt to force and enforce sharing, in an act of consciousness-raising about greed. The point was to enlighten the miser.

As special conservators of the land, the women controlled the gift economy, because doing all the farming put them in charge of all food, along with preparing and distributing it.[96] Western sexism has long misconstrued these facts as evidence of Indian women's oppression, but they were evidence of women's high economic status in the Woodlands. Men feasted when the women let them. A major purpose of the gift economy was to quell fighting. Just as the original Muskogee in the Southeast took in multifarious new groups, such as the Natchez fleeing the French, they also treated them as equals, so as to bring them into peaceful relations, as the Tomochichi did once the Muskogee first arrived in their lands. In sharing what they had, the Tomochichi engulfed the Muskogee, just as the Muskogee later attempted to engulf the Europeans. Upon first meeting, gifts were lavished on the newcomers, who (under Indigenous rules) had the reciprocal responsibility to return with extravagant gifts of their own. A failure to return with gifts was a declaration of hostile intent. By the same token, gifts given in return were taken as the intention to set up a peaceful gifting relationship.

Thus, for instance, as far as the Muskogee traditionals were concerned, through long dealings with the Spaniards of Louisiana and Florida, they had established a gifting circle, which was why it was natural for the traditionalist Red Sticks to have received weapons from Spanish Pensacola at the outbreak of the Muskogee Civil War.[97] This also explains why the Choctaw fully expected gifts from the Spanish every time they visited Spanish Mobile or New Orleans, and not, as Milfort had it, because they were "cowards, lazy and slovenly" beggars.[98] Instead of grasping the obligation to give, the persistence of the "beggar" stereotype continued from Milfort through Hawkins and into most Western history books, a problem only beginning to be corrected today.[99]

Because U.S. officials understood gifting as a failed sort of exchange, they were intent on controlling it as such. With the ratification of the U.S. Constitution in 1789, all treaty making with the Indian nations was formally handed to the United States under Article I, Section 8, Number 3, and Article VI, Number 2. Southern states, with their heavily land-depleting crops, chafed under these provisions, so that one main stimulus behind the Intercourse Act of 1790 was the need to slap them down, especially in Georgia, by establishing an exclusively federal right to deal with the Indians. Congress refined this concept with "An Act for Establishing Trading Houses with the Indian Tribes" (1796) by appropriating $50,000 in 1795 and another $150,000 in 1796 to "carry on trade with the Indians." Only U.S.- not state-licensed merchants were allowed to "trade" with the Indigenous peoples, while Europeans were prohibited from having any business dealings at all with the Indians. Indian Affairs were put under the War Department, a signal that could hardly have been more obvious.[100] Here is seen one of the first acts of successful massacre: isolating the intended victim from outside aid, in this instance, economically.

The official U.S. intention behind the factories was to drain the Indians of their resources. In a letter of February 27, 1803, to William Henry Harrison, then governor of the Northwest Territory, President Thomas Jefferson articulated this twist on trade. The furs and leathers of commerce were supplied by overhunting the land. Knowing this, Jefferson reasoned that the resultant "decrease of game" would necessarily force the Indians into the small farming of the European peasant class. Once confined to the "culture of a small piece of land," the Indians would "perceive how useless to them" their "extensive forests" were and "be willing to pare them off from time to time in exchange for necessaries for their farms and their families." Consequently, the United States should "push" its "trading uses and be glad to see the good and influential individuals run into debt, because we observe that when these debts get beyond what the individuals can pay, they become willing to lop them off by a cession of lands."[101]

The factory system thus established was even more insidious than Jefferson had laid out, for in its initial stages, it looked to the Muskogee—and to all Woodlanders—to have been the seating of a gift alliance with the United States. During traditional giveaways, parties showed their good intentions by coming laden down with goods, which were displayed at a pre-established spot. Then, each party selected what it wanted from the goods displayed by the other side. No matter how large or small the gifts on either side, a gifting alliance was considered to have been launched, with regular giveaways conducted periodically, thereafter.[102] To the Indians, then, the U.S. factories looked at first blush to have been operating the same way, for upon arriving at a U.S. factory, the Indians would deposit their goods in one place, and then select whatever they wanted from the factor's table in another place. It took some time for the Indians to realize that factories did not represent gifting councils.[103] The United States was well aware of this confusion, however, and knew that factories could be used as peace devices with the Indians simultaneously with robbing them. Thomas Jefferson acknowledged as much to Andrew Jackson in a letter of February 16, 1803.[104]

Once the *talwa* system was prone and panting, the factory trap was sprung. Factors began demanding that tabs be paid in full, confronting the Indians with incredible levels of debt, which factors claimed they had run up, its interest carefully compounded. As early as 1798, the Choctaw were, for instance, presented with a bill for $12,000. Their chiefs smelled fraud, especially in the calculation of interest, which they could in no wise audit, but in 1805, the Choctaw were forced to pay off the full amount in land.[105] The same unaudited sleight-of-hand was perpetrated against the Muskogee, but in even higher due bills. In 1803, the bill presented to the Muskogee chiefs was an astounding $113,512 with Hawkins on the scene to help sell lands to settle the debt.[106] In the fall of 1812, a factor presented himself at Tuckabatchee—the same town that *Tecumseh* had just visited the year before—to insist that the Muskogee fork over land in lieu of a claimed debt of $40,000.[107] None of this was accidental. The U.S. government and its traders knew perfectly well that the Indians had no concept of calculating capital, let alone, interest.[108] The United States *counted* on it. In his February 16, 1803, letter to Jackson, Thomas Jefferson directly admitted that "obtaining lands" was a primary purpose behind the factory system.[109] As a method of land appropriation, it was proving quite fruitful, with the settlers fully earning their Muskogee name of *Ecunnaunuxulgee* or "people greedily grasping after all lands."[110]

As Jefferson predicted, the factories had the dire effect of game extinction, but it was not entirely from Indian hunting, as too many Western texts suggest. The invading squatters exacerbated the problem, dramatically. Instead of taking just what they needed and leaving the rest untrammeled, they rampaged through the landscape, wasting resources and leaving a barren husk behind. What the European squatters regarded as "living off the land," the Muskogee complained of bitterly as the destruction of their assets in the game taken, the fish decimated, the water sources polluted, and the forests cut down.[111] The demise of the game made it just that much easier for the settlers to bring in their farm animals, whose pens and corrals the Woodlanders saw as animal "prisons," unlike the free-range animals of the forest preserves traditionally maintained by the Indigenous men.[112]

At the same time as the squatters moved in, the trading post factors accustomed the Young Men to the use of metal arms and gunpowder, specifically to increase the kill rate. Worse, from the Red Sticks' point of view, was the environmental degradation caused by European livestock brought in after the game animals were dead, making a sustainable recovery of the environment for the Indigenous game impossible. These were the direct reasons that the Red Sticks both began their campaign by killing the 8,000 head of intrusive European livestock and forewent firearms in favor of the less efficient hunting tools of arrows and clubs.[113] Instead of presenting these acts as the foolishness of primitivism, historians need to start understanding them, as did the Red Sticks, as the necessary initial steps to restoring the natural environment.[114]

A point usually lost in the headlong rush to the battles of the Creek War is that, when the Muskogee Civil War erupted, it was not directed at settlers, at all, but was internecine among the Muskogee, pitting the assimilated Lower Creeks against the traditionalist Upper Creeks. Due to invasionary pressures, the small, privileged cadre of Muskogee in the South was by now adopting European religion, politics, social organization, and economics (including slavery) all on its own, specifically to benefit its members without regard to the well-being of fellow Muskogee. As the assimilants' fortunes soared under this imitation of the European order, the vast majority of the Muskogee farther north became increasingly impoverished.[115] This development seriously upended the traditional goal of feeding, clothing, and supplying all the people, equally, as was done under the old gift economy. The Muskogee Civil War was about the traditionalist Red Sticks' goal of reseating an accurate reflection of the cosmic order, as they perceived it, thus restoring their cultural, spiritual, political, and economic well-being.

No less than the settlers, the Muskogee had to gear themselves up for hostilities by degrees, meeting the preconditions of war, as defined by their own culture. As among all Indigenous Americans, the cosmic balance, or the West-called "spirituality" of the "tribes," was the reference point of all activity, so that herbalists (using Blood medicine) and visionaries (using Breath medicine) were important actors in any town. In Western records, women's Blood medicine is typically ignored or, if noted at all, denigrated as fortune-telling. By contrast, men's Breath medicine is elevated to the whole of the shamanic business.[116] Among traditional Muskogee holy men and women, however, there was (and is) a distinction between healers, who used herbs, snakes, and dreams, or things of Blood medicine, and those whom Westerners call "prophets," who used song, fire, and visions, or things of Breath medicine. Western sources are extremely unclear, mixing these two types of medicine with abandon, but traditionals were (and are) always clear as to, for example, the distinction between dreams (Blood) and visions (Breath).[117] They did not and do not confuse the types.

In times of danger, skilled Blood workers can cause a host of problems for their enemies, from casting disease on them to causing a rain to wash away the Muskogee's tracks while bogging the enemy down, lost, in a swamp. Breathmen can shape-shift into eagles to spy on enemy movements or, in another sort of shape-shifting, turn "the human body into a sieve," through which arrows and bullets will travel ineffectually.[118] Strong holy people, whether male or female, can "mix medicines" to impressive effect. For example, earthquakes, which are echoed in stomp dancing, belong to snaky Blood medicine, whereas comets and eclipses, which belong to Breath medicine, can devastatingly affect Blood earth.[119] Bringing on the two together, exhibits the highest possible interface with the Twinned Cosmos in harmony, suggesting great virtue in the holy worker.

The Red Sticks' (traditionalists') war was guided by three Breathmen: Paddy Walsh, *Hellis Hajo*, and *Himollemico*. Originally, Walsh was the premiere of the three, until after his bulletproofing sieve medicine failed to work at Fort Mims. After Mims, *Hellis Hajo* (also called "Francis" by the settlers as, confusingly enough, was *Tenskwatawa*) was probably the most influential of the three Muskogee Breathmen. One officer in Jackson's army, General John B. Rodgers, recalled *Hellis Hajo* as "a handsome man, six feet high," weighing perhaps "one hundred and fifty pounds." Of "pleasing manners," *Hellis Hajo* "conversed well in English and Spanish." Moreover, he was "humane in his disposition" and "by no means barbarous—withal, a model chief."[120] Perhaps because, unlike *Hellis Hajo*, *Himollemico* escaped Jackson's hangman to fight again later in Florida, Rodgers less charitably presented him as the war hawks' poster boy for feral violence. In the language of phrenology, then regarded as tight science by the settlers, Rodgers painted *Himollemico* as "a savage-looking man, of forbidding countenance, indicating cruelty and ferocity."[121] Notwithstanding, it was the humane man of pleasing manners who, on his march to the army gallows, was barely thwarted in his attempt to assassinate Jackson, using a cleverly concealed weapon.[122]

There was a reason for the ghastly losses among the Red Sticks in their "successful" attack on Fort Mims: part of Red Sticks' agenda was to abandon all Western weapons, so that the Red Sticks attacked with arrows and hatchets, whereas the defenders in the fort replied with bullets.[123] This has to do with Western armament, which are heavily Blood-based in their metals for muskets and balls and whose gunpowder even came from the earth but whose bullets cut through the air (Breath) to kill noisily at a distance. For traditionals, this represented a wild imbalance of Blood and Breath. The old implements of the hunt were made from wood and the sinew of forest game, both Breath (trees are lungs). The flint usage goes back to Mound Builder times, with Muskogee flint-tipped arrows later able to penetrate Spanish armor, while sweating before and after arrow usage restored the imbalance thus created.[124]

This same low-tech armament had served the Red Sticks well enough at Burnt Corn, where a vastly outnumbered Muskogee force with only thirteen guns to its name suffered but two casualties in defeating a heavily armed U.S. militia.[125] This tale was told and retold throughout Muskogee Country, as evidence of the easy vincibility of the Europeans.[126] Before the Mims assault, the Red Sticks had been assured by Walsh that he would put the same spirit shield around the Muskogee's lead attackers at Fort Mims as he had at Burnt Corn, which shield, bullets could not penetrate.[127] The failure of Walsh's spirit shield at Mims cost him his following, the angry Red Sticks not caring that Walsh, himself, had suffered three bullet wounds in the attack.[128] Until recent days, Western accounts have disregarded such Muskogee thinking as Walsh's, unless to denigrate it under the "silly savage" analysis.

In the mid-twentieth century, the diction of "silly savage" changed, yet the content remained remarkably stable. In 1956, Anthony F. C. Wallace proffered his gentler approach of "cultural revitalization" or the attempts of a conquered people to recapture a nostalgic past through religion.[129] The Wallace proposition had the advantage of putting the entire onus of disaster on the victims of invasion. Even in *Sacred Revolt* (1991), which purportedly looked at the spiritual content of the Red Sticks movement from an Indian point of view, author Joel Martin immediately framed the Red Sticks' beliefs and actions in terms of Foucaultian psychology on the role of religion in resisting oppression.[130] (At last notice, Michel Foucault was not Muskogee.) Thus, instead of listening to the Indigenous reasoning behind Indigenous actions, mainstream Western historians eagerly seized on explanations featuring the spiritual thrashings of doomed peoples in their futile attempts to root out the European, in favor of their own, lesser, culture.

Meantime, off to the left, but still working from a purely Western set of definitions, Marxists looked solely at the economic "progress" of settlement in accumulating its way from feudalism to industrialism.[131] Over in psychology, the favored distancing technique was to demean Indian medicine as "magical thinking."[132] Until the 1990s, it was customary for Western scholars just to snicker at Indian holy men such as Paddy Walsh as "jugglers" (from the French, *jongleur*, or trickster)—in other words, to finger them as *frauds*, who knowingly perpetuated illusion for the sake of securing personal power.[133] Interestingly, it is still strictly taboo to use the same psychological rubric of "magical thinking" to evaluate the role of the settlers' Christian mythology of Manifest Destiny in perpetrating their massacres, let alone, to refer to settler ministers and priests as *jongleurs*.

Taken together, Western intellectualizing screened the blood on the ground from settler view, in the sort of scholarship that, in 2001, Christopher Barnard correctly exposed as "Isolating the Knowledge of the Unpleasant."[134] By the twenty-first century, the rising, guilty purpose of much mainstream history had become to submerge from sight the shame of collective wrongdoing in massacre for the purpose of seizing North America from the Indians, so that Indigenous peoples had become bit players in the story of their own displacement from the continent. Nevertheless, when push comes to shove, the "savagery" of such reasoning as the Red Sticks' resistance remains the underlying presumption in refusing to weigh Indigenous purposes.

Western isolation of the unpleasant aside, the Muskogee Civil War was not about capitalism driving out feudalism or righteous invasion after a "savage" attack, nor did it rest on a pathetic Muskogee fantasy of recapturing a romanticized past by means of shamanic snake oil. The Red Sticks movement emerged, instead, from a pragmatic comparison of European and Muskogee cultural structures, resulting in a conscious choice of the traditional Muskogee, over the Western European, form. The Red Sticks rejected Western:

- governance by extraneous, brute force;
- raiding culture economics; and
- Christianity

in favor of the following:

- governance by Muskogee-recognized leadership,
- the Indigenous gift economy, and
- the traditional spiritual system of the Twinned Cosmos.

Moreover, knowing that *Tenskwatawa* was gathering the people in the north and that his brother, *Tecumseh*, was planning to come south to the Muskogee with his invitation to join the pan-Indian resistance, they were ready to listen.

Fully "nine-tenths" of living Muskogee in 1813 were officially known to have thus rejected Western in favor of Indigenous culture.[135] Just because the Red Sticks did not prevail in the subsequent war does not mean that their analysis was ridiculous. It means that the total U.S. population in 1813 hovered around 7,200,000, whereas heading into the Creek War, the entire Muskogee population including the Seminole of Florida was 17,750 (see Table 4.1). Of this number, the Red Sticks' population hit 4,800 to 5,000, out of which 202 were slaughtered at the outset of the Muskogee Civil War at Fort Mims.[136] Invasion is a numbers game, and the Muskogee clearly lacked numbers compared to settlers.

The four events that gave the Red Sticks the confidence to move forward rattled the superstitious settlers every bit as much as they electrified the Muskogee. One of these events rattled the settlers quite literally: the series of devastating New Madrid earthquakes of 1811 and 1812. The second event was the appearance of a comet, the Great Comet of 1811 (Comet C/1811 F1), which continued being seen into 1812. The third and fourth were two "Black Suns," or eclipses, the 1806Jun16 Corona-Ferrer solar eclipse and the annular eclipse of September 17, 1811.[137] There was a whole lot of shaking going on, and more than just the Red Sticks felt the vibrations.

Beginning in the wee hours of December 16, 1811, with its initial tremors, the New Madrid series of earthquakes and aftershocks was of dimensions terrifying to the Europeans. First around 2:00 A.M., again around 7:00 A.M., and finally around 11:00 A.M., in the small settler regions around New Madrid, Missouri, the ground shook violently, emitting sulfurous stenches, water, rocks, and from eyewitness reports, coal. Quakes and tremors continued through January 23, 1812.[138] Scientists today think that the various quakes and aftershocks bounced between 7.8 and 7.9 on the Richter scale.[139] Had the quakes squarely hit the large, east-coast towns, the devastation of the new United States would have been complete, but New Madrid was in the boonies, as far as the settlers were concerned. Even so, the Mississippi River became utterly fractious and impossible to navigate, seeding terror up and down its length by running previously unknown courses and dropping the bottoms out of islands until the trees on them were level with the ground.[140] The soil liquefied, and for the *coup de grâce*, the Mississippi River ran backwards.[141] Hysteria reigned among the spooked settlers.

Among those leaving first-hand accounts of "the alarm which has recently been excited here, by that dread phenominon of Nature, an Earthquake," was William Charles Cole Claiborne, governor of Louisiana. The night of December 16, 1811, "a trembling of the Earth interrupted the Gaiety of the Season, & many Ladies retired from a Ball Room seriously affrighted." Then, on January 7, 1812, "a like trembling, more than the one preceding, excited our apprehensions." Claiborne was "attending (at that time) a Theatrical Representation." The "unusually serene" night was disrupted suddenly by "the vibration of the Chandeliers," which "attracted every Eye:—The whole House undulated:—The Comedians ceased to act;—after a moment of most profound silence, a General expression of fear was heard from the Ladies, & an anxiety for *their safety*, filled me with *Inquietude.—It* however was of short duration, for in about a Minute & a half the Earth became composed" (all italics in the original).[142]

However glad he was to have been affrighted only on behalf of the ladies, Claiborne was not "without serious apprehensions, that elsewhere, the *Shock*" had been "more terrible, & attended perhaps with consequences," to have been "regretted by all, who can feel a sympathy for human woe" (italics in the original).[143] Consequences were, indeed, regretted, not the least of them being two years' worth of the "Visitations of providence against which no human foresight could have guarded," that effectively "blasted" the settlers' cotton crops, with "the fertile bottoms of the Mississippi" between 1812 and 1814 having been "destroyed by the unusual inundations of that River."[144]

This level of panic and dismay among the settlers had first been aroused even before the earthquakes, by the two-tailed comet, C/1811 F1, which had appeared in the fall of 1811, filling many settlers with a sense of foreboding as a supposed harbinger of bad luck.[145] (They did not miss that the New Madrid earthquakes soon followed.) The comet did not just strike terror in Euro-Americans but unsettled continental Europeans, as well. The Europeans called it "Napoleon's comet," since under its light, Napoleon assembled the troops for his ill-fated Russian campaign.[146] This was a comet that boded no good in the Western mind.

Neither were comets and earthquakes without meaning to the Woodlanders.[147] Traditionally, comets and asteroids are panthers, and panthers have mysterious properties, not the least of them being the vertical pupils of their eyes, which connect them with the dreaded Stone Giants, who also had vertical eyes in Muskogee tradition.[148] Panthers are Breath creatures, beautiful and swift but dangerous, with comets and asteroids commonly referred to as "Sky Panthers." In fact, the word *Tecumthé* (*Tecumseh*) means "Sky Panther," for his birth in 1768 was announced by the appearance of the comet for which his mother named him.[149] In traditional Woodlands lore, spirit Panthers are seen as crouching in wait. For instance, *erie* means "panther," so that Lake Erie is construed as a Water Panther, her twitching tail dangling down as the Miami of the Lake (the Maumee River), as she crouches to pounce on Lake Ontario. By the same token, Sky Panthers dash across the sky, pouncing on the earth. There are Iroquoian traditions of Sky Panthers falling on towns, destroying them, such as the "blazing star"—an asteroid—that came down onto a palisaded town along the St. Lawrence River in Mohawk Country "and destroyed the people," just as *Tecumseh* planned to fall upon settler towns.[150]

At least as important as *Tecumseh* to the pan-Indian alliance was his holy brother, *Tenskwatawa*. Woodlanders were well aware that *Tenskwatawa* had been born a triplet.[151] Three being the number of warning in the eastern Woodlands, they knew to watch him closely for extraordinary things. Not to disappoint, he became an "Open Door" of the Sky, that is, a Breathman, *par excellence*.[152] Possessing the power of the spheres, he could "destroy the white people at any time," he announced. Anyone doubting him was threatened with the combined weight of Breath and Blood: "the spirits of the air, and great snakes under the earth" would do them in, for *Tenskwatawa* could "take down the sun and the moon" bringing about "great darkness," that is, he could call forth "Black Suns," or total eclipses while causing "Snakes" in the ground, that is, earthquakes fissures.[153]

When William Henry Harrison challenged *Tenskwatwa* to predict a comet, expecting to expose him as a fraud, *Tenskwatawa* took him up on the test, gathering the Shawnees at Tippecanoe in the spring of 1806 to witness the 1806Jun16 Corona-Ferrer eclipse.[154] The impression of his prowess only increased when he repeated the feat on September 17, 1811. *Tenskwatawa* was once more and spectacularly vindicated when he predicted the two-tailed, blood-red C/1811 F1 comet that streaked the sky. U.S. sources have long smirked that the British had to have clued *Tenskwatawa* in on the approach of the 1811 Napoleon comet, but there is absolutely no evidence of this, whereas predicting celestial events had been part of the Breathmen's stock-in-trade since Mound Builder times, thousands of years earlier.[155]

The settlers were getting restless. U.S. leaders began looking to dampen the rising mood of hysteria, for the appearance of the two-tailed comet had as seriously unnerved the Europeans as it had heartened the Indians. Worse, from the U.S.

perspective, jittery settlers were also crediting *Tenskwatawa* and *Tecumseh* with bringing about the New Madrid earthquake series that coincided with the 1811 comet. It was not accidental or incidental that three weeks later, on November 7, 1811, Harrison fell on Tippecanoe. By the spring of 1811, Harrison had already determined to attack the town, so that aside from timing his attack to coincide with *Tecumseh*'s absence and an Indian harvest to be destroyed, Harrison might well have timed his attack to insinuate that the C/ 1811 F1 comet presaged a settler, not an Indian, victory.

The fame of *Tecumseh* and his holy brother preceded *Tecumseh*'s visit to the Muskogee, then, raising the hopes of the coalescing Red Sticks, while frightening the bejesus out of both the settlers and the Muskogee assimilants at Tensaw. Five thousand Muskogee, mostly Red Sticks, assembled to hear *Tecumseh*.[156] Arriving at Tuckabatchee, the Muskogee capital, in October 1811, during the national council meeting, *Tecumseh* walked into an already steaming situation. Benjamin Hawkins's top man, *Tastanagi Tako* ("Big Warrior"), did not want *Tecumseh* there, whereas the roiling Red Sticks were eagerly awaiting *Tecumseh*.[157] Anxious to ensure that no hanky-panky ensued, Hawkins hung about the fringes as a U.S. spy on the uneasy proceedings.

Each day, *Tecumseh* appeared in traditional garb, but his twenty-four men merely and wordlessly danced the War Dance of the Lakes each night in front of their Stranger House or visitors' lodgings.[158] After day had succeeded day, with no talk materializing, Hawkins left in disgust, arrogantly insisting that nothing bad would happen, for the Muskogee "were entirely under his control."[159] His absence was apparently the event that *Tecumseh* and his impressive retinue had awaited, for as soon as Hawkins was gone, *Tecumseh* deigned to speak.[160] No out-siders were present for that talk, so—despite the multifarious versions of it afloat in settler lore—there is no reliable text of his speech. Compiled from the memory of those Muskogee present, Stiggins left only this summary:

> Tecumseh had said to many in private, and to the national council, that he was determined to war with the Americans. He stated the great supernatural powers he possessed. He said if he was to beat the white people they would know it by the following sign: he would ascend to the top of a mountain about four moons [months] from that time and there he would whoop three unbounded loud whoops, slap his hands together three times, and raise his foot and stamp it on the earth three times. By these actions, he could make the whole earth trem-ble, which would be a sign of his success in the undertaking. If such did not happen, they would know that he was to fail in the enterprise.[161]

Perhaps the best, blow-by-blow account of *Tecumseh*'s appearance and speech comes from Samuel Dale, an illiterate, backwoods settler and U.S. translator among the Muskogee, who was a semi-insider. He claimed to have been present at the October 1811, annual Muskogee council meeting to hear *Tecumseh*, leaving an account of it, as written up in 1860 by John Francis Hamtramck Claiborne, of the Mississippi Claibornes, in a story picked up from the settler historian Albert Pickett.

In 1858, the contemporary Muskogee source, *Chula Tarla Emathla*, having seen some of Pickett's "sketches" of the Muskogee, claimed that Albert Pickett was in error to have used Dale as an informant. A personal acquaintance of Dale, *Chula Tarla Emathla* was quite skeptical that Dale had been present on the grounds, claiming that Hawkins would not have allowed him to have been. In another supposition, *Chula Tarla Emathla* held that *Tecumseh* and his followers would also not have countenanced the presence of any settlers during his visit to Tuckabatchee.[162]

There is another dimension to this issue, however. *Chula Tarla Emathla* was riled that a European setter, Pickett, had set himself up as an authority on the Muskogee, superior to either himself or George Stiggins, who were both Muskogee. In his memoirs, *Chula Tarla Emathla* missed not a single chance to quibble archly with Pickett about his information and authority.[163] *Chula Tarla Emathla*'s resistance to Dale's version must be understood, therefore, as part and parcel of his turf war with Pickett. To add insult to injury, *Chula Tarla Emathla* was unable to get hold of Stiggins's handwritten memoir, although he knew that Pickett had seen and used it, adding to his anti-Pickett umbrage.[164] On the one hand, exasperated Indians can quickly line up behind *Chula Tarla Emathla*, in his pique at a settler presuming to set himself up as a greater authority on Indigenous people than the Indigenous people, themselves. Moreover, it is quite unlikely that *Tecumseh* would have willingly spoken in the presence of a known settler. This consideration is large enough for some historians to decide that Dale's report had to have been a sheer fabrication.[165]

On the other hand, *Chula Tarla Emathla*'s specifics are not necessarily persuasive. First, Hawkins was clearly not the puppet master of the Muskogee that he liked to boast that he was. Second, Hawkins had left before *Tecumseh* spoke, so that whether Hawkins "allowed" Dale to sit in is beside the point. Finally, many backwoodsmen had been raised by Indians, and thus dressed, spoke, and behaved as Indians. They might easily have been mistaken for such by a visiting dignitary, like *Tecumseh*. (It is a racist stereotype to insist that all Indians, everywhere, instinctively recognize one another.) Whether Dale was personally present might be negligible, in any case. The account gleaned from Muskogee who had personally heard *Tecumseh* was then in circulation, courtesy of Stiggins. As "Indianized," Dale had many Muskogee friends—including *Chula Tarla Emathla*. The version that Dale passed along could easily have been compounded from reports he gathered later from his Muskogee friends and then passed along, with a sly grin, as his own.

There is no question that Dale's version was heavily filtered through Claiborne and Pickett and therefore includes obvious settler interpolations, such as the threat of digging up the dead. Indians avoided (and still avoid) cemeteries; digging up the dead was a militia tactic. Similarly, the contempt expressed for women and the terminology of "white" and "red" to indicate the races instead of alluding to the Cosmic Twinship also certainly echo Western biases. Finally,

Dale voiced the settler fear that Spain and England might enter the war in support of the Red Sticks, a U.S. talking point that the Muskogee knew was ungrounded. Nevertheless, Dale's account echoes in essentials those versions by bruited about by contemporary Muskogee, while also recording authentic Muskogee sentiments, such as the Indigenous refusal to be enslaved, and ceremonial details, such as repetition by threes, which carry profound ritual meaning not generally known to settlers. I therefore, with reservations, accept Dale's version in outline, as recounted below.

Although unhappy over *Tecumseh*'s appearance at the council, Woodlands etiquette forced *Tastanagi Tako* to welcome *Tecumseh* and his men officially with a peace pipe.[166] This gave *Tecumseh* speaking rights in the circle, allowing him to stride into the council, his retinue walking directly behind him, in his footsteps, while offering crumbled tobacco and poison sumac to the four directions, three times.[167] These were meaningful actions. Walking directly in the footsteps of the man before was a Woodlands war march (to hide the size of the war party from enemy scouts), while the tobacco (Breath) and sumac (Blood) offerings called for success in war and the triple repetition required the attention of the audience. *Tecumseh* was clearly signaling the thrust of his speech to the assembly of 5,000, while inviting the spirits into the circle, a gesture creating a ceremonial consensus around his message. No wonder *Tastanagi Tako* felt uncomfortable.

Approaching the circle of council, *Tecumseh* gave the *Yee-Haw*! battle cry of the Shawnee, which each of his men repeated.[168] Once in the circle, he offered his own peace pipe (which *Tastanagi Tako* had to accept) and wampum, showing that he had been deputed a speaker of the Great Lakes Elders by the Grandmothers to deliver their words to the Muskogee. Then, *Tecumseh* spoke to a hushed crowd.[169]

Here is the speech, as Pickett took it from the lips of Dale, as represented by Claiborne:[170]

In defiance of the white warriors of Ohio and Kentucky, I have traveled through their settlements, once our favorite hunting grounds. No war-whoop was sounded, but there is blood on our knives. The Pale-faces felt the blow, but knew not whence it came.

Accursed be the race that has seized on our country and made women of our warriors. Our fathers, from their tombs, reproach us as slaves and cowards. I hear them now in the wailing winds.

The Muscogee was once a mighty people. The Georgians trembled at your war-whoop, and the maidens of my tribe, on the distant lakes, sung the prowess of your warriors and sighed for their embraces.

Now your very blood is white; your tomahawks have no edge; your bows and arrows were buried with your fathers. Oh! Muscogees, brethren of my mother, brush from your eyelids the sleep of slavery; once more strike for vengeance—once more for your country. The spirits of the mighty dead complain. Their tears drop from the weeping skies. Let the white race perish.

They seize your land; they corrupt your women; they trample on the ashes of your dead!

Back, whence they came, upon a trail of blood, they must be driven.

Back! back, ay, into the great water whose accursed waves brought them to our shores!

Burn their dwellings! Destroy their stock! Slay their wives and children! The Red Man owns the country, and the Pale-faces must never enjoy it.

War now! War forever! War upon the living! War upon the dead! Dig their very corpses from the grave. *Our* country must give no rest to a white man's bones.

This is the will of the Great Spirit, revealed to my brother, his familiar, the Prophet of the Lakes. He sends me to you.

All the tribes of the north are dancing the war-dance. Two mighty warriors across the seas will send us arms.

Tecumseh will soon return to his country. My prophets shall tarry with you. They will stand between you and the bullets of your enemies. When the white men approach you the yawning earth shall swallow them up.

Soon shall you see my arm of fire stretched athwart the sky. I will stamp my foot at Tippecanoe, and the very earth shall shake.

Well might this speech have affrighted the ladies, especially because, even as *Tecumseh* was on his way home, the C/1811 F1 comet appeared and the New Madrid earthquake series began. With the aid of *Tenskwatawa*, his Breathman brother, *Tecumseh* was seen to have stretched his panther arm across the sky and stamped his foot to call up the snakes of the earth.

On August 30, 1813, the Muskogee saw the comet as predicting a Red Sticks victory at Fort Mims, in the action that precipitated and was promptly used to justify the U.S. military invasion of Muskogee Country. In the full scope of the war's events, the attack by the Red Sticks at Mims was in no way as destructive of the settlers as the subsequent U.S. attacks were of the Muskogee. When regarded in isolation, however, a significant number of U.S.-aligned people—130—lost their lives in one day at Fort Mims.[171] This fact was, of course, treated as a pure gift by the war hawks, who had long itched for exactly such a justification by which to take Muskogee land. Meantime, never mentioned in the U.S. war drive and, in fact, almost never mentioned to this day, is that, of the total number of people killed during the attack, the vast majority were Muskogee. Personally taking casualty counts from Muskogee Country "heads of towns" seventeen years after the attack on Mims, the memoirist Stiggins tallied up 202 Red Sticks attackers dead, while inside the fort, modern historian Gregory Waselkov has counted up 26 U.S.-aligned Muskogee dead.[172]

Waselkov's casualty counts mean that, although 130 U.S.-aligned people did die inside the fort, not all of them were Euro-Americans. In addition to the twenty-six Muskogee, thirty more of the lost were African slaves, hardly present on Muskogee lands of their own volition, so that only seventy-four of the dead were European settlers.[173] Thus, of those inside the fort who were documented to have died, 20 percent were Muskogee, 23 percent were Africans, and 57 percent were European settlers.[174] Overall, of the total of 332 dead on both sides, only 22 percent of the casualties from the Fort Mims attack were settlers, and most of them were demonstrably soldiers.

Despite having been long and relentlessly presented in Western history as a surprise, the attack on Fort Mims was anticipated with martial preparations made in advance, so that on the day of the attack, Fort Mims was top heavy with military men, sent in as reinforcements before the attack. A major force of 175 were U.S. Army soldiers, there under Major Daniel Beasley, with another sixteen U.S. soldiers arriving under Spruce McCall Osborne, dispatched from, most probably, Fort Stoddert. A further ten were mounted "dragoons" (cavalry). A final seventy-six formed a Muskogee "home militia," which meant that it consisted of the assimilant Muskogee. Thus, 277 of the 553 people in the fort were *soldiers*, with seventy-six of the 277 soldiers officially dubbed "half-breeds," that is, Muskogee assimilants.[175] Stiggins claimed that all 122 men killed were soldiers, meaning that of the 130 settler-aligned casualties, 94 percent were military men.[176] Moreover, the Red Sticks knew full well another largely ignored fact, that "a great many" of those U.S. soldiers at Mims had been the selfsame men ambushing the Muskogee at Burnt Corn, an added incentive for the Red Sticks' fury.[177]

Western records lack a clear count of the actual number of dead Red Sticks, partly because the Muskogee acknowledged carrying off their wounded to die among their friends, as was the Woodlands custom.[178] In counting up their casualties later, Stiggins reported that the Red Sticks found that, of the 726 attacking, "fully half were killed or disabled or wounded" at Mims.[179] Of the 363 in that condition, 202 died of their wounds, leaving open exactly how many lay on the ground at Mims, but on mop-up detail after the attack, U.S. captain Joseph P. Kennedy personally counted almost 100 Red Sticks dead on the ground at Mims.[180] Thus, including the dead Muskogee among the fort's defenders, at least 228 of the total 332 dead in the action, or 69 percent, were Muskogee. These statistics also bring home the fact that the Creek War started as a civil war between traditionalists and assimilants.

Undaunted, well into the twentieth century, settler historians cheerfully took the Muskogee losses in stride: "Exterminating wars," however "dreadful," were also "needful," as Henry S. Halbert and Timothy H. Ball, settler historians of the Muskogee War, calmly opined in 1895.[181] Similar equanimity is never displayed over counts of settler dead at, say, the beaches at Normandy on D-day in 1944. Of the 73,000 U.S. soldiers who landed, the best estimate lists 1,465 U.S. dead, which is but 2 percent of the total, yet in weepy movies like *Saving Private Ryan* (1998), this loss is still grieved as incomprehensible, with the World War II population extolled as *The Greatest Generation* for having fought through such things as the egregious losses there.[182] The differential in responses based on the race of the deceased is telling and, worse, continuing.

The realpolitik of the propaganda in 1813 was that the United States needed to clear the "just war" hurdle. Consequently, it could not linger on the fact that the primary casualties at Mims were Muskogee, for dead Indians simply did not justify an invasion and subsequent war. Neither did dead Africans. Moreover, the authorities knew full well that "half-breeds" were heavily in the mix of casualties inside the fort and that the majority of the dead settlers were army soldiers.[183] Notwithstanding, for best effect, the war hawks gussied up the in-fort casualty count from the actual 130 to a sensational 350, while carefully ignoring the ethnicities and professions of the victims to portray them all as helpless, "white" farmers, widows, and orphans.[184] This antique propaganda proved so effective that many historians, relying on William Charles Cole Claiborne's fudged figures, still cite his sensational head count, without examining the identities of the dead. Only Gregory Waselkov honestly sorted out the in-fort statistics in 2006.[185]

The probable reason that the Red Sticks won the bloody Fort Mims confrontation at all was because the military commander at the station, Major Daniel Beasley, blithely ignored three direct warnings of impending attack, even savagely beating as liars two African slaves who brought in the word.[186] In addition, Beasley failed to keep the fort's east gate in closeable repair. Indeed, the gate was so little attended to, as to have been permanently jammed open with eroded sand. For his grand finale, at the moment of attack, Beasley was stinking drunk and playing cards. (On the day prior to the attack, a Sunday, a "fresh supply of whiskey" had arrived for the soldiers.) Settlers later consoled themselves for Beasley's stunning failures by noting that he was one of the first struck down in the attack, as he finally, and far too late, tried to close the gate.[187] His fiasco was later glossed as owing to "inexperience," leading one to wonder how he had become a major.[188] The Red Sticks were not, then, fools for faith, as typically depicted. They had a political, social, and economic analysis. At Mims, 202 prime men were lost, with as many more wounded, and the Red Sticks could count. They continued to the bitter end at Horseshoe Bend, not because they were deluded, but because their struggle was just, and a man "could die but once."[189]

NOTES

1. Gatschet, 1884, vol. 1, 244.

2. Mann, 2016, 48–49, 166. The Hopi are very direct about their Ant People taking them to live underground, Waters, 1963/1997, 16; Mandan traditional story of living underground near a huge lake, Clark *et al.*, 1814/1893, vol. 1, 208. Other such traditions exist without its being recognized what they are about, Mann, 2016, 48–49, 165–67.

3. Deloria, 1997, 204.

4. Lewis and Maslin, 2015, 171–80.

5. Gatschet, 1884, vol. 1, 245–46.

6. Mann, 2016, 85–87.

7. Gatschet, 1884, vol. 1, 246.

8. Speck, 1943, 325–26.

9. For international relationships, Aupaumut, 1827, 76–77. For Europeans as "younger brothers," McElwain, 2001, 113–14.

10. Gatschet, 1884, vol. 1, 247.

11. Crane, 1918, 339.

12. Waselkov, 2006, 6; Hewitt, 1939, 129.

13. Thunderbirds in tradition, Mann, 2016, 70–73.

14. Gatschet, 1884, vol. 1, 247.

15. Oldmixon, 1741, vol. 2, 444.

16. Mann, 2016, seasonal shifts, 52; death and reincarnation, 214.

17. Gatschet, 1884, vol. 1, 248.

18. Ibid., vol. 1, 249–50.

19. Ibid., vol. 1, 250.

20. Webb *et al.*, 1988, 254, 313.

21. For Choctaw, Peet, 1892, vol. 1, 128; for Salish and Kootenai, Smithsonian Institution,1978–2008, vol. 12, *Plateau*, 312.

22. West, 1904, 54.

23. Gatschet, 1884, vol. 1, 250.

24. Hewitt, 1939, 129; as trader-initiated, Adair, 1775, 46–47; Ethridge, 2003, 93–94.

25. See Mann, 2016, 41–77.

26. Mann, 2010, 29–48.

27. Typically, what Western anthropologists call "clans," Native Americans just call "families." Hewitt, 1939, 128–29.

28. Hewitt, 1939, vol. 124, no. 2, 124.

29. USC, 1907, vol. 2, 1250.

30. Milfort, 1802/1959, 128.

31. Hewitt, 1939, 125; Adair, 1775, as red/white "imperial seats," 30, 31, 99.

32. Owsley, 1985, 282; Halbert and Ball, 1895, 247.

33. Crane, 1918, 340; Waselkov, 2006, 5; for various ethnic groups of Muskogee, see Stiggins, 1989, 27–48.

34. Waselkov, 2006, 5–6.

35. Ethnic groups, Stiggins, 1989, 27–47.

36. Gatschet, 1884, vol. 1, 251.

37. Mann, 2016, 85–89.

38. Hupka *et al.*, 1997, Table 2, 164. Because college psychology students were subjects in each country (Hupka *et al.*, 1997, 160), those attending the elite "National University of Mexico" (National Autonomous University of Mexico) necessarily derived from the privileged, Euro-Mexican sector.

39. For "stages of history" stone age to metal age and tool-creating demarcations, Goguet, 1758/1975, vol. 1, 135–37; for popularization of the idea, Lubbock, 1865/1913/1969; for the arch-"scientific" articulation, Morgan, 1877.

40. Ethridge, 2003, 140.

41. Glasser *et al.*, 2001, 37–41.

42. Bartram Trail Conference, 1979, 68.

43. Bartram, 1791/1928, 51.

44. Bartram Trail Conference, 1979, 68.

45. Ethridge, 2003, 154.

46. For the original mounds survey, Squier and Davis, 1848/1965.

47. Bartram, 1791/1928, 13–14.

48. Swanton, 1928/2000, 481–82.

49. Bossu, 1768, 51, 108.

50. Ibid., 225; Swanton, 1928/2000, 490; Haas and Hill, 2015, 722.

51. Bossu, 1982, 101, holy woman of the snake, 111–12.

52. Literally, *"ils s'étoient promit et de ne point se survivre"* is: "they had solemnly promised one another not to outlive each other." Translation mine. Pratz, 1758, vol. 3, 28.

53. Pratz, 1758, vol. 3, 36–37.

54. Milfort, 1802/1959, 157.

55. Ibid., 158; examples of in action, Stiggins, 1989, 119, 125

56. Milfort, 1802/1959, for preparation, 152–53; for honors, 154–55.

57. For cannibal charge, Milfort, 1802/1959, 13, 59, 97.

58. Stiggins, 1989, 107–8; Hewitt, 1939, 140.

59. Milfort, 1802/1959, 147.

60. Ibid., 148.

61. Adair, 1775, 46–47.

62. Hewitt, *Notes on the Creek Indians*, 125.

63. Bossu, 1982, 92–93.

64. Accounts of the *cacica* of Cofitachique, in Bourne, 1905, vol. 2, 13–14, 99–101.

65. Adair, 1775, 146.

66. For quotation, Milfort, 1802/1959, 150; for women calling for war, Bossu, 1962, 62.

67. Gatschet, 1884, vol. 1, 244.

68. Brinton, 1885/1999, 144; Heckewelder, 1820/1876/1971, 47–53.

69. Bourne, 1905.

70. Spanish presumption precipitated its own major revolts, Mann and Grinde, 2001, 1–33.

71. Grenke, 2005, 174.

72. *Chula Tarla Emathla*, 1959, 16.

73. Stiggins, 1989, for Natchez, 25, 33, 37–44; de Soto, 34–36 passim; 42.

74. *Chula Tarla Emathla*, 1959, for "Nitches" people, 16, 18, 23, 30; for de Soto, 14–17 passim; 2–29 passim; 64–69; for Cortez, 15, 18, 23, 68.

75. Milfort, 1802/1959, 153.

76. Miller *et al.*, 2010; Newcomb, 2008.

77. Saunt, 1999, 192, 196; *ASPIA*, 1832, McGillivray treaty signature, vol. 1, no. 12, 81– 82; Milfort, 1802/1959, 91, 92.

78. Hawkins, 2003, 102.

79. Ibid., 24.

80. Ibid., 67s–71s.

81. Saunt, 1999, 179–80; Ethridge, 2003, 231–32.

82. Hawkins, 2003, 68s; Henri, 1986, 216–17.

83. See collaboration with Charles Weatherford to upend Augustus Bowles' scheme of empire, Waselkov, 2006, 44; for the Western-style Muskogee "elite," see Ethridge, 2003, 64, 79, 85, 162, 181.

84. Stiggins, 1989, 103.

85. Waselkov, 2006, 22–23, 27, 48; Milfort, 1802/1959, 22.

86. Mauelshagen and Davis, 1969, 66, and note 47, 66; Henri, 1986, 271.

87. Waselkov, 2006, 10.

88. Owsley, 1985, 276.

89. Henri, 1986, 212.

90. Henri, 1986, 217.

91. Stiggins, 1989, 51–54.

92. Milfort, 1802/1959, 17–18.

93. Stiggins, 1989, 52.

94. Milfort, 1802/1959, note*, 126.

95. Ibid., note*, 126.

96. Ibid., 129, 150.

97. Carter, 1934–1975, Holmes to Armstrong, vol. 6, letter 8/30/1813, 396; *ASPIA*, 1832, letter, Hawkins to Armstrong, vol. 1, no. 139, letter 9/21/1813, 854.

98. Milfort, 1802/1959, 177.

99. Hawkins, 2003, 57, 399; Harmon, 2010, 60.

100. USC, 2008; *ASPIA*, 1832, Dearborn to Jefferson, vol. 1, no. 93, letter 12/8/1801, 654–55.

101. Jefferson, 1903–1907, Jefferson to Harrison, vol. 10, letter 2/27/1803, 369–70; Miller, 2012, 34–35.

102. The gift economy worked in the same way across the Woodlands. For gifting alliance-making, Mann, 1998, 129–32.

103. Ethridge, 2003, 195–214.

104. Jefferson, 1903–1907, Jefferson to Jackson, vol. 10, letter 2/16/1806, 375.

105. John Forbes and Company, 1930, 132, 134–40.

106. Hawkins, 2003, 408–10; Henri, 1986, 235; Mauelshagen and Davis, 1969, note 26, 44.

107. Henri, 1986, 273–74.

108. Ibid., 275.

109. Jefferson, 1903–1907, Jefferson to Jackson, vol. 10, letter 2/16/1803, 357.

110. O'Brien, 2003, 8.

111. Hawkins, 203, for game 57, 164, 198, 386; by August, 1798, catching only "a few" fish, although the whole town turned out to fish, 490; for settlers raiding resources, Milfort, 1802/1959, 38–39; for missionaries simply helping themselves to forests for logging, see Mauelshagen and Davis, 1969, 16–17, 18; also see Henri, 1986, 272.

112. For farm animals as imprisoned, see the speech of *Sadekanakte* (Onondaga) in Richter, 1992, 184.

113. Waselkov, 2006, 86.

114. Remini, 2001, 80.

115. Waselkov, 2006, 24–26, 73.

116. See, for instance, how the subject is handled in Hewitt, 1939, 133.

117. Mann, 2016, 104–31.

118. Hewitt, 1939, 156.

119. Mann, 2016, 93–94; for comets and meteors, Hewitt, 1917, 435.

120. Parton, 1860/1870, vol. 2, 457.

121. Ibid., vol. 2, 458.

122. Ibid., vol. 2, 457.

123. For lack of weapons, see *Chula Tarla Emathla*, 1959, 89.

124. Swanton, 1922, 233.

125. Stiggins, 1989, 100; Owsley, 1985, 279.

126. Stiggins, 1989, 101, 102; *Chula Tarla Emathla*, 1959, 75, 85.

127. Stiggins, 1989, 110.

128. Ibid., 114–15.

129. Wallace, 1956, 264–81.

130. Martin, 1991, x.

131. Rogin, 1975. Rogin's data is good, but his analysis is ardently non-Indigenous.

132. Duran and Duran, 1995, 41; as believing in "magic methods of warfare," Rogin, 1975, 150.

133. For instance, Owsley, 1985, 274. French missionaries long dubbed Indigenous holy people "*les charlatans ou les jongleurs*," meaning charlatans or con artists, here 1650, in Thwaites, 1899, vol. 35, 240. Thus, it seemed "natural" to the Frenchman Bossu to apply "jongleur" to the Muskogee holy men, in Bossu, 1768, 190.

134. Barnard, 2001, 519–30. Barnard specifically looked at the Japanese case, but the dynamic is obviously at work in standard American histories.

135. *ASPIA*, 1832, Blount to Flournoy, vol. 1, no. 139, letter 12/15/1813, 855.

136. For U.S. population, U.S. Third Census of 1810; for entire Muskogee population, Swanton, 1922, 443; for the Red Sticks head count, see Stiggins, 1989, 94. Stiggins's editor (Stiggins, 1989, note 77, 160) implied that 4,800 was merely a portion of the Red Sticks' complement but 5,000 was also Sam Dale's on-the-spot head count of the total number of Muskogee who turned out to hear *Tecumseh* speak, Claiborne, 1860, 51. Dale's 5,000 included Hawkins's "national" council members, so I trust Stiggins's count of 4,800 Red Sticks.

137. Espenak, 2008; Espenak, 2003.

138. Bagnall, 1996, 22–23. The Moravian missionaries in Muskogee country at the time recorded the major events, in Mauelshagen and Davis, 1969, 67, 68.

139. Hough, 2007, 130.

140. Bagnall, 1996, 42–43, 82.

141. Feldman, 2005, 146.

142. Claiborne, 1917, Claiborne to "A Lady," vol. 6, letter 2/9/1812, 52.

143. Ibid., Claiborne to "A Lady," vol. 6, letter 2/9/1812, 52.

144. Carter, 1934–1975, Territorial Legislature to Congress, vol. 6, letter 1/11/1814, 408.

145. Bagnall, 1996, 27.

146. Olson and Pasachoff, 1998, 144.

147. Valencius, 2013, 106–44.

148. Swanton, 1928/2000, 497; Mann, 2016, 132–61.

149. Sugden, 1997, 23. Other translations include Blazing or Shooting Star. *Tecumthé* literally translates as "I Cross the Way," a reference to the motion of the comet.

150. Cusick, 1827, 11.

151. Cave, 2006, 64.

152. Ibid., 69.

153. Ibid., 101.

154. Edmunds, 1983, 46, 48–49; Cave, 2006, 109.

155. For the settler allegation of fraud, see Claiborne, 1860, 61 note*.

156. Claiborne, 1860, 51.

157. Sugden, 1997, 243.

158. Claiborne, 1860, 51, 52. Woodlanders kept "Stranger Houses" for the use of visiting dignitaries, Mann, 2000, 206.

159. Claiborne, 1860, 53.

160. Ibid., 53.

161. Stiggins, 1989, 85–86.

162. *Chula Tarla Emathla*, 1959, 73–74.

163. Ibid., for instance, 72, 81, 90, 101, 102–3.

164. Ibid., 8, 13, 52, 111.

165. Henri, 1986, 269.

166. Claiborne, 1860, 52.

167. Ibid., 54.

168. For "*Yee-Haw*" as the Shawnee cry, see "Bowman's Campaign of 1779," 1913, 504–505.

169. Claiborne, 1860, 55; for *Tastanagi Tako* accepting *Tecumseh*'s calumet, see Stiggins, 1989, 85.

170. Claiborne, 1860, 59–61.

171. Writing in 1830, Muskogee historian Stiggins said that 303 in the fort were killed (Stiggins, 1989, 113), but this was based on settler records, which deliberately inflated head counts and most probably included those taken prisoner as deceased. Waselkov has the best modern research into the events at Fort Mims. His in-fort casualty numbers yielded 130, Waselkov, 2006, 192–93, 229–57.

172. Stiggins, 1989, 113; Waselkov, 2006, Table 2, 192.

173. Waselkov, 2006, Table 2, 192.

174. Ibid., Table 6.1, 191. Waselkov lists the Muskogee inside of Mims as "Metís," which is just French for "half," as in "half-breed," terms I find noxious. In traditional Woodlands culture, one was 100 percent of whatever one's mother was. Western records were not kept in this way, but nearly all of the intermarriage occurred between European men and Muskogee women.

175. Halbert and Ball, 1895, 148; Waselkov, 2006, 106. Osborne's men might also have come from Fort Vernon, but Stoddert was the main fort of the area. Halbert and Ball estimated the home force at seventy, but Stiggins said that the home militia numbered seventy-six, Stiggins, 1989, 112. Halbert and Ball, 1895, 148 counted the total of soldiers at 275, but the total was 277.

176. Stiggins, 1989, 112. Waselkov also counted 122 dead but simply listed them as "men," in Waselkov, 2006, Table 2, 192.

177. Stiggins, 1989, 106.

178. Waselkov, 2006, 190, 192.

179. Stiggins, 1989, 114. Halbert and Ball, 1895, 153, estimated of 1,000 attackers, but they were working from hysterical settler reports, which probably lumped in with the Mims force the 200 to scout a second fort, Waselkov, 2006, 112.

180. Stiggins gave these statistics, and I see no legitimate reason to doubt information that he received directly from Muskogee "heads of towns," Stiggins, 1989, for 726, 108; for 202, 113; Waselkov, 2006, 192.

181. Halbert and Ball, 1895, 163.

182. The best statistic for U.S. casualties on D-Day have 6,603 total, with 1,465 killed, 1,954 captured or missing, and 3,184 wounded, Mitchell, 1997, 94; Brokaw, 1998.

183. For knowledge of "half-breed" presence, see *ASPIA*, 1832, Hawkins to Unk, vol. 1, no. 139, letter 9/17/1813, 853; Hawkins to Eustis, vol. 1, letter 9/21/1813, 853; Hawkins to Floyd, vol. 1, letter 9/30/1813, 854.

184. Claiborne, 1917, "Circular to Militia Colonels," vol. 6, 9/8/1813, 265.

185. Waselkov, 2006, 33, 100–12, 192, 229–57. I do not understand why Waselkov did not use Stiggins's head counts on Muskogee, however.

186. Halbert and Ball, 1895, 150–51; Waselkov, 2006, 112–13.

187. Halbert and Ball, 1895, quotation, 151, whole account, 151–52; Parton, 1860/1870, vol. 1, 414–16.

188. Carter, 1934–1975, Toulmin to Lattimore, vol. 6, letter 12/1815, 588.

189. Stiggins, 1989, quotation, 124; reiterated as "man is born to die" and "can lose his life but once," 131.

CHAPTER 6

❦

"We Now Shot Them Like Dogs": The Massacre of the Muskogee, 1813–1814

The pretext of Fort Mims having been offered, the seizure of Muskogee Country began in earnest, with the machinery of invasion kicking into gear under the cover of the War of 1812. Despite the supposed enemy having been the British, the settlers had in place a military road for access to Muskogee Country, a fifth column of Muskogee "allies" in Tensaw, outside allies in the Cherokee, and the inevitable militias impatiently stamping their feet to move on the Red Sticks. Meantime, any effective aid to the Red Sticks from the Spanish had been cut off, while the public had been whipped into a furor against the Red Sticks as a dire threat to U.S. borders.

Just as crucially by 1813, the settlers had collected data on the size and whereabouts of all Muskogee towns and villages. During his many years of residence with the Muskogee, Benjamin Hawkins had created a map, although his data lacked overall organization while being limited to towns along the Chattahoochee River.[1] Realizing its deficiency, Hawkins gave considerable aid and comfort to two Moravian missionaries scooting about Muskogee Country from 1807 to 1813. By 1813, just in time for the war, the Moravians had improved on Hawkins's work with an up-to-date, full-blown list and accompanying map of habitations in most of Muskogee Country, with all the towns carefully pinpointed along their rivers.[2] The towns and rivers of the Red Sticks were so deftly noted that the list and map could not have been incidental to the ability of U.S. armies and militias to march directly to the Red Sticks' towns for purposes of destruction.

No congressional declaration of war against the Muskogee was ever made. Instead, President James Madison simply, if unconstitutionally, ordered the action.[3] From the first, Tennessee, Georgia, and Mississippi, the states and territories that stood to gain the most from the invasion of Muskogee Country, pressed for action, with Tennessee dispatching armies even before the War of

1812 was federally declared. Although U.S. Army major general Thomas Pinckney theoretically oversaw the action, Andrew Jackson conducted the strikes against the Muskogee, pretty much at will.[4]

The subsequent conquest was swift and bloody. As a direct result of the U.S. invasion, fully sixty towns and villages of the Muskogee people were destroyed. Except at Burnt Corn and Fort Mims, the U.S. Army with its state auxiliaries completely overwhelmed the Red Sticks, in what can only be described as slaughters, for the Red Sticks, using bows and arrows, were in no way capable of repulsing heavily armed, mounted, and federally supplied armies, whose numbers were literally ten times those of Muskogee whom they attacked. Despite the fact that there had been, at their height, 5,000 Red Stick "warriors," Congress had authorized a standing U.S. Army of 25,000 regulars with an increase of 50,000 one-year-enlisted volunteers and another 100,000 six-month-enlisted militia, all purportedly toward the War of 1812, but with many thousands siphoned off to throw against the Muskogee.[5] Jackson, alone, raised 2,500 men to march against the Red Sticks from Tennessee.[6] Throughout the war, the Red Sticks' soldiers found themselves heavily outnumbered by the U.S. troops.

Eleven engagements are traditionally considered significant in the Creek War, including Burnt Corn and Fort Mims (see Table 6.1).

 1. Burnt Corn, July 27, 1813
 2. Fort Mims, August 30, 1813
 3. Tallushatchee, November 3, 1813
 4. Talladega, November 9, 1813
 5. Hillabee, November 18, 1813
 6. Autosse (Multiple, Combined Actions), November 29, 1813
 7. Econochaca ("Holy Ground"), December 23, 1813
 8. Emuckfau Creek, January 22, 1814
 9. Enitachopco, January 24, 1814
10. Calabee Creek, January 27, 1814
11. Tohopeka ("Horseshoe Bend"), March 27, 1814

It will not be necessary for our purposes to go into exquisite detail on every assault of the war, but three of the eleven attacks deserve a closer look than the other eight: Tallushatchee, Hillabee, and Tohopeka. These three particularly illustrate, on the one hand, the extent of the cultural permission the settlers granted themselves to commit atrocities and, on the other hand, the complete mismatch of the contending forces.

On November 3, 1813, Jackson's brother-in-law, Brigadier General John Coffee of Tennessee, raced into the Muskogee town of Tallushatchee with 900 Americans, destroying it in a massacre that only became more revolting the next day.[7] This was an action taken by the "volunteers" of the State of Tennessee. Although a state action in a congressionally undeclared war, Coffee's attack was countenanced by the U.S. Army. Both militia and volunteer army actions are counted today as U.S. military actions.[8]

Table 6.1 Significant Engagements of the Creek War (1813–1814)

Dates	Places	Red Sticks		United States	
		Killed	Wounded	Killed	Wounded
July 27, 1813	Burnt Corn	2	5	5	15–20
August 30, 1813	Fort Mims	202	161	130	Unknown
November 3, 1813	Tallushatchee	186–200	Unknown	5	41
November 9, 1813	Talladega	290+	Unknown	18	84
November 18, 1813	Hillabee	64	Unknown	0	0
November 29, 1813	Autosse (combined)	200–300	100+	50 (K & W)	
December 23, 1813	Econochaca (Holy Ground)	30	Unknown	1	6
January 22, 1814	Emuckfau Creek	93	Unknown	9	Several
January 24, 1814	Enitachopco	200	Unknown	15	71[a]
January 27, 1814	Calabee Creek	40	Unknown	22	147
March 27, 1814	Tohopeka (Horseshoe Bend)	850	19	69	195

[a] Combined statistics from Emuckfau Creek and Enitachopco.

Table 6.1 lists the major conflicts and their casualties.

Sources: Brannan, 1823, Econochaca, 295; Emuckfau, 300–4; Enitachopco, 304; Calabee Creek, 296–97; Hillabee, 255–56; Tallushatchee, 255, 256, 265, 466; Brewer, 1872, Calabee Creek, 338; Carter, 1934–1975, vol. 6, Burnt Corn, 396–97; Moser et al., 1980–2013, Econochaca, vol. 3, 18; Emuckfau, vol. 3, 18–19; Enitachopco, vol. 3, 20; Hillabee, vol. 2, 462; Tallushatchee, vol. 2, 466; Tohopeka, vol. 3, 52–55; O'Brien, 2003, Burnt Corn, 41; Stiggins, 1989, Autossee, 127; Burnt Corn, 100–1; Calabee Creek, 129, 132; Fort Mims, 112–13; Waldo, 1820, Tallushatchee, 73–74, 88; Adams, 1894, Autosse and Tallushatchee, 639; Waselkov, 2006, Burnt Corn, 100, note 12, 304; Fort Mims, 192–93, 229–57; Williams, 1815, Hillabee, 240–41; Autosse, 242–44.

The dawn attack on the sleeping town surprised the Muskogee, who nevertheless offered "all the resistance that an overpowered soldier could," according to Coffee's report of November 4, 1813, to his commanding officer, Major General Andrew Jackson. The Muskogee's "destruction was very soon completed," Coffee recounted, as the soldiers "rushed up to the doors of the houses, and in a few minutes killed the last warrior of them." Coffee characterized the Muskogee as fighting "with savage fury," without anyone's asking to have been "spared," resisting, instead, "as long as they could stand or sit." Because the assault was really on the homes of a sleeping, civilian town, "in killing the males," the Tennesseeans also "killed and wounded a few of the squaws and children."[9] "Squaw" is an Iroquoian word. It does not mean "woman" but "cunt."[10]

Coffee held that killing the women and children, although "regretted," could not have been "avoided," but that was not quite how Davey Crockett saw it.[11] According to Crockett, who was one of the enlisted men present on the scene, "most" of the townspeople "wanted us to take them prisoners; and their squaws and all would run and take hold of any of us they could, and give themselves up. I saw seven squaws have hold of one man."[12] Crockett and his companions "took all the prisoners that came out to us in this way," but when they saw forty-six men dash into a house for cover, the soldiers "pursued them until we got near the house," where they saw a woman, who was "sitting in the door," place "her feet against the bow she had in her hand." Taking an "arrow, and, raising her feet, she drew with all her might, and let fly at us, and she killed a man," whose death "so enraged us all, that she was fired on, and had at least twenty balls blown through her." After thoroughly killing the woman, Crockett recalled, "We now shot them like dogs; and then set the house on fire," burning alive the forty-six men inside.[13]

During this massacre, Crockett also witnessed a twelve-year-old boy shot down, the bullet breaking his arm and thigh in felling him "so near the burning house that the grease was stewing out of him. In this situation he was still trying to crawl along; but not a murmur escaped him." Crockett expended no pity on this lad, instead pouring the scene through the sieve of racism. The natural horror at the desperation of an adolescent boy's being shot and then roasted alive was deflected by an anthropological lecture from Crockett. So "sullen" was "the Indian, when his dander is up," Crockett assured his readers, "that he had sooner die than make a noise, or ask for quarter."[14]

Crockett recalled another tidbit of Tallushatchee that did not make it into Coffee's official report. After hightailing it back to the safety of Fort Strother, the soldiers soon felt the lack of rations there, because the United States would not furnish Jackson with supplies for a war not yet called officially.[15] Consequently, on November 4, 1813, "all as hungry as wolves," Crockett and crew "went back to our Indian town," Tallushatchee, to scavenge for food. There, "many of the carcasses of the Indians were still to be seen," looking "very awful, for the burning had not entirely consumed them, but given them a very terrible appearance, at least what remained of them." Discovering that the burned house "had a potatoe cellar under it," the militiamen made "an immediate examination" of the cache that unearthed a "fine chance of potatoes." The potatoes had been neatly cooked by the "oil of the Indians we had burned up on the day before," until they "looked like they had been stewed with fat meat." Although Crockett "had a little rather not," he joined the other soldiers in devouring the potatoes, roasted in human fat.[16]

It is instructive to pause here to dissect massacre rationales in the raw. First, it is to be remembered that Crockett's 1834 memoirs constituted his political biography, concocted in the service of the 1835 U.S. congressional election. (He lost to Jackson's man.) Crockett was a humorist, whose above recital would have been read by its audience in 1834 as a rollickin' parody. His comedy was famed for its gut-splitting asides, as in the quip "at least what remained of them," regarding the burned bodies, and in the straight-faced announcement that he "had a little rather not" have eaten the potatoes. Perpetrators' laughing at their target in its extremities is a common feature of racist propaganda.

Second, the settler seal of approval affixed firmly to shooting down determined women and escaping boys, even as both witnessed the brutal murders of beloved family members under assault. The resourceful courage of the seated woman, who had had to use her legs to be strong enough to draw a man's bow, brings up Coffee's oblique comment in his official report on the Red Sticks' having fought as long as they could *sit* or stand, especially since Coffee next admitted to having killed women. Further, Crockett presented the woman's pluckiness as an outrage. The fact that Indigenous women actively defended themselves against settler attack, rather than whimper masochistically at its sadism, was typically interpreted as supporting evidence of the settler charge of "Indian savagery."[17] Meantime, the notion iterated by both Coffee and Crockett, that sullen Muskogee would not ask quarter, was directly controverted by Crockett's sketch of desperate Muskogee women begging American soldiers for quarter.

Some of the army's unadmitted purpose in its massacre of Innocents was to eliminate the witnesses. (*"Innocents"* is the traditional Woodlands term for non-combatants.[18]) Another purpose was preemptive. The murder of Indian children had long been excused by the settler slogan, hatching during King Philip's War (1675–1676), that "nits make lice," that is, that a vermin-boy would grow into man-lice, whom the settlers would just have to kill later on.[19] This was a commonly voiced rationale of soldiers who murdered children, a situation of which many examples beyond Crockett's exist.[20] Because killing Indigenous children was so commonplace among settlers, Jackson's having taken an infant—the only survivor of his Muskogee family at Tallushatchee—to send the baby to his wife to keep is typically depicted as an act of compassion, instead of what it was, a racial act of child-stealing as trophy-taking.[21]

Third, the disparity here between participant accounts and formal reports is hardly isolated. The official versions of events so regularly glossed their unsavory details, that the strategic silences could only have been deliberate. There is considerable evidence for this assertion. It is clear, for instance, that direct evidence of wrongdoing was "disappeared," never to surface again, after the ghastly massacre of Lenape and Mahican—U.S. allies at the time—at Goschochking, Ohio, in 1782.[22] In another instance, circumlocutions gingerly gilded crimes, such as occurred against the New York Onondagas in 1779. After an unprovoked attack, U.S. soldiers gang-raped female and child prisoners throughout a celebratory, drunken afternoon, as distraught Onondaga relatives watched from the hills, powerless to intervene.[23] How often militias and regular soldiers gang-raped their prisoners is not recorded, but I suspect that it was not an infrequent occurrence.

Fourth, settlers regularly projected their own misdeeds onto the Indians, accusing their targets of what they, themselves, had done and then punishing the Indians for those crimes. In this instance, there was a settler slur of long-standing against the Muskogee as "cannibals," but Tallushatchee begs the question of just who literally ate whom.[24] This is one of the most spectacular instances I have ever encountered of reverse accusations, but it is hardly the only one. It was a standard tactic to foist a war on various Indian nations, and then, post-conquest, force those nations to pay "reparations" to the United States for the cost of the war. Indeed, this happened in the Treaty of Fort Jackson, which ended the

Creek War by taking as reparations all Muskogee lands, including those of the Lower Muskogee, the assimilants who had been allies of the United States.[25]

Finally, an extreme disparity in casualties was a regular feature of the Creek War. According to U.S. sources, between 186 and 200 Muskogee were killed outright at Tallushatchee, with an uncounted number wounded, against five U.S. soldiers killed and forty-one wounded.[26] Coffee stated that he took eighty-four Muskogee prisoners.[27] Tallushatchee had about 400 inhabitants, which comports with the combined totals of those executed and captured, with a small, uncounted number either wounded or having escaped. Thus, whereas 0.55 percent—less than 1 percent—of Coffee's force was killed, between 47 percent and 50 percent of the Tallushatchee Red Sticks were killed, many of them not soldiers but civilians. This is hardly surprising, because Coffee had attacked with a complement of 900 militiamen against a civilian town of 400, including women, children, and the elderly.

Following up on Tallushatchee on November 7, 1813, with 2,000 of the Tennessee volunteers, Jackson attacked the Red Sticks at Talladega. Jackson gave varying reports of his and the Red Sticks' casualties. In his November 11, 1813, report to Tennessee governor Willie Blount, he announced that he had suffered seventeen killed and eighty-five wounded.[28] In his report of December 3, 1813, to the head of the U.S. military general Thomas Pinckney, however, Jackson cited fifteen U.S. killed on the spot, with eighty-seven wounded, three of whom died.[29] Using the final December count, after Jackson had gathered all his statistics, puts the split of U.S. killed to wounded at 18:84. Against this statistic, Jackson reported to both Blount and Pinckney that the Red Sticks saw 290 of their men die, with an uncounted number of wounded, although to Pinckney, he added that it was "since well ascertained" that the 290 count fell "far short of the number really killed."[30] There could not have been more than 400 Red Sticks at Talladega, against Jackson's force of 2,000.

In the annals of official U.S. history, the Talladega action has incredibly gone down as an American defeat for having forced the Tennessee volunteers into a retreat.[31] However, the incongruence of casualties and the lasting damage done to the Red Sticks at Talladega make this a Pyrrhic victory, at best. Personally, I suspect that Talladega has been moved into the Red Sticks' column as a "win" to help disguise the fact that the entire Creek War was a massacre.

There is no possible way to characterize the actions at Hillabee as anything short of deliberate massacre. After Talladega, so close on the destructive heels of Tallushatchee, the Red Sticks were in shock. Working from survivors' testimony about fifteen years after the war, the Muskogee memoirist George Stiggins recorded that, especially after the horrors of Tallushatchee, the Red Sticks began "to think how they might evade a total annihilation of their nation." They saw "the impropriety of having a war at the door of every town" and that "even their largest towns would be inevitably overthrown." If they went up against the "well equipped army of white people" town by town, then the "nation would be consumed piecemeal." Many of the Red Sticks' towns, especially Autosse and Hoithlewaulee, therefore looked to coalesce into a unit, although the most that these two towns could muster between them as a joint army was 1,500 men: a thousand from Autosse and 500 from Hoithlewaulee. Other towns just looked to cut their losses immediately through surrender.[32] Lacking supplies, let alone arms, on November 13, 1813, the three Hillabee towns officially offered Jackson "to lay down their arms, and to join in peace and amity" with the United States, even as the Red Sticks were "evacuating their War Camps, and flying in every direction," now before the invading army of Georgia.[33]

Simultaneously with these developments, President James Madison finally issued his general order to Pinckney, commander of U.S. armies, to proceed with a war against the Muskogee, thus formalizing as a federal action what had, up till then, been Jackson's private war.[34] Meantime, because of his premature march to Muskogee Country from Tennessee, Jackson was hurting for food and equipment at Fort Strother. Consequently, on November 7 and 13, 1813, he ordered his subordinate commanders, Major General John Cocke and General James White, to move directly to Fort Strother, further ordering Cocke on November 18, 1813, to bring supplies with him.[35] In concert with these developments, on November 17, 1813, Jackson accepted the Hillabee offer, laying out the terms for their surrender.[36]

Even as Jackson's reply to the Hillabee was in progress, White acted on orders of November 11, from his commander John Cocke, to run his men to Hillabee not to Strother. On November 18, 1813, the day after Jackson accepted the Hillabee towns' surrender and the same day that he gave Cocke specific orders to bring supplies, White attacked the satellite towns around Hillabee proper, without warning or pretext. Immediately taking prisoner five "hostile" Muskogee men, whom he "supposed to be spies," White proceeded to burn to the ground the 123 houses in the two Hillabee bedroom communities of Okfuscooche and Auchenauulgau. He spared the twenty-five-house village of Nitty Chaptoa, thinking it "might possibly be of use at some future period," presumably as a U.S. military or militia camp.[37]

Then, White turned to Hillabee proper. In his report to Cocke, he noted that "so complete was the surprise" of his attack that he "succeeded in surrounding the town, and killing and capturing almost (if not entirely) the whole of the hostile Muskogee assembled there, consisting of about 316, of which number about sixty warriors were killed on the spot, and the remainder made prisoners."[38] In his own, unaddressed report (presumably to his commanding officer, Jackson) on the matter, composed nine days after the event, Cocke upped White's count of Red Sticks killed to sixty-four, suggesting that four of the five captive "spies" had been dispatched. Cocke also added the figure of 256 prisoners, including twenty-nine men, whom he inevitably described as "warriors."[39] It is unrecorded how many men White had with him but Cocke's full complement was 1,500 men.[40]

Both White and Cocke crowed that these feats were accomplished without spilling "one drop" of White's blood.[41] Of course, not. No one in Hillabee was expecting an attack to result the day after its surrender had been accepted. After this attack, the survivors of the Hillabee massacre became some of the most dedicated of the Red Sticks fighters. Meantime, according to Stiggins, their fellow survivors of Talladega and Hillabee predicted "that the white people intended to press" on the Red Sticks "all at once and crush them with overwhelming force," which was exactly what played out.[42]

There has since been debate among U.S. historians about whether Cocke and White knew of the surrender that had been negotiated, with many historians claiming that poor communications had hampered Cocke's decision-making. Jackson's early biographer, James Parton, even palliated Hillabee by fabricating out of whole cloth the story that Jackson felt "grief and rage" upon learning of White's actions under Cocke's orders, but this story is completely without foundation.[43] Not only did Jackson never mention the Hillabee incident in any report to his commander, Pinckney, but he also never reprimanded Cocke for ordering it, despite having written to Cocke on December 6, 1813, eighteen days *after* the Hillabee attack, by which time Jackson certainly knew of it.[44] Personally, I suspect that plundering Hillabee was how Cocke and White intended to round up the supplies that Jackson had commanded them to bring with them to Fort Strother. There was a reason that the U.S. Army and its associated state militias consistently timed their attacks for the fall, instead of the summer, months: to raid Indigenous harvests, thus to feed their armies.

Even as Jackson attacked from Tennessee, Georgians moved west on the Muskogee, from the Atlantic coast. According to his official report to Pinckney, in late November 1813, General John Floyd of Georgia proceeded to Autosse, with "950 of the Georgia militia, accompanied by between 3 and 400 friendly Indians," for a total force of 1,350.[45] (James Tait, who marched with Floyd, put the number of Indigenous allies at 500.[46]) Stiggins reported that the Red Sticks had "long expected" the attack, so that as Floyd approached, "an instant order" went out to move "the infirm old men" and to take the "women, children, and Negroes and disperse them into places of safety" below Hoithlewaulee.[47] The Red Sticks gave sanctuary to "runaway Negros," that is, escaped slaves, bringing in intelligence on militia and U.S. troop movements.[48]

At 6:30 A.M. on November 29, 1813, the Georgians assembled to attack, only to have been surprised to find that "a second town" of some significance lay at the site, with the Red Sticks determined to keep Floyd's army from their holy "hickory ground," about eighteen miles away. Surrounding both places, Floyd plied his artillery and bayonets against Red Sticks who, lacking both, nevertheless "presented themselves at every point, and fought with the desperate bravery of real fanatics."[49] Departing from this official line in his journal, Tait described, instead, a "truly strange" battle, consisting of "passive" people sitting in their houses, simply "suffering themselves to be slain without resistance," while others "scampered" out of their houses "like so many ants."[50]

None of this detail was included by Floyd, who simply noted that, by 9:00 A.M., he had prevailed, with the Red Sticks "completely driven from the plain" and the 400 houses of both towns "wrapped in flames." In this encounter, Floyd slaughtered at least 200 Red Sticks, although from "their making no effort to molest" Floyd's "return," he assumed that Red Sticks casualties were "probably greater."[51] Here, James Tait put the Red Sticks casualties as high as 300.[52] In the Autosse attack, alone, Stiggins held that eighty Red Sticks were killed, with "more than a hundred wounded."[53] The Georgians suffered but fifty casualties, an undifferentiated number comprising both killed and wounded Georgians, with a "number not exactly known" but including "several killed and wounded" among the "friendly Indians."[54]

Here, besides the clear lack of concern for Floyd's Indigenous allies, we see again the typical, heavy imbalance of casualties. Disguising the massacre by pretending that it was a regular military engagement, Floyd gave mixed signals on the exact count of Red Sticks. On the one hand, he intimated that he had faced a large force by citing intelligence "from some of the chiefs" that "warriors from eight towns" had rushed forward to defend Autosse, which suggests a great number of Red Sticks. On the other hand, he acknowledged that his having killed the 200-odd Red Sticks had been sufficient to prevent their pursuit of his men's hasty retreat to Chatahouche after the attack.

Floyd finalized his gloss with the vague assertion that it was "difficult to determine the strength of the enemy."[55] James Tait estimated the head count of Red Sticks "engaged" at "between 1,500 and 2,000," but then, he also claimed that the Red Sticks' army totaled "9,000 fighting men," a statistic that more than doubled the whole, which in January 1814, Jackson estimated at 4,000—number already down 800 from the count of 4,800 just a few months before.[56] Had Tait's 2,000 Red Sticks at Autosse been more than camp gossip, Floyd would certainly have crowed over having defeated so superior a force. Again, George Stiggins, whose information came directly from fellow Muskogee, including the handful of survivors of the war, put the Autosse fighting force at 1,000 at its height.[57]

The way cleared for him by Floyd, on December 23, 1813, Brigadier General Ferdinand L. Claiborne rushed east, bringing a militia from Mississippi, "a party of Choctaw," and part of the Third U.S. regiment of infantry, with which he "charged" Econochaca, one of the Holy Grounds of the Red Sticks. The town was easily overcome as the Red Sticks, "flying precipitately," had "barely time to remove their women and children" out of harm's way, as Claiborne destroyed 200 houses. Thirty Red Sticks were killed during the charge, while "judging from every appearance, many were wounded." Meantime, Claiborne suffered one dead and six wounded. The next day, Claiborne destroyed the second town of sixty houses, killing three "Indians of some distinction."[58]

With an army of 930, on January 22 and 24, 1814, Jackson assaulted Emuckfau and Enitachopco, respectively. The main target was Enitachopco, but a rear guard of Red Sticks attacked Jackson at Emuckfau, to cover the retreat of their fellows "carrying off their women and children." This guard was "completely routed at every point," leading Jackson's men on a two-mile "pursuit," in a diversion common to Indigenous troops, which traditionally lured attackers diametrically away from the escaping Innocents. Over the two-mile run, the Red-Stick decoys sustained a "considerable slaughter" of forty-seven men.[59]

Another chase of three miles resulted in another forty-five Red Sticks slain.[60] In addition, one scout was killed before Jackson's attack, bringing the total counted as Red Stick dead at Emuckfau to ninety-three.[61] In a letter to Rachel Jackson dated January 28, 1814, Jackson claimed nine casualties on his side, but in his report to Pinckney, composed the next day, he claimed just four casualties.[62] It seems here that Jackson gave casualties only for the second chase in his letter to

Pinckney but casualties for both chases in his letter to Rachel. Moreover, in his letter to Pinckney, it is obvious that Jackson did not fill in his full casualty count, so I use nine as the casualty count in Table 6.1.[63]

Two days later at Enitachopco, Jackson "rejoiced," predicting that he "could slaughter the whole" of the Red Sticks' army facing him, which he put at "upwards of 500 Indians in view," 200 of whom, he estimated that his army had killed.[64] This kill boast came in a letter to his wife, in which he also lamented the cowardice of two officers, which had prevented him from killing "most of these barbarians without half the loss" that he suffered there.[65] When he reported later to his commanding officer Pinckney, however, he slimmed down the total Red Sticks' casualties in both encounters to 189 confirmed dead—that is, his men physically counted them lying on the battlefield—although he added that the statistic "must fall considerably short of the number really killed."[66] Stiggins was silent on this set of engagements, but because it was a cultural habit of all Woodlanders to carry both dead and wounded off a battlefield if at all possible, I believe that Jackson's assertion of the high number was true. Thus, I use 200 as the number of Red Stick casualties at Enitachopco. As for his own casualties, Jackson was vague, summing up all the skirmishes and the two main actions into one bundle, to report "twenty killed and seventy-five wounded, four of whom" died of their wounds, for a split of dead to wounded at 24:71.[67] Removing the nine U.S. dead at Emcukfau yields fifteen U.S. dead at Enitachopco, the statistic I use in Table 6.1.

By this point, the Red Sticks were desperate. Stiggins recorded that in the aftermath of Hillabee, the Red Sticks "were determined to meet the foe despite all hazards and take death if so ordained, for a man could die but once."[68] The signal losses that followed at Autosse, Econochaca, Emuckfau, and Enitachopco did not alter this mind-set. In preparing for the next large engagement, at Calabee near modern-day Tuskegee, Alabama, Red Sticks leaders again cheered themselves forward with the thought that "man is born to die and that he could lose his life but once."[69] This courage line was a standard sentiment among all Indigenous North Americans, its best publicized permutation having been uttered in 1876 by the Lakota war chief, *Tȟašúŋke Witkó* ("Crazy Horse"): *Hókahéy*, "It's a good day to die."[70]

According to *Chula Tarla Emathla*, who fought as a Muskogee ally of the United States, the Red Sticks at Calabee were "without ammunition" and had "but little to eat," with no help in the offing from the Spanish at Pensacola, even as they faced "armies marching in from all quarters." In this circumstance, he said, they formed a plan to watch the ongoing retreat of Floyd, thinking to secure arms and supplies by raiding his forces.[71] Stiggins described 1,274 Red Sticks grouping for the joint effort, "stripped and painted red, all in readiness" to give Floyd "a night encounter."[72] On January 27, 1814, they struck Floyd before dawn, at 5:20 A.M., inflicting considerable damage, before Floyd's cavalry could constitute and charge. As Floyd's Indigenous allies interestingly "remained inactive" behind his lines, the cavalry dispersed the attackers with bayonets, with the Red Sticks retreating into the swamps, all but one of them shaking loose of Floyd's pursuit. Broken and damaged, Floyd quit the field after Calabee.[73]

Floyd suffered 17 settlers and 5 Indigenous allies dead, with 132 wounded among the settlers and another 15 Indigenous allies wounded, for a total of 22 dead and 147 wounded.[74] His men counted 37 Red Sticks dead on the field and another 15 who had been "sabred" as they fled. Floyd supposed "from the effusion of blood" and discarded "head-dresses and war-clubs" that "their loss must have been considerable, independent of the wounded."[75] Stiggins gives as 40 the number of Red Sticks killed, but survivors could not even estimate the number of wounded.[76] I use here the total of 40 dead. For once, the settlers bore the brunt of the destruction, the probable reason that it is almost impossible to-day to find any mention of the Calabee battle in primary or secondary Western sources.

Because Floyd gave up the fight and returned to Georgia after this engagement, Alabama historian Willis Brewer awarded the "practical results" of Calabee "wholly" to the "brave natives."[77] By contrast, Stiggins recorded Calabee as "fatal" to the Red Sticks.[78] Thereafter, many lower Red Stick towns retreated permanently from the fight, with their chiefs "paralyzed and inattentive to national affairs."[79] According to *Chula Tarla Emathla*, by the end of January 1814, the Red Sticks still had 1,800 to 2,000 men (down from Jackson's count of 4,000 at the outset of January 1814) but many "were without guns, and only had war-clubs and bows and arrows."[80] Serving as one of Floyd's so-called friendly Indians in the Calabee encounter, *Chula Tarla Emathla* later recorded that, during the Calabee action, he had overheard the Red Sticks begging one another, "give me some bullets—give me powder."[81]

It was in this condition that the remaining Red Sticks either left for Florida or fortified themselves at Tohopeka, at the bend of the Tallapoosa River. Not just "warriors" but all the Red Stick Innocents as well—women, children, the infirm, and the elderly—hunkered together about 1,200-strong, there to weather the attack of the combined forces of the settlers bearing down on them. An important leader, *Menewa*, the war chief of Okfuskee, breathed new hope into the diehards at the bend by agreeing to hold out at Tohopeka.[82] They industriously set about creating formidable fortifications. Jackson later reported to his governor, Willie Blount, that taking a solid, natural location, the *"barbarians"* had *"never rendered one more secure by art"* (italics in the original).[83] In his report to Pinckney, he elaborated on this theme, adding that it was "difficult to conceive a situation more eligible for defence than the one they had chosen, or one rendered more secure by the skill with which they had erected their breastworks."[84]

Jackson's Tennessee regiments had been significantly bolstered in January with 5,000 men, all told, to give him a more than four-to-one advantage over the Red Sticks.[85] By March 21, 1814, Jackson had sent scouts to "scour the surrounding country," as he searched for the Red Sticks.[86] Six days later, he found them at Tohopeka on the Tallapoosa. "Determining to exterminate them," Jackson strategized a multipronged attack, having realized that, if the Tohopeka breastworks provided a cover, then they also provided a prison, from which the Red Sticks could not easily escape a surrounding army.[87] He forthwith surrounded them and proceeded with his plans for an extinction-making attack.

Jackson's later report of the numbered slaughtered changed as his information improved. Writing in excitement to Pinckney on March 28, 1814, the day after his attack, he claimed 557 "left dead" on the spot and a "great number" more "killed by the horsemen," with not more than twenty escaping his onslaught, sixteen of whom his men tracked down and killed. He took 250 prisoners, all but two or three being women and children. For his troops in this report, he claimed twenty-six dead and 106 wounded.[88] In his letter to Blount, also of March 28, he augmented these numbers, adding eighteen Cherokee and five Muskogee allies killed, with eleven Indian allies wounded. Among other regiments, Jackson counted a total of 20 dead with 53 wounded, for a grand total on Jackson's side of 69 dead and 195 wounded.[89]

In a letter to Rachel dated April 1, 1814, Jackson described the *"carnage"* as *"dreadfull,"* again citing the 557 dead by head count but adding another 300 who died, attempting to escape across the river, for a total "slain" of 857. He believed that only "19 wounded Indians alone escaped" his attack. In addition to the final head count on the deceased, he upped his prisoner count to 350, including three "warriors."[90] Since Jackson had had four intervening days in which to perfect his enumerations, and Muskogee tradition claims that all were killed or captured at Tohopeka, I believe and use Jackson's second set of figures.

It should be noted that whereas settler histories traditionally have described everyone killed as "warriors," in fact, Tohopeka was the last bastion of the Red Sticks. Women, children, the elderly, and the incapacitated were among those at Tohopeka, so that they were also perforce among the slain. Particularly, those killed in the river attempting to escape necessarily included Innocents, despite the propaganda of "warriorizing" all the dead and pretending that the 350 taken prisoner, for sale into slavery, represented "warriors," the prisoners were women and children.

Stiggins stated that, having totally lost the best fortifications that could have made at the same time as killing the Red Sticks' best war chiefs and prophets, the horrible slaughter at Tohopeka had "sunk" the traditionals "in their opinion of themselves." Any still alive after Jackson's horrendous assault "appeared desirous to get out of the reach of harm and to live neutrally upon neutral grounds." Broken, the few remaining Red Sticks "made their way to Pensacola" for succor and sanctuary.[91] Knowing that the shattered remnants of the Red Sticks were "flying in consternation" to Pensacola, Jackson ruthlessly pursued them.[92] Still intent on "exterminating" them, he even attempted unilaterally to widen the War of 1812 by invading Florida in pursuit of survivors. The U.S. government, however, already in main war with England, was in no mood to widen its troubles to include Spain. Jackson was, consequently, forced to pull back (although he returned to invade Florida in 1818). In the aftermath of Tohopeka, Jackson offered extravagant public congratulations to his settler militiamen as "brave men" who "came to chastise an insolent foe," those "Barbarians" so woefully "ignorant of the influence of civilization & of government, over human powers."[93]

Demonstrating grace in victory was never Jackson's long suit, and the treaty that ended the war in August 1814, involved the shortest suit in his closet.

First, Jackson wrested complete power to negotiate the "treaty" with the Muskogee from Pinckney.[94] Worse, even by the low standards of coerced Indian treaties, that imposed at Fort Jackson was reprehensible. It flagrantly controverted the provisions of the 1814 Treaty of Ghent, which halted the War of 1812. In Article IX of the Ghent Treaty, the Americans agreed to restore the Indians to the "possessions, rights and privileges they may have enjoyed or been entitled to" in 1811, that is, to return all lands seized during the war.[95] Instead of returning Muskogee Country to the Muskogee, however, Jackson extracted 23,000,000 acres of Muskogee land, basically all of Muskogee Country, now the State of Alabama. This brazen land theft was styled a just reimbursement to the United States for the costs of the war, that is, as reparations.[96] While he was at it, Jackson also stripped his Muskogee allies of their land, included in the 23,000,000 acres grabbed, while taking from his Cherokee allies 4,000,000 acres of their land. This latter robbery of allies was accomplished under the threat that, if the Muskogee and Cherokee delegates to the treaty council did not sign, then Jackson would prosecute a new war against them.[97] This certainly set a new low for the treatment of allies, but it made Jackson popular among the settlers.

No Red Sticks were present at this treaty council, but even *Tastanagi Tako*, Hawkins's right-hand man from the get-go, objected to the treaty, trying to persuade Hawkins to intervene on behalf of the Muskogee.[98] (Interestingly in this regard, *Chula Tarla Emathla*'s asserted that *Tastanagi Tako* had always been a Red Stick in his heart, if only he had had the courage to join the Red Sticks on the ground.[99]) Neither Hawkins nor Jackson cared much what the Muskogee or Cherokee thought, however, with the result that *Tastanagi Tako* gave Hawkins and Jackson lands in addition to what they had already extracted, in a show of contempt through the traditional practice of "sacred clowning," a form of Indigenous satire used as exposé.[100] Hawkins and Jackson took the land and ignored the rebuke.

Massacre does not happen just by direct murder of inconvenient peoples. It also occurs through the exposure of survivors to the elements after the destruction of their habitations and through the direct starvation of survivors after the seizure of their harvests. The Creek War achieved these objectives handily, leaving nearly all the Muskogee shivering, homeless, and hungry. Jackson ethnically cleansed the upper Muskogee Country of Muskogee, while the subsequent Treaty of Fort Jackson demonstrated the true object of the war from the beginning: depopulation in the service of land seizure.

Although the eleven engagements canvassed are typically cited as the substance of the Creek War, this focus on "battles" leaves the unsupportable supposition, first, that they were evenly matched battles rather than massacres and, second, that the damage was confined to those eleven places. They were neither battles nor so confined. Fully sixty towns and villages were wiped clean from the face of the earth, with twelve of them evacuated before military action could sweep over them, and the remaining forty-eight left to invasion and conflagration as the desperate inhabitants fled for their lives. This included the towns of the "friendly" as well as those of the "hostile" Muskogee, for the Red Sticks raided U.S.-"friendly" towns. (See Table 6.2.)

Table 6.2 Muskogee Towns Destroyed, 1813–1814

No.	Date	Town/Village (or Abandoned)
1	July 1813	Hatchechubba Village
2	July 1813	Kialigee Town
3	July 1813	Tuchabatchee Town
4	July 1813	Thlathlagulgau Village
5	August 1813	Chattacchufaulee Village or "Peter McQueen's Town"
6	August 1813	Aubecooche Town (Abandoned)
7	August 1813	Coosa Town (Abandoned)
8	August 1813	Eufaula Town (Abandoned)
9	August 1813	Nauchee Village (Abandoned)
10	August 1813	Tallassee Town (Abandoned)
11	October 1813	Unnamed Village above "Black Warrior's" Town
12	October 1813	"Black Warrior's Town"
13	October 3, 1813	Yuchi Town
14	October 28, 1813	Littafuches Village
15	November 3, 1813	Tallushatchee Village
16	November 16, 1813	"Mad Warrior's Village"
17	November 17, 1813	Nuyaka Village
18	November 1813	Okfuscooche Town or "Little Okfuskee"
19	November 1813	Auchenauulgau or Genalga Village
20	November 18, 1813	Hillabee Town
21	November 29, 1813	Autossee Town
22	November 29, 1813	"Town adjoining Autossee"
23	December 23, 1813	Eccanachaca or "Holy Ground" Town
24	December 24, 1813	"Town eight miles" above "Holy Ground"
25	January 20, 1814	Enotachopco Village
26	January 22, 1814	Emuckfau Village
27	March 21, 1814	Woccoccoie Village 1
28	March 21, 1814	Woccoccoie Village 2
29	March 22, 1814	Unchaula Village
30	March 23. 1814	Wehoofka Village 1 or "Muddy Creek Town"
31	March 23, 1814	Wehoofka Village 2
32	March 27, 1814	Tohopeka Town, or "Horseshoe Bend"
33	April 11, 1814	Wewokee Town, or "Falling Creek"
34	April 13, 1814	Foushatchee Town, or "Bird Creek"
35	April 13, 1814	Columee Town
36	April 14, 1814	Hoithlewaulee Town, or Cluwalee Town
37	April 15, 1814	Ecunhatke Town, or "White Ground"

(*continued*)

Table 6.2   (Continued)

No.	Date	Town/Village (or Abandoned)
38	April 15, 1814	Muclassee Town
39	April 15, 1814	Sausanogee Town, or "Shawnee Town"
40	April 29, 1814	Lower Penoolau Town
41	April 29, 1814	Upper Penoolau Town
42	April/May 1814	Coosaudee Town
43	April/May 1814	Ecunchata Village, or "Alabama Village"
44	April/May 1814	Toowassa Village, or "Alabama Village"
45	April/May 1814	Pauwacta Village, or "Alabama Village"
46	April/May 1814	Attaugee Village, or "Alabama Village"
47	May 1, 1814	Oschooco Village
48	May 1, 1814	Tullavaligau Village, or "Mad Town"
49	May 3, 1814	Unnamed Village
50	May 3, 1814	Unnamed Village
51	May 3, 1814	Unnamed Village
52	May 3, 1814	Unnamed Village
53	May 3, 1814	Unnamed Village
54	July 1814	Hookchoi Town
55	July 1814	Hookchoioochee Town
56	July 1814	Kahaubah Village
57	July 1814	Ocheobofau Town
58	July 1814	Okfuskee Town
59	July 1814	Opilthlucco Village
60	July 1814	Tuskeegee Town

Table 6.2 Muskogee Towns Destroyed, 1813–1814. This is a list, organized by date, of the sixty Creek towns destroyed during the Creek War. This table includes towns of not only Red Sticks but also the "Lower Creeks," who were "allies" of the United States. The list distinguishes between towns and villages. It also shows those towns abandoned by the Creeks in anticipation of imminent attack.

Sources: Brannan, 1823, passim; Crockett, 1834/1973, 87–99; Moser *et al.*, 1980–2013, vols. 2 and 3, passim; Mauelshagen and Davis, 1969, 12–13; Remington, 1999, vol. 1; Waldo, 1820, passim; Waselkov and Wood, 1986, 12–14; Williams, 1815, combined vols. 1 and 2, 240–41, 262–63.

All but a literal handful of Red Sticks men were killed in the Creek War, with nearly all the women and children seized for sale into slavery, while the official U.S. source, *Report on Indians Taxed and Indians Not Taxed in the United States*, listed the total number of Euro-American regulars known to have been killed as seventy-four, with another 333 who were "killed or wounded."[101] My review of the eleven major engagements of the Creek War, including volunteer, militia, and allied Indigenous casualties, yields 159 U.S. killed with 600 or so wounded. There were more casualties, on both sides, from the remaining assaults on the other thirty-seven towns attacked, but the percentages and breakdowns for the United States at those places were better than for those at these eleven sites.

Clearly, the Creek War was never a contest of equals. When the troops dedicated to the one side quadruple the entire male population on the other, while the dead are 159 on the one side but 4,800 on the other, what is at hand is not a war but a baby seal hunt. The most notable aspect of a baby seal hunt is that the seals are not armed. Thus, historians cannot rationalize the carnage simply by demonstrating that the Red Sticks were as anti-settler, as the settlers were anti-Muskogee. False moral equivalencies exist to excuse, not to comprehend, massacre. To understand the massacre of the Muskogee, what is required is a clear grasp of the lethality of the categories and rationales used by the United States.

Along with Jackson's victory at New Orleans, the Creek War helpfully cleared the settler mind of Jackson's missteps in the Burr Conspiracy, at least during his first run at the presidency, which he grasped at unsuccessfully in 1824. When Jackson began making strides in a presidential direction through his election as the U.S. senator from Tennessee, Kentucky representative and speaker of the House Henry Clay and his circle were horrified. Notwithstanding, by April, Jackson's name was being bandied about as a serious candidate. On October 20, 1823, Clay intoned with a straight face that he had been given to understand that Jackson had turned over a new leaf, to "become extremely gentle," having "extinguished some of his most antient and bitter enemies," while seeking to "reconcile himself" with his current "enemies" (of whom, Clay was one).[102] By October 29, 1823, Clay was strategizing heavily to stymie Jackson's election as president by pitting him against either John Quincy Adams, then secretary of state, or William Harris Crawford, then secretary of the treasury, and ultimately, himself.[103] Clay worried through the problem for the rest of 1823.

Jackson was apparently aware of Clay's dangerous opposition and tried to "bury the hatchet" with him, but it did him little good.[104] Jackson was up against some of the best-known and most honored names in the United States, so that his mere Indian-killing—and British-killing—credentials did not necessarily catch the fancy of East Coast voters. In fact, on December 2, 1823, Ohio had the gall to name him as a vice presidential candidate to DeWitt Clinton's presidential candidacy, a development that, as a Clay-colleague later snickered, Jackson could not have considered a "compliment on the part of the People of Ohio."[105] Meantime, Jackson's real competition for the Democratic nomination was John C. Calhoun of South Carolina, whom Jackson ultimately beat out for the honor on February 18, 1824.[106] Both Jackson and Calhoun were dedicated supporters of plantation slavery.

As Jackson made unexpected strides in popularity, a friend of Clay's fumed, "How is it no one speaks freely of this man?" Jackson was a "contemptible seeker after popularity." A "victim of strong passions and prejudices," he was "violent when irresponsible, cautious when differently situated, ambitious, vain and hasty, a fit instrument for others to work upon, subject to be governed by flatterers," hating anyone who opposed or saw through him. If he were "classed as an animal," he would be a "kind of monkey-tiger," and if he and his supporters were on Barataria (stronghold of the pirate Jean Lafitte), then Jackson would "be their King."[107] More than a frightened few agreed with this assessment, and once the election was thrown into the House of Representatives in December 1824, after no candidate acquired a majority of electoral votes, a despairing Clay declared that the presidency must go either to Jackson or Quincy Adams. "And what an alternative that is!" he cried.[108] Unsurprisingly, he came down for Adams.[109] From the powerful Speaker of the House, Clay's preference had consequences for Jackson.

Because Jackson had actually won the popular vote, his chances of prevailing were strong, despite Speaker Clay. On January 28, 1825, as the matter lingered amidst hectic politicking, Clay "interrogated his conscience" and the result was widely distributed in the newspapers. As a "friend of liberty" and of the "permanence of our institutions" yet in their infancy, he simply could not help elect a "military chieftain," thereby giving the "strongest guaranty" that the United States would "march in the fatal road" that had "conducted every other republic to ruin." This roused Jackson to a predictable explosion of fury against Clay in his own publicly released letter, dressing Clay down for "never" having "risked himself for his country." Continuing in tones of innocence outraged for the length of a lurid paragraph, he ended by intimating that Clay was the "Demogague."[110] Then on January 29, things became really unfriendly, when Clay shot back that he would never willingly have selected Adams, had his other choice not been a mere "Military Chieftain" whose qualification for the presidency apparently consisted of "killing 2,500 Englishmen at N. Orleans."[111] Enough seasoned pols agreed with Clay that it was hardly a surprise, when on February 9, 1825, Clay's choice, John Quincy Adams, was elected president by a vote in the House.[112]

Jackson was back for the next election, however, as it was fairly clear that few wanted Adams to receive the nod a second time. This did not indicate that Jackson would enjoy clear sailing to the presidency, however. As Jackson's biographer James Parton noted, the campaign season quickly degenerated into a war of personalities.[113] In the summer of 1827, an old enemy of Jackson's from an 1813 duel, Dr. James L. Armstrong, brother of John Armstrong, secretary of war under Madison and a U.S. congressman in 1796, came out with a pamphlet, *Reminiscences, or Catalogue of General Jackson's Juvenile Indiscretions between the Ages of 23 and 60.*[114] The title, alone, indicated that, as a sexagenarian, Jackson was as puerile and unfiltered as a child. Judgments against Jackson simply increased with Armstrong's elucidation of his fourteen "indiscretions," from his first barroom brawl in East Tennessee; through the Robards affair, although as a gentleman, Armstrong spared Rachel Jackson's reputation; and ending with Jackson's intemperate challenges and duels, including those with Sevier, Dickinson, and Samuel Jackson, the latter of whom Jackson ran through with his cane sword.[115]

Regarding Colonel Thomas Benton's duel (indiscretion number thirteen), Armstrong quoted Benton's assessment of the Jackson coterie as "the meanest wretches under heaven to contend with; liars, affidavit-makers, and shameless cowards." His life in danger, Benton realized that "nothing but a decisive duel" could "save" him.[116] In the end, Jackson and his posse waylaid Armstrong and his brother, Jesse, rushing upon Armstrong firing, with Jackson personally pistol-whipping him, while Jesse was stabbed by one Jackson acolyte and pistol-whipped by another. Then, in 1824, both Benton and Jackson found themselves in the U.S. Senate, seated together and placed on the same committees, but Benton turned into one of the "antient enemies" that Jackson now determined to win over with courtesy visits and dinners. Armstrong ended by noting in disgust that, at his last count upon writing, Jackson had engaged in 100 duels.[117]

In particular, the Ohio publication, the *Truth's Advocate and Monthly Anti-Jackson Expositor*, took Jackson to task for his actions against the Muskogee, publishing his war-mongering letter after the Duck Creek affair and detailing such travesties as his 1814 treaty seizing the lands of his Muskogee allies and pointing out that he had taken advantage of a "conquered people."[118] The periodical brought up the wanton attack on the Hillabee, after the people had been "subdued; had laid down their arms and sought peace."[119] Jackson's involvement in the Burr campaign was also generally leveraged against him during his 1828 presidential bid.[120] The *Truth's Advocate*, especially, had a field day detailing his part in the Burr Conspiracy.[121]

Although alone in its ire, the *New York American* denounced Jackson's slaveholding, depicting his slaves as "taxed to the uttermost" just so that Jackson might "add another race-horse to his stud."[122] This marked one of the initial entries of abolitionists into the larger political fray. For its part, the Washington *National Journal* took direct aim at Rachel Jackson, picking up the call from the *Truth's Advocate*, with Charles Hammond, the editor of the *Advocate*, producing a separate pamphlet on the matter. "Ought a convicted adulteress and her paramour husband to be placed in the highest office of this free and Christian land?" Hammond demanded. (The pro-Jackson *United States Telegraph* got even, concocting a scurrilously untrue story about the Adamses locked in steamy premarital relations.[123]) The Anti-Masons also got into the act. Andrew Jackson had been a Mason since at least 1798, having joined the Grand Lodge of North Carolina, while from 1823 to 1824, he had served as the Grand Master of the Grand Lodge of Tennessee.[124] In Vermont in 1824, Anti-Masons had supported the Anti-Masonic Adams over Jackson, and in 1828, now strengthened as a political party, they again rallied to the Clay faction, even though as president, Adams had remained fairly neutral toward the Masons.[125] The reasons for the Anti-Masonic distrust of Jackson were not entirely crackpot. Like Clay, the Anti-Masonic standard-bearer, William Wirt, feared that Jackson had the makings of a tyrant, were he offered commander-in-chief powers.[126]

With those excoriations abroad amid many more, all in cheery derogations of Jackson's flammable personality and violent tendencies, Quincy Adams expected to be reelected. Like Armstrong, Adams had little use for Jackson, annoyed that Jackson's "Central Committee" was deciding whom he would fire on December 15, 1828, before anyone had been elected.[127] Adams's disgust rose on January 20, 1829, when he was shown a pamphlet that Jackson had sent an acquaintance of Adams, containing Jackson's "passionate and illiterate" remarks, handwritten on a blank page of it.[128] Thus, Adams was stunned on

February 11, 1829, when Jackson was declared the new president, and on February 17, 1830, his alarm rose when William Henry Harrison called, suggesting that Jackson intended to make himself "King or Emperor."[129]

It was not as though Jackson's ardent supporters did not know of all the charges against him. They knew. Apparently, those were the things they liked about Jackson: blood and soil. Once president, Jackson set to coalescing one signature program applauded by his "common man" supporters: Indian Removal.

NOTES

1. Foster, 2003, 25s, 51s–66s, 33–35, 168–74.

2. Mauelshagen and Davis, 1969, map and list, 11–13.

3. Moser *et al.*, 1980–2013, Pinckney to Jackson, vol. 2, letter 11/16/1813, 455; Remini, 2001, 43–46.

4. Moser *et al.*, 1980–2013, Jackson to Cocke, vol. 2, letters 12/12/1813, 478; Jackson to Tennessee First Brigade, vol. 2, letter 12/13/1813, 482; Jackson to Blount, vol. 2, letter 12/15/1813, 487.

5. Tucker, 2012, 149; Claiborne, 1860, 51.

6. Moser *et al.*, 1980–2013, vol. 2, note 2, 433; Crockett, 1834/1973, 75.

7. Brannan, 1823, Coffee to Jackson, letter 11/4/1813, 255.

8. Adams, 1894, 639.

9. Waldo, 1820, 73–74.

10. Mann, 2000, 19–22.

11. Waldo, 1820, 74.

12. Crockett, 1834/1973, 88.

13. Ibid., 88.

14. Ibid., 89.

15. Moser *et al.*, 1980–2013, Jackson to Blount, vol. 2, letters 10/28/1813, 442; S. Flournoy to Jackson, vol. 2, letter 11/9/1813, 447; Jackson to Blount, vol. 2, letter 11/14/1813, 453; Pinckney to Jackson, vol. 2, letter 11/16/1813, 456; Remini, 2001, 68–69.

16. Crockett, 1834/1973, 89–90.

17. For the settler attitude toward "Muskogee masculinity and femininity as direct assaults on 'civilization'," Saunt, 1999, 268.

18. Heckewelder, 1820/1876/1976, note 1, 136.

19. Levene, 2005, 26; Churchill, 1997, 129–288.

20. Remini, 2001, 77.

21. Taking the child, Moser *et al.*, 1980–2013, Jackson to Rachel Jackson, vol. 2, letter 11/4/1813, 444; as compassionate, Remini, 2001, 64.

22. Mann, 2005, 167.

23. Ibid., 31.

24. Milfort, 1802/1959, 13, 59, 97.

25. Kappler, 1904, "Treaty with the Creeks," vol. 2, 108.

26. Brannan, 1823, Coffee to Jackson, Coffee cited 200 dead, letter 11/4/1813, 256; Adams, 1894, 639; Moser *et al.*, 1980–2013, Jackson to Jackson, Jackson said Coffee counted 180 dead on the ground, but that "there is no doubt but 200 was killed," vol. 2, letter 11/4/1813, 444; in his later official report to Pinckney, Jackson cited 186 dead and 80 taken prisoner, Jackson to Pinckney, vol. 2, letter 12/3/1813, 466. I use Coffee's direct head count in his official report of eighty-four as prisoners.

27. Brannan, 1823, Coffee to Jackson, letter 11/4/1813, 256.

28. Ibid., report, Jackson to Blount, letter 11/11/1813, 265.

29. Moser *et al.*, 1980–2013, Jackson to Pinckney, vol. 2, report, 12/3/1813, 466.

30. Brannan, 1823, Jackson to Blount, report, 11/11/1813, 265; Moser *et al.*, 1980–2013, Jackson to Pinckney, vol. 2, report, 12/3/1813, 466.

31. Remini, 2001, 74.

32. Stiggins, 1989, 123. Stiggins wrote Hoithlewaulee as "Othlewallee."

33. Moser *et al.*, 1980–2013, Grierson to Jackson, vol. 2, letter 11/13/1813, 451–52.

34. Ibid., Pinckney to Jackson, vol. 2, orders, 11/16/1813, 455–56.

35. Ibid., White to Jackson, vol. 2, letters 11/7/1813, 446–47; Jackson to Jackson, vol. 2, letter 11/12/1813, 448; Jackson to Cocke, vol. 2, orders, 11/16/1813, 454–55; Jackson to Cocke, vol. 2, orders, 11/18/1813, 457–58.

36. Moser *et al.*, 1980–2013, Jackson to Grierson, vol. 2, letter 11/17/1813, 456–57.

37. Williams, 1815, White's report, 240–41.

38. Ibid., 241.

39. Moser *et al.*, 1980–2013, Cocke to Jackson, vol. 2, report, 11/27/1813, 462.

40. Ibid., Jackson to Cocke, vol. 2, letter 12/6/1813, 469.

41. USDI, 1894b, claimed that 60 Red Sticks were killed at Hillabee, 639. However, the formal report on the expedition listed sixty-four dead, Moser *et al.*, 1980–2013, Cocke to Jackson, vol. 2, report, 11/27/1813, 462.

42. Stiggins, 1989, 124.

43. Parton, 1860/1870, vol. 1, 453.

44. Brannan, 1823, Jackson to Pinckney, report, 1/29/1814, 298–305; for Cocke, Moser *et al.*, 1980–2013, Jackson to Cocke, vol. 2, letter 12/6/1813, 469–70.

45. Williams, 1815, report, 242.

46. Tait, 1924, 234.

47. Stiggins, 1989, 125.

48. Ibid., 124.

49. Williams, 1815, report, 243.

50. Tait, 1924, 235.

51. Williams, 1815, report, 242–44.

52. Tait, "Journal," 234.

53. Stiggins, 1989, 127.

54. For the Georgian casualty count, see USDI, 1882/1894, 639; for the allied Indigenous casualties, see Williams, 1815, 244.

55. Williams, 1815, report, 243.

56. Tait, 1924, for 2,000, 234; for 9,000, 235; for Jackson's estimate of 4,000, see Moser *et al.*, 1980–2013, Jackson to Pinckney, vol. 3, report, 1/9/1814, 12.

57. Stiggins, 1989, 123.

58. Brannan, 1823, Claiborne to Armstrong, letter 1/1/1814, 295; for the number "slaughtered," see Moser *et al.*, 1980–2013, vol. 3, 18.

59. Brannan, 1823, Jackson to Pinckney, report, 1/29/1814, 300–1.

60. Ibid., Jackson to Pinckney, report, 1/29/1814, 302; Moser *et al.*, 1980–2013, Jackson to Jackson, vol. 3, letter 1/28/1814, 18.

61. Ibid., Jackson to Pinckney, report, 300.

62. Moser *et al.*, 1980–2013, for five, Jackson to Jackson, vol. 3, letter 1/28/1814, 18; for four, Jackson to Jackson, vol. 3, letter 1/28/1814, 19; to Pinckney, Brannan, 1823, Jackson to Pinckney, letter 1/29/1814, 302.

63. Brannan, 1823, Jackson to Pinckney, letter 1/29/1814, 304.

64. Moser *et al.*, 1980–2013, Jackson to Jackson, prediction, vol. 3, letter 1/28/1814, 19; numbers, vol. 3, 20.

65. Ibid., Jackson to Rachel Jackson, vol. 3, letter 1/28/1814, 20.

66. Brannan, 1823, Jackson to Pinckney, report, 1/29/1814, 304.

67. Ibid., Jackson to Pinckney, report, 1/29/1814, 304.

68. Stiggins, 1989, 124.

69. Ibid., 131.

70. Black Elk *et al.*, 1932/2008, 11, 111.

71. *Chula Tarla Emathla*, 1959, 88.

72. Stiggins, 1989, 129.

73. Brannan, 1823, Floyd to Pinckney, report, 1/27/1814, 296–97.

74. Brewer, 1872, 338.

75. Brannan, 1823, Floyd to Pinckney, report, 1/27/1814, 297.

76. Stiggins, 1989, 132.

77. Brewer, 1872, 338.

78. Stiggins, 1989, 132.

79. Ibid., 132.

80. *Chula Tarla Emathla*, 1959, 89.

81. Ibid., as with Floyd, 128; conversation overheard, 89.

82. Stiggins, 1989, 133.

83. Brannan, 1823, Jackson to Blount, letter 3/28/1814, 322.

84. Moser *et al.*, 1980–2013, Jackson to Pinckney, vol. 3, report, 3/28/1814, 52.

85. Ibid., Doherty to Jackson, vol. 3, letter 3/2/1814, note 4, 38–39.

86. Ibid., Jackson to Pinckney, vol. 3, report, 3/23/1814, 50.

87. Ibid., Jackson to Pinckney, vol. 3, report, 3/28/1814, 52.

88. Ibid., Jackson to Pinckney, vol. 3, report, 3/28/1814, 53.

89. Brannan, 1823, Jackson to Blount, letter 3/28/1814, 321–23.

90. Ibid., Jackson to Jackson, vol. 3, report, 4/1/1814, 54–55.

91. Stiggins, 1989, 133.

92. Moser *et al.*, 1980–2013, Jackson to Blount, vol. 3, letter 4/18/1814, 64.

93. Ibid., Jackson to Tennessee Troops, vol. 3, circular, 4/2/1814, 58.

94. *ASPIA*, 1832, Pinckney to Jackson, vol. 1, no. 139, orders, 4/23/1814, 857–58; Hawkins to Armstrong, vol. 1, letter 7/19/1814, 860.

95. Prucha, 1994, 132.

96. Kappler, 1904, "Treaty with the Creeks," 1814, vol. 2, 107–10.

97. Remini, 2001, 89–90; Wright, 1986, 180.

98. Moser *et al.*, 1980–2013, vol. 3, 373.

99. *Chula Tarla Emathla*, 1959, 34, 83, 101.

100. *ASPIA*, 1832, Agreement, vol. 1, no. 139, 8/9/1814, 837–38; Henri, 1986, 303–4; for sacred clowning, Mann, 2016, 2–3, 63, 220.

101. USDI, 1882/1894, 639.

102. Spelling as in the original. Clay, 1959–1993, Clay to Leigh, vol. 3, letter 10/20/1823, 501.

103. Ibid., Clay to Hammond, vol. 3, letter 10/29/1823, 505.

104. Ibid., Clay to Porter, vol. 3, letter 12/11/1823, 535.

105. Ibid., vol. 3, note 2, 546; Fletcher to Clay, vol. 4, letter 1/2/1824, 601.

106. Ibid., vol. 3, note 3, 646.

107. Ibid., Hammond to Clay, vol. 3, letter 4/1824, 730.

108. Ibid., Clay to Erwin, vol. 3, letter 12/13/1824, 895.

109. Ibid., Clay to McClure, vol. 3, letter 12/28/1824, 906.

110. Ibid., Clay to Brooke, vol. 4, letter 1/28/1825, note 1, 45–46.

111. Ibid., Clay to Blair, vol. 4, letter 1/29/1825, 47.

112. Ibid., Clay to Brooke, vol. 4, letter 2/10/1825, 62. For Henry Adam's blow-by-blow description of events, Adams, 1882/1894, 284–87.

113. Parton, 1860/1870, vol. 3, 140.

114. For James L. Armstrong, see Tucker, 2018, vol. 1, 39.

115. Armstrong, 1828, 4–5, for Samuel Jackson, 8. Parton dated this pamphlet to 1824, but Jackson was not 60 till 1827. The pamphlet is generally agreed to date from 1828. Parton, 1860/1870, vol. 3, 48.

116. Armstrong, 1828, 7.

117. Ibid., for Benton, 7; for 100 duels, 8.

118. "Literature & Principles," 1828, 201–3; Hammond, February, 1828, 43, 47.

119. Hammond, *Truth's Advocate*, April, 1828, 136–37.

120. Moser *et al.*, 1980–2013, vol. 2, editorial commentary on incriminating Jackson letter on 9/25/1806, 110; for numerous other damaging documents and testimony injured Jackson's presidential bid, especially vol. 2, note 14, 114; document, vol. 2, 11/1806, 115–16; strange letter to Claiborne, vol. 2, 11/12/1806, 116–17.

121. "Jackson and Burr," 1828, 203–5; "True Character of General Jackson," 1828, 216; Hammond, June, 1828, 218–23; "Remarks," 1828, 289–93; Buchanan, 1828, 311–14; "Further Illustrations of General Jackson's True Character," 1828, 389–92.

122. Parton, 1860/1870, vol. 3, 145.

123. Boller, 1998, 66.

124. Burstein, 2004, 39.

125. Vaughn, 2009, for Vermont, 70; for Adams as neutral, 119.

126. Ibid., 62.

127. Adams, 1874–1877, vol. 8, entries, 12/15/1828, 82–83.

128. Ibid., vol. 8, entries, 1/20/1829, 93.

129. Ibid., vol. 8, entries, 2/11/1829, 101; vol. 8, 2/17/1830, 190.

PART III

~

Zachary Taylor, 1784–1850, Admin., 1849–1850

CHAPTER 7

❧

"Inch by Inch": Zachary Taylor, "Old Rough and Ready"

If schoolchildren are allowed to forget Zachary Taylor outright after the test ("Who was the twelfth president of the United States?"), then mainstream historians mainly pull him up as a handy prop in minimizing the less-than-glorious aspects of American history. Shunting aside everything but Taylor's sixteen months as president, they can emphasize Taylor's support of the Union over sectionalism and his opposition to Henry Clay's slavery-favoring 1850 Compromise, while studiously ignoring the pesky theorists over in the corner talking out loud about Taylor's curious death.

This Euro-American belief at being able to tout Taylor as an "anti-slavery" president a decade before Abraham Lincoln hurries historians past mention of his large slave plantations in the Deep South. The battle of Buena Vista during the Mexican-American War is sloughed off, even in discussions of the Mexican-American War, despite Taylor's kill count in the thousands of *latinx*. Rating even less mentioned is the brutality of Taylor's Indian wars in Wisconsin and Florida. Just because Taylor did not, like Andrew Jackson, murder 5,000 Indians in one, six-month blitz spectacular enough to capture an adolescent's attention, does not mean that the Sauk, Mesquaki, Seminole, and Africans killed piecemeal in his Indian wars do not matter. Taken together, the deaths mount up. What Taylor engaged in were "fractal massacres," multiple mini-massacres, with each fractal replicating in miniature the sweep of the whole. Taken together, fractal massacres tuck into the overall pattern of genocide.[1]

Zachary Taylor did not appear in the White House one day from nowhere. He hailed from the "Dark and Bloody Ground" of "Kentucke," as valorized by John Filson in 1784 and painted from life by Elias Pym Fordham in 1818.[2] The settler push into Kentucky was canonized in Filson's "Dan'l Boon" hagiography. It was Filson who first popularized the terms, "Dark and Blood Ground" and "Middle Ground," in direct reference to settler Kentucky.[3] Ignoring all the earlier French

presence, Filson presented European intrusion into Kentucky as beginning with
the English in 1754, during the French and Indian War, with James McBride
and John Finley entering in 1767, followed by Daniel Boone in 1769. Because,
however, the Shawnee were not done living in Kentucky, they put up quite a fight
to kick the squatters back out. The settlers deeply resented it. Continually portraying themselves as the victims despite their status as invaders, ferocious
Kentucky militias made regular attacks on the Shawnee in Kentucky and Ohio.[4]
Filson sang a lullaby to the settler soul, and Taylor grew up hearing it.[5]

A generation later, Fordham chronicled his travels in Kentucky, primarily for
British interests. An educated and decently well-off Englishman who emigrated to
the United States in 1817, Fordham ended up in Illinois, amidst a large contingent
of immigrant Englishman. Although he ultimately returned to England in 1818, as
a civil engineer, Fordham was a surveyor of the Northwest Territory, carefully
assessing Indian lands for their worth to the British.[6] In the process, Fordham
imbibed and then regurgitated the Filson catechism: Kentucky was a "bloody field"
that had been "won inch by inch from the Indians" and, at that, by "just a few enterprising men"—or, as Fordham later specified, Daniel Boone—"unaided by governments, unorganized, for the most part poor." Moreover, Kentucky was "not the
property" of any particular "tribe of Savages" but just a "hunting ground of many."[7]

Not quite. The Shawnee did, in fact, live in Kentucky, and had for a very long
time. The first French intruders found the Shawnee very much living there, along
the Cumberland River, running through Tennessee and Kentucky. The Shawnee
had been in Kentucky long enough for modern archaeologists to call their fore-
bearers, those creators of impressive rock art, "proto-Shawnee."[8] The Shawnee
were also living along the Ohio River where, in fire alliance with the Cherokee
of southeastern Ohio, they patrolled the Ohio River during the Revolution. The
Shawnee had been in southwestern Ohio long enough to create the precontact
Fort Ancient culture, with Ohio Mound Builder culture stretching back thousands of years.[9]

Filson calculated that by 1784, there were 30,000 settlers in Kentucky. He
characterized them as "polite, humane, hofpitable, and very complaifant," but
this is not what Fordham found, thirty-four years later.[10] Kentucky was an "off-
slip" (colony) of Virginia, said Fordham, even as Tennessee had been a colony
of North Carolina and Missouri would later be as a colony of Kentucky.[11] By
and large, this meant that the established states were staking out western
territory, initially as a garbage dump for their unwanted populations. Held in
contempt by dainty easterners, these settlers were scorned as the "off-scourings
of the earth, fugitives from justice" whom the east was "well rid of," said a 1785
report.[12] In November 1817, calling Kentucky the "verge of the habitable world,"
Fordham went into a mite more detail, categorizing the four levels of Kentucky
society as consisting of:[13]

1. The "hunters, a daring, hardy race of men who live in miserable cabins,
   which they fortify in times of War with Indians," that is, they erected the
   "forts" that dotted the lands set for seizure. Although hating the Indians, they

aped Indian "dress and manners," while their "wars with the Indians" had made them "vindictive."

2. "First settlers," who were essentially "hunters and farmers" albeit a little better off than the hunters, above. Nevertheless, they were "a half barbarous race" that sold out to move on the minute the area became "well settled."

3. The professionals, "Young doctors, Lawyers, Storekeepers, farmers, & mechanics" from Virginia, who came in to "speculate in land, and begin the fabric of Society," although the "general tone of Social manners" was "yet too relaxed," with the "Law" lacking the "energy to prevent violence."

4. Finally, "the old settlers," who included "rich, independent farmers," typically meaning slave plantation owners, and "wealthy merchants," both with some level of education and "military taste," that is, the ability to organize anti-Indian militias. Most were veterans of the American Revolution. They were also "great duelists," said Fordham. Although forestalled by strengthened anti-dueling laws in 1817, they always carried their "dirks," or knives, with them and "sometimes decided a dispute on the spot." (In January 1818, Kentuckians repealed the law against dueling.[14]) Having been "irritable and dissipated in youth," they were "generally steady and active in Manhood." Risk-takers, they were stoic when they lost, big.

Fordham brought up a point often lost in modern recitals, to wit, that the post-Revolutionary War veterans rushing into the Old Northwest waiving their land warrants were battle-hardened by a cruel, seven-year-long war. Some were even veterans of the preceding French and Indian War, 1754–1763. They were thus well versed in violence. In Kentucky, militia action was constant, with large Kentucky militia participation in the 1774 Lord Dunmore's War over Ohio.[15] According to John Heckewelder, Kentuckians, especially, ambushed Indians they wanted gone by inviting them to parties, only to fall upon and kill their guests, once arrived.[16] In all instances, killing Indians was a highly regarded activity, with racially fixated serial killers like Lewis Wetzel, David Owens, Timothy Murphy, and David Williamson celebrated as heroes on the so-called frontier, although today, they are mainly hushed up as footnotes.[17] Notwithstanding, from the French and Indian War on, settler solidarity was created through such shared activities as killing Indians and enslaving Africans.[18]

As yet another scion of slavery, Zachary Taylor was raised in this Kentucky landscape of ferocious settlers, trapped slaves, and desperate Indians. He sprang from what passed in the settlements for aristocratic roots, the Taylors of Virginia having been in the Americas 150 years before Zachary was born. Thus, Taylor's father, Richard, could boast of his Old Virginia wealth. On the preferment of fellow Virginian George Washington, when the Revolution began, Richard Taylor was appointed a captain in the Revolutionary Navy of Virginia, receiving as pay not only land warrants for "several thousand acres" but also a pension of $300 a year, worth about $7,000 today.[19]

Considerable ink has been spilled on the Revolution as the first European war of liberation, but the seamier side of the Revolution has been gingerly avoided.

There were reasons that so many rich, southern slavers, including George Washington, Thomas Jefferson, James Madison, James Monroe, and Richard Taylor, took part against British dominion, and those reasons were not all about taxation or quartering (forced, free boarding of British soldiers). Primary if unsung reasons for colonists' entering the war included the British Proclamation of 1763 and the Mansfield Decision of 1772.

The Proclamation of 1763 was an outgrowth of the French and Indian War, as ended by the 1763 Treaty of Paris. Rather schizophrenically, on the one hand, it set the tone of plundering the Indians for land, while on the other hand, it outlawed colonists' squatting on Indian land. In the first instance, to "testify" to Britain's "Royal Sense and Approbation" of the conduct of its officers in the war, it handed out vast acreages to them, so long as they saw to the "Conditions of Cultivation and Improvement." Each "Field Officer" of the army was granted 5,000 acres; each captain, 3,000 acres; and so forth down the ranks to "every Private Man," who received fifty acres. Moreover, colonial "Governors" and "Commanders in Chief" were empowered to hand out land to naval officers. Five thousand acres to each field officer is a truckload of land, almost eight square miles of it. It moved battle-tested European men into Indian country Because Indian cooperation was still needed for the fur trade, however, Britain wished to stay on the good side of, especially, the powerful Iroquois League. It therefore decreed that the "several Nations or Tribes of Indians" living under the Crown's "Protection" were not to have been "molested or disturbed" in their "Possession" of any "Hunting Grounds" existing in supposedly British "Dominions and Territories" that had not yet been "ceded to or purchased by" the British.[20]

Importantly, the lands in question were already "cultivated," having been intensively farmed by the Indians, who lived in towns larger than those of Europe, facts that had been common knowledge since the first French arrivals. In 1536, Jacques Cartier saw "*belles grandes campagnes pleines de blé, qui est comme du mil de Brésil, aussi gros de que du pois: les habitants en vivent comme nous de froment*" (big, beautiful fields full of corn [lit. wheat], which is like that of Brazil, as big as peas; the inhabitants live like us, from grain).[21] From July 14 to 24, 1687, while warring against the Seneca, Jacques-René de Brisay, Marquis de Denonville reported to his minister of war that he had destroyed four towns of "14 to 15 thousand souls," each, including their stored grain and associated fields of standing corn, which existed "in such great abundance" that the total burned was later calculated at "400 thousand minot of Indian corn," or 1,200,000 bushels of corn.[22] On August 27, 1779, during the massive Revolutionary Army's summer sweep through Iroquoia, Major John Burrowes cited crops that grew in ways unparalleled in his state of New Jersey. One field of "100 acres" contained "beans, cucumbers, Simblens [melons], watermelons, and pumpkins in such quantities" as to have been "almost incredible to a civilized people."[23]

The same obtained in the South. In 1770, Jean Bernard Bossu described southeastern harvests "*de patates, d'ignames, et de mais, ou bled d'Inde*" (of potatoes, yams, and maize, or Indian wheat [corn]).[24] In 1791, traveling the South, William Bartram found that towns all had a "large district of excellent, arable land adjoining."

On this excellent land, the Muskogee peoples planted "Corn, Potatoes, Beans, Squash, Pumpkins, Citruls [watermelons], Melons, etc." If nothing was nearby, the town chose "such a convenient fertile spot at some distance."[25]

Although clearly preposterous, the "hunting grounds" fiction was heavily pushed by the British, and later, the United States, because the European rationale for land seizure held that only "civilized" people, that is, Europeans, "cultivated" (farmed) or "improved" the land by, say, putting up fences. These rubrics referred back to England's emendation of the papal Doctrine of Discovery, which originally pertained solely to Catholics. As a Protestant country, England rationalized that by planting and fencing, settlers had a right to the land.[26] After the American Revolution, U.S. settlers continued the hunting-grounds masquerade for two reasons. First, they had inherited and continued the Protestant-friendly version of the Doctrine of Discovery, later wedded into U.S.-Indian law by John Marshall.[27] Second, "hunting ground" was a term that speculators used to describe whatever Indian lands were just then being eyed for seizure and sale to incoming settlers, by way of calming buyers' jitters over potential Indian objections.

The majority of the Proclamation was what really infuriated the Revolutionaries, for it guaranteed the various Indian nations that their land, stretching from the Appalachian Mountains to just west of the Mississippi River, and from Wisconsin in the north to Mississippi in the south, was safe from settler infringement. The "Loving subjects" of Britain were cautioned not to try taking the land—without royal "leave and Licence," anyhow. Squatters were advised "forthwith to remove themselves," for "all Officers" and "Military as those Employed in the Management and Direction of Indian Affairs" were ordered "to seize and apprehend all Persons" intruding on Indian land. Woe betided any settlers fleeing "Justice" for crimes of "Treason, Murders, or other Felonies or Misdemeanors" by seeking "Refuge in the said Territory." Such miscreants would be arrested and taken under "proper guard to the Colony where the Crime was committed" to stand trial for their offenses.[28] This last bore tacit witness to the reputation of western settlers as "off-scourings," the worst of the worst of settler culture.

As a guarantee of Indian land rights, the Proclamation fomented anger among the settlers along the borderlands, with anger only intensified by the British reinforcement of the Proclamation's land guarantees in the Fort Stanwix Treaty of 1768, as reiterated in the Treaty of Pittsburg, 1775, following repudiation of Lord Dunmore's War for Ohio.[29] Squatting proliferated, notwithstanding. Mainstream historians often describe the settlers as "land-hungry" and leave their analysis at that, with the lingering impression that the settlers were, somehow, victims rushing understandably for succor. "Land hunger" euphemizes and disguises the fact that the reasons the settlers "needed" land was their own fecklessness and greed. Militantly ignorant of land management techniques (most came from the poorest urban centers of England), their very sloppy agricultural practices along with their nutrient-sucking cotton and tobacco crops quickly depleted the land. Instead of conserving their land or improving their practices, plantation owners simply moved west to grab cheap, "fresh" land.[30]

The mythology of the North presented its settlers as mild-mannered agrarians, each industriously farming his little estate with yeomanly resolution, but land greed was as steep in the north as in the south. After the Revolution, in the "West" of the eighteenth century, the DeLanceys and the van Rensselaers in the north, as much as the Harrisons and the Taylors in the south and the West, were exemplars of land greed, busily replicating the landed-wealth model of Europe.[31] In the north, great estates developed, their overlords loathe to share yet speculating and renting rapaciously, ultimately bringing the Anti-Rent Wars of New York on themselves in the 1840s.[32] From the time the Taylors arrived in America, they participated in this land greed. Because they saw land as wealth, in the old European way, they set about laying hold of as much of it as they could.[33]

Landed aristocracy might have flown in the face of Revolutionary principles, but north or south, east or west, becoming rich and powerful through landed wealth motivated the settlers. In the Carolinas, Maryland, Georgia, and Virginia, slave plantation owners presented themselves as aristocrats, yet the majority of what, in 1865, President Andrew Johnson termed the "slave aristocracy" were simply living out their peasants' fantasy of aristocracy as the ability to mistreat "inferiors" with impunity.[34] Reconstructing feudalism in the slave South, they lived out their illusions of wealth and nobility, donning fine clothes and erecting McManor Houses, while perpetuating the crudest conceptions of wealth, servants, and privileges. In 1818, Fordham thus found planters living "in a bad house with a plentiful table," which was "covered three times a day with a great many dishes," with "Brandy, Whisky, and Rum ... always standing at a side table." Planters were "hospitable, but rather ostentatious." Politically, they were "rather apt to censure than to praise," and withal, were "rather bigoted" politically.[35]

The slaveholders' self-concept as feudal nobility was why, in 1822, literary critic William Howard Gardiner urged James Fenimore Cooper to take the romantically feudal model of a Walter Scott novel, for said Gardiner, such a society actually existed in "the high-minded, vainglorious Virginian, living on his plantation in baronial state, an autocrat among his slaves, a nobleman among his peers."[36] It was why Taylor's son, Richard (Dick) Taylor, likened slave-naming to feudal customs.[37] It supplied the illiterate pretensions satirized by Missouri native, Mark Twain, in *Pudd'nhead Wilson*, in the pompously noble names affected by Twain's Missouri settlers: York Leicester Driscoll, Cecil Burleigh Essex, Percy Northumberland Driscoll, Pembroke Howard, and Thomas à Becket Driscoll.[38] Playacting at perquisites, per the enabling tenets of racism, Euro-Southerners concocted chivalric rituals like that detailed in *The House Behind the Cedars*, holding faux medieval pageants featuring a ("white," only) "Queen of Love and Beauty," a title chivalrously bestowed by a local "Sir" This or That.[39] The southern penchant for dueling at the drop of a hat was part of this Wii-play.

The flip side of this pretense was craven fawning over perceived "superiors." Fordham reported that Kentuckians' respect for "talent," "superior knowledge," "age," and "wealth," generally meant that, their "rough and democratic" ways notwithstanding, they toadied to the upper classes, with a "respect even more marked" than met with in England.[40] The real question was, "Shall we have civilization and refinement, or sordid manners and semi-barbarism, till time shall produce so much inequality of condition that the poor man must serve the rich man for his daily bread?" Fordham was not opposed to this outcome.[41]

Western historians portray the Proclamation of 1763 as hand-wringingly unenforceable, but whether its lax implementation stemmed from a lack of ability or a lack of will is debatable. When the British did evict squatters, the Proclamation became a flashpoint of Revolutionary ire because of its supposed "leniency" toward the Indians. In 1763, at the end of the French and Indian War, the Euro-colonists wanted all the Indians killed, not welcomed back into the good graces of Great Britain.[42] The settlers perversely interpreted the Proclamation as Parliament siccing the Indians on them, partly accounting for Thomas Jefferson's wild allegation in the Declaration of Independence that King George III had "endeavored to bring on the inhabitants of our frontiers, the merciless Indian savages."

The Mansfield Decision of 1772 simply added fuel to the Revolutionary fire, but it was neither a bolt from the blue nor intended as a slap at the colonists. The precedents for the Mansfield Decision were set in much earlier rulings by Lord Chief Justice of the King's Bench, Sir John Holt. In 1692, Holt determined that "so soon a negro lands in England, he is free" and then reiterated this tenet in his 1702 decision that "there is no such thing as a slave by the law of England."[43] American settlers were dodging Holt's decisions when they took to calling their slaves, "servants."[44] The next ruling was a mite harder to skirt, however. Lord Mansfield (William Murray, first earl of Mansfield) sat on the King's Bench as Lord Chief Justice from 1756 to 1788, taking his famous swing at slavery in the 1772 case of *Stuart v. Somerset*.

James Somersett, usually given as Somerset, was a slave held by Charles Steuart, typically simplified to Stuart or misspelled as Stewart. Little is known of Somerset. One text characterized him as having been "apprehended in the wilds of Africa by slave dealers and carried to Virginia," where the Virginia slaveholder, Stuart, bought him.[45] In 1769, Stuart took Somerset to London, where abolition sentiment ran high, enabling Somerset to escape only to be retaken by an angry Stuart, who placed him on a slave ship for resale in Jamaica. Refusing to accept his fate, the determined Somerset had managed to make English friends, who sued on his behalf. The case came before Judge Mansfield, who issued a writ of *habeas corpus*, forcing Somerset's removal from the hold of the slave ship.[46]

From 1771 to 1772, the case was vigorously debated, with both parties refusing to settle out of court. Finally on June 22, 1772, based on the precedents of Holt and crying, "*fiat justitia, ruat cœlum*" (let justice be done, though the heavens should fall), Mansfield rendered his decision: "The state of slavery is of such a nature that it is incapable of being introduced on any reasons, moral or political, but only by positive law," which law Mansfield found to be "so odious, that nothing can be suffered to support it." In no uncertain terms, Mansfield declared that slavery was neither "allowed nor approved by the law of England," and thus ordered that "the black must be discharged."[47] Somerset became a free man in that moment.

Legally speaking, Mansfield's *Somerset* decision was a narrow ruling on two scores. First, it made it illegal for a master forcibly to transport a slave from the British realm against the slave's will. Second, the slave in question had the legal right to a writ of *habeas corpus* to prevent a forced removal elsewhere.[48] In neither case was slavery abolished in either Great Britain or its colonies, as Benjamin Franklin observed in eloquent disgust to a friend, an ardent Quaker abolitionist.[49] In 1821, dismissing the Mansfield Decision as flimsy, "moderate" editor of the prestigious and conservative *North American Review*, American Edward Everett sniffed that the *au courant* phrase, "the air of England is too pure for a slave" simply implied that "tobacco and cotton, sugar and coffee" could not be cultivated in Norfolk, England, but that when it could grow in a British colony, Englishmen felt no "scruple" in "resorting to the labor of slaves."[50]

Notwithstanding, across the American colonies, Mansfield was popularly understood to have abolished slavery. Southern slaveholders went berserk. Up to forty-three articles appeared in twenty different papers, with the *Virginia Gazette* alone publishing six stories in 1772, covering the proceedings from the first hearings to the final decision, aghast the whole way. Of course, the gist of the planter argument was that *Somerset* had been wrong-**wrong**-WRONGLY decided.[51] Still, slavers held their breath. Not only did their colonial charters allow them to pass only those laws that comported with British law, as their slave laws now did not, but also the 1766 Declaratory Act had given Parliament complete power to overrule the colonies' laws. Thus, should Parliament follow up on Mansfield by outrightly abolishing slavery—a possibility, given abolition sentiment in London at the time—Southern planters would have gone immediately bankrupt.[52] As late as 1862, slavers were still fuming about Mansfield, declaring *Somerset* to have been an "apt illustration of the inconsistency and effrontery" that had "characterized abolitionism from that day to this."[53]

For their part, the slaves were electrified. They began escaping to England, as did John Christian, rejecting his slave name of Bacchus and changing "a purse of dollars" to a "five Pound Bill," to finance his flight.[54] Some did not even bother with England but simply fled. In 1772, a slave snidely called "Mr. Dublin" by his sometime master, John Riddell, told "the other servants" (that is, slaves) that he had a letter from "Uncle Sommerset" saying that "Lord Mansfield had given them their freedom, received" and that he intended to take it. Riddell was miffed not only that Dublin had departed with his own clothes ("which I don't know he had any right to," snarled Riddell) but also that he had left "without even speaking" to him. Riddell left undisclosed why an escaping slave should confide his plans to his master.[55]

In this hysteria of "white" entitlement defied, the Declaration of Independence erupted in Jefferson's accusation against King George III for having "excited domestic insurrections amongst us." Jefferson's original draft went into considerable detail over this charge. In the ever-popular mode of settler victimhood, Jefferson raged that Great Britain had forced African slavery on the settlers, thereafter (in Mansfield) treacherously "exciting those very people"—the slaves—"to rise in arms among us, and to purchase that liberty of which he ha[d] deprived them, by murdering the people upon whom he ha[d] obtruded them." Jefferson's fellow Revolutionaries made him tone this passage down in the final version, so as not to alienate northern abolitionists like Ben Franklin and John Adams.[56] All the nattering, aside, everyone in the colonies knew that what Judge Mansfield had done was to date-stamp slavery in America so long as Britain ruled it, thus explaining the heavy involvement of southern slavers in the American Revolution. It was not for nothing that the Revolutionary Army was under the command of George Washington, a Virginia planter reportedly holding 400 slaves on 10,000 acres in 1797.[57]

Zachary Taylor's Revolutionary father, Richard Taylor, was as proslavery as his fellow southerners. Originally living on the Hare Forest plantation in Orange County, Virginia, once the war was concluded, like so many fellow veterans, Richard Taylor, now using the militia title of "Colonel," took his 8,163-acre pay of Virginia land warrants to the Dark and Bloody Ground of Kentucke. Using his original down payment of 1,000 warrant acres, Richard Taylor purchased 324 acres of farm land at Beargrass Creek, near Louisville, Kentucky, to start a plantation.[58] His wife Sarah Dabney Strother joined him in 1785, after a grueling, 700- mile trek, crossing the Alleghenies and then navigating two rivers by flatboat while toting three young children, of whom the infant, Zachary, was probably still nursing.[59]

By 1797, the Taylor family plantation consisted of 1,650 acres in Jefferson County, worked by twenty-six slaves.[60] In 1800, Richard Taylor acquired 10,000 acres besides his plantation, and although biographers like to cite the Taylors's log cabin phase, it very quickly gave way to a "large white mansion" called Springfield, which consisted of painted brick.[61] By 1819, Richard Taylor had thirty-seven slaves.[62] While surveying the Old Northwest, Fordham described the typical "wealthy Kentucky farmer" as having 2,000 to 3,000 acres, "but only about 500 cleared for farming," acreage, worked by twenty to thirty slaves.[63] Based on Fordham's description of Kentucky wealth, with 10,000 acres and twenty-six slaves, the Springfield estate made the Taylors some of the richest people in the state and, indeed, in the west.

In Louisville, Richard Taylor added to his martial reputation by becoming a great, so-called Indian-fighter, part of the inch-by-inch conquest of Kentucky.[64] Thereafter, as an upper-crust Virginian turned Kentucky colonel, he took his turn as judge, tax collector at the Port of Louisville, and delegate to the Kentucky State Constitutional Convention. A member of the state electoral college in 1812, he was able to help vote his cousin, James Madison—with whom he was on free, letter writing terms—into presidential office and later cast votes for fellow southerners James Monroe in 1816 and 1820 and Henry Clay in 1824.[65] All of these were slave-booster votes.

Zachary Taylor thus entered manhood elite, yet slimly educated. As his first biographer, Henry Montgomery, put it, in the early nineteenth century, even wealthy Louisville afforded "but few" opportunities to acquire "a practical, much less an ornamental or classical education," by which Montgomery meant a mastery of Latin and Greek.[66] (At the time, a little arithmetic, theology, and reading of "the ancients" in their original Latin or Greek was construed as a gentleman's education.) Although practically no one in Kentucky had a better education than that provided young Taylor by his Connecticut tutor, the first known of Taylor's surviving letters, from June 6, 1808, seconded Montgomery's observation. Accepting Taylor's original commission as a first lieutenant in the Seventh Regiment of the U.S. Army, this letter was "rough and full of misspellings."[67] Taylor was not the only literacy-challenged yet privileged settler around. The U.S. Senate *Journal* recording his commission as first lieutenant in the U.S. Army rendered his name as "Zachariah Taylor."[68] By the time he was promoted to captain in March 1811, someone had corrected the mistake.[69] As time went on and his military duties required letters and reports, Taylor learned to write somewhat creditably, although those of his adjuncts who were genuinely literate, particularly Captain William Bliss, composed the clear and vigorous dispatches signed by Taylor.[70]

Due to the Taylors' "powerful family connections," in 1808, then president Thomas Jefferson awarded Taylor his first lieutenant's commission in the U.S. Army, despite the fact that Taylor was entirely untrained as a soldier at the time.[71] By 1812, Taylor was serving under another untried officer, General William Henry Harrison, in the Northwest Territories. During the War of 1812, Taylor was promoted to captain by then president James Madison, Taylor's second cousin.[72] (Robert E. Lee, later general of the Confederacy, was Taylor's third cousin.[73]) In his new military post in 1809, Taylor wound up in New Orleans under General James Wilkinson, that mammoth of iniquity, theoretically, to help thwart dark British designs on the city.[74] In fact, the army was present as part of the preliminaries to the Creek War, thus dropping Taylor squarely into the feverish camp of the southern land-jobbers, just as one of their most ambitious schemes was underway. In 1811, Taylor even traveled to Frederick, Maryland, to act as a character witness for Wilkinson during the court-martial for his part in the Burr Conspiracy.[75] Before Americans learned to stay mum about their unearned legs up on power, such oligarchic "connections" as Taylor's were considered lineal points of personal merit.

Taylor inherited his parents' taste for slave plantation ownership as well as his father's 324 acres at Beargrass Creek upon his marriage on June 21, 1810, to Margaret (Peggy) Mackall Smith, the educated daughter of a prominent Maryland family.[76] It is probable that in marrying Taylor, Smith had thought that she was setting up eventual life as a plantation wife, but Peggy Taylor wound up traipsing about from post to backcountry post as an army spouse, bearing five daughters and one son. During what was supposed to have been a respite at Taylor's Louisiana plantation in 1820, she came down with a "bilious fever," which today is equated with malaria. By September 8, she was almost dead, and two of her daughters did die of the 1820 malaria. Peggy Taylor never fully recovered but for the rest of her life remained in delicate health.[77]

For a brief interlude from 1815 to 1816, Taylor did attempt to farm at Beargrass Creek. Although some biographers present this career switch from army officer to planter as an active choice, in fact, it signaled trouble for Taylor in the army.[78] Taylor had made it to the rank of brevet major on February 1, 1815, when his clear sailing to promotion was socked in the jaw.[79] Although it is true that Congress severely reduced army forces from 10,000 regulars and 50,000 volunteers down to just 10,000 regulars following the War of 1812, it is not true that this was why Taylor was also reduced in rank to captain. He was always regular army, so his rank reduction was not attendant upon those rescissions.[80] Instead, Taylor had been "busted" back down to captain pretty clearly because of his superior officer, the peevish colonel William P. Anderson.

In a letter of October 14, 1815, to Secretary of War James Monroe, Anderson slammed Taylor as lightly countermanding his orders, after Taylor was accused of hampering recruiting efforts by Anderson's buddy, Captain W. N. Wilkinson, a personal enemy of Taylor.[81] Taylor inquired of the adjutant general whether Anderson had permanently shredded his reputation with the War Department and received the quizzical reply on November 19, 1815, that "no complaints" had been received from anyone who had the ability to ruin Taylor's "good reputation." The adjutant general then directly named Anderson, saying that Anderson was being sent south and Taylor north, thus separating the two in a backhanded acknowledgment that Anderson was not well regarded and had, indeed, been the rub.[82]

Not willing to take his demotion lying down, Taylor visited Washington, D.C. in company with two fellow officers to pursue the matter of their rank reductions. Taylor defended himself, bringing his cause to the attention of his cousin, President Madison.[83] Madison stood up for Taylor, questioning the Military Board of the Organization of the Army, which had lowered Taylor's rank. Writing on May 10, 1815, to Alexander James Dallas, then acting secretary of war, Madison noted that he was returning letters, including one from "Major Taylor," going on to remind Dallas that Taylor was "the first officer that was breveted" in the war, that is, Taylor had received a battlefield promotion for meritorious conduct for his "defence of Fort Harrison." Although achieved "on an obscure theatre" of war, Taylor's accomplishment had "probably not been exceeded in brilliancy by any affair that ha[d] occurred." Wrapping up, and sounding a mite piqued, Madison proclaimed that, had Taylor been more conspicuously assigned, he would have "obtained" an even "higher grade" than brevet major.[84] Madison's appeal had no immediate effect, although it did grind through the bowels of the bureaucracy with eventual consequence.

Family feeling had led Madison to gush somewhat over the top in claiming that no other action had exceeded Taylor's brilliance at Fort Harrison (Thermopylae springs to mind), but Taylor did prove himself in that engagement. Because William Henry Harrison had previously described "Captain Z. Taylor" as "amiable" and a "good officer," who had made the previously disastrous Fort Knox "defensible," on March 7, 1812, Secretary of War William Eustis informed Harrison that he had sent Taylor to take command of Fort Harrison.[85] By May 1812, Taylor was informing Harrison that *Tenskwatawa* was in the vicinity with 500 Indians, his forces steadily growing.[86] On August 9, at some risk to his messengers, Taylor sent warning to Harrison of impending attack.[87]

Messengers whom Harrison sent with a reply were entirely unable to pass through to Fort Harrison.[88] On September 2, somewhat prematurely, Taylor reported to John Gibson, acting governor of Indiana Territory, that all was quiet around his fort.[89]

On September 3, the attack on Fort Harrison opened with the killing of two locals making hay about 400 yards distant from the fort. This was followed "late on the 4th" by about forty Shawnee, including women, who approached the fort, under a white flag, their speaker requesting their food annuity.[90] Under orders from Harrison to be stingy, Taylor had refused to supply the Miami chiefs on August 9, 1812, even though a large enough supply was on hand "to feed a considerable body of Indians for a month," Taylor assured Harrison.[91] Interestingly, following the attack on October 14, on orders from Eustis, Gibson reported having distributed "part of the Indian Annuities" to the regiment at Fort Harrison.[92] This strongly suggests that the attack came largely due to Harrison's refusal to distribute annuity goods in August.

Fort Harrison must have appeared to be an easy target. Taylor's militiamen were ill, with only "10 or 15" of them able-bodied at the time, while Taylor himself was just recovering from "a very severe attack of the fever" which left him barely ambulatory on September 3.[93] The Miami and Shawnee were not in much better shape, as "a severe famine afflicted" the Wabash nations through the spring of 1812, turning Harrison's refusal of food in August downright sinister.[94] Having adhered to his orders to withhold the food, Taylor was awakened, "about 11 o'clock" the night of the fourth, by a sentinel's rifle fire. Rushing out of his quarters and into the fort's yard, Taylor learned from his sergeant that the Indians had just set fire to the "lower block house," where the "property of the contractor," that is, the refused annuities, were stored.[95]

Because the ground-level part of the blockhouse held the salt rations, farm animals had previously "licked several holes" in it to get at the salt. It was through these cavities that the Shawnee, Wea, and Miami introduced the fire, which quickly roared up to the roof. As a pitched battle raged, Taylor organized a bucket brigade to douse the flames, but rattled by the word, "fire," the soldiers panicked and in their confusion were "very slow" to obey his orders, proving worse than useless, as much from despair as from illness. Now, Taylor saw the flames reaching for the barracks. It flashed on him that, were the roof of that portion of the fort thrown off and its joists heavily watered, the flames could not proceed through it. This would leave only the twenty-foot gap of what had been the blockhouse as an access point for the attackers, a space that might be effectively defended by his fifteen active men, were barricades thrown up. Rousing the soldiers from their lethargy with a pep talk, Taylor put this plan into effect, and it worked, although fighting continued till morning.[96]

For all the fire and fury, Taylor reported only three casualties, with one dead and two wounded.[97] Taylor believed that the Indians "suffered smartly" but had no casualty count on them, because they were "so numerous"—indeed, "several hundred"—as to have been able to carry away all their dead and wounded.[98] This casualty estimate is very likely, as *Tenskwatawa* frowned upon Western weapons, so that the starving Indians had primarily brought bows, arrows, and knives to the fight, whereas Taylor's men had firearms.

The fact that the salt reserves were the first burned must have gratified *Tenskwatawa's* followers, given his interdictions of salt. Unable to access the fort, the attackers killed all the settlers' horses and "a number of the hogs," in full view of those in the fort, for another part of *Tenskwatawa's* philosophy was to destroy the settlers' environmentally intrusive animals. Finally, the Miami Confederacy fighters made off with all sixty-five head of cattle, along with uncounted oxen, apparently making this exception to *Tenskwatawa's* "kill" policy on farm animals because they were desperate for food. This war on farm animals left the settlers with nothing to eat but "green corn."[99]

The attack seems to have been more intent on obtaining the denied food than on destroying the fort. When the Miami Confederacy left, the settlers were the ones without food. Although Westerners have been slow to realize this, it is a standing convention of Indigenous etiquette to teach offenders the harm that they have caused by doing unto the perpetrators what the perpetrators had just done unto them.[100] It should be noted that, in keeping with this convention, the original forty delegates embodied a warning of what was to come should the delegation leave without its annuity food, but nothing in Taylor's report indicated that he understood that. Apparently, Eustis did get the point, however, as in effect, he countermanded Harrison by ordering the annuities distributed following the attack.[101]

This action notwithstanding, at least for the time being, and with Taylor unwilling to serve at the lowered rank of captain, with his honorable discharge of June 15, 1815, in hand, he left the army to live at Beargrass as a corn- and tobacco-raising, slave plantation master.[102] Although biographer Elbert Smith found Taylor's assertions of planter bliss at Beargrass "entirely credible," the descent from major to captain pretty clearly rankled him.[103] His neighbor and childhood playmate, George Croghan, who had accomplished a similar, nearly impossible defense of Fort Stephenson—in violation of direct orders, no less— had ascended to, and remained, a colonel, after all.[104] Taylor might have brought the Croghan example up in Washington, D.C. accounting for Madison's allusion to commanders of better known forts receiving more consideration than Taylor for similar feats.

Taylor nevertheless tried to put a good face on the matter in public. His letter of April 25, 1816, remarked on the corn and tobacco he had planted, as he assured a relative that he did not "regreat" having abandoned the army for the Beargrass plantation.[105] In isolation, this sounds upbeat, but in context, the relative in question was U.S. Army major Taylor Berry, which rank had just been actively denied Taylor, leaving the contentment to sound suspiciously like face-saving.[106] Inklings of Taylor's resentment are reinforced by another letter written on April 12, 1817— after he had regained his rank—in which he essentially confessed to boredom with farming, a topic he found insufficiently interesting to discuss.[107]

On May 17, 1816, the U.S. Army announced vacancies, and Madison compiled his preferences for filling them, including Zachary Taylor at the proposed rank of major in the Third Regiment of the U.S. Army.[108] This list had yet to receive

Senate consideration or confirmation, so Richard Taylor embarked on a full-court press on behalf of his son, appealing to Cousin Madison. He sent his young son, Joseph, to Washington, D.C. with a letter dated July 10, from their mutual cousin, James Taylor, an even closer relative of Madison than himself, assuring Madison that, should Zachary Taylor accept the new appointment, he would re-present an "acquisition to the service."[109] On July 23, 1816, fearful that Joseph was too "young & Inexperienced" to manage the lobbying effectively on his own, Richard Taylor reiterated to Madison that his son, Zachary, although retained by the army, had been shunted from "the Infantry to the Artillery" and at a "Lower grade" than he had held in the infantry. "I confess to a wish," said Taylor, "if he reejons" the army, that it be at his former rank of major.[110] These efforts bore fruit on December 9, 1816, when Madison's list of recess appoint-ments, including Taylor at the rank of major, was formally submitted to the Senate and then approved by it, six days later. Taylor was offered reinstatement in the army at the rank of major, with seniority in the rank backdated to May 15, 1814, and he took it in a heartbeat.[111]

Thus began Taylor's sojourns in Wisconsin and Florida, where his primary actions included the Black Hawk War of 1832 and the second Seminole War, in which he served from 1837 to 1840, both treated in the chapters to follow. Regarding his Wisconsin and Florida military service, Taylor has been cried up as one of those ubiquitous, settler-anointed "friends of the Indian." A twentieth-century biographer praised Taylor's "Indian Policy" while president as "both real-istic and fair."[112] A different twentieth-century biographer characterized Taylor as "uniformly fair and firm" in his dealings with the "aborigines" while he was U.S. Indian agent at Prairie du Chien, otherwise known as a homeland of the Sauk, Meskwaki, and Lakota peoples.[113] A eulogy from 1850, claimed that Taylor had "not only conquered the Indians, but he secured their good will, and by protect-ing their rights, made them feel that he was their friend."[114] Claiming friendship toward the Indians was a standard bamboozlement, which should not be taken at face value, today, for even Andrew Jackson, in his Second Annual Message of Congress of December 6, 1830, had the audacity to claim that "no one" could "indulge a more friendly feeling" toward the Indians than he.[115] All Western eval-uations of Taylor regarding Indian affairs need to be revisited, using Indian over settler input, not the least because "fair" and "firm" are authoritarian descriptors assuming settler rights over Indian lives.

In comparison with rabid "Indian-haters"—an authentic and proud self-designation of the day—Taylor was not as frightening as some, because full-on Indian-haters were homicidal maniacs. Fulsome praise was nonetheless heaped on them in settler tracts. Indian killers were described as in "Judge" James Hall's *Indian Hater* (1829) as nobly motivated, or excused as poor things simply in need of a wife, hearth, and home to quiet their murderous impulses, as in Herman Melville's purportedly funny "Metaphysics of Indian-hating" (1857).[116] To insist, therefore, that others caused the Indians more harm than Taylor, ergo Taylor was good, is to minimize with energy by conjuring up a "least worst" argument. Yes, in contrast to racially motivated, psychopathic killers like Wetzel, Owens,

Murphy, and Williamson, any sane person comes as a relief, but the valid comparison of rectitude is not to culturally enabled serial killers. The proper comparison is to civil norms of ethics and morality, while considering all injury to Others as focal, not incidental. At that point, Taylor's multiple military assaults on the Indians, including in the War of 1812, the Black Hawk War, and the second Seminole War mount up to something other than friendly paternalism toward the Indians.

In support of Taylor as Indian-friendly, modern biographers call up his supposedly benign actions, like creating a "school" for Ho-Chunk ("Winnebago") children in Wisconsin.[117] Context obviates insinuations of kindly intent, however. In the Ho-Chunk instance, Taylor was not making any personal, charitable choice in establishing a school for Ho-Chunk children, for its creation was attendant upon Article 4 of the 1832 Winnebago Treaty. It provided an annual $3,000 (of Ho-Chunk money) over twenty-seven years for "clothing, board, and lodging" of those Ho-Chunk children "voluntarily" sent. The school was to teach skills "according to" the children's "sexes," such as "arithmetic" and "agriculture" to the boys and "carding, spinning, weaving, and sewing" to the girls, along with "such other branches of useful knowledge as the President of the United States" might "prescribe."[118] The president of the United States in 1832 was Andrew Jackson.

Almost exclusively under the direction of missionaries, with the willingness of children's families to send them forth residing entirely in the eye of the beholder, these governmental "Indian schools" forced Christianity and Westernization on Indians. The children were separated from their families for long periods, up to the entirety of their formative years, which is why these were boarding, not day, schools. Children were typically treated brutally, in a pattern set well before Richard Henry Pratt ever envisioned his 1879, military-style Carlisle Indian School.[119] This was why, in 1842, the Sauk chief *Keokuk* vehemently resisted the institution of "Indian" schools. In a speech to Hartley Crawford, then commissioner of Indian Affairs, *Keokuk* rejected "with concentrated bitterness" a proposed school, calling it *"Kichee-Waleshi—very, very bad!"* There were "no English words" able to "convey the indignant, utter scorn and hatred" that *Keokuk* "threw into his words," said a witness to the scene.[120] Thus, however laudable "school" may sound to the Western ear, to Indians, past and present, it is a trauma trigger. Using the forced assimilation of Indian boarding schools to put Taylor in the least-worst category is disingenuous.

The sweep of Taylor's life needs to be considered, as well. He was not the "gentleman farmer" of biographical lore but a large-scale, slave plantation owner and high-ranking army officer whose job it was to kill people, primarily Indians, in the way of U.S. expansion.[121] It was no accident that the highest-ranking officers were almost all slaveholders, for expansion from 1783 to 1850 primarily benefited the slavocracy. As an army officer, Zachary Taylor was in the constant company of pro-slavery soldiers and settlers, some of them well known to history.

In his command capacity at Fort Crawford, Taylor was, for instance, the superior officer of Lieutenant Jefferson Davis, future president of the Confederacy, who married Taylor's daughter, Sarah Knox Taylor (Knox) in 1835. Young Mrs. Davis died of malaria within three months of their marriage, but Davis remained close to his brother-in-law, elevating Taylor's son, Dick Taylor, to the rank of brigadier general of the Confederate Army. Rising from there to lieutenant general, Dick Taylor was the dead last Confederate general to surrender when the South was defeated in the Civil War.[122] At last report, a monument to him stands outside of an American Legion Post in Pleasant Hill, Louisiana. Zachary Taylor's grandson and Dick Taylor's nephew, John Taylor Wood, became a Confederate naval officer. Wood was "the last man to leave Jefferson Davis" before his 1865 capture by the Union Army.[123] The Taylors were up to their eyebrows in plantation slavery and its slave aristocracy.

A least-worst defense for Taylor here holds that an enduring animosity existed between Zachary Taylor and Jefferson Davis, a tale seeded by the fact that Taylor initially objected to Davis marrying his daughter, Knox. Because Taylor's opposition to his daughter's marriage with a future Confederate president plays well today, some stretch the story to claim that Taylor despised Davis, outrightly.[124] On the contrary, one of Taylor's only known letters mentioning the proposed marriage undercuts claims of his supposed personal antagonism toward Davis. In it, Taylor went out of his way to state that he had "no personal objections to Lieutenant Davis."[125] Facts support this claim. Taylor had made West-Point graduate Davis his acting adjutant at Fort Crawford and, during the Black Hawk War, charged Davis with guarding the all-important chief, *Makataimeshekiakiak* ("Black Hawk"), then captive at Black Rock.[126] Davis was with Taylor during the Mexican-American War, at Monterrey and Buena Vista.[127] When Taylor "accidentally" ran into Davis in Baton Rouge on February 25, 1845, the two were friendly, with Taylor offering his congratulations to Davis on his second marriage to Varina Howell.[128] In the spring of 1847, Taylor visited the plantations of both Jefferson Davis and his brother, Joseph Davis.[129] Finally, Davis attended Taylor's state funeral in 1850.[130]

As Taylor told his friend, "Colonel" Hercules Louis Dousman, part owner of the American Fur Company, his concern was not about Davis but for his daughter, Knox, Taylor's favorite, whom he had carefully educated in Cincinnati.[131] He knew the regret, he said, of having "scarcely" known his children, or they, him, essentially having left his wife to raise them all alone.[132] Besides, Knox was used to a graceful life, increasing Taylor's anxiety about her living in rough-hewn forts, married to a poor lieutenant lacking hope of promotion in peacetime.[133] Taylor did not wish to see Knox dragged from one miserable post to the next, as his own wife had been. He had already watched with anxiety the wedded life of another daughter, Anne Mackall Taylor, who had married a post surgeon, Robert C. Wood in 1829.[134]

After these initial fears abated, and Knox's affection for Davis remained, the Taylors relented. An extant letter shows Peggy Taylor actively helping Knox put together her trousseau, and it was Taylor, himself, who arranged for Knox to have been married at her Aunt Elizabeth Taylor's plantation, Beechland, in Louisville, where Knox was attended by her sister Margaret Wood. Knox and her mother continued in an "affectionate" relationship thereafter.[135] Davis resigned from the army before the wedding to take up plantation life upon his marriage, that is, he accommodated all of the Taylors' objections.[136] Dousman attested, "for a fact" that Taylor "held Lieut. Davis in high regard and had given his consent" to Knox's marriage. Dick Taylor remained a lifelong friend of Davis, while Knox's sister, Betty, directly stated that there was "never any estrangement" between the Taylors and the Davises.[137] An 1846 letter from Zachary Taylor displayed no animosity, whatsoever.[138] In fact, Taylor relented so much on his stance against his daughters as army wives that he did not even try to stop his remaining daughter, Elizabeth (Betty), from likewise marrying into army life.[139] Direct, primary evidence simply does not support sensational rumors that Taylor despised Davis.

Tales of Taylor behaving like the boneheaded father of Gothic literature came from the major bonehead in the affair, Davis. In a strange, nearly unreadable "love" letter to Knox composed in the purplest of prose on December 16, 1834, Davis depicted her as a "sacrifice" to her parents' desire that she marry someone else, whom she must "despise."[140] Humorless, Davis always overreacted—for instance, fainting dead away many years after Knox's death upon finding a slipper of hers in an old trunk—and he pretty regularly projected his reactions onto others.[141] All of the overwrought depictions of the affair came from him and the then-young people of his coterie at Fort Crawford, eagerly playing out the script of young lovers evading despotic fathers to meet clandestinely at friends' army tents, culminating in a desperate elopement that assuredly never happened.[142]

Davis's second wife, Varina, further muddied the historical record by relating these exaggerated tales from her husband and his friends as straightforward facts. This included her claim that the Taylor family rift that had "never" been "healed during the life of Mrs. Davis."[143] Other claims had some slim basis in fact but were hyped into melodrama. The Davis faction held, for instance, that the supposed chasm between Taylor and Davis had opened during a court-martial taking place a little after Taylor had nixed Davis's proposal to Knox. As one of the sitting "judges," on one question of the proceedings, Lieutenant Davis had sided against Taylor and with an enemy of Taylor's.[144]

Taylor could take offense, as shown in the Anderson affair, but it would not have been unlike Davis to have sided against Taylor out of sheer spite, whereas the Anderson business was of a decidedly different, harmful, and potentially permanent nature, deserving of the alarm it aroused. More likely, if it was a court-martial that made Taylor hesitate over Davis, then it was Davis's own February 1835, court-martial for gross insubordination, of which he was found not guilty after a six-day trial. It was not Taylor who had laid the charges. Nevertheless, if anything, the description of the charges supports an interpretation of young Davis as rash, flying off the handle at the merest provocation without regard to place or propriety.[145] Another story told to "St. Louis newspapers" by John Gibson in 1890 reinforces this sense of Davis as headlong and injudicious. Upon Taylor's initial refusal of Davis as a son-in-law, the young man intended to challenge the reluctant Taylor to a duel. Davis was dissuaded from this only when the man he asked to act as his second, Captain Samuel MacRee (also rendered "McRee"), pointed out that it was "absurd to plan the death" of his proposed father-in-law.[146] Given Davis's impetuosity, this story is not unlikely.

A final, fairly sordid tale of Davis published in 1878 by Nehemiah Matson has been picked up ever since by Taylor and Davis biographers. It is illustrative of both men in regard to Indians. Shortly before the Black Hawk war, a French fur trader Pierre Bulbena and his Potawatomi wife were celebrating their mixed-race daughter's marriage with a large dance, to which four officers belonging to Fort Smith were invited on the spur of the moment. A guest at the Bulbena reception, named Kilgore, told Matson that two of the officers were Taylor and Davis. The dance was partly Potawatomi and partly French, and a Potawatomi niece of Mrs. Bulbena in attendance performed Potawatomi dances "with much grace."[147]

With the reception heading into the wee hours, Davis fell somewhat into his cups and began to dance with the niece. Although dances followed a set order at the time, Davis ignored that, substituting waltzes for quadrilles, because the waltz allowed him to embrace the niece around the waist, but he also occasionally broke free to leap, holler, and otherwise insultingly pretend to dance, "Indian-style." Taylor and his captain were supposed to have sat in the corner, "splitting their sides with laughter" at Davis's antics. At some point, Davis began groping the niece. Insulted, she immediately pulled away, finding her brother to appeal for help. Also drunk, the brother accosted Davis, pulling his nose and apprising him of his bad behavior. Pushing the brother, Davis drew his pistol, to which the brother replied by pulling out his knife. Of course, the entire party was thrown into confusion, ending only when Taylor jumped between the men, separating them. Essentially tossed out of the party (although Matson made the departure sound like the officers' idea), they quickly left to continue their entertainment at a nearby establishment.[148] Clearly, this story did no honor to any of the officers involved, although in 1878, settlers were supposed to construe it as hilarious.

In 1955, Davis biographer Hudson Strode dismissed this story as "decidedly suspect," claiming that Davis never overindulged in liquor, but that did not stop Strode from retelling the tale.[149] Similarly, Davis biographer Felicity Allen dredged up and summarized the story, only to reject it as "highly dubious," this time, based on Davis's religiosity.[150] Since then, modern Taylor biographers have either carefully avoided it or canvassed it only to wave it off as "fantastic" or "unconfirmed," while offensively characterizing the Potawatomi niece as a "squaw," a word from the Iroquois meaning "cunt" not "woman."[151] Notwithstanding Western reluctance to take the tale seriously, there are cultural and religious ideologies, social permissions, and practices of the day regarding drink, religion, and seigneurial rights that lend the story weight.

First, spurning distilled alcohol was often socially affected at this time as an outward signal of class standing, although how well the pose stuck, especially at late-night, mixed-race, drunken parties out West, is highly questionable. Forced on men of standing in the east, this teetotaler convention was called "The Pledge." Essentially, men signed a contract solemnly promising never to touch liquor. In practice, this worked out about as well as the "Purity Pledges" of sexual abstinence taken by modern teenagers. Taylor contemporary James Fenimore Cooper railed against The Pledge as the purest hypocrisy, declaring that a "man may be as abstemious as an anchorite, and get no credit for it, unless 'he sign the pledge;' or signing the pledge, he may get fuddled in corners, and be cited as a miracle of sobriety."[152] Moreover, there were strong differences in attitude toward The Pledge between rural and urban populations, generally, with rural areas greatly relaxed about it.[153] Thus, to offer a *prima facie* defense of Davis as a teetotaler is to be a bit credulous.

Second, planters had their own version of Christianity, one specifically justifying slavery.[154] "Bound labor," pronounced one defense of planter Christianity, was "not disapproved by true Christianity." It was only false, "English Christianity" that "meddled" with the true variety to push (British) abolition. The "pernicious influence" of such "Christian Don Quixotism" needed to be checked promptly by the clergy, for slavery was the law, and "Christ came not to destroy the law, but to fulfill it."[155] Being overtly Christian was thus political for southerners. Planters played vigorously at piety as a slave-boosting tactic, its intensity of display flowering in proportion to their slaveholding. Notably, when slaves attempted to hold their own, northern-style evangelical services—the "Don Quixote" variety of Christianity—planters firmly outlawed the services.[156] Davis's purported piety, then, had fraught contextual dimensions that the religious defense ignores, for motives other than virtue were at stake in Davis's public displays of devotion to Southern Christianity.

Third and most importantly to the Davis-Taylor-Bulbena niece affair, due to pervasive racist ideology, all Indian women were viewed as sexually available, through an extension of "white" male privilege. In particular, the rape of "inferior" Others was construed as part of the settlers' feudal seigneurial rights.[157] The right of rape might have been one *droit de cuissage* not mentioned in polite company, but it was one, nevertheless, eagerly taken up by slave masters. Under *le droit de cuissage*, the "seigneur" (noble) had a "right" to any virgin peasant woman on his lands, typically on or before her wedding night, that is, the noble had first crack at her, before her fiancé.[158] Although this "right" theoretically "fell into disuse" (*"tombé en désuétude"*) with the rise of the rights of man in the latter eighteenth century, among atavistic Southern planters, this "right" made slave and Indian women constant objects of sexual assault, from the moment they turned fourteen.[159]

High incidences of settler, especially soldier, rape making recurrent stories like Matson's of Indian women being sexually assaulted by drunken settlers during public events fairly commonplace.[160] Notably, when Taylor intervened, it was not as the young woman was being assaulted but only when Davis was confronted about his assault by an Indian man with a weapon. It is common, if too-seldom discussed, knowledge that rape of Indian women, as well as kidnap of Indian women for the purpose of rape and murder, was "common practice on every American frontier."[161] Matson's story has, then, cultural weight behind it, so that lightly waving it off based solely on the supposed character of the officers involved effectively lets prominent, upscale settler men off the hook without inquiry.

Seigneurial rights was prominent throughout the South, so that rape was an open secret on slave plantations. When pressed, as were Thomas Jefferson and his kin from 1802 to 1807 about "Dusky Sal" Hemings's children, it was common to mumble, be affronted, and as a last resort, throw the blame on feckless nephews, for the planter was never acknowledged to have fathered children with his "plantation wife."[162] As Confederate diarist Mary Boykin Miller Chesnut recorded in 1861, even when the "unfortunate results" of the slaver's "bad ways" were not promptly sold, his "wife and daughters" were "supposed never to dream" of what was "as plain before their eyes as sunlight," so that the patriarch might continue being praised as "the model of all saintly goodness."[163]

For all the minimizing of Taylor's Southernness, it would appear that he, too, had a plantation wife, Sally. "Granny Coates," the grandmother of William Arthur Taylor (b. 1944), retained her family slave narratives, telling her grandson that while in New Orleans, Zachary Taylor purchased a Caribbean "mulatto" woman. She gave birth in 1835 to a boy named William Henry Taylor, who was eventually to become the valet of his father, Zachary Taylor. When Taylor became president, William Henry was not allowed to accompany him to Washington, D.C. said Granny Coates. Instead, Taylor sent his son to Ontario, Canada, with some traveling diplomats. William Henry remained in Canada to marry and raise his family, whose descendants included his daughter, Granny Coates, and his great-grandson, William Arthur Taylor. Attempting to locate Zachary Taylor's plantation records, William Arthur Taylor discovered what all biographers had found before him, that Taylor's papers had been destroyed by the Union Army. William Arthur Taylor did, however, find records of his great-grandfather in Canada and a Census confirming that William Henry Taylor was black and born in the United States around 1835.[164]

Interestingly in this regard, Zachary Taylor did not typically keep house slaves, putting all but two in his fields. These two, named Sally and Will, he always had with him. According to an eyewitness account, Will had considerable latitude of behavior allowed him, although this Will was around thirty years old in 1829.[165] Especially in the Deep South, it was commonplace for children fathered by the slaver to be presented as the children of their mother's slave husband.[166] This again followed the old feudal custom of *le droit de cuissage* or seigneurial rights.

Importantly in this regard, Taylor was a large-scale plantation owner and slaver. Throughout his army career, Taylor invested heavily in land, his seed money for the ventures originally acquired by selling his Beargrass plantation "at a handsome profit."[167] In two payments in 1823 and 1824, he purchased his 163-acre Feliciana plantation, straddling the border of Mississippi and Louisiana.[168] By 1830, Taylor was so rich from the slave system that, despite having lost $20,000 (or about $548,000 in today's money) in the Panic of 1819 by cosigning for friends' debts, he did not go under financially but simply had to rearrange his planned retirement from the military.[169] In 1831, Taylor purchased 130 acres in Wilkinson County, Mississippi, near the Feliciana plantation.[170] In 1841, he consolidated his Deep South plantations by purchasing a plantation outside of Rodney, Mississippi.[171] Although floods wiped out his cotton crops and prices collapsed, making this Mississippi plantation a failure, he still owned it at his death.[172]

Taylor also made his son, Dick, a large-scale plantation master. As an eight-year-old at Fort Crawford during the Knox affair, Dick was described as a "lubberly sort of a boy."[173] Apparently, he was not more promising at twenty-one. Worried because his adult son was living a life of aimless leisure, in 1846, Taylor wrote his wife that although he would "do all" in his "power" to help his son, he urgently wanted him to be "engaged in some pursuit or other." Taylor ended by crying, "Anything but idleness!"[174] During Taylor's brief tenure as president, the idleness had not abated, so in conjunction with his son (and for his son) he bought, yet another plantation, this one the 1,000-acre Fashion sugar plantation in Louisiana, which he turned over entirely to Dick.[175] Dick Taylor not only ran his father's Cypress Grove plantation but quickly took over the sugar plantation for himself.[176] When Taylor died in office, his estate was worth $140,000 or almost $5,000,000, today.[177] This considerable wealth allowed him to keep his unproductive plantation in Mississippi while financing his son's ascent to plantation slaveholding as a Confederate general.

Although skirted by Taylor's biographers as pure land investments, these plantations represented quite an investment in chattel slavery. There is no precise count—all of Taylor's records were burned by the Union Army when it destroyed Dick Taylor's Baton Rouge plantation, where they were stored—but it is known that, when he died, Taylor "owned" up to 150 slaves, scattered among his plantations.[178] In an additional least-worst contention, Euro-biographers downplay Taylor's trafficking in human beings with the gloss of Taylor as a "compassionate master," who although not freeing his slaves in his will, required in it that they be neither overworked nor neglected in old age.[179] It is not unimportant, however, that all the testimony about Taylor's paternal nurture came from settlers and European visitors disposed to praise him. By way of nuance, in describing the settlers of Kentucky in 1818, despite his general assertion of gentle slavery, Fordham remarked that the "Respectable families from Kentucky" were "accustomed to treat their Slaves with severity."[180] The Taylors were a primary example of Kentucky-bred slaveholders, while Mississippi was not known for its considerate masters.

Accounts of Kentucky slavery second Fordham on its severity. Harry Smith of Nelson County, Kentucky, was born in 1815 and lived as a slave on the plantation of Misha Midcalf, a planter who maintained a large "hotel" to accommodate slave traders and the chained slaves they dragged with them to and from New Orleans.[181] As a child, Smith watched Midcalf take Smith's mother, along with Midcalf's own son by a slave and two other young slaves, to strip and whip them all, in full view of the local highway. Smith recalled his mother, tied to a locust tree, "begging Massa not to kill her" as he mercilessly beat her. Terrified, young Harry took up the same pleading that Midcalf not kill his mother, but to no avail. Midcalf delivered 100 lashes to the sobbing woman, before turning with equal cruelty on the children.[182]

Smith also described the omnipresent Kentucky "patrols" or roving bands of vigilantes, typically composed of drunken, lower-class settlers. As described by Kentucky slave Francis Fedric, patrolmen were deputized annually to roam about, policing and beating any slaves they found without a "pass," that is, a planter's permission to be off-plantation.[183] Smith described the patrols as perfectly willing to beat slaves who had the passes, as well. When Smith was a young man at one dance of about 150 slaves in Louisville, patrols seized and whipped fifty of them, *en masse*, alleging that they were without passes. One of the patrol's favorite tools, which patrolmen always carried with them, said Smith, was the "cane," being "an iron rod with a large head to knock negroes down with."[184]

Then, there was the slave born in 1814 in Bowling Green Circuit, Kentucky, whom it amused someone to name Andrew Jackson. After being shuttled about from master to master, for such reasons as to settle debts idiotically incurred by the planter, Jackson was put into the tobacco fields and ordered "to enrich" the planter by producing "a family of young slaves" with a slave woman.[185] Should Jackson refuse to bring babies into the criminal system of slavery, he was to be sold to a chain gang for transport to a slave market in the Deep South. Refusing to suffer the indignities of his lot any longer, Jackson escaped, only to have been run down by dogs accompanied by patrolmen on horseback. The drunken patrol first compelled him to pray for them. Then, during Jackson's forced march back to slavery, the patrolmen "drank freely" and "to amuse themselves or to torture me," Jackson recounted, "made me run, or rack along, with cords around my knees, and my arms fastened behind, laughing and harrassing my feelings as much as possible whenever they met any one."[186] Many, many more such accounts exist, and none of them portray the easy, friendly slavery conjured up by apologists for slavery. From early infancy on, Taylor grew up on one of these Kentucky slave plantations and became a Deep South plantation owner, himself.[187]

As compared to Kentucky, the conditions of slavery in the Deep South were only worse. In his slave narrative, Charlie Moses recalled that his planter, Jim Rankin, put all of his slaves into the field, because he had paid "good money" for them, and "Niggers" were "meant to work." It is not unimportant here to recall that Taylor, likewise, kept all but two of his slaves in the field. There was no "meaner man in the world," said Moses. Rankin would "beat, knock, kick, kill" his slaves. He whipped his slaves until some just "lay down to die." After the whippings, Rankin would kick his victims "'round in the dust." Moses cried out, "I hates him! I hates him!"[188]

In his narrative, William Wells Brown gave a sampling of news clippings from Mississippi and environs. One advertisement for a runaway woman and her two children casually stated that shortly before they fled, the planter had "burnt her on the left side of her face," trying to brand an "M" on her cheek. She successfully resisted. Her eldest boy, seven years old, was a "mulatto," meaning the planter's or his kin's son, but the five-year-old was "black." This information was given to the *North Carolina Standard* by way of identification not as comprehension of why she might have escaped with her boys.[189] Children were not immune from extreme cruelty, as St. Louis newspapers revealed. One little girl, whose age was not disclosed, was "tied to a tree from Monday to Friday" denied food yet left exposed to the elements the whole time, while being "whipped daily." The inquest found "the flesh on her back and limbs was beaten to jelly," with evidence of blunt-force trauma to her head. The child died in agony. The wife of the planter "renting" the child was known to have been responsible for the murder but was acquitted at trial.[190] Wells also included news stories of the sorts of punishments visited on slaves in Mississippi accused of murder: the men were burned alive. One in Union County, Mississippi, who managed to pull free of his bindings and leap from the flames, was "picked up by two or three" spectators and "thrown again into the fire and consumed."[191]

All of this, despite the laws of Mississippi, as a Territory in 1807, as a state in 1822, and as consolidated law in 1848, declaring that "no cruel or unusual punishment shall be inflicted on any slave within this territory" (on pain of a $200 fine in 1807, upped to $500 by 1848).[192] Importantly, it was not Taylor, but Taylor's son, Dick, who was in charge of running the Mississippi and Louisiana Taylor plantations, and in his book, Dick Taylor sneered at the "imaginary woes of the Africans," while playing up the idyll of faithful slaves as friends and willing servants.[193] All this puts a light on Taylor-style slavery that is quite different from the *prima facie* interpretation of Zachary Taylor's kindness per his will. Will-makers do not prohibit something like overworking slaves or leaving the elderly to die, unless they know that it is likely to happen. It was the leisure-loving Dick Taylor, not the workaholic Zachary Taylor, who ran the plantations, so that calling up as evidence the overseers who "served for long periods of time" might more reflect Dick Taylor's inertia than Zachary Taylor's alleged "respect and affection" for his slaves.[194] The legal words of the Mississippi statute against cruelty, reiterated identically three times, were but a pretty, public wrapping for the ugly, personal reality of slavery in the Deep South.

Taylor did not run for president on his slaveholding credentials, however—at least, not openly—but on something every settler, north, south, or west, could get behind: the U.S. seizure of Indian land. The tacit point of the U.S. Army's maintaining various "frontier" forts was to enlarge U.S. territory, which Zachary Taylor certainly accomplished in the Black Hawk War and in the second Seminole War. These undertakings were extolled as great achievements in their own right, while leading into his 1848 presidential run, his return as "the hero of the Mexican War" played well (even though Taylor shared the heroic sobriquet with General Winfield Scott—who also used it in his runs for the Whig nomination in the 1848 and 1852 elections).

To privilege the hero view of Taylor is, however, to ignore that the U.S. war on Mexico was really targeting North American Indian land (Texas, New Mexico, and California). The war was, moreover, decried at the time by progressives, eloquently including Transcendentalist Henry David Thoreau, who condemned it as "the work of comparatively a few individuals using the standing government as their tool."[195] Thoreau went on to censure the "thousands" of Americans who were, *in opinion,* opposed to slavery and the war" but who would nevertheless "do nothing to put an end to them." They preferred, instead, to "sit with their hands in their pockets," idly boasting that they would like the government to try and "order" them "out to help put down an insurrection of the slaves, or to march to Mexico" and just see whether they would do it.[196] There was a reason that Thoreau lumped slavery into his disquisition on Mexico. Everyone knew perfectly well that the impetus behind the war was land seizure for the expansion of slavery.

For all Thoreau's "thousands" in opposition to the war, the war hawks were in official ascendancy, with expansionism in the driver's seat. Accordingly, during the buildup to hostilities in 1845, U.S. newspapers intensified their rhetoric.[197] *Annex Texas!* was the cry, in full knowledge that such unilateral annexation of northern Mexico was pure provocation to bring on war. Indeed, the term "Manifest Destiny" was coined in a convoluted, 1845 argument from the Proustian pen of John L. O'Sullivan in anticipation—and justification—of the seizure of northern Mexico in a war:

> Why, were other reasoning wanting, in favor of now elevating this question of the reception of Texas into the Union, out of the lower region of our past party discussions, up to its proper level of a high and broad nationality, it surely is to be found, found abundantly, in the manner in which other nations have undertaken to intrude themselves into it, between us and the proper parties to the case, in a spirit of hostile interference against us, for the avowed object of thwarting our policy and hampering our power, limiting our greatness and checking the fulfillment of our *manifest destiny* to overspread the continent allotted by Providence for the free development of our yearly multiplying millions.[198] (Italics mine.)

O'Sullivan's points seemed to have been that Mexico could not have the land because the United States wanted it, and anyway, the United States was the victim here. Besides, the settler god liked Protestant America best, so the United States should go help itself to the land.

U.S. politicians presented part of the necessity of their war as to rescue Mexico from the foul clutches of the treacherous Indians, who were purportedly ravaging it, overwhelming the feeble ability of the Mexican authorities to put those red menaces in their place. It became standard to "denigrate the Indians that had 'overrun' the Mexican north," although how it was possible for the Comanche, Kiowa, Apache, and Navajo to overrun their own land was left unaddressed.[199] Never mind, though the Indians were Bloodthirsty Savages who had to be stopped to Save Civilization, echoing the official appeal preceding every U.S. seizure of Indian land, the only difference in the Mexican-American War being that Euro-Mexican leaders were likewise looking to "annihilate" the Indians.[200] The Comanche, Kiowa, Apache, and Navajo were thus caught in a pincer between the two Euro-settler sides, neither of which recognized their sovereignty over their own lands.

As early as August 31, 1845, President James K. Polk's Cabinet discussed sending Taylor in to occupy Texas, which order was issued on September 7, 1845.[201]

The United States was attempting, rather unilaterally, to incorporate Texas as a U.S. slave state, thus compounding the aggravation, so that the international situation grew quite dicey. Taylor had already moved into action before these steps had been taken, stationing himself as ordered, directly across the Rio Grande from Mexico in clear provocation.[202] His sheer presence at the Rio Grande nudged matters over the edge. When his men were predictably attacked on April 26, 1846, it was a Mexican gift to the United States, for through early May, the cabinet had been actively anxiously awaiting word of Mexican-initiated hostilities (to legitimize U.S. attack).

President Polk received the happy news on May 9.[203] On May 11, he brought his declaration of war on Mexico to Congress, citing "long-continued and unredressed wrongs and injuries committed by the Mexican government on citizens of the United States, in their persons and property."[204] Notably, these were exactly the charges used against Indians in announcing the various wars on them. For good measure, in Congress on July 9, 1846, Texas representative David Spangler Kaufman feminized Mexico as an uppity woman getting ahead of herself in *"her obstinate and faithless refusal to negotiate"* with the United States (that is, to cede Texas). She needed to be slapped down for *"sending her army across the Rio Grande to commence the attack,"* instead of giving in, like a lady. She had brought the beating on herself by victimizing the United States.[205]

Mr. Kaufman notwithstanding, the Mexican-American War was as naked a land grab as any other Indian war, as New York Whig representative Hugh White made clear in Congress on August 8, 1846. White insisted that everyone knew that President Polk's war had been orchestrated for "territory," and he would vote for the administration's $2,000,000 war appropriation only if the legislation included his own amendment "to forever preclude the possibility of extending the limits of slavery."[206] If the United States has been reticent till quite recently about acknowledging the skullduggery to which White alluded, Mexican historians were onto it from the beginning. An 1848 Mexican history was fairly straightforward in proclaiming that *"el verdadero origen de la guerra,"* was that *"la [había] ocasionado la ambicion insaciable de los Estados Unidos"* that had *"desde los primeros dias de su independencia adoptaron el proyecto de estender sus dominios"* ("the true origin of the war" was that "it [had been] occasioned by the insatiable ambition of the United States" that had "from the first days of its independence adopted the project of extending its dominions").[207]

Of course, O'Sullivan's, Polk's, and Kaufman's hype did not have to work with the Indians, the Mexicans, or even Thoreau and White, but only with the American *homo politicus*. Across the country, men responded to the call for national volunteers, resulting from the May 13, 1846, act of Congress authorizing the war.[208] Made a colonel on June 13, 1846, for instance, Jefferson Davis sprang into action, raising a detachment to rush to the aid of America.[209] In July 1846, Davis composed a verbose missive to "the People of Mississippi," explaining why he had abandoned his post as Mississippi representative to the U.S. Congress to join in the fight, pointedly blaming Mexico for the war, using what had by now become the standard charge against Mexico, of its "crossing the Rio

Grande to attack the forces of General Taylor."[210] Throughout the hoopla, the fact that Texas had been unilaterally declared U.S. territory in the first place was completely obliterated from the public mind.

In a blitz on May 8–9, 1846, Taylor pushed from Palo Alto through Resaca de la Palma, twice defeating General Mariano Arista and his army, which included "half-trained Indian conscripts."[211] Taylor's victory owed largely to the superiority of his armaments.[212] Thereafter, Taylor penetrated as far as Monterrey, the fallback position of the Mexican Army, and from September 20 to September 24, he conducted his siege of the city. Albeit at a cost of 394 men, Taylor claimed Monterrey due to the surrender of General Pedro de Ampudia.[213] Taylor soared in public approval ratings, his own huge casualty count notwithstanding.

At that point, having just been shellacked over the war in the midterm elections by Thoreau's "thousands," it dawned on President Polk that, for all his slaveholding southern plantations and expansionism, Taylor might not be a fellow Democrat.[214] Given Taylor's growing accolades, Polk saw that Taylor might even run against him in the next election, so Polk elevated General Winfield Scott over Taylor (in a move that Polk soon came to regret).[215] Although not directly acknowledging his motives for Winfield's elevation over Taylor, Polk clearly hoped to reduce Taylor's appeal to the electorate by removing him from the spotlight. The move backfired as Taylor's friend, General Edmund Pendleton Gaines, most probably with Taylor's knowledge, published in the newspapers a November 9, 1846, Taylor's letter from Monterrey (the site of Taylor's most recent victory), and the letter was quite critical of the Polk Administration.[216] Polk was furious, calling in the heads of the military to watch him dress down General Gaines. Polk realized with a thud that Taylor was "in the hand of political managers."[217]

Alas for Polk's demotion of him, Taylor pulled another rabbit out of the hat by holding off a furious attack on Buena Vista by General Antonio López de Santa Anna from February 22 to February 23, 1847. Although seriously outnumbered by Santa Anna's 20,000–22,000 men to his own 5,000 (and violating his orders in pursuing Santa Anna), Taylor prevailed, costing Santa Anna 20 percent of his army, with 594 killed outright, 1,039 wounded, and 1,854 missing, for a total of 3,487 men out of commission.[218] Congratulated warmly by Secretary of War William L. Marcy, Taylor learned of the "general joy which the intelligence of this success" had "spread through the land," despite Taylor's own heavy losses of 450 dead and twenty-six missing in action.[219]

In Washington, D.C. Polk was pressured to order the firing of a "salute in honor of Gen'l Taylor for the Battle of Buena Vista," which Polk resented and resisted mightily. "It would be embarrassing," he admitted in his diary, and then went on rather venomously to credit the "indomitable bravery of our army" over Taylor's generalship for the victory.[220] By April 16, Polk was absolutely fuming at the Whig newspapers for "boldly" attributing all the victories of the war to Taylor, whether or not they were his, and "proclaiming him to be their candidate for the Presidency."[221] Quitting while the quitting was good—the Buena Vista victory would have been hard to beat, while someone might have begun to notice his heavy sacrifice of other men's lives—Taylor essentially cooled his heels at his headquarters in Monterrey until requesting and receiving a six-month leave of absence to return to the United States, where he was in December 1847.[222] Of course, the purpose of the leave was to explore his Whig presidential run.

Taylor's campaign came as one of the last, happy gasps of the Whig Party, which settled on him as its 1848 candidate on the fourth ballot.[223] The mere sobriquet, "Old Rough and Ready" indicated Taylor's warrior status, so the Democrats put up their own noted general, Lewis Cass, the second governor of Michigan, U.S. ambassador to France, and Jackson's secretary of war, the very man who had engineered Jacksonian Removal. Cass's 1848 campaign biographer, his protégé Henry Rowe Schoolcraft, sought to one-up Taylor's Indian-fighting credentials by portraying Cass as a great Indian-killing machine. In one melodramatic passage, Cass was shown witnessing his mother-in-law being "stabbed . . . in several places" as she stood in front of his "temporary log hut." (Getting a log cabin into the mix had been *de rigueur* since William Henry Harrison's 1840 campaign.) Pictured as "forgetting all personal danger" to fly to her defense, Cass "seized two young Indians by their hair" and "hurled them to the ground," although neither of them had been involved in the stabbing, a point that Schoolcraft lightly skipped over. The next day, the "assassin" of no one—the woman had survived—was dragged to the top of a mound, where he was stripped and then dressed in a petticoat, supposedly to the jeers of all Indians witnessing the punishment.[224] This sort of pulpy sensationalism was standard in antebellum depictions of Indians, although Schoolcraft's scene affronted real Indian norms.

The cultures of the eastern Woodlands, especially in the Ohio Valley, where this crime and punishment supposedly occurred, were (and are) matriarchal. For Woodlanders, it was the job that was gendered, not the person. Male speakers of the women, for instance, proudly wore skirts in the course of their duties, a fact that scandalized Europeans from the first Jesuit priests on the scene on, who assumed in horror that the men were gay.[225] Furthermore, Indians do not approach ceremonial mounds lightly—or burial mounds, at all. In Indiana, the setting of this story, mounds were almost all for ceremonies or burials. The claimed hollering of the Indians was, then, much more likely to have been occasioned by the desecration of sacred space than by putting a skirt on a man. If the shouting had anything to do with the skirt, it would have been about the violation of a soldier, a job gendered male, by the wearing of a skirt, which indicated men who were judges or speakers of the women, jobs gendered female. This was as profound a violation of social signals as would be a Baptist minister showing up to conduct services in a micro-bikini while sipping his third martini. Actual Indian lore was not the point of political campaigns, however. Puffing a hero who killed and humiliated Indians was.

Taylor's own 1848 campaign biographies likewise extolled (and exaggerated) his exploits against the villainous Indians. One such Taylor biography ominously presented the "encroachments" of the Miami Confederacy of Indians in the War of 1812, as though it were they who were stealing the land. At "every opportunity," the Miami Confederacy "would fall on the settlers, murdering all, without distinction of age or sex," it screamed, parroting the settler justification of all

Indian wars: Indian savagery falling on settler innocence. The biography's description of Taylor's Fort Harrison battle began with the starving Shawnee delegation, claiming that it only "pretended to be greatly in want of provisions."[226] Another 1848 campaign biography of Taylor characterized the Indians' losses at Fort Harrison as a "great slaughter" by Taylor, which was seen as a recommendation for the job of president.[227]

Of the horrific butchery of the Sauk and Mesquaki in 1832, one of Taylor's campaign biographies claimed that Old Rough and Ready never "failed" in pursuit of the Indians, through the marshes and the swamps. The scene ending at Bad Axe, where Taylor ran down the starving, terrified, and exhausted men, women, and children fleeing for their lives, was given in celebration of "Anglo-Norman" racism. "At last the very Indians themselves, whom Taylor thus desperately pursued from day to day, and week to week, began to sink from fatigue and exhaustion: they were found by our men stretched beside the trails," that is, lying dead on the road. By contrast, the "good Anglo-Norman blood of Taylor's band held out amid sufferings, in the wilderness, which the child of the forest himself could not endure."[228] Another campaign biography presented the Indians as great malefactors, stoked by "their implacable aversion" to the "peaceful encroachments" of the settlers, who were again depicted as victims "forced to arms and the work of destruction as acts of simple self-defence." If "the same reason" could not "be asserted" for the Black Hawk War, the text conceded, then once it started, "the security of all parties demanded its termination by the most vigorous measures."[229]

Even though the Seminole have the rare distinction of never having been conquered by the United States, the Battle of Okeechobee was inexorably exalted as a Taylor victory. The "Americans," said the text, "charged the swamp, and drove out the enemy." The fight was "long and severe—the Indians disputing the ground inch by inch, and yielding only to the bayonet." Taylor pursued them all night, racking up 138 casualties in the process, yet the text assured the reader, in that battle, "the Indians had learnt to fear him." Taylor would ride about, ahead of his men, unconcernedly eating lunch while exposed under a tree, but "[n]o matter how many Indians were prowling about"—Indians always prowled, whereas settlers marched—"the old general seemed unconscious that they would harm him."[230] Although presented as a ringing endorsement of his nerve, Taylor's survival was perhaps just a measure of his luck, as a similar nonchalance would get Armstrong Custer killed.

Another political panegyric to Taylor at Okeechobee demanded to know whether any "answer" could "be found" to the burning question of why the soldiers went through all their suffering at Okeechobee, unless it were due to "the valour, the endurance, the inspiring presence" of Taylor? Well, yes, direct orders from their superior officer could also have had that effect, with no valor required, but never mind; it was obviously Taylor's "thrilling voice and flashing eye" that gave his troops hope of victory.[231] These accounts comprise little more than a litany of racist tenets, yet they worked on the settler mind to exalt Taylor.

For political purposes in his run for the presidency, Taylor was portrayed as "neutral" on the point of slavery but in context, slavery was reduced by everyone but the radical abolitionists to a sideshow in the carnival of sectionalism versus nationalism. Happily, Taylor's position could be interpreted either way in a neat, vote-getting strategy. On the one hand, Taylor was a U.S. Army officer, who had pledged his honor to the federal Union, not to his southern section of the country. On the other hand, he was a slave-owning, large-scale Mississippi and Louisiana planter. Of course, expansionism encompassed both goals—expansion of territory and of slavery—so that as an army officer, Taylor extended national lands for sectional slavery or for sectional free soil, depending on which set of settlers was voting at the moment. Confusion worked. When the electoral votes came in, it was clear that killing both Indians and Mexicans had vaulted Taylor over Lewis Cass by an electoral count of 163 to 127 or 56 percent for Taylor, although the popular vote showed a narrower gap of 53 percent to 47 percent.[232] Either way it went, however, the election remained a loss for both the Indians and the slaves.

Of course, slavery sizzled up as an issue during Taylor's presidency, through the Wilmot Proviso, first brought forth in 1846 by "free" Pennsylvania's representative David Wilmot, who attached a rider to an appropriations bill that would have banned slavery in the newly grabbed Southwest. Predictably, Southern planters frothed, apoplectic. Even though Wilmot's proviso was removed from the 1846 bill, its ghost hung about the halls of Congress, periodically jumping out to scare Southern congressmen.[233] It was resuscitated in 1849. President Taylor interpreted the Wilmot Proviso as intensifying sectionalism, at the same time he urged California and New Mexico to apply for statehood outright, without first waiting as federal territories for a congressional enabling act. In Taylor's mind, this approached evaded fistfights in Congress over territorial slavery laws.[234] Of course, California and New Mexico petitioned for entry as Free States, allowing Taylor to adhere to the Whig Party platform, which called for "no extension of slave territory."[235] Southern planters now realized that, when push came to shove, Taylor stood for the Union over sectionalism, even though it meant sacrificing slavery.

Chaos erupted. Southerners cried foul, the chorus led by South Carolina senator John C. Calhoun from 1849 to 1850, the period of Taylor's Whig presidency. Calhoun proposed a sectional solution to the woes of the agrarian South, just then locked in losing economic competition with the industrial and commercial north. Basically, the idea was for the incoming southwest to join with the original South to form a block caucus based on region and supporting slavery. To anyone paying attention, the Southern caucus was a clear prelude to outright secession.[236] Given the extreme aggressiveness of southerner planters, successful secession would set up a European-style set of rivalries in North America, leading to endless, internecine warfare, a nightmare of the Founding Fathers. Now, Henry Clay, senator from Kentucky, stepped forward with his proposal offering eight, interlocking resolutions that, in aggregate, favored slavery.[237] Fraught negotiations followed on an Omnibus Bill combining Clay's resolutions into one package, but that failed in Congress due to a circular firing squad, so Clay organized his eight resolutions into five separate laws, which were then passed, one by one.[238] Taylor opposed Clay (who had challenged him for the 1848 Whig nomination, after all) as well as Clay's Resolutions and Bills.[239]

Given the clear tensions here, Taylor's unexpected demise on July 9, 1850, in the midst of opposing Clay's slavery-accommodating 1850 Compromise has since led to questions about whether Taylor was assassinated by irate Southerners playing with arsenic. In 1988, Ph.D. historian Elbert Smith conjectured that Taylor had suffered from "mild sunstroke" on July 4. Smith also gave probably the best biographical rundown on the progress of Taylor's illness from July 4 to July 9, noting that the remedies he was given—calomel (powdered mercury), opium, and quinine—could not have helped a man with "gastroenteritis."[240] However, in 1991, Clara Rising, a novelist with a Ph.D. in English, proposed that Taylor had been deliberately assassinated by poison. She pressed for a forensic analysis of his remains, so in 1991, William Ross Maples, a Ph.D. forensic anthropologist, examined Taylor's exhumed body and found that the arsenic levels were normal for a long-buried corpse and well below the level required for poisoning.[241] In 1998, a Ph.D. political (not forensic) scientist, Michael Parenti, conducted an intensive inquiry into Maples' report, its methods and processes, finding the latter to have been cavalier and somewhat sloppy. Although Parenti could not declare that Taylor was certainly poisoned, he did not accept the 1991 study or its conclusion as reliable.[242]

Today, historians mostly sidestep the issue, simply citing cholera as the cause of death. In his 2007 biography of Taylor, Elbert Smith credibly noted not only that others, including Henry Clay, were already ill with suspected cholera before the July 4 celebration, but also that cholera was not an unlikely culprit, given the "primitive water supply and sewage systems."[243] To date, no one has attempted to explain the high levels of antimony also found in Taylor's system, a second peg on which Parenti hung his hat, although it is worth mentioning that, as "tartar emetic," antimony was then considered medicinal under the crackbrained theories of "elemental medicine" abroad in Western medicine.[244] People in 1850 were entirely aware that antimony could be poisonous, for it was used to commit murder, although those who wanted to be sure of killing the victim mixed antimony and strychnine.[245] Strychnine was not found in Taylor's remains.

However, Taylor died, the Whig eulogist Richard Tolman rhapsodized that, whereas other commanders in chief might have "driven away the Indians, and conquered the Mexicans," only Taylor could have "put the curb on the fiery fanatics of the South."[246] In eleven years, those fiery fanatics broke loose, after all, firing on Fort Sumter.

NOTES

1. Mann, 2013, 167–82.

2. Montgomery, 1847, 14.

3. Filson, 1784, 7–8.

4. See, for instance, from George Rogers Clark reports on militia attacks on Shawnee towns, "Gen. Rogers Clark to Gov. Harrison," 1875–1893/1968, vol. 3, 381; Nelson, 1986, 219–51.

5. Taylor was born on November 24, 1784, at the Montebello plantation in Orange County, Virginia, because his mother could not travel while pregnant. Taylor and his mother came to Louisville in the spring of 1785, Groover, 1978, 42.

6. Colyer, 1913, 44–45.

7. Fordham, 1906, 177.

8. Coy *et al.*, 1997, 152.

9. Mann, 2003, Cherokee, 155–67; Shawnee, 118–27.

10. Filson, 1784, 28–29.

11. Fordham, 1906, 93.

12. Williams, 1933, Cage and Carter to Martin, report, 3/22/1785, 63.

13. Fordham, 1906, habitable world, 131; categories, 125–27.

14. Fordham, 1906, 148.

15. Thwaites and Kellogg, 1905, x–xviii, 4–9, 20–88; 108–36 passim; 164–25 passim; 239, 242, 269–80 passim; 344, 348, 374, 387, 420, 429.

16. Heckewelder, 1820/1971, 130–31.

17. For Wetzel, Kellogg, 1912/1977, note 2, 379–80; for Owens, Silver, 2008, note 69, 358; Mann, 2005, for Murphy, note 473, 94, 118, 213; for Williamson, 151–70 passim.

18. Silver, 2008, 125–29, 241–44.

19. John M. Gresham Company, 1896, 393.

20. George, 1763/2018.

21. Cartier, 1929, 35.

22. O'Callaghan, 1850, Denonville to Minister of War, vol. 1, report, 8/25/1687, 147.

23. Cook, 1887, 44.

24. Bossu, 1778, 98.

25. Bartram, 1791/1928, 400.

26. Miller *et al.*, 2010, 7.

27. Ibid., 54–56.

28. George, 1763/2018.

29. For 1768 Fort Stanwix Treaty, Butler, 1834/2010, 378–90; Mann, 2004, 140–42; for 1775 Treaty of Pittsburg, Morris and Kellogg, 1908.

30. Kulikoff, 2000, 144, 153.

31. For intensive interconnections among elites, Pessen, 1973, van Rensselaers, 211–13; DeLanceys, 102–3, 211–12; Harrisons, 206, 231.

32. Huston, 2000.

33. Hamilton, 1941, 22.

34. Johnson, 1865, 21.

35. Fordham, 1906, 180.

36. Gardiner, 1822, 252.

37. Taylor, 1879, 62.

38. Twain, 1894/1981, 3, 8.

39. Chesnutt, 1900/2007, 36–40.

40. Fordham, 1906, 134.

41. Ibid., 229.

42. Wilson, 1998, 127.

43. Greeley *et al.*, 1860, 50.

44. Fordham noted the Kentucky habit calling the slave a "servant," Fordham, 1906, 125.

45. Gresham, 1917, vol. 1, 37.

46. "Somerset's Case," 1862, 171–72. Stuart spelled as "Stewart." For the original spell-ings as Steuart and Somerset, Gikandi, 2011, 92. Unfounded rumor stated that Stuart was from Boston (Gikandi, 2011, 92), but this rumor was most likely based on Mansfield's con-tempt for Massachusetts and perhaps an effort to tweak the abolitionists there. Gresham, 1917, Massachusetts, vol. 1, 36. For the Capel Lofft transcript of arguments, see 1 Lofft 1, 98 ER 499.

47. Gikandi, 2011, 92. The legal precept, *fiat justitia, ruat cœlum*, is attributed to Governor Lucius Calpurnius Piso Ceasonius and is shorthanded as "Piso's justice." Rivlin, 2015, 93. Piso was justifying his own major injustice at the time he uttered it, but Mansfield did not seem to be using the phrase sarcastically. He realized what the ruling would mean to Englishmen, everywhere.

48. Wiecek, 1974, 87.

49. Franklin, 1906, Franklin to Benezet, vol. 5, letter 8/22/1772, 431–32.

50. Everett, 1821, 45–46.

51. Blumrosen and Blumrosen, 2005, 15.

52. Ibid., 30.

53. "Somerset's Case," 1862, 171.

54. Blumrosen and Blumrosen, 2005, 24–25.

55. Gilbert, 2012, 8.

56. Jefferson, 1903–1907, vol. 12, vii.

57. Hirschfeld, 1997, 56.

58. Bauer, 1985, 2; for "Hare Forest," Groover, 1978, 39.

59. Smith, 2007, 9–10.

60. Bauer, 1985, 1, 3–4.

61. Jillson, 1926, Richard Taylor deeds: at Otter Creek, Lincoln County, 400 acres, 1780, 66; at Floyd's Fork, Jefferson Co., 1,000 acres, 1780, 295; at Ohio River, Jefferson County, 1,000 acres, 1780; at May & Thompson Watercourse, 1,000 acres, 1780, 295; 1,000, Floyd's Fork, 1783., 295; military warrants, for three years' Naval service, 5,333⅓ acres, Warrant #133, 1783, 364; for Lieutenant Colonel of the "Virginia line," Warrant #1734, 6,000 acres, 1783, 364; Court of Appeals, Deeds Granted, at Rough Creek, 1,000 acres, 1786, 454; Smith, 2007, 10; "Zachary Taylor Home."

62. Smith, 2007, 12.

63. Fordham, 1906, 180.

64. Montgomery, 1847, 13–15.

65. Smith, 1988, 26.

66. Montgomery, 1947, 16.

67. Eisenhower, 2008, 3. A photo of the 1808 acceptance letter, Hamilton, 1941, between 36 and 37; Connecticut tutor, Groover, 1978, 42.

68. USS, 1828, Jefferson to Senate, vol. 2, communication, 1/25/1809, 97; Recess Appointments, "Zachariah Taylor," vol. 2, 105; vol. 2, 1/30/1809, 107; vol. 2, 2/2/1809, 107.

69. USS, 1828, Eustis to Senate, vol. 2, communication, 2/25/1811, 169; Seventh Regiment, vol. 2, 171; as Captain, vol. 2, 172; Senate confirmation, vol. 2, 3/1/1811, 173.

70. Dyer, 1946, 172.

71. Montgomery, 1847, 17–18.

72. For promotion, Montgomery, 1847, 19; for cousin, Taylor, 1908, viii.

73. Taylor, 1908, viii.

74. Bauer, 1985, 6.

75. Ibid., 10.

76. Ibid., 9.

77. Deppisch, 2015, 45–47; for New York schooling, see Graff, 1997, 635.

78. For instance, assertion that Taylor "loved farming," in Smith, 2007, 13.

79. Most sources cite Taylor's date of promotion to major as May 15, 1814, the date that he was notified that it was in the works, but it did not actually go through till January 2, 1815, Dyer, 1946, 35.

80. USC, 1836a, Pierce speech, 6/30/1836, 4575; for reduction in rank, Heitman, 1890, 634.

81. For major declined, Heitman, 1890, 634; for Anderson letter, Hamilton, 1941, Anderson to [Monroe], letter 10/14/1814, 55–56.

82. Dyer, 1946, 34.

83. Bauer, 1985, 27.

84. Dallas and Dallas, 1871, Madison to Dallas, letter 5/10/1815, 412.

85. Esarey, 1922, Harrison to Eustis, vol. 1, letter 8/6/1811, 548; Carter, 1934–1975, Eustis to Harrison, vol. 8, letter 3/7/1812, 170.

86. Ibid., Harrison to Eustis, vol. 2, letter 5/13/1812, 49.

87. Ibid., Taylor to Harrison, vol. 2, letters 8/9/1812, 82; Harrison to Eustis, vol. 2, letter 8/12/1812, 89; for risk, Taylor to Harrison, vol. 2, letter 9/13/1812, 134.

88. Ibid., Harrison to Eustis, vol. 2, letter 9/11/1812, 130.

89. Carter, 1934–1975, Gibson to Eustis, vol. 8, report, 9/2/1812, 198.

90. Esarey, 1922, Taylor to Harrison, vol. 2, report, 9/10/1812, 124–25.

91. Ibid., Taylor to Harrison, vol. 2, report, 8/9/1812, 83.

92. Carter, 1934–1975, Gibson to Eustis, vol. 8, report, 10/14/1812, 209.

93. Esarey, 1922, Taylor to Harrison, vol. 2, report, 9/10/1812, 125, 126; for Taylor's men as militia, Carter, 1934–1975, Park to Eustis, vol. 8, letter 2/22/1813, 288.

94. Beckwith *et al.*, 1880, 16.

95. Esarey, 1922, Taylor to Harrison, vol. 2, report, 9/10/1812, 125–26.

96. Ibid., Taylor to Harrison, vol. 2, report, 9/10/1812, 126–28 passim.

97. Ibid., Taylor to Harrison, vol. 2, report, 9/10/1812, 127.

98. Ibid., Taylor to Harrison, vol. 2, report, 9/10/1812, 128.

99. Ibid., Taylor to Harrison, vol. 2, report, 9/10/1812, 127, 128.

100. For example of this teaching technique, Mann, 2009, 98.

101. Carter, 1934–1975, Gibson to Eustis, vol. 8, report, 10/14/1812, 209.

102. Heitman, 1890, 634.

103. Smith, 2007, 26.

104. Dyer, 1946, playmate, 10–11; Croghan as Colonel, 33.

105. Ibid., 38.

106. Hamilton, 1941, Taylor to Berry, letter 4/25/1816, 59.

107. Bauer, 1985, 29.

108. "United States Army," *Niles*, vol. 10, 6/15/1816, 352.

109. Taylor, 1936, Taylor to Madison, letter 7/10/1816, 325.

110. Taylor and Taylor, 1938, Taylor to Madison, letter 7/23/1816, 338.

111. USS, 1828, recess appointments submitted, vol. 3, 12/9/1816, 56; appointments confirmed, vol. 3, 12/17/1816, 62.

112. Smith, 1988, 70.

113. Hamilton, 1941, 114.

114. Upham and Silsbee, 1850, 20.

115. Richardson, 1897, vol. 2, 1083.

116. Hall, 1829/1989, 63–73; Melville, 1857, 201–12.

117. For school to Taylor's credit, Hamilton, 1941, 114; Smith, 1988, 29; Roberts, 2005, 48; for establishment of school, see Carter, 1934–1975, Harris to Dodge, vol. 27, letter 7/29/1836, 629.

118. Kappler, 1904, "Treaty with the Winnebago," Article IV, vol. 2, 346.

119. Coleman, 2008, vol. 1, 181–84.

120. Italics in the original. Street, 1904, 365.

121. For "gentleman farmer," Eisenhower, 2008, 1.

122. Davis, 1971–2015, vol. 1, note 2, 443/347; for marriage of Sarah Knox Taylor, Davis to Taylor, vol. 1, letter 12/16/1834, 443/345–47; Taylor to Taylor, vol. 1, letter 6/17/1835, 483/406–7; for death of Sarah Knox Taylor, note 4, 483/410, and Fleming, 1912, 34; for Confederacy, Taylor, 1879; for Dick Taylor as Confederate general, see Davis, 1971–2015, vol. 1, note 11, 483/408–9.

123. Fleming, 1912, 23.

124. See, for instance, Wait, 1999, 89; Harmon, 2014, 5.

125. Hamilton, 1941, 101.

126. Davis, 1971–2015, Davis as acting adjutant, muster roll, vol. 1, 8/31/1834, 424/333; court martial, vol. 1, 2/13/1835, 456/363; court martial, vol. 1, 2/14/1835, 456/372; note 21, 373; Davis dispatched to Black Rock, vol. 1, note 2, 334/252–53; Post Return, vol. 1, 9/30/1832, 339/258; for West Point, McElroy, 1937, vol. 1, 11.

127. Hamilton, 1941, Monterrey, 209–10; Buena Vista, 237–38.

128. Strode, 1955, 136; Bauer, 1985, 113–14.

129. Dyer, 1946, 259–60.

130. Bauer, 1985, 328.

131. Fleming, 1912, 23.

132. Hamilton, 1941, 101; for wife's and daughter's sufferings, Davis, 1971–2015, vol. 1, note 8, 408.

133. Fleming, 1912, 24–25.

134. Davis, 1971–2015, vol. 1, note 5, 408.

135. For trousseau and sister, Davis, 1971–2015, Davis to Taylor, vol. 1, letters 6/17/1835, 483/406–407; Davis to Taylor, Appendix I, vol. 1, letter 8/11/1835, 475; for Taylor arranging the marriage at his sister Elizabeth's house, Fleming, 1912, 31. Mrs. John Gibson Taylor was Elizabeth Taylor, Taylor's sister who had married a Taylor cousin, Strode, 1955, 95. John Gibson Taylor was deceased at the time of the Knox-Davis marriage, Davis, 1971–2015, vol. 1, note 7, 487.

136. Davis, 1971–2015, Arbuckle to Jones, vol. 1, letter 3/10/1835, 470/396.

137. Ibid., vol. 1, note 8, 408.

138. Fleming, 1912, 35.

139. Ibid., 25.

140. Davis, 1971–2015, Davis to Knox, vol. 1, letter 12/16/1834, 443/346.

141. Fleming, 1912, for slipper, 35; for humorless, 24.

142. Ibid., secret meetings, 26–27; alleged elopement, 29–30.

143. Davis, 1890, vol. 1, 162.

144. Ibid., vol. 1, 95–96.

145. Davis, 1971–2015, including description of the precipitating event, court-martial, vol. 1, 2/12/1835, 454/357–62; court martial, vol. 1, 2/13/1835, 456/363; court martial, vol. 1, 2/14/1835, 456/372; court martial, adjourned for illness of judge, vol. 1, 2/17/1835, note 373; court martial, vol. 1, 2/17/1835, 457/373–75; court martial, vol. 1, 2/19/1835, 458/376–81.

146. McElroy, 1937, vol. 1, 23. The farthest back I can track this story is to Fleming, 1912, citing "Charles Gibson in the *St. Louis* newspapers of January 5, 1890," italics in the original, note 5, 26.

147. Matson, 1880, 67–70.

148. Ibid., 70–73.

149. Strode, 1955, 62.

150. Allen, 1999, 72.

151. For "fantastic" and "squaw," Hamilton, 1941, 102; for "unconfirmed" and "squaw," Smith, 2007, 51; for Iroquoian meaning of "squaw," Mann, 2000, 19–22.

152. Cooper, 1848/1877, 367.

153. Armstead, 2012, 136; Stewart, 2010, 328, 330–31.

154. Douglass, 1849, 118–25.

155. Juge, 1854, 27–28.

156. Harvey, 2016, 71–72.

157. Brownmiller, 1975, 153–69; McLaurin, 1991, 97.

158. Louis, 1994, 15–17.

159. Ibid., 19; Louis also argues that instead of dying, the feudal custom transmuted into new forms under capitalism, Jacobs, 1861/1987, 51; Wayne, 2018, vol. 1, 215.

160. Brownmiller, 1975, 140–53; Shire, 2016, 117–23; Amnesty International, 2007.

161. Peavy and Smith, 1998, 67.

162. For "Dusky Sal," see Brodie, 1974, 354–55, 361, 419, 540–54; for the "nephew" lie, see Lewis and Onuf, 1999, 13; for "plantation wife," see Egerton, 2002, 182.

163. Chesnut, 1906, 115.

164. Taylor, 2001.

165. Lehman, 2011, 64, 66.

166. Burton, 1985, 188–89.

167. Bauer, 1985, 9.

168. Hamilton, 1941, 72.

169. Hamilton, 1949, 101; Smith, 1988, 27.

170. Hamilton, 1941, 81–82.

171. Dyer, 1946, 262.

172. Ibid., price collapse, 260; floods, 261, and Hamilton, 1978, 23.

173. Fleming, 1912, 23.

174. Dyer, 1946, 259.

175. Ibid., 262; Hamilton, 1941, 143.

176. Ibid., 262–63.

177. Smith, 1988, 27.

178. Finkelman, 2011, 51; Eisenhower, 2008, destruction of records, 138–39.

179. Smith, 2007, 13

180. Fordham, 1906, 125.

181. Smith, 1891, 15–16.

182. Ibid., 10.

183. Fedric, 2010, 30.

184. Smith, 1891, 23.

185. Jackson, 1847, 7–8.

186. Ibid., 19.

187. Groover, "The Taylor Family of Virginia," 42.

188. Moses, 2005, 113–15.

189. Brown, 1850, 139.

190. Ibid., 141–42.

191. Ibid., 140.

192. The Territory of Mississippi, 1807, Section 16, 385; The State of Mississippi, 1848, "Master and Servant—Slaves, Free Negroes, and Mulattoes," 510–42; for 1822 consolidation in 1848, 512; for prohibition on cruelty, Article 2, paragraph 44, 519.

193. Taylor, 1879, imaginary woes, 236; idyll of slavery, 62–63, 210.

194. Smith, 2007, 13.

195. Thoreau, 1903, 7.

196. Italics in the original. Thoreau, 1903, 13, 17.

197. DeLay, 2008, for 1845, 220–21.

198. O'Sullivan, 1845, 5.

199. DeLay, 2008, xvii–xviii, 183, 240.

200. Ibid., 168, 174, 242.

201. Polk, 1910, 8/31/1845, 12; vol. 1, 9/7/1845, 20.

202. Dyer, 1946, 170.

203. Polk, 1910, waiting, vol. 1, 5/5–6/1846, 379–80; vol. 1, 5/9/1846, 386.

204. Taylor *et al.*, 1848, Executive Document No. 60, 5/11/1846, 4; Polk, 1910, vol. 1, 5/12/1846, 394.

205. Italics in the original. USC, 1846, Kaufman speech, 7/9/1846, 805.

206. USC, 1846, White Speech, 8/8/1846, 1214.

207. Trans. mine. Alcarez, 1952, 2.

208. USC, 1862, Mexican War Act, vol. 9, 5/13/1846, 9–10.

209. Davis, 1971–2015, vol. 2, 6/13/1846, note 4, 694.

210. Ibid., "To the People of Mississippi," vol. 3, 7/13/1846, 8; originally published in 7/22/1846, Jackson *Mississippian*.

211. Bauer, 1985, 154.

212. Dyer, 1946, 173.

213. Bauer, 1985, 178–84; casualty count, 181; Taylor *et al.*, 1848, Taylor to War Department, letter 9/25/1846, 345–46.

214. Polk, 1910, for Polk's "embarrassment" over "present officers" (Taylor and Scott), 12/14/1846, vol. 22, 75–76; for Taylor's "lack of sympathy toward the government," Polk, vol. 2, 12/19/1846, 282; for midterm elections, DeLay, 2008, 286.

215. Polk, 1910, vol. 2, 2/27/1847, 394.

216. Ibid., vol. 1, 1/25/1847, note 1, 353, 357.

217. Ibid., vol. 2, 1/25/1847, 354–55; as published by Gaines, vol. 2, 1/26/1847, 356.

218. For 20 percent of Santa Anna's army, Bauer, 1985, 205–6; for comparative sizes of the armies, Carleton, 1848, Santa Anna to Taylor, letters 2/22/1847, 36, 183; Taylor *et al.*, 1848, Marcy to Taylor, letter 4/3/1847, 1118; Polk, 1910, vol. 2, 4/1/1847, 451.

219. Taylor *et al.*, 1848, Marcy to Taylor, letters 4/3/1847, 1117–18; for losses, Taylor to Marcy, letter 2/27/1847, 1115.

220. Polk, 1910, vol. 2, 4/7/1847, 462.

221. Ibid., vol. 2, 4/16/1847, 479.

222. Ibid., vol. 3, 12/31/1847, 270; leave requested by Taylor, vol. 3, 1/2/1848, 275.

223. Ibid., vol. 3, 6/9/1848, 488.

224. Schoolcraft, 1848, 49.

225. Lafitau, 1724/1974, vol. 1, 298–99.

226. *Taylor and Fillmore*, 1848, 4.

227. Thorpe, 1848, 10.

228. *Taylor and Fillmore*, 1848, 5.

229. Fry and Conrad, 1848, 32.

230. *Taylor and Fillmore*, 1848, 6–8.

231. Fry and Conrad, 1848, 44.

232. Bauer, 1985, Table, "Voting Patterns," 246.

233. Taylor, 1848.

234. Dyer, 1946, 371–74.

235. Greeley *et al.*, 1860, 15.

236. Ames, 1918, 19–50.

237. USC, 1850, Clay speech, 1/29/1850, 244–47.

238. Hamilton, 1964/2005.

239. Fafoutis, 2012, vol. 1, 367–68.

240. Smith, 1988, 156.

241. Maples and Browning, 1994, 223–37.

242. Parenti, 1998, vol. 20, no. 2, 141–58. Parenti returned to these themes in Parenti, 1999, 209–29.

243. Smith, 2007, 251.

244. Graham, 1827, 30, 102–3, 288, 557.

245. Buckingham, 2008, antimony, alone, to murder, 147; as mixed with strychnine to murder, 119, 151, 160.

246. Tolman, 1850, 8.

CHAPTER 8

~

"All Nations Call Me Sauk!": The Black Hawk War, 1831–1832

Western sources are still promoting the "Bering Strait crossing" for the peopling of the Americas, dating entry from 10,000 to 8,500 BCE.[1] This proposition has us trudging behind herds of bison across Siberia, into Alaska, and then across and down through Canada into the central Great Plains of the United States. The ancestors of the Sauk ("Sac") and Meskwaki ("Fox") are included in the groups that supposedly hiked in this way, but as Vine Deloria Jr. demonstrated rather witheringly in 1997, as a theory, the Bering Strait crossing has some explaining to do.

First, even supposing a starting point in Siberia, just to arrive at the Bering Strait, the theory's herders would have had to trek up to the Arctic Circle, where they would run face-first into two mountain ranges, the Kolyma Range (elevations up to 6,437′) and Chukotskoye Nagor'ye Range (up to 1,316′). Second, having crossed these heights to reach the easternmost tip of Siberia, the bison and footsore humans would next have had to cross ten additional mountain ranges, two of them just to leave the Alaskan Arctic Circle, the Baird Mountains (up to 4,700′) and the Brooks Range (up to 4,000′). Having at last emerged from the Arctic Circle, our intrepid travelers would have encountered the Endicott Mountains (elevations up to 7,775′), the Shublik Range (up to 5,880′), and the Kushkokwim Range (up to 2,575′). Finally, at the southern border of Canada, the herders and bison would have run into the Richardson Range (up to 4,067′), the Rocky Mountains (up to 14,439′), the Ogilvie Range (up to 7,749′), the MacKenzie Range (up to 9,751′), and the Franklin Range (up to 7,192′). At this point, our frostbitten herders and their bison would have found a flat plain. Unfortunately, at the time proposed for this crossing, it was covered by a mile-thick glacier.[2]

Indigenous Americans have never bought into this theory, and not just because of the dozen mountain ranges but also because, culturally, on the Steppes of Central Asia and on the North American plains, people migrated along a north-south axis, not an east-west axis.[3] Moreover, a 4,200-mile trek implies certain foreknowledge that the grassy Great Plains lay ahead. If true, such knowledge might motivate humans, but they were supposedly following, not leading, the herds of bison, who are not noted for either their mountain-climbing prowess or their geological surveys of the world's grasslands.[4] Even were the trek bovinely possible, what were those mountain-climbing bison eating? Everything along the route was under mile-deep glaciers. Ice-grazing bison seem even more fantastic than mountain-climbing bison-geographers.

The holes in the Bering Strait theory are not the only problem with the supposed Sauk and Meskwaki arrival. Recorded in 1820, the Sauk origin story has them created in situ on Turtle Island, at *Moneac* (Montreal), where the four First People were made. The two original men were made from dirt, and the two original women were created from ribs, one from each man. The Christian contribution to this Adam's Rib-off is obvious, but the necessity of four (in reference to the cosmic directions) is Indigenous: a female pairing, the north-south axis, referencing the First Women, and a male pairing, the east-west axis, referencing the First Men. Because this was a Blood creation story only—Breath creation involves stars not dirt—it was necessarily picked up from Sauk women. Breath is traditionally considered older than Blood—the stars were created before the earth— so the creation order of male/Breath and female/Blood is also traditional.[5]

In a counterpart Breath story from 1671, a Meskwaki man claimed that "his ancestor had come from Heaven," that is, the stars, and "spoke of a God who had made all the other Gods." The "Gods" of the tale were supplied by the Jesuits (Indigenous spirits are not gods), but the story of descent from a Star Being is a very typically male, complementing the female creation from soil.[6] In this outlay, the Sauk form the Blood half, and the Meskwaki, the Breath half of the nation. The Sauk-Meskwaki halved whole always traveled together, with phratry duties halved again, although settlers recorded only the male positions involved. In 1820, the twinned chiefs, two each of the Meskwaki and of the Sauk, totaled the sacred four. The Sauk and Meskwaki intermarried, used the same language, and were "considered as the same nation."[7]

Although early French chroniclers typically meant the Meskwaki when they mentioned the "Outagamis," they also might mean both the Sauk and Meskwaki, as in 1722, when Bacqueville de la Potherie used "*Outagamis*" to indicate both. Describing them as springing from "*deux extractions*" (two extractions), he was certainly indicating their twinned halves, not separate nations. The *Outagami*, he said, paired themselves as the "*Renards*" against their "*parens*" (relatives) opposite, the "*Terre-Rouge*." "*Renard*" is simply French for "fox," indicating the Meskwaki, while their "*parens*," the "*Terre-Rouge*," were the "Red-Earth People," the Sauk.[8] In 1820, Sauk civil chief *Masco*, insisted that they had never been called by any name other than "Sau-kie," while Meskwaki civil chief *Wahballo* stated that they had never been called anything but "Mus-quak-kie."[9] By and large, the Meskwaki handled foreign affairs, and the Sauk, civil affairs.

The Sauk and Meskwaki also claimed close relations with the Potawatomi and the Kickapoo. In 1820, *Wahbollo* claimed that numerous Sauk and Meskwaki lived with the Potawatomi, while the Kickapoo spoke a dialect of the Sauk-Meskwaki language.[10] The Sauk and Meskwaki had also allied themselves with the Iowa nation, because the Iowa were terrible people, too mean to oppose, reflecting a standard Indigenous reasoning about alliances that Western historians should keep in mind when touting Indian "allies" of the United States.[11]

One really old migration tradition had the Sauk and Meskwaki both originally traveling up from the south, "a great distance below Detroit." According to this tradition, the Shawnee were originally part of the same people as the Sauk and Meskwaki, but the Shawnee broke from the main group following a quarrel over which chief should be served a delicacy, that is, a dispute over which subgroup had leadership rights over the whole.[12] Interestingly, this Shawnee connection necessitates a mutual south-to-north migration, well in advance of the European arrival. *Moneac* was nevertheless the place where the Sauk and Meskwaki "first saw white men," possibly Verrazano (1524) but more likely Cartier (1535).[13] Like all northeastern Woodlanders, the Sauk and Meskwaki recognize the Lenape as the Grandfather (elder) nation, also suggesting this migration.[14] As the first nation through the "eastern door" into Dawnland, along the Delaware River, the Lenape necessarily "opened the door" to nations arriving after them.[15] Newcomers being welcomed by people already in the place is an important Indian ritual, legitimizing the travelers' presence. It is akin to receiving a green card in the United States.

When the Sauk and Meskwaki later sighted the Europeans sailing in, the lookouts were puzzled by what was coming over the horizon, first mistaking the white blob they saw for a "great bird." As it drew near, however, they recognized it as a "monstrous canoe" loaded with strange people. (Southern Indians had sails, apparently bringing them to the north.[16]) These new people, originally created lower than the Shawnee and placed "beyond the great water," proceeded to take over Turtle Island.[17] Sauk chief *Makataimeshekiakiak* ("Black Sparrow Hawk," "Black Hawk") opined that instead of bringing "*poisonous liquors, disease and death*," the Europeans "should have remained on the island where the Great Spirit first placed them."[18] "Great Spirit" may be a Euro-Christian interpolation, but the sentiment is entirely Indigenous.

Because of the Euro-Christian ideology of female inferiority and prejudices surrounding sex roles, European chroniclers simply overlooked the fact of female leaders. Notwithstanding, female clan chiefs certainly existed among the Sauk and Meskwaki, for offhand mentions of them appear throughout settler records.[19] The most informed sources accorded women the title of chief, but usually, women in leadership roles were Europeanized as the "daughter" or the "queen" of a sitting male chief.[20] In all Woodland nations, however, women ran the domestic (Blood) affairs. A woman was not the "dusky queen" of the "wigwam" but the clan mother who managed the farm. This, and not sexism, was why *Makataimeshekiakiak* mentioned that women "cheerfully" kept to their set of tasks and "*never*" interfered with "*business belonging to men.*"[21] Conversely, men cheerfully attended to their Breath tasks, never interfering with Blood business of women.

Like all Woodlanders, the Sauk and Meskwaki were primarily farmers, their fields of "corn, squashes, beans, and tobacco" noted by the earliest missionaries.[22] Women were the "sole mistresses" of the household and the fields, their Blood tasks, including child-rearing, "cultivating their fields," and fetching water. They raised corn, squash, pumpkins, melons, gourds, beans, peas, sweet potatoes, and by the early 1800s, white potatoes, as well. There was an abundance of nuts, including hazel nuts, hickory nuts, walnuts, chestnuts, and pecans, along with licorice, anise, and sweet myrrh. Their crops included strawberries, gooseberries, and whortleberries, along with black and dew berries, as well as plums and "a great variety of grapes."[23] In the 1830s, the Sauk and Meskwaki were remarkable for their fields boasting "great quantities" of corn, beans, and melons.[24] A two-mile span of fields sat outside of Saukenuk, about 800 acres of crops—and this was just for that one town. In going through Sauk and Meskwaki Wisconsin in 1766, Jonathan Carver passed through Saukenuk, seeing fields "adjacent to their houses" all "neatly laid out" and producing "great quantities of Indian corn, beans, melons, &c."[25]

The women created this bounty, yet this very fact made settlers contemptuous of Sauk and Meskwaki culture, for in Europe, only men farmed, and it marked them indelibly as peasants.[26] Like Michigan governor Lewis Cass, American propagandists denounced Indian men as living "in the rudest condition of society, wandering from place to place" and living on "a little corn by the labor of their women," devoured with "true savage improvidence." Otherwise, the men "subsisting" on the "precarious supplies" garnered by hunting and fishing.[27] If we remove the heavy racist sneer, Cass had the facts right: women supplied the vegetal (Blood), and men, the protein (Breath) halves of the national diet.

Carver described 1766 Saukenuk as a prosperous town of ninety longhouses, constructed of "hewn plank, neatly jointed, and covered with bark, so compactly as to keep out the most penetrating rains," with "each large enough for several families." Saukenuk's streets were "regular and spacious," a common feature of Indian roads.[28] This description closely matched that of Peter Pond in 1773, who noted that roofs were constructed by arching, bent-over saplings.[29] Alas for propaganda picturing grubby "wigwams," Satterlee Clark described the dwellings of the 1830s as "more like houses," meaning settler houses, "covered in white cedar bark" as shingles.[30]

Carver also stopped at a main Meskwaki town in 1766, seeing fifty longhouses, but "mostly deserted," due to an "epidemical disorder that had lately raged among them," undoubtedly referring to the massive smallpox outbreak attendant on the deliberate settler smallpox distribution in 1763.[31] The epidemic had "carried off more than half of the inhabitants." Those still healthy had moved into the woods, separating themselves to avoid the contagion.[32] In 1773, Peter Pond found that a "Sweapeing Sicknes" had likewise "a Shorte time Before" carried off "Grate Numbers of Inhabitans" of the companion Sauk town. Although the pox had "Abated," there were still "Sum Sick" when he visited.[33]

Pond encountered the Sauk and Meskwaki in Wisconsin along the Fox River, which runs into Green Bay, living "in a Close Connection among themselves."

He saw the usual crops but complained of an insufficient variety of lake fish, while (given the fur trade's ravishes) the game were just "Sum Rabits & Patreageis, a small Quantaty of Vensen [venison]." In the swamps near Lake Winnebago, "Just in the Canoe track," the "Wilde Oates," rice, "ware so Thick" that the canoes could barely pass. Although all settlers treated Indian berry patches and rice paddies as serendipitous acts of nature, Indians carefully tended these sites. Even as devastated by the fur trade, the September landscape afforded "Eavery artickel of Eating in thare way In abundans."[34]

Although American histories almost never canvass as much, the Sauk and Meskwaki were deeply attenuated by 1800, following debilitating interfaces with Europeans well before the American enterprise disturbed Wisconsin. At contact, the Sauk and Meskwaki lived along the northern shores of the St. Lawrence River, with French sources tracing their being pushed west, past Lakes Ontario and Erie, past Detroit, around the Upper Great Lakes, and down into Wisconsin. Thus, they were hardly untouched by Europeans before William Henry Harrison forced his land grabbing, 1804 Treaty of St. Louis on them. Moreover, French attacks had significantly thinned the populations, while the rapacious fur trade had devastated the environment.

From 1656 through 1667, interacting with the Iroquois, the Sauk and Meskwaki were already west of Montreal in towns along the St. Laurence River, between Lakes Ontario and Erie.[35] From 1670 on, Jesuits regularly encountered Sauk and Meskwaki at Sault Ste. Marie, Michilimackinac, around Lake Michigan, and at Green Bay, Wisconsin.[36] By 1674, a Jesuit mission was established west of Green Bay, specifically for the "Outagami."[37] Thereafter, mentions of the Meskwaki and Sauk located them primarily around Green Bay or along Lake Michigan, although they were still mentioned as being near Lake Erie as late as 1676.[38]

The Sauk and Meskwaki had obviously come to the west only recently, for they told Potherie that the early French trader Nicolas Perrot (ca. 1644–1717) was "*le premier François qui ait ouvert la porte*" (the first Frenchman who had opened the door), that is, welcomed them into the west. Clearly, this welcome came from the French, not the Ho-Chunk ("Winnebago"), Dakota, or Menominee, whose land this was. Still, that Perrot had welcomed them indicates that the French had been out and about in the west before the Sauk and Meskwaki arrived.[39]

A major draw for the French were the copper deposits long mined by the peoples around the Upper Great Lakes, although the lead deposits came as something of a surprise to them. Both led to trouble when, on June 14, 1671, in the "name of the Most High, Most Mighty, and Most Redoubtable Monarch," Louis XIV, the French decreed themselves owners of the copper mines. With the same effect, if a less narcissistic flair on May 8, 1689, Perrot took possession of the "Bay des Puants," meaning Stinky-Water Bay (so-called due to fish die-offs).[40] Now, the Ho-Chunk there became "*Puants*" (Stinkards) under the French pen.

The fur trade directly brought on war against the French from 1681 to 1683 and then again from 1689 to 1698. Plundering the plunderers, the Sauk and Meskwaki killed the missionaries and no longer traded in Montreal, resulting in considerable French losses.[41] Then, as so often happened whenever Europeans were losing an "Indian" war, *"une maladie contagieuse,"* or a contagious disease, mysteriously appeared in Green Bay, causing *"beaucoup de mortalité, ce fleau les affligea extrêmement; ceux qui en rechaperent se trouverent presque tous incommodez, les jeunes gens sur tout"* (great mortality, this scourge afflicting them very severely; those in recuperation found themselves almost totally incapacitated, the Young Men most of all). The French blamed the Indians' own *"crimes seuls"* (crimes, alone) for bringing such a *"châtiment"* (punishment) down on themselves.[42]

Following an uneasy 1683 truce, the war kettle boiled over again in 1689, around the fur and copper trades. Forcing a Jesuit blacksmith to resharpen their battle-dulled hatchets, the Sauk and Meskwaki, along with Kickapoo, Miami, and Illini allies, intercepted French supply boats and assailed the Dakota (*Nadouaissioux*), French trading partners.[43] Meantime, Perrot rushed about, playing both ends against the middle, assuring each side that the other was out to destroy it. Somehow, quiet descended, and the French goal came into focus: access to a lead mine that they had learned about, just before hostilities erupted.[44]

Fearing British influence, to prevent 900 Meskwaki from moving to the Wabash to live with Miami allies, in 1711, the French governor general Pierre de Rigaud de Vaudreuil invited the Sauk and Meskwaki to reside at Detroit.[45] Once the Sauk and Meskwaki arrived, however, Vaudreuil dressed them down in a public shaming, falsely claiming that the Meskwaki had come to Detroit to destroy the Miami and the Wyandot ("Huron") there.[46] Meantime, wanting Michigan back, the Ottawa and Potawatomi of the Three Fires Confederacy attacked the French, with Meskwaki joining in against Detroit, as the Sauk decamped west, for traditionally, the Meskwaki handled war.[47] On October 15, 1712, as the Meskwaki were in the act of surrendering, the French killed almost 1,000 "of both sexes," taking 200 prisoner as slaves.[48] Under pressure from superiors to explain the massacre, Vaudreuil blamed a conspiracy cooked up by Ottawa chief *Saguina*.[49] Amazingly, Western historians take Vaudreuil's word for it, yet the sweep of events read *en suite* instead of piecemeal in multiple, scattered French sources, show that the French had set a deliberate trap to eliminate the Meskwaki.[50] Unsurprisingly angry, the Sauk and Meskwaki now aligned themselves squarely with the Iroquois League, doing as much damage as possible to the French at Green Bay.[51]

French trader militias took over in 1745, in a war drive against the "haughty, imperious" Meskwaki. Striding into a Sauk town, their Captain de Velie demanded that the Sauk hand over the Meskwaki, but the Sauk "old woman" (that is, a chief) flatly refused.[52] At that, Velie pulled his pistol and killed a male chief. When the stunned Sauk still hesitated to comply, Velie casually shot down a second Sauk chief, and a third, apparently planning to continue till the Sauk complied with his order. A twelve-year-old Sauk boy, *Makautapenase* ("Black Bird"), later a renowned Sauk chief, returned fire, killing Velie. Using Velie's death as their opening, the French reinforced immediately, attacking the Sauk.[53]

Next, a fur trader cum militia officer, Captain Morand, executed a sneak attack on the Meskwaki, killing a large number and tracking those escaping as far as

Oshkosh, killing many more, all the way to the mouth of the Wisconsin River.[54] Tracking refugees 200 miles through the snow, Morand mounted his final assault, killing "some" and taking the remaining twenty men and a "large number of women and children" prisoner. One bold Meskwaki woman in the rear waited until only one French-allied "chief" was guarding them. Although bound at the wrists, she grabbed him by the penis with both hands, as he was stooping down to drink from the river. Twisting and squeezing while forcing his head into the river, she held him fast till he died. Next untangling herself, she expeditiously released her cohort, who made their escape. For her quick-thinking bravery, the Meskwaki elevated her to a chieftainship.[55]

The Sauk and Meskwaki decimated by 1747, the French finally erected their permanent trading fort, forcing the Sauk and Meskwaki into trading partnerships.[56] The French ascendency was pretty nigh over, however. Under the onslaught of the British in the French and Indian War, by 1761, the French had conclusively lost all their forts.[57] As full-time enemies of the French and sometimes allies of the British-accommodating Iroquois, the Sauk and Meskwaki hailed the British arrival in 1763, to the point of providing an armed escort for the military and associated British traders coming to Green Bay, not realizing that the peace treaty of February 10, 1763, gave the "French" Northwest to the British.[58] Their accommodating attitude conclusively evaporated once the British began scouting out the copper and lead mines around Lake Superior, with the honeymoon conclusively over by 1769, as British settlers began forcing their way in, despite the Royal Proclamation of 1763, bringing on the successful attack on Fort Chartres, on the Illinois River on May 14, 1769.[59]

When Peter Pond came through Green Bay and down the Fox River in September 1773, he characterized the Meskwaki as having earlier been driven from Detroit "for thare misbehaver," the standing settler gloss of the French massacre of the Meskwaki in 1712. It also remained standard to denigrate the Meskwaki as "insolent" for turning the tables on British traders. "Inclineing Cheaterey," Pond growled, the Meskwaki would "Git Creadit from the trader in the fall of ye Year to Pay in the spring after they Have Made thare Hunt." Then, "When you Mete them in Spring" to "ask for your Pay," they "Speake in thare One Langeuge if thay Speake at all Which is not to be understood or Other ways thay Will Look Sulkey and Make you no answer and you loes your Debt."[60] Pond found the Sauk more to his liking as a people of "Good Sise [sense]" and "Les Inclind to tricks and Bad manners than thare Nighbers."[61]

Clearly, the Meskwaki were not interested in dealing with British traders, so the Spanish thought that they saw their chance. By 1773, the Spanish were conducting a bustling trade with the Sauk, to the growing concern of the British.[62] The Revolution intensified Indian efforts to dislodge the British thorn in their side, despite the British sending two "Bostonnise" (Revolutionary) scalps and wampum to entice the Sauk and Meskwaki in 1780, while threatening all-out war against them, should they not become British proxy fighters. At the same time, discouraging any alliance with the Revolutionaries, the Potawatomi assured the Sauk and Meskwaki that American settlers were the "meanest of wretches."[63]

By 1783, those mean wretches had won the Revolution, obtruding yet a third hostile, foreign presence on them.

European presumption continued in the September 3, 1783, Treaty of Paris, in which the British willy-nilly ceded the Old Northwest to the United States.[64] On October 23, 1782, British general Frederick Haldiman acknowledged that, throughout the Revolution, the Indian nations had staunchly resisted all American efforts to "dispossess" them of it, "their Most Valuable Country." Worse, the treaty fell "So far short" of what the British had assured them was happening in Paris, that they were righteously "Thunder Struck" at the "accommodation" made, for not one of the Indian nations of the Old Northwest had ever agreed to give up any of their land.[65] As Shawnee war chief *Kekewepellethy* put it to U.S. commissioners in 1786, "you never conquered any of us."[66]

Since 1535, the Sauk and Meskwaki had not been able to catch a break, and things were about to deteriorate. With the Louisiana Purchase forcing their Spanish allies to leave St. Louis on March 9, 1804, President Jefferson's governor of the Old Northwest, William Henry Harrison, set about seizing 14,803,520 acres of their land in his very fishy Treaty of St. Louis.[67] Chillingly laying out the steps of U.S. invasion in his 1833 autobiography, *Makataimeshekiakiak* rightly despised St. Louis Treaty as the "origin of all our difficulties."[68] Article 9 of that treaty pledged to "put a stop to the abuses and impositions" of the private traders—by establishing a U.S. trading post that cut off Sauk and Meskwaki access to British and Spanish trade, while physically hedging them in.[69]

Four years later in 1808, the U.S. "factory" or trading post sat at the Des Moines rapids, promising "very cheap" goods. What *Makataimeshekiakiak* called a U.S. "war party" arrived, chopping down the Indians' trees to build their "houses" (Fort Madison), shouldering weapons everywhere, and acting for all the world as if they were in "an enemies' country." As Indians came from all around to see what was happening, some young men played a prank on the settlers, essentially sneaking up on them and shouting, "Boo!" just to watch them drop their weapons and run. Fort Madison's commandant overreacted, firing back with cannons.[70] The Sauk and Meskwaki were now left either at the mercy of the rapacious American Fur Company or turning to the British traders at Malden. They chose Malden, so that Fort Madison closed in 1812, even as *Tenskwatawa* sent his moccasins (messengers) to alert everyone to settler encroachment methods.[71]

U.S. war hawks promptly cooked up a conspiracy theory, featuring the steely-eyed British manipulating the air-headed *Tenskwatawa* and *Tecumseh* into a war against the United States. On July 18, 1810, head war hawk Harrison rang alarm bells over a report that the Sauk and Meskwaki had "received the Tomahawk" and were merely awaiting *Tenskwatawa*'s go-ahead to "strike." In the next breath, Harrison worried that a "considerable number" of Sauk had gone to the British at Malden, implying insidious intent, although he admitted that all the Miami received at Malden were their "accustomed donation of goods," that is, their annuities. In August 1810, the Sauk were likewise "liberally supplied" at Malden in dealing peacefully with British, not American, fur traders. Notwithstanding, Harrison asserted in 1811 that the Sauk had to be talked out of attacking the United States, although *Makataimeshekiakiak* claimed that he went to the British only because the United States at Fort Madison stiffed his people of their annuities, on orders from Washington, D.C.[72]

The Sauk and Meskwaki did ally with *Tecumseh* and *Tenskwatawa* (not the British) against the United States throughout the War of 1812. *Makataimeshekiakiak* supplied 200 men who took part in the sieges of Fort Meigs and Fort Stephenson and engineered two major defeats of the Americans. *Makataimeshekiakiak* spotted six major barges, three armed, retreating down the river on July 22, 1814, as Americans withdrew from the siege of British Fort McKay (later U.S. Fort Crawford) at Prairie du Chien. On July 21, the first set of barges docked for the night at Rock River, where early the next morning, *Makataimeshekiakiak* attacked the third armed barge, killing 100 soldiers, taking five cannons, and then setting the barge aflame. His Sauk, Meskwaki, and Potawatomi Young Men included women warriors, armed with hoes. They leapt onto the barge, some "breaking heads" or cutting holes in the barge to sink it, while others set it on fire. Seeing the destruction in progress, the other barges scrambled to depart. *Makataimeshekiakiak* lost three people in this fight, two men and one woman, two of them in attacking a second barge, as it fled. On the first barge, *Makataimeshekiakiak* found "several barrels of whiskey" (which he emptied onto the ground), along with guns, clothing, tents, and "a box full of small bottles and packages" containing the kind of "*bad medicine*" that settler doctors used "to kill white people when" they were "sick." In reporting this important action, the British officer at Fort McKay, Lieutenant-Colonel William McKay, termed it "one of the most brilliant actions fought by the Indians" in the whole war.[73]

Makataimeshekiakiak followed up this triumph on September 4, 1814, in the Battle of Rock Island Rapids. In this action, identifying the Sauk as those responsible for the barge disaster, the army sent Major Zachary Taylor and 430 men specifically to destroy the Sauk capital of Saukenuk at Rock Island. Meantime, complimenting his July victory, the British supplied *Makataimeshekiakiak* with a "*big gun*," that is, a three-pounder, or cannon, along with two swivels. Bedding them along the Rock River, *Makataimeshekiakiak* dispatched "spies" to watch for Americans coming down the river from Prairie du Chien. Landing on September 3 on a "small willow island"—unwittingly putting him directly across the river from *Makataimeshekiakiak* and British engineers—Taylor made camp for the night. Quickly moving their cannon into best position, *Makataimeshekiakiak* and the British opened fire as Taylor prepared to depart the next morning, hitting fourteen Americans, three of whom later died. Taylor beat a hasty retreat.[74]

Proceeding to a high bluff, where Warsaw, Illinois, now stands, despite the "numerous" Sauk there, Taylor busied himself building Fort Johnson, leaving on October 1, 1814, before the fort was completed. Not wishing "to see a fort" in his "best hunting ground," on July 17, *Makataimeshekiakiak* took what remained of the four kegs of his British gunpowder and set out for Fort Johnson. The night before he arrived, he had a strong dream (Blood potency) directing him to a hollow tree near where Fort Johnson was in the making.

There, he was to look for a large snake, and he would find the "enemy close by, and unarmed."[75]

Scrupulously following the dream's directions, *Makataimeshekiakiak* and one Young Man found the hollow tree and spied "a large snake with his head raised, looking across the creek," to where two American "war chiefs" walked "arm-in-arm, without guns" before the fort's "men at work." *Makataimeshekiakiak's* Young Man shot their sentinel, sending panicked soldiers scattering every which way. There being but two of them, *Makataimeshekiakiak* decided that discretion was the better part of valor. He and his Young Man returned to the full war party, which went home to Saukenuk. Fort Johnson proved unsustainable for the Americans, for even without a full-on attack by *Makataimeshekiakiak*, it could not be supplied from St. Louis. In late October, Taylor had the fort burned, and his men, withdrawn.[76] So far, *Makataimeshekiakiak* was besting Taylor.

At the close of the War of 1812, the United States forced a series of new treaties on the Sauk and Meskwaki, each of them coercing recognition of the repudiated 1804 treaty. On September 13, 1815, those Sauk who had remained aloof from the Tecumseh War pledged to shun the veterans. On September 14, 1815, Article 4 of a treaty specific to the Meskwaki reinstated the 1804 Treaty of St. Louis. On May 13, 1816, Article 1 of the newest "Treaty with the Sauk" likewise re-established the 1804 Treaty of St. Louis, its Article 2 requiring reparations for the war, with Article 3 pledging to withhold Sauk annuities if they did not ante up. Neither *Makataimeshekiakiak* nor *Keokuk* signed either Sauk treaty, although the pushover *Quashquame* signed the 1815 Sauk Treaty.[77] Treating separately with the Sauk and Meskwaki this way was part of a deliberate strategy of the United States to pulverize Indian confederacies. It had the same devastating effect as Ohio's making independent treaties with foreign powers would have on the U.S.

The main draw of Wisconsin for settlers was its lead and copper mining, so that the 1804 Treaty of St. Louis was largely about acquiring the lead mines, whose deposits were so vast as to encourage forced sales and federal squabbles over ownership through 1811. Importantly, the Sauk and Meskwaki had spent the war years blocking settler access to the mines, succeeding in keeping the settlers out until the postwar treaties forced them to stand down.[78] Such homeland defense was always cried up as "Indian depredations" but just who was despoiling whom deserves to be considered.

Subsequent to these treaties, Fort Armstrong was built very near the Sauk capital of Saukenuk on Rock Island. Under the cover of a trading post from which the promised annuities were distributed, it was actually a U.S military staging ground. By September 1819, Colonel Henry Leavenworth was gathering up men and supplies to begin building what, in 1820, became Fort Snelling, at the mouth of the St. Peter's River.[79] The United States was spreading out a web of forts across the upper Northwest that would prove fatal to the Sauk and Meskwaki in the trumped-up Black Hawk War of 1832.

Around 1819, the local Indian agent informed the Sauk and Meskwaki that they soon had to move west of the Mississippi River, per the terms of the 1804 treaty. Stunned, *Makataimeshekiakiak* asked the British to parse out the law for him. *Quashquame*, who had signed the fatal 1804 treaty as well as the 1815 treaty, assured *Makataimeshekiakiak* that he "never had consented to the sale" of Saukenuk. The civil chief *Keokuk* had made a deal to sell a different strip of land, in the forced, September 3, 1822, treaty concluded at Fort Armstrong. Both *Keokuk* and *Quashquame* signed this hasty treaty, but *Makataimeshekiakiak* did not. Although encompassing the Sauk and Meskwaki as a unified group, the 1822 document again required signatories to recognize the 1804 treaty.[80]

As settler invasion caused the land and game to grow scarce, friction erupted among the nations of the area, so on August 4, 1824, proclaiming a need to "remove all future cause of dissesions" over boundaries, the United States seized all the land in a new treaty, signed by *Keokuk* but not by *Makataimeshekiakiak*. Article 1 required the Sauk and Meskwaki to "cede, relinquish, and forever quit claim" to all their lands in northern Illinois and the eastern third of Missouri, except for a small strip belonging to the "half-breeds." The fraudulent 1804 treaty was clearly the rub there, but the U.S. presumption of authority over Dakota land was even more dubious, although the United States somehow dictated its boundary lines, too, on August 19, 1825.[81]

The next order of invasion was to establish U.S. roads. The southern portion of Wisconsin was the most heavily populated by the Mound Builders and their descendant nations. Settler mythologies about a mysteriously "white race" of Mound Builders aside, mound building was Indigenous and continued into the era of European contact.[82] Networks of roads connected the mound complexes, so the settlers simply took over the Indians' wide roads and regular water routes, including fords.[83] Using Indian guides, first the French and then the British entered through and usurped the established routes. The War of 1812 brought the Wisconsin-Fox River portage strongly to U.S. attention.[84] By 1814, the roads connecting Green Bay with the surrounding areas were being mentioned in U.S. settler letters.[85]

The 1820s saw the real burst of activity, as lead miners linked themselves to markets, particularly after 1821, when the president was authorized to lease area lead mines as supervised by the War Department, spurring an enormous mining output and concomitant settler population boom (see Table 8.1).[86] Over extant Indian roads, miners connected Fort Armstrong, where the Sauk capital lay, with mining towns at Galena and Mineral Point and from Galena to Chicago. At the same time, Dixon's Ferry ran across the Sauk's Rock River. The General Survey Act of 1824 next empowered surveying for roadbuilding as governmentally deemed necessary, "in a commercial or military view."[87]

Surveys commenced immediately in Michigan, Arkansas, and Florida, although Iowa and Wisconsin lagged. Two important roads emerged, however, along the Meskwaki's Fox River, the one connecting to Fort Winnebago, and the other, to Fort Howard. Constructed in 1827, "Kellogg's Trail," a U.S. mail route, linked Galena with Peoria and on to the southern and eastern Illinois.[88] U.S. orders came down to connect the Fox and Wisconsin Rivers to the Mississippi, militarily, because of high-volume shipping through Green Bay,

Table 8.1 Population of Territories of Michigan and Illinois and of the Sauk and Meskwaki

Years	Settlers			Indians[a]	
	Michigan (MI) Territory[b]	Illinois (IL) Territory		Sauk	Meskwaki
	Free	Slave[c]	Free		
1666–1667					4,000
1716	600				3,500
1728					800
1736				800	
1752		595	785		
1758					1,000
1764				1,600	
1777				1,600	1,400
1786				1,600	1,400
1800	3,757		2,458		
1804				2,000	
1806					1,750[d]
1810	4,762		12,282		
1818				4,800	2,000
1820	7,452		55,211		
1829				5,000	
1830	28,004		157,445		
1834				2,500	
1836					1,600
1840	212,267		476,183		

[a] Settler sources typically listed "warrior" head counts, standardly considered one-fourth of total population. Based on that formula, the whole population is calculated here.

[b] Includes Wisconsin and Iowa.

[c] Includes both Indian and African slaves.

[d] Actual head count.

Table 8.1 shows the change in settler, slave, Sauk, and Meskwaki populations from 1666 to 1840.

Sources: For Meskwaki, for 1666–1667, Thwaites, 1899, vol. 51, 43; for 1716, Charlevoix, 1903, vol. 5, 82; for 1728, Hodge, 1907–1910, vol. 1, "Foxes," 474; for 1758, Krzywicki, 1934, 454; for 1777, Houck, 1909, vol. 1, 146; for 1806, Schoolcraft, 1853, vol. 3, 562; for 1786, Thwaites, 1908, 365; for 1811, Morse, 1822, 363; for 1836, Krzywicki, 1934, 455; for Sauk, Schoolcraft, 1853, vol. 3, in 1736, 554, in 1764, 559; for 1777, Houck, 1909, vol. 1, 146; for 1786, Thwaites, 1908, 365; for 1804, *ASPIA*, 1832, vol. 1, 711; for 1818, Morse, 1822, 363; for 1829, Krzywicki, 1934, 470; for 1834, Hodge, 1907–1910, vol. 2, "Sauk," 479; for Settlers, Michigan Territory, for 1716, Peterson, 1985, 46; for 1800, 1810, 1820, 1830, and 1840, USDC, 1996, 4; for Settlers, Illinois Territory, for 1752, Ekberg, 2000, 152; for 1810, 1820, 1830, and 1840, USDC, 1996, 4.

1828–1829.[89] In May 1830, Congress appropriated $2,000 for the Wisconsin Road, a military road, bisecting Wisconsin to position the army for attack on area Indians.[90] In 1831, Jefferson Davis was dispatched to build a military road between Fort Winnebago to Fond du Lac.[91] In October 1830, and again in March 1832, miner conglomerates pressed hard for two formal roads, the one from the Illinois line to Green Bay through Fort Winnebago and the other from Prairie du Chien (Fort Crawford) to the Blue Mounds, the heart of the mining district.[92]

By 1832, there were "travelled roads" connecting Fort Crawford to just about all points in the region, with regular water travel supplementing land travel. Now, it was just a matter of consolidation, so on July 14, 1832, Congress appropriated $5,000 for a federal road connecting Forts Howard, Winnebago, and Crawford, traversing Wisconsin, east to west.[93] This road was delayed, however, because *Makataimeshekiakiak* had already made other plans, marching his people home that spring, so the Wisconsin Road could not be constructed until 1836.[94]

Roads and forts went hand-in-hand. Settler militia forts and fur traders' forts, usually armed with cannons, already dotted the area (as shown in Table 8.2). On the premise of establishing U.S. "factories" or trading posts, a bevy of military forts were sneaked in. By 1829, a plan was hatched to carve a proposed "Huron Territory" from what had been Western Michigan Territory, with Green Bay its headquarters, and its extent running west to Prairie du Chien, where Fort Crawford sat, but the plan was stymied by simultaneous Removal plans to dump the Oneida at Green Bay as complicated by an insufficient settler population to form a separate territory.[95]

Since 1828, settler expansion had been squeezing the Sauk and Meskwaki ever farther west onto Menominee and Dakota lands, heating up friction among them over resources. Stuffing Indian nations together this way on an attenuated land base was quite consciously done from the first. As Secretary of War Henry Knox observed on June 15, 1789, to President George Washington, Indians "removed from their usual hunting grounds ... must necessarily encroach on the hunting grounds of another tribe," which would "not suffer the encroachment with impunity—hence they destroy each other."[96] The hostilities then offered a pretext for U.S. interference, as in 1829 in U.S.-forced "peace" negotiations.[97] Honest enough to name the precipitating "evil" as the squatters, John Quincy Adams looked to quiet the Wisconsin hubbub by removing them, but one of the first moves of the Jackson administration was to belay that order, instead beefing up the militias of Michigan Territory.[98]

Trying to live with the unlivable, the Sauk and Meskwaki continued their traditional ways of the women's agriculture in the summer and the men's hunt in the winter, but knowing that they could get away with any crime against Indians, squatters began moving into Sauk and Meskwaki towns, once the people left on their winter hunt. Used to returning to a perfectly undisturbed abode, *Makataimeshekiakiak* was shocked in 1819–1820 to find squatters living in it. He immediately acquired a U.S. writ removing these intruders, but over the winter of 1823–1824, additional squatters arrived, with the U.S. government

Table 8.2 Forts Heading into the Black Hawk War, 1832

Dates	Fort Names	Locations	Usage	Notes
1832	Apple River Fort	Elizabeth, Illinois	Settler fortification	Single Blockhouse
1832	Blue Mounds Fort	Dane County, one mile south of Eastern Mound	Militia fort	Built in two weeks for Black Hawk War; also "Fort Blue"
1832	Buffalo Grove Fort	Buffalo Grove, Illinois	Militia fort	Activated for Black Hawk War
1816–1863	Fort Armstrong	Rock Island, Illinois	U.S. Army fort	Arsenal; staging ground, Black Hawk War; first encamped, 1804
1832	Fort Cassville	Cassville, Wisconsin	Settler fortification	Lead miners' fort; also called "Fort Cass"
1816–1856	Fort Crawford	Prairie du Chien, Wisconsin; mouth of Wisconsin River	U.S. Army fort	Rebuilt, 1829, by Zachary Taylor
1832	Fort Clark	White Oak Springs, Wisconsin	Militia fort	100′ × 50′ stockade
1803–1871	Fort Dearborn	Chicago, Illinois	U.S. Army fort	Rebuilt 1816 after burned in 1812
1832	Fort Defiance	Mineral Point, Wisconsin	Settler fortification	Lead Miners' blockhouses
1832	Fort Diamond Grove	Diamond Grove, Wisconsin	Settler fortification	John B. Terry's Farm
1832	Fort Dodge	Platteville, Wisconsin	Militia fortification	Also called "Roundtree's Fort," built for Black Hawk War
1832	Fort Ebersol	Hardscrabble Prairie, Wisconsin	Settler fortification	Miners' log fort at Ebersol mansion; also "Ebersol's Fort"
1832	Fort Funk	Monticello, Wisconsin	Settler fortification	Town originally "Wiley's Grove"; for Black Hawk War

(continued)

Table 8.2 (Continued)

Dates	Fort Names	Locations	Usage	Notes
1832	Fort Galena	Galena, Illinois	Militia encampment	Built for Black Hawk War
1832	Fort Gratiot	Gratiot's Grove, Wisconsin	Settler fortification	Lead Miners' stockade
1832	Fort Hamilton	Wiota, Wisconsin	Settler fortification	Miners' fort built for Black Hawk War
1816–1841	Fort Howard	Green Bay, Wisconsin	U.S. Army fort	Rebuilt briefly, 1852, 1861–1863
1827–1832	Fort Independence	Old Shullsburg, Wisconsin	Militia fort	Stockade; also called "Fort Shull"
1832	Fort Jackson	Mineral Point, Wisconsin	Settler fortification	Stockade for Black Hawk War
1832	Fort Justus	Elk Grove, Wisconsin	Settler fortification	Miners' stockade built for Black Hawk War; also called "Fort DeSeelhorst"
1832	Fort Kindle	Lafayette Co., Wisconsin	Settler fortification	Stockade for Black Hawk War
1832	Fort Koshkonong	Fort Atkinson, Wisconsin	Temporary Army stockade	Named for nearby Lake Koshkonong
1814–1895	Fort Mackinac	Mackinac Island, Michigan	U.S. Army fort	Acquired from British, 1814; personnel deployment point, Black Hawk War, 1832
1832	Fort Napoleon	Linden, Wisconsin	Settler fortification	Also called "Fort Bonaparte"
1832	Fort Parrish	Montfort, Wisconsin	Settler fortification	Blockhouse; Built by Thomas Parrish; first called "Wingville"
1827–1832	Fort Plattville	Near Plattville, Wisconsin	Settler fortification	Blockhouse
1832	Fort Union	Dodgeville, Wisconsin	Militia fort	Wisconsin State Militia HQ
1828–1845	Fort Winnebago	At portage of Fox and Wisconsin	U.S. Army fort	Medical post till stockade built 1832 for Black Hawk War

1826	Jefferson Barracks	St. Louis, Missouri	U.S. Army fort	First actual use in Black Hawk War
1832	Jones' Blockhouse	Sinsinawa, Wisconsin	Settler fortification	Not to be confused with 1844 structure at Sinsinawa Mound Center
1832	Journey's Fort	White Oak Springs, Wisconsin	Settler fortification	100′ × 50′ stockade

Table 8.2 enumerates and describes the settler forts ringing Sauk and Meskwaki lands leading into the Black Hawk War.

Sources: Generally, see Hannings, 2006, 616–19; **Apple River**, Trask, 2006, 220–23; Matteson, 1893, 245; Birmingham, 2014, 99; **Blue Mounds**, Birmingham, 2014, 99; Matteson, 1893, 242–43, 219; Smith, 1854, vol. 1, 215; **Buffalo Grove**, Matteson, 1893, 245; Smith, 1854, vol. 1, 147–48, 171, 179; **Armstrong**, Flagler, 1877; Dyer, 1946, 68, 82–84; **Cassville**, Smith, 1854, vol. 1, 216; Birmingham, 2014, 99; **Clark**, Western Historical Company, 1881, 471, 564; Smith, 1854, vol. 1, 216; Birmingham, 2014, 99; Payette, 2010, "American Forts, Wisconsin"; **Crawford**, Mahan, 1926; Smith, 1854, vol. 1, 184–85; Payette, *op. cit.*; **Dearborn**, Blanchard, 1898–1900, vol. 1, 334–38, 386–88, 489–92, 549–620 passim; **Defiance**, Western Historical Company, 1881, 472–76, 609; Smith, 1854, vol. 1, 215; Birmingham, 2014, 99, 102–3; Payette, *op. cit.*; **Diamond Grove**, Smith, 1854, vol. 1, 216; Western Historical Company, 1881, 471; **Dodge**, Matteson, 1893, 243; Birmingham, 2014, 99; Payette, *op. cit.*; **Ebersol**, Birmingham, 2014, 99; Butterfield, 1881, 785–86; **Funk**, Western Historical Company, 1881, 429, 471; Payette, *op. cit.*; **Galena**, Birmingham, 2014, 99; Smith, 1854, vol. 1, 180–81; **Gratiot**, Smith, 1854, vol. 1, 215; Western Historical Company, 1881, 429, 437, 457; Birmingham, 2014, 99; Wisconsin Historical Society, 1828; **Hamilton**, Matteson, 1893, 244; Smith, 1854, vol. 1, 215; Western Historical Company, 1881, 428; Birmingham, 2014, 99; Wisconsin Historical Company, 1881, 44, 221; Matteson, 1893, 152; **Independence**, Smith, 1854, vol. 1, 216; Western Historical Company, 1881, 471; Birmingham, 2014, 99; **Jackson**, Smith, 1854, vol. 1, 215; Birmingham, 2014, 27, 64, 66, 69, 99, 102–3; **Justus**, Western Historical Company, 1881, 471; Smith, 1854, vol. 1, 216; Birmingham, 2014, 99; **Kindle**, Birmingham, 2014, 99, 113; **Koshkonong**, as "Fort Koshkonong"; Matteson, 1893, 219; **Mackinac**, Jung, 2018, 139–40; **Napoleon**, Prairie Farmer Publishing Copmany, 1929/1986, 16; Birmingham, 2014, 99; **Parrish**, Smith, 1854, vol. 1, 215; Holford, 1900, 723; Birmingham, 2014, 99; **Plattville**, Smith, 1854, vol. 1, 216; Payette, *op. cit.*; **Snelling**, DeCarlo, 2017; **Union**, Smith, 1854, vol. 1, 215; Birmingham, 2014, 99, 102–3; **Winnebago**, Matteson, 1893, 170–72; **Jefferson Barracks**, Grassino and Schuermann, 2011; **Jones' Blockhouse**, Birmingham, 2014, 99; Payette, *op. cit.*; **Journey's Fort**, Birmingham, 2014, 99; Western Historical Company, 1811, 584.

disregarding its guarantee to remove them. Emboldened, squatters used "sticks" to assault Indians coming home and "cheated" them of the hunt's peltries. During one winter, squatters set fire to forty homes. Other intruders plied the Sauk with illegal whiskey (an old trick for getting Indians to sign over land) and beat any and all Indians, at will. They ripped up Sauk fencing, ploughed under their planted fields, and raped the women.[99]

At first, *Makataimeshekiakiak* allowed no one to respond in kind, hoping that it might sink in that the Sauk were peaceful, but the squatters promptly beat a Sauk to death. Next, they complained to U.S. authorities that the Sauk were the "*intruders*" and themselves, "the *injured* party." Still hoping to settle matters quietly, *Makataimeshekiakiak* approached two semi-officials, James Hall, a territorial judge, and Edward Coles, who had been governor of Illinois, 1822–1826, only to find that they had no power over the squatters. Finally, *Makataimeshekiakiak* checked with the U.S. Indian agent, who had the worst news: the government was selling Saukenuk land to individual settlers, so that he and his followers had to vacate the premises.[100]

There was nowhere to go. With the February 1830 U.S.-forced "peace" negotiations stumbling, the Dakota ("Sioux"), Menominee, and Ho-Chunk were planning an "exterminating war" against the Sauk and Meskwaki. Fur trader Robert Stuart blamed the tensions on the failure of the United States to establish the Indian nations' "boundary lines." The "game" having nearly "disappeared" from Sauk and Meskwaki lands had left the people desperate and "reckless," he added, not connecting the fauna extinction to the European fur trade or the overcrowding to Jacksonian Removal.[101]

On the pretext of ending the warfare against the Sauk and Meskwaki, the United States imposed a "peace" on July 15, 1830, that simply packed the Sauk, Meskwaki, Omaha, Iowa, Dakota, Otoe, and Missouria in even tighter. By February 9, 1831, the Menominee were forced to fork over land around Green Bay as the Removal home of the Oneida.[102] Meanwhile, the U.S. "peace" treaty had the uncanny effect of zeroing in on the Sauk and Meskwaki concerning "ceded and unceded" lands, running boundary lines around Rock River, Fox River, and Fort Winnebago, all Sauk and Meskwaki land.[103] Article 2 specifically seized the strip of Sauk and Meskwaki land twenty miles wide running from the Mississippi to the Des Moines River, land that had been specifically retained by the Sauk and Meskwaki under an 1825 treaty. Thus, the "peace" treaty was, in fact, a Sauk and Meskwaki Removal treaty. It was signed by *Keokuk* but not by *Makataimeshekiakiak*.[104]

Although the United States presented *Keokuk* as speaking for all the Sauk, it was not unaware of the opposition of *Makataimeshekiakiak*. The 1830 treaty commissioners had plenty of advance notice of his position that the Sauk had never sold their homeland and would not, therefore, abandon it. Officials were consequently sent to pressure *Makataimeshekiakiak* to "give up" and move across the river with *Keokuk*, but *Makataimeshekiakiak* refused to leave Saukenuk.[105] The government next turned to its "good" chief, *Keokuk*, smearing *Makataimeshekiakiak* as the leader of ominous "British Band." Western historians have since presented the distance between *Keokuk* and *Makataimeshekiakiak* as personal, but this diminishes both men, for the distance was governmental. *Keokuk* was the civil chief, charged with maintaining peace, whereas *Makataimeshekiakiak* was the war chief, charged with defense of sovereignty. Each did his job, and were it not for European invasion, the two would have operated in traditional tandem, with each position checking and balancing the other.

Western historians miss this interface because they tend not to realize how much and how casually Europeans lie. Neither do they know that lying, not murder, is the highest crime for traditional Indians, for a murderer cannot shred the fabric of a society, but a liar can. That is why a wampum ritual exists to quell the disruption caused by murder, but there is no wampum to repair the damage done by lying.[106] Throughout his autobiography, *Makataimeshekiakiak* evinced visceral shock each time he realized that the settlers, whether U.S. or British, had deceived him.[107] Devotion to truth was why he remained at Saukenuk in the face of U.S. threats, because he knew that their basis, the 1804 treaty, was a web of lies, and he expected the truth to prevail. *Keokuk* knew the same but did not expect honor to guide settler actions. Both men were trying to protect the people, each from his own standpoint.

Because *Makataimeshekiakiak* never acted without first seeking counsel, he called councils of the whole of his people before he responded to the 1830 treaty. The women's councils reported that the planting was poor, and the crop yields, scanty, at *Keokuk*'s Removal site, the hard ground breaking their hoes. Meantime, the men's councils declared that, if they were going west, then it would have to be by force. *Makataimeshekiakiak* also contacted both the Michigan territorial governor and the British governor at Malden, Ontario, specifically asking the British about the Western legalities of the matter. The British reassured him that, so long as the Sauk had not sold their lands, the settlers could not oust them.[108] Of course, the United States claimed that the land was sold and seized on *Makataimeshekiakiak*'s trips to Canada as proof that he led the "British band" of Sauk.[109]

Finally, *Makataimeshekiakiak* approached trader George Davenport, who was "fond of talking." Unsurprisingly, Davenport defended the Removal treaty, pressing *Makataimeshekiakiak* to try for "some terms" consistent with honor that would allow him to remove. "After thinking some time" on the suggestion, *Makataimeshekiakiak* decided to assent to his own, separate treaty with the United States, if the "Red Headed Chief" at St. Louis (William Clark) were willing. ("Red-Head" was an allusion to the cannibal giants of tradition.[110]) Far from reacting with grace, the "great chief" Clark growled that he would make no such deal, that if *Makataimeshekiakiak* did not "remove immediately," then he would be *"drove off!!"*[111] A slit-eyed settler rumor ascribed *Makataimeshekiakiak*'s resistance to a ruse to force the United States to ante up, enabling the Sauk to settle their debts. Just suggesting the deal had torn *Makataimeshekiakiak* to the core, however. Not really wanting the treaty in the first place, he was actually relieved by Clark's reply, although had Clark agreed, *Makataimeshekiakiak* would have "removed peaceably" for the sake of the "women and children."[112]

Keokuk used his "smooth tongue" to cajole those at Saukenuk into coming west, while the lesser orator *Makataimeshekiakiak* consoled himself with the thought that all the women supported him as the United States stepped up its pressure on *Makataimeshekiakiak* to leave, immediately.[113] The Ho-Chunk holy man who would go on to become his primary civil chief, *Wabokieshiek* ("White Cloud") assured him that he would not be removed, however, so *Makataimeshekiakiak* again tried for peaceful coexistence, the women planting their spring fields at Saukenuk, only to see the fractious settlers rip them up. Determined to "put a stop to it," once and for all, *Makataimeshekiakiak* gave the settlers one day to clear out of Saukenuk. The "worst left within the appointed time," he said.[114]

The worst did not accept their eviction, however. Presenting themselves as the "residents" of Rock Island, on April 30, 1831, they wrote to Illinois governor John Reynolds, demanding immediate "protection" against the Sauk, whom they charged with destroying their crops in the fall of 1830. Claiming that "Black Hawk" had "six or seven Hundred" men under him, they alleged that the Potawatomi and Ho-Chunk had joined *Makataimeshekiakiak*. On May 19, abetted by a deposition of May 26, the "Sitizens of rock river" reiterated their complaints, again demanding protection. This time, *Makataimeshekiakiak* supposedly led 300 men.[115] As the settlers were known "thieves, counterfeiters, cut-throats," as well as "social outlaws from the east," there was more than elite concern for the backwoods citizenry behind Reynolds's May 26 order calling up 700 militia to remove the "Sock Indians ... forcibly if they must." By May 28, *Makataimeshekiakiak*'s band had become a hostile, invading force, *Makataimeshekiakiak*'s stand attributed to the effects of "whiskey" on the Indian brain. On May 29, U.S. Army general Edmund Pendleton Gaines notified Reynolds that he had ordered six companies of regular soldiers to replace the Illinois militia.[116] Within two weeks, a mole hill had swelled into the Himalayas.

Seeing the settler frenzy, *Makataimeshekiakiak* went again to *Wabokieshiek* for insight. The holy man had dreamed that Gaines approached solely to frighten him into fleeing Saukenuk, which was, in fact, true. Having heard of a U.S. pledge not to harm peaceful Indians (a probable reference to Article 9 of the 1814 Treaty of Ghent guaranteeing the Indians "all the possessions, rights, and privileges" they had held in 1811), *Makataimeshekiakiak* trusted the dream and stayed put.[117]

A settler war drive ensued, circulating spurious stories of *Makataimeshekiakiak* gathering up "from 5 to 800 fighting men" at Saukenuk. By June 9, 1831, Governor Reynolds was preparing for war and generally presenting *Wabokieshiek*'s intercourse with Saukenuk as war planning. By mid-June, settler rumors had 100 Kickapoo, Potawatomi, and Ho-Chunk visiting Saukenuk.[118] The second week of May 1831, Colonel Willoughby Morgan, then commander at Fort Crawford, ordered the Sauk and Meskwaki to appear at talks. On June 4–7, the settlers' lead "war chief," General Gaines threatened and cajoled *Makataimeshekiakiak*, and *Keokuk* attempted to defuse the situation. Indian culture teaches that the best way not to be attacked is to appear strong and unafraid. Consequently, *Makataimeshekiakiak* and his people arrived at the talks in war regalia, singing war songs. Predictably, this left settlers tittering that they had never before seen "so strong a demonstration of hostility."[119]

As talks opened on June 4, Gaines charged the Sauk with "improper conduct" and openly fumed over the cost of sending U.S. troops, while ordering *Makataimeshekiakiak* to move west, forthwith. *Makataimeshekiakiak* replied that they had never sold their land, cleverly pointing out that the United States had had never paid his people any annuities, legally meaning that they were not party to the treaties of 1804, 1815, and 1816, and thus could not have sold Saukenuk. Interestingly, Gaines never mentioned the 1830 Removal treaty, which stealthily took the strip of land in question. These telling points somehow did not appear in the U.S. minutes. In fact, the U.S. minutes barely recorded *Makataimeshekiakiak* as speaking for the Sauk, instead, featuring as speaker *Quashmaquilly* ("Jumping Fish").[120] Also omitted from the U.S. minutes was Gaines leaping up in frustration, shouting, "Who is *Black Hawk?* Who is *Black Hawk?*"

"I am a *Sac!*" *Makataimeshekiakiak* shot back. "My forefather was a SAC! and all nations call me SAC!"[121]

Of this contretemps, the official minutes only recorded *Makataimeshekiakiak* as demurely agreeing that he was Sauk, but in a personal letter, the session's recording secretary portrayed *Makataimeshekiakiak* as responding pretty much as *Makataimeshekiakiak* had it, desiring to "remain" where the ancestors' "bones" were "laid," the traditional way of referring to one's homeland.[122] Gaines was apparently upset that *Makataimeshekiakiak* had undeniable standing and determined support, with speakers *Quashmaquilly* and *Akiniconisot* ("Man Who Strikes First") strongly seconding his message. Indeed, *Makataimeshekiakiak* threw Gaines an astute curve, asking whether the settlers wanted the land so urgently because they had just found additional mineral deposits.[123] The first day's talks ended in vexation all around.

That night, *Makataimeshekiakiak* consulted *Wabokieshiek* on how to break the deadlock. In a dream, *Wabokieshiek* had seen an unnamed clan chief, given only as the "daughter of *Matatas*," unfortunately left unnamed in the sources. (*Matatas* was a civil chief generally regarded as "friendly" by U.S. treaty commissioners.) She was to take her "stick" (planting hoe, a sign of office) and go to the "war chief" Gaines with the words of the women, first reminding Gaines of *Matatas*'s long-standing cooperation with the United States. She was to ask whether the women could stay at Saukenuk long enough to gather their harvest, without which the "little children must perish with hunger." Accordingly, this female chief, properly accompanied by an entourage of Young Men, entered the fort, approaching Gaines with *Wabokieshiek*'s dream speech. Arrogantly patriarchal, Gaines replied coldly that the president sent him neither "to make treaties with women, nor to hold council with them!" He threw the Young Men out of the fort, although bidding her to remain, "if she wished."[124] The U.S. minutes included none of this authorized speech.

Apparently, Gaines and Reynolds had decided on action immediately following the first day's resistance, for by the second day of the conference, the United States was preparing for war, with Gaines rumoring to Reynolds that

Makataimeshekiakiak was gathering an army. On June 5, the second day, *Keokuk* met ex parte with Gaines, asking for military calm as he plied his own tactic to "draw" Saukenuk families to his side of the river, *Makataimeshekiakiak* recounted. Already, fifty households had joined *Keokuk*, and he expected his efforts soon to pull over additional families. Thus, gradually, he would hollow out the Saukenuk holdouts, till all were safely west—if only Gaines and the United States would hold off on hostilities. If the U.S. government would use its muscle to prevent Dakota and Menominee raiding against removed Sauk and Meskwaki, *Keokuk* intimated, then all Rock Island families would likely join him. Gaines acceded to his requests.[125]

The June 7, 1831, minutes recorded women's speeches, with both the minutes and a personal letter noting that several female chiefs came forward accompanied by *Makataimeshekiakiak*, who presented their words. It is a standing Woodlands practice for women's councils to send male speakers to male councils (and vice versa).[126] Culturally, what the Sauk would have heard in Gaines's disdain for *Matata*'s daughter was a rebuke for not presenting the women's words to a male council through a male speaker. Thus, the female chiefs returned *en masse* on June 7, bringing their male speaker, *Makataimeshekiakiak*. Now in recorded minutes, the women said that they had worked hard to render Saukenuk valuable farmland, only now to be told they must leave it. A female chief styled the "daughter of a great chief"—probably *Matatas*—then reiterated that the women had no intention of leaving, as the land had never been sold. *Makataimeshekiakiak* requested food for the women. Because Gaines did reply to the women on June 7, this was probably their second attempt, the primarily male speaker forcing their talk into the minutes.[127]

According to the U.S. minutes, the June 7 minutes ended on a concession from *Makataimeshekiakiak*. As the meeting broke up, Gaines again pressed for removal west with *Makataimeshekiakiak* agreeing to make no further opposition, should all of the chiefs agreed to remove.[128] On June 8, Gaines reiterated this claim and a week later, announced that *Makataimeshekiakiak* was removing by June 18.[129] In his memoirs, *Makataimeshekiakiak* said that Gaines had threatened him with removal by force if the Sauk did not leave by the U.S. deadline. At this ultimatum,*Makataimeshekiakiak* remarked disconsolately, "All our plans were now defeated." It is a chief's job to ensure that all the people are provided for and safe, which seemed to be *Makataimeshekiakiak*'s concern. Removal rations being notoriously inadequate, *Makataimeshekiakiak* recalled a treaty guarantee of farming assistance, so he asked for it, with settlers casting this request as a hostile act. Meantime, Gaines had sent heavily armed gunboats to haze Rock Island, as the children played along the shoreline.[130]

In accordance with his pledge to Gaines, *Makataimeshekiakiak* withdrew across the Mississippi. Close on his heels, the settler militia sacked the Saukenuk cemetery, disinterring fifteen to twenty corpses, pulling one entirely from its grave to throw in a fire. (Not only did settler militias regularly scalp the deceased for the scalp bounties, but from 1823 on, Indian skulls were "collected" by "scientists," who paid handsomely for the "best" skulls.[131]) The settlers also began taking free shots at any Indians "peaceably" going down river, seizing, stealing, or destroying their canoes. They waylaid one Indian with a pass to retrieve a settler-stolen horse and "gave him a severe whipping."When informed of the occurrences, Reynolds intoned that "all good men" would be "shocked"—but he took no action.[132] Perhaps this was because Reynolds presented the Sauk as basely refusing to leave land that they "had sold to the General Government." Albeit the preferred settler narrative, after Gaines's conference, horrified U.S. officials realized that *Makataimeshekiakiak* had been correct. The "residents" had had no legal right to Rock Island, even under U.S. law. The preemption (squatters') act of April 30, 1830, required them to have "occupied" the land by April 30, 1830, and have "cultivated" it in 1829, conditions never met by the squatters.[133]

Fretting, commander in chief of the Army Alexander Macomb ordered an independent review of the situation by Captain Richard H. Bell. On August 16, 1831, Bell significantly corrected the settler version of events at Saukenuk, forthrightly attributing their bad behavior to a "rooted animosity" toward all Indians "at all times." In 1832, settler Charles Whittlesey presented the facts leading to the Black Hawk War as so "variously stated," that it was "difficult to come at the truth," but Bell's facts were pretty clear: "Cupidity" animated the settler stance, "allways." Backed by the military might of the U.S. war apparatus, the settlers would accept nothing less than war. *Makataimeshekiakiak* had 120 "warriors," at best, said Bell, charging settlers with "extravagant exaggeration" but not for reasons of fear. Instead, they were excited by the prospect of the U.S. government paying them to act as militiamen, supplied with government-issue ammunition with which to "get" the Rock Island "lands."[134] And there it was: "getting" Indian lands was ever the bottom line for settlers, especially if they could inveigle the United States to pay them to do it. Settler militias were the Brownshirts of U.S.-Indian policy, achieving U.S. goals while allowing the government plausible deniability for their crimes.

Bell was drowned out. The war justification that Indian agent James Boyd offered on July 23, 1832, mirrored the official U.S. explication of the war: A "crisis" had arrived, cried Boyd, which "if not promptly and gallantly met by all entrusted with authority for the public good," would "cause this fair & infant portion of the union to mourn for devastations by the scalping knife." The ruin would be "scarcely inferior" to that which, "by the Scourging hand of an Almighty Providence," the 1832 cholera pandemic was about to unleash. The cholera pandemic took around 150,000 U.S. lives, whereas seventy-seven settlers, including civilian and military, died in the Black Hawk War.[135] This sort of wild overstatement characterized all contemporary commentary on the Black Hawk War.

Soldier John Allen Wakefield offered up rationales for the massacre of the "wretched wanderers," that regurgitated settler ideology of "right by civilization" to Indian lands. After all, said Wakefield, the Sauk and Meskwaki had "had no home in the world" but were "like the wild beasts more than man." Settlers wrote at narcissistic length, blowing events wildly out of proportion, for instance, inflating a tiny, June 16, skirmish into the grand "Battle of Pecatonica," replete with a "controversy" that arose over whose recollections were accurate.[136]

Makataimeshekiakiak was thus on thin ice figuratively as well as physically when he crossed over the Mississippi River on spring's last frozen water early in 1832, traveling east to see *Wabokieshiek*.[137] Because his father was Sauk, *Wabokieshiek* enjoyed informal influence with many Sauk, becoming the refugees' civil chief.[138] *Wabokieshiek* urged *Makataimeshekiakiak* not to give up Saukenuk, lest the squatters "plough up" the ancestors' "bones."[139] To be sure, the militia had dug up the Saukenuk cemetery, but *Wabokieshiek* was referencing an Indian commonplace about the people's sacred connection to Spirits of Place, where Earth is made of their ancestors, the first five feet down. This is why *Makataimeshekiakiak* repeatedly referenced ancestral bones and why the Three Fires Confederacy and the Ho-Chunk were willing to support the Sauk claim to Saukenuk.[140] When *Wabokieshiek* invited the Sauk to La Crosse, *Makataimeshekiakiak* was elated, for he had, after all, made no promise to the United States about La Crosse. Undeterred even after some Meskwaki assured him that he was being imposed upon by liars, *Makataimeshekiakiak* gathered up as many people as he could to "make corn" at La Crosse.[141] His mind was made up.

On April 5, 1832, to "rescue" Saukenuk, the sixty-five-year-old war chief *Makataimeshekiakiak* did cross the river at Rock Island with 1,200 Sauk and Meskwaki and 400 Potawatomi, Ho-Chunk, and Kickapoo followers. Comprised of men, women, and children, the cadre of 1,600 intended to live peacefully, if not at Saukenuk, then at La Crosse. The moment that they entered Rock River, however, *Makataimeshekiakiak* realized they were being hunted, so he had them beat their drums and sing their songs, "to show the Americans" that they "were not afraid."[142]

Far from a rescue of Saukenuk, what followed was the sustained massacre called the Black Hawk War. For the next 119 days, the people ran for their lives through the forests, through the swamps, evading the militias and dodging the army, desperate to recross the river to supposed safety. They did not make it. Nearly all of them were murdered. The most elegant settler rationalization for the slaughter was that *Makataimeshekiakiak*'s "generalship" had "prolonged the contest five months, without any offers of surrender."[143] Aside from blaming the victim, this spin ignored the fact that on four separate and specific occasions, the Sauk and Meskwaki attempted to surrender:

1. The night of May 14, 1832, to the Fourth Illinois Militia Regiment under Isaiah Stillman
2. On July 21, 1832, to militia "General" Henry Dodge, immediately following the "battle" at Wisconsin Heights
3. On August 1, 1832, to Captain Joseph Throckmorton
4. On August 2, 1832, in the very midst of the Bad Axe massacre

Following the "war," the first thing *Makataimeshekiakiak* attempted to clarify was precisely this point.[144] It deserves to be highlighted in every account of the Black Hawk War.

After the massacre, on December 4, 1832, Zachary Taylor impatiently questioned why the U.S. Sixth Infantry was reassigned from Fort Leavenworth to Jefferson Barracks instead of reinforcing Fort Armstrong in the spring of 1832.[145] Why, indeed, for "several months previous to Black Hawk & his band crossing," his plan was common knowledge and reported as such in March 1832.[146] The United States ever sought the appearance of the moral high ground preparatory to a massacre, and *Makataimeshekiakiak*'s return provided its pretext. Three days after *Makataimeshekiakiak* crossed the river, General Henry Atkinson called up the Sixth Army from Jefferson Barracks, and on April 20, Illinois governor Reynolds called up 3,250 militia. Even as these massive call-ups occurred, at St. Louis, General William Clark was entirely aware that *Makataimeshekiakiak* had only "600 fighting men."[147]

From this point forward, militias and the U.S. Army attacked without a second thought. Army general Henry Atkinson, commander of the Second U.S. Army, led the war effort, with his second in command, Colonel Zachary Taylor.[148] On May 13, 1832, five U.S. Army scouts spotted *Makataimeshekiakiak*. Majors David Bailey and Isaiah Stillman of the Illinois Fourth Militia Regiment eagerly "besought" Atkinson to "grant them the privilege" of attacking, and because neither of their militia units had "done much service," Reynolds sent them out under Stillman to "coerce" the "hostile Indians" into "submission." Leaving the morning of May 14, Stillman marched 275 militiamen to Sycamore Creek, where they made camp for the night.[149] Official reports omit a salient fact of the encampment. Treating their "pursuit" of the Sauk and Meskwaki as one, "big frolic," the brigade traveled well supplied with whiskey, the men drinking till all were significantly "intoxicated."[150] In mock astonishment, *Makataimeshekiakiak* quipped, "I had understood that all the *pale faces* belonged to the *temperance societies!*" In his memoir, Reynolds ruefully acknowledged that Stillman's utter route owed at least partially to the "empty kegs" of "fire water" later found.[151]

Given the condition of Stillman's brigade and the militiamen's attitude toward their prey, the night of May 14, 1832, was hardly the best time for *Makataimeshekiakiak* to attempt a peace parley. Not realizing as much, he sent three unarmed men to the brigade under a white flag to sue for peace, saying that he had "given up all intention of going to war." The drunken militiamen immediately took the three prisoner, murdering them all. Five additional men, originally sent to watch and report back, next approached the camp for a look-see. When the drunken militiamen noticed them, they killed two. The other three made it back with their story to where *Makataimeshekiakiak* waited with forty men.[152] Regardless of the clear evidence of the white flag, a large number of mounted militia ran out "in full gallop" upon *Makataimeshekiakiak*, who quickly stationed his men in the bushes and tall grass. They expected to jump up, fire, and be dead in the next moment. Instead, incredibly, they won. The second that the Stillman's brigade took fire, the militiamen ran away in skedaddle so epic that Zachary Taylor later drubbed it as the "most shameful" that any "troops" were ever "known to do, in this, or any other country."[153]

Makataimeshekiakiak gave chase, as the militiamen ran screaming into their camp, causing a "stampede," at which commotion, the remaining militia sped off "in an inglorious panic," running all the way back to headquarters. Major Timothy Perkins and Captain John G. Adams attempted a small, rearguard action with fifteen men, but to little avail. It was only because Stillman had attacked in the dark, said Taylor, that "a very large proportion of the whites" were not killed. As it was, Stillman suffered casualties "considerable enough" as to have been "quite serious." On the other side, "I was never so surprised," said *Makataimeshekiakiak*. Not in "all the fighting" he had seen as a war chief had anything equaled forty men on foot defeating 275 mounted men. In the end, the militia lost eleven men, and *Makataimeshekiakiak*, five.[154] No longer trusting the Illinois militia, by May 19, U.S. Army general Henry Atkinson had taken control.[155] Taylor later claimed that Stillman's "shameful" attack had "brought on the war."[156]

After the Stillman fiasco, the Sauk and Meskwaki separated into small groups for safety, traveling separately through the swamps in making for the Mississippi River. Massive U.S. "alarm & distress" followed the guerrilla raids by which *Makataimeshekiakiak* fed the people, further stoking settler self-righteousness about war.[157] Regarding the Stillman embarrassment as *Makataimeshekiakiak*'s declaration of war, Reynolds promptly called up another 2,000 militia.[158] (Militia served only one month per call-up.[159]) Illinois, alone, fielded 2,700 men against the entirety of *Makataimeshekiakiak*'s initial cadre of, at best, 1,600 people, most of them noncombatant males, women, and children.

The Western unifocus on *Makataimeshekiakiak* has submerged historical recognition that other Indigenous actors on the ground took advantage of his presence to attain unrelated goals, for instance, in an attack on the sawmill settlement of William Davis north of modern-day Ottawa, Illinois. It had long infuriated Indian nations that settlers, missionaries, fur companies, and the U.S. Army simply set themselves up on Indian land to strip it of its assets. Sawmills were particularly hated.[160] Consequently, on May 22, 1832, thirty Potawatomi (with three Sauk) attacked, burning out the settlement, killing all its livestock, while dispatching and mutilating fifteen settlers, capturing the sisters Rachel and Sylvia Hall.[161] *Makataimeshekiakiak* was cleverly implicated when they were brought to his camp at Lake Koshkonong, yet the Hall sisters were released for $2,000 in ransom to Ho-Chunk chief *Kaukishkaka* ("White Crow"), who was running his own game.[162] Another dubious instance included the May 23, discovery of interpreter and U.S. agent Felix St. Vrain among the dead and scalped at Kellogg's Grove.[163] There were indications that the raid had been mounted by the Ho-Chunk.[164] Not unimportantly, St. Vrain operated a sawmill in Ho-Chunk territory.[165]

The identities of the raiders notwithstanding, the Hall event, especially, was emblazoned abroad, with the Hall sisters becoming the three-hanky poster children of the settlers' war. The strident Indian-hater Wakefield emoted over the sisters as "suffering everything but death with those Indian barbarians."[166] (EVERYTHING BUT DEATH was period code for rape, yet Woodlands men eschewed rape.[167]) U.S. officialdom knew that the "intelligence" it was receiving from settlers on these incidents was "greatly exaggerated," with "much of it, the mere vision of fancy," birthed in the overwrought minds of "a few individuals."[168] Settler men saw "an Indian in every bush, or behind every tree stump," Taylor quipped, with the "panic & distress" following the sawmill attack "not confined to women and children."[169]

On June 16, 1832, the "Battle of Pecatonica," at modern-day Wiota, Wisconsin, was little more than a militia slaughter. Militia major William Daviess recorded that after a man was killed near Fort Hamilton, militia general Henry Dodge, replete in his "buck-skin hunting shirt," raced off on horseback with a posse of twenty-eight men. In an all-day chase, Dodge used a hunting dog to track down eleven Sauk and Meskwaki on foot, his mounted militia chasing the "Red-Skins" to ground. Hiding in a thicket and out of options, the Sauk and Meskwaki fired into Dodge's onslaught, hitting three or four militiamen, before throwing down their spent weapons to make a run for it. Dodge and his crew then killed nine from a range of about twenty-five feet, along with two others as they swam the river.[170]

The starving Sauk and Meskwaki fled, pushed ever north through May and June. On June 24, 1832, *Makataimeshekiakiak* and his Young Men raided various outposts. Seeing that he could not get at the combatants in Apple River Fort without burning it, he instead seized all the flour, provisions, cattle, and horses that his men could carry off. Accidentally running into a militia at Kellogg's Grove, *Makataimeshekiakiak* did not expect great problems given Stillman, but the militia put up a determined fight, with *Makataimeshekiakiak* losing nine men with five wounded, while the militia suffered five dead and three wounded.[171] One motive of *Makataimeshekiakiak*'s raids was to forestall the massed militias from finding the body of his people. He succeeded in slowing down the settler advance, but he could not stop it.[172]

On July 14, 1832, the *Niles Register* screamed that 5,000 Sauk and Meskwaki fighters had amassed, with Army general Atkinson "determined to bring on a decisive battle."[173] By late July, *Makataimeshekiakiak*'s fearsome band consisted of 800 women, children, old folks, and eighty Young Men, all desperately digging up swamp roots, eating tree bark, and in danger of dying *"from hunger!"*[174] Fixated on martial triumph, settler reports crowed over each armed success, and if they mentioned the misery of the Sauk and Meskwaki, at all, then it tended to be in jubilation at their suffering.

The "Battle of Wisconsin Heights" on July 21, 1832, thus inspired settler celebration not mercy. To draw off the militias while *Makataimeshekiakiak* made for the Wisconsin River, his secondary civil chief *Neapope* ("Broth") and twenty men formed a rear guard. Still, Dodge's militia closed in.[175] The terrified people ran into the Wisconsin River, with *Makataimeshekiakiak* herding them to an island, the best protection he could manage on a moment's notice. As the militia neared, *Makataimeshekiakiak* quickly assembled fifty young men to rush it or "sacrifice our wives and children to the fury of the whites!"[176]

Militia accounts rejoiced in the clear desperation of the fleeing families. Wakefield calmly remarked that their trail was "strewed with Indian trinkets, such as mats, kettles, &c." Instead of reflecting on the fact that they were discarding household goods to lighten a horrified flight, Wakefield outlined his militia's battle array against "Indians" raising the "war-whoop, screaming and yelling hideously." Directing the unfolding action from a bluff, perched on his white pony, *Makataimeshekiakiak* issued a string of stentorian orders in "one of the best voices for command" that Wakefield had "ever heard" before calling a retreat.[177] Dodge claimed glorious victory, but *Makataimeshekiakiak* held out only long enough to ensure that "our women and children" had crossed to safety.[178]

Lieutenant Jefferson Davis described the women during this engagement, tearing "bark from the trees," hastily fashioning small boats on which they "floated their papooses" across to the island. Half next swam to the island, turning to open fire on the militia to cover the retreat of their sisters trapped on the river bank, now slipping into the water to swim. In his report, such as it was, Dodge gave no description of the "battle," merely noting that it capped a one-hundred-mile pursuit. Based on scalps taken, he claimed to have killed "about 40 of them," wounding "many" others, and predicted overtaking them all at Prairie du Chien on the Mississippi River, given their "crippled situation."[179]

Dodge's forty were not a complete count of the Sauk and Meskwaki dead. Dodge later announced that the Sauk and Meskwaki were in such "starving condition" that his troops found "many of them" lying "dead on their trail, or at their camp, perfectly emaciated." On July 23, James Henry added that bodies were "scattered over a large tract" of forest and besides, "many of the dead were removed" afterward, "during the night." Wakefield recorded sixty-eight found dead, with another twenty-five gravely wounded, while on August 5, and again in his summary report of August 25, Atkinson reiterated that sixty-eight Sauk and Meskwaki had perished at Wisconsin Heights.[180] Meanwhile, the militia had suffered one man killed and eight wounded.[181]

Makataimeshekiakiak had only fifty men fighting, losing but six of them.[182] This begs the question of how many of the sixty-eight Sauk and Meskwaki dead were women and children. The answer was left gingerly unspoken in military accounts, for the pretense was that the United States never fired on women and children. However, given *Makataimeshekiakiak*'s six dead men against the militia claim of sixty-eight dead Indians, the official silence strongly suggests that sixty-two of the dead were women and children. Disproportions of casualties and careful silences, especially against a militia death toll of just one man, evidence a massacre, not a battle.

The night of July 23, 1832, *Neapope* called out loudly to the militia from the Wisconsin Heights bluff, using Ho-Chunk on the misimpression that the militia's Menominee scouts could understand him. Explaining that the women and children "were starving," *Neapope* pled for peace, promising that, if the settlers would just "let them pass over the Mississippi," then they "would do no more mischief." All that he elicited was panic in the militia camp.[183] No surrender transpired. To *Makataimeshekiakiak*'s dismay, having failed in his peace embassy, *Neapope* now "retired," taking refuge at *Wabokieshiek*'s town until after the war.[184] The militia sleeping instead of pursuing, the main body of refugees escaped its clutches overnight, leaving only the "sign of a few horse tracks."[185]

Settler histories linger over Taylor's "forced march of nearly thirty days" to catch up, as his men "suffered every privation & hardship" traversing the swamps on inadequate supplies.[186] Anything that Taylor was doing, however, starving women, children, old folks, and dwindling numbers of men were doing on no supplies, whatsoever, under conditions of exposure. Beyond desperation, "worn out with travelling," children and elders died on the path. *Makataimeshekiakiak* allowed clear Innocents to move ahead of the main group to the Mississippi River under two Ho-Chunk guides, for only those making it across the Mississippi stood a chance.[187]

This breakaway contingent was most likely that found by army Lieutenant Joseph Ritner on July 29, 1832. Patrolling the Wisconsin River, he encountered "four canoes" overloaded with people, apparently ramming Ritner's barge by accident in the night. Despite the complete darkness, Ritner insisted that they were all "naked and painted warriors," thus justifying his opening fire. Three of the four canoes capsized, with Ritner sure that "nearly all" of the Sauk and Meskwaki were "killed or disabled." In his summary report, Atkinson recorded thirty-two women and children, along with four men, captured, with fifteen prisoners murdered. One week later, Ritner's commander, Captain Loomis, upped the count to five canoes, adding that Ritner had found "fresh tracks" of a multitude of women and children near the Bad Axe River.[188]

Forced by the United States "to dig up the tomahawk" against their traditional Sauk and Meskwaki allies, on the night of August 1, 1832, Ho-Chunk scouts directed by Indian agent Joseph Street brought in fourteen "women boys and small children," along with one scalp. "Wasted, to mere skeletons" and "clothed in rags," the children had "starved so long" that it was iffy whether they could be "restored." The next morning, the Menominee brought in eight scalps and nine children and women, including *Keokuk*'s sister. At Fort Crawford, Colonel Zachary Taylor threatened to seize these "women & children prisoners," although Street cautioned against it as "calculated to produce unhappy results, extensively."[189] In other words, it was unwise to murder those wretched prisoners.

Reaching the Mississippi River, *Makataimeshekiakiak* determined for the third time to surrender. Forty miles down the Mississippi from his location ran the civilian steamboat *Warrior*, as captained by an acquaintance from happier days, Joseph Throckmorton. Assembling an entourage of sixty or more men, women, and children, *Makataimeshekiakiak* deposited the remainder of his people at the confluence of the Bad Axe and Mississippi Rivers, as he trekked to a landing spot near the *Warrior*'s route. Stepping out of the trees and into plain sight at the *Warrior*'s approach, *Makataimeshekiakiak* unraveled a white flag in an obvious attempt to surrender to Throckmorton.[190]

Unbeknownst to *Makataimeshekiakiak*, U.S. Army captain Gustavus Loomis had taken over the *Warrior*, emplacing a "six-pounder," that is, a cannon, on board, to prevent any "escape by water."[191] In forced alliance with the United States, the Ho-Chunk aided the Sauk and Meskwaki whenever they thought it might be safe. Consequently, when *Makataimeshekiakiak* called out from the river-bank, the Ho-Chunk interpreter aboard the *Warrior* urgently shouted, *"run and* hide" because "*the whites were going to shoot.*" One Young Man was about to swim a second white flag to the *Warrior*, but in light of this news, another quickly pulled him back. No settlers aboard the *Warrior* understood this exchange, so Loomis's boss, Colonel Reuben Holmes, later commended the Ho-Chunk for displaying the "utmost coolness & intrepidity" by shouting in the face of the enemy.[192]

The later, preferred settler story was that those "hostile Sacs and Foxes" attacked the *Warrior*, although testimonies disagreed.[193] Lieutenant James Kingsbury claimed to have ordered *Makataimeshekiakiak* to "send aboard" a white flag, or he would shoot, at which the Sauk and Meskwaki opened fire, but this strains credulity.[194] Holmes, not Kingsbury, was in charge, and Indians never brought women and children to a battle. Throckmorton declared that *Makataimeshekiakiak* was given fifteen minutes to clear the area of women and children before the *Warrior* fired, but on August 9, 1832, George Boyd reported that Holmes immediately ordered his men to open fire. Holmes himself claimed that he fired rather promptly, having seen Sauk and Meskwaki "preparing their guns and selecting trees" for cover. Both Throckmorton and Holmes claimed that the white flags were a ruse, with Holmes "Suspicious" of the Sauk's "appearance & intentions," as a woman on board "who knew their language" (probably the "Indian squaw prisoner" he also mentioned) told them that the Indians were Sauk. I doubt that her information was volunteered; notably, she did not give away the Ho-Chunk interpreter.[195]

The *Warrior* steered to shore as if to shore to parley but, instead, sent "a shower of cannister," that is, shot the cannon, at the Sauk and Meskwaki. Agent Street said that Holmes shot "9 or 10 times with a 6 pounder," although soldier John Fonda had the volley repeating thrice, "each time mowing a swath clean through them." Caught off guard, the Sauk and Meskwaki threw themselves on their stomachs. The only reason the cannonade ended was that the *Warrior* ran out of "cannister-shot." Small arms then strafed those along the shore.[196] *Makataimeshekiakiak* stated that "few" of his men were killed by the first canister, but after the two-hour-long attack, twenty-three had died, with many more wounded. Throckmorton took thirty-six women and children prisoner.[197] Clearly, Throckmorton had allowed Holmes to shoot a cannon from his ship, point blank at women and children.

Following the *Warrior*'s attack, *Makataimeshekiakiak* was disconsolate, his only hope now being refuge as with the Anishinabe of Three Fires Confederacy of his Potawatomi followers. He welcomed any who wished to accompany him to the Anishinabe, but any still wishing to cross the Mississippi could do that, too. Some immediately chose the river, although "three lodges" elected to go to the Anishinabe. Under later interrogation, the Sauk *Weesheet* stated that the rest disliked being without *Makataimeshekiakiak* but proceeded to the river, nonetheless.[198]

The *Niles Register* exulted that *Makataimeshekiakiak* had "absconded," seeding the long-lived spin of a cowardly "Black Hawk" abandoning his people to "their fate," but instead expecting the army to make a beeline for him while ignoring the rest, *Makataimeshekiakiak* was distraught to learn that his latest misdirection had failed. Determining to die with his people at the river, he reversed course but did not make it to the Mississippi in time to share their fate or witness his people being "slaughtered" in the waters. By August 3, 1832, when he heard about the attack from a survivor, the people were already butchered.[199]

On August 2, 1832, the main body of the fugitives was trapped at the confluence of the Bad Axe and Mississippi Rivers, just north of Fort Crawford at Prairie du Chien. Dakota scouts estimated their numbers at 400, but they were more likely to have been around 600.[200] Two swampy islands stood in the Bad Axe River, where it dumped into the Mississippi. The people were in the act of island-hopping to the Mississippi when, first, Dodge's militia; second, the *Warrior*, bearing Zachary Taylor with his troops; and finally, Atkinson fell upon them. Very few Young Men remained to defend the refugees, but when the massacre began, and they saw that the settlers were indiscriminately "murdering helpless women and little children," they decided to *"fight until they were killed."*[201] They did.

This final U.S. assault was no spur-of-the-moment attack. On August 1, 1832, Atkinson had ordered his 1,300 men to ready their equipment for a 2:00 A.M. attack on August 2, knowing that the Sauk and Meskwaki were at the Bad Axe River.[202] Dodge was already in place at the river.[203] In his statement on the action, Captain James B. Estes directly stated that the U.S. troops had "driven" the Sauk and Meskwaki onto the two islands.[204] Still deployed, the *Warrior* wheeled from the Mississippi into the Bad Axe River, coming upon the first of the islands on August 2. The soldiers aboard heard gunfire raging ahead. Throckmorton cried, "Dodge is giving them hell!" as, indeed, Dodge was.[205]

Atkinson had ordered Taylor to the wrong side of the Bad Axe River, so Taylor quick-marched 250 of his 400 men a mile to where they could see the Sauk and Meskwaki already crossing the Mississippi. Due to his misplacement, Taylor had his men scramble down the steep banks into the water, to wade around to the rear of the hintermost island, up to their waists in muck. The militia had begun its attack "a few minutes" earlier, so Taylor took heavy fire from the handful of Young Men holding the island in a rearguard action orchestrated from the island ahead. Taylor ordered his men to drive them from that island. The ensuing fight was "severe," but grossly outnumbered, the few remaining Young Men could not long cover the fleeing women and children. Taylor reported that his men "killed every Indian that presented himself on land or who endeavored to seek safety by swimming the river."[206] Fonda recalled Taylor's charging "through the island to the right and left," taking only a "few prisoners," primarily women and children. The rest were killed, regardless of sex or age. All but one of those remaining on the small island were "shot in the water attempting to cross the Mississippi," while that one man swam "to the opposite shore." Coming late to the party, the *Warrior* aided Taylor's slaughter by turning the six-pounder on the people in the river, so that "Horses and Men fell like grass before the scythe," leaving the river "spotted with Indians and horses" floating by.[207]

The remaining Sauk and Meskwaki fought with a "desperation" that "surpassed everything" Fonda had ever seen—and he had, he said, "seen more than one" action. The Young Men held off the *Warrior* by lying under the water, with only their nostrils and mouths exposed, jumping up and firing only when they had a clear shot. The *Warrior* strafed them so intensively that they were forced to run, all killed in their retreat. Afterward, it was seen that the men on the islands had but one canoe among them, forcing them to swim between the islands, with many later found drowned. Notwithstanding, the firing on the *Warrior* continued to be "severe." The resultant carnage was so massive that the Mississippi River "current" was "perceptibly tinged with the blood of the Indians," said Street. Taylor calculated that, on the islands, alone, he had killed "about a hundred," along with their horses, while taking "fifty or sixty prisoners" and "destroying a large portion of their baggage."[208] The late-arriving *Warrior* ferried Taylor's remaining 150 men to the larger of the two islands, but the firing was nigh over. Because the men who had waded to the island had not "taken refreshments" since 2:00 A.M., Taylor ordered his fresh troops to sweep the islands for survivors. They found and killed "several" who had "endeavored to secret themselves by climbing trees &tc."[209]

Once the soldiers had murdered everyone on the islands, they moved to the mainland, to which the horrified people had fled. Positioned on a bluff, Dodge's militia fired on them as they gained land. To escape, many "Men Women & children" jumped back in the river, but Dodge's men "threw in a heavy fire which killed great numbers." One Sauk elder and his sons, personally known to Fonda, stationed themselves halfway up the bluff to return fire "with deadly aim," the old man reloading his sons' firearms as fast as they could discharge them. They held off Dodge as long as they could, but his militia "poured over the bluff," killing them. After scalping the "braves" who had held them off, militiamen cut "two parallel gashes" down the back of each, stripping them of their still "quivering flesh." Such "hide" was turned into souvenirs, shoes, and shaving strops. Fonda breezily announced that he had claimed a strip of "hide" from the old man and his sons.[210]

Trapped and encircled, the remaining people made their final attempt at surrender, but in a pure bloodbath, the United States spared no one.[211] Settler reports are full of militiamen who, like Captain Price and his fifteen men, rushed at "full speed of horses" upon stragglers, killing most while taking twelve prisoner.[212] Dodge's 900 mounted militiamen killed every last person they encountered. As the last of the people were closed in on, surviving women quickly hid their children while they fashioned makeshift canoes.[213] It did them little good. Women and children were among the dead, with Robert Anderson blaming the Sauk and Meskwaki for hiding "in the high grass and behind logs and the banks of the ravines and rivers." He did not reveal where the women and children should have hidden, instead.[214] Present for the slaughter was Illinois militiaman Wakefield, whose account showed not the slightest remorse, despite some sadistic crocodile tears over the "horrid sight" of children (still given as the "enemy") in "excruciating pain" from their wounds.[215] The U.S. Army and militias "all joined in the work of death," he reported, "for death it was. We were by this time fast getting rid of these demons in human shape."[216]

Accounts showed women and children being deliberately targeted.[217] One young mother was shot very carefully through the heart while her four-year-old daughter, later found sheltered by her dead body, lay wounded. The toddler's arm was shattered as the bullet passed through her tiny elbow and into the heart of her mother. Her damaged arm was amputated. Estes reported that she ate a biscuit during the operation, "apparently unconcerned, and insensible to pain." (Standing racist propaganda held that Indians and Africans felt no pain.) The traumatized orphan was eventually handed over to *Keokuk*'s Sauk.[218] Another small, naked boy, whose shot-up arm was dangling by a thread, crawled out of hiding, motioning Fonda for food. Fonda had the humanity to take the boy aboard the *Warrior* to give him bread. His arm was also amputated.[219]

Following Bad Axe, some questioned the massacre of women and children. Wakefield justified it as a "mistake" yet insisted that it was their fault, for failing to "surrender themselves prisoners of war" on the morning of the massacre.[220] Kentucky recruit Robert Anderson wormed around the issue by declaring, "When the fact is known, that the women urged their warriors to an opposition to the U. States," and that some of the women shot back, then people might "think it less to be regretted" that they were killed.[221] Based on a long acquaintance with the settlers, the women feared that, if captured, then enslavement, rape, and castration of their boys would follow. Although in 1970, Anthony F. C. Wallace downplayed these fears as "fantasies," period documents show that Indians were, indeed, enslaved, with men castrated, while women and girls were raped.[222]

Wakefield estimated that the Army and militias had killed roughly 150 at Bad Axe, taking about fifty prisoners.[223] Also citing 150 dead, the *Niles Register* added that "a large number of Indians were killed or captured in the river."[224] However, by August 5, 1832, Atkinson confidently reported having killed "300 of Black Hawk's band." In his summary report of August 25, Atkinson hedged. A true count of the dead was impossible, because "the greater portion was slain after forced into the river."[225] Against this, U.S. losses at Bad Axe totaled twenty-seven in killed and wounded.[226]

Another 300 Sauk and Meskwaki made it across the Mississippi River.[227] They were ruthlessly hunted down. On August 3, 1832, the U.S. Army sent 100 Dakota under *Wáȟpe-šá* (*Wabasha*, "Falling Leaf"), along with Menominee parties under *L'Arc* ("Lark"), after the refugees.[228] Although most settler accounts were not very careful to distinguish between the two, it was the Dakota who tracked them into Iowa, with "very few" escaping.[229] By August 21, 1832, almost the "whole" of those remaining of "Black Hawk's band" had been "killed, drowned, or captured" by the Dakota.[230] On August 22, Dakota reported to Taylor that they had killed 200, mostly women and children.[231] Taylor doubted the head count due to the slight number of scalps brought in, but five days later, Sauk chief *Weesheet* verified that 200 were murdered.[232] Over the five-month duration of the Black Hawk War, up to 1,500 Sauk, Meskwaki, Potawatomi, Ho-Chunk, and Kickapoo followers of *Makataimeshekiakiak* died, whereas total settler losses, military and civilian, amounted to seventy-nine.[233]

Makataimeshekiakiak and *Wabokieshiek* were in the federal custody by August 27, 1832, along with 118 others, mostly women and children, dragged to Taylor at Fort Crawford.[234] Taylor coerced the Ho-Chunk into turning over both. When *Chaashjan-ga* brought them in, he directly eyed Taylor, saying, "You said, if these two were taken by us and brought to you, there would never more a black cloud hang over" the Ho-Chunk. "That one," said *Chaashjan-ga* indicating *Wabokieshiek*, "is my relation—if he is to be hurt, I do not wish to see it." Looking from his uncle to eye Taylor, *Chaashjan-ga* continued: "Soldiers sometimes stick the ends of their guns (bayonets), into the backs of Indian prisoners." *Chaashjan-ga* trusted that that would "not be done to these men."[235] Anyone who knows Young Men knows that this was a threat, uttered with a steadfast gaze. *Makataimeshekiakiak* was dragged east for imprisonment, becoming a show-and-tell war trophy, displayed around the country.[236]

Bad Axe was one of the great "victories" touted during Taylor's presidential campaign.[237]

NOTES

1. Ritzenthaler, 1985, 29.
2. Deloria, 1997, 73.
3. For established north-south migration patterns, Deloria, 1997, 75; Mann, 2016, 52.
4. Deloria, 1997, 76, 84–85.
5. Morse, 1822, 138; four of traditional thought, Mann, 2016, 98–99, 197, 213–15.
6. Thwaites, 1899, vol. 55, 221; Mann, 2016, Breath, 53–54, 115, 193–97.
7. Morse, 1822, Meskwaki, 129; Sauk, 130; Carter, 1934–1975, Bell to Macomb, vol. 12, letter 8/16/1831, 333.
8. Potherie, 1722/1753, vol. 2, 174–75.
9. Morse, 1822, 121–22.
10. Ibid., 122, context includes the Sauk here.
11. Ibid., 122.
12. Ibid., 122, 123.
13. Ibid., 138.
14. Ibid., 123.
15. Mann, 2003, Lenapes, 140–54.
16. Forbes, 2007, 64–65, 68–72.
17. Busby, 1886, 51–52; for sails, Forbes, 2007, 2, 48.
18. Italics in the original. *Makataimeshekiakiak* and Patterson, 1839, 35.
19. Clemmons, 2003, 3.
20. Grignon, 1904, female chief, vol. 3, 210; Busby, 1886, "queen," 35; *Makataimeshekiakiak*, 1916, "daughter," 124.
21. Busby, 1886, 213; *Makataimeshekiakiak*, 1916, 65.
22. Thwaites, 1899, vol. 51, 43; vol. 54, 207.
23. Hunter, 1823, 257; Trask, 2006, 33.
24. *Makataimeshekiakiak* and Patterson, 1839, 44–45; as "Black Sparrow Hawk," Thwaites, 1892, vol. 12, 219.
25. Carver, 1779, 39, 47.
26. *Makataimeshekiakiak*, 1916, crops, 96.
27. Cass, 1826, 53.

28. Carver, 1779, 46–47.

29. Pond, 1908, 335.

30. Clark, 1879, note *, 313.

31. Mann, 2009, 8–18.

32. Carver, 1779, 48.

33. Pond, 1908, 337.

34. Brackets mine. Pond, 1908, 330–32, 335.

35. Thwaites, 1899, vol. 44, 217; vol. 50, 309

36. Ibid., Sault Ste. Marie, vol. 54, 215–17; Michilimackinac, vol. 55, 103; and Green Bay, vol. 55, 183; Lake Michigan, vol. 51, 43, 45; vol. 54, 221.

37. Ibid., west of Green Bay, vol. 58, 41; hunt, vol. 58, 44.

38. Ibid., Green Bay, vol. 60, 199–201; vol. 62, 193; Lake Michigan, vol. 62, 203; vol. 67, 161; Lake Erie, vol. 67, 215.

39. Potherie, 1753, vol. 2, 173.

40. Thwaites, 1888, 28, 35.

41. Potherie, 1753, vol. 2, 142–43, 149.

42. Translations mine; Potherie, 1753, vol. 2, 150–51.

43. Potherie, 1753, vol. 2, 245–47, 251–52, 258–62.

44. Ibid., vol. 2, 263–68; present, 251, 260; mine, 270, 310.

45. Ibid., vol. 2, 314; "Report from M. de Vaudreuil," 1905, 9/8/1711, 532.

46. "Cadillac Papers," 1904, "Memorandum," 3/10/1711, 500–501; verbal abuse, 505; Mann, 2001, "Delusional," 49.

47. Ibid., Dubuisson to Vaudreuil, letter 6/15/1712, 281; Thwaites, 1902, "French Regime, I," 293.

48. Ibid., Meskwaki losses, Vaudreuil report, 10/15/1712, 570; Dubuisson to Vaudreuil, letter 6/15/1712, 267–84; casualties "of both sexes," Brodhead, 1855, Vaudreuil to Pontchartrain, vol. 9, letter 11/6/1712, 863; Thwaites, 1902, "French Regime, I," enslavement of survivors, 294–95.

49. Brodhead, 1855, Vaudreuil to Pontchartrain, vol. 9, letter 11/6/1712, 863.

50. Kellogg bought Vaudreuil's innocence plea, Kellogg, 1908, note 76, 160; Hebberd, 1890, 81–89.

51. Thwaites, 1902, "French Regime, I," Ramezey and Bégon, 9/13 and 9/16/1715, 321.

52. Grignon, 1904, 204–5; Thwaites, 1906, "French Regime, II," Beauharnois, supply shortages, 10/24/1745, 449.

53. Ibid., dating, 200–201; "old woman," 205–6.

54. Ibid., 207–8.

55. Ibid., 209–10.

56. Thwaites, 1906, "French Regime, II," Sious, Jonquière and Bigot, 10/9/1749, 33; fort, "Agreement," 4/10/1747, 452.

57. Thwaites, 1908, "British Regime," 223–29.

58. Gorrell, 1903, 6/18/1763, 40–41; Thwaites, 1908, "French Regime, III," Ethrington to Gladwin, letter 7/18/1763, 255; Thwaites, 1888, "Important Papers," proposed, Article 2, 37–38; final, Article 4, 41–42.

59. Thwaites, 1908, "British Regime," copper, Johnson to Hillsborough, letter 12/20/1768, 293–95, and Butricke, 6/27/1769, 297; Carver, 1779, 138, 528; Henry, 1809, note*, 231–34; Carver, 1779, lead, 48–49, 528, 535; Henry, 1809, 230, 232.

60. Pond, 1908, 330.

61. Brackets mine. Pond, 1908, 335.

62. Thwaites, 1908, "British Regime," Report, Rios y Morales, 3/9/1769, 300; Vattas to Haldiman, letter 6/16/1773, 311.

63. Ibid., "British Regime," Prévost to Clark, letter 2/20/1780, 404–6.

64. USC, 1871, "Treaty of Peace" Article 2, 9/3/1783, 315–16.

65. Haldiman, 1888, Haldiman to Townsend, letter 10/23/1782, 662–63.

66. McKee, 1792, 9.

67. Jung, 2012, 29.

68. *Makataimeshekiakiak*, 1916, 40.

69. Kappler, 1904, vol. 2, Article 9, Sauk and Foxes Treaty, 76.

70. *Makataimeshekiakiak*, 1916, 40–43.

71. *Makataimeshekiakiak* and Patterson, 1839, 62; Prucha, 1986, 124.

72. Esarey, 1922, Harrison to Eustis, vol. 1, letters 7/18/1810, 446–47; Johnson to Eustis, vol. 1, letter 8/7/1810, 459; Harrison to Eustis, letter 9/17/1811, vol. 1, 575; *Makataimeshekiakiak*, 1916, 51.

73. *Makataimeshekiakiak* and Patterson, 1839, 79–80; Jung, 2012, 40; Brymner, 1888, McKay to McDougall, letter 7/27/1814, 269–70; italics in the original, *Makataimeshekiakiak*, 1916, 74–75.

74. Italics in the original. *Makataimeshekiakiak*, 1916, 76–77; 1985, 23–24.

75. *Makataimeshekiakiak*, 1916, 77–78; gunpowder distribution, Forsyth, 1888, Forsyth to Edwards, letters 9/3/1814, 329; and Forsyth to Edwards, letter 9/12/1814, 330; four kegs of pounder, Brymner, 1888, McKay to McDougall, letter 7/27/1814, 269; Bauer, 1985, 25.

76. *Makataimeshekiakiak*, 1916, 78–79; Hamilton, 1941, 54.

77. Kappler, 1904, Sauk Treaty, vol. 2, 9/13/1815, 121; "Foxes" Treaty, vol. 2, 9/14/1815, 122; Sauk Treaty, vol. 2, 5/13/1816, 127–28.

78. Zee, 1915, 13, 25, 27–29; *Makataimeshekiakiak* and Patterson, 1839, 86.

79. *Makataimeshekiakiak* and Patterson, 1839, 88; Forsyth, 1908, Leavenworth, 217; annuity, Forsyth to Clark, letter 9/23/1819, 215.

80. Anderson, 1888, 145–46; *Makataimeshekiakiak*, 1916, 102–4; Kappler, 1904, Sauk and "Foxes" Treaty, 9/3/1822, vol. 2, 202–203.

81. Kappler, 1904, Sauk and "Foxes" Treaty," vol. 2, 8/4/1824, 207–8; Sioux Treaty, vol. 2, 9/19/1825, 250–55.

82. Mann, 2003, 54–88.

83. Hulbert, 1902–1905, vol. 1, 25; Thomas, 1894, 47–98

84. Thwaites, 1899, vol. 59, 101–7; Hulbert, 1902–1905, vol. 7, 186.

85. Dickson and Grignon, 1888, Dickson to Law, letter 3/31/1814, 300.

86. Carter, 1934–1975, "Memorial," vol. 12, 12/15/1829, 93; transfer to War Department, *ASPPL*, 1834–1861, Exhibit A, vol. 4, no. 466, 2/7/1826, 370; mine output and population increases, 1825–1829, see Strong, 1908, 251.

87. USC, 1845–1875, U.S. Chapter 46, vol. 4, 4/30/1824, 22–23.

88. Thwaites, 1892, 228–29.

89. Carter, 1934–1975, Cross to Macomb, vol. 12, letter 9/23/1829, 62; "Petition," vol. 12, 9/25/1829, 70.

90. Durbin and Durbin, 1984, 8.

91. Matteson, 1893, 171.

92. Carter, 1934–1975, Dodge, "Minutes," and "Petition," vol. 12, 10/5/1830, 201–6; "Memorial," vol. 12, 3/12/1832, 448–49.

93. Whittlesey, 1903, 75–76; USC, 1832, 7/14/1832, 206.

94. Carter, 1934–1975, Cass to Whiting, vol. 12, letter 9/1/1832, 520; Nelson, 1955, Cass and Michigan, 7–8; Green Bay, 10.

95. Ibid., Cass to Benton, vol. 12, letters 1/26/1829, 13–14; McKenney to Ogden, vol. 12, letter 1/26/1829, 14–15; "Minutes," vol. 12, 10/5/1830, 201–2; "Petition," vol. 12, 10/1830, 202–6; "Huron," *Niles*, vol. 35, 1/24/1829, 346.

96. *ASPIA*, 1832, letter, vol. 1, no. 1, 13.

97. Carter, 1934–1975, Stuart to McKenney, vol. 12, letters 8/15/1829, 59–60; McKenney to Stuart, vol. 12, letter 11/3/1829, 87.

98. Ibid., McKenney to Cass, vol. 12, letters 2/17/1829, 23–24; McKenney to Cass, vol. 12, letter 7/2/1829, 53; militia appointments, Cass to Jackson, vol. 12, letter 3/6/1829, 27–28.

99. *Makataimeshekiakiak*, 1916, 105, 110; *Makataimeshekiakiak* and Patterson, 1839, 108–10.

100. Italics in the original. *Makataimeshekiakiak*, 1916, 108–11.

101. Carter, 1934–1975, Stuart to Eaton, vol. 12, letter 2/9/1830, 125–26.

102. Kappler, 1904, Menominee Treaty, vol. 2, 2/8/1831, 319–20; Carter, 1934–1975, McKenney to Eaton, vol. 12, letter 5/18/1830, 170–71; Cass to Lewis, vol. 12, letter 11/30/1830, 215–16; "Resolution," vol. 12, 2/24/1831, 259; Eaton to Stambaugh, vol. 12, letter 4/23/1831, 279–81; Whittlesey, 1903, note *, 68.

103. Carter, 1934–1975, Lyon to Lytle, vol. 12, letters 6/12/1830, 178–79; Mullett to Lytle, vol. 12, letter 8/12/1830, 193–94; Lyon to Lytle, vol. 12, letter 9/17/1830, note 90, 199–200.

104. Kappler, 1904, Sauk and "Foxes" Treaty, vol. 2, 7/15/1830, 305–10.

105. For Forsyth, Trask, 2006, 74; *Makataimeshekiakiak*, 1916, 105.

106. Marsh, 1900, 138; *Makataimeshekiakiak*, 1916, 100. The penalty for murder in Woodland cultures was formalized by the Iroquois as Twenty Wampum or Twenty Matters, Mann, 2000, note 20, 252, 448–49.

107. *Makataimeshekiakiak*, 1916, 52, 85–86, 89, 110, 137, 145.

108. Ibid., 109–14.

109. Thwaites, 1892, 221.

110. Mann, 2016, 142.

111. Italics in the original. *Makataimeshekiakiak*, 1916, 118–19; for "Red Heads" and giant lore, Mann, 2016, 144–47, 156–57; for Clark as "Red-Headed" chief, Trask, 2006, 11.

112. For rumor, Carter, 1934–1975, Bell to Macomb, vol. 12, letter 8/16/1831, 334; *Makataimeshekiakiak*, 1916, 119.

113. *Makataimeshekiakiak*, 1916, 117; Whitney, 1973–1975, St. Vrain to Clark, vol. 2, part II, letter 5/15/1831, 7.

114. *Makataimeshekiakiak*, 1916, 117–21; *Wabokieshiek*'s position, Whitney, 1973–1975, Minutes, vol. 2, part II, 8/27/1832, 1056.

115. Whitney, 1973–1975, Citizens to Reynolds, vol. 2, part I, letter 4/30/1831, 3; Rock River citizens to Reynolds, vol. 2, part I, letter 5/19/1831, 11; Pike, deposition, vol. 2, part I, 5/26/1831. 12.

116. Thwaites, 1892, 230; Whitney, 1973–1975, Reynolds to Clark, vol. 2, part I, letters 5/26/1831, 13; Clark to Reynolds, vol. 2, part I, letter 5/28/1831, 19; Reynolds to Gaines, vol. 2, part I, letter 5/28/1831, 20; Vrain to Clark, vol. 2, part I, letter 5/28/1831, 21; Gaines to Reynolds, vol. 2, part I, letter 5/29/1831, 22–23; Reynolds, 1855/1879, 208.

117. *Makataimeshekiakiak*, 1916, 121; Treaty of Ghent, 1814, British-American Diplomacy, Avalon Project, 2008.

118. Whitney, 1973–1975, Cutler to Munn, vol. 2, part I, letters 6/9/1831, 38; Reynolds to Buckmaster, vol. 2, part I, letter 6/9/1831, 39; Gratiot to Gaines, vol. 2, part I, letter 6/11/1831, 46; Gaines to Jones, vol. 2, part I, letter 6/14–15/1831, 47.

119. Whitney, 1973–1975, Burnett to Clark, vol. 2, part I, letters 5/18/1831, 9; McCall to McCall, vol. 2, part I, letter 6/17/1831, 55; *Makataimeshekiakiak*, 1916, 121–22; Gaines as "great war chief," 121.

120. Whitney, 1973–1975, "Memorandum," vol. 2, part I, 6/4/1831, 27–28; Gaines to Reynolds, vol. 2, part I, letter 6/5/1831, 35; for *Neapope*'s as "the leading chief," Whitney, 1973–1975, Council, vol. 2, part I, 4/13/1832, 253; *Neapope* later identified as secondary civil chief, "Minutes," vol. 2, part I, 8/27/1832, 1056, and Anderson, Memoranda, vol. 2, part I, 8/27/1832, 1058; Whittlesey, 1903, *Neapope* as the "Head Chief," that is, civil chief, 72, and "ruling chief" (civil chief), 84; *Makataimeshekiakiak*, 1916, 122–23; Kappler, 1904, Sauk and "Foxes" Treaty, vol. 2, 7/15/1830, 308.

121. *Makataimeshekiakiak*, 1916, 123.

122. Whitney, 1973–1975, McCall to McCall, vol. 2, part I, letter 6/17/1831, 57; "Memorandum," vol. 2, part I, 6/4/1831, 29.

123. Ibid., "Memorandum," vol. 2, part I, 6/4/1831, 27–29.

124. *Makataimeshekiakiak*, 1916, 123–24.

125. Whitney, 1973–1975, Davenport to Chouteau, vol. 2, part I, letter 6/5/1831, 33; Gaines to Reynolds, vol. 2, part I, letter 6/5/1831, 35; "Memorandum," vol. 2, part I, 6/5/1831, 29–30; *Makataimeshekiakiak*, 1916, 124.

126. Whitney, 1973–1975, McCall to McCall, vol. 2, part 1, letter 6/17/1831, 57; speakerships, Mann, 2000, 165–70.

127. Whitney, 1973–1975, "Memorandum," vol. 2, part I, 6/7/1831, 30.

128. Ibid., "Memorandum," vol. 2, part I, 6/7/1831, 30.

129. Ibid., Gaines to Jones, vol. 2, part I, letters 6/8/1831, 37; Gaines to Jones, vol. 2, part I, letter 6/14–15/1831, 47.

130. *Makataimeshekiakiak*, 1916, 124–27; Whitney, 1973–1975, Wells Deposition, vol. 2, part I, 6/10/1831, 43; for insufficient Removal rations, Mann, 2009, 32–33, 38.

131. Mann, 2003, skull collecting, 30–48; cemetery scalping, Mann, 2005, 127.

132. Whitney, 1973–1975, St. Vrain to Clark, vol. 2, part I, letters 7/23/1831, 112; Reynolds to Clark, vol. 2, part I, letter 8/5/1831, 124.

133. Reynolds, 1855/1879, 202; Carter, 1934–1975, Moore to Van Buren, vol. 12, letter 10/12/1830, 207.

134. Whittlesey, 1903, 71; Carter, 1934–1975, Bell to Macomb, vol. 12, letter 8/16/1831, 332–33.

135. Boyd, 1892, Boyd to Porter, letter 7/23/1832, note 1, 272, 278; Gómez-Díaz, 2008, 99; Smith, 1998/2018.

136. Wakefield, 1834/1908, 136; Bracken and Parkinson, 1903, 365–92.

137. For *Wabokieshiek*'s position, Whitney, *The Black Hawk War*, "Minutes of an Examination of Prisoners," vol. 2, part 2, 8/5/1832, 1056.

138. *Makataimeshekiakiak Life*, 1916, note 23, 105–6; Thwaites had a skewed version of *Wabokieshiek*, in Thwaites, "Story of Black Hawk," note 1, 224.

139. *Makataimeshekiakiak, Life*, 1916, 106.

140. Seton, 1936, 58–59; *Makataimeshekiakiak*, 1916, 90, 106, 111, 117, 119; Whitney, 1973–1975, *Wabokieshiek*, "Minutes," vol. 2, part II, 8/27/1832, 1056.

141. *Makataimeshekiakiak*, 1916, 130–31; "make corn," 135.

142. Jung, 2008, number at Saukenuk, 60. Some authors simply split the difference, giving 1,400 as crossing, Fredriksen, 2001, 54; date, 54; *Makataimeshekiakiak*, 1916,

132, 134; Whitney, 1973–1975, "Minutes," Kickapoo with the group, vol. 2, part II, 8/19/1832, 1028; Ho-Chunk, vol. 2, part II, 1029.

143. Whittlesey, 1903, 83–84.

144. Whitney, 1973–1975, *Makataimeshekiakiak*, speech, vol. 2, part II, 9/4/1832, 1103.

145. Ibid., Taylor to Jesup, vol. 2, part II, letter 12/4/1832, 1223

146. Beers, 1935, 84.

147. Whitney, 1973–1975, Atkinson orders, vol. 2, part II, 4/8/1832, 233; Reynolds orders, vol. 2, part II, 4/20/1832, 284–85; Clark to Reynolds, vol. 2, part II, letter 4/20/1832, 284

148. Taylor's position, Hamilton, 1941, 90.

149. Whitney, 1973–1975, Stillman to Reynolds or Atkinson, vol. 2, part I, letters 5/21/1832, 400–401; Homes to Atkinson, vol. 2, part I, letter 5/22/1832, 405–6; Holmes to McCary, vol. 2, part I, letter 5/23/1832, 414–15; Reynolds, 1855/1879, 230; Elliott and Illinois, 1882, xvii.

150. Strong, 1908, 268–69.

151. Italics in the original. *Makataimeshekiakiak*, 1916, 143; Reynolds, 1855/1879, 235.

152. *Makataimeshekiakiak*, 1916, three sent, 139; quotation, 141–43; Reynolds, 1855/1879, 232. Reynolds claimed that six approached, but *Makataimeshekiakiak* was the more likely to that he dispatched five men.

153. Ibid., 140; Whitney, 1973–1975, Taylor to Lawson, vol. 2, part II, letter 8/16/1832, 1014.

154. Elliott and Illinois, 1882, xviii; Whitney, 1973–1975, Taylor to Lawson, vol. 2, part II, letters 8/16/1832, 1014; Whiteside and Reynolds to Atkinson, vol. 2, part II, letter 5/15/1832, 372; *Makataimeshekiakiak*, 1916, for five dead, 141; for surprise, 144; Reynolds, 1855/1879, 233; militia casualties, Elliott and Illinois, 1882, xviii; Whitney, 1973–1975, [Marsh], from *Missouri Republican*, vol. 2, part I, 5/23/1832, 424–25. The militia account claimed seven Indians killed (Elliott and Illinois, 1882, xviii), but militia records also promoted officers, willy-nilly, referring to Timothy Perkins as "Major" in the summary, although he was on the rolls as "Lieutenant" and Stillman as "Brigadier General" (Elliott and Illinois, 1882, Perkins, xviii, 124; Stillman, xvi, xvii, 152.

155. Reynolds, 1855/1879, 237.

156. Whitney, 1973–1975, Taylor to Lawson, vol. 2, part II, letters 8/16/1832, 1014; Taylor to Jesup, vol. 2, part II, letter 12/4/1832, 1223.

157. Ibid., Taylor to Lawson, vol. 2, part II, letters 8/16/1832, 1015; "alarm and distress," Holmes to McCary, vol. 2, part I, letter 5/23/1832, 415.

158. Reynolds, 1855/1879, 235.

159. Whitney, 1973–1975, Taylor to Lawson, vol. 2, part II, letter 8/16/1832, 1015.

160. Mann, 2009, 97–98.

161. Whitney, 1973–1975, Holmes to McCary, vol. 2, part I, letter 5/23/1832, 415.

162. Thwaites, 1892, 242–43.

163. Whitney, 1973–1975, Strode to Reynolds and Atkinson, vol. 2, part I, letter 5/23/1832, 421; vol. 2, part II, 5/23/1832, note 39, 1312; Parkinson, 1903, 241, 352; Strong, 1908, 273; Reynolds, 1855/1879, 243; Armstrong, 1887, 415.

164. Armstrong, 1887, 415; Quaife, 1925, note 24, 403.

165. Trask, 2006, 89.

166. Wakefield, 1834/1908, imagination, 101; Hall sisters, 96.

167. Mann, 2000, 27, 76, 277–78.

168. Trask, 2006, 203.

169. Whitney, 1973–1975, Taylor to Lawson, vol. 2, part II, letter 8/16/1832, 1015.

170. Salisbury, 1908, 404–5; Dodge claimed three men hit (Strong, 1908, 278), whereas Davis said that four were down (Salisbury, 1908, 405).

171. *Makataimeshekiakiak*, 1916, 149–51; Strong, 1908, 279.

172. Trask, 2006, 258.

173. "Indian War," *Niles*, vol. 42, 7/14/1832, 353.

174. Italics in the original. *Makataimeshekiakiak*, 1916, 153.

175. For *Neapope* as "Broth," Whitney, 1973–1975, Scott to Cass, vol. 2, part I, letter 8/20/1831, 1026.

176. *Makataimeshekiakiak*, 1916, 153–54.

177. Wakefield, 1834/1908, 110–12. Wakefield misidentified the shouter as *Neapope*; *Makataimeshekiakiak* was the man on a "fine horse," shouting orders in a "loud voice," *Makataimeshekiakiak*, 1916, 154.

178. *Makataimeshekiakiak*, 1916, 154–55.

179. Davis, 1971–2015, item 322, vol. 1, note 4, 241–42; controversy over Davis's presence at Wisconsin Heights, vol. 1, note 4, 240–41; Whitney, 1973–1975, Dodge to Loomis, vol. 2, part II, letter 7/22/1832, 845.

180. Whitney, 1973–1975, Henry to Atkinson, vol. 2, part II, letter 7/23/1832, 860; Atkinson to Scott, vol. 2, part II, letter 8/5/1832, 935; Stevens, 1903, Atkinson to Macomb, letter 8/25/1832, 228; Wakefield, 1834/1908, 113; for Dodge, "Letter from Fort Howard," *Niles*, vol. 42, 424.

181. Whitney, 1973–1975, Dodge to Loomis, vol. 2, part II, letter 7/22/1832, 845.

182. *Makataimeshekiakiak*, 1916, 154.

183. Wakefield, 1834/1908, 134; Stevens, 1903, 218; Salisbury, 1908, 405–6.

184. *Makataimeshekiakiak*, 1916, 156.

185. Wakefield, 1834/1908, 116.

186. Whitney, 1973–1975, Taylor to Lawson, vol. 2, part II, letter 8/16/1832, 1015; Dyer, 1946, 80; *Taylor and Fillmore*, 1848, 5.

187. *Makataimeshekiakiak*, 1916, departing group, 155; quotations, 155, 157; starvation, 157; confirmatory information, Whitney, 1973–1975, Stambaugh to Scott, vol. 2, part II, letters 8/11/1832, note 5, 988–89; information amended, Stambaugh to Scott, vol. 2, part II, letter 8/13/1832, 996.

188. Ritner's men saw four, but he saw only three canoes, in Whitney, 1973–1975, Ritner to Loomis, vol. 2, part II, letter 7/23/1832, 903; Loomis to Atkinson, vol. 2, part II, letter 7/30–31/1832, 906; Atkinson to Scott, vol. 2, part II, letter 8/5/1832, 936.

189. Ho-Chunk as forced, *Washington Constitution*, 1907, 307; Whitney, 1973–1975, Street to Clark, vol. 2, part II, letter 8/1–2/1832, 913–14.

190. Distance from Bad Axe, Wakefield, 1834/1908, 136; Whitney, 1973–1975, "Minutes," vol. 2, part II, 8/27/1832, 1056.

191. Fonda, 1907, 261; Whitney, 1973–1975, Dodge to Loomis, vol. 2, part II, letters 7/22/1832, 845; Loomis to Atkinson, vol. 2, part II, letter 7/28/1832, 900; Report, Throckmorton, vol. 2, part II, 8/3/1832, 927; Buchanan, vol. 2, part II, 8/5/1832, 937.

192. Italics in the original. *Makataimeshekiakiak*, 1916, 157–58; Boyd, "Papers," Boyd to Porter, letter 8/9/1832, 287; Whitney, *Black Hawk War*, Reuben Holmes to Atkinson, vol. 2, part 2, letter 8/5/1832, 938–39; "Minutes of an Examination of Prisoners," 8/27/1832, 1056.

193. Whitney, *Black Hawk War*, letter, Street to Clark, vol. 2, part 2, 8/2/1832, 917.

194. Wakefield, *Wakefield's History*, 135.

195. Boyd, 1892, Boyd to Porter, letter 8/9/1832, 287–88; Whitney, 1973–1975, statement, Throckmorton, vol. 2, part II, 8/3/1832, 928; Holmes to Atkinson, vol. 2, part II, letter 8/5/1832, 938–39.

196. Whitney, 1973–1975, Street to Clark, vol. 2, part II, letter 8/2/1832, 917; Fonda, 1907, 261–62.

197. *Makataimeshekiakiak*, 1916, 158; Whitney, 1973–1975, statement Throckmorton, vol. 2, part II, 8/3/1832, 928; Holmes to Atkinson, vol. 2, part II, letter 8/5/1832, 938–39.

198. Whitney, 1973–1975, "Minutes," vol. 2, part II, 8/27/1832, 1056.

199. "The North West," *Niles*, vol. 42, 8/21/1832, 450; for coward, Kingston, 1903, 332; *Makataimeshekiakiak*, 1916, 158–59; Whitney, 1973–1975, "Minutes," vol. 2, part II, 8/27/1832, 1056.

200. For 400, Whitney, 1973–1975, statement, Throckmorton, vol. 2, part II, 8/3/1832, 927.

201. Italics in the original. *Makataimeshekiakiak*, 1916, 159.

202. For readiness, Wakefield, 1834/1908, 128; Stevens, 1903, 222; for Atkinson's 1,300 men, Whitney, 1973–1975, Atkinson to Scott, vol. 2, part II, letters 8/5/1832, 938; Atkinson to Macomb, vol. 2, part II, letter 8/25/1832, 228; *ASPMA*, 1832–1861, vol. 5, no. 532, 11/1832, 30.

203. Wakefield, 1834/1908, 131.

204. Smith, 1854, statement, Estes, vol. 3, 230; Whitney, 1973–1975, statement, Throckmorton, vol. 2, part II, 8/3/1832, 927.

205. Fonda, 1907, 262.

206. Whitney, 1973–1975, Street to Clark, vol. 2, part II, letter 8/3/1832, 926; report, Taylor, vol. 2, part II, 8/5/1832, 942; Taylor's total regiment at 400, Stevens, 1903, Atkinson to Macomb, letter 8/25/1832, 228.

207. Fonda, 1907, 263–64; Whitney, 1973–1975, Street to Clark, vol. 2, part II, letter 8/3/1832, 926; report, Taylor, vol. 2, part II, 8/5/1832, 942; Smith, 1854, Estes, vol. 3, 230.

208. Fonda, 1907, 262; Smith, 1854, Estes statement, vol. 3, 231; Whitney, 1973–1975, Street to Clark, vol. 2, part II, letters 8/3/1832, 926; Taylor to Lawson, vol. 2, part II, letter 8/16/1832, 1016.

209. Whitney, 1973–1975, report, Taylor, vol. 2, part II, 8/5/1832, 942; Smith, 1854, Estes statement, vol. 3, 230; Stevens, 1903, Atkinson to Macomb, letter 8/25/1832, 228.

210. Fonda, 1907, 263; Whitney, 1973–1975, quotation, Johnston, vol. 2, part II, 8/2/1832, 1321; for Dodge's 900, letter, Modecai to Macomb, vol. 2, part II, letter 8/3/1832, 922; standard militia usages of Indian "hide," Mann, 2005, as shaving strops, 165; as shoes, 86.

211. *Makataimeshekiakiak*, 1916, 159; Smith, 1854, *Galena Gazette*, vol. 3, 8/6/1832, 232; Wakefield, 1834/1908, 131.

212. Smith, 1854, *Galena Gazette*, vol. 3, 8/6/1832, 232.

213. Wakefield, 1834/1908, 131; Trask, 2006, 283.

214. Whitney, 1973–1975, Anderson to Anderson, vol. 2, part II, letter 8/5/1832, 933.

215. Wakefield, 1834/1908, 133.

216. Ibid., 131.

217. Trask, 2006, 285.

218. Smith, 1854, Estes statement, vol. 3, 232; "Scene at the Battle of Bad Axe," *Niles*, vol. 43, 11/3/1832, 147; Whitney, 1973–1975, Anderson to Anderson, vol. 2, part II, letter 8/5/1832, 933.

219. Fonda, 1907, 263–64.

220. Wakefield, 1834/1908, 133.

221. Whitney, 1973–1975, Anderson to Anderson, vol. 2, part II, letter 8/5/1832, 933.

222. Wallace, 1970, 41, 42; Somerville, 1997, 74–89, Indian slaves, Wallenstein, 1997, 57–73.

223. Wakefield, 1834/1908, 132, 133.

224. "The North West," *Niles*, vol. 42, 8/21/1832, 450.

225. Stevens, 1903, Atkinson to Macomb, letter 8/25/1832, 228; Whitney, 1973–1975, Atkinson to Beall, vol. 2, part II, letters 8/5/1832, 934; Atkinson to Scott, vol. 2, part II, letter 8/5/1832, 935.

226. Whitney, 1973–1975, "War New from Galena," vol. 2, part II, 8/6/1832, 955.

227. Ibid., Scott to Cass, vol. 2, part II, letter 8/10/1832, 980.

228. Ibid., Scott to Cass, vol. 2, part II, letter 8/6/1832, 980; Hall, 2007, note 15, 167.

229. Fonda, 1907, 264; Curtis-Wedge, 1917, 44.

230. Whitney, 1973–1975, Scott to Cass, vol. 2, part II, letter 8/21/1832, 1027.

231. Ibid., Taylor to Galt, vol. 2, part II, letter 8/22/1832, 1043.

232. Ibid., "Minutes," vol. 2, part II, 8/27/1832, 1056.

233. Smith, 1998/2018.

234. Whitney, 1973–1975, Pilcher to Scott, vol. 2, part II, prisoners of war, letter 8/18/1832, 1020–21; Fort Crawford, Galt to Taylor and Street, vol. 2, part II, letter 8/25/1832, 1047.

235. Parentheticals in the original. "Indian War Over," *Niles*, vol. 43, 9/29/1832, 79.

236. Trask, 2006, 299–302.

237. Montgomery, 1847, 29–32; *Taylor and Fillmore*, 1848, 5.

CHAPTER 9

❧

"Is This the White Men's Faith?":
Seminole, Maroons, and Settlers,
1835–1840

Modern Americans suffer from Acute Historical Amnesia (AHA) about the Spanish presence in "La Florida," which extended from Port Royal, South Carolina, south through Florida, from the mid-sixteenth century into the French and British periods. Sloppy vocabulary usage does not aid comprehension. In sheerly practical terms, absent prior understanding of the Spanish word *cimarrón*, Americans find themselves flailing for comprehension upon encountering the terms *cimarrón*, "Seminole," and "Maroon" tossed about as though everyone were born knowing where they came from and what they meant.

In fifteenth-century Spain, *cimarrón* indicated either a domesticated animal or a slave fled into the countryside, supposedly running wild. This concept of *cimarrón* was transported to the Americas during the Spanish conquest of the Antilles, where originally, it indicated only imported animals that escaped, but soon enough it was also applied to Taino, Arawak, and Africans on the lam from Spanish cruelty, all rushing to the interior of the Islands.[1] *Cimarrón* continued morphing on the North American mainland, through a convoluted series of events connected with invasion, internecine European competition, Indian resistance, and African slavery.

The Muskogeean Guale were some of the original peoples of what is now coastal Georgia extending into Florida, and from 1597 to 1601, they orchestrated a uniquely successful, military repulsion of Spanish invasion.[2] The Guale were aided by African slaves of the Spanish, when in 1597, Africans escaped Spanish clutches "to join the rebellious" Guale.[3] Similarly, during the Yamasee War (1715–1716), an Indian attempt to end the European slave trade, the Yamasee freed "hundreds of slaves" in the British Carolinas. The British made the mistake of arming their slaves against the Yamasee, which made the Africans quite effective fighters, once they defected, arms in tow.[4] Clearly, Africans had been escaping European slavery to join Muskogeean groups for centuries before the southern slaveholders of the U.S. period arose. These Indian and African freedom fighters were called *cimarrones*.

Having murdered all the peninsular Apalachee during Queen Anne's War (1702–1713), the Spaniards of La Florida realized that they were naked of people between them and their rivals, the British, in North America. The Spanish solution to this problem was to invite the anti-British Muskogee onto old Apalachee land, seeing them as body blocks against British encroachment. Five Muskogeean towns agreed to migrate, so that the Apalachicola, Oconee, Hitchiti, Sawokli, and Yuchi became the nucleus of a new nation.[5] Around the same period, the Yamassee lost their war, the British killing or enslaving captured Yamassee.[6] A trickle of Yamassee remnants fled south, becoming one of the additional strains incorporated into the Seminole nation. The transplanted Muskogee and their incorporated remnant nations were all *cimarrones*, alike, to the Spaniards.

Meantime, the transplanted Muskogee picked up on the Spanish term, *cimarrón*, turning it into what is now treated as a Muskogeean word, *simanóli* (or its dialect variant, *simanóni*). *Simanóli* was, however, nothing other than a Muskogee attempt to pronounce the Spanish word, *cimarrón*, in a language containing no "r."[7] Hearing *simanóli* with Anglophonic ears, the British and their colonists then decided that "Seminole" was self-name for this Florida nation. It is a mistake to think that throughout these transitions, the original Spanish meaning of *cimarrón* as wild-eyed runaway transferred intact. Instead, *simanóli* are "wanderers," "strayed people" who "failed to return" to their parent group or, even, "pioneers."[8] These translations all struggle to indicate those traditionally called "Walkaways." Whenever a significant portion of a nation was displeased with the national direction, custom called on the dissenters to leave, forming their own nation to avoid cultural disruption within the parental group. Thus did *Makataimeshekiakiak* and his band walk away from *Keokuk*'s town in 1832, because they refused to accept the 1830 Sauk and Meskwaki Removal Treaty.

It is mistaken to present national remnants such as the Gaule and Yamassee as incorporated by the Seminole as second-class citizens. Writing in 1967, John Mahon did exactly that, presenting the Yamassee as enslaved and raped by the Muskogee, a proposition twisted by Western expectations of "primitive" behavior.[9] First, rape was firmly against Woodlands law, with rapist liable to be killed by the woman's relatives—if not by her.[10] Second, Woodlanders had formal steps to citizenship, something like the U.S. Green Card progression, with any non-Muskogee marrying in granted immediate Muskogean rights, and their children, outright citizenship.[11] The rest worked their way up, like the Yamasse "slaves" William Bartram mentioned seeing in 1774 in the Alachua town of Cuscowilla. Well-dressed, these Yamasee were "mild, peaceable, and tractable," in contrast to the "bold, active, and clamorous" Alachua.[12] The incumbents for citizenship had to mind their P's and Q's. It sounds as if this was what Bartram saw: people on suffrage in Cuscowilla, behaving themselves.

The British also picked up on the term *cimarrón*. As first published in 1628 and produced in 1659, Philip Nichols's play, *The History of Sir Francis Drake*, included in its Dramatis Personae, the "King of the Symerons," "Pedro, *A Symeron*," and "The Symerons," in dramatizing the *cimarrón* community's 1572–1573 victory over the Spanish in Panama (recalling it as Drake's, of course).[13] In its next English incarnation during the seventeenth century, *cimarrón* slimmed down to its handy Castilian suffix, *arrón*, retaining only the "m" of its stem, "*cim*," to become "Maroon."[14] By the eighteenth century, the English slang "Maroon" had completely replaced "Symeron," especially as the Jamaican Maroon revolution stretched on and on.[15]

Further confusing the issue, *cimarrón* later bifurcated in American English, with one denotation playing off the archaic Spanish usage and the other constricting to apply solely to escaped slaves. By 1844, typically omitting the accent mark, U.S. documents connected "*cimarron*" with "*carnero*" (ram), as "*carnero cimarron*" or "wild rams." This term was presented as Spanish for the bighorn sheep of the Rocky Mountains, with the U.S. Congress picking up on "*cimarron*," alone, to indicate "bighorn" in 1850.[16] In its other life in the United States, by the nineteenth century, "Maroon" had come solely to mean militant escaped slaves, organized for self-defense, whereas Seminole solely meant Florida Indians.

Although Seminole clans were recorded, it was not in such a way as to enlighten anyone concerning the outlay of the phratries. On the Blood side, the Otter Clan seemed primary, and interestingly, instead of the Wind sitting as Breath primary, as it was farther north among the Muskogee, the Tiger led the Breath half, with both the Tiger and Otter phratries "of descent" having been clung to "through a long and tragic past."[17] The second half of the Tigers were the Wind in the two-town Breath setup recorded in 1886, with the northernmost town led by the Tiger, while its counterpart, the Big Cypress town was led by the Wind.[18] Otters clearly led the Blood half. Alligators are also very Blood-based, and from their importance in the Second Seminole War, it can be inferred that the Alligators stood as the second half of the Otters in the Blood half.

Culturally, the Seminole derived from a matriarchal clan base. Even after two centuries of brutal Spanish patriarchy punishing any signs of matriarchy, the Seminole retained the Blood/woman focus of their clan structure. Clan identity emphatically followed the mother's line, with lineage titles deriving exclusively through the women.[19] The great holy man and war chief of the Second Seminole War, *A-Cee-Yahola* (*Osceola*), claimed to be fully Seminole, and under Woodlands law, he was, because his mother was Seminole. Unable (or unwilling) to grasp that the construction of identity in matriarchies runs solely through the mother, during *Osceloa's* lifetime, the settlers insisted on calling him "Powell" after his mother's sometime mate, the trader William Powell, who might well have been a one-night stand.[20] Insisting on "Powell" might have made the settlers feel so much better about being defeated by *Osceola*, but it did not erase his Seminole ancestry. He likely also enjoyed an African heritage. Of his two wives, his favorite, *Chechola* ("Morning Dew"), was a Black Seminole.[21]

Mikko (chief) titles ran through mothers to daughters, leaving Western sources perplexed to grasp how *mikko*-ship operated. Among other problems, although "*cacias*" or female chiefs were commonly recorded by the Spaniards, English sources ignored them.[22] Consequently, *Ahaya Secoffee Mikko* ("Cowkeeper") of the Alachua Seminole is falsely presented as paternal uncle of his successor, Payne *Mikko*. Instead, it was *Ahaya Secoffee*'s unnamed mother who held the lineage titles, and when he died, his mother having no more sons, the title descended through her daughter, *Ahaya Secoffee*'s sister. The daughter's son, Payne *Mikko*, was thus the grandson of the female line. When Payne *Mikko* died, the title reverted to his mother, who gave it to her second son, *Halpuda Mikko* ("Alligator Chief," nicknamed "Billy Bowlegs"). When *Halpuda Mikko* passed on, the title returned to his mother's bundle, from whence it descended to her daughter, the sister of *Halpuda Mikko*. She bestowed it on her son, *Micanopy Mikko*.[23] In other words, the title went from mother to daughter in a standard matriarchal pattern.

It has been customary, since the first Spanish priests expressed horror over multiple Guale women passing one man around, for European men to present multiple marriage as a male arrangement, styling the Muskogee men as polygamous. Consequently, in 1562, René de Laudonnière described "kings" (*mikko*) as having "two or three" wives, primarily honoring the first, whose children inherited.[24] This view was slightly refined in 1887 by Clay McCauley, who asserted that "several Seminole families" had "duogamy" or one man and two women as one marriage, the style of marriage that *Osceola* had.[25]

The duogamy was an expression of matriarchy. Women held all the titles, which were preferably kept together. Sisters of a lineage thus married the same man, neatly keeping the position titles in their line, with inheritance running through the elder sister's line, first.[26] The idea of two women initiating possession of the same man was inconceivable to Europeans, so they literally did not conceive of it, but it was an Indigenous variation of the polyandry, farther north.[27] The Spanish attempt to wipe out duogamy greatly helped to bring on the Guale revolt, for the first thing the Guale did upon victory was to restore their matrilineal duogamy.[28]

Again, like all Woodlanders, the Seminole lived in fixed, light and airy dwellings, often open-sided to catch breezes in the heat and sitting stilts to snake-, alligator-, and flood-proof the floor.[29] Describing the Alachua town of Cuscowilla, eighteenth-century naturalist William Bartram said that each housing unit actually consisted of two houses. One was walled and divided down the middle, with kitchen and "common hall" on one half and living quarters on the other. Each house half was thirty feet long by twelve feet wide, reaching up another twelve feet in height, to the ceiling. The second house, of the same dimensions but two stories tall, was the lineage family dwelling. Open-air on three sides, the second-floor loft was accessed by a movable staircase. Catching the breezes, the loft created a "cool" and "airy" family room where the chief received his guests. The other half of this house was closed in on all sides, with the lower half, a potato cellar, and the upper half, a granary. In all, the town boasted thirty of these dual dwellings.[30] The doubled halves clearly honored the Twinned Cosmos.

Towns typically sat next to cultivated fields, farmed by the women. Traveling into Florida in 1774, Bartram saw the women's created soil, the land's "very upper surface" having been purposely intermingled with the "ashes of burnt vegetables" to create *terra preta* fertility, in this instance, supporting a forest.[31] Seminole women grew corn, "in considerable quantity," along with potatoes and "much praised melons and pumpkins," while tending rice paddies in the swamp.[32] Food supply depending on landscape, the Seminole also grew a palmetto "cabbage" and a very starchy root, Koonti, something like Bermuda arrowroot, that was dug like potatoes and pounded into flour. The large reservoirs of cane in Florida were rendered for their sugar.[33] Fruit of all kinds abounded: oranges, limes, lemons, guavas, pineapples, grapes, and plums.[34] For their part, Seminole men engaged in the "winter" hunt, supplying protein through rabbit, squirrel, venison, pork, fish, bear, land turtles, and fowl of all sorts, plus less obvious meat-bearers such as opossum.[35] Had it not been for 300 years' worth of unremitting settler despoliation, life in Florida would have been paradisiacal.

Cuscowilla was the "capital town" of the Alachua Seminole, Bartram noting its lake and "fine fruitful orange grove," although right next to the town, he saw only modest gardens with the usual corn, beans, "Citruls" (watermelons), and tobacco.[36] The large-scale "plantation" sat "two miles distant." Farmed in common by "the whole community," each clan had its own section, for which it was responsible and whose fruits it claimed. However, all clans contributed a portion of their harvest to the "public granary," sitting in the midst of the fields.[37] Surplus was stored as a national food supply for use during public gatherings such as ceremonies, councils, and festivals.[38] Bartram was describing the gift economy, common to all Woodland cultures. Such communal storage included all items necessary to life, from food to hides to tools, with Joseph François Lafitau in 1724, rather accurately regarding this warehousing system as a public treasury.[39]

The daytime job of the youngsters was to act as living scarecrows, and the nightly task of adult men was to patrol the fields, keeping off the wildlife that would otherwise have eaten all the corn, in particular.[40] The townspeople served Bartram a feast including Spanish milk and honey, as well as the traditional "venison stewed with bear's oil," hominy, and corn cakes.[41] He watched men on horseback tending "several herds of cattle," which belonged to *Ahaya Secoffee Mikko*, who had the finest of the cattle slaughtered to provide for a town feast.[42] Such gifting as the feast honoring Bartram was required of chiefs, for any who hoarded would not long be chief.

Important to the men was the Black Drink, in common usage (under various names) among the Algonkin and Muskogee Woodlanders. A hallucinogen, it was (and is) a spiritual cleanser, as well as vision medium for those of talent. The men regularly used the Black Drink at Green Corn, the main harvest festival.[43] Traditionally, the Seminole used two different versions of the Black Drink, the Blood honoring made from the button snakeroot (*Eryngium synchaetum*) and the Breath honoring made from inner willow bark (*Salix amphibia*).[44] Rituals were conducted under the watchful guidance of the *A-Cee-Yahola*

("Black Drink Singers"), the holy men, who "sang" the Black Drink, in long, haunting cries. Amusingly, "Yahola" was one of the terms wildly misappropriated in 1775 by James Adair, as his smoking-gun proof that the Indians had descended from the "Ten Lost Tribes of Israel."[45]

Sources offer next to no information on the Africans with the Seminole before the U.S. annexation of Florida in 1821.[46] This did not stop settler sources from insisting that the Seminole kept Blacks as slaves. For instance, Payne *Mikko*, himself at least partially African, was closely connected with the Alachua "Negro Town" of 300 people, inevitably dubbed "slaves" by Western historians.[47] Settler-style slavery did not occur, however, until the twenty-year period that the British held Florida, from 1763 to 1783. African slavery was accepted only by certain chiefs who noticed the "prestige" of slaveholding in British culture. They allowed chiefs with forty head of cattle to acquire a slave, and the British began handing out slaves as perquisites to their hip-pocket chiefs.[48]

In 1821, U.S. Army captain John H. Bell also described Africans living with the Seminole as their "slaves," but what he went on to detail was hardly slavish. The "slaves" lived in "separate families" and raised their own crops on their own land. Their "surplus" yields "went to the master," said Bell, but this seems to have been a misconstruction of the Seminole gift economy.[49] Like all Seminole, adopted Black Seminole owned their own fields and harvests and were expected only to kick into the public granary, their chiefs occasionally slaughtering a hog or a cow to share, just like everyone else.[50] It was standard that, upon adoption, the person and even whole groups acquired a job for the clan and nation. It appeared that the job that the Seminole commonly assigned to adopted Blacks was foreign affairs, acting as interpreters and advisers in matters relating to the fractious U.S. Southerners.[51] What Bell described, then, was not slavery and was not oppression. It was acceptance. He saw Black Seminole.

It was during the U.S. period that the insistence on southern Indians as slave masters arose, based on such avatars as the U.S.-anointed "chief" of the Muskogee, *Hoboi-Hilr-Miko* ("Alexander McGillivray"). As Removal sentiment heated up, other assimilants joined him to prove to the settlers that they were "civilized," for rumor had it that, if the settlers saw Indians as "civilized," then the government would not remove them. Acting "civilized" meant to dress, eat, talk, act, and take slaves like the settlers. It did not forestall Removal one whit, but it did permanently attach the moniker, "Five Civilized Tribes," to the Cherokee, Choctaw, Chickasaw, "Creek," and Seminole.

The Seminole were famed as "the least civilized" of this cadre, owing to their rejection of forced assimilation.[52] During the period of U.S cultural interference with the Muskogee under Benjamin Hawkins, the Seminole attracted Muskogee Walkaways from Hawkins's "Creek laws," whereas his collaborators were deemed "civilized."[53] This is the light in which to read Indian agent William Ward's announcement that "the least civilized of the Five Civilized Tribes" were the "old Indians," the Seminole who did not "take kindly to the new ideas and ways."[54]

Even as late as 1886, when Clay McCauley surveyed the Seminole, settler accounts had the Blacks among them "still held as slaves." Writing for the

Smithsonian, McCauley disputed this southern fantasy, for he had not seen or heard of "anything that could justify" such a "statement."[55] Instead, Seminole and "negress" marriages were not uncommon, with resultant "half-breed" Seminole openly acknowledged and accepted as Seminole.[56] Indigenous Seminole women lived "in apparent terms of perfect equality" with the "two negresses" among them.[57] In 1894, the Census Bureau listed 1,761 Seminole in "Indian Country," separating out the 806 "of Negro descent." A companion schedule, segregated by racist standard, at least correctly listed the total number of Seminole in "Indian Country" as 2,739, of whom 933 were mixed race, 127 of them of settler, and 806 of them of African, admixture.[58] The Seminole regarded all, regardless of racial heritage, as Seminole. The fact that the Seminole were horrified when urged to sell their Black members, leaves the settler story of Seminole slavery looking politically motivated.[59]

The settler history of Florida went through four stages:

1. The first Spanish phase, 1565–1763
2. The British phase, 1763–1783
3. The second Spanish phase, 1783–1821
4. The U.S. phase, 1821, to Statehood in 1845

The Spanish first attempted colonization in 1513 under Ponce de Leon, with Spanish slave raids along the southeastern coast starting up in 1514, followed by Hernan de Soto rampaging murderously through the southeast, starting in 1539.[60] The Spanish famously created St. Augustine in 1565. African slaves accompanied the first Spaniards. By 1687, escaping ferocious British slavery in the Carolinas, Africans ran to Spanish Florida, where they enjoyed some freedom; for lacking Spanish settlers and having killed significant numbers of Indians, it dawned on Spanish authorities that *los cimarrones* afforded an easy way to beef up their colony. Consequently, on November 7, 1693, Charles II, the Austrian King of Spain, declared that slaves escaping to St. Augustine were free, so long as they became Catholic. By 1704, Florida governor José de Zúñiga y Cerda amplified this decree with his own Orders for Apalachee Province, specifying that Black refugees from the Carolinas were free, upon entering Florida, whether or not they were Christian.[61]

Originally, the Spanish government reimbursed British slaveholders for their losses, but so many slaves flooded Florida that, in 1731, the Council for the Indies in Madrid ended the payments.[62] Not only was the expense unsustainable, but also, given the Guale experience, the Spanish did not wish to pay for their own defeat by African forces combining with the Indians against them. Thus, they co-opted the escapees to their own purposes in 1739, by training and arming them as the Spanish guard against the British at Gracia Real de Santa Teresa de Mosé. This became the legendary Fort Mosé.[63]

British colonists frothed over Florida's slave refuge. In 1738, the lieutenant governor of South Carolina described armed Africans as "more Dreadful" to English settler "Safety than any Spanish Invaders." Moreover, the ex-slaves acted as agents, forging alliances with the southern Indian nations, who were as liable as Africans to be enslaved. Whether those agents were connected to the great and bloody insurrection against the British colonists in 1739 is unclear, but with the Carolina Maroons, Spanish Africans clearly wanted to destroy slavery.[64] Although the enraged British attempted in 1740 to expropriate escaped Africans through an invasion of Florida, the Africans prevailed in 1745, when Fort Mosé supplied troops for the Spanish counter-invasion of the Carolinas.[65] The Spanish and British were eventually both displaced, but "Fort Mose" was resurrected as the "Negro Fort," anathema to U.S. slavers.

The second period of Floridian colonial history was brief and British. It ran from 1763 to 1783, resulting directly from the British victory in the French and Indian War. Article 19 of the Treaty of Paris ending that war gave Spain full rights to Cuba, while Article 20 ceded Florida to the British.[66] One upshot of Article 20 was that the Spanish evacuated Fort Mosé's Black troops to Cuba with them, burning the old fort.[67] This hardly emptied Florida of Maroons, however. Throughout the British period, slaves continued escaping to the Seminole. Not able to beat the trend, during the American Revolution, the British joined it, promising British freedom to entice slaves of the Revolutionaries to the British side of the war. At the 1779 British siege of Savannah, "thousands" of slaves took the British up on their offer. At the end of the Revolution, African rebels left with the British, but a significant number remained in Florida, using their British arms and training to mount raids on slaveholders. This continued until 1786, when the Georgia militia drove them from their fort at Bear Creek.[68]

The third period of Floridian colonial history was the second period of Spanish rule, started under Article 2 of the 1783 Treaty of Paris, which drew U.S. boundaries as north of the Floridian peninsula and panhandle.[69] In Article 8 of a separate Paris Treaty between Britain and Spain, negotiated in January 1783, Florida was restored to the Spanish.[70] Frustrated by the strength of the Florida Seminole and desirous of ending the refuge flow bleeding it dry of slaves, the United States negotiated the 1795 Treaty of San Lorenzo el Real with Spain. Disguised as a measure restraining Indian hostilities against either Spain or the United States, its Article 5 essentially pledged that neither the United States nor Spain would use armed Indian proxies against one another. In effect, Article 5 stripped the Seminole of their ability to gain arms with which to defend themselves against U.S. depredations.[71]

A major U.S. hope was to regain custody of free Blacks in Florida through the treaty, but the War of 1812 dashed that wet dream. Spanish Florida became a British staging ground. In 1814, the British rebuilt and greatly enlarged a fort along the Apalachicola River, near the ruins of old Fort Mosé. After the war, upon departing Florida, the British ceded the new fort at Mosé to the Maroons.[72] This formidable fort was what all U.S. documents angrily dubbed the "Negro Fort." It was not until this period that the United States became fully aware that the Seminole, more than the Spanish, welcomed the escaped slaves, while the Spanish picked up where they left off, employing Maroons as intermediaries with the Seminole.[73] Much of the later U.S. determination to seize Florida reflected its "need" to cut off the Maroon refuge for escaped slaves.

As European powers blindly raged against one another between 1763 and 1815, the Florida Seminole emerged forcefully as a unified power, by their own count in 1822, numbering 4,883, with 600 to 1,000 allied Maroons.[74] (For obvious reasons, Maroons would not allow a real census of themselves.) The growing unification of Maroon and Seminole deeply disturbed U.S. officials, and on more than one score. Both economics and ideology entered the equation. Economically, the resale value of the Maroons was a prime consideration for southern slaveholders, apparent as early as Article 3 of the first U.S.-Creek Treaty. Cooked up in 1790 between George Washington and his hip-pocket "chief" *Hoboi-Hilr-Miko*, it bound the Alabama Muskogee to turn over all "prisoners," whether "white" or "negroes."

Oddly, no "negroes" were forthcoming. Article 3 empowered the governor of Georgia to "claim and receive" the "negroes" at the Oconee River in June 1791, but even federal assists from May through September 1791, failed to return anyone to slavery.[75] The pattern of Black refuge among the Muskogee and the Seminole might well have played into Andrew Jackson's determination to invade the Muskogee in his Creek War (1813–1814), and it certainly animated his invasion of Florida in the First Seminole War (1816–1818). There was, however, much more to Jackson & Co.'s furious Muskogee and Seminole wars than just the potential for financial gain.

Psychological factors were also at work. Ideologically, slavery and "civilization" went hand-in-hand in the settler script, so that free-standing, self-governing, and prosperous Seminole and Maroon towns caused massive cognitive dissonance for slavers. Their cultural story-frames would not let them see a black without assuming that she should be enslaved or an Indian without assuming that she should be dead. Thus, the splendid existence of Maroon and Seminole communities unhinged the settler mind. Already facing abolitionist opposition to their "Peculiar Institution," heading into the nineteenth century, it became vital for settlers "scientifically" to isolate Africans and Indians from Euro-humanity, for the only alternative was the unthinkable: ending slavery and, worse, abandoning Manifest Destiny.

Enter, "scientific" stories of African-Orangutan mating. In 1775, German naturalist Johann Frederick Blumenbach tackled the thorny question of "hybridity," which under his pen, slopped over into interspecies dating. In 1795, he repeated as factual the preposterous tale of African women being raped by "lascivious male apes."[76] In the United States, Thomas Jefferson helped promote this inane story in his *Notes on the State of Virginia*, by way of proving that the "lower" entity just naturally lusted to mate with its "superior." In the same way that the "Oranootan" show a marked "preference" for "black women over those of their species," Jefferson wrote, African men made a beeline for European women.[77] In 1789, Jefferson offhandedly referred to himself as "an animal of a warm climate, a mere Oran-ootan," most probably in oblique (and confused) allusion to himself and Sally Hemings.[78]

The offspring of alleged ape-human mating and, soon enough, European-African mating, was purported to be infertile—hence the "mule" in "mulatto"—

with any progeny being "degenerations" from "Caucasian" perfection.[79] A corollary of this fantastic theorem posited the various races as natural enemies, fighting to the death if thrown together, unless the master race controlled events. In "all ages and all places," Indians and Africans had been shown to be "inferior to the Caucasians," thundered Josiah Nott, proud discoverer of the "science" of "Niggerology."[80] History could not "designate a time when the Caucasian was a savage," he proclaimed.[81] Happily, the Caucasian would "eat out" all others, pushing them to extinction.[82] Given these "scientific facts," the successful Seminole-Maroon alliance outraged settler ideology in just about every way conceivable.

Disturbed by this threat to its systems, the United States looked to end its migraines by displacing Spain entirely in Florida, beginning a circuitous play for the peninsula that continued till 1821. In 1803, the Louisiana Purchase handed over large chunks of Indian country to the United States, but in 1806, a major tumult ensued over whether the Florida Panhandle was included in the treaty, occasioning "bitter" congressional "vaporing against Spain," as John Quincy Adams put it.[83] In 1810, President James Madison stepped up the Panhandle efforts.[84] Direct land seizure was now an option, with just such a Floridian enterprise urged on Andrew Jackson as early as 1810 by his nephew, Donelson Caffrey.[85] On January 3, 1811, Madison asked Congress to authorize executive action declaring West Florida (the Panhandle) U.S. territory, a move that greatly angered Spanish governor Vincente Folch.[86] Madison next felt out whether the Spanish might cede East Florida to the United States, thus ending the easy slave access to Florida. Recommended as a solid backdoor go-between, Madison handed Floridian George Mathews secret orders in September 1810, to feel out Folch on his proposed cession. Negotiations continued through November 10.[87]

Jackson used the heat of war with Great Britain in 1812 to pursue the seizure of Florida, entirely, as a necessary part of his Creek War, although in light of his prior communications with his nephew, he had a land deal on his mind, as well.[88] If citizen Jackson somehow felt empowered to make U.S. foreign policy, then citizen Mathews took empire building to new heights, forming a private militia to march on Amelia Island and declare East Florida U.S. territory. He did not bother mentioning the plan to Madison until April 16, 1812, however. By then, Mathews was actually contemplating taking St. Augustine.[89] On April 24, 1812, Madison confided to Jefferson his dismay at the "strange comedy" that Mathews was "playing, in the face of common sense," by greatly exceeding "his instructions" and, thereby, placing the United States in a "most distressing dilemma."[90]

This sort of cowboy attitude toward Florida continued unabated, even after the War of 1812. Once the Treaty of Ghent ended the war, angry about its loss of slaves, Georgia began dispatching militias into—still Spanish-claimed—Florida, intending to root out its safe haven for escapees and, not incidentally, to drag as many as possible back into U.S. slavery. Settlers also snarled that survivors of the Creek War had made their way to the "Negro Fort" after Jackson's massacre at Tohopeka. Few survived Tohopeka, however, so that the twenty-five Seminole that the United States claimed were in the "Negro Fort" in 1816 were probably the Red Sticks surviving the Calabee massacre.[91]

The fort was connected with a nearby Maroon town, supported by farms running up and down the Apalachicola River. In undisputed charge of the settlement and fort was a man variously called García or Garçon ("Boy").[92] Sallying out of their fort under García's command, the Maroons conducted raids, freeing as many slaves as possible. Between 250 and 300 free Blacks defended the "Negro Fort," causing heartburn among the southern slavers.[93] Promoted to commander of the U.S. Army, Southern Division, for his services in the War of 1812, General Andrew Jackson was now in a position to push for an all-out Florida war. More cautious than Jackson, however, the new president, James Monroe, ordered the matter resolved through diplomacy with Spain, instead.[94]

Insubordinate as ever, on April 8, 1816, Jackson ordered General Edmund Pendleton Gaines to destroy the "Negro Fort," more than two weeks before Florida governor Mauricio de Zuñiga replied to his diplomatic inquiries.[95] On April 23, Jackson pushed the lackadaisical Zuñiga for his answer, rationalizing his pending attack on the fort as necessary and demanding to know immediately whether it were a Spanish- or Maroon-initiated fort.[96] In his May 14 orders to Edmund Pendleton Gaines, Jackson indicated that Benjamin Hawkins had already deployed various chiefs and "Warriors" to attack the fort on a bounty-hunting junket. They were to deliver the "negroes" to Hawkins for a fee of "50$ each."[97] Finally, on May 26, Zuñiga agreed that "Destroying" the "Negro Fort" and "returning" the Maroons to their "Lawful owners" sounded like a jim-dandy idea to him, although he could not agree to it officially without orders from his own captain general.[98]

Under Jackson's orders to take the fort, Gaines turned the matter over to his lieutenant colonel Duncan Lamont Clinch. Carting in two eighteen-pound cannons, a five-and-a-half-inch Howitzer, and a "quantity of ordnance" with which to blow up the fort, Clinch's regiment set off along with Hawkins's 150 to 200 Muskogee proxies for the Apalachicola River.[99] By July 25, 1816, Clinch had set up a battery and commenced his attack on the "Negro Fort." Joined on July 27 by river warships under Captain Jarius Loomis, stationed opposite the fort on the river, Clinch resumed bombarding the fort, with Loomis aiming for the fort's magazine.[100] Throughout, García refused Clinch's demand for surrender, sneering at the United States, and threatening to "sink any American vessels" in the river and "blow up the fort if he could not defend it." Hoisting a revolutionary red flag atop the fort's old Union Jack, the fort's defenders returned fire from their own thirty-two pounder.[101]

A "hot shot" from one of Loomis's ships hit the fort's magazine dead-on, bringing about a terrific explosion that left a "scene horrible beyond description," said Clinch.[102] There were 334 men, women, and children in the fort, including 25 Seminole and 309 Maroons. Only "100 effective men," defended it, yet 227 died instantly.[103] Shedding a crocodile "tear" for the "sufferings" of the women and children, Clinch cried that soldiers must "acknowledge that the Great Ruler of the Universe" had used them as his "instruments in chastising the blood-thirsty and murderous wretches" defending the fort.[104]

Clinch promptly appropriated the fort's surviving military equipment, estimated as worth $200,000, while Loomis delivered the remaining equipment valued between $10,000 and $12,000 to the army at New Orleans. Reporting that the Seminole and Maroon corn fields extended "fifty miles up the river," Clinch concluded gloomily that "their numbers were daily increasing."[105] The Seminole taken alive were promptly murdered by Hawkins's Muskogee mercenaries, while the real point of the whole exercise, the surviving, $50–per-head Maroons, were handed over to Forbes and Company for auction.[106] An undisclosed number of survivors were thus dragged into U.S. slavery, although many had been born free in Florida.[107] On September 7, 1816, Jackson got around to notifying the secretary of war of Clinch's "Capture & destruction of the negro Fort."[108]

Jackson's First Seminole War was on. Furious, the Seminole replied by attacking militias along the Georgia border. Tit for tatting followed, with Gaines burning down neutral Fowltown (near modern-day Bainbridge, Georgia) in November 1817, ostensibly because Mikasuki chief *Neamathla* did not respond to his imperious order to take his people to a Muskogee reservation. The unspoken reason for Gaines's attack was that "Negro Fort" survivors had fled to Fowltown, while another 400 escapees from Georgia were in the vicinity, along with 2,000 "hostile warriors."[109]

Retaliating for Fowltown, 500 Seminole lay siege to reinforcements heading up the Apalachicola River to U.S. Fort Scott.[110] Of course, as Congressman Timothy Fuller of Massachusetts scathingly pointed out, the United States had no business, at all, building forts, patrolling rivers, or in conducting raids in Spanish territory, but Jackson was never a stickler for the rules.[111] As it turned out, neither was Congress, which ignored Virginia congressman Charles Fenton Mercer, who observed that there had been no military "necessity" behind destroying the "Negro Fort."[112] In a political dodge, not the destruction of the "Negro Fort," but the Fowltown attack was fingered as initiating the First Seminole War.[113] On December 26, 1817, Secretary of War John Caldwell Calhoun ordered Jackson to Fort Scott in command of 800 U.S. Army and 1,000 Georgia militia against the Seminole, while sending Gaines to Amelia Island, Florida.[114]

In his violent element, Jackson immediately did as much damaged as possible to the Seminole (whom he persisted in calling "Red Sticks"), reducing neutral Mikasuki towns "to ashes." On April 8, 1818, he berated the Spanish commander at St. Augustine Francisco Caso y Luengo, accusing him of arming and supplying "Indians and Negroes." Because St. Marks (the fort at St. Augustine) was in a "defenceless" state, Jackson seized it, "on the universal principal of self defence," missing the contradiction in his own rationale.[115] Soon based at St. Mark's, on April 12, Jackson's men killed thirty-seven Ecofina Seminole, while taking six men and ninety-seven women and children prisoner. At the Suwanee River on April 15, they killed another man and took one man, one woman, and two children prisoner. Jackson's primary target was a major Black and Seminole town on the

Suwanee River, which he attacked on April 16, his forces causing "considerable injury." There was no casualty count other than the eleven Seminole later found dead, nine of them being Black Seminole. Two unfortunate Black Seminole were taken prisoner. Although plundering the settlement of its corn and cattle, Jackson's men could not catch the townsfolk, who were in full retreat. The best they could do was capture another fourteen Seminole, five of them being Black.[116]

Next fixating on the Spanish town of Pensacola, Jackson began building his case to Calhoun about the weak Spanish, cowed by and unable to stem the tide of the "Outlaws of the old red stick party" and their Maroon allies. The only remedy for Spanish treachery in supplying the Seminole and Maroons was the U.S. occupation of Pensacola.[117] Western Florida governor and military commander José Mascot mightily protested Jackson's invasion but to no avail. Jackson plied his usual rhetoric of "all the horrors of a cruel and savage War" against innocent U.S. settlers.[118] In a note (which he closed with "Respectfully yrs."), Jackson threatened the military commander at Pensacola lieutenant colonel Louis Piernas with the murder of every last soldier under Piernas's command, should his men open fire. Jackson then took Pensacola.[119]

Jackson's international banditry was rewarded with the Adams-Onís Treaty with Spain, signed on February 22, 1819, halting the First Seminole War by setting new Spanish-U.S. boundaries. Although not ratified until 1821, Adams-Onís, in fact, ceded Florida to the United States.[120] This is tawdry story that marks the official beginning of the U.S. territorial period in Florida. Now a U.S. territory, on paper, anyhow, U.S. officials immediately turned their efforts to securing Florida with roads and forts.

Ever since the Spanish arrival, Europeans had tried, and failed, to establish routes into and around Florida. The Indians of Florida experienced no such difficulty, however, for the usual access routes connected the mound cities that dotted the peninsula. Indeed, later settler towns like Gainesville were constructed at or near the sites of the old mounds.[121] De Soto's forces followed Timacuan roads, moving easily from town to town, planting their crosses atop mounds.[122] Later Europeans finding themselves every bit as bewildered by the Floridian landscape as the Spaniards had been, it was not until July 1822 that U.S. military road building was proposed for the peninsula, the first effort connecting Pensacola with St. Augustine.[123] Despite Florida territorial lobbying, it was winter 1823, before the House floated H.R. 275 to appropriate funding.[124] The ball rolling, ambitious plans hit the drawing board to connect not only Pensacola to St. Augustine but also to Colerain, Georgia, itself connected to Crawford (later, Jacksonville), Florida. From there, the old British highway was relaid through St. Augustine to New Smyrna. The military geared up for the projects in March 1823, although Congress would not fund the Pensacola–St. Augustine route till March 1824, with the contract for this first road awarded in December.[125]

By October 1823, new roads "important" both "in promoting Settlement of the Territory" and for "military purposes" were proposed among Pensacola, Mobile, and other "important points & Towns" in Alabama.[126] In April 1824, military roads were surveyed, one from Pensacola to Fort Mitchell, in southern Alabama;

another from Pensacola all the way south to Cape Sable, at the southwestern tip of Florida in the Everglades; and a third branching off of the Pensacola-St. Augustine Road, running south to Tampa.[127] By 1828, the significant Pensacola-Mobile route was declared an exclusively military highway.[128]

From there, an 1825 road connected Tampa and Coleraine, Georgia.[129] By November 1825, routes to connect Tallahassee with the Montgomery mail route were afloat, and by May 1826, the road from Tallahassee to St. Augustine was underway, although rather badly constructed and not really passable till the fall of 1830.[130] In 1827, King's Road from the Georgia line through St. Augustine to New Smyrna was gotten up, although difficulties slowed its completion till 1831.[131] A post road ran from St. Mary's to Jacksonville, with another connecting Pensacola to Blakely, Georgia, in 1827, with three routes planned to Blakely by 1828, the main road completed in October 1829, with the military appropriating one for its exclusive use.[132] The St. Augustine-Tampa Bay route was completed by the summer of 1832.[133] The Jacksonville project acquired a military road to Alachua in 1832, the project completed in 1833, while in 1838, a second road was ordered from Jacksonville to Tallahassee.[134] In 1836, a road was run from the Alabama line to Apalachicola.[135]

A flurry of fort construction accompanied the roadbuilding. Some like the Spanish-*cum*-British Fort of St. Marks became the U.S. staging grounds of St. Francis Barracks (the St. Augustine presidio) at U.S. Fort Marion. Others were newly built structures of varying elegance and multiply named—like Fort Alabama, which became Fort Foster—to supply depots or rude posts for military communications. Some fort names were wildly spelled in official documents ("Keais," "Keas," "Keys"), while still others were mentioned offhandedly, perhaps once in the sources (Fort "Jennings"). Whatever their condition or usage, more than eighty-five posts quickly sprang up around the Second Seminole War (1835–1842), signaling the importance of the exercise in the settler mind (see Table 9.1).

Once the roads and the forts were in place, the Second Seminole War could commence. Like all "Indian Wars," the Second Seminole War was a war of choice for the United States, its war drive featuring the standard rhetoric of "Indian depredations," including "wanton and unprovoked" murders of settlers, requiring immediate military attention.[136] The anti-Indian tattoo of these war drums helped to mask the twinned reason behind the Second Seminole War: the threat to American Slavery posed by the Seminole-aided existence of Maroons not only as living in complete freedom in Florida but also as actively rescuing fellow Blacks from chains. To its impotent disgust, settler officialdom was perfectly aware that "the negroes of the Seminole Indians" were "wholly independent, or at least regardless of the authority" of their supposed Seminole "masters." They were "Slaves but in name," fumed the Florida Indian agent Gad Humphreys in 1827, working "only when it suit[ed] their inclination." They were also their own "Judges," concerning "what portion, of the product of their labour" should go to the Seminole. They were "indolent in the extreme," Humphreys cried, and altogether a bad influence on the Seminole. It was, therefore, "necessary to withdraw" the Maroons "as fast as practicable from their erratic and idle habits."[137]

Table 9.1 Primary Forts Heading into the Second Seminole Wars (1835–1842)

Dates	Fort Names	Locations	Usage	Notes
1835–1836	Addison Blockhouse	National Gardens	South Carolina militia fort	Burned by Seminole
1836–1838	Fort Alabama	Tampa, Florida	U.S. Army depot	Stockade; later called Fort Foster
1837–1838	Fort Ann	Near Titusville, Florida	U.S. Army	Outpost
1838–1840	Fort Andrews	Hampton Springs, Florida	U.S. Army	Burned by Seminole
1832–1866	Apalachicola Arsenal	Chattahoochee, Florida	U.S. Army arsenal	Completed in 1836
1836–1837	Fort Armstrong	Bushnell, Florida	U.S. Army	Temporary Headquarters
1839	Fort Atkinson	Day, Florida	Florida militia	At Atkinson's Lake
1837–1841	Fort Barbour	Gadsden, Florida	U.S. Army	Also given as "Fort Aspagala"; perhaps consecutive forts
1840?–1841	Fort Barker	Near Natural Bridge Spring, Florida	U.S. Army	Post in line of communications; burned by Seminole, 1841
1837–1850	Fort Basinger	Highland Co. at Kissimmee River	U.S. Army supply depot	Established by Zachary Taylor; also as "Bassinger"
1823–1883	Fort Brooke	Tampa, Florida	Settler fortification to U.S. Army	Also called Cantonment Brooke
1838–1839	Fort Butler	Astor, Florida	U.S. barracks	Log structure, for line of communications
1818–1898	Fort Clinch	Old Fernandina, Florida	U.S. Army garrison	On Amelia Island; Spanish fortification since 1686
1836	Fort Cooper	Near Inverness, Florida	U.S. Army	Temporary encampment; resuscitated in Civil War
1836–1838	Fort Call	Volusia, Florida	U.S. Army	Small post, abandoned as unhealthy in 1838
1835–1842	Fort Center	Glades County, Fisheating Creek, Florida	U.S. Army	Small, palisaded post

(continued)

Table 9.1 (Continued)

Dates	Fort Names	Locations	Usage	Notes
1838?–1842	Fort Christian	Pass Christian, MI	U.S. Marine post	Troop transport by water and gunboat port
1837–1838	Fort Christmas	Western tip, Lake Okechobee, Florida	U.S. Army	Supply depot
1838?–1842	Fort Cross	Cape Sable, Florida	U.S. Army	Possibly Marine post
1839–1842	Fort Cummings	Lake Alfred, Florida	U.S. Army	Line of communications
1837–1838	Fort Dade	Pasco County, Florida	U.S. Army	Abandoned following loss to Seminole
1836–1842	Fort Dallas	Miami, Florida	U.S. Army	Resuscitated in Third Seminole War and Civil War
1835–1836	Fort Defiance	Micanopy, Florida	Florida militia	Sometimes call "Micanopy"
1837–1841	Fort Denaud	Denaud, Florida	U.S. Army	Converted trading fort; also "Deyneaud"
1841–1842	Fort Doane	Six miles west of St. Rte. 29, Collier County, Florida	U.S. Army	Also as "Dunne," "Doune," mistakenly marked "Fort Keais" by historic markers
1840–1841	Fort Downing	East edge of Mallory Swamp, west of Florida 349	U.S. Army	Burned by Seminole
1835–1836	Fort Drane	Micanopy, Florida	U.S. Army	Artillery post; also "Drain"
1838–1841	Fort Dulaney	Punta Rassa, Florida	U.S. Army supply depot	Destroyed in hurricane; also given as "Dulany"
1838–1843	Fort Fanning	Fanning Springs, Florida	U.S. Army supply depot	First called "Fort Palmetto; burned, 1842; repaired
1838–1842	Fort Floyd	Okeechobee Co., Florida	U.S. Army	Zachary Taylor created; also given as "Fort Lloyd"
1836–1842	Fort Foster	Near Zephyrhills, Florida	U.S. Army supply depot	First as garrison; in 1837, as supply depot; also given "Camp Foster"
1836–1840	Fort Frank Brooke	Lower Steinhatchee River	U.S. Army	Established by Zachary Taylor; burned by Seminole

Dates	Fort	Operator	Location	Notes
1837–1838	Fort Fraser	U.S. Army	Just north of Bartow, Florida	Established by Zachary Taylor; also "Frazer," "Frazier"
1838–1843	Fort Gamble	Settler fort; to U.S. Army	East of Wacissa, Florida	In 1839, taken over by army; also called "Fort Welaunee"
1837–1842	Fort Gardiner	U.S. Army temporary HQ	Tioti, Florida	Established by Zachary Taylor; also as "Gardner"
1838–1841	Fort Gilmer	SC militia GA	Southwest of Fargo, North Dakota	Used by Zachary Taylor, 1838 as key to Okefenokee
1840–1841	Fort Griffin	U.S. Army Eugene, Florida	Three miles south of Eugene, Florida	Burned by Seminole
1840–1841	Fort Halbert	U.S. Army	Blue Springs, Florida	Zachary Taylor established or used; burned, 1841; also given as "Hulbert"
1839–1842	Fort Harney	Trading post	Calooshatchee	Used by U.S. Army
1839	Fort Harlee	Settler fort	Suwanee River, East Florida	Army stopover; also as "Harle"
1841	Fort Harrison	U.S. Army	Clearwater, Florida	Army hospital; some garrisons
1841–1842	Fort Harvie	U.S. Army	Fort Myers, Florida	Built to replace Fort Dulaney in less hurricane-prone location
1836–1842	Fort Heileman	U.S. Army supply depot	Middleburg, Florida	Occasional garrison; rebuilt stockade from First Seminole War
1836–1841?	Fort Izard	U.S. Army	Between Branford and Loraville, Florida	Also as "Camp Izard"
1822–1846	Fort Jesup	U.S. Army	Twenty-two miles west of Natchitoches, Louisiana	Established by Zachary Taylor; also given as "Cantonment Jesup"
1838?	Fort Jennings	U.S. Army	By Newton, Florida	Still being excavated
1838–1842	Fort Jupiter	U.S. Army, HQ at times	Jupiter, Florida	Prison and holding camp for captured Seminole and Blacks

(continued)

Table 9.1 (Continued)

Dates	Fort Names	Locations	Usage	Notes
1837–1842	Fort Keais	South of Ft. Denaud	U.S. Army	Line of Communications; also as "Keys" and "Keas"
1825–1835/ 1844	Fort King	Ocala, Florida	Settler fortification to U.S. Army HQ	Also as "King Cantonment"; Seminole burned, 1835; rebuilt
1837–1840	Fort Kingsbury	Enterprise, Florida	U.S. Army	Adjunct post of Fort Mellon
1837–1838	Fort Lane	Ten miles south of Fort Mellon	Militia to U.S. Army	Abandoned by Army in 1838
1838/1839–1842	Fort Lauderdale	Fort Lauderdale, Florida	Tennessee militia; U.S. Army	Promptly burned by Seminole; rebuilt by Army
1839–1842	Fort Macomb (#1)	Natural Bridge Spring, Florida	U.S. Army	Primary Fort Macomb; not to be confused with #2
1839	Fort Macomb (#2)	South of Rose, Florida	U.S. Army	Secondary Fort Macomb, #2
1841–1842	Fort Many	Near Wakulla Springs, Florida	U.S. Army	Line of communication
1672–1865	Fort Marion	St. Augustine, Florida	U.S. Army HQ	Castillo de San Marcos; U.S. acquired, 1821; included St. Francis Barracks
1835–1842	Fort McClure	Near Coleman, Florida	U.S. Army	Also called "Camp Wendell"
1838?	Fort McRae	Eastern shore of Lake Okechobee, Florida	South Carolina militia fort	Used as way station by U.S. Army; also "Camp M'Crae"
1837–1947	Fort McRee	East end, Perdido Key, Florida	U.S. Army	Confused with Fort McRae
1836–1842	Fort Mellon	Sanford, Florida	U.S. Army HQ of line	Originally "Camp Monroe"; line of communications and supply
1837–1842	Fort Micanopy	Micanopy, Florida	U.S. Army	Replaced destroyed Fort Defiance

Date	Fort	Operator	Location	Notes
1814–1841	Fort Mitchell	Georgia militia; U.S. Army	North of Sadler, Florida	Usurped by army for Seminole Wars
1838–1842	Fort Moniac	U.S. Army; Florida militia	Hogan's Ferry, Florida	Burned by Seminole, 1840, and rebuilt by army
1819–1846	Fort Morgan	U.S. Army	Mouth, Mobile Bay, Alabama	Marine Base, departure pt., troop transport to Florida
1839–1842	Fort Noel	U.S. Army	Near Covington, Florida	Line of communications
1838–1842	Fort Norton	Settler fortification to U.S. Army	Blunt's Ferry, Georgia	First as "Norton's Station"; also as "Fort Repose" and "Fort Rosa"
1840–1843	Fort Ocilla	U.S. Army	SW of Lamont, Florida	Also spelled "Auscilla"
1837–1841	Fort Peyton	U.S. Army	Seven miles south of St. Augustine, Florida	Line of communications; first as "Fort Moultrie"; abandoned and burned
1829–1947	Fort Pickens	U.S. Army	Pensacola, Florida	Early line of Pensacola defense
1838–1842	Fort Pierce	U.S. Army HQ	Fort Pierce, Florida	Primary supply depot; also given as "Pearce"
1828–1890	Fort Pike	U.S. Army	New Orleans, Louisiana	Staging ground; troop departure point
1838–1842	Fort Pleasant	U.S. Army	Twenty-two miles up from mouth of Econfina River	Established by Zachary Taylor; also as "Pleasants"
1838–1843	Fort Robert Gamble	Settler fortification	Twenty-eight miles from Tallahassee, Florida	Used by Army as way station; confused with Fort Gamble
1839–1842	Fort Russell	Settler fortification to U.S. Army	Island Grove (Marion Co.), Florida	Army withdrew, 1842
1841–1842	Fort Simmons	U.S. Army	North bank, Caloosa River opposite Ft. Denaud, Florida	Silted badly; abandoned for Fort Denaud
1835–1843	Fort Stansbury	Settler fortification to U.S. Army	Between St. Marks and Tallahassee, Florida	Army appropriated, 1842 as a HQ
1838–1842	Fort Taylor	U.S. Army	West bank of Lake Winder, Florida	Founded by Zachary Taylor; also as "Fort Zach"
1838–1842	Fort Thompson	U.S. Army	7½ miles above Fort Denaud	Supply depot

(continued)

Table 9.1 (Continued)

Dates	Fort Names	Locations	Usage	Notes
1836–1836	Fort Volusia	Volusia, Florida	South Carolina militia	Badly constructed and poorly defended; rebuilt as "Fort Barnwell"
1837–1842	Fort Wacassassa	West mouth of Wacassassa River	U.S. Army	Mostly stabling of horses; way station
1840–1842	Fort Watkahoota	Seven miles from Blue Peter Spring, Florida	U.S. Army	Mostly a way station; also as "Wacahoota"
1840–1842	Fort Wheelock	Near Orange Lake, Florida	Florida militia	Used as stopover and reference point by army
1836–1842	Fort White	Four miles west of Fort White, Florida	U.S. Army	Troop gathering facility
1820–1871	Fort Wood	Western shore of Chef Mentor Pass, Louisiana	U.S. Army	Staging ground; became Fort Macomb, in 1851
1839–1842	Oklawaha District Post	Eastpoint, Florida	Communications post	Associated with Fort King; also "Ocklawaha"

Table 9.1 shows the settler forts ringing the Seminole leading into the Second Seminole War. It is a partial list because many forts are still in the process of being identified and excavated.

Sources: Generally, see Hannings, 2006, Florida, 54–81; **Addison Blockhouse**, Griffin, 1952, 276–93; **Alabama**, Sprague, 1848/1964, 131, 144, 147; **Ann**, McGovern, 2007, 127; **Andrews**, Mahon, 1967, 261, 263; Sprague, 1848/1964, 434; **Apalachicola Arsenal**, Carter, 1934–1975, vol. 25, 40; Payette, 2010, "American Forts, Middle Florida"; **Armstrong**, Mahon, 1967, 196–98; Sprague, 1848/1964, 167, 170, 279, 455; for map, Lossing, 1876, 289; **Atkinson**, Payette, *op. cit.*; **Barbour**, Payette, *op. cit.*; **Barker**, Sprague, 1848/1964, 398, 434; **Fort Basinger**, Mahon, 1967, 219, 227, 229, 238, 241, map appended; Sprague, 1848/1964, 193; **Brooke**, extensive references in Carter, 1934–1975, vols. 23–26; map appended, Mahon, 1967; map, Shire, 2016, 150; McGovern, 2007, 124; Sprague, 1848/1964, 52; Wright, 1986, 241, 245; **Brooks**, map appended, Mahon, 1967; **Butler**, "Fort Butler," Historical Marker Project, 2018; **Call**, Carter, 1934–1975, vol. 25, 386; **Center**, McGovern, 2007, 127; Sprague, 1848/1964, 378–82, 387 passim; **Christian**, Sprague, 1848/1964, 190; **Christmas**, McGovern, 2007, 127; map appended, Mahon, 1967; **Clinch**, Carter, 1934–1975, vol. 25, 346; Norton, 1892, 128; Sprague, 1848/1964, 223, 256, 432, 433; map appended, Mahon, 1967; map, Lossing, 1876, 289; **Cooper**, Sprague, 1848/1964, 131, 278, 455; **Cross**, Van Blarcom, 2011, 240–41; McGovern, 2007, 127; map, Lossing, 1876, 289; Sprague, 1848/1064, 254, 435, 455; **Cummings**, map appended, Mahon, 1967, 285; Sprague, 1848/1964, 223–24, 258, 260, 271, 292, 260, 324; **Fort Dade**, Mahon, 1967, 197, 199, 200, 248, and map appended; Norton, 1892, 74; Sprague, 1848/1964, 172, 177, 187, 191, 278–79; map, Lossing, 1876, 289; **Dallas**, Mahon, 1967, 282–84, 304; Sprague, 1848/1964, 223–24, 280, 307, 334, 348, 383, 490; **Defiance**, Sprague, 1884/1964, 158–61; Carter, 1934–1975, vol. 25, 300, 336–37; **Denaud**, McGovern, 2007, 127; map appended, Mahon, 1967, 304; Sprague, 1848/1964, 303; **Doane**, Van Barclom, 2011, 241–45; Sprague, 1848/1964, 368, 371–72, 374; **Downing**, Sprague, 1848/1964, 434; **Drane**, Carter, 1934–1975, vol. 25, numerous mentions; map appended, Mahon, 1967, 107, 111, 173–77 passim, 180–84 passim; Sprague, 1848/1964, 110, 160–61; map, Lossing, 1876, 289; **Dulaney**, McGovern, 2007, 128; Sprague, 1848/1964, 332; **Fanning**, map appended, Mahon, 1967; Sprague, 1848/1964, 255–56, 261, 280, 423, 435, 446; **Floyd**, map appended, Mahon, 1967; Sprague, 1848/1964, 420; **Foster**, map appended, Mahon, 1967, 196–97, 202; Sprague, 1848/1964, 371–72, 374–75, as "Fort Lloyd," 198, 509; **Frank Brooke**, Briggs, 2010, 6–12; Sprague, 1848/1964, 434; **Frazier**, Sprague, 1848/1964, 204, 209, 211; Van Blarcom, 2011, 32; **Gamble**, Payette, *op. cit.* 2010; Sprague, 1848/1964, 308; **Gardiner**, map appended, Mahon, 1967, 219, 226, 229, 241; Sprague, 1848/1964, 203, 211, 257; **Gilmer**, Sprague, 1848/1964, 413, 415, 421–23 passim; **Griffin**, Payette, *op. cit.* 2010; Sprague, 1848/1964, 434; **Halbert**, Payette, *op. cit.* 2010; Sprague, 1848/1964, 434; **Harlee**, Carter, 1934–1975, vol. 25, 625; McGovern, 2007, 128; Sprague, 1848/1964, 434; **Harney**, Sprague, 1848/1964, 375; **Harrison**, Sprague, 1848/1964, 307; Mahon, 1967, 300; **Harvie**, McGovern, 2007, 128; Sprague, 1848/1964, 348, 375–76, 435; **Heileman**, Carter, 1934–1975, vol. 25, 609; map appended, Mahon, 1967, 281; Sprague, 1848/1964, 180, 541, 545; **Izard**, ASPMA, 1832–1861, map following vol. 7, 434; Mahon, 1967, 174, 149–51 passim, 166–67; Sprague, 1848/1967, 97, 127, 132, 139, 147, 273, 279, 473; **Jennings**, Payette, 2014; "American Forts, East Florida"; Van Blarcom, 2011, 109, 121; for map (as "Jennigs"), Lossing, 1876, 289; **Jesup**, Sprague, 1848/1964, 331, 529; **Jupiter**, Carter, 1934–1975, vol. 25, 489, 492–93; Sprague, 1848/1964, 190, 193, 196, 199, 333; **Keais**, McGovern, 2011, 128; Sprague, 1848/1964, 352, 355, 357, 360; **King**, Carter, 1934–1975, vol. 23, 873; multiple mentions, vol. 25; McGovern, 2011, 125; map, Shire, 2016, 150; map appended, Mahon, 1967; Sprague, 1848/1964, 68, 88–89, 109–10, 118–23 passim, 188–91 passim; Wright, 1986, 253–54, 256; map, Lossing, 1876, 289; **Kingsbury**, Sprague, 1848/1964, 224; **Lane**, McGovern, 2007, 128; map appended, Mahon, 1967; **Lauderdale**, Carter, 1934–1975, vol. 25, 635; McGovern, 2007, 125; map appended, Mahon, 1967, 233; Sprague, 1848/1964, 223–24, 348, 392–93, 436, 490; **Macomb (#1)**, Sprague, 1848/1964, 262, 398, 408; **Macomb (#2)**, Payette, *op. cit.* 2014; **Many**, Wakula County Chamber of Commerce, 2013; Sprague, 1848/1964, 434; **Marion**, Carter, 1934–1975, vol. 25, 130, 549; Norton, 1892, 157; Sprague, 1848/1964, 337–38, 341–42; **McClure**, Carter, 1934–1975, vol. 25, 211, 276, 279; map, Lossing, 1876, 289; **McRae**, Carter, 1934–1975, vol. 25, 494; Griffin, 1952, 289–90; **McRee**, McGovern, 2007, 125; Payette, 2016; "American Forts, Pensacola Bay"; **Mellon**, Carter, 1934–1975, vol. 25, 386, 612; map appended, Mahon, 1967; Sprague, 1848/1964, 178, 187–88, 190–91, 222–28 passim, 275–76, 307–8, 316, 325, 391, 435, 455, 465–66; **Micanopy**, Sprague, 1848/1964, 160–61; **Mitchell**, Monaco, 2000, 1–25; map appended, Mahon, 1967; Sprague, 1848/1964, 179, 434; **Moniac**, Sprague, 1848/1964, 406–10, 413–14, 421, 487; **Morgan**, Carter, 1934–1975, vol. 25, no. 30, 188; Sprague, 1848/1964, 179; **Noel**, Sprague, 1848/1964, 434; **Norton**, Payette, 2010, "American Forts, Southern Georgia"; Sprague, 1848/1964, 420, for 1838, 536, as "Fort Rosa," 409–10; **Ocilla**, Payette, *op. cit.* 2010; "Middle Florida"; Sprague, 1848/1964, 262, 434, 486; **Peyton**, Mahon, 1967, 214, 224; Sprague, 1848/1964, 186–87, 217–19; **Pickens**, Carter, 1934–1975, vol. 25, no. 30, 188; McGovern, 2007, 125; Sprague, 1848/1964, 179, 480, 484; **Pierce**, Carter, 1934–1975, vol. 25, 493; map appended, Mahon, 1967; map, Shire, 2016, 150; Sprague, 1848/1964, 190, 192, 198, 220, 223–24, 260–62, 277, 307, 325; **Pike**, Carter, 1934–1975, vol. 25, no. 30, 188, no. 77, 210; Sprague, 1848/1964, 407, 434, 486; **Pleasant**, Sprague, 1848/1964, 262, 307, 394, 406, 436; **Robert Gamble**, map, Shire, 2016, 150; Sprague, 1848/1964, 348, 351, 360, 367–68, 375–76, 378; Sprague, 1848/1964, 280, 486, 506, 539; **Taylor**, Winn, 452; **Simmons**, Norton, 1892, 266; Sprague, 1848/1964, 348, 351, 360, 367–68, 375–76, 378; **Stansbury**, Sprague, 1848/1964, 307–8, 391, 2003, 30–31; map appended, Mahon, 1967; Norton, 1892, 153, 154; Sprague, 1848/1964, 192, 391; **Thompson**, Carter, 1934–1975, vol. 25, 555; Sprague, 1848/1964, 377; **Volusia**, Payette, *op. cit.* 2014; "Central Florida"; Sprague, 1848/1964, 249–50, 307, 309, 435, 446, 457, 470–71, 484, 545; **Wheelock**, Carter, 1934–1975, vol. 25, 609; **Watkahoota**, map appended, Mahon, 1967; Sprague, 1848/1964, 398, 406, 418; **Wood**, Carter, 1934–1975, vol. 25, no. 30, 188; Sprague, **White**, map, Shire, 2016, 150; map appended, Mahon, 1967; Sprague, 1848/1964, 252, 392. 1848/1964, 484; **Oklawaha District**, Sprague, 1848/1964, 484;

The propaganda phase of war drive complete, the forced treaty phase began with the Treaty with the Florida Tribes of Indians (1823), usually called the Treaty of Moultrie Creek, and the Treaty with the Seminole (1832), typically called the Treaty of Payne's Landing. Article 2 of the Treaty of Moultrie Creek sought to confine the Seminole to one reservation of about 4,000,000 acres concentrated in central Florida, on swampy land that the settlers did not immediately want. Article 9 of the treaty agreed that the reservation's northern border could be stretched.

In return, in Article 1, the Seminole gave up all claim to the rest of Florida and any communication with any power other than the United States, while Article 4 reserved U.S. rights of way through the reservation. Article 7 called upon the Seminole to capture and return to Gad Humphreys any escaped slaves, for a small finder's fee. The usual gaggle of cherry-picked chiefs and U.S. commissioners signed Florida away from all the Seminole, with a sweetheart "Additional Article" appended after the signing. It granted U.S.-favored Apalachicola signatories their own reservations of about four or eight square miles on the Panhandle, outside of the main reservation.[138] By 1827, settlers could pass through the reservation at will, but the Seminole could not leave the reservation without penalty.

Aggrieved by the Treaty of Moultrie Creek, ordinary Seminole disregarded it and its boundaries, walking about as they liked, prompting the brutal Florida law of January 29, 1827, "For the Prevention of Indians Roaming at Large throughout the State." Roamers were condemned to "thirty-nine stripes" on the "bare back," although U.S. officials were entirely aware that such actions simply provoked hostilities (most probably, the intent).[139] Concerned about this law, U.S. secretary of war James Barbour advised governor of Florida William P. DuVal not to enforce it, as the Seminole would "hardly submit" to its ordered "chastisement ... without seeking to be revenged," resulting in the "destruction of many lives." Instead of settler savagery, Barbour recommended settler "forbearance and kindness" toward the "miserable and perishing" Seminole.[140]

Barbour was dismissed as soft on savages. Two years earlier, he had pushed for incorporating all Indians as citizens of the United States in preference to murdering them all. Henry Clay kicked aside Barbour's "impracticable" plan, declaring it "impossible to civilize" the Indians, for "full blooded" Indians never "took to civilization." It was simply "not in their nature," explaining why they were "destined to extinction." As it turned out, they were just not "a race, worth preserving," being "essentially inferior to the Anglo-Saxon race," which was happily "taking their place" in North America. Because Indians were not an "improvable breed," their "disappearance from the human family" would constitute "no great loss to the world." Besides, they "were rapidly disappearing," anyhow, and in "fifty years," there would probably not "be any left."[141] Clay had just perfectly recited the catechism of Manifest Destiny, whose effect was to disguise the agency of the settlers in the Indian vanishing act.

The sneaking suspicion that the Seminole continued to harbor escaped slaves raised settler dander so much that by 1826, Secretary of War Barbour was receiving ominous warnings about the "unsettled State of the Indians" and the "outrages" that they had "recently committed" against Florida settlerdom, which had no militias in the field, despite a surfeit of militia officers.[142] In 1828, as enthusiasm for Removal schemes heated up nationally, Florida governor DuVal nudged Barbour about the "Semminole." He assured Barbour that they could be "induced to emigrate" west of the Mississippi River, arguing for the scheme on the three-hanky plea that, otherwise, they would "in a few years become extinct," the humanitarian contention of the day no doubt intended to move Barbour.[143]

Nine months later, in October 1828, Gad Humphries excitedly reported to the War Department that annuity Seminole chiefs, some of whom had visited with officials in Washington, D.C. in 1826, were planning to trek west, to see their proposed Removal territory.[144] By March 1829, Andrew Jackson was in the presidential way, and Removal took off like a big bird. Awareness that he had not actually conquered the Seminole in the First Seminole War was the sort of thing to stick in Jackson's craw, so upon assuming office as president, he set about fixing his little Seminole problem. Floridians were delighted. DuVal freely admitted to Jackson's first secretary of war John Eaton that it had "long been a favorate [object] of the people of Florida to [have] the Indians removed," which hope DuVal had communicated to Barbour "several" times, to dead silence.[145]

DuVal's and Humphries's enthusiasm aside, Removal was clearly more thrust upon than invited by the Seminole chiefs. In January 1832, Florida's territorial delegate to the U.S. House of Representatives, Joseph M. White, attempted the sympathy approach to Removal, assuring Eaton that "no country can afford a paralel of the fraud, oppression, and inhumanity" to which the Seminole had been subjected. They had been "reduced to the utmost extremities" with some having starved to death, making White sure that they would gladly go west.[146] Again, crocodile tears covered the pre-softening plan behind the deliberate starvation of the Seminole.

By May 1832, the Payne's Landing Treaty was imposed on the Seminole, in all confidence that it would take, given their starving condition. Its preamble (after praising Jackson's "solicitude" for Seminole well-being) announced that four chiefs would travel west to inspect their Removal home—on Osage land already granted to the Muskogee (without consulting the Osage). Article 1 relinquished all of Florida to the settlers for $15,400, just nine years after all but 4,000,000 of their acreage was seized. Article 5 confiscated all of the Seminole's cattle for the settlers, in exchange either for replacement cattle or sums to be decided once out west, although Article 6 demanded that payment be skimmed off the top of the sums to settle all settler claims of losses due thefts and destruction of property. Article 7 required the Seminole to be leaving by 1833, with all gone west by May 1836. The usual gaggle of co-opted chiefs signed, looking to share the $15,400 among themselves, as per Article 2.[147]

The treaty was repudiated immediately by the Seminole, who flatly refused deportation. Escaped slaves continued running to Florida. In January 1832, settlers around Micanopy, Florida, complained loudly to President Jackson about the 1,100 "Slaves" (Maroons) and 1,600 "Warriors" of the Seminole freely crossing north, out of the 1823 reservation, committing aggressions against them and fomenting "insurrection" among the settlers' slaves. They demanded the immediate assignment of U.S. troops to Fort Brooke or Fort King to defend them.[148] Major General

Alexander Macomb, commander of the U.S. Army, was ordered to investigate the situation at once, "on account of the Indians and Negroes amongst" the settlers.[149] By March, indignant over "depredations" and the Maroons sheltered by the Seminole, settlers demanded that Congress remove the Seminole, forthwith.[150]

Given its military might, the U.S. government was not expecting big problems when it sent General Wiley (Willie) Thompson to Fort King to implement Seminole Removal in October 1834. From the moment of his arrival, however, the chiefs gave Thompson a hard time, refusing to meet till tardy delegates arrived (lateness being a sign of resistance) and interrupting Thompson when he tried to speak (a grave signal of contempt). Tone deaf, Thompson portrayed the Seminole as "awestruck" when he threatened their utter destruction, should they prove recalcitrant. (Listening in grim silence is an Indigenous sign of displeasure.) Old hip-pocket chiefs of the United States, representing perhaps one-third of the Seminole, declared their intent to remove, but their lives were threatened by the other two-thirds. Importantly, the Seminole refused not only on their own account but also on account of the Maroons, for the encroaching settlers "manifest[ed] a restless desire to obtain" them as slaves, immediately as the Seminole left.[151]

Originally, the solution that Humphreys had proposed in 1827 to the government's perceived Maroon problem was to induce the Seminole to "sell their Slaves at a reasonable and fair price" to slave speculators (like, say, Humphreys).[152] In 1835, the federal government decided to give this proposal a try, for it saw detaching the Indian and Black Seminole from each other as vital. Thompson was to inveigle the Seminole into selling their "slaves," for as it turned out upon inquiry, no law existed against Indians selling slaves.[153] The answer Thompson received from the Seminole was, however, a resounding, "No."

Then, things turned really nasty on January 22, 1835, when brevet brigadier general Duncan L. Clinch—the same Clinch who had destroyed the "Negro Fort"—was sent to Fort King to oversee Seminole Removal. He informed Macomb that the operation would require heavy artillery at Forts King (Ocala, Florida) and Brooke (Tampa Bay), for a "large majority of this nation have not the most distant idea of going west."[154] General Wiley Thompson was ordered on January 1, 1835, to round up the Seminole for involuntary transport west and the Maroons for sale into slavery.[155] Although in April, a happy-faced letter to Washington, D.C. announced that Clinch and Thompson had acquired agreement to leave from "at least half" of the chiefs (meaning half of the U.S.-loyal chiefs), even they insisted on leaving with their Black "slaves."[156] The remaining Seminole and Maroons had quite other ideas.

The settlers simply could not conceive of self-directed Indians. If there were no Spanish, French, or British directing them, then it must have been the Maroons. Consequently, in his report of April 27, 1835, Thompson advised Secretary of War Lewis Cass that Humphreys's plan would not bear fruit, for the "slaves" had "great influence" with the Seminole. They lived in their own towns, "remote" from their supposed "owners," keeping their own farm cattle, horses, and hogs. Moreover, they "dread[ed] the idea of being transferred from their present state of ease and comparative liberty to bondage and hard labor under overseers, on sugar and cotton plantations." Worse, a Seminole "would almost as soon sell his child" as turn over the Blacks, with the "malcontent" Seminole agreeing among themselves that this whole scheme was a ruse of Thompson's to acquire slaves for himself. This suspicion was quickly substantiated for the Seminole when a group of settlers came in looking to buy up the slaves, even as Thompson was broaching the plan to the Seminole.[157] In view of these propositions, the Seminole and Maroons knew that they had to act fast to prevent separation.

Western history books still call what followed the "Dade massacre." Cocky and feckless, Major Francis Langhorne Dade was oblivious of his surroundings when, on December 23, 1835, he moseyed his 100 men out of Fort Brooke on his way north to Fort King, about 100 miles distant. Meantime at Fort King on December 28, *Osceola* and his party were just outside of the fort, busily killing Wiley Thompson. Incredibly, Thompson had strolled out of the fort and lit up a cigar. Perhaps he thought his companion Lieutenant Constantine Smith would protect him, but both were thoroughly shot, with Thompson hit by twenty-four bullets.[158] (It was a convention of Indian communalism for all to shoot simultaneously, so that no one person could disruptively claim credit.) According to *Otee Emathla* ("Jumper"), *Osceola* was to join the party attacking Dade right after he had taken care of *"his friend"* Thompson, but *Osceola* did not arrive in time to join in the Dade attack.[159]

Marching on obliviously, Dade presented an easy target for a second war party led by *Micanopy*, *Otee Emathla*, and *Halpuda Mikko* (called "Chief Alligator," for his clan). Like old Roman roads, which led attackers in as effortlessly as Roman soldiers out, the military road to Fort King allowed this war party of 180 to track Dade's every move and then wait for him to pass through Wahoo Swamp, the planned point of attack. As Dade came within twenty yards of them, the Seminole jumped into the open and fired, taking down "more than half of the white men" in their first volley, while Dade's cannon was panic-aimed too high, its balls whizzing harmlessly over the Seminole's heads. A small group of soldiers scurried behind logs, fighting bravely till their ammunition ran out. Ninety-seven of Dade's men were killed in battle, and "after a conversation in English," the Maroons killed the three survivors of the firefight. The Seminole lost three men with five wounded. The main war party left, as the Maroons lingered on the field, "looking at the dead men."[160] With tidings of this event, President Jackson decided that the Second Seminole War was on.[161]

Osceola soon emerged as the primary war chief. According to *Halpatta Tustenuggee*, *Osceola* had been considering options and laying plans for the resistance since the winter of 1834, as Florida Removal heated up.[162] U.S. military estimates put the entire Florida Seminole population, including the Maroons, at 3,000, of whom, 1,400 were calculated to be men of fighting age.[163] By April 30, 1836, General Winfield Scott downscaled that number, reporting that "the whole force of the enemy, including the negroes" could not "exceed 1200 fighting men." Not more than 500 of them coalesced for any one action, with most war parties not exceeding 130 men. At the same time, "parties from ten to thirty" were encountered "everywhere."[164] (See Table 9.2.) Clearly, *Osceola* was

Table 9.2 Populations of Spanish Florida and Florida Territory (1761–1842)

Years	Group		
	Seminole	Black	Settlers
1761	3,080[a]		
1774	1,500[b]		
1784		574	1,418
1814		1,779	1,302
1821	3,000–5,000[c]		5,000
1830		16,345	18,385
1834	4,883[d]		
1840		26,534	27,913
1841	3,765		
1847	370[e]		

[a] Based on head count of 770 "hunters" (men) present in each town, multiplied by four, per the standing settler formula.

[b] Only one Yuchi town.

[c] Included sixty black Seminole

[d] Seminole self-enumeration.

[e] Reflects post-Removal total.

Table 9.2 shows the change in Seminole, black, and settler populations in Florida from the Spanish through the U.S. periods to statehood.

Sources: For 1761, Candler, 1904–1986, vol. 8, Apalachicola as "Pallachocolas," 522; Oconee, 522; Hitchiti as "Hitchetaws," Sawokli as "Chewallees," and Yuchi as "Euchees," 522–24; for 1774, Bartram, 1791/1928, 312–13; for 1784, Landers, 1999, 82; for 1814, Landers, 1999, 82; for 1822, *ASPIA*, 1832, vol. 2, 411–12; for 1834, *ASPIA*, 1832, vol. 2, 439; for 1841, Swanton, 1922, 443; for 1847, Swanton, 1922, 443; for 1830, USBC, 1918, 45.

conducting a guerilla campaign, for he knew his numbers could not possibly match what the U.S. Army would throw against him. By April, using his intimate knowledge of the landscape, he had strategically deployed small groups, carefully unconcentrated and mobile. Able, cooperating leaders could act independently. This was exactly the kind of war that the U.S. Army did not know how to fight.

Before he died sick and imprisoned on January 30, 1838, *Oscoela* managed to send four U.S. commanders home, the first three, in disgrace:

1. U.S. general Edmund Pendleton Gaines, who lasted all of twenty days in the field in 1836
2. U.S. general Winfield Scott, whose March to April 1836, campaign was also a stunning failure
3. Florida militia brigadier general and governor Richard Keith Call, whose campaign from July to December 1836, embarrassed everyone
4. U.S. general Thomas Jesup, who lasted from January 1837 to April 1838

Zachary Taylor was called in, after Jesup likewise flopped.

General Scott had been assigned to lead the army in Florida, but upon hearing of Dade's defeat and without notifying Scott, Gaines wrote Clinch that by February 8, 1836, he would arrive at Fort Brooke with 700 men of the 1,100 men he was bringing from New Orleans.[165] (Gaines later claimed, unbelievably, that he had no inkling that Scott was his superior officer.[166]) After reaching Fort Brooke but not Clinch (who was actually at Fort Drane), Gaines continued on to Fort King, burning abandoned Seminole towns along the way. Passing the Dade battleground and finding the broken bodies of the 100 men, most scalped but otherwise unmutilated, Gaines ordered them buried.[167] Improvidently, he had dragged out his 700 men with only ten days' worth of supplies, because he expected to meet a supply shipment at Fort King. Once there, however, he found nothing much but rations sufficient for the few men stationed at Fort King.[168]

Humiliated, Gaines was returning to Fort Brooke when he was waylaid by a Seminole war party as he forded the Withlacoochee River. Gaines attempted to hold off the attack, while sending for Clinch to come rescue him.[169] Gaines reported that 1,400 to 1,500 Seminole and Maroons had attacked, although Lieutenant Colonel Ethan Allen Hitchcock testified that their number was about 1,300 and Captain George A. McCall claimed that only 800 attacked.[170] In light of *Osceola*'s game plan, even the 800 seems like a face-saving inflation of the real numbers.

Pinned down at his makeshift breastwork, praying for Clinch, Gaines was instead confronted with a siege continuing from March 1 to March 5, 1836. Already quite hungry due to poor planning, Gaines's men desperately ate horses that had been shot during the Withlacoochee skirmish.[171] On the fifth, John Caesar, a Maroon claiming to come from *Osceola*, called a parley for noon, the next day.[172] At the council under civil chief *Micanopy*, Gaines and his men were informed that, if they withdrew from the Withlacoochee area, then the attack would cease.[173] Later, Seminole and Maroons in the know claimed that Caesar had called the talks without authorization from the primary war chiefs, so probably the civil chief *Micanopy* had sent Caesar.[174]

Armed with irate letters from Scott regarding Gaines's sortie, Clinch arrived during the talks with about 600 heavily armed men, 150 of them mounted. He instantly attacked the Seminole delegation, now variously estimated at 800, 600, or 400, scattering them precipitously.[175] (Even 400 was unlikely.) Perhaps unsurprisingly, Gaines was forced to turn his command over to Clinch on March 9, 1836, as a furious president Jackson ordered an inquiry into Gaines's conduct, throughout.[176] After lengthy proceedings, the court found that Gaines's campaign had failed "for want of the means of subsistence" to see it through.[177]

Even as the Gaines disaster was unfolding, General Winfield Scott took to the field, flying high on self-importance. Following the Dade Massacre, Georgia had called up 3,000 militia troops, to which were added around 800 Alabama militia, 600 South Carolina militia, and 190 U.S. Army soldiers.[178] Gearing up in

January 1836, Scott confided to Colonel William Lindsay that he did not believe that many troops were required to undo the Seminole, greatly reduced by Jackson's Seminole war.[179]

Heading out, Scott did little more than repeat Gaines's errors, however. Taking minimal supplies, Scott also bogged down at the Withlacoochee River from February to March, as a "severe storm" (perhaps a hurricane) hit the area with rains so intense that "the whole country was under water."[180] Scott's troops aimlessly slogged about, firing signal cannon, which mainly apprised the Seminole of their location, while *Osceola*'s war parties fired on them, inducing them to use up their ammunition in reply, to no avail.[181] Scott finally reached out for rescue to Clinch at Fort Drane, his plea arriving almost simultaneously with Gaines's. About to pursue probable Seminole decoys, Scott received a note from Gaines that he was holding a peace council, so Scott belayed all his own actions.[182] Clinch was left in the dark. Coordination did not seem to be the army's long suit.

With two bumbling generals on his hands, Clinch triaged, bringing in and feeding Gaines's starving men. This inclined Scott to continue in the field, despite his own lack of provisions, although thanks to Gaines, all provisions at Fort King had been consumed, with those at Fort Drane "reduced to the last extremity." Scott then realized that against *Osceola*, "whose plan was concealment and retreat," he possessed insufficient supplies to sustain his expedition. Dispatching a detail to fetch "friendly Creek warriors" to come act as his human "bloodhounds" in tracking down the Seminole, Scott backtracked along the Withlacoochee. On March 26, for opaque reasons, he split his forces—he with his right wing, heading vaguely for Tampa, burning abandoned towns along the way, and his left wing shadowing him, to no particular purpose. On March 30, Scott was lured by a "small party of Indians" into the labyrinthian swamps, where they stranded Scott, who was lost yet pretending to have driven the Seminole into the arms of his left wing. (That did not happen.[183])

Now, his supplies almost gone, Scott left a detachment of Georgia militia as a rearguard with twelve-to-fifteen days' worth of supplies in a half-baked blockhouse on the Withlacoochee River, while he pushed on toward Tampa.[184] An attempt to supply this blockhouse was dashed, when Captain Gustavus S. Drane was assured that the militia "could take care of themselves" until Scott's return.[185] This left the Georgians at the blockhouse not only starving but also sitting ducks. As Clinch dryly observed, as "good soldiers," the Seminole and Maroons attacked only when they enjoyed a "decided advantage," and the enfeebled detachment met this stipulation.[186] Essentially deserted by Scott, who gave confused, tardy, and silly orders, the blockhouse's major was killed going for help, after a six-week siege.[187]

Meantime in Tampa, Scott could not round up any supplies, for common rumor had it that Gaines had called off the war, having "beat the enemy."[188] Cooling his heels from April 6 to April 14, 1836, finding no "friendly Creeks" (who would just have deliberately led him astray, anyhow), Scott at last managed to scrounge up a few supplies.[189] Reentering the wetlands, scoutless, Scott broke his forces into multiple small units to fight guerrilla with guerrilla. Far more adept at the tactic than Scott, the Seminole and Maroons led his forces on a series of wild goose chases. In the end, testified James Gadsden, "we found ourselves in the same position from whence we started—the enemy unsubdued, because he could not be found."[190]

Having crashed and burned even more spectacularly than Gaines, Scott faced his own Court of Inquiry, charged with needless delay and lack of accomplishment, despite consuming valuable supplies.[191] In the end, the Court of Inquiry put Scott's failure down to lack of time (due to militias' short enlistments), lateness of the season, weather conditions, poor supply lines, and Scott's ignorance of the landscape against the skill of the "enemy" operating within it.[192] Notwithstanding the court's soft-peddling of his incompetence, Scott was relieved of duty, and on June 28, 1836, by order of President Jackson, General Thomas S. Jesup assumed command.[193]

In the absence of named commanders while the inquiries were on, U.S. Army officers conducted their own independent actions. On June 10, 1836, Major Julius F. Heileman pursued 150–200 Seminole for two miles near Micanopy, attacking in a twenty-minute firefight in which he lost one man and then died, himself, on June 27. On August 12, at 2:00 A.M., Major Benjamin F. Pierce chased 300 Seminole under *Osceola*, he claimed, about three-quarters of a mile, killing 10, while losing 1 man and suffering 16 wounded for his pains. So many Seminole were together around Fort Drane, where these attacks occurred, because large Seminole farms lay there. The 500 people being attacked were therefore women, tending their crops and bringing in their sugarcane and corn.[194]

Florida governor and militia "general" Richard Call next rushed into the leadership void. The first thing Call did was run face-first into Jesup, who had actually been assigned to the duty. Puzzled by the duplication, Jesup joined Call on October 25, 1836, while nonplussed letters flew back and forth from Washington, D.C.[195] Meantime, like Gaines and Scott, the unprepared Call managed little other than to pressure the army's inadequate supplies, for his post on the Withlacoochee with its 2,000 men proved unable to locate any Seminole to attack. On November 4, Acting Secretary of War Benjamin Butler ordered Jesup to take over from Call forthwith and mount "vigorous" attacks on Seminole "strongholds" along the Withlacoochee River.[196]

The Keystone Generals now on the way out and his confidence still exuding that new command smell, Jesup predicted on November 6, 1836, that should the "Indian fight," then the war would "soon be ended" by his "500 regulars" at Tampa Bay, increased by the arrival of 120 Alabama militia, soon joined by 180 additional men, along with 400 mounted men. By luck on December 3, Jesup stumbled across a Maroon town, which his men destroyed, capturing forty-one for enslavement. Later, on January 10, 1837, Jesup "surprised" a Black Seminole town, taking sixteen prisoners, no doubt as slaves. Having found a promising area, Jesup kept at it, two days later attacking another Black Seminole town, this time, taking thirty-six, while receiving the exciting intelligence that *Osceola* was at the Withlacoochee, "sick" and able to collect only "100 warriors." Jesup's mood soon sank, however, when another sweep of the Withlacoochee turned up no *Osceola* and only three Seminole, although his men did take another fifty-two Maroons. Pumping the prisoners for information, he learned that *Osceola* was constantly on the move, "flying from one hiding place to another" in the Maroon camps, accompanied by only three Seminole.[197]

Pursuit with firefights continued through February 1837, with additional prisoners, primarily Black Seminole and Maroon, reported seized.[198] The unspoken purpose behind the Seminole Wars snaps into focus with Jesup's "Registry of Prisoners Captured," drawn up in July 1837. It contained the most detailed, precise data he submitted during his entire tenure in Florida. Although the Removal of the Seminole is still listed as the cause of the war, the prisoners taken from Jesup's arrival in 1836 to July 1837 were all Black and categorized as stolen property to be returned to claimants. Blacks went to the firstcomers, for settler claims to escaped slaves were not verified with the same zeal as were the age, sex, and identity of the captured Blacks. As many actions were mounted to retake escaped slaves as to round up the Seminole, with orders directly from Secretary of War Joel Poinsett to take "Great care" of the Blacks, possibly confining them in Charleston, South Carolina, till the war's end.[199]

Their councils divided as the war intensified, *Otee Emathla* and *Halpatta Tustenuggee* agreed to Jesup's offer on February 7, 1837, to meet in a council on February 18.[200] Notwithstanding, Jesup continued his attacks, unabated, with one "handsome affair" on February 8 at Lake Monroe, destroying eight towns and driving off a "superior force," probably meaning the towns' evacuees, although Jesup assumed that they were martial reinforcements. Realizing that the February 8 action would probably scuttle his February 18 conference, Jesup shrugged, incongruously sighing that at least he had "afforded them the opportunity to come in."[201] Despite Jesup's bad faith, by February 25, *Halpatta Tustenuggee*, *Yaholoochee* ("Cloud"), and *Holah Touchee* showed up, speaking for *Micanopy*.[202] By March 6, Jesup had negotiated their terms of surrender and agreement to remove to Indian Territory.[203] *Micanopy* had always been the most "timid" of the Seminole chiefs.[204]

This initial burst of activity was the best that Jesup had to offer during his entire tenure. By June 5, 1837, he was completely frustrated by his inability to make any headway in the ordered roundups, reporting sardonically to adjutant general Roger Jones that he had the "honor to report that this campaign" had "entirely failed," as far as Seminole Removal was concerned, for the negotiating chiefs proved unable to persuade anyone to leave. Jesup recommended, therefore, that the Seminole be left alone in the swamps and he, relieved of Florida duty, forthwith, a request he reiterated on July 25, eliciting a nova of words from President Martin Van Buren. Their essential import was Buck Up.[205] Jesup bucked down, however, not moving again.

Noticing the quiet along the settler front, *Osceola* urged his people to hide and watch, till they saw what the settlers planned to do next. Tired of the struggle, on July 7, Seminole around St. Augustine, including people from *Osceola*'s camp, assembled for deportation.[206] On August 3, *Tuckabatchee Hajo* ("John Hicks") informed the army at Fort King that yet more planned to come in and that *Osceola* was near Fort Mellon. Jesup doubted their good faith, yet people came, although not as many as anticipated.[207]

Before the army would allow Jesup out of Florida, he had to provide it with some claim to fame, for the war was coming under scrutiny for its duration and cost. Thus, in early May, 1837, when the main war chiefs, including *Osceola*, were to assemble at Fort Mellon to call a truce, Jesup misrepresented their purpose as *Osceola*'s surrender, announcing it as such to Secretary of War Poinsett on May 8.[208] Word that Jesup had *Osceola* at Fort Mellon spread around the Washington military establishment like wildfire, with U.S. adjutant general Jones on May 31 excitedly expecting *Osceola* to be among those sent to Tampa for Removal.[209] *Osceola* did not attend the parley, however, so no *Osceola* later appeared in Tampa, putting Jesup under enormous pressure to make good on his premature boast.

Jesup did not take well to public humiliation, especially any engineered by an Indian, and *Osceola* had been denting his reputation for the last year. Into the fall, frustrated and irate, Jesup strategized to grab *Osceola* by fair means or foul, tending to the foul. Acting for Jesup on October 20, 1837, Florida militia "general" Joseph Hernandez lured *Osceola* to Fort Peyton on the pretext of talks that *Osceola* had requested under a *"white plume"* (white flag).[210] Arriving for the talks, accompanied by four Maroons and seventy-seven Seminole (including six women), on Jesup's direct order, they were "closed in on" as prisoners, their goods looted.[211] Settler tradition had it that when *Osceola* saw the double-cross that was afoot, he rose to his full height, a large tear coursing down his cheek, as he demanded, "Is this the white men's faith?"[212]

Receiving word of Hernandez's coup, Jesup dispatched "a party of mounted men" to commandeer *Osceola* and his party, accompanying them to St. Augustine. Although Jesup's betrayal of trust was hotly condemned by some as "dishonorable," war hawks took indignant exception to the characterization, falsely claiming that *Osceola* had signed the Payne's Landing Removal Treaty, started the war, and killed "white" men. Thus, *Osceola*'s white plume was but a ploy to cover his "intended treachery," they glowered, slit-eyed.[213] *Osceola* was gravely ill at the time he was taken and died in prison at Fort Moultrie, South Carolina, on January 30, 1838, not yet thirty-four years old.[214]

Osceola's "capture" notwithstanding, public opinion turned against the expensive, endless war. To recover their reputations, both Jesup and the U.S. Army needed a "win," preferably one of the spectacular variety as led by a celebrated Indian-killer—say, the hero of Bad Axe. In pursuit of this goal, the War Department decided to throw everything it had at the Seminole, amassing 6,000 men, 3,750 of whom were to be in the field, reassigning regulars out west to Florida.[215] Zachary Taylor's First Infantry was, therefore, moved to Florida via General Order No. 50 issued on July 31, 1837; colonels, including Taylor, were to be in Tampa between October 10 and 15.[216] With people in the know doubtful of Order No. 50's impact, Poinsett was determined to pull the war to a speedy, dazzling close. (His reputation was at stake, too.) Taylor was placed under Jesup, with the intent to relieve Jesup to move Taylor into the command, should he measure up.

During his tenure, Jesup had killed 30 Seminole and deported 500, while returning 103 people to slavery (5 of whom promptly died).[217] From the time Jesup arrived, these represented 8 percent of the Seminole and about 17 percent of the Maroons (and/or Black Seminole—the records did not distinguish between them). Consequently, the Seminole and Maroons were already worn down by ceaseless attack, their homes and crops burned for the last three years running. Essentially, Taylor was to mount a mop-up operation.

With new talks set along the Kissimmee River, hope ran high that the Seminole, at least, would finally throw in the towel. On December 20, 1837, Taylor met with primary chiefs, including *Otee Emathla*, fifteen Young Men, Maroons, and their families, amounting all told to sixty-three people, at nearby Fort Gardiner as guided by "friendly" Cherokee, themselves playing a precarious double game, assuring the holdouts that, if they just stood pat, then they could remain in Florida. Encouraged, *Halpuda Mikko* was coalescing with the Mikasuki Seminole, embittered by Jackson's wanton attack on them in the First Seminole War. The resistance was further enlarged by a recent, large-scale escape of Seminole prisoners from St. Augustine (perhaps with Cherokee assistance), their arrival among the Mikasuki breathing new life into the resistance.[218]

Heading into talks on December 19, Taylor received sudden word from Jesup that he had fired the Cherokee for their "interference." In high dudgeon, Jesup ordered Taylor to attack the Seminole, forthwith, especially the Mikasuki and the holdouts under *Apiaka* (*Abiaka*, "Sam Jones"), the holy man who had worked closely with *Osceola*, from the beginning of the resistance.[219] Mustering 1,032 men, including 180 Missouri militia, and planning to force the Seminole to fight a European-style war, Taylor set off on December 20, 1837, down the Kissimmee River traveling southeast toward Lake Istokpoga, setting up crude blockhouses as he went. First, he intended to sweep up "hostiles" whom he believed lay in that direction; second, he thought that Jesup might be driving the Mikasuki into his arms at Lake Okeechobee; and finally, he figured that his 1,032 men would "overawe" the Seminole into giving up on the spot. The "hostiles" Taylor took prisoner along the way were actually those like *Otee Emathla*, who had already surrendered, so Taylor was artificially inflating his roundup numbers by counting them as fresh captures. He failed to encounter *Halpuda Mikko* and his 380 men, however.[220]

Sending a message to *Halpuda Mikko*, Taylor demanded a meeting, but an "old Indian," not *Halpuda Mikko*, arrived instead, bearing what Taylor characterized as a "very equivocal" response. *Halpuda Mikko* assured Taylor that the Mikasuki were exactly where they had been all along and were "determined to fight" Taylor, the implication being: if he could find them. Such impudence did not improve Taylor's mood, so he set about "indulging" the Mikasuki, "as soon as practicable." Leaving his baggage and his sick at a hasty base camp, he set out but without the Lenape and Shawnee who had been his "guides," because they flatly refused to budge. Their legs and moccasins had been torn up by the saw grass along the trail, they said, but like the Cherokee before them, they appeared as intent on sabotaging as on aiding the expedition.[221]

Irritated at having no scouts and "finding no enemy to oppose" him, Taylor pressed the elderly messenger into guiding him to the Mikasuki, much to the reluctance of the old man. He led Taylor to mostly evacuated camps, finding old folks, a few youths, women, and children who professed to have been coming in. The number of cattle Taylor saw slaughtered roundabout suggested another story, so he supposed that a very large group was nearby. Perhaps realizing that the elder was not actually leading him to the Mikasuki, Taylor "dismissed" him in favor of "four warriors" whom he "captured." In fact, the four lads had simply been seized from the camps of folks already on their way in. Taylor did not reveal by what method he encouraged the youths to lead him to *Halpuda Mikko* and *Apiaka.*[222]

The boys were somehow worse guides than the Shawnee, Lenape, and the aged Seminole had been. They led Taylor directly into a "dense cypress swamp" and then, working on his soldiers' nerves as they made camp, warned them that the army was liable to be attacked. During the night, two "friendly Indians" came by, informing Taylor that the Mikasuki were not where the boys said but at a place three miles distant. Starting out the next day, Taylor took an actual Young Man, interrogating him to learn that the Mikasuki were hovering one mile away, ready to attack.[223] The changing stories on "enemy" location were clearly disinformation, although Taylor swallowed each whole as fact, while the spooky warnings of imminent attack were obviously psychological operations.

Still in search of the summary battle that all U.S. Army officials were convinced would end the war, Taylor pressed forward. "Capturing" another Young Man, Taylor learned that the Seminole were awaiting him, dead ahead. Pressing his advance on the "enemy," Taylor's men found camps with "evidence" that "several hundred" had cleared out "in a great hurry," for their campfires were still burning and meat that had been about to be cooked was abandoned on the ground.[224] Taylor was obviously close now, although evacuation, not attack, was the Seminole and Maroon response to his presence, so far.

The morning of December 25, 1837, found Taylor disposing his men in battle array at the "enemy" location pointed out by the most recent Young Man. Ready for action by 11:00 A.M., Taylor found to his chagrin that, once more, there was "no enemy to oppose" him. Magically, another suspiciously available Young Man wandered by and, "captured" by Taylor, directed him now to a "dense hammock" (grove of trees) another mile away. There, the Seminole had set a deliberate trap, into which they had been drawing Taylor, incrementally. They were stationed on the hammock just across from that to which the Young Man had sent Taylor.[225]

Between the Seminole's and Taylor's hammocks lay a swamp of fairly impassable stands of palmetto and saw grass. *Halpuda Mikko, Coacoochee,* and *Apiaka* had had the palmetto and saw grass cut down to half size in strategically placed, narrow lanes of passage between the hammocks. From experience, they knew that in a charge, Taylor's men would be siphoned through those precut passages in a steady file. At the same time, the massed Seminole had their own, quick and easy egress across flat, sandy areas. *Halpuda Mikko* put his 180 men front and center of the Seminole hammock, with Lake Okeechobee to his back. *Coacoochee* ("Wild Cat") had his eighty men on *Halpuda Mikko*'s left, while the remaining 120 under *Apiaka* were stationed to his right. Ten lookouts were posted in the tallest trees to give notice to those on the ground as to which way the army was tending, while Seminole sharpshooters were posted behind carefully notched trees, to pick off Taylor's officers, one by one. When the firefight commenced, *Apiaka* moved to a distance to commence holy ceremonies, to aid the Young Men, as per Woodlands convention.[226]

Not seeming to catch on that he was being set up, Taylor repositioned his men based on the latest Young Man's information. For some reason, he stationed the 180 untried Missouri militiamen on his front lines, where they took the brunt of the opening fire. The militiamen then did what militiamen had long been famous for doing upon meeting actual resistance: They screamed in panic, threw down their weapons, and "retired in disorder," as Joel Poinsett discreetly had it, running back to camp as fast as their legs could carry them. Their militia colonel killed in the first volley, they refused to return to action.[227]

Taylor claimed that, post-militia panic, the Seminole were "promptly checked," but this does not seem to have been the case. True, the Seminole did not advance against Taylor, as a European army would have done, but began a staged retreat, carefully picking off all but one of Taylor's officers, along with "most" of the non-commissioned officers, as they lured Taylor's army forward into the prepared paths.[228] Next, a company of 160 of Taylor's men took the front and "drove"— or more likely, simply followed—the Seminole, all the way to Lake Okeechobee, where the body of Seminole now scattered in small clusters in every direction, guerrilla-style. *Coacoochee* later said that none of the Young Men fell back until Taylor's men ran whooping at them through the choke points that the Seminole had created in the palmetto and saw grass. Then, the Seminole broke into small units, retreating separately into the Everglades. *Coacoochee* added that the total Seminole casualties in the action consisted of twelve men, including one Maroon. Nine others were wounded, with two later dying.[229]

At Lake Okeechobee sat a now-evacuated Mikasuki camp that ran a mile along the shore. The action ended there, Taylor's men "nearly exhausted." From the first skedaddle of the Missourians to the final chase to Okeechobee, the firefight had lasted from 12:30 P.M. to 3:00 P.M.[230] Omitted from Taylor's report were the "signs," that is, the message left in the sand after the battle by *Halpuda Mikko*, which the army's translator, a Black man name Abraham, could read. The message said that the Seminole intended "to war to the death."[231]

It is unclear from his battle report whether Taylor realized what had just happened. Of course, he claimed total victory—just before eulogizing all the officers who had been killed. December 26, 1837, was spent burying the dead and sending a litter train of the wounded to Tampa Bay. When Taylor moved the next day, he took with him 600 head of Seminole cattle and 100 head of Seminole horses. In all, he suffered twenty-six dead, among them his "most valuable officers," and shipped back in pieces his 112 wounded, one of whom later died. His men found only ten Seminole dead, although he speculated, quite inaccurately, that many more had been carried off the field, as was "customary with them."[232] Some victory.

At first, the *Niles Weekly Register* reported Taylor's battle with dismay. "We learn with the greatest pain," said the editors, "that this was one of the most disastrous battles" of the war, as indeed, it was for the United States.[233] For his part, Missouri senator Thomas Hart Benton was enraged by Taylor's official report, which described the Missouri militia's backward sprint. On February 14, 1838, Benton demanded to know why Taylor had placed them in "the fore-front of the battle," alleging that they had been a sacrifice "to draw the fire of the hidden enemy, and to absorb their bullets," noting that Taylor had held his best troops, the regulars, in reserve, as second and third lines. By the time Benton had finished blasting Taylor, the well of the Senate was on fire.[234]

The Van Buren administration was determined, however, to rebrand the Battle of Okeechobee as the glorious victory that it needed to justify its expensive Florida adventure. After the emotional dust had settled on February 22, 1838, both President Van Buren and Commanding General of the Army Alexander Macomb publicly expressed national thanks to Colonel Zachary Taylor. With a nod to Taylor's officers, Van Buren pointedly praised the U.S. regulars for their "discipline and bravery," while carefully avoiding mention of the militia. Macomb offered his "high commendation" for Taylor's "triumph of success," sad-facing yet downplaying the high casualty count.[235]

The national tone set, in his final report as Florida commander, issued July 7, 1838, Jesup extolled Taylor's Okeechobee action as "one of the best fought battles known" to all of U.S. history. Taylor had "gained a complete victory," Jesup cried.[236] This became the official history of the Battle of Okeechobee, repeated relentlessly thereafter, until quite recently, with Taylor promoted to brevet brigadier general in recognition of his "distinguished service" at "Kissimmee" (Okeechobee).[237] Probably some of Jesup's excessive praise came as an exhale of relief that the Florida mess had just been handed to Taylor, as he finally relinquished command of his odious duty on April 10, 1838.[238]

As it turned out, Okeechobee was the only combat of Taylor's command in Florida, for the Seminole and Maroons were hardly foolish enough to fight a European-style war. This left Taylor's actual tasks—to remove the Seminole and ship the Maroons into slavery—but they proved as elusive of accomplishment as massed battle. Although enjoying as little success as had Gaines, Scott, Call, and Jesup before him, Taylor was not one to give up, even as guerilla attacks resumed, with "friendly" Seminole hanging with U.S. forces only long enough to spread disinformation, especially to Macomb, when he showed up in person.[239]

Desperate for an alternative to chasing ghosts through swamps, Taylor changed tactics. As early as May 25, 1837, Jesup had brought up the possibility of using bloodhounds from Cuba, even threatening *Osceola* with them.[240] Based on War Department correspondence, on June 6, 1838, and again on July 28, 1838,

Taylor wrote to Secretary of War Poinsett requesting permission to use blood-hounds to track down the Seminole and Maroons. Interestingly, the June 6 letter has disappeared, but happily, war memorialist John Titcomb Sprague and abolitionist and U.S. congressman from Ohio Joshua R. Giddings preserved the July 28 letter to adjutant general Roger Jones.[241] In it, Taylor announced that he had received a "communication," most probably from Thomas F. Hunt, on the "subject of procuring blood-hounds" from Cuba to "aid the army in its operations against the hostiles" of Florida, presumably including the Maroons. As "decidedly in favor of the measure," Taylor requested official approval of the idea as the "only means of ridding this country of Indians." Should approval and "necessary authority" be granted him, Taylor would immediately open communications with Cuba through Hunt, the "Quarter Master at Savannah," Georgia.[242]

Escaped slaves were regularly dogged in the South, so there was a reason for acquiring dogs specifically from Cuba. Turning ferocious hounds loose on the Indians, to tear them to shreds, had been a practice starting with the first Spanish invaders. Theirs were the original "dogs of war," which the Spanish equipped with armor and raised on a diet of human flesh.[243] During the French and Indian War, Pennsylvania assemblyman John Hughes had urged the British command to use dogs the same way, to "Enable ye Soldiers to kill the Indians at pleasure."[244] The British were open to the suggestion, agreeing that a "few instances of Indians Seized and worried by Dogs" would "deter" them "more effectually from a war with us, than all the Troops we could raise."[245] Not much had changed by 1838. The governor of Florida, Raymond R. Reid, referred to the Seminole as "beasts of prey."[246] This sort of attitude helped make hunting dogs feel acceptable to settlers. Poinsett endorsed Taylor's idea, writing on the letter of July 28 that he had "always been of the opinion that dogs ought" to have been "employed" in the Seminole War to "protect the army" from ambush and to "track the Indian to his lurking place."[247]

"Every slaveholder understood the habits of these ferocious dogs," Giddings spat out in disgust, adding that everyone also understood that the real purpose of the long Florida war had always been "*to obtain slaves* rather than *to fight Indians*."[248] Giddings was right. Southern slavery was facing labor shortages due to Article 1, Section 9, paragraph 1 of the U.S. Constitution, as solidified by the Act Prohibiting Importation of Slaves (2 Stat. 426, March 2, 1807). Both had cut off the foreign slave trade as of 1808, with the Founders assuming that absent newly imported Africans, slavery would die out in the United States. They assumed wrongly. Aside from the semi-legal method of purchasing Africans through Cuba or the outrightly illegal method of smuggling in Africans—both very expensive—southern planters came up with two frugal ways around the prohibition: first, "breeding," that is, the forced mating of extant slaves to increase slave populations, and second, the rape of the "plantation wives" with their "unfortunate results" or what Ralph Ellison bitingly called "Mammy made" children.[249] With the acquisition of Florida, another means of obtaining "fresh" slaves had popped up: hunting down Maroons and Black Seminole. Better and better, the army would finance it, explaining the urgency in securing Florida.

Under pressure to explain himself, by December 30, 1839, Poinsett was obfuscating for all he was worth. Acknowledging the use of dogs, he pulled up the hoary, all-purpose justification of "helpless women and children" set upon by "ruthless savages," insisting that "every means possible" had to be "resorted to in order to protect" innocent settlers. Ever since his appointment to the War Department, he said, he had been receiving letters urging the use of bloodhounds in Florida. Given these reasons, he had authorized Taylor to "obtain as many dogs" as he thought necessary to his purpose.[250] Notwithstanding, Giddings brought the issue to the floor of the U.S. Congress, in relation to an appropriations bill to fund the "Indian Department."[251]

On January 26, 1840, still pressured, Poinsett reported that "a pack of bloodhounds" had been imported into Florida from Cuba. To quiet accusations that they were to kill Seminole or track Maroons, Poinsett ordered that they be muzzled and used solely to track Seminole, ignoring the fact of Black Seminole.[252] On January 26, 1840, Taylor replied that he was scrupulously following Poinsett's instructions on the usage of the dogs.[253] By January 28, protest against the scheme was hardening, especially among abolitionists, so that details on the dogs were released. Totaling thirty-four in number and "well trained," they looked like an "ordinary pack barking about a planter's dwelling." Still, when "any living thing" approach one of the older dogs, "his eyes" would "flash" he would roar with "rage, and twist like a serpent to escape his chains." The pack was kept "in subjection" by the Cuban keepers, delivering "heavy blows with a cudgel."[254] Oddly, abolitionists were not quieted by this information.

The back-and-forth debate became extremely heated in Congress. On March 9, 1840, now a U.S. representative from Massachusetts John Quincy Adams introduced a resolution calling upon the secretary of war to give specifics about the bloodhounds, particularly as to how they were trained to tell the difference between the "blood of the freeman" and that of an escaped slave or a Seminole.[255] On February 9, 1841, U.S. representative from Georgia Edward Junius Black sneered at abolitionist charges of "negro-stealing" and using "Florida blood-hounds" to maul the Seminole as nothing other than the "miserable cant" of the "modern philanthropist."[256] Adams and Giddings were, indeed, human rights advocates, but Black's sneer produced no resolution of the bloodhound issue that I can find in the records, other than a half-hearted attempt to use it against Taylor's presidential run. This suggests that the bloodhounds continued being used, with the congressional debate no more than a pressure relief valve on the slavery issue.

The only upshot of the furor was that Taylor decided to get out of Florida while the getting was good. In 1839, his reputation was still intact as the great, Indian-fightin' hero of the glorious Bad Axe and Okeechobee triumphs. Thus, on May 6, 1839, Taylor formally requested to be relieved of command in Florida.[257] Poinsett and Macomb pretended not to notice. By 1840, however, as the bloodhound drama began to coagulate around Taylor, rather than watch one of his best generals pilloried in public, on April 21, 1840, Macomb issued General Order, No. 42, extricating Taylor from his Florida quagmire by transferring the hopeless job to General Walter K. Armistead.[258] By August 14, 1842, with the United States in a hole for the Second Seminole War to the tune of 1,466 soldiers dead and $30,000,000–$40,000,000—over one billion dollars, today—the U.S. Army simply declared victory and left.[259]

Taylor's prowess as the hero of Okeechobee became a selling point during his presidential bid.[260]

The Seminole and the Maroons won the war.

NOTES

1. Arrom, 1983, esp. 47–57.
2. Mann and Grinde, 2001, 1–33.
3. Landers, 1997, 85; Mann and Grinde, 2001, 1–33.
4. Gallay, 1996, 10–11.
5. Sturtevant, 1987, 101–2.
6. Ivers, 2016.
7. Sturtevant, 1987, 105.
8. Ibid., as "pioneers," 105; USDI, 1894b, for "strayed people" definition, 28; for "wanderers," 65.
9. Mahon, 1967, 3; for the racist term "primitive," 14.
10. Mann, 2000, note 41, 27, 76, 367.
11. As citizenship process example, Mann, 2000, 175–77.
12. Bartram, 1928, 164.
13. Italics in the original. Nichols, 2002, 270; Twyman, 1999, 24–25.
14. Arrom, 1983, 48; Price, 1996, xi–xii.
15. Campbell, 1988.
16. Gregg, 1844, "*carnero cimarron,*" 194–95; for USS, 1850, "bighorn," vol. 14, no. 64, 201.
17. McCauley, 1887, 481.
18. Town as "Camp," McCauley, 1887, 507.
19. Mahon, 1967, 10.
20. Wright, 1986, 60–61; "Osceola, of Florida," 1838, 364; Sprague, 1848/1964, 100.
21. Wright, 1986, 80, 251.
22. Mann and Grinde, 2001, vol. 2, 7–8.
23. Mahon, 1967, 10.
24. French, 1869, 172.
25. McCauley, 1887, 495.
26. Mann and Grinde, 2001, note 69, 11, 28.
27. Mann, 2000, 284–85.
28. Mann and Grinde, 2001, 11.
29. McCauley, 1887, 499–501.
30. Bartram, 1791/1928, 168.
31. Ibid., 153.
32. McCauley, 1887, 504, 510.
33. Ibid., cabbage, 504; Koonti, 499, 513–14; sugar, 499, 511.
34. Ibid., 504.
35. Morse, 1822, 309; McCauley, 1887, 504, 512–13.
36. Bartram, 1791/1928, orange grove, 160; Alachua capital, 168; garden, 169.

37. Ibid., 169–70.

38. Mann, 2000, 236–37.

39. Lafitau, 1724/1974, vol. 1, 294, 312.

40. Bartram, 1791/1928, 169–70.

41. Ibid., 164.

42. Ibid., 167.

43. McCauley, 1887, 522–23; Mann, 2016, 108.

44. Capron, 1953, 189–90.

45. Wright, 1986, 26–27, 160; Willoughby, 2012, *A-Cee-Yahola*, 15; Adair, 1775, 49–50; Mann, 2016, 23–24; Mann, 2003, Ten Lost Tribes, 10, 18–19.

46. Porter, 1951, 253.

47. McReynolds, 1957, 97.

48. Porter, 1951, 251–52.

49. Morse, 1822, 309.

50. Porter, 1951, 252–53.

51. Ibid., 253.

52. USDI, 1894b, 69–70.

53. Foreman, 1989, 268.

54. USDI, 1894b, 69–70.

55. McCauley, 1887, 526.

56. Ibid., intermarriage, 526; "half-breeds," 489–90.

57. Ibid., 526.

58. USDI, 1894b, 4, 7.

59. *ASPMA*, 1832–1861, Thompson to Cass, vol. 6, no. 690, letter 4/27/1835, 534.

60. Mann and Grinde, 2001, 4–8.

61. Mulroy, 2007, note 10, 8, 331.

62. Twyman, 1999, 32–33; Mulroy, 2007, 8.

63. Deagan and McMahon, 1995.

64. Porter, 1951, 250.

65. Mulroy, 2007, 9–10.

66. "Treaty of Paris, 1763," 2008.

67. Mulroy, 2007, 10.

68. Porter, 1951, 252.

69. "Treaty of Paris, 1783," 2008.

70. Davenport and Paullin, 1917–1937, vol. 4, no. 170, 151.

71. USS, 1795.

72. USDI, 1995, 47.

73. Mulroy, 2007, 11.

74. Twyman, 1999, 80–81; *ASPIA*, 1832, self-count, vol. 2, no. 198, 439.

75. Kappler, 1904, "Treaty with the Creeks," vol. 2, 8/7/1790, 26; *ASPIA*, 1832, vol. 1, no. 19, 125–29.

76. Blumenbach and Hunter, 1865, 81, 201.

77. Jefferson, 1785/1832, 145.

78. Quoted in Brodie, 1974, 299.

79. Blumenbach and Hunter, 1865, "Causes" of "Degeneration," 207, *et seq.*; Caucasian, 264–65.

80. Nott, 1844, 35; for "Niggerology," Stanton, 1960, 118.

81. Nott, 1844, 37.

82. Fitzhugh, 1854, 31.

83. Adams, 1874–1877, vol. 1, 1/17/1806, 386; vol. 1, 2/7–8/1806, 404–6.

84. Madison, 1900–1910, Madison to Smith, vol. 8, letter 7/17/1810, 105.

85. Moser *et al.*, 1980–2013, Caffrey as nephew, vol. 2, 5/20/1810, 246; Florida breaking from Spain, vol. 2, 7/20/1810, 251.

86. Madison, 1900–1910, Message to Congress, vol. 8, 1/3/1811, 130–31.

87. USDS, 1897, 98.

88. Moser *et al.*, 1980–2013, Jackson to Claiborne, vol. 2, letter 1/5/1813, 352.

89. Mathews, 2018, Mathews to Madison, letter 4/16/1812.

90. Madison, 1900–1910, Madison to Jefferson, vol. 8, letter 4/24/1812, 190.

91. Stiggins, 1989, 132; Covington, 1990, 79.

92. Wright, 1986, 183.

93. Moser *et al.*, 1980–2013, Crawford to Jackson, vol. 4, letter 3/15/1816, 15.

94. Ibid., Crawford to Jackson, vol. 4, letter 3/15/1816, 15–16.

95. Fuller, 1906, note 3, 229. Later sanitizing changed the date on the letter, but the original date seems to have been 4/8/1816.

96. Moser *et al.*, 1980–2013, Jackson to Zuñiga, vol. 4, letter 4/23/1816, 22–23.

97. Ibid., Gaines to Jackson, vol. 4, letter 5/14/1816, 31.

98. Ibid., Zuñiga to Amelung, vol. 4, letter 5/26/1816, 42.

99. Clinch, 1819, armament, 186; 150 Muskogee, 187; 200 Coweta Muskogee, 188; Giddings, 1858, 38.

100. Clinch, 1819," 187; Giddings, 1858, 40–41.

101. Clinch, 1819, 187; *ASPNA*, 1834, vol. 1, no. 159, 3/24/1818, 502.

102. Clinch, 1819, 187.

103. Ibid., called Seminole, "Choctaw," 187; Giddings, 1858, 41–42.

104. Ibid., 187.

105. *ASPNA*, vol. 1, no. 159, 3/24/1818, 502; Clinch, 1819, 187; Giddings, 1858, 41–42.

106. Clinch, 1819, 188.

107. Giddings, 1858, 42.

108. Moser *et al.*, 1980–2013, Jackson to Crawford, vol. 4, letter 9/7/1816, 60.

109. Bassett, 1926–1935, Gaines to Jackson, vol. 2, letter 8/21/1817, 323–24; Moser *et al.*, 1980–2013, Gaines to Jackson, vol. 4, letter 11/21/1817, 151; Cave, 2017, 83–84; *ASPMA*, 1832–1861, Report, Mitchell, vol. 1, no. 16, 2/22/1819, 748–49.

110. Moser *et al.*, 1980–2013, vol. 4, 149; Gaines to Jackson, vol. 4, letter 12/2/1817, 153–54.

111. USC, 1855, 2/1819, 989.

112. USC, 1819, Speech of Charles Fenton Mercer, 804.

113. *ASPMA*, 1832–1861, Report, Mitchell, vol. 1, no. 16, 2/22/1819, 749.

114. Moser *et al.*, 1980–2013, Calhoun to Jackson, vol. 4, letter 12/26/1817, 163.

115. Ibid., Jackson to Caso y Luengo, vol. 4, letter 4/8/1818, 186–87.

116. Ibid., Jackson to Calhoun, vol. 4, letter 4/20/1818, 193–95.

117. Ibid., Jackson to Calhoun, vol. 4, letter 5/5/1818, 197–200.

118. Ibid., Mascot to Jackson, vol. 4, letter 5/23/1818, 205–6; Jackson to Mascot, vol. 4, letter 5/23/1818, 206–9.

119. Ibid., Jackson to Piernas, vol. 4, letter 5/24/1818, 210.

120. Loveman, 2010, 36.

121. Thomas, 1894, 328.

122. Clayton *et al.*, 1993, vol. 1, 272.

123. Carter, 1934–1975, Duval to Calhoun, vol. 22, letter 7/18/1822, 492.

124. Ibid., Walton to Burch, vol. 22, letter 1/30/1823, 608; roads, vol. 22, 2/5/1823, 634–35.

125. Ibid., Hernandez to Williams, vol. 22, letter 2/1823, 633–34; Calhoun to Hernandez, vol. 22, letter 3/19/1823, 651–52; Calhoun to Walton, vol. 22, letter 3/26/1823, 654; Jesup to Burch, vol. 22, letter 5/1/1823, 676; Gadsden to Calhoun, vol. 22, letter 3/16/1824, 902; road contract, vol. 23, 12/21/1824, note 94, 128–32.

126. Carter, 1934–1975, Burch to Jesup, vol. 22, letter 10/5/1823, 764–65.

127. Ibid., Jesup to Burch, vol. 22, letter 4/4/1824, 924; Jesup to Clark, vol. 22, letter 4/14/1824, 924–25; to Fort Mitchell, completed, Burch to Jesup, vol. 23, letter 9/1/1824, 64; Cape Sable, Humphries to Calhoun, vol. 23, letter 3/2/1825, 202; Cutts to Jesup, vol. 23, letter 9/8/1825, 315.

128. Carter, 1934–1975, White to Jesup, vol. 23, letter 12/25/1827, 958; Burch to Jesup, vol. 23, letter 3/10/1828, 1039.

129. Ibid., Jesup to Burch, vol. 23, letter 3/22/1825, 227; Burch to Jesup, vol. 23, letter 6/17/1825, 266.

130. Ibid., McLean to Crane, vol. 23, letter 11/29/1825, 363; Rodman to Pierce, vol. 23, letter 5/11/1826, 543; Burch to Jesup, vol. 23, letter 5/18/1826, 552–53; Macomb to McLean, vol. 23, letter 8/23/1826, 633; L'Engle to Jesup, vol. 24, letter 8/1/1830, 437.

131. Ibid., Jesup to Brown, vol. 23, letter 3/26/1827, 804; L'Engle to Jesup, vol. 24, letter 9/15/1830, 441–42; L'Engle to Jesup, vol. 24, letter 1/9/1831, 481.

132. Ibid., McLean to Prior, vol. 23, letter 9/8/1826, 640; Advertisement, vol. 23, 12/4/1827, 940–41; Burch to Jesup, vol. 23, letter 3/10/1828, 1040–41; Burch to Jesup, vol. 24, letter 10/16/1829, 279.

133. Ibid., advertisement, vol. 24, 7/24/1832, 724.

134. Ibid., Jesup to L'Engle, vol. 24, letter 8/3/1832, 725; L'Engle to Jesup, vol. 24, letter 10/12/1832, 742; L'Engle to Jesup, vol. 24, letter 6/6/1833, 828; Albert to Guion, vol. 25, letter 7/17/1838, note 89, 524.

135. Ibid., Albert to Graham, vol. 25, letter 1/25/1836, 228.

136. *ASPIA*, 1832, Walton to Barber, vol. 2, letter 5/26/1825, 629; Humphreys to Walton, vol. 2, letter 4/6/1825, 630.

137. Carter, 1934–1975, Humphries to McCarty, vol. 23, letter 9/6/1827, 911.

138. Kappler, 1904, "Treaty with the Florida Tribes," vol. 2, 9/18/1823, 203–7.

139. State of Florida and Thompson, 1847, note (a), 547.

140. Carter, 1934–1975, Barbour through McKenney to DuVal, vol. 23, letter 3/22/1827, 801.

141. Adams, 1874–1877, vol. 7, 12/22/1825, 89–90.

142. Carter, 1934–1975, Rodman to Barbour, vol. 23, letter 7/11/1826, 604–5.

143. Ibid., DuVal to Barbour, vol. 23, letter 1/28/1828, 1013–14.

144. Ibid., Humphreys to McKenney, vol. 24, letter 10/28/1828, 92.

145. Brackets in the original. Carter, 1934–1975, DuVal to Eaton, vol. 24, letter 5/4/1829, 210.

146. Carter, 1934–1975, White to Eaton, vol. 24, letter 1/23/1832, 637.

147. Kappler, 1904, Treaty with the Seminole, vol. 2, 5/9/1832, 344–45.

148. Carter, 1934–1975, Proceedings, vol. 24, 1/23/1832, 644.

149. Ibid., Macomb to McIntosh *et al.*, vol. 24, letter 2/23/1832, 663.

150. Ibid., Memorial, vol. 24, 3/26/1832, 678–80; Petition, vol. 24, 3/26/1832, 680–82.

151. Ibid., letter, Thompson to Herring, vol. 25, 10/28/1834, 58–60.

152. Ibid., Humphries to McCarty, vol. 23, letter 9/6/1827, 911.

153. *ASPMA*, 1832–1861, Thompson to Cass, vol. 6, no. 690, letter 4/27/1835, 533.

154. Carter, 1934–1975, Clinch to Macomb, vol. 25, letter 1/22/1835, 99–100.

155. Ibid., vol. 25, note 41, 61.

156. Ibid., Fanning to Jones, vol. 25, letter 4/29/1835, 133.

157. *ASPMA*, 1832–1861, Thompson to Cass, vol. 6, no. 690, letter 4/27/1835, 533–34.

158. Sprague, 1848/1964, 89; *ASPMA*, 1832–1861, date of departure, vol. 6, no. 638, 57.

159. Italics in the original. Sprague, 1848/1964, 90.

160. Sprague, 1848/1964, 90–91.

161. *ASPMA*, 1832–1861, Jackson to Congress, vol. 6, no. 638, message, 2/9/1836, 56.

162. Sprague, 1848/1964, 90.

163. *ASPMA*, 1832–1861, Jones to Cass, vol. 6, no. 638, letter 2/9/1836, 58.

164. Sprague, 1848/1964, 131.

165. *ASPMA*, 1832–1861, "Hitchcock Testimony, vol. 7, no. 738, 370; Court Opinion, vol. 7, 3/21/1837, 464.

166. Ibid., Gaines, "He was never authorized to command me," vol. 7, no. 738, 2/1837, 401.

167. Sprague, 1848/1964, Hitchcock to Gaines, letter 2/23/1836, 108–9; *ASPMA*, 1832–1861, Hitchcock Testimony, vol. 7, no. 738, 1/12/1837, 367–68; McCall Testimony, vol. 7, 1/17/1837, 374–75.

168. *ASPMA*, 1832–1861, McCall Testimony, vol. 7, no. 738, 1/17/1837, 375; Gaines, vol. 7, 2/1837, 401; Scott to Clinch, vol. 7, letter 3/1/1836, 402–3; Scott to Clinch, vol. 7, letter 3/4/1837, 403.

169. *ASPMA*, 1832–1861, McCall Testimony, vol. 7, no. 738, 1/17/1837, 373; Thistle Testimony, vol. 7, 1/17/1837, 376; Mitchell Testimony, vol. 7, 1/27/1837, 383; Gaines, vol. 7, 2/1837, 401.

170. *ASPMA*, 1832–1861, Hitchcock Testimony, vol. 7, no. 738, 1/12/1837, 369, 372–73; McCall Testimony, vol. 7, 1/17/1837, 373–74; Thistle Testimony, vol. 7, 1/17/1837, 375–76; Gaines, vol. 7, 2/1837, 401.

171. *ASPMA*, 1832–1861, Hitchcock Testimony, vol. 7, no. 738, 1/12/1837, 369–70.

172. Ibid., Hitchcock Testimony, vol. 7, no. 738, 1/12/1837, 368; Hitchcock Testimony, vol. 7, 1/14/1837, 371–72; McCall Testimony, vol. 7, 1/17/1837, 373; Smith Testimony, vol. 7, 2/10/1837, 389; name, John Caesar, Sprague, 1848/1964, 112.

173. *ASPMA*, 1832–1861, Thistle Testimony, vol. 7, no. 738, 1/18/1837, 376.

174. Sprague, 1848/1964, 112.

175. *ASPMA*, 1832–1861, "Proceedings," Hitchcock Testimony, letter from Scott, vol. 7, no. 738, 1/12/1837, 370, Clinch's force, vol. 7, 371; McCall Testimony, vol. 7, 1/17/1837, 373; Thistle Testimony, vol. 7, 1/18/1837, 376; Scott to Clinch, vol. 7, letter 2/12/1836, 378; Scott to Clinch, vol. 7, letter 3/1/1836, 378–79; Scott to Clinch, letter 3/4/1836, 379; Clinch's 600 men, Scott to Jones, vol. 7, letter 3/14/1837, 381; Scott to Jones, vol. 7, letter 3/14/1836, 405.

176. *ASPMA*, 1832–1861, McCall Testimony, vol. 7, no. 738, 1/17/1837, 373.

177. Ibid., Court Opinion, vol. 7, no. 738, 3/21/1837, 465.

178. Ibid., Lindsay Testimony, vol. 7, no. 738, 12/7/1836, 137; Alabama, Lindsay Testimony, vol. 7, 12/8/1836, 140; South Carolina and U.S. Army, Eustis Testimony, vol. 7, 12/8/1836, 141.

179. Ibid., Lindsay Testimony, vol. 7, no. 738, 12/7/1836, 138.

180. Ibid., storm, Van Buren Testimony, vol. 7, no. 738, 1/16/1836, 157; flood, Eustis Testimony, vol. 7, 12/9/1836, 143.

181. Ibid., Thurston Testimony, vol. 7, no. 738, 12/9/1836, 144–45.

182. Ibid., Gadsden Deposition, vol. 7, no. 738, 133.

183. Ibid.

184. Ibid.

185. Ibid., quotation, Drane Testimony, vol. 7, no. 738, 12/26/1836, 153; resupply effort, Clinch Deposition, vol. 7, 1/20/1837, 159–59.

186. Ibid., Clinch Testimony, vol. 7, no. 738, 12/22/1836, 154.

187. Ibid., 1832–1861, Gadsden Deposition, vol. 7, no. 738, 134; Scott through Gadsden to McLemore, vol. 7, 3/25/1836, 134.

188. Ibid., 1832–1861, Gadsden Deposition, vol. 7, no. 738, 133; De Peyster Testimony, vol. 7, 12/12/1836, 148; Bankhead Testimony, vol. 7, 12/17/1836, 150, 151; quotation, Green Testimony, vol. 7, 12/16/1836, 148.

189. Ibid., Lindsay Testimony, vol. 7, no. 738, 12/8/1836, 140; Thurston Testimony, vol. 7, 12/10/1836, 145.

190. Ibid., Gadsden Deposition, vol. 7, no. 738, 134; chief of staff, Eustis Testimony, vol. 7, 12/8/1836, 142.

191. Ibid., Memoranda, Part Second, No. 2, vol. 7, no. 738, 125.

192. Ibid., Court Opinion, vol. 7, no. 738, 1/30/1837, 159.

193. Ibid., Macomb to Scott, vol. 7, no. 760, letter 6/28/1836, 795.

194. Sprague, 1848/1964, farms, 160; Heileman to Eustis, letter 6/10/1836, 158–59; Pierce to unknown, letter 8/12/1836, 160–61.

195. *ASPMA*, 1832–1861, Jones to Jesup, vol. 7, no. 760, letter 12/36/1836, 798; Jesup to Dallas, vol. 7, no. 738, letter 10/25/1836, 187.

196. Ibid., Poinsett to Jesup, vol. 7, no. 760, letter 8/3/1837, 812; Butler to Jesup, vol. 8, letter 11/4/1836, 807; Jesup to Butler, vol. 7, letter 12/5/1836, 819–20.

197. Ibid., Jesup to Butler, vol. 7, no. 760, letter 11/6/1836, 817; Jesup to Jones, vol. 7, letter 12/5/1836, 820; Jesup to Butler, vol. 7, letter 12/9/1837, 820; Jesup to Jones, vol. 7, letter 1/10/1837, 825; Jesup to Jones, vol. 7, letter 1/12/1837, 825; Jesup to Jones, vol. 7, letter 1/17/1812, 825–26; Jesup to Jones, vol. 7, letter 1/19/1837, 826; Jesup to Jones, vol. 7, letter 1/20/1837, 826.

198. Ibid., Maroons and Seminoles taken, Jesup to Jones, vol. 7, no. 760, letter 7/20/1837, 842; detailed schedule of Blacks taken, 1836–1837 Registry, Jesup, vol. 7, 851–52.

199. Ibid., Hernandez to Jesup, vol. 7, no. 760, letter 9/17/1837, 849–50; Poinsett to Jesup, vol. 7, letter 10/7/1837, 853.

200. Ibid., Jesup to Jones, vol. 7, no. 760, letter 1/21/1837, 827; councils divided, Jesup to Butler, vol. 7, letter 1/21/1837, 827; Jesup to Butler, vol. 7, letter 2/7/1837, 827.

201. Ibid., Jesup to Jones, vol. 7, no. 760, letter 2/17/1837, 830.

202. Ibid., Jesup to Jones, vol. 7, no. 760, letter 2/25/1837, 833.

203. Ibid., signed surrender, Jesup to Jones, vol. 7, no. 760, letter 3/6/1837, 834.

204. Sprague, 1848/1964, 90.

205. *ASPMA*, 1832–1861, Jesup to Jones, vol. 7, no. 760, letter 6/5/1837, 838–39; Jesup to Jones, vol. 7, letter 7/25/1837, 843–44; Poinsett to Jesup, vol. 7, letter 7/25/1837, 811–12.

206. Ibid., Miller to Jesup, vol. 7, no. 760, letter 7/8/1837, 840; Childs to Linnard, vol. 7, letter 7/7/1837, 840–41; Galt to unknown, vol. 7, letter 8/8/1837, 846.

207. Ibid., Childs to Jesup, vol. 7, no. 760, letter 8/3/1837, 845; Jesup to Jones, vol. 7, letter 8/13/1837, 845–46; Galt to Jesup, vol. 7, letter 8/11/1837, 846–47; Jesup to Jones, vol. 7, letter 9/27/1837, 848; Jesup to Jones, vol. 7, letter 10/2/1837, 848–49.

208. Ibid., Jesup to Poinsett, vol. 7, no. 760, letter 5/8/1837, 870–71.

209. Ibid., Jones to Jesup, vol. 7, no. 760, letter 5/31/1837, 803.

210. Italics in the original. Sprague, 1848/1964, *"white plume,"* 216; Jesup to Hernandez, letter 10/21/1837, 218; Hernandez to Jesup, letter, no date, 218–19; *ASPMA*, 1832–1861, Jesup to Poinsett, vol. 7, no. 760, letter 10/221837, 886; Mahon, 1967, 214–15.

211. Mahon, 1967, 216.

212. USC, 1860, Stevens, 4/19/1860, 1806.

213. USC, 1840, Butler Speech, 6/11/1840, 665.

214. Mahon, 1967, 218.

215. *ASPMA*, 1832–1861, Poinsett to Jesup, vol. 7, no. 760, letter 7/25/1837, 811–12.

216. "Army General Order—Official," *Niles*, vol. 52, 8/12/1837, 373; Taylor as Colonel, First Infantry, *ASPMA*, Report, vol. 7, no. 745, 11/1837, 597.

217. *ASPMA*, 1832–1861, Jesup to Poinsett, vol. 7, no. 760, letter 11/1837, 588; "Registry of Negro Prisoners," vol. 7, 851–52.

218. Ibid., Jesup to Armistead, vol. 7, no. 745, letter 12/25/1837, 894.

219. Ibid., Taylor Report, vol. 7, no. 789, 12/25/1837, 986.

220. Ibid., Taylor Report, vol. 7, no. 789, 12/25/1837, 986; Seminole strength, Sprague, 1848/1964, 213.

221. Ibid., Taylor Report, vol. 7, no. 789, 12/25/1837, 987.

222. Ibid.

223. Ibid.

224. Ibid.

225. Ibid.

226. Sprague, 1848/1964, 213–14.

227. *ASPMA*, 1832–1861, Taylor Report, vol. 7, no. 789, 12/25/1837, 987; letter, Poinsett to Johnson, vol. 7, 2/20/1838, 986.

228. Ibid., Taylor Report, vol. 7, no. 789, 12/25/1837, 988.

229. Sprague, 1848/1964, 214; in 1838, Jesup claimed that the Seminole "acknowledged a loss of fourteen killed," "Florida War," *Niles*, vol. 55, 9/8/1838, 30.

230. *ASPMA*, 1832–1861, Taylor Report, vol. 7, no. 789, 12/25/1837, 988.

231. "Important from Florida," *Niles*, vol. 53, 1/13/1838, 305.

232. *ASPMA*, 1832–1861, Taylor Report, vol. 7, no. 789, 12/25/1837, 988. Taylor listed 26 dead and 112 wounded but one of the wounded later died, Sprague, 1848/1967, Returns, 213.

233. "Important from Florida," *Niles*, vol. 53, 1/13/1838, 305.

234. USC, 1838, 2/14/1838, 182.

235. "Official: General Order No. 4," *Niles*, vol. 53, 2/20/1838, 401.

236. "Florida War," *Niles*, 9/8/1838, 55, 30.

237. Heitman, 1903, 949.

238. "General Orders—No. 7," *Niles*, Item V, vol. 54, 4/14/1838, 97.

239. Sprague, 1848/1964, continued attacks, 233–36; Macomb to Poinsett, disinformation, letter 5/22/1839, 230–31.

240. USC, 1841, 350.

241. Dyer, 1946, note 58, 116. This is not the first time I have encountered sanitization of the official record, Mann, 2009, xiv–xv, 8–9, 14–17, 74–77.

242. Giddings, 1858, 267; Sprague, 1848/1967, 241.

243. Varner and Varner, 1983, 36–39, 192–93.

244. Bouquet, 1940/1994, 304–5.

245. Bouquet, 1940/1994, 295.

246. Giddings, 1858, 263.

247. USC, 1840, 204.

248. Italics in the original. Giddings, 1858, 265.

249. For forced mating, Douglass, 1849, 62–63; for "plantation wife," Egerton, 2002, 182; for "results," Chesnut, 1906, 115; for "Mammy made," Ellison, 1947/1995, 227.

250. Sprague, 1848/1964, Poinsett to Wise, letter 12/30/1839, 240–41.

251. USC, 1841, 12/23/1840, 51.

252. *Army and Navy Chronicle*, 1840, Poinsett to Taylor, vol. 10, no. 8, letter 1/26/1840, 116.

253. Ibid., Taylor to Poinsett, vol. 10, no. 9, letter 2/27/1840, 135.

254. Ibid., bloodhounds, vol. 10, no. 8, 124.

255. USC, 1840, Adams Resolution, 3/9/1840, 252.

256. USC, 1841, 165.

257. Carter, 1934–1975, Macomb to Poinsett, vol. 25, letter 5/6/1839, 610.

258. Sprague, 1848/1964, General Order No. 42, Jones for Macomb, 4/21/1840, 243.

259. Vandervort, 2006, 130.

260. Montgomery, 1847, 34–59; *Taylor and His Generals*, 1847, 23–39; *Taylor and Fillmore*, 1848, 6–8; Fry and Conrad, 1848, 37–68.

Conclusion: Men of Which People?

∿

Nul mot n'est plus vague et n'a permis de commettre des
plus grandes iniquités que celui de civilisacion.[1]
(No word is more vague or has permitted the commission
of greater crimes than that of civilization.)
—Charles Salomon (1889)

Cultural heroes matter. Their gender matters. Their ethnic origin matters. Their lived values as authorized by their religion, science, and caste and class mythology matter. What is promulgated of heroes expresses what the dominant culture defines as the "civilization" to be imposed on the rest of us.

The way in which any necessary allusion is made to these heroes also matters. When casually referring to a mass murderer as an "Indian-fighter" still raises no Euro-Christian eyebrows, when large-scale human trafficking by a wealthy slaveholder and slave trader is reduced to a quick-and-dirty mention of him as a "southern gentleman," and when state-orchestrated massacres of inconvenient people are purveyed as the triumphs of a prestigious military career, then official history is failing miserably to represent ALL the people.

Instead of acknowledging the gaping wounds left on the shared American consciousness by the massacre of Indians and the enslavement of Africans, the "mainstream" employs linguistic dodges. Students are assured that historical massacres of Indians and enslavement of Africans were real "tragedies," all right—except that they were not tragedies. A tragedy is an untoward event occurring without human agency, thrust upon people unawares by circumstances beyond their control. Tornadoes, landslides, earthquakes, and pyroclastic flows qualify, but massacre and slavery do not, for they require human agency, prior planning, and strategy to pull off. Thus, one human population murdering a second human population to steal its land and enslave a third human population to work that land is not a series of independent tragedies. It is a crime spree.

Every effort is made to ignore that elephant in the rotunda, because the Euro-Christian self-image is at stake. Selective sympathy is the latest dodge. It acknowledges that the poor settlers behaved badly, but doggone it, they were just afraid. Fear of impending Indian attack or slave revolt drove them to cruelty.[2] This tack elevates settler anxiety over the terror and pain daily experienced by those being massacred, those being enslaved. I realize that Euro-Christian Americans are simply "Isolating the Knowledge of the Unpleasant," again, but Native Americans and African Americans do not much appreciate being categorized as The Unpleasant.[3]

As told to date, American history is a carefully concocted myth, faithfully following Plato's well-known schemata as outlined in *The Republic*. Positing knowledge as power, Plato then carefully distinguished between knowledge and belief.[4] Belief was an emotional trait that his Philosopher Kings were to avoid themselves yet instill in their functionaries, whose education was to have been dream-induced mythology. Meanwhile, all actual knowledge, which Plato conflated with goodness, was to be reserved to themselves.[5] The *Republic*'s Philosopher Kings were to be strictly portrayed to the public as unique, having sprung from gold, the sheer force of their innate greatness, alone, propelling them forward, although in reality, they were to be selected, given every advantage, and nurtured into their positions.[6]

Ideally, the justifying myths of the resultant Republic were repeated endlessly to the succeeding generations as an essential prop of the Republic's—or, at least, the Philosopher Kings's—existence.[7] Only those accounts of history that extolled those gods and heroes useful to the Republic were to be fed to the functionaries, with no contrary views aired, lest the functionaries stop believing in the government.[8] Lies were to have been deliberately manufactured and promulgated, as the need arose, for the supposed good of the Republic.[9] It looked "as though our rulers" would "have to employ a great many lies and deceptions for the benefit of those they rule," Plato sighed to Glaucon.[10]

The degree to which the so-called West continues to follow Plato's prescriptions is almost spooky. It can be observed in the numbing repetitions of Euro-America's exceptionalism, glorifying as superheroes those who promoted vaguely defined American values. A simple walk through the local bookstore's history section demonstrates as much, with the endless tomes on America's "Founding" demigods and latter-day heroes. Purportedly self-made golden boys stride onto the stage from the nowhere of log cabins and hinterland forts, propelled forward by their innate greatness, alone—and just in the nick of time to win this war or support that manifestly destined cause. Postmodernists may sniff all they like that Plato's *Republic* lost its power sometime since, as a creaking absolute in relative-minded times, but they miss the structural degree to which Plato's *Republic* is baked into the Euro-American script.

If nineteenth-century America turns out to have been a crime scene, then what is a Philosopher King to do? Hopefully, retreat to his mansion, there quietly to sip his favorite beverage, while the rest of America chucks the euphemisms, tunes out the myths, and cleans up the oligarchic mess he made.

Cultural heroes matter. Hopefully, twenty-first-century America chooses wisely. Maybe someone will even remember that the original Greek Hero was a woman.

NOTES

1. Salomon, 1889, 195.
2. Owen, 2015, 4–5.
3. Barnard, 2001, 519–30.
4. Plato, 1985, 477a–d.
5. Ibid., education, 414d, 505b–c, 514a; philosophers, 473d, 484–485a, 519d.
6. Ibid., gold, 415a; 535a–537a.
7. Ibid., 415a–e.
8. Ibid., 377b5–378e, 380a–c, 381b–c5, 389b, 607a5.
9. Ibid., 414c.
10. Ibid., 459d.

Bibliography

Adair, James. *The History of the American Indians: Particularly Those Nations Adjoining to the Mississippi, East and West Florida, Georgia, South and North Carolina, and Virginia.* London: Printed for Edward and Charles Dilly, 1775.

Adams, Henry. *John Randolph.* 1882. Boston: Houghton Mifflin Company, 1894.

Adams, John, Abigail Adams, and Thomas Jefferson. *The Adams-Jefferson Letters: The Complete Correspondence between Thomas Jefferson and John and Abigail Adams.* Edited by Lester J. Cappon. Chapel Hill: University of North Carolina Press, 1959.

Adams, John Quincy. *Memoirs of John Quincy Adams, Comprising Portions of His Diary from 1795 to 1848.* Edited by Charles F. Adams. 12 vols. Philadelphia: J. B. Lippincott, 1874–1877.

Adams, Richard. C. "History." In *Report on Indians Taxed and Not Taxed in the United States (except Alaska) at the Eleventh Census, 1890,* 297. Washington, D.C.: Government Printing Office, 1894.

Alcarez, Ramón. *Apuntes para la historia de la guerra entre México y los Estados Unidos.* 1848. Ciudad de México: D. F. Editoria Nacional, 1952.

Alexander, Edward P. "Chats with the Editor." *Wisconsin Magazine of History* 28, no. 1 (September 1944): 1–6.

Allen, Felicity. *Jefferson Davis, Unconquerable Heart.* Columbia: University of Missouri Press, 1999.

Allen, Thomas M. *A Republic in Time: Temporality and Social Imagination in Nineteenth-century America.* Chapel Hill: University of North Carolina Press, 2008.

Allen, William C. *History of the United States Capitol: A Chronicle of Design, Construction, and Politics.* Washington, D.C.: Government Printing Office, 2001.

Allison, Harold. *The Tragic Saga of the Indiana Indians.* Paducah, KY: Turner Publishing Company, 1986.

American State Papers, Class II: *Indian Affairs* (ASPIA). 2 vols. Washington, D.C.: Gales and Seaton, 1832.

American State Papers, Foreign Relations (ASPFR). 6 vols. Washington, D.C.: Gales and Seaton, 1832–1859.

American State Papers, Military Affairs (ASPMA). 7 vols. Washington, D.C.: Gales and Seaton, 1832–1861.

American State Papers, Miscellaneous (ASPMISC). 2 vols. Washington, D.C.: Gales and Seaton, 1834.

American State Papers, Naval Affairs (ASPNA). 4 vols. Washington, D.C.: Gales and Seaton, 1834.

American State Papers, Public Lands (ASPPL). 8 vols. Washington, D.C.: Gales and Seaton, 1834–1861.

Ames, Herman V. "John C. Calhoun and the Secession Movement of 1850." *American Antiquarian Society*, n.s. 28 (April 1918): 19–50.

Amnesty International. *Maze of Injustice: The Failure to Protect Indigenous Women from Sexual Violence in the USA*. New York: Amnesty International USA, 2007.

Anderson, Thomas Gummersall. "Papers of T. G. Anderson, British Indian Agent." In *Report and Collections of the State Historical Society of Wisconsin*, vol. 10, 142–49. Madison: State Historical Society of Wisconsin, 1888.

Andrews, Edward Deming. "The Shaker Mission to the Shawnee Indians." *Winterthur Portfolio*, no. 7 (1972): 113–28.

Armstead, Myra B. Young. *Freedom's Gardener: James F. Brown, Horticulture, and the Hudson Valley in Antebellum America*. New York: New York University Press, 2012.

Armstrong, James L. *Reminiscences, or, An Extract from the Catalogue of General Jackson's 'Juvenile Indiscretions' between the Ages of 23 and 60*. 1828.

Armstrong, Perry A. *The Sauks and the Black Hawk War, with Biographical Sketches, Etc.* Springfield, IL: H. W. Rokker, 1887.

Army and Navy Chronicle 10, nos. 8–9 (1840).

"Army General Order.—Official." *Niles Weekly Register* 52, no. 1350 (August 12, 1837): 373.

Arrom, José Juan. "*Cimarrón: Apuntes sobre sus primeras documentaciones y su probable origen.*" *Revista española de antropología Americana* 13 (1983): 47–57.

Article 1: "Review of Wilkinson's *Memoirs*." *Literary and Scientific Repository* 1, no. 1 (June 1820): 1–24.

Aupaumut, Hendrick. Letter of May 21, 1805. "Hendrick Aupaumut to Henry Dearborn." *National Archives, Records of the Office of the Secretary of War*, Record Group 107. Shawnee Series. Great Lakes-Ohio Valley Ethnohistory Collection, Glenn A. Black Laboratory of Archaeology, Indiana University, Bloomington.

Aupaumut, Hendrick. "A Narrative of an Embassy to the Western Indians, from the Original Manuscript of Hendrick Aupaumut, 1791 and 1793." *Memoirs of the Historical Society of Pennsylvania* 2, no. 1 (1827): 9–131.

Averill, James P. *Fort Meigs: A Condensed History of the Most Important Military Point in the Northwest, Together with Scenes and Incidents Connected with the Sieges of 1813, and a Minute Description of the Old Fort and Its Surroundings, as They Now Appear*. Toledo, OH: Blade Printing and Paper Co., 1886.

Axelrod, Alan. *A Chronicle of the Indian Wars from Colonial Times to Wounded Knee*. New York: Prentice Hall General Reference, 1993.

Babbitt, Irving. *Literature Cultures, and Religion*. Edited by George A. Panichas. New Brunswick, NJ: Transaction Publishers, 2006.

Babcock, Elkanah. *A War History of the Sixth U.S. Infantry, from 1798 to 1903, with Rosters and Memorials of the Curan and Philippine Campaigns*. Edited by S. T. Fiske Jr. Kansas City, MO: Hudson-Kimberly Publishing Co., 1903.

Badger, Joseph. *A Memoir of Rev. Joseph Badger, Containing an Autobiography and Selections from His Private Journal and Correspondence.* Hudson, OH: Sawyer, Ingersoll and Co., 1851.

Badollet, John, and Albert Gallatin. *The Correspondence of John Badollet and Albert Gallatin, 1804–1836.* Edited by Gayle Thornbrough. Indiana Historical Society Publications, vol. 22. Indianapolis: Indiana Historical Society, 1963.

Baggett, Ashley. "Domestic Violence." In *The World of Antebellum America: A Daily Life Encyclopedia,* edited by Alexandra Kindell, vol. 1, 210–13. 2 vols. Santa Barbara, CA: Greenwood, an Imprint of ABC-CLIO, LLC, 2018.

Bagnall, Norma Hayes. *On Shaky Grounds: The New Madrid Earthquakes of 1811–1812.* Columbia: University of Missouri Press, 1996.

Baires, Sarah E. *Land of Water, City of the Dead: Religion and Cahokia's Emergence.* Tuscaloosa: University of Alabama Press, 2017.

Baldwin, Charles Candee. "Early Maps of Ohio and the West." *Western Reserve and Northern Ohio Historical Quarterly,* no. 25 (1875): 1–23.

"Banks and Banking." *Niles Weekly Register* 17, no. 425 (October 30, 1819): 139.

Barnard, Christopher. "Isolating Knowledge of the Unpleasant: The Rape of Nanking in Japanese High-School Textbooks." *British Journal of Sociology of Education* 22, no. 4 (2001): 519–30.

Barnett, Jim, and H. Clark Burkett. "The Forks of the Road Slave Market at Natchez." *Mississippi History Now* (2017). Mississippi Historical Society. Accessed December 26, 2017. http://www.mshistorynow.mdah.ms.gov/articles/47/the-forks-of-the-road-slave-market-at-natchez.

Barton, Benjamin Smith. *New Views of the Origin of the Tribes and Nations of North America.* 1798. Reprint. Millwood, NY: Kraus Reprint Co., 1976.

Bartram Trail Conference. *Bartram Heritage: A Study of the Life of William Bartram by the Bartram Trail Conference.* Montgomery, AL: The Bartram Trail Conference, 1979.

Bartram, William. *The Travels of William Bartram.* Edited by Mark Van Doren. 1791. New York: Dover Publications, 1928.

Bassett, John Spencer, ed. *The Correspondence of Andrew Jackson.* 7 vols. Washington, D.C.: Carnegie Institution of Washington, 1926–1935.

Bassett, John Spencer. *The Life of Andrew Jackson.* 2 vols. Garden City, NY: Doubleday, Page, & Company, 1911.

Bateman, Newton, Paul Selby, and Charles A. Church. *Historical Encyclopedia of Illinois.* 2 vols. Chicago: Munsell Publishing Co., 1916.

Bauer, K. Jack. *Zachary Taylor: Soldier, Planter, Statesman of the Old Southwest.* Baton Rouge: University of Louisiana Press, 1985.

Beatty, Charles. *The Journal of a Two Months Tour.* London: William Davenhill and George Pearch, 1768.

Beauchamp, William M., and Onondaga Historical Association, eds. *Moravian Journals Relating to Central New York, 1745–66.* Syracuse, NY: Dehler Press, 1916.

Beckwith, H. W., J. H. Beadle, and S. B. Gookins. *History of Vigo and Parke Counties, together with Historic Notes on the Wabash Valley Gleaned from Early Authors, Old Maps and Manuscripts, Private and Official Correspondence, and Other Authentic, though, for the Most Part, Out-of-the-way Sources.* Chicago: H. H. Hill and N. Iddings, 1880.

Beers, Henry Putney. *The Western Military Frontier, 1815–1846.* Philadelphia: University of Pennsylvania, 1935.

Bellfy, Philip C. *Three Fires Unity: The Anishnaabeg of the Lake Huron Borderlands*. Lincoln: University of Nebraska Press, 2011.

Berthrong, Donald J. *Indians of Northern Indiana and Southwestern Michigan: An Historical Report on Indian Use and Occupancy of Northern Indiana and Southwestern Michigan*. New York: Garland Publishing, 1974.

Beveridge, Albert Jeremiah. *The Life of John Marshall*. Vol. 3, *Conflict and Construction, 1800–1815*. New York, NY: Cosimo, Inc., 2005.

Biggs, William. *Narrative of the Indian Captivity of William Biggs among the Kickapoo Indians in Illinois in 1788*. Heartman's Historical Series No. 37. Metuchen, NJ: C. F. Heartman, 1922.

Birbeck, Morris. "An Appeal on the Question of a Convention." In *Papers in Illinois History and Transactions*, 147–63. Publication No. 10. Part III, Contributions to State History. Springfield: Illinois State Historical Society, 1906.

Birmingham, Robert A. *Life, Death, and Archaeology at Fort Blue Mounds: A Settlers' Fortification of the Black Hawk War*. Madison: Wisconsin Historical Society Press, 2014.

Black, Elk, John G. Neihardt, and Raymond J. DeMallie. *Black Elk Speaks: Being the Life Story of a Holy Man of the Oglala Sioux*. 1932. Albany: State University of New York Press, 2008.

Blanchard, Rufus. *Discovery and Conquests of the North-West, with the History of Chicago*. 2 vols. Chicago: R. Blanchard and Company, 1898–1900.

Blennerhassett, Harman, and William Harrison Safford. *The Blennerhassett Papers, Embodying the Private Journal of and the Hitherto Unpublished Correspondence of Burr, Alston, Comfort, Tyler, Devereaux, Dayton, Adair, Miro, Emmett, Theodosia Burr Alston, Mrs. Blennerhassett, and Others, Their Contemporaries; Developing the Purposes and Aims of Those Engaged in the Attempted Wilkinson and Burr Revolution; Embracing Also the First Account of the "Spanish Association of Kentucky" and a Memoir of Blennerhassett*. Cincinnati: Moore, Wilstach & Baldwin, 1864.

"Bloodhounds, The." *Army and Navy Chronicle* 10, no. 8 (February 20, 1840): 114–16, 124.

Blumenbach, Johann Friedrich. *Beyträge zur Naturgeschichte*. 3 vols. 1790. Göttingen: Heinrich Dietrich, 1806.

Blumenbach, Johann Friedrich. *De Generis Humani Varietate Nativa*. 3rd ed. 1775. Gottingae: apud Vandenhoek et Ruprecht, 1795.

Blumenbach, Johann Friedrich, and Joannes Hunter. *The Anthropological Treatises of Blumenbach and Hunter*. London: Longman, Green, Longman, Roberts, & Green, 1865.

Blumrosen, Alfred W., and Ruth G. Blumrosen. *Slave Nation: How Slavery United the Colonies and Sparked the American Revolution*. Naperville, IL: Sourcebooks, Inc., 2005.

Boller, Paul F., Jr. *Presidential Wives: An Anecdotal History*. 2nd ed. New York: Oxford University Press, 1998.

Bonney, Catharina V. R. *A Legacy of Historical Gleanings*. 2nd ed. 2 vols. Albany, NY: J. Munsell, 1875.

Book of American Indians Containing the Most Interesting Narratives of Indian Chiefs and Indian Wars Now Extant with 40 Wood Engravings. 1853. Reprint. Dayton, OH: Moore, Clarke & Co., 1854.

Booker, Margaret Moore. "Native North American Art: Beadwork and Shell Work." In *The Grove Encyclopedia of American Art*, edited by Joan Marter, vol. 1, 457–61. 5 vols. New York: Oxford University Press, 2011.

Bossu, Jean-Bernard. *New Travels in North America by Jean-Bernard Bossu, 1770–1771*. Edited by Samuel Dorris Dickinson. Natchitoches, LA: Northwestern State University Press, 1982.

Bossu, Jean-Bernard. *Nouveau Voyages aux Indies Occidentales, Premiere Partie*. Paris: Le Jay, 1768.

Bossu, Jean-Bernard. *Nouveaux voyages dans l'Amérique Septentrionale: contenant une collection de lettres écrites sur les lieux, par l'auteur; à son ami, M. Douin, Chevalier, Capitaine dans les Troupes du Roi ci-devant son camarade dans le Nouveau Monde. Nouvelle édition*. Amsterdam et à Paris: Veuve Duchesne, 1778.

Bossu, Jean-Bernard. *Travels in the Interior of North America, 1751–1762*. Edited by Seymour Feiler. 1768. Norman: University of Oklahoma Press, 1962.

Bouquet, Henry. 1940. *The Papers of Henry Bouquet*. Edited by Louis M. Waddell. Harrisburg: The Pennsylvania Historical and Museum Commission, 1994.

Bourne, Edward Gaylord. *Narratives of the Career of Hernando de Soto in the Conquest of Florida*. 2 vols. London: David Nutt, 1905.

Bowes, John P. *Land Too Good for Indians: Northern Indian Removal*. Norman: University of Oklahoma Press, 2016.

"Bowman's Campaign of 1779." *Ohio Archaeological and Historical Publications* 22 (1913): 502–19.

Boyd, James M. "The Papers of Indian Agent Boyd, 1832." In *Collections of the State Historical Society of Wisconsin*, edited by Reuben Gold Thwaites, vol. 12, 266–98. Madison: State Historical Society of Wisconsin, 1892.

Bracken, Charles, and Peter Parkinson Jr. "The Pekatonika Battle Controversy." In *Collections of the State Historical Society of Wisconsin*, vol. 2, 365–92. Madison: State Historical Society of Wisconsin, 1903.

Brady, Cyrus Townsend. *The True Andrew Jackson*. Philadelphia: J. B. Lippincott, 1906.

Brands, Henry William. *Andrew Jackson, His Life and Times*. New York: Anchor Books, 2006.

Brannan, John, ed. *Official Letters of the Military and Naval Officers of the United States during the War with Great Britain in the Years 1812, 13, 14, & 15*. Washington, D.C.: Way & Gideon, 1823.

Brasser, T. J. "Mahican." In *Handbook of North American Indians*, edited by Bruce G. Trigger, vol. 15, 198–212. *Northeast* Washington, D.C.: Smithsonian Institution, 1978.

Brewer, Willis. *Alabama, Her History, Resources, War Record, and Public Men from 1542 to 1842*. Montgomery, AL: Barrett & Brown, 1872.

Briggs, Deane R. "Fort Frank Brook." *Florida Postal History Journal* 17, no. 3 (October 2010): 6–12.

Brinton, Daniel Garrison. *The Lenâpé and Their Legends: The Complete Text and Symbols of the Walam Olam, A New Translation, and Inquiry into Its Authenticity*.1885. Reprint. Lewisburg, PA: Wennawoods Publishing, 1999.

British-American Diplomacy. Avalon Project. Yale Law School. Lillian Goldman Law Library, 2008. Accessed November 27, 2018. http://avalon.law.yale.edu/subject_menus/brtreaty.asp.

Brodhead, John Romeyn. *Documents Relative to the Colonial History of the State of New York: Procured in Holland, England and France*. Edited by Edmund Bailey O'Callaghan. 14 vols. Albany, NY: Weed, Parsons and Company, 1855.

Brodie, Fawn. *Thomas Jefferson: An Intimate History*. New York: W. W. Norton & Company, Inc., 1974.

Brokaw, Tom. *The Greatest Generation*. New York: Random House, 1998.

Brown, Charles R. *The Old Northwest Territory: Its Missions, Forts, and Trading Posts.* Kalamazoo, MI: Brown, Moore, & Quale, 1875.

Brown, Matthew. *The Struggle for Power in Post-Independence Columbia and Venezuela.* New York: Palgrave Macmillan, 2012.

Brown, Robert C., and J. E. Norris. *History of Portage County, Ohio: Containing a History of the County, Its Townships, Towns, Villages, Schools, Churches, Industries, etc.: Portraits of Early Settlers and Prominent Men, Biographies: History of the Northwest Territory, History of Ohio, Statistical and Miscellaneous Matter, etc., etc.* Chicago: Warner, Beers, & Co., 1885.

Brown, William Wells. *Narrative of William W. Brown, an American Slave: Written by Himself.* London: Charles Gilpin, 1850.

Brownmiller, Susan. *Against Our Will: Men, Women, and Rape.* New York: Fawcett Books, 1975.

Brunson, Alfred. "Memoir of Thomas Pendleton Burnett." In *Collections of the State Historical Society of Wisconsin*, vol. 2, 233–325. Madison: State Historical Society of Wisconsin, 1903.

Brymner, Douglas. "Capture of Fort McKay, Prairie du Chien, 1814." *Collections of the State Historical Society of Wisconsin*, vol. 11, 254–70. Madison, WI: State Historical Society of Wisconsin, 1888.

Brymner, Douglas. *Report on Canadian Archives, 1893.* Vol. 1. Ottawa: E. Dawson, 1894.

Buchanan, Joseph. "Burr's Conspiracy." *Truth's Advocate and Anti-Jackson Expositor* (August 1828): 311–14.

Buckingham, John. *Bitter Nemesis: The Intimate History of Strychnine.* New York: CRC Press, 2008.

Buckley, Jay H. "Bellfontaine, Fort." In *The Louisiana Purchase: A Historical and Geographical Encyclopedia*, edited by Junius P. Rodriguez, 29–30. Santa Barbara, CA: ABC-CLIO, LLC, 2002.

Buell, Augustus C. *History of Andrew Jackson, Pioneer, Patriot, Soldier, Politician, President.* 2 vols. New York: Charles Scribner's Sons, 1904.

Bunn, Mike, and Clay Williams. *Battle for the Southern Frontier: The Creek War and the War of 1812.* Charleston, SC: Arcadia Publishing Inc., 2008.

Burr, Samuel Jones. *The Life and Times of William Henry Harrison.* New York: L. W. Ransom; Philadelphia: R. W. Pomeroy, 1840.

Burstein, Andrew. *The Passions of Andrew Jackson.* New York: Vintage Books, 2004.

Burton, Clarence M. *History of Detroit, 1780 to 1850: Financial and Commercial.* Detroit, MI: n.p., 1917.

Burton, Clarence Monroe, William Stocking, and Gordon K. Miller, eds. *The City of Detroit, Michigan, 1701–1922.* 2 vols. Chicago: S. J. Clarke Pub. Co., 1922.

Burton, Harold H. " 'Justice the Guardian of Liberty:' John Marshall at the Trial of Aaron Burr." *American Bar Association* 57 (October 1951): 735–38.

Burton, Orville Vernon. *In My Father's House Are Many Mansions: Family and Community in Edgefield, South Carolina.* Chapel Hill: University of North Carolina Press, 1985.

Busby, Allie B. *Two Summers among the Musquakies, Relating to the Early History of the Sac and Fox Tribe, Incidents of Their Noted Chiefs, Location of the Foxes, or Musquakies, in Iowa, with a Full Account of Their Traditions, Rites and Ceremonies, and the Personal Experience of the Writer for Two and a Half Years among Them.* Vinton, IA: Herald Book and Job Rooms, 1886.

Buss, James Joseph. *Winning the West with Words: Language and Conquest in the Lower Great Lakes.* Norman: University of Oklahoma Press, 2011.

Butler, Mann. *A History of the Commonwealth of Kentucky.* 1834. Reprint. Bedford, MA: Applewood Books, 2010.

Butterfield, Consul Wilshire. *History of Grant County, Wisconsin Containing an Account of Its Settlement, Growth, Development, and Resources, and Extensive and Minute Sketch of Its Cities, Towns and Villages, Their Improvements, Industries, Manufactures, Churches, Schools, and Societies; Its War Record, Biographical Sketches, Portraits of Prominent Men and Early Settlers; the Whole Preceded by a History of Wisconsin Statistics of the State and an Abstract of Its Laws and Constitution and of the Constitution of the United States.* Chicago: Western Historical Company, 1881.

"Cadillac Papers." In *Collections and Researches Made by the Michigan Pioneer and Historical Society,* vol. 33, 36–748. Lansing, MI: Robert Smith Printing Co., State Printers and Binders, 1904.

Callendar, Charles. "Central Algonkin Moieties." In *North American Indian Anthropology: Essays on Society and Culture,* edited by Raymond J. DeMallie and Alfonso Ortiz, 108–24. Norman: University of Oklahoma Press, 1994.

Callendar, Charles. "Miami." In *Handbook of the North American Indians,* edited by Bruce G. Trigger, 681–89. 15 vols. Washington, D.C.: Smithsonian Institution, 1978.

Calloway, Colin. "The Proclamation of 1763: Indian Country Origins and American Impacts." In *Keeping Promises: The Royal Proclamation of 1763, Aboriginal Rights, and Treaties in Canada,* edited by Terry Fenge and Jim Aldridge, 33–48. Montreal & Kingston, CA: McGill-Queen's University Press, 2015.

Campbell, Mavis Christine. *The Maroons of Jamaica, 1655–1796: A History of Resistance, Collaboration, & Betrayal.* Granby, MA: Bergin & Garvey, 1988.

Camper, Pieter. *Oeuvres qui ont pour object l'histoire naturelle, la physiologie et l'anatomie compare.* 3 vols. Paris: H. J. Jansen, 1803.

Candler, Allen D., ed. *The Colonial Records of the State of Georgia: Journal of the Proceedings of the Governor and Council, March 8, 1759 to December 31, 1761, Inclusive.* 31 vols. Atlanta, GA: The Franklin-Turner Company, 1904–1986.

Capron, Louis. *Medicine Bundles of the Florida Seminole and the Green Corn Dance.* Anthropological Papers Nos. 33–42, 155–210. Smithsonian Institution. Bureau of American Ethnology. Bulletin 151. Paper No. 35. Washington, D.C.: Government Printing Office, 1953.

Carleton, James Henry. *The Battle of Buena Vista, with the Operations of the "Army of Occupation" for One Month.* New York: Harper & Brothers, 1848.

Carr, Edson I. *The Carr Family Records.* Rockton, IL: Herald Printing House, 1894.

Carter, Clarence Edwin. *The Territorial Papers of the United States.* 28 vols. Washington: United States Government Printing Office, 1934–1975.

Cartier, Jacques. *Trois voyages au Canada: Jacques Cartier, voyages fait en la Nouvelle France en 1535 et 1536, et S[amuel] de Champlain, voyages fait en la Nouvelle France en 1608 et 1611; Fr. Gabriel Sagard, Le grand voyage fait en pays des Hurons en l'an 1624.* Paris: Editions du Carrefour, 1929.

Carver, Jonathan. *Travels through the Interior Parts of North America, in the Years 1766, 1767, and 1768.* London: William Richardson, 1779.

Cass, Lewis. "The Indians of North America." *North American Review* 22 (January 1826): 53–119.

Cave, Alfred A. *Prophets of the Great Spirit: Native American Revitalization Movements in Eastern North America.* Lincoln: University of Nebraska Press, 2006.

Cave, Alfred A. *Sharp Knife: Andrew Jackson and the American Indians.* Santa Barbara, CA: Praeger, 2017.

Cave, Alfred A. "The Shawnee Prophet, Tecumseh, and Tippecanoe: A Case Study of Historical Myth-Making." *Journal of the Early Republic* 22, no. 4 (Winter 2002): 637–73.

Cayton, Andrew R. L. *Frontier Indiana.* Bloomington: Indiana University Press, 1996.

Cayton, Andrew R. L. *The Frontier Republic: Ideology and Politics in the Ohio Country, 1780–1825.* Kent, OH: Kent State University Press, 1986.

Charlevoix, Pierre-François-Xavier de. "Charlevoix's Account of de Louvigny's Expedition." In *Collections of the State Historical Society of Wisconsin,* vol. 5, 81–85. 31 vols. Madison: State Historical Society of Wisconsin, 1903.

Cheathem, Mark R. *Andrew Jackson and the Rise of the Democrats: A Reference Guide.* Santa Barbara, CA: ABC-CLIO, LLC, 2015.

Chesnut, Mary Boykin Miller. *A Diary from Dixie.* Edited by Isabella D. Martin and Myrta L. Avary. New York: D. Appleton and Company, 1906.

Chesnutt, Charles Waddell. *The House behind the Cedars.* 1900. Mineola, NY: Dover Publications, 2007.

Christian, Thomas. "Sortie at Fort Meigs." *Western Reserve and Northern Ohio Historical Society* 1, no. 23 (October 1874): 4–7.

Chula Tarla Emathla ("Thomas Simpson Woodward"). *Reminiscences of the Creek, or Muscogee Indians.* Montgomery, AL: Barrett & Wimbish, 1959.

Claiborne, John Francis Hamtramck. *The Life and Times of Gen. Sam Dale, the Mississippi Partisan.* New York: Harper & Brothers Publishers, 1860.

Claiborne, William Charles Cole. *Official Letter Books of W. C. C. Claiborne, 1801–1816.* Edited by Dunbar Rowland. 6 vols. Jackson, MS: State Department of Archives and History, 1917.

Clanin, Douglas E., ed. *The Papers of William Henry Harrison, 1800–1815.* 10 Reels. Typescript. Indianapolis: Indiana Historical Society, 1993.

Clark, Daniel. *Proofs of the Corruption of General James Wilkinson and of His Connection with Aaron Burr.* Philadelphia: William Hall Jr., and George W. Pierie, Printers, 1809.

Clark, Ella E. *Indian Legends of the Pacific Northwest.* 1953. Reprint. Berkeley: University of California Press, 1997.

Clark, Jerome ("Jerry") E. *The Shawnee.* Lexington: University Press of Kentucky, 1977.

Clark, Meriwether, William Lewis, and Elliott Coues. *History of the Expedition under the Command of Lewis and Clark to the Sources of the Missouri River, Thence across the Rocky Mountains and Down the Columbia River to the Pacific Ocean, Performed during the Years 1804–5–6, by Order of the Government of the United States.* 4 vols. 1814. New York: F.P. Harper, 1893.

Clark, Satterlee. "Early Times in Wisconsin, and Black Hawk War Reminiscences." In *Collections of the State Historical Society of Wisconsin,* vol. 8, 309–21. Madison: State Historical Society of Wisconsin, 1879.

Clay, Henry. *The Papers of Henry Clay.* Edited by Robert Seager II. 11 vols. Lexington: The University Press of Kentucky, 1959–1993.

Clay, Henry. *The Private Correspondence of Henry Clay.* Edited by Calvin Colton. Boston: Frederick Parker, 1856.

Clayton, Lawrence A., Edward C. Moore, and Vernon James Knight, eds. *The De Soto Chronicles: The Expedition of Hernando de Soto in North America in 1539–1543.* 2 vols. Tuscaloosa: University of Alabama Press, 1993.

Clayton, W. Woodford. *History of Davidson County, Tennessee, with Illustrations and Biographical Sketches of Its Prominent Men and Pioneers.* Philadelphia: J. W. Lewis & Co., 1880.

Cleaves, Freeman. *Old Tippecanoe: William Henry Harrison and His Time.* Newton, CT: American Political Biography Press, 1990.

Clemmons, Linda. "Sauk and Meskwakie Women in Eighteenth- and Nineteenth-Century Northern Illinois." *Illinois History Teacher* 10, no. 2 (2003): 2–5.

Clifton, James A. *The Prairie People: Continuity and Change in Potawatomi Indian Culture, 1665–1965.* Iowa City: University of Iowa Press, 1998.

Clinch, Duncan L. "Negro fort on Appalachicola [sic]." *Niles Weekly Register* 17, no. 428 (November 20, 1819): 186–88.

Cockrum, William Monroe. *Pioneer History of Indiana: Including Stories, Incidents, and Customs of the Early Settlers.* Oakland City, IN: Press of the Oakland City Journal, 1907.

Cohen, Benjamin R. "The Moral Basis of Soil Science and Geology: What Antebellum Farmers Knew and Why Anyone Cared." *Physics and Chemistry of the Earth* 35 (2010): 860–67.

Coker, William S. "The Papers and History of Panton, Leslie and Company, and John Forbes and Company." *Florida Historical Quarterly* 73, no. 3 (January 1995): 353–58.

Cole, Cyrenus. *A History of the People of Iowa.* Cedar Rapids, IA: The Torch Press, 1921.

Cole, Cyrenus. *I Am a Man: The Indian Black Hawk.* Iowa City: State Historical Society of Iowa, 1938.

Coleccion de documentos relativos a la vida publica del libertador de Colombia y del Peru, Simon Bolívar para servir a la historia de la independencia del Suramérica, vol. 19. Caracas: Imprenta de Devisme hermanos, 1829.

Coleman, Michael C. "Treaties and American Indian Schools in the Age of Assimilation, 1794–1930." In *Treaties with American Indians: An Encyclopedia of Rights, Conflicts, and Sovereignty,* edited by Donald L. Fixico, 179–91. 2 vols. Santa Barbara, CA: ABC-CLIO, LLC, 2008.

Collins, Gail. *William Henry Harrison.* The American Presidents Series. New York: Henry Holt and Company, Times Books, 2012.

Colyer, Walter. "The Fordhams and La Serres of the English Settlement in Edwards County." *Transactions of the Illinois State Historical Society for the Year 1911.* Publication No. 16. Illinois State Historical Library. Springfield: Illinois State Journal Co., State Printers, 1913.

Combs, Leslie. *Dudley's Defeat Opposite Fort Meigs, May 5, 1813: Official Report from Captain Leslie Combs to General Green Clay.* Cincinnati: Spiller & Gates, 1869.

Cook, Frederick, ed., *Journals of the Military Expedition of Major General John Sullivan against the Six Nations of Indians in 1779.* Auburn, NY: Kapp, Peck & Thomson, 1887.

Cooper, James Fenimore. *Jack Tier, or The Florida Reefs.* 1848. New York: D. Appleton and Co., 1877.

Cooper, James Fenimore. *Oak Openings, or the Bee Keeper.* 1848. New York: D. Appleton and Company, 1883.

Countryman, Edward. *Americans: A Collision of Histories.* New York: Hill and Wang, 1996.

Covington, James W. "The Negro Fort." *Gulf Coast Historical Review* 5 (1990): 79–91.

Cox, Isaac Joslin, ed. "Selections from the Torrence Papers, III." *Quarterly Publication of the Historical and Philosophical Society of Ohio* 2, no. 3 (July–September 1908): 97–120.

Cox, Isaac Joslin, ed. "Selections from the Torrence Papers, IV." *Quarterly Publications of the Historical and Philosophical Society of Ohio* 3, no. 3 (July–September 1908): 69–102.

Cox, Isaac Joslin. *The West Florida Controversy, 1798–1813: A Study in American Diplomacy.* Baltimore: Johns Hopkins Press, 1918.

Cox, Isaac Joslin. "Western Reaction to the Burr Conspiracy." In *Transactions of the Illinois State Historical Society for the Year 1928*. Springfield, IL: Phillips Bros., 1928.

Coy, Fred E., Jr., Thomas C. Fuller, Larry G. Meadows, and James F. Swauger. *Rock Art of Kentucky*. Lexington: University of Kentucky Press, 1997.

Crane, Verne W. "The Origin of the Name of the Creek Indians." *Mississippi Valley Historical Review* 5, no. 3 (December 1918): 339–42.

Crockett, David. *A Narrative of the Life of David Crockett of the State of Tennessee*. Edited by James A. Shackford and Stanley J. Folmsbe. 1834. Knoxville: The University of Tennessee Press, 1973.

Cruikshank, Ernest Alexander. *Documentary History of the Campaign upon the Niagara Frontier in the Year 1813*. The Lundy's Lane Historical Society. 9 vols. Welland, NY: Tribune, 1902–1908.

Curtis, Benjamin Robbins, Alexander James Dalls, William Cranch, Henry Wheaton, and Richard Peters. *Reports of Decisions in the Supreme Court of the United States [1790–1854]: With Notes and a Digest*. Boston: Little Brown, 1864.

Curtis-Wedge, Franklyn. *History of Trempealeau County, Wisconsin*. Edited by Eben D. Pierce. Chicago: H. C. Cooper Jr. & Co., 1917.

Cushing, Daniel. *Fort Meigs and the War of 1812: Orderly Book of Cushing's Company, 2nd U.S. Artillery, April 1813–February 1814, and Personal Diary of Captain Daniel Cushing, October 1812–July 1813*. Edited by Harlow Lindley, vol. 11. Ohio Historical Collections. 2nd ed. Columbus: The Ohio Historical Society, 1975.

Cusick, David. *David Cusick's Sketches of Ancient History of the Six Nations*. Lewiston, NY: Printed for the Author, 1827.

Dallas, Alexander James, and George Mifflin Dallas. *Life and Writings of Alexander James Dallas*. Philadelphia: J. B. Lippincott & Co., 1871.

Davenport, Frances G., and Charles Oscar Paullin. *European Treaties Bearing on the United States and Its Dependencies*. Publications of the Carnegie Institution of Washington. Papers of the Department of Historical Research. No. 254. Washington, D.C.: Carnegie Institute, 1917–1937.

Davidson, Cathy N. *Revolution and the Word: The Rise of the Novel in America*. New York: Oxford University Press, Inc., 2004.

Davidson, Victor. *History of Wilkinson County*. Macon, GA: John Ball Chapter, Daughters of the American Revolution, 1930.

Davis, Jefferson. *The Papers of Jefferson Davis*. Rev. ed. Edited by Haskell M. Monroe Jr. and James McIntosh. 12 vols. Baton Rouge: Louisiana State University Press, 1971–2015.

Davis, Varina. *Jefferson Davis, Ex-president of the Confederate States of America: A Memoir*. 2 vols. New York: Belford Company, 1890.

Dawson, Moses. *A Historical Narrative of the Civil and Military Services of Major-General William H. Harrison and a Vindication of His Character and Conduct as a Statesman, a Citizen, and a Soldier with a Detail of His Negotiations and Wars with the Indians, until the Final Overthrow of the Celebrated Chief Tecumseh and His Brother, the Prophet*. Cincinnati: M. Dawson, 1824.

Deagan, Kathleen A., and Darcie A. McMahon. *Fort Mose: Colonial America's Black Fortress of Freedom*. Gainesville: University Press of Florida, 1995.

DeCarlo, Peter. *Fort Snelling at Bdote: A Brief History*. St. Paul: Minnesota Historical Society Press, 2017.

Delaney, Martin R. *Blake, or the Huts of America*. 1852–1853. Boston: Beacon Press, 1970.

DeLay, Brian. *War of a Thousand Deserts: Indian Raids and the U.S.–Mexican War*. New Haven, CT: Yale University Press, 2008.

Deloria, Vine, Jr. *Red Earth, White Lies: Native Americans and the Myth of Scientific Fact.* Golden, CO: Fulcrum Publishing, 1997.

Deloria, Vine, Jr. "The Subject Nobody Knows." *American Indian Quarterly* 19, no. 1 (Winter 1995): 143–47.

Deloria, Vine, Jr., and Raymond J. DeMallie. *Documents of American Indian Diplomacy: Treaties, Agreements and Conventions, 1775–1979.* 2 vols. Norman: University of Oklahoma Press, 2000.

Deppisch, Ludwig M. *The Health of the First Ladies: Medical Histories from Martha Washington to Michelle Obama.* Jefferson, NC: McFarland & Company, Inc., Publisher, 2015.

"Descendants of Joseph Cornhill." Generation 3. Item 8. Accessed September 13, 2018. http://dts.scott.net/~dtscott/i/Creeks/DescendantsOfJosephCornhill.pdf.

Despatches, Correspondence, and Memoranda of Field Marshal Arthur Wellesley, Duke of Wellington. Edited by Arthur Richard Wellesley and Duke of Wellington. 8 vols. London: John Murray, 1867–1880.

Diamond, Jared. *Guns, Germs, and Steel: The Fates of Human Societies.* New York: W. W. Norton & Co., 1999.

Dickson, Robert, and Louis Grignon. "Dickson and Grignon Papers, 1812–1815." In *Collections of the State Historical Society of Wisconsin*, vol. 11, 271–315. Madison: State Historical Society of Wisconsin, 1888.

Dillon, John B. *The History of Indiana, from the Earliest Exploration by Europeans to the Close of the Territorial Government in 1816, Comprehending a History of the Discovery, Settlement, and Civil Affairs and Military Affairs of the U.S. Northwest of the River Ohio and a General View of the Progress of Public Affairs in Indiana from 1816 to 1856.* Indianapolis: Bingham and Doughty, 1859.

Doster, James F. "Early Settlements on the Tombigbee and Tensaw Rivers." *Alabama Review* 12 (1959): 83–94.

Douglass, Frederick. *Narrative of the Life of Frederick Douglass, an American Slave.* Boston: Anti-slavery Office, 1849.

Dowd, Gregory Evans. *A Spirited Resistance: North American Indian Struggle for Unity, 1745–1815.* Baltimore: Johns Hopkins University Press, 1992.

Downes, Randolph C. *Council Fires on the Upper Ohio: A Narrative of Indian Affairs in the Upper Ohio Valley until 1795.* Pittsburgh: University of Pittsburgh Press, 1968.

Drake, Samuel Gardner. *Indian Biography.* Carlisle, MA: Applewood Book, 1832.

Drexler, Robert W. *Columbia and the United States: Narcotics Traffic and a Failed Foreign Policy.* Jefferson, NC: McFarland & Company, Inc., 1997.

Dunn, Jacob Piatt, Jr. *Indiana: A Redemption from Slavery.* Rev. ed. New York: Houghton-Mifflin, 1888.

Dunn, Jacob Piatt, Jr. *True Indian Stories, with a Glossary of Indiana Indian Names.* Indianapolis: Sentinel, 1909.

Duran, Eduardo, and Bonnie Duran. *Native American Postcolonial Psychology.* Albany: State University of New York Press, 1995.

Durbin, Richard D., and Elizabeth Durbin. "Wisconsin's Old Military Road: Its Genesis and Construction." *Wisconsin Magazine of History* 68, no. 1 (Autumn 1984): 2–42.

Dyer, Brainerd. *Zachary Taylor.* New York: Barnes & Noble, 1946.

Eaton, Joseph H., compiler. *Returns of Killed and Wounded in Battles or Engagements with Indians and British and Mexican Troops, 1790–1848.* 1850–1851. Washington, D.C.: National Archives and Records Administration Microfilm Publications, 2000.

Edmunds, R. David. "*Main Poc*: Potawatomi *Wabeno.*" *American Indian Quarterly* 9, no. 3 (Summer 1985): 259–72.

Edmunds, R. David. *The Potowatomis: Keepers of the Fire.* Norman: University of Oklahoma Press, 1978.

Edmunds, R. David. *The Shawnee Prophet.* Lincoln: University of Nebraska Press, 1983.

Egerton, Douglas R. *Rebels, Reformers, and Revolutionaries: Collected Essays and Second Thoughts.* New York: Routledge, 2002.

Eisenhower, John S. D. *Zachary Taylor: The 12th President, 1849–1850.* The American Presidents Series. New York: Times Books, Henry Holt and Company, 2008.

Ekberg, Carl J. *French Roots in the Illinois Country: The Mississippi Frontier in Colonial Times.* Chicago: University of Illinois Press, 2000.

Ekberg, Carl J., and Sharon K. Person. *St. Louis Rising, The French Regime of Louis St. Ange de Bellerive.* Chicago: University of Illinois Press, 2015.

Elliott, Isaac H., and Illinois Office of the Adjutant General. *Record of the Services of Illinois Soldiers in the Black Hawk War, 1831–32, and in the Mexican War, 1846–8 Containing a Complete Roster of Commissioned Officers and Enlisted Men of Both Wars, Taken from the Official Rolls on File in the War Department, Washington, D.C., with an Appendix, Giving a Record of the Services of the Illinois Militia, Rangers and Riflemen, in Protecting the Frontier from the Ravages of the Indians from 1810 to 1813.* Springfield, IL: H.W. Rokker, State Printer, 1882.

Ellison, Ralph. *Invisible Man.* 1947. New York: Vintage Books, 1995.

Ely, James W., and Theodore Brown Jr., ed. *Legal Papers of Andrew Jackson.* Knoxville: University of Tennessee Press, 1987.

"Enclosure, Schedule of Property, 9 July 1799." Item b. Founders on Line. National Archives. Accessed January 3, 2018. https://founders.archives.gov/documents/Washington/06-04-02-0404-0002.

Esarey, Logan, ed. *Governors Messages and Letters: Messages and Letters of William Henry Harrison.* 2 vols. Indianapolis: Indiana State Historical Commission, 1922.

Esarey, Logan. *History of Indiana from Its Exploration to 1922.* 4 vols. Dayton, OH: Dayton Historical Publishing Company, 1922–1924.

Espenak, Fred. "Major Solar Eclipses Visible from Chicago IL, 0001 CE to 3000 CE." National Aeronautics and Space Administration. March 11, 2003. Accessed August 2, 2018. https://eclipse.gsfc.nasa.gov/SEcirc/SEcircNA/ChicagoIL2.html.

Espenak, Fred. "Solar Eclipses of Historical Interest." National Aeronautics and Space Administration. July 2008. Accessed September 21, 2012. https://eclipse.gsfc.nasa.gov/SEhistory/SEhistory.html.

Ethridge, Robbie. *Creek Country: The Creek Indians and Their World.* Chapel Hill: The University of North Carolina Press, 2003.

"Events of the War: British Official Account, February 8, 1813." *Niles' Weekly Register* 4 (March 6, 1813): 10–13.

Everett, Edward. "On the Complaints in America against the British Press: An Essay in the New London Monthly Magazine for February, 1821." *North American Review*, n.s., 4, 13, no. 32 (July 1821): 20–47.

Ewbank, Lewis B., and Dorothy L. Riker, ed. *The Laws of the Indiana Territory, 1809–1816.* *Indiana Historical Collections*, vol. 20. Indianapolis: Indiana Historical Bureau, 1934.

Executive Journal of Indiana Territory, 1800–1816. Edited by William Wesley Woollen, Daniel Wait Howe, and Jacob Piatt Dunn. Indianapolis, IN: The Bowen-Merrill Co., 1900.

Fafoutis, Dean. "Zachary Taylor, 12th President of the United States." In *Chronology of the U.S. Presidency*, edited by Mathew Manweller, vol. 1, 357–94. 4 vols. Santa Barbara, CA: ABC-CLIO, LLC, 2012.

Fairbanks, Charles H. "The Ethno-Archaeology of Florida Seminole." In *A Seminole Source Book*, edited by William C. Sturtevant, 163–93. New York: Garland Publishing, Inc., 1987.

Farmer, John S., and W. E. Henley. *Slang and Colloquial English*. 7 vols. London and New York: E. P. Button & Co., 1889–1905.

Farrow, Anne, Joel Lang, and Jenifer Frank. *Complicity: How the North Promoted, Prolonged, and Profited from Slavery*. New York: Hartford Courant Company, 2005.

Federal Writers' Project. *WPA Guide to Indiana: The Hoosier State*. San Antonio, TX: Trinity University Press, 2014.

Fedric, Francis. *Slave Life in Virginia and Kentucky: A Narrative by Francis Fedric, Escaped Slave*. Edited by C. L. Innes. Baton Rouge: Louisiana State University Press, 2010.

Feldman, Jay. *When the Mississippi Ran Backwards: Empire, Intrigue, Murder, and the New Madrid Earthquakes*. New York: Free Press, 2005.

Filson, John. *The Discovery, Settlement, and Present State of Kentucke*. Wilmington, DE: John Adams, 1784.

Findling, John E., and Frank W. Thackeray, eds. *Events That Formed the Modern World: From the European Renaissance through the War on Terror through the Seventeenth Century*. Vol. 1, 237–45. Santa Barbara, CA: ABC–CLIO, LLC, 2011.

Finkelman, Paul. *Millard Fillmore: The American Presidents Series: The 13th President, 1850–1853*. New York: Times Books, 2011.

Fitzhugh, George. *Sociology for the South, or the Failure of Free Society*. Richmond, VA: A. Morris Publisher, 1854.

Flagler, Daniel Webster. *A History of the Rock Island Arsenal from Its Establishment in 1836 to December, 1876; and of the Island of Rock Island, the Site of the Arsenal, from 1804 to 1863; Prepared under the Instructions of Brig. Gen. Stephen V. Benet*. Washington, D.C.: Government Printing Office, 1877.

Fleming, Walter L. "Jefferson Davis' First Marriage." *Mississippi Historical Society* 12 (1912): 21–36.

Fletcher, Alice C., and Washington Matthews. "Ethics and Morals." In *Handbook of the American Indians North of Mexico*, edited by Frederick W. Hodge, vol. 1, 441–42. 2 vols. Smithsonian Institution. Bureau of American Ethnology. Bulletin No. 30. Washington, D.C.: Government Printing Office, 1912.

Fletcher, Robert, and Terry Cameron. "Serpent Mound: A New Look at an Old Snake-in-the-Grass." *Ohio Archaeologist* 38, no. 1 (1988): 55–61.

"Florida War." *Niles Weekly Register* 55, no. 1406 (September 8, 1838): 29–31.

Florida, State of, and Leslie A. Thompson. *A Manual or Digest of the Statute Law of the State of Florida: Of a General of Public Character, in Force at the End of the Second Session of the General Assembly of the State on the Sixth Day of January, 1847*. Boston: Charles C. Little and James Brown, 1847.

Fonda, John H. "Reminiscences of Wisconsin." In *Collections of the State Historical Society of Wisconsin*, vol. 5, 205–84. Madison: State Historical Society of Wisconsin, 1907.

Forbes, Jack D. *The American Discovery of Europe*. Chicago: University of Illinois Press, 2007.

Ford, Worthington Chauncey. *Some Papers of Aaron Burr*. Dorchester, MA: American Antiquarian Society, 1920.

Fordham, Elias Pym. *Personal Narrative of Travels in Virginia, Maryland, Pennsylvania, Ohio, Indiana, Kentucky; and of a Residence in the Illinois Territory, 1817–1818*. Cleveland, OH: A. H. Clark & Co., 1906.

Foreman, Grant. *The Five Civilized Tribes: Cherokee, Chickasaw, Choctaw, Creek, Seminole*. 1934. Norman: University of Oklahoma Press, 1989.

"Forsyth Manuscript." In Kinzie, Juliette, *Wau-Bun: The Early Day in the Northwest*, 381–86. Philadelphia: J. B. Lippincott & Co., 1875.

Forsyth, Thomas. *An Account of the Manners and Customs of the Sauk and Fox Nations of Indian Tradition*. 1827. In *The Indian Tribes of the Upper Mississippi Valley and Region of the Great Lakes*, translated and edited by Emma H. Blair, vol. 2, 183–245. Cleveland, OH: Arthur H. Clark Company, 1912.

Forsyth, Thomas. "Letter-Book of Thomas Forsyth—1814–1818." In *Collections of the State Historical Society of Wisconsin*, vol. 11, 316–55. Madison: State Historical Society of Wisconsin, 1888.

Forsyth, Thomas. Letter of December 23, 1812. "Thomas Forsyth to William Clark." In *Indian Tribes of the Upper Mississippi Valley and the Region of the Great Lakes*, edited and compiled by Emma Helen Blair, vol. 2, 273–79. Cleveland, OH: Arthur H. Clark Company, 1912.

Forsyth, Thomas. Letter of September 23, 1819. "Thomas Forsyth to William Clark." In *Collections of the State Historical Society of Wisconsin*, edited by Reuben Gold Thwaites, vol. 6, 215–19. Madison: State Historical Society of Wisconsin, 1908.

"Fort Butler." Historical Marker Project. 2018. Accessed December 12, 2018. https://www.historicalmarkerproject.com/markers/view.php?marker_id=HMKZ8.

"Fort Koshkonong: A Fortification That May Not Have Existed." Wisconsin Historical Society. 2018. Accessed November 7, 2018. https://www.wisconsinhistory.org/Records/Article/CS295.

Fowke, Gerard. *Archaeological History of Ohio: The Mound Builders and Later Indians*. Columbus, OH: Fred J. Heer Press, 1902.

Franklin, Benjamin. *The Writings of Benjamin Franklin*. Edited by Albert Henry Smyth, vol. 5. New York: The Macmillan Company, 1906.

Franklin, Wayne. *James Fenimore Cooper: The Early Years*. New Haven, CT: Yale University Press, 2007.

Franquelin, Jean Baptiste Louis. *Carte contenant une part. du Canada & les terres qui s'estend-ent depuis 44. jusqu'à 61^d. de latitude et de longitude depuis 247 jusqu'à 296, Cette carte est une de quatre parties de la description general du Canada et des terres qui s'estendent depuis 27 degrez jusqu'à 61 de latitude septentrionale et depuis 246 degrez jusqu'à 338 de long. A Québec en la Nouvelle France le 10 Setptembre 1681, par Jean Louis Franquelin*. MSS. 1681. Paris: *Bibliothèque du service hydrographique de la marine*. 4040B, no. 2, Reproduction, APC H-3-900-1681.

Franquelin, Jean Baptiste Louis. *Carte de la Louisiane ou des voyages du Sr. De La Salle*, as *Franquelin's map of Louisiana*. 1684. S.l to 1901, 1896. Map. https://www.loc.gov/item/2001620469/.

Fredriksen, John C. *American Military Leaders from Colonial Times to the Present*. 2 vols. Santa Barbara, CA: ABC-CLIO, LLC, 1999.

Fredriksen, John C. *America's Military Adversaries: From Colonial Times to the Present*. Santa Barbara, CA: ABC-CLIO, LLC, 2001.

Frelinghuysen, Theodore. *Speech of Mr. Frelinghuysen, of New Jersey, in the United States Senate, April 6, 1830*, 3–28. Washington, D.C.: The National Journal, 1830.

French, Benjamin Franklin. *Historical Collections of Louisiana and Florida*. New York: J. Sabin & Sons, 1869.

Fry, Joseph Reece, and Robert T. Conrad. *A Life of Gen. Zachary Taylor, Comprising a Narrative of Events Connected with His Professional Career Derived from Public Documents and Private Correspondence by Joseph Reese Fry and Authentic Incidents of His Early Years from Materials Collected by Robert T. Conrad*. Philadelphia: Grigg, Elliott & Co., 1848.

Fuller, Hubert Bruce. *The Purchase of Florida: Its History and Diplomacy*. Cleveland, OH: The Burrows Brothers Company, 1906.

Fur, Gunlög. *A Nation of Women: Gender and Colonial Encounters among the Delaware Nations*. Philadelphia: University of Pennsylvania Press, 2009.

"Further Illustrations of General Jackson's True Character." *Truth's Advocate and Anti-Jackson Expositor* (October 1828): 389–92.

Gallatin, Albert. *Laws, Treaties, and Other Documents, Having Operation and Respect to the Public Lands, Collected and Published pursuant to an Act of Congress Passed April 27, 1810*. Washington, City: Roger C. Weightman, 1811.

Gallay, Alan. "African Americans." In *Colonial Wars of North America, 1512–1763: An Encyclopedia*, edited by Alan Gallay, 10–11. New York: Garland, 1996.

Galle, Jillian E. "Designing Women: Measuring Acquisition and Access at the Hermitage Plantation." In *Engendering African American Archaeology: A Southern Perspective*, edited by Jillian E. Galle and Amy L. Young, 39–72. Knoxville: University of Tennessee Press, 2004.

Gardiner, William Howard. "Article XII." *North American Review* 15 (July 1822): 250–82.

Gatschet, Albert Samuel. *A Migration Legend of the Creek Indians*. 2 vols. Philadelphia: D. G. Brinton, 1884.

Gaynwawpiahsika (Thomas Wildcat Alford). "Shawnee Story of Creation." *Indians at Work* 2, no. 18 (1935): 7–8.

"Gen. Rogers Clark to Gov. Harrison." *Calendar of Virginia State Papers and Other Manuscripts, 1652–1781*, vol. 3, 381. 1875–1893. Reprint. New York: Kraus, 1968.

"General Orders—No. 7." *Niles Weekly Register* 54, no. 1385 (April 14, 1838): 97.

"General Wayne's Orderly Book." In *Michigan Pioneer and Historical Society*, vol. 34, 341–660. Lansing, MI: Wynkoop Hallenbeck Crawford Company, 1905.

George R. "By the King, A Proclamation." London: Mark Baskett, Printer to the King's Most Excellent Majesty, 1763. At "Royal Proclamation, 1763." Indigenous Foundations, 2018. https://indigenousfoundations.arts.ubc.ca/royal_proclamation_1763/.

Giddings, Joshua R. *The Exiles of Florida, or, the Crimes Committed by Our Government against the Maroons Who Fled from South Carolina and Other Slave States, Seeking Protection under Spanish Law*. Columbus, OH: Follett, Foster and Co., 1858.

Gifford, C. H. *History of the Wars Occasioned by the French Revolution, from the Commencement of Hostilities in 1792, to the end of the Year 1816*. 2 vols. London: W. Lewis, 1817.

Gikandi, Simon. *Slavery and the Culture of Taste*. Princeton, NJ: University of Princeton Press, 2011.

Gilbert, Alan. *Black Patriots and Loyalists: Fighting for Emancipation in the War for Independence*. Chicago: University of Chicago Press, 2012.

Gilbert, Ed, and Catherine Gilbert. *Cowpens, 1781: The Turning Point of the American Revolution*. New York: Osprey Publishing, 2016.

Gilje, Paul A. *Free Trade and Sailors' Rights in the War of 1812*. New York: Cambridge University Press, 2013.

Gilpin, Alec R. *The War of 1812 in the Old Northwest*. East Lansing: Michigan State University, 2012.

Gipson, Henry Lawrence. *The Moravian Indian Mission on the White River: Diaries and Letters 5 May 1799 to 2 November 1806*. Translated from the original German manuscript by Harry E. Stocker, Herman T. Freuauff, and Samuel C. Zeller. Indianapolis: Indiana Historical Bureau, 1938.

Girty, Catherine (Mrs. Prideaux Girty). Draper Manuscripts, Reel S-17, 194.

Glasser, Bruno, Ludwig Haumaier, Georg Guggenberger, and Wolfgang Zech. "The 'Terra Preta' Phenomenon: A Model for Sustainable Agriculture in the Humid Tropics." *NaturWissenschaften* 88, no. 1 (January 2001): 37–41.

Goddard, William Giles. *An Address in Commemoration of the Death of William Henry Harrison, President of the United States, Delivered before the City Council and Citizens of Providence, on the National Fast, May 14, 1841*. Providence: Knowles & Voce, Printers, 1841.

Goebel, Dorothy Burne. *William Henry Harrison: A Political Biography*. Indianapolis: Historical Bureau of the Indiana Library and Historical Department, 1926.

Goguet, Antoine-Yves. *The Origin of Laws, Arts, and Sciences, and Their Progress among the Most Ancient Nations*. 3 vols. 1758. English translation and Reprint. New York: AMS Press, 1975.

Gómez-Díaz, Donato. "Cholera: First through Third Pandemics, 1816–1861." In *Encyclopedia of Pestilence, Pandemics, and Plaques*, edited by Joseph P. Byrne, vol. 1, 96–105. 2 vols. Westport, CT: Greenwood Press, 2008.

Goodrich, De Witt Clinton, and Charles Richard Tuttle. *An Illustrated History of the State of Indiana: Being a Full and Authentic Civil and Political History of the State from Its First Exploration down to 1875*. Indianapolis: Richard S. Peale & Co., 1875.

Gopnik, Adam. "Faces, Places, Spaces: The Renaissance of Geographic History." *New Yorker*, October 29 and November 5, 2012.

Gordon, Armistead Churchill. *Monument to John Tyler, Address Delivered in Hollywood Cemetery, at Richmond, Va., on October 12, 1915 at the Dedication of the Monument Erected by the Government to John Tyler, Tenth President of the United States*. Washington, D.C.: Government Printing Office, 1916.

Gorrell, James. "Lieut. James Gorrell's Journal." In *Collections of the State Historical Society of Wisconsin*, edited by Rueben Gold Thwaites, vol. 1, 24–48. Madison: State Historical Society of Wisconsin, 1903.

Graff, Henry F. *The Presidents: A Reference History*. New York: Macmillan Library References, USA, 1997.

Graham, Thomas John. *Modern Domestic Medicine, or a Popular Treatise Illustrating the Character, Symptoms, Causes, Distinction, and Correct Treatment, of All Diseases Incident to the Human Frame; Embracing All the Modern Improvements in Medicine, with the Opinions of the Most Distinguished Physicians*. London: Simpkin and Marshall, 1827.

Grassino, Sandie, and Art Schuermann. *Jefferson Barracks*. Images of American Series. Charleston, SC: Arcadia Publishing, 2011.

Greeley, Horace, John F. Cleveland, and John Fitch. *A Political Text-Book for 1860, Comprising a Brief View of Presidential Nominations and Elections: Including All the National Platforms Ever Yet Adopted; Also, a History of the Struggle Respecting Slavery in the Territories, and of the Actions of Congress as to the Freedom of the Public Lands, with the Most Notable Speeches and Letters of Messrs. Lincoln, Douglas, Bell, Cass, Steward, Everett, Breckenridge, H. V. Johnson, Etc. Etc., Touching the Questions of the*

Day; And Returns of All Presidential Elections since 1836. New York: Published by the Tribune Association, 1860.

Green, James Albert. *William Henry Harrison, His Life and Times.* Richmond, VA: Garrett & Massie, Inc., 1941.

Greene, George E. *History of Old Vincennes and Knox County, Indiana, Volumes 1 and 2.* Chicago: S. J. Clarke Publishing Company, 1911.

Gregg, Josiah. *Commerce of the Prairies: Or, The Journal of a Santa Fé Trader, during Eight Expeditions across the Great Western Prairies, and a Residence of Nearly Nine Years in Northern Mexico.* New York: H.G. Langley, 1844.

Gregory, Ben Thomas. *A Gregory Colonial Family.* Pensacola, FL: New South Press, 1986.

Grenke, Arthur. *God, Greed, and Genocide: The Holocaust through the Centuries.* Washington, D.C.: New Academia Publishing, 2005.

Gresham, Matilda. *Life of Walter Quintin Gresham, 1832–1895.* 2 vols. Chicago: Rand McNally & Company, 1917.

Greve, Charles Theodore. *Centennial History of Cincinnati and Representative Citizens.* 2 vols. Chicago: Biographical Publishing Company, 1904.

Griffin, James Bennett. "Culture Periods in Eastern United States Archaeology." In *Archaeology of Eastern United States*, edited by James Bennett Griffin, 352–64. Chicago: University of Chicago Press, 1952.

Griffin, James Bennett. *The Fort Ancient Aspect.* University of Michigan Anthropological Papers No. 28. Ann Arbor, MI: Museum of Anthropology, 1943.

Griffin, James Bennett. "Fort Ancient Has No Class: The Absence of an Elite Group in Mississippian Societies in the Central Ohio Valley." *Archaeological Papers of the American Anthropological Association* 3, no. 1 (June 28, 2008): 53–59.

Griffin, John W. "The Addison Blockhouse." *Florida Historical Quarterly* 30, no. 3 (January 1952): 276–93.

Grignon, Augustin. "Seventy-Two Years' Recollections of Wisconsin." In *Collections of the State Historical Society of Wisconsin*, edited by Lyman Draper, vol. 3, 197–295. Madison: State Historical Society of Wisconsin, 1904.

Grinde, Donald A., Jr., and Bruce Elliott Johansen. *Exemplar of Liberty: Native American and the Evolution of Democracy.* Los Angeles: American Indian Studies Center, UCLA, 1990.

Grinnell, George Bird. *The Cheyenne Indians: War, Ceremonies, and Religion.* 2 vols. New York: New Haven Press, 1924.

Groneman, William, III. *David Crockett: Hero of the Common Man.* New York: Forge Books, 2005.

Groover, Mary-Agnes Brown. "Pilgrim Ancestors of Revolutionary Soldiers, No. 7: The Taylor Family of Virginia." *Mayflower Quarterly* (May 1978): 39–44.

Gue, Benjamin F. *History of Iowa, from the Earliest Times to the Beginning of the Twentieth Century.* 4 vols. New York: The Century History Company, 1903.

Gunderson, Robert G. "William Henry Harrison: Apprentice in Arms." *Northwest Ohio Quarterly* 65, no. 1 (Winter 1993): 3–29.

Haas, Mary R., and James H. Hill. *Creek (Muskogee) Texts.* Translated and edited by Jack B. Martin, Margaret McKane Mauldin, and Juanita McGirt. Oakland: University of California Press, 2015.

Halbert, Henry S., and Timothy H. Ball. *The Creek War of 1813 and 1814.* Chicago: Donohue & Henneberry, 1895.

Haldiman, Frederick. "The Haldiman Papers." In *Collections and Researches Made by the Pioneer and Historical Society of the State of Michigan*, vol. 10, 210–672. Lansing, MI: Thorp & Godfrey, State Printers and Binders, 1888.

Hall, James. "The Indian Hater." In *Stories of the Early American West*, edited by Peter Bischoff, 63–73. *Arbeiten zur Amerikanistik*. Band 3. 1829. Essen: *Verlag Die Blaue Eule*, 1989.

Hall, James. *Memoir of the Public Services of William Henry Harrison, of Ohio*. Philadelphia: Key & Biddle, 1836.

Hall, John William. "Friends Like These: The United States' Indian Allies in the Black Hawk War." Diss., University of North Carolina, Chapel Hill, NC, 2007.

Halsey, John R. *Miskwabik—Red Metal: The Roles Played by Michigan's Copper in Prehistoric North America*. Eagle Harbor, MI: Keweenaw County Historical Society, 1992.

Hamilton, Holman. *Prologue to Conflict: The Crisis and Compromise of 1850*. 1964. Lexington: The University Press of Kentucky, 2005.

Hamilton, Holman. *Three Presidents—Lincoln, Taylor, Davis*. Lexington: University of Kentucky Press, 1978.

Hamilton, Holman. "Zachary Taylor and Minnesota." *Minnesota History* 30, no. 2 (June 1949): 97–110.

Hamilton, Holman. *Zachary Taylor: Soldier of the Republic*. 1st ed. New York: Bobbs-Merrill Company, 1941.

Hamilton, Peter J. "Indian Trails and Early Roads." In Alabama Historical Society's *Report of the Alabama History Commission to the Governor of Alabama, December 1, 1900*, edited by Thomas M. Owen, vol. 1, 422–29. *Publications of the Alabama Historical Society, Miscellaneous*. Montgomery, AL: Brown Printing Co., 1901.

Hammond, Charles. "Jackson and Burr." *Truth's Advocate and Anti-Jackson Expositor* (June 1828): 218–23.

Hammond, Charles. "Life of General Jackson." *Truth's Advocate and Anti-Jackson Expositor* (February 1828): 41–49.

Hammond, Charles. "Six Militiamen." *Truth's Advocate and Anti-Jackson Expositor* (April 1828): 127–42.

Hannings, Bud. *Forts of the United States: An Historical Dictionary, 16th through 19th Centuries*. Jefferson, NC: McFarland & Company, Inc., Publishers, 2006.

Hannings, Bud. *The War of 1812: A Complete Chronology with Biographies of 63 General Officers*. Jefferson, NC: McFarland & Co., 2012.

Hardin, Benjamin. *Speech of Mr. Hardin of Kentucky, on Mr. Adams's Resolutions, concerning the Loss of the Fortification Bill in the Last Session, Delivered in the House of Representatives on Jan. 28, 1836*. Washington, D.C.: National Intelligencer Office, 1836.

Hardman, Clark, Jr., and Marjorie H. Hardman. "The Great Serpent and the Sun." *Ohio Archaeologist* 37, no. 3 (1987): 34–40.

Hardy, Stella Pickett. *Colonial Families of the Southern States of America*. New York: Tobias A. Wright, 1911.

Harmon, Alexandra. *Rich Indians: Native People and the Problem of Wealth in American History*. Chapel Hill: University of North Carolina Press, 2010.

Harmon, Stanley M. *Irrepressible Conflict: The Cause of the American Civil War, and the Sad, Tragic Story of It Resulting in the Deaths of So Many*. Bloomington, IN: AuthorHouse, LLC, 2014.

Harrell, Kevin. "Federal Road in Alabama." *Encyclopedia of Alabama*. Posted December 22, 2010. Accessed September 14, 2018. http://www.encyclopediaofalabama.org/article/h-2999.

Harrington, James. *Oceana and Other Works of James Harrington, Esq*. 3rd ed. London: A. Millar, 1737.

The Harrison Log Cabin Song Book of 1840. Columbus, OH: A. H. Smythe, 1888.

Harrison, J. Scott. *Pioneer Life at South Bend: An Address by Hon. J. Scott Harrison Delivered before the Whitewater and Miami Valley Pioneer Association at Cleves, Ohio, Sept. 8, 1866.* Pamphlet. Cincinnati: Robert Clarke & Company, 1867.

Harrison, Simon. *Dark Trophies: Hunting and the Enemy Body in Modern War.* New York: Berghahn Books, 2012.

Harrison, William Henry. *An Address Delivered before the Hamilton County Agricultural Society, at Their Annual Exhibition, Held on the 15th and 16th of June, 1831.* Cincinnati: The Hamilton County Agricultural Society, 1831.

Harrison, William Henry. Letter of January 24, 1817. "William Henry Harrison to James Findlay." *Quarterly Publication of the Historical and Philosophical Society of Ohio* 2, no. 3 (July–September 1907): 104–7.

Harrison, William Henry. Letter of July 20, 1939. "William Henry Harrison to Erastus Brooks." In *Manuscripts Collection.* New-York Historical Society.

Harrison, William Henry. "Selections from the Torrence Papers, IV: The Political and Personal Career of William Henry Harrison from 1830 to 1841, as Illustrated by the Findlay Letters." *Quarterly Publication of the Historical Society of Ohio* 3, no. 3 (July–September 1908): 66–102.

Harvey, Paul. *Christianity and Race in the American South: A History.* Chicago: University of Chicago Press, 2016.

Hauser, David R. *The Only True America: Following the Trail of Lewis and Clark.* New York: Writer's Showcase, 2000.

Hawkins, Benjamin. *The Collected Works of Benjamin Hawkins, 1796–1810.* Edited by Thomas Foster. Tuscaloosa: The University of Alabama Press, 2003.

Hawkins, Benjamin. "Letters of Benjamin Hawkins, 1796–1806." In *Collections of the Georgia Historical Association,* vol. 9. Savannah: Georgia Historical Society, 1916.

Haywood, John. *The Natural and Aboriginal History of Tennessee, up to the First Settlements Therein by the White People in the Year 1768.* Nashville, TN: George Wilson, 1832.

Heath, William. *William Wells and the Struggle for the Old Northwest.* Norman: University of Oklahoma Press, 2015.

Hebberd, Stephen Southric. *History of Wisconsin under the Dominion of France.* Madison, WI: Midland Publishing Co., 1890.

Heckewelder, John. *History, Manners, and Customs of the Indian Nations Who Once Inhabited Pennsylvania and the Neighboring States.* The First American Frontier Series. 1820. 1876. Reprint. New York: Arno Press and *The New York Times,* 1976.

Heckewelder, John. *A Narrative of the Mission of the United Brethren among the Delaware and Mohegan Indians from Its Commencement, in the Year 1740, to the Close of the Year 1808.* 1820. Reprint. New York: Arno Press, 1971.

Heckewelder, John. *Thirty Thousand Miles with John Heckewelder.* Edited by Paul A. W. Wallace. Pittsburgh: University of Pittsburgh Press, 1958.

Heim, Joe. "Recounting a Day of Rage, Hate, Violence and Death." *Washington Post,* August 14, 2017.

Heitman, Francis Bernard. *Historical Register and Dictionary of the United States Army,* vol. 1. Washington, D.C.: Government Printing Office, 1903.

Heitman, Francis Bernard. *Historical Register of the United States Army, from Its Organization, September 29, 1789, to September 29, 1889.* Washington, D.C.: National Tribune, 1890.

Henri, Florette. *The Southern Indians and Benjamin Hawkins, 1796–1816.* Norman: University of Oklahoma Press, 1986.

Henry, Alexander. *Travels and Adventures in Canada and the Indian Territories, between the Years 1760 and 1776.* New York: I. Riley, 1809.

Herring, George C. *From Colony to Superpower: U.S. Foreign Relations since 1776*. New York: Oxford University Press, 2008.

Hess, Stephen. "William Henry Harrison." In *America's Political Dynasties: From Adams to Clinton*, 223–47. Washington, D.C.: Brookings Institution Press, 2016.

Hewitt, John Napoleon Brinton. "Ethnological Studies among the Iroquois Indians." *Smithsonian Miscellaneous Collections* 78 (1927): 237–47.

Hewitt, John Napoleon Brinton. "North America." *American Anthropologist*, n.s., 19 (1917): 429–38.

Hewitt, John Napoleon Brinton. *Notes on the Creek Indians*. Anthropological Papers No. 10. Smithsonian Institution. Bureau of American Ethnology. Washington, D.C.: Government Printing Office, 1939.

Hewitt, John Napoleon Brinton. "*Some Esoteric Aspects* of the League of the Iroquois." *Proceedings of the International Congress of Americanists* 19 (1915): 322–26.

High, Ellesa Clay. "West Virginia." In *Native America: A State-by-State Historical Encyclopedia*, edited by Daniel S. Murphree, vol. 3, 1219–46. 3 vols. Santa Barbara, CA: Greenwood, an Imprint of ABC-CLIO, LLC, 2012.

Hildreth, Richard. *The People's Presidential Candidate, or, The Life of William Henry Harrison, of Ohio*. Boston: Weeks, Jordan and Co., 1840.

Hirschfeld, Fritz. *George Washington and Slavery: A Documentary Portrayal*. Columbia: University of Missouri Press, 1997.

Hively, Ray, and Robert Horn. "Geometry and Astronomy in Prehistoric Ohio." *Archaeoastronomy* 4 (1982): 1–20.

Hively, Ray, and Robert Horn. "Hopewellian Geometry and Astronomy at High Bank." *Archaeoastronomy* 7 (1984): 85–100.

Hoagland, William. *The Whiskey Rebellion: George Washington, Alexander Hamilton, and the Rebels Who Challenged America's Newfound Sovereignty*. New York: Simon & Schuster Paperbacks, 2006.

Hodge, Frederick Webb. *Handbook of American Indians North of Mexico*. 2 vols. Smithsonian Institution, Bulletin 30. Washington, D.C.: Government Printing Office, 1907–1910.

Hodge, J. P. *Vincennes in Picture and Story: History of the Old Town, Appearance of the New, including George Rogers Clark's Own Account of the Capture of the Village (Revolutionary War)*. Bedford, MA: Appleton, 1902.

Holford, Castello N. *History of Grant County, Wisconsin, Including Its Civil, Political, Geological, Mineralogical, Archaeological and Military History, and a History of the Several Towns*. Lancaster, WI: Teller Print, 1900.

Houck, Louis. *The Spanish Régime in Missouri: A Collection of Papers and Documents Relating to Upper Louisiana Principally within the Present Limits of Missouri during the Dominion of Spain, from the Archives of the Indies at Seville, Etc., Translated from the Original Spanish into English, and Including Also Some Papers Concerning the Supposed Grant to Colonel George Morgan at the Mouth of the Ohio, Found in the Congressional Library*. 2 vols. Chicago: R. R. Donnelley & Sons Company, 1909.

Hough, Susan Elizabeth. *Richter's Scale: The Measure of an Earthquake, Measure of a Man*. Princeton, NJ: Princeton University Press, 2007.

Howells, William D. "Gnadenhütten." In *Three Villages*, 117–98. Boston: James R. Osgood and Company, 1884.

Hudson, Angela Puelley. *Creek Paths and Federal Roads: Indians, Settlers, and Slaves and the Making of the American South*. Chapel Hill: University of North Carolina Press, 2010.

Hulbert, Archer Butler. *Historic Highways of America*. 16 vols. Cleveland, OH: The A. H. Clark Company, 1902–1905.

Hunter, John Dunn. *Memoirs of a Captivity among the Indians of North America, From Childhood to the Age of Nineteen, with Anecdotes Descriptive of Their Manners and Customs, to Which Is Added Some Account of the Soil, Climate, and Vegetable Productions of the Territory Westward of the Mississippi.* London: Longman, Hurst, Rees, Orme, and Brown, 1823.

Hupka, Ralph B., Zbigniew Zaleski, Jurgen Otto, Lucy Reidl, and Nadia V. Tarabrina. "The Colors of Anger, Envy, Fear, and Jealousy." *Journal of Cross-Cultural Psychology* 28, no. 2 (March 1997), 156–71.

"Huron." *Niles Weekly Register* 35, no. 906 (January 24, 1829): 346.

Hurt, R. Douglas. *The Ohio Frontier: The Crucible of the Old Northwest, 1720–1830.* Bloomington: University of Indiana Press, 1996.

Huston, Reeve. *Land and Freedom: Rural Society, Popular Protest, and Party Politics in Antebellum New York.* New York: Oxford University Press, 2000.

Illinois State Historical Library. *Collections of the Illinois State Historical Library.* Vol. 19, *George Rogers Clark Papers, 1781–1784,* vol. 2. Springfield: Illinois State Historical Library, 1926.

"Important from Florida." *Niles Weekly Register* 53, no. 1372 (January 13, 1838): 305.

Indian Claims Commission and Native American Rights Funds. *Indian Claims Commission Decisions,* vol. 27. Boulder, CO: Native American Rights Fund, 1973.

Indian Territory. *Laws of the Indiana Territory, 1809–1816. Indiana Historical Collections,* vol. 20. Indianapolis: Indiana Historical Bureau, 1934.

"Indian War." *Niles Weekly Register* 42, no. 1086 (July 14, 1832): 353.

"Indian War Over." *Niles Weekly Register* 43, no. 1097 (September 29, 1832): 78–79.

Indiana Territory. *Laws of the Indiana Territory, Comprising Those Acts Formerly in Force, and as Revised by Messrs. John Rice Jones, and John Johnson and Passed (after Amendments) by the Legislature; and the Original Acts Passed at the First Session of the Second General Assembly of the Said Territory.* Vincennes, IN: Stout & Smoot, 1807.

Irwin, Lee. *Coming Down from Above: Prophecy, Resistance, and Renewal in Native American Religions.* Norman: University of Oklahoma Press, 2008.

Ivers, Larry E. *This Torrent of Indians: War on the Southern Frontier, 1715–1728.* Columbia: University of South Carolina Press, 2016.

Jablow, Joseph. *Indians of Illinois and Indiana: Illinois, Kickapoo, and Potawatomi Indians.* American Indian Ethnohistory: North Central and Northeastern Indians: A Garland Series. Edited by David Agee Horr. New York: Garland Publishing, Inc., 1974.

"Jackson and Burr." *Truth's Advocate and Anti-Jackson Expositor,* 203–5. June 1828.

Jackson, Andrew. *Legal Papers of Andrew Jackson.* Edited by James W. Ely and Theodore Brown Jr. Knoxville: University of Tennessee Press, 1987.

Jackson, Andrew. "The Massacre at the Mouth of Duck." Account dated July 8, 1812. *Clarion* section in *Democratic Clarion & Tennessee Gazette* 5, no. 286 (July 7, 1812).

Jackson, Andrew. *Narrative and Writings of Andrew Jackson, of Kentucky; Containing an Account of His Birth, and Twenty-Six Years of His Life While a Slave; His Escape; Five Years of Freedom, Together with Anecdotes Relating to Slavery; Journal of One Year's Travels; Sketches, etc. Narrated by Himself; Written by a Friend.* Syracuse, NY: Daily and Weekly Star Office, 1847.

Jackson, Donald. "Old Fort Madison, 1808–1813." *Palimpsest* 47, no. 1 (1966): 1–62.

Jackson, Isaac Rand. *General William Henry Harrison, Candidate for the President of the United States.* Baltimore: Samuel Sands, 1840.

Jackson, Isaac Rand. *The Life of Major-General William Henry Harrison: Comprising a Brief Account of His Important Civil and Military Services, and an Accurate Description of the Council at Vincennes with Tecumseh, as Well as the Victories of Tippecanoe, Fort Meigs, and the Thames.* Philadelphia: Grigg & Elliot, 1840.

Jacobs, Harriet A. *Incidents in the Life of a Slave Girl, Written by Herself.* Edited by Jean F. Yellin. 1861. Cambridge: Harvard University Press, 1987.

Jacobs, James Ripley. *Tarnished Warrior: Major-General James Wilkinson.* New York: The Macmillan Company, 1938.

Jay, John, Landa M. Freeman, Sarah Livingston Jay, Louise V. North, and Janet M. Wedge. *Selected Letters of John Jay and Sarah Livingston Jay: Correspondence by or to the First Chief Justice of the United States and His Wife.* Jefferson, NC: McFarland & Co., 2010.

Jaynes, Gerald David. *Encyclopedia of African American Society.* 2 vols. London: Sage, 2005.

Jefferson, Thomas. *Notes on the State of Virginia.* 1785. Boston: Lilly and Wait, 1832.

Jefferson, Thomas. *The Writings of Thomas Jefferson.* Edited by Albert Ellery Bergh. 20 vols. in 10. Washington, D.C.: Thomas Jefferson Memorial Association of the United States, 1907.

Jennings, Jonathan. *Unedited Letters of Jonathan Jennings.* Annot. Dorothy Riker. Indiana Historical Society Publications, vol. 10, no. 4. Indianapolis: Indiana Historical Society Publications, 1932.

Jillson, Willard Rouse. *Old Kentucky Entries and Deeds: A Complete Index to All of the Earliest Land Entries, Military Warrants, Deeds and Wills of the Commonwealth of Kentucky.* Louisville, KY: The Standard Printing Company, 1926.

Johansen, Bruce Elliot. " 'By Your Observing the Methods Our Wise Forefathers Have Taken, You Will Acquire Fresh Strength and Power': Closing Speech of Canassatego, July 4, 1744, Lancaster Treaty." In *Native American Speakers of the Eastern Woodlands: Selected Speeches and Critical Analyses*, edited by Barbara A. Mann, 83–105. Westport, CT: Greenwood Press, 2001.

Johansen, Bruce Elliot. *Forgotten Founders: Benjamin Franklin, the Iroquois, and the Rationale for the American Revolution.* Ipswich, MA: Gambit Inc., 1982.

Johansen, Bruce Elliot. "Review: State Propaganda in China's Entertainment Industry." *Journalism & Mass Communication Quarterly*, March 26, 2018. Accessed July 20, 2018. http://journals.sagepub.com/doi/full/10.1177/1077699018758725.

Johansen, Bruce Elliott, and Barbara Alice Mann, eds. *Encyclopedia of the Haudeonsaunee (Iroquois League).* Westport, CT: Greenwood Press, 2000.

John Cleves Symmes. "Letter of John Cleves Symmes to Elias Boudinot of January 12 and 15, 1792." *The Quarterly Publication of the Historical and Philosophical Society of Ohio* 5, no. 3 (1910): 95.

John Forbes and Company. "John Forbes & Co., Successors to Panton, Leslie & Co., vs. The Chickasaw Nation: A Journal of an Indian Talk, July, 1805." *Florida Historical Quarterly* 8, no. 3 (January 1930): 131–42.

The John M. Gresham Company. *Biographical Cyclopedia of the Commonwealth of Kentucky, Embracing Biographies of Many of the Prominent Men and Families of the State.* Chicago: John M. Gresham Company, 1896.

Johnson, Andrew. *Life, Speeches, and Services of Andrew Johnson, Seventeenth President of the United States.* Philadelphia: T. B. Peterson & Brothers, 1865.

Johnson, David R., and Lynette Schneider. *Fort Amanda, 1790–1814: A Historical Redress.* Wapakoneta, OH: David R. Johnson, 2017.

Johnson, Willis Fletcher. *Life of Wm. Tecumseh Sherman, Late Retired General, U.S.A.: A Graphic History of His Career in War and Peace; His Romantic Youth, His Stern and Patriotic Manhood, His Calm and Beautiful Old Age, a Marvelous March from the Mountain of Time to the Sea of Eternity.* Philadelphia: Edgewood Publishing Company, 1891.

Jones, David. *A Journal of Two Visits Made to Some Nations of Indians on the West Side of the River Ohio in 1772 and 1773.* Burlington, VT: Isaac Collins, 1774.

Jordan, Ryan P. *Church, State, and Race: The Discourse of American Religious Liberty, 1750–1900.* Lanham, MD: University Press of America, Inc., 2012.

Jortner, Adam. *Gods of Prophetstown: The Battle of Tippecanoe and the Holy War for the American Frontier.* New York: Oxford University Press, 2012.

Juge, M. A. *The American Planter, Or The Bound Labor Interest in the United States.* New York: Long and Brother, 1854.

Jung, Patrick J. *The Black Hawk War of 1832.* Norman: University of Oklahoma Press, 2008.

Jung, Patrick J. "Lonely Sentinel: A Military History of Fort Madison, 1808–1813." *Annals of Iowa* 75 (Summer 2016): 201–33.

Jung, Patrick J. "Toward the Black Hawk War: The Sauk and Fox Indians and the War of 1812." *Michigan Historical Review* 38, no. 1, Special Issue: The War of 1812 (Spring 2012): 27–52.

Kappler, Charles Joseph. *Indian Affairs: Laws and Treaties.* 2 vols. Washington, D.C.: Government Printing Office, 1904.

Karr, Jean Baptiste Alphonse. *Les guêpes.* 6th ed. New ed. 1839. Paris: Michel Lévy frères, 1867.

Karsner, David. *Andrew Jackson: The Gentle Savage.* New York: Bretano's, 1929.

Keating, Ann Durkin. *Rising up from Indian Country: The Battle of Fort Dearborn and the Birth of Chicago.* Chicago: University of Chicago Press, 2012.

Keiger, Dale. "What Killed Bolívar?" *John Hopkins Magazine,* September 3, 2010. Accessed February 19, 2018. http://archive.magazine.jhu.edu/2010/09/what-killed-bolivar/.

Kellogg, Louise Phelps. "The Fox Indians during the French Regime." In *Proceedings of the State Historical Society of Wisconsin at Its Fifty-Fifth Annual Meeting Held November 7, 1907,* 142–88. Madison: State Historical Society of Wisconsin, 1908.

Kellogg, Louise Phelps, ed. *Frontier Retreat on the Upper Ohio, 1779–1781.* 1912. Millwood, NY: Kraus Reprint, 1977.

Kelton, Dwight H. "Ancient Names of Rivers, Lakes, etc." In *Annals of Ft. Mackinac,* 117–21. Island Edition. Detroit: *Detroit Free Press,* 1884.

Kenny, James. "Journal of James Kenny, 1761–1763." Part I. Edited by John W. Jordan. *Pennsylvania Magazine of History and Biography* 37, no. 1 (1913): 1–47.

King, Charles C., Dan Atzenhoefer, and Ohio Department of Natural Resources. *A Legacy of Stewardship: The Ohio Department of Natural Resources, 1949–1989.* Columbus: Ohio Department of Natural Resources, 1990.

Kingston, John T. "Early Western Days." In *Collections of the State Historical Society of Wisconsin,* vol. 7, 297–344. Madison: State Historical Society of Wisconsin, 1903.

Kline, Mary Jo, ed. *The Political Correspondence and Public Papers of Aaron Burr.* 2 vols. Princeton, NJ: Princeton University Press, 1983.

Krzywicki, Ludwik. *Primitive Society and Its Vital Statistics.* London: Macmillan, 1934.

Kulikoff, Allan. *From British Peasants to Colonial American Farmers.* Chapel Hill: University of North Carolina Press, 2000.

Lafitau, Joseph François. *Customs of the American Indians Compared with the Customs of Primitive Times.* Translated and edited by William N. Fenton and Elizabeth L. Moore. 2 vols. 1724. Toronto: The Champlain Society, 1974.

Lakomäki, Sami. *Gathering Together: The Shawnee People through Diaspora and Nationhood, 1600–1870.* New Haven, CT: Princeton University Press, 2014.

Landers, Jane. "Africans in the Spanish Colonies." *Historical Archaeology* 31, no. 1 (1997): 84–103.

Landers, Jane. *Black Society in Spanish Florida*. Urbana: University of Illinois Press, 1999.

Lanman, Charles. *Biographical Annals of the Civil Government of the United States: During Its First Century*. Washington, D.C.: James Anglim Publisher, 1876.

Law, John. *The Colonial History of Vincennes, under the French, British and American Governments, from Its First Settlement down to the Territorial Administration of General William Henry Harrison, Being an Address Delivered before the Vincennes Historical and Antiquarian Society, February 22nd, 1839*. Vincennes, IN: Harvey, Mason & Co., 1858.

Ledbetter, Mark David. *America's Forgotten History: Part Two—Rupture*. Morrisville, NC: Lulu Enterprises, Inc., 2007.

Lehman, Christopher P. *Slavery in the Upper Mississippi Valley, 1787–1865: A History of Human Bondage in Illinois, Iowa, Minnesota and Wisconsin*. Jefferson, NC: MacFarland & Company, Inc., Publishers, 2011.

"Letter from Fort Howard." *Niles Weekly Register* 42, no. 1090 (August 11, 1832): 424.

"Letter of William Henry Harrison to Harmar Denny of Pittsburgh." *Western Pennsylvania Historical Magazine* 1, no. 3 (March 1918): 144–51.

Levene, Mark. *The Rise of the West and the Coming of Genocide, II: Genocide in the Age of the Nation State*. New York: Palgrave Macmillan, 2005.

Lewis, James E., Jr. *The Burr Conspiracy: Uncovering the Story of an Early American Crisis*. Princeton, NJ: Princeton University Press, 2017.

Lewis, Jan, and Peter S. Onuf. "Introduction." In *Sally Hemings & Thomas Jefferson: History, Memory, and Civic Culture*, edited by Jan Lewis and Peter S. Onuf, 1–16. Charlottesville: University of Virginia Press, 1999.

Lewis, Simon L., and Mark A. Maslin. "Defining the Anthropocene." *Nature* 519 (March 12, 2015): 171–80.

Libby, Dorothy. "An Anthropological Report on the Piankeshaw Indians." Indian Claims Commission. Consolidated Docket, no. 315. In *Piankashaw and Kaskaskia Indians*, 27–341. New York: Garland Publishing, Inc., 1974.

Linneaus, Carolus. *Systema naturae per regna tria naturae, secundum classes, ordines, genera, species cum characteribus differentiis, synonimis, locis*. 10th ed. 3 vols. Holmaie: Laurentii Salvii, 1758.

"Literature & Principles." *Truth's Advocate and Anti-Jackson Expositor* (June 1828): 201–3.

Little, Lucius P. *Ben Hardin: His Times and Contemporaries*. Louisville, KY: Courier-Journal Job Printing Company, 1887.

Lofft, Capel. "Somerset Arguments." 1 Lofft 1, 98 ER 499.

Lossing, Benson John. *An Outline History of the United States, for Public and Other Schools, from the Earliest Period to the Present Time*. New York: Sheldon & Company, 1876.

Lossing, Benson John. *The Pictorial Field-book of the War of 1812: Or, Illustrations, by Pen and Pencil, of the History, Biography, Scenery, Relics, and Traditions of the Last War for American Independence*. New York: Harper & Brothers, 1869.

Louis, Marie-Victoire. *Le droit de cuissage: France, 1860–1930*. Paris: Editions de l'Atelier/ Editions ouvrières, 1994.

Loveman, Brian. *No Higher Law: American Foreign Policy and the Western Hemisphere since 1776*. University of North Carolina Press, 2010.

Lowther, Minnie Kendall. *History of Ritchie County, with Biographical Sketches of Its Pioneers and Their Ancestors, and with Interesting Reminiscences of Revolutionary and Indian Times*. Wheeling, WV: Wheeling News Litho. Co., 1911.

Lubbock, John. *Prehistoric Times as Illustrated by Ancient Remains and the Manners and Customs of Modern Savages*. 1865. 1913. Reprint. New York: Humanities Press, 1969.

M'Lean, John. *Sketch of Rev. Philip Gatch*. Cincinnati: Swormstedt & Poe, 1854.

MacLean, John Patterson. "Shaker Mission to the Shawnee Indians." In *Ohio Archaeological and Historical Publications*, vol. 9, 215–29. Columbus: Fred J. Heer, 1903.

Madison, James. *The Writings of James Madison, Comprising His Public Papers and His Private Correspondence*. Edited by Gaillard Hunt. 9 vols. New York: G. P. Putnam's Sons, 1900–1910.

Madison, James, William T. Hutchinson, William M. E. Rachal, Robert A. Rutland, and University of Virginia Press. *The Papers of James Madison*, vol. 7. Chicago: University of Chicago Press, 1962–1991.

Mahan, Bruce Ellis. *Old Fort Crawford and the Frontier*. Iowa City: State Historical Society of Iowa, 1926.

Mahon, John K. *History of the Second Seminole War, 1835–1842*. Gainesville: University of Florida Press, 1967.

Mahudel, Nicolas. *Dissertattion historique sur les monnoyes antiques d'Espagne*. Paris: Le Mercier, 1725.

Makataimeshekiakiak (Black Hawk). *Life of Black Hawk: Ma-ka-tai-me-she-kia-kiak*. Edited by Milo Milton Quaife. Chicago: Lakeside Press, 1916.

Makataimeshekiakiak (Black Hawk), and John Barton Patterson. *Life of Ma-ka-tai-me-she-kia-kiak, or Black Hawk*. Cincinnati: George Conclin, 1839.

Makwa, Ogimaa (Jerome Fontaine). "*gi-mi-ni-go-wi-ni-nan o-gi-ma-wi-win zhigo o-gi-ma-win* (The Gifts of Traditional Leadership and Governance)." Diss. Indigenous Studies, PhD Graduate Program, Trent University, Peterborough, Ontario, CA, 2013.

Mann, Barbara Alice. " 'Are You Delusional?' Kandiaronk on Christianity." In *Native American Speakers of the Eastern Woodlands*, edited by Barbara A. Mann, 35–81. Greenwood Publishing Group, 2001.

Mann, Barbara Alice. "Economics of the Haudenosaunee." In *Encyclopedia of Native American Economic History*, edited by Bruce Johansen, 120–34. Westport, CT: Greenwood Publishing Group, 1998.

Mann, Barbara Alice. "A Failure to Communicate: How Christian Missionary Assumptions Ignore Binary Patterns of Thinking within Native-American Communities." In *Remembering Jamestown: Hard Questions about Christian Mission*, edited by Amos Young and Barbara B. Zikmund, 29–48. Eugene, OR: Pickwick Publications, 2010.

Mann, Barbara Alice. "Foreword: 'And Then They Build Monuments to You'." In *Wielding Words like Weapons: Selected Essays in Indigenism, 1995–2005*, edited by Ward Churchill. Oakland, CA: PM Press, 2017.

Mann, Barbara Alice. "Fractal Massacres in the Old Northwest: The Example of the Miamis." *Journal of Genocide Research* Special Issue 15, no. 2 (2013): 167–82.

Mann, Barbara Alice. *George Washington's War on Native America*. Westport, CT: Praeger Press, 2005.

Mann, Barbara Alice. "The Greenville Treaty: Pen-and-Ink Witchcraft in the Struggle for the Old Northwest." In *Enduring Legacies: Native American Treaties and Contemporary Controversies*, edited by Bruce E. Johansen, 135–201. Westport, CT: Praeger, 2004.

Mann, Barbara Alice. " 'I Hope You Will Not Destroy *What* I Have Saved': Hopocan before the British Tribunal in Detroit, 1781." In *Native American Speakers of the Eastern*

Woodlands, edited by Barbara Alice Mann, 145–64. Greenwood Publishing Group, 2001.

Mann, Barbara Alice. *Iroquoian Women: The Gantowisas*. New York: Lang Publishing, 2000.

Mann, Barbara Alice. *Native Americans, Archaeologists, and the Mounds*. New York: Lang Publishing, 2003.

Mann, Barbara Alice. *Spirits of Blood, Spirits of Breath: The Twinned Cosmos of Indigenous America*. New York: Oxford University Press, 2016.

Mann, Barbara Alice. *The Tainted Gift: The Disease Method of Frontier Expansion*. Santa Barbara, CA: Praeger, 2009.

Mann, Barbara Alice. " 'Where Are Your Women?' Missing in Action." In *Unlearning the Language of Conquest: Scholars Expose Anti-Indianism in America*, 120–33. Austin: University of Texas Press, 2006.

Mann, Barbara Alice, and Donald A. Grinde Jr. " 'Now the Friar Is Dead': Sixteenth-Century Spanish Florida and the Guale Revolt." In *Native American Speakers of the Eastern Woodlands: Selected Speeches and Critical Analyses*, 1–33. Westport, CT: Greenwood Publishing Group, 2001.

Mann, Barbara Alice, and Jerry L. Fields. "A Sign in the Sky: Dating the League of the Haudenosaunee." *American Indian Culture and Research Journal* 21, no. 2 (August 1997): 105–63.

Maples, William R., and Michael Browning. *Dead Men Do Tell Tales: The Strange and Fascinating Cases of a Forensic Anthropologist*. New York: Doubleday, 1994.

Marsh, Cutting. "Documents Relating to the Stockbridge Mission, 1825–1848." In *Collections of the State Historical Society of Wisconsin*, edited by William Ward Wright and Reuben Gold Thwaites, vol. 15, 39–204. Madison: State Historical Society of Wisconsin, 1900.

Marshall, Humphrey. *The History of Kentucky, Exhibiting an Account of the Modern Discovery, Settlement, Progressive Improvement, Civil and Military Transactions, and the Present State of the Country*. 2 vols. Frankfort, KY: Geo. S. Robinson, Printer, 1824.

Martin, Joel W. *Sacred Revolt: The Muskogees' Struggle for a New World*. Boston: Beacon Press, 1991.

Masterson, William H. "Land Speculator of the West: The Role of William Blount." *East Tennessee Historical Society Publications* 27 (1955): 3–8.

Mathews, George. Letter of April 16, 1812. George Mathews to James Madison. *Founders Online*. National Archives. Last modified June 13, 2018. https://founders.archives.gov/documents/Madison/03-04-02-0341.

Matson, Nehemiah. *Memories of Shaubena: With Incidents Relating to Indian Wars and the Early Settlement of the West*. Chicago: Donnelley, Gassette & Loyd, Printers, 1880.

Matteson, Clark S. *The History of Wisconsin from Prehistoric to Present Periods: The Story of the State in Interspersed with Realistic and Romantic Events*. Milwaukee: Wisconsin Historical Publishing Company, 1893.

Mauelshagen, Carl, and Gerald H. Davis, eds. and trans. *Partners in the Lord's Work: The Diary of Two Moravian Missionaries in the Creek Indian Country, 1807–1813*. Research Paper No. 21. Atlanta: Georgia State College, 1969.

Mayor, Adrienne. *Fossil Legends of the First Americans*. Princeton, NJ: Princeton University Press, 2005.

McAfee, Robert Breckinridge. *History of the Late War in the Western Country*. 1816. Bedford, MA: Applewood Publishing, 1919.

McBride, James. "The James McBride Manuscripts: Selections Relating to the Miami University." In *Quarterly Publication of the Ohio Historical and Archaeological*

Society, edited by John Ewing Bradford, vol. 1, no. 4, 50–54. Cincinnati: Press of Jennings and Graham, 1909.

McCafferty, Michael. *Native American Place-Names of Indiana*. Chicago: University of Illinois Press, 2008.

McCauley, Clay. "The Seminole Indians of Florida." In *Fifth Annual Report of the Bureau of Ethnology to the Secretary of the Smithsonian Institution, 1883–'84*, edited by John Wesley Powell, 469–531. Washington, D.C.: Government Printing Office, 1887.

McCoy, Robert R., and Steven M. Fountain. *History of American Indians: Exploring Diverse Roots*. Santa Barbara, CA: Greenwood, an Imprint of ABC-CLIO, LLC, 2017.

McElroy, Robert. *Jefferson Davis: The Unreal and the Real*. 2 vols. New York: Harper & Brothers, 1937.

McElwain, Thomas. " 'Then I Thought I Must Kill, Too:' Logan's Lament, A 'Mingo' Perspective." In *Native American Speakers of the Eastern Woodlands: Selected Speeches and Critical Analyses*, edited by Barbara Alice Mann, 107–22. Westport, CT: Greenwood Press, 2001.

McGovern, Bernie. *Florida Almanac, 2007–2008*. Gretna, FL: Pelican Publishing, 2007.

McKee, Alexander. *Minutes of Debates in Council on the Banks of the Ottawa River (Commonly Called the Miamis of the Lake), November, 1791*. Philadelphia: William Young, Bookseller, 1792.

McMichael, Francis Andrew. *Atlantic Loyalties: Americans in Spanish West Florida, 1785–1810*. Athens: University of Georgia Press, 2008.

McNab, David T. " 'The Land Was to Remain Ours': The St. Anne Island Treaty of 1796 and Aboriginal Title and Rights in the Twenty-first Century." In *Native American Speakers of the Eastern Woodlands: Selected Speeches and Critical Analyses*, edited by Barbara Alice Mann, 229–50. Westwood, CT: Greenwood Press, 2001.

McReynolds, Edwin C. *The Seminoles*. Norman: University of Oklahoma Press, 1957.

Meacham, John. *American Lion: Andrew Jackson in the White House*. New York: Random House, 2008.

Meek, Basil. *Twentieth Century History of Sandusky County, Ohio: And Representative Citizens*. Chicago: Richmond-Arnold Publishing Co., 1909.

Melton, Alonza. *Celia, A Slave: A True Story of Violence and Retribution in Antebellum Missouri*. Athens: University of Georgia Press, 1991.

Melton, Buckner F., Jr. *Aaron Burr: Conspiracy to Treason*. Hoboken, NJ: John Wiley & Sons, 2001.

Melton, Buckner F., Jr. *The First Impeachment: The Constitution's Framers and the Case of Senator William Blount*. Macon, GA: Mercer University Press, 1999.

Melville, Herman. "The Metaphysics of Indian-Hating." In Herman Melville, *The Confidence Man: His Masquerade*, 201–12. London: Longman, Brown, Green, Longmans, & Roberts, 1857.

Mendoza, Patrick M., Ann Strange Owl-Raben, and Nico Strange Owl. *Four Great Rivers to Cross: Cheyenne History, Culture, and Traditions*. Englewood, CO: Teacher Ideas Press, 1998.

Meynard, Virginia G. *The Venturers: The Hampton, Harrison, and Earle Families of Virginia, South Carolina, and Texas*. Easley, SC: Southern Historical Press, 1981.

Middleton, Stephen. *The Black Laws: Race and the Legal Process in Early Ohio*. Athens: Ohio University Press, 2005.

Milfort, Louis (Jean-Antoine Le Clerc). *Memoirs, or a Quick Glance at My Various Travels and My Sojourn in the Creek Nation*. Translated and edited by Ben C. Gary. 1802. Kennesaw, GA: Continental Book Company, 1959.

Mill, James. *The History of British India.* 10 vols. 1817. London: James Madden and Co., 1858.

Miller, Jay. "The 1806 Purge among the Indiana Delaware: Sorcery, Gender, Boundaries, and Legitimacy." *Ethnohistory* 41, no. 2 (Spring 1994): 245–66.

Miller, Robert J. "The International Law of Colonialism: A Comparative Analysis." *Lewis & Clark Law Review* 15, no. 4 (2011): 847–922.

Miller, Robert J. *Native America, Discovered and Conquered: Thomas Jefferson, Lewis & Clark, and Manifest Destiny.* Westport, CT: Praeger, 2006.

Miller, Robert J. *Reservation "Capitalism:" Economic Development in Indian Country.* Santa Barbara, CA: Praeger, 2012.

Miller, Robert J. "Treaties between the Eastern Shawnee Tribe and the United States: Contracts between Sovereign Governments." In *The Eastern Shawnee Tribe of Oklahoma: Resilience through Adversity*, edited by Stephen Warren in Collaboration with the Eastern Shawnee Tribe of Oklahoma, 107–48. Norman: University of Oklahoma Press, 2017.

Miller, Robert J., Jacinta Ruru, Larissa Behrendt, and Tracey Lindberg. *Discovering Indigenous Lands: The Doctrine of Discovery in the English Colonies.* New York: Oxford University Press, 2010.

Monaco, Chris. "Fort Mitchell and the Settlement of the Alachua Country." *Florida Historical Quarterly* 79, no. 1 (Summer 2000): 1–25.

Monette, John Wesley. *History of the Discovery and the Settlement of the Valley of the Mississippi, by the Three Great European Powers, Spain, France, and Great Britain, and the Subsequent Occupation, Settlement and Extension of Civil Government by the United States until the Year 1846.* 2 vols. New York: Harper & Brothers Publishers, 1846.

Monsalve, José Dolores. *El ideal político del libertador Símon Bolívar*, vol. 2. Madrid: Editorial-América, 1916.

Montesquieu, Charles-Louis de Secondat, baron de La Brède et de. *Esprit des lois par Montesquieu, avec les notes de l'auteur et un choix des observations de Dupin, Crevier, Voltaire, Mably, La Harpe, Servan, etc.* 1748. Paris: Firmin Didot frères, 1862.

Montgomery, Henry. *The Life of Major General Zachary Taylor, Twelfth President of the United States.* Buffalo, NY: Derby & Hewson Publishers, 1847.

Mooney, James. "Myths of the Cherokee." In *Nineteenth Annual Report of the Bureau of American Ethnology, 1897–1898, Part 1*, 3–548. Washington, D.C.: Government Printing Office, 1900.

Mooney, James. "Shawnee." In *Handbook of the American Indians North of Mexico*, edited by Frederick Webb Hodge. 2 vols. Smithsonian Institution. Bureau of American Ethnology. Bulletin No. 30. Washington, D.C.: Government Printing Office, 1912.

Moreno de Angel, Pilar. *José María Córdova. Academia Colombiana de historia. Biblioteca de historia nacional*, vol. 137. Bogotá, Colombia: Editorial Kelly, 1977.

Morgan, Henry Lewis. *Ancient Society, or Researches in the Lines of Human Progress from Savagery through Barbarism to Civilization.* Chicago: Charles H. Kerr & Company, 1877.

Morris, Lewis, and Louise Phelps Kellogg. *Report of a Treaty with the Western Indians: Conducted at Pittsburgh September 12–October 21, 1775 and Now for the First Time Published.* Madison: Wisconsin Historical Society, 1908.

Morse, Jedidiah. *A Report to the Secretary of War of the United States on Indian Affairs, Comprising a Narrative of a Tour Performed in the Summer of 1820, under a*

Commission from the President of the United States, for the Purpose of Ascertaining, for the Use of the Government, the Actual State of the Indian Tribes in Our Country. New Haven, CT: S. Converse, 1822.

Morton, Samuel George. *Crania Americana, or a Comparative View of the Skulls of the Various Aboriginal Nations of North and South America, to Which Is Prefixed an Essay on the Varieties of the Human Species.* Philadelphia: J. Dobson, 1839.

Moser, Harold D., Sharon Macpherson, David R. Hoth, and George H. Hoemann, eds. *The Papers of Andrew Jackson.* 10 vols. Knoxville: The University of Tennessee Press, 1980–2013.

Moses, Charlie. "Charlie Moses, Brookhaven, Mississippi." In *Slave Narratives from the Federal Writers' Project, 1936–1938: Mississippi.* Library of Congress. 1972. Reprint. Bedford, MA: Applewood Books, 2005.

Mulroy, Kevin. *The Seminole Freedmen: A History.* Norman: University of Oklahoma Press, 2007.

Nasatir, Abraham Phineas, ed. *Before Lewis and Clark: Documents Illustrating the History of the Missouri, 1785–1804.* Norman: University of Oklahoma Press, 2002.

National Cyclopaedia of American Biography, Being the History of the United States as Illustrated in the Lives of the Founders, Builders, and Defenders of the Republic, and of the Men and Women Who Are Doing the Work and Moulding the Thought of the Present Time, vol. 11. New York: James T. White & Company, 1901.

Nawahtahtha ("George Bluejacket"). "A Story of the Shawanoes." MSS. October 29, 1839. Translated and edited by John Allen Raynor. Ohio Historical Society. 1886. Library. Ohio History Connection. Typescript, Call # 970.92 R218.

Naylor, Isaac. "Judge Isaac Naylor's Description of the Battle of Tippecanoe." In State of Indiana, Tippecanoe Battle-Field Monument Commission, United States, Tippecanoe Battle-Field Monument Commission, and the Tippecanoe Battle-Field Monument Association. *The Tippecanoe Battle-Field Monument: A History of the Association Formed to Promote the Enterprise, the Action of Congress and the Indiana Legislature, the Work of the Commission and the Ceremonies at the Dedication of the Monument,* complied by Alva O. Reser, 146–51. Indianapolis: W.B. Burford, State Printing and Binding, 1909.

Nelson, Harold L. "Military Roads for War and Peace, 1791–1836." *Military Affairs* 19, no. 1 (Spring 1955): 1–14.

Nelson, Paul David. *Anthony Wayne: Soldier of the Early Republic.* Bloomington: Indiana University Press, 1985.

Nelson, Paul David. "General Charles Scott, the Kentucky Mounted Volunteers, and the Northwest Indian Wars, 1784–1794." *Journal of the Early Republic* 6, no. 3 (Autumn 1986): 219–51.

Newcomb, Steven T. *Pagans in the Promised Land: Decoding the Doctrine of Christian Discovery.* Golden, CO: Fulcrum Publishing, 2008.

Nichols, Philip. *The History of Sir Francis Drake.* In *Drama of the English Republic, 1649–1660,* edited by Janet Clare, 270–93. Manchester, UK: Manchester University Press, 2002.

"The North West." *Niles Weekly Register* 42, no. 1092 (August 21, 1832): 450.

Norton, Charles Ledyard. *Handbook of Florida.* Rev. 3rd ed. New York: Longmans, Green & Co., 1892.

Nott, Josiah. *Two Lectures, on the Nature History of the Caucasian and Negro Races.* Mobile, TX: Dade and Thompson, 1844.

Noyelle, Nicolas Joseph de. "De Noyelle's Expedition against the Sauk and Foxes." In *Collections of the State Historical Society of Wisconsin*, edited by Reuben Gold Thwaites, vol. 17, 221–30. 31 vols. Madison: Wisconsin State Historical Society, 1906.

Nunnally, Michael N. *American Indian Wars: A Chronology of Confrontations between Native Peoples and Settlers and the United States Military, 1500s–1901.* Jefferson, NC: McFarland and Company, Inc., Publishers, 2007.

O'Brien, Sean Michael. *In Bitterness and in Tears: Andrew Jackson's Destruction of the Creeks and Seminoles.* Westport, CT: Praeger, 2003.

O'Callaghan, Edmund Bailey, ed. *Documentary History of the State of New-York.* 4 vols. Albany, NY: Weed, Parsons & Co., 1850.

O'Sullivan, John L. "Annexation." *The United States Magazine and Democratic Review* 17, no. 85 (July–August 1845): 5–10.

Oberholtzer, Ellis Paxson. *Robert Morris, Patriot and Financier.* New York: Macmillan Company, 1903.

Oberly, James Warren. *Sixty Million Acres: American Veterans and the Public Lands before the Civil War.* Kent, OH: Kent State University Press, 1990.

"Official: General Order No. 4." *Niles Weekly Register* 53, no. 1348 (February 20, 1838): 401.

Ogle, Charles. *Speech of Mr. Ogle, of Pennsylvania, on the Regal Splendor of the President's Palace: Delivered in the House of Representatives, April 14, 1840.* Campaign Pamphlet. Washington, D.C., 1840.

Oldmixon, John. *The British Empire in America: Containing the History of the Discovery, Settlement, Progress and State of the British Colonies on the Continent and Islands of America.* 2 vols. London: J. Brotherton, J. Clarke, 1741.

Olmstead, Earl P. *David Zeisberger: A Life among the Indians.* Kent, OH: Kent State University Press, 1997.

Olson, Roberta J. M., and Jay M. Pasachoff. *Fire in the Sky: Comets and Meteors, the Decisive Centuries, in British Art and Science.* Cambridge: Cambridge University Press, 1998.

"Osceola, of Florida." In *Literary Gazette and Journal of the Belle Lettres, Arts, Sciences, & c.,* no. 1116, 364. London, Saturday, June 9, 1838.

Owen, Thomas McAdory, and Marie Bankhead Owen. *History of Alabama and Dictionary of Alabama Biography.* 4 vols. Chicago: S. L. Clark Publishing Company, 1921.

Owens, Robert M. "Jeffersonian Benevolence on the Ground: The Indian Land Cession Treaties of William Henry Harrison." *Journal of the Early Republic* 22, no. 3 (Autumn 2002): 405–35.

Owens, Robert M. *Mr. Jefferson's Hammer: William Henry Harrison and the Origins of American Indian Policy.* Norman: University of Oklahoma Press, 2007.

Owens, Robert M. *Red Dreams, White Nightmares: The Pan-Indian Alliances in the Anglo-American Mind, 1765–1815.* Norman: University of Oklahoma Press, 2015.

Owsley, Frank Lawrence, Jr. "Prophet of War: Josiah Francis and the Creek War." *American Indian Quarterly* 9, no. 3 (Summer 1985): 273–93.

Parenti, Michael. *History as Mystery.* San Francisco, CA: City Lights Books, 1999.

Parenti, Michael. "The Strange Death of Zachary Taylor: A Case Study in the Manufacture of Mainstream History." *New Political Science* 20, no. 2 (1998): 141–58.

Parker, Arthur Caswell. *The Code of Handsome Lake, the Seneca Prophet,* 1–148. New York State Museum Bulletin 163. Education Department Bulletin. No. 530, 1913.

Parker, Arthur Caswell. "The Constitution of the Five Nations." *New York State Museum Bulletin,* no. 184 (April 1916): 7–158.

Parker, Arthur Caswell. "Iroquois Uses of Maize and Other Food Plans." *New York State Museum Bulletin*, no. 144 (April 1910): 1–118.

Parkinson, Daniel M. "Pioneer Life in Wisconsin." In *Collections of the State Historical Society of Wisconsin*, vol. 2, 326–64. Madison: State Historical Society of Wisconsin, 1903.

Parton, James. *The Life of Aaron Burr, Lieutenant-Colonel in the Army of the Revolution, United States Senator, Vice President of the United States, etc.* Expanded Edition. 2 vols. 1857. New York: Houghton Mifflin Company, 1892.

Parton, James. *The Life of Andrew Jackson.* 3 vols. 1860. Boston: Fields, Osgood, and Co., 1870.

Paullin, Charles O. *Atlas of the Historical Geography of the United States.* Edited by John D. Wright. Carnegie Institution of Washington. Publication no. 401. Washington, D.C.: Carnegie Institution of Washington and the American Geographical Society of New York, 1932.

Payette, Pete. "American Forts, Central Florida." *American Forts Network*, 2014. https://www.northamericanforts.com/East/flcentral.html.

Payette, Pete. "American Forts, East: Alabama." *American Forts Network*, 2010. https://www.northamericanforts.com/East/al.html.

Payette, Pete. "American Forts, East Florida." *American Forts Network*, 2014. https://www.northamericanforts.com/East/fleast.html.

Payette, Pete. "American Forts, East: Indiana." *American Forts Network*, 2010. https://www.northamericanforts.com/East/in.html#half.

Payette, Pete. "American Forts, Middle Florida." *American Forts Network*, 2010. https://www.northamericanforts.com/East/flmiddle.html#sem.

Payette, Pete. "American Forts, Northern Alabama." *American Forts Network*, 2018. https://www.northamericanforts.com/East/alnorth.html.

Payette, Pete. "American Forts, Pensacola Bay." *American Forts Network*, 2016. https://www.northamericanforts.com/East/flpen.html.

Payette, Pete. "American Forts, Southern Georgia." *American Forts Network*, 2010. https://www.northamericanforts.com/East/ga-south.html.

Payette, Pete. "American Forts, Wisconsin." *American Forts Network*, 2010. https://www.northamericanforts.com/East/wi.html.

Peavy, Linda S., and Ursula Smith. *Pioneer Women: The Lives of Women on the Frontier.* Norman: University of Oklahoma Press, 1998.

Peeler, Elizabeth H. "The Policies of Willie Blount, as Governor of Tennessee, 1809–1815." *Tennessee Historical Quarterly* 1, no. 4 (December 1942): 309–27.

Peet, Stephen Denison. *The Mound Builders: Their Works and Relics*, vol. 1. Chicago: Office of the *American Antiquarian*, 1892.

Perling, Joseph Jerry. *Presidents' Sons: The Prestige of Name in a Democracy.* New York: Odyssey Press, 1947.

Pessen, Edward. *Riches, Class and Power before the Civil War.* Lexington, MA: D. C. Heath, 1973.

Peterson, Jacqueline. "Many Roads to Red River: Métis Genesis in the Great Lakes Region, 1680–1815." In *The New Peoples: Being and Becoming Métis in North America*, edited by Jacqueline Peterson and Jennifer S. H. Brown, 37–72. 1985. St. Paul: Minnesota Historical Society Press, 2001.

Philbrick, Francis S. *The Laws of the Indiana Territory, 1801–1809*, vol. 21. Law Series, vol. 2. Springfield: Trustees of the Illinois State Historical Library, 1930.

Pigeon v. McCarthy et al. No. 9700. In *Reports of Cases Argued and Determined in the Supreme Court of Judicature of the State of Indiana, with Tables of the Cases Reported and Cases*

Cited and an Index. Vol. 82, Containing Cases Decided at the May Term, 1882, Not Reported in Vol. 81, edited by Francis M. Dice, 321–30. Indianapolis: Carlon & Hollenbeck, 1883.

Pilling, James Constantine. *Bibliography of the Algonquian Languages*. Bulletin no. 13. Bureau of Ethnology. Smithsonian Institution. Washington, D.C.: Government Printing Office, 1891.

Pirtle, Alfred. *The Battle of Tippecanoe, Read before the Filson Club, November 1, 1897*. Louisville, KY: J. P. Morton and Co., 1900.

Plato. *The Republic*. Translated by Richard C. Sterling and W. C. Scott. *ca.* 360 BCE. New York: W. W. Norton, 1985.

Polk, James K. *Diary of James K. Polk during His Presidency, 1845 to 1849: Now First Printed from the Original Manuscript Owned by the Society*. Edited by Milo Milton Quaife. Chicago Historical Society's Collections. 4 vols. Chicago: A. C. McClurg & Co., 1910.

Pond, Peter. "Journal of Peter Pond." In *Collections of the State Historical Society of Wisconsin*, edited by Reuben Gold Thwaites, vol. 18, 314–54. Madison: State Historical Society of Wisconsin, 1908.

Porter, Kenneth Wiggins. "Negroes and the Seminole War, 1817–1818." *Journal of Negro History* 36, no. 3 (July 1951): 249–80.

Porter, Kenneth Wiggins. "Negroes and the Seminole War, 1835–1842." *Journal of Southern History* 30, no. 4 (November 1964): 427–29.

Portrait of Sarah Cutler Dunn. By Gilbert Stuart. Oil on canvass. 1809. Risd Museum. Museum Appropriation Fund 31.273. Rhode Island School of Design. Accessed January 3, 2018. https://risdmuseum.org/art_design/objects/2472_portrait_of_sarah_cutler_dunn?context=19&type=galleries.

Potherie, Bacqueville de la, Claude Charles le Roy. *Histoire de l'Amerique Septentrionale*. 4 vols. 1722. Paris: chez Nyon Fils, 1753.

Prairie Farmer Publishing Company. *Prairie Farmer's Home and County Directory of Iowa County, Wisconsin*. 1929. Kokomo, IN: Selby Publishing, 1986.

Pratt, G. Michael. "The Battle of Fallen Timbers: An Eyewitness Perspective." *Northwest Ohio Quarterly* 67, no. 1 (Winter 1997): 4–34.

Pratt, Julius W. *Expansionists of 1812*. Gloucester, MA: Peter Smith, 1957.

Pratz, Le Page du. *Histoire de la Louisiane: contenant la decouverte de ce vaste pays; sa description geographique; un voyage dans les terres; l'histoire naturelle, les moeurs, coutumes & religion des naturels, avec leurs origines; deux voyages dans le nord du nouveau Mexique, dont un jusqu'a la mer du Sud*. 3 vols. Paris: de Bure, l'aîné, 1758.

Price, Richard. *Maroon Societies: Rebel Slave Communities in the Americas*. 3rd ed. 1979. Baltimore: Johns-Hopkins University Press, 1996.

Prucha, Francis Paul. *American Indian Treaties: The History of a Political Anomaly*. Berkeley: University of California Press, 1994.

Prucha, Francis Paul. *Atlas of American Indian Affairs*. Lincoln: University of Nebraska Press, 1990.

Prucha, Francis Paul. *The Great Father: The United States Government and the American Indians*. Lincoln: University of Nebraska Press, 1986.

Quaife, Milo Milton. "Journals and Reports of the Black Hawk War." *Mississippi Valley Historical Review* 12, no. 3 (December 1925): 392–409.

Quimby, George Irving. *Indian Life in the Upper Great Lakes, 11,000 B.C. to A.D. 1800*. Chicago: University of Chicago Press, 1960.

Rafert, Stewart. *The Miami Indians of Indiana: A Persistent People, 1654–1994*. Indianapolis: Indiana Historical Society, 1996.

Rainwater, Percy Lea, ed. "The Siege of Fort Meigs." *The Mississippi Valley Historical Review* 19, no. 2 (September 1932): 261–63.

Ranck, James B. "Andrew Jackson and the Burr Conspiracy." *Tennessee Historical Magazine*, Series II, 1, no. 1 (October 1930): 17–28.

Rappleye, Charles. *Robert Morris: Financier of the American Revolution*. New York: Simon & Schuster, 2010.

Ratner, Lorman A. *Andrew Jackson and His Tennessee Lieutenants: A Study in Political Culture*. Westport, CT: Greenwood Press, 1997.

Raymond, Ethel T. *Tecumseh: A Chronicle of the Last Great Leader of His People*. Chronicles of Canada Series. Vol. 17. Part 5. *The Red Man in Canada*. Series edited by George M. Wrong and Hugh H. Langton. Toronto: Glasgow, Brook, & Company, 1922.

Records Relating to the 1811 and 1815 Courts-Martial of Maj. Gen. James Wilkinson, 1811 and 1815. M1523. National Archives Identifier 301659. Record Group 153: Records of the Office of the Judge Advocate General (Army), 1792–2010.

Reid, Basil A. *Myths and Realities of Caribbean History*. Tuscaloosa: University of Alabama Press, 2009.

"Remarks." *Truth's Advocate and Anti-Jackson Expositor*, 289–93, August 1828.

Remington, W. Craig. *Historical Atlas of Alabama*. Vol. 1, *Historic Locations by County*. Tuscaloosa: Department of Geography, University of Alabama Press, 1999.

Remini, Robert V. *Andrew Jackson*. New York: Twayne Publishers, Inc., 1966.

Remini, Robert V. *Andrew Jackson & His Indian Wars*. New York: Viking, 2001.

Remini, Robert V. *Andrew Jackson: The Course of American Democracy, 1833–1845*. Baltimore: Johns Hopkins University Press, 1984.

Remini, Robert V. *Andrew Jackson: Lessons in Leadership*. New York: Palgrave Macmillan, 2008.

Remini, Robert V. *The Life of Andrew Jackson*. New York: Harper & Row Publishers, 1988.

"Report from M. de Vaudreuil of the Condition of the Colony." *Michigan Pioneer and Historical Society*, vol. 33. 301–14. Lansing, MI: Wynkoop Hallenbeck Crawford Company, 1905.

Reynolds, John. *Reynolds' History of Illinois: My Own Times, Embracing Also the History of My Life*. 1855. Chicago: Chicago Historical Society, 1879.

Reynolds, William R., Jr. *The Cherokee Struggle to Maintain Identity in the 17th and 18th Centuries*. Jefferson, NC: McFarland & Company, Inc., Publishers, 2015.

Ricard, Serge. *The Manifest Destiny of the United States in the 19th Century, Ideological and Political Aspects*. Collection CNED-Didier concours Series. Paris: Didier Erudition, CNED, 1999.

Richard, Carl J. *The Founders and the Classics: Greece, Rome, and the American Enlightenment*. Cambridge: Harvard University Press, 1994.

Richardson, Darcy G. *Others: Third Party Politics from the Nation's Founding to the Rise and Fall of the Greenback-Labor Party*. Vol. 1. New York: iUniverse, 2004.

Richardson, Henry J., III. *Origins of African American Interests in International Law*. Durham, NC: Carolina Academic Press, 2008.

Richardson, James D., ed. *A Compilation of the Messages and Papers of the Presidents*. 10 vols. Washington, D.C.: Bureau of National Literature, 1897.

Richardson, John. *War of 1812, First Series, Containing a Full and Detailed Narrative of the Operations of the Right Division of the Canadian Army*. Brockville, Ontario: New Era, 1842.

Richter, Daniel K. *Ordeal of the Longhouse: The Peoples of the Iroquois League in the Era of European Colonization*. Chapel Hill: University of North Carolina Press, 1992.

Ritenour, John S. "Logan, Michael Cresap, and Simon Girty." In Joseph Doddridge, Narcissa Doddridge, John S. Ritenour, and William T. Lindsey, *Notes on the Settlement and Indian Wars of the Western Parts of Virginia and Pennsylvania from 1763 to 1783, Inclusive, Together with a Review of the State of Society and Manners of the First Settlers of the Western Country.* Pittsburgh: John S. Ritenour and Wm. T. Lindsey, 1912.

Ritzenthalen, Robert E. *Prehistoric Indians of Wisconsin.* Reviewed by Lynee G. Goldstein. 3rd ed. Milwaukee, WI: Milwaukee Public Museum, 1985.

Rivlin, Geoffrey. *First Steps in the Law.* Oxford: Oxford University Press, 2015.

Roberts, Jeremy. *Zachary Taylor.* Minneapolis: Lerner Publications Company, 2005.

Robertson, R. S. "A Curious and Important Discovery in Indiana: Chief of the Miamis." In *Magazine of American History with Notes and Queries,* edited by Martha J. Lamb, vol. 24, 45–51. New York: J. J. Little & Co., 1890.

Robinson, Solon. *Me-Won-I-Talk: A Tale of Frontier Life and Indian Character, Exhibiting Traditions, Superstitions, and Character of a Race That Is Passing away, a Romance of the Frontier.* 1864. New York: New York News Company, 1867.

Rochefoucauld-Liancourt, François-Alexandre-Frédéric, duc de la. *Voyage dans les États-Unis d'Amérique fait en 1795, 1795, et 1797.* 8 vols. Paris: *Du Pont, Impremeur-Libraire, l'an VII du République,* 1798.

Rogin, Michael Paul. *Fathers and Children: Andrew Jackson and the Subjugation of the American Indian.* New York: Alfred A. Knopf, 1975.

Ronda, James P. "Forgotten Removals: The Life and Times of Hendrick Aupaumut." In Minnestrista Council for Great Lakes Native American Studies. *1991–1992 Proceedings of the Woodland National Conference,* 103–6. Muncie, IN: Minnestrista Cultural Center and Ball State University, 1993.

Ross, Frank E. "The Fur Trade of the Ohio Valley." *Indiana Magazine of History* 34, no. 4 (1938): 417–42.

Rothman, Adam. *Slave Country: American Expansion and the Origins of the Deep South.* Cambridge, MA: Harvard University Press, 2005.

Rubin, Julius H. *Tears of Repentance: Christian Indian Identity and Community in Colonial Southern New England.* Lincoln: University of Nebraska Press, 2013.

Russell, Don. "How Many Indians Were Killed? White Man versus Red Man: The Facts and the Legend." *The American West: The Magazine of Western History* 10, no. 4 (July 1973): 42–42, 61–63.

Salisbury, Albert. "Green County Pioneers." In *Collections of the State Historical Society of Wisconsin,* vol. 6, 401–15. Madison: State Historical Society of Wisconsin, 1908.

Salomon, Charles. *L'occupation des territoires sans matre: étude de droit international.* Paris: A. Girard, Libraire-Éditeur, 1889.

Sankey, Margaret. "Jay's Treaty (1796)." In *The American Economy: A Historical Encyclopedia,* edited by Cynthia Clark Northrup, vol. 1, 163. 2 vols. Santa Barbara, CA: ABC-CLIO, LLC, 2003.

Satz, Ronald N. *Tennessee's Indian Peoples: From White Contact to Removal, 1540–1840.* Knoxville: University of Tennessee Press, 1979.

Saunt, Claudio. *A New Order of Things: Property, Power, and the Transformation of the Creek Indians, 1833–1816.* Cambridge, UK: Cambridge University Press, 1999.

Sayre, Robert Woods. *Modernity and Its Other: The Encounter with American Indians in the Eighteenth Century.* Lincoln: University of Nebraska Press, 2017.

"Scene at the Battle of Bad Axe." *Niles Weekly Register* 43, no. 1102 (November 3, 1832): 147.

Schoolcraft, Henry Rowe. *Historical and Statistical Information Respecting the History, Condition, and Prospects of the Indian Tribes of the United States, Collected and Prepared under the Direction of the Bureau of Indian Affairs per Act of Congress of March 3rd, 1847.* 6 vols. Philadelphia: Lippincott, Grambo & Company, 1853.

Schoolcraft, Henry Rowe. *Outlines of the Life and Character of Gen. Lewis Cass.* Albany, NY: J. Munsell, Printer, 1848.

Schoolcraft, Henry Rowe. *Travels in the Central Portions of the Mississippi Valley: Comprising Observations on Its Mineral Geography, Internal Resources, and Aboriginal Population.* New York: Collins and Hannay, 1825.

Schweinitz, Edmund de. *The Life and Times of David Zeisberger, the Western Pioneer and Apostle of the Indians.* Philadelphia: J. B. Lippincott & Co., 1870.

Scott, Rebekah. "Human Bones Quietly Moved from Dig Site at Fort Meigs." *Toledo Blade,* April 12, 2002. A1, A9.

Scovell, Josiah Thomas, and the Fort Harrison Centennial Association. *Fort Harrison on the Banks of the Wabash, 1812–1912.* Terre Haute, IN: The Moore-Langen Printing Co., 1912.

Seaver, James Everett. *A Narrative of the Life of Mrs. Mary Jemison.* Canandaigua, NY: J. D. Bemis and Co., 1824.

"Selections from the Torrence Papers, III." *Quarterly Publication of the Cincinnati Historical Association* 2, no. 3 (July–September 1907): 97–120.

Seton, Ernest Thompson. *The Gospel of the Red Man: An Indian Bible.* Garden City, NY: Doubleday, Doran & Company, Inc., 1936.

Shaw, John. "Sketches of Indian Chiefs and Pioneers of the Old North-West." In *Collections of the State Historical Society of Wisconsin,* vol. 10, 213–22. Madison: State Historical Society of Wisconsin, 1888.

Sheppard, Si. *The Partisan Press: A History of Media Bias in the U.S.* Jefferson, NC: McFarland & Co., 2008.

Shire, Laurel Clark. *The Threshold of Manifest Destiny: Gender and National Expansion in Florida.* Philadelphia: University of Pennsylvania Press, Inc., 2016.

Shreve, Royal Ornan. *The Finished Scoundrel: General Wilkinson, Sometime Commander-in-Chief of the Army of the United States, Who Made Intrigue a Trade and Treason a Profession.* Indianapolis: Bobbs-Merrill Company, 1933.

Silver, Peter Rhoads. *Our Savage Neighbors: How Indian War Transformed Early America.* New York: W.W. Norton, 2008.

Singer, Alan J. *New York and Slavery: Time to Teach the Truth.* Albany, NY: SUNY, Excelsior Editions, 2008.

Skaggs, David Curtis. "Aftermath of Victory: The Perry-Elliott Controversy." *Naval History Magazine* 21, no. 1 (February 2014). https://www.usni.org/magazines/navalhistory/2014-01/aftermath-victory-perry-elliott-controversy.

Skeen, C. Edward. *Citizen Soldiers in the War of 1812.* Lexington: University of Kentucky Press, 1999.

Slade, William. "Abolition Petitions: Speech of Mr. Slade." In United States Congress. Twenty-Sixth Congress, First Session. *Appendix to the Congressional Globe* 8, no. 6 (January 7, 1840): 844–57.

Slocum, Charles Elihu. *History of the Maumee River Basin from the Earliest Account to Its Organization into Counties.* Defiance, OH: Charles Elihu Slocum, 1905.

Smith, Adam. *An Inquiry into the Nature and Causes of the Wealth of Nations.* 2 vols. 1776. Dublin: N. Kelly for P. Wogan, 1804.

Smith, Elbert B. *The Presidencies of Zachary Taylor and Millard Fillmore.* Lawrence: University of Kansas, 1988.

Smith, Elbert B. *President Zachary Taylor: The Hero President.* New York: Nova Science, 2007.

Smith, Harry. *Fifty Years of Slavery in the United States of America.* Grand Rapids: West Michigan Printing Co, 1891.

Smith, Hubbard Madison. *Historical Sketches of Old Vincennes: Founded in 1732: Its Institutions of Churches, Embracing Collateral Incidents and Biographical Sketches of Many Persons and Events Connected Therewith.* Indianapolis: W. B. Buford, 1903.

Smith, Linda Tuhiwai. *Decolonizing Methodologies: Research and Indigenous Peoples.* 2nd ed. London: Zed Books, 2012.

Smith, Robert B. "Black Hawk War." *Military History Magazine,* February 1998. Posted HistoryNet. 2018. Accessed November 22, 2018. http://www.historynet.com/black-hawk-war.

Smith, William Henry, ed. *The St. Clair Papers: The Life and Public Services of Arthur St. Clair.* 2 vols. Cincinnati: R. Clarke & Co., 1882.

Smith, William Rudolph. *The History of Wisconsin in Three Parts, Historical, Documentary, and Descriptive.* 3 vols. Madison, WI: Beriah Brown, Printer, 1854.

Smithsonian Institution. *Handbook of North American Indians.* Edited by William C. Sturdevant. 17 vols. Washington, D.C.: Smithsonian Institution, 1978–2008.

Snyder, Timothy. *Bloodlands: Europe Between Hitler and Stalin.* New York: Basic Books, 2012.

"Somerset's Case." *De Bow's Review* 32, nos. 3–4 (March–April 1862): 171–87.

Somerville, Diane Miller. "Rape, Race, and Castration in Slave Law in the Colonial and Early South." In *The Devil's Lane: Sex and Race in the Early South,* edited by Catherine Clinton and Michele Gillespie, 74–89. New York: Oxford University Press, 1997.

Southerland, Henry deLeon, Jr., and Jerry Elijah Brown. *The Federal Road through Georgia, the Creek Nation, and Alabama, 1806–1836.* Tuscaloosa: University of Alabama Press, 1989.

Speck, Frank Gouldsmith. "Ceremonial Songs of the Creek and Yuchi Indians." *University of Pennsylvania Anthropological Publications* 1, no. 2 (1911): 157–245.

Speck, Frank Gouldsmith. "Ethnology of the Yuchi Indians." *University of Pennsylvania Anthropological Publications* 1, no. 1 (1909): 1–154.

Speck, Frank Gouldsmith. "The Wapanachki Delawares and the English: Their Past as Viewed by an Ethnologist." *Pennsylvania Magazine* 67, no. 4 (October 1943): 319–44.

Spencer, Jaob. "Shawnee Folk-Lore." *Journal of American Folk-Lore* 22 (1909): 319–26.

Spencer, Jaob. "The Shawnee Indians: Their Customs, Traditions, and Folklore." *Transactions of the Kansas State Historical Society* 10 (1908): 382–402.

Spitzer, Nicholas. "Cajuns and Creoles: The French Gulf Coast." *Southern Comfort* 4, no. 2. Part II. "The Long Journey Home." (Summer/Fall 1978): 140–55.

Sprague, John Titcomb. *The Origin, Progress, and Conclusion of the Florida War.* 1848. Reprint. Gainesville: University of Florida Press, 1964.

Squier, Ephraim George, and Edwin H. Davis. *Ancient Monuments of the Mississippi Valley: Comprising the Results of Extensive Original Surveys and Explorations. Smithsonian Contributions to Knowledge,* vol. 1. 1848. Reprint. New York: Johnson Reprint Corporation, 1965.

Stanton, William. *The Leopard's Spots: Scientific Attitudes toward Race in America, 1815–59.* Chicago: University of Chicago Press, 1960.

The State of Mississippi. *Code of Mississippi, Being an Analytical Compilation of the Public and General Statutes of the Territory and State, with Tabular References to the Local and Private Acts, from 1798–1848.* Edited and compiled by Anderson Hutchinson. Jackson, MS: Price and Fall, State Printers, 1848.

State of Ohio. General Assembly. Senate. *Journal of the Senate of the United States, Being the First Session of the Eighteenth General Assembly.* Columbus, OH: P. H. Olmstead, 1820.

Steele, Robert Wilbur, and Mary Davies Steele. *Early Dayton, with Important Facts and Incidents from the Founding of the City of Dayton, Ohio to the Hundredth Anniversary, 1796–1896.* Dayton, OH: W. J. Shuey, 1896.

Stevens, Frank Everett. *The Black Hawk War: Including a Review of Black Hawk's Life.* Chicago: Frank E. Stevens, 1903.

Stewart, Bruce E. " 'The Forces of Bacchus Are Fast Yielding': The Rise and Fall of Anti-Alcohol Reform in Antebellum Rowan County, North Carolina." *North Carolina Historical Review* 87, no. 3 (July 2010): 310–38.

Stiggins, George. *Creek Indian History.* Edited by Virginia Pounds Brown. Birmingham, AL: Birmingham Public Library Press, 1989.

Stocker, Harry Emilius. *A History of the Moravian Mission among the Indians on the White River in Indiana.* Bethlehem, PA: Times Publishing Company, 1917.

Stout, David Bond. "The Piankashaw and Kaskaskia and the Treaty of Greene Ville." In *Piankashaw and Kaskaskia Indians.* Indian Claims Commission. Consolidated Docket no. 315, 343–75. New York: Garland Publishing, Inc., 1974.

Street, Ida M. "A Second Chapter of Indian History." *Annals of Iowa: A Historical Quarterly,* 3rd series, 6, no. 5 (April 1904): 364–75.

Strode, Hudson. *Jefferson Davis: American Patriot, 1808–1861.* New York: Harcourt, Brace, 1955.

Strong, Moses McCure. "The Indian Wars of Wisconsin." In *Collections of the State Historical Society of Wisconsin,* vol. 8, 241–86. Madison: State Historical Society of Wisconsin, 1908.

Sturtevant, William C. "Creek into Seminole." In *A Seminole Source Book,* edited by William C. Sturtevant, 92–128. New York: Garland Publishing, Inc., 1987.

Sugden, John. *Tecumseh: A Life.* New York: Henry Holt and Company, 1997.

Sullivan County Historical Society. *History of Greene and Sullivan Counties, State of Indiana.* Chicago: Godspeed Bros. & Co., 1884.

Sullivan, James, ed. *The Papers of Sir William Johnson Papers,* vol. 3. Albany: The University of the State of New York, 1921.

Swanton, John Reed. *Creek Religion and Medicine.* 1928. Reprint. Lincoln: University of Nebraska Press, 2000.

Swanton, John Reed. *Early History of the Creek Indians and Their Neighbors.* Smithsonian Institution. Bureau of Ethnology. Washington, D.C.: Government Printing Office, 1922.

Sweet, Roland. "A Vote for Logs." *Log Home Living* 27, no. 10 (November–December 2010): 24.

Swiney, P. D. "The Glorious Revolution in America, 1688–1689: Interpretive Essay." In *What Happened? An Encyclopedia of Events that Changed America Forever,* vol. 1: *Through the Seventeenth Century.* 237–45. John E. Findling and Frank W. Thackeray, ed. *Bottom of Form Santa Barbara,* CA: ABC–CLIO, LLC, 2011.

Symmes, John Cleves. Letter of January 12 and 15, 1792. "John Cleves Symmes to Elias Boudinot." In *Ohio Historical and Philosophical Society, Quarterly Publications* 5, no. 3 (July–September 1910), 93–101.

Symmes, John Cleves, Anna Tuthill Symmes Harrison, and Beverley W. Bond Jr. *The Intimate Letters of John Cleves Symmes.* Edited by Beverley W. Bond Jr. Cincinnati: Historical and Philosophical Society of Ohio, 1956.

Symmes, John Cleves, Johnathan Dayton, and Peter Gibson Thomson. *The Correspondence of John Cleves Symmes, Founder of the Miami Purchase, Chiefly from the Collection of Peter G. Thomson.* Edited by Beverley W. Bond Jr. New York: The Macmillan Company, 1926.

Tait, James A. "The Journal of James A. Tait for the Year 1813." *Georgia Historical Quarterly* 8, no. 3 (1924): 229–39.

Tasler, Nick. *The Impulse Factor: An Innovative Approach to Better Decision-Making.* New York: Fireside, 2008.

Taylor and Fillmore: The Life of Major-General Zachary Taylor with Characteristic Anecdotes and Incidents. Philadelphia: T. K. & P. G. Collins, 1848.

Taylor and His Generals: A Biography of Major-General Zachary Taylor; and Sketches of the Lives of Generals Worth, Wool, and Twiggs, with a Full Account of the Various Actions of Their Divisions in Mexico up to the Present Time; together with a History of the Bombardment of Vera Cruz, and a Sketch of the Life of Major-General Winfield Scott. Philadelphia: Published by E.H. Butler & Co. 1847.

Taylor, James. "Letters of James Taylor to the Presidents of the United States (Concluded)." Edited by James A. Padgett. *Register of the Kentucky State Historical Society* 34, no. 109 (October 1936): 318–46.

Taylor, Richard, Jr. *Destructions and Reconstruction: Personal Experiences in the Late War in the United States.* London: William Blackwood and Sons, 1879.

Taylor, Richard, and Richard Taylor. "Letters of Colonel Richard Taylor and of Commodore Richard Taylor to James Madison, with a Sketch of Their Lives." *Register of the Kentucky State Historical Society* 36, no. 117 (October 1938): 330–44.

Taylor, William Arthur. "Re: Zachary Taylor: Illegitimate Children?" Forum. Posted January 30, 2001. Accessed October 15, 2018. https://www.genealogy.com/forum/surnames/topics/taylor/15098/.

Taylor, Zachary. *General Taylor and the Wilmot Proviso.* Boston: Wilson & Darnell, 1848.

Taylor, Zachary, James K. Polk, Winfield Scott, Nicholas Philip Trist, and United States War Department. *Messages of the President of the United States, with the Correspondence, Therewith Communicated, between the Secretary of War and Other Officers of the Government, on the Subject of the Mexican War.* Washington, D.C.: Wendell and Van Benthuysen, Printers, 1848.

Tello, Pilar León. *Documentos Relatives a la Independencia de Norteamérica Existentes en Archivos Españoles,* vol. 4. Madrid: Ministerio de Suntos Exteriores, 1980.

"Tenskwatawa." In *Encyclopedia of American Indian History,* edited by Bruce E. Johansen and Barry M. Pritzker, vol. 1, 684–85. 4 vols. Santa Barbara, CA: ABC-CLIO, LLC, 2008.

The Territory of Mississippi. *The Statutes of the Mississippi Territory, Revised and Digested by the Authority of the General Assembly.* Edited and compiled by Harry Toulmin. Natchez, MS: Samuel Terrell, 1807.

Teyoninhokarawen (John Norton). *The Journal of Major John Norton.* Edited by Carl F. Klinck and James J. Talman. Publications of the Champlain Society. 2nd ed., vol. 72. 1970. Toronto: Champlain Society, 2011.

Thomas, Cyrus. "Report on the Mound Explorations of the Bureau of Ethnology." In *Twelfth Annual Report of the Bureau of Ethnology to the Secretary of the Smithsonian Institution, 1890–'91,* edited by John W. Powell, 17–730. Washington, D.C.: Government Printing Office, 1894.

Thomas, Cyrus. *The Story of a Mound; or, the Shawnees in Pre-Columbian Times.* Washington, D.C.: Judd & Detweiler, 1891.

Thomas, Jacob, with Terry Boyle. *Teachings from the Longhouse.* Toronto: Stoddart Publishing Co., Ltd., 1994.

Thomas, Louis R. "Newport Barracks." In *The Kentucky Encyclopedia,* edited by John E. Kleber, 680. Lexington: University Press of Kentucky, 1992.

Thoreau, Henry David. *On the Duty of Civil Disobedience.* London: The Simple Life Press, 1903.

Thornbrough, Gayle, ed. *Letter Book of the Indian Agency at Fort Wayne, 1809–1815.* Indianapolis: Indiana Historical Society, 1961.

Thornbrough, Gayle, ed. *Outpost on the Wabash, 178–1791, Letters of Brigadier General Josiah Harmar and Major John Francis Hamtramck and Other Letters and Documents from the Harmar Papers in the William L. Clements Library.* Indiana Historical Society Publications, vol. 19. Indianapolis: Indiana Historical Society, 1957.

Thorpe, Thomas Bangs. *The Taylor Anecdote Book: Anecdotes and Letters of Zachary Taylor.* New York: D. Appleton & Company, 1848.

Thwaites, Rueben Gold, ed. "British Regime in Wisconsin—1760–1800." In *Collections of the State Historical Society of Wisconsin,* vol. 18, 223–464. Madison: State Historical Society of Wisconsin, 1908.

Thwaites, Rueben Gold, ed. "French Regime in Wisconsin—I, 1624–1727." In *Collections of the State Historical Society of Wisconsin,* vol. 16, 1–380. Madison: State Historical Society of Wisconsin, 1902.

Thwaites, Rueben Gold, ed. "The French Regime in Wisconsin—II, 1727–1748." In *Collections of the State Historical Society of Wisconsin,* vol. 17, 1–518. Madison, WI: State Historical Society of Wisconsin, 1906.

Thwaites, Rueben Gold, ed. "The French Regime in Wisconsin—III, 1743–1760." In *Collections of the State Historical Society of Wisconsin,* vol. 18, 1–469. Madison, WI: State Historical Society of Wisconsin, 1908.

Thwaites, Rueben Gold, ed. "Important Western State Papers." In *Collections of the State Historical Society of Wisconsin,* vol. 11, 26–63. Madison, WI: Democrat Printing Company, State Printers, 1888.

Thwaites, Rueben Gold, ed. *The Jesuit Relations and Allied Documents.* 73 vols. Cleveland, OH: Burroughs Brothers Publishers, 1899.

Thwaites, Reuben Gold. "The Story of the Black Hawk War." In *Collections of the State Historical Society of Wisconsin,* edited by Reuben Gold Thwaites, vol. 12, 216–65. Madison: State Historical Society of Wisconsin, 1892.

Thwaites, Reuben Gold, and Louise P. Kellogg, eds. *Documentary History of Dunmore's War, 1774.* Madison: Wisconsin Historical Society, 1905.

Todd, Charles Stuart, Benjamin Drake, and James H. Perkins. *Sketches of the Civil and Military Services of William Henry Harrison.* Cincinnati: J.A. & U.P. James, 1847.

Tolman, Richard. *A Funeral Oration on the Death of President Zachary Taylor.* Boston: Press of T. R. Marvin, 1850.

Tooker, Elisabeth. *An Ethnography of the Huron Indians, 1615–1649.* Syracuse, NY: Syracuse University Press, 1991.

Toth, Andrew L. *Missionary Practices and Spanish Steel: The Evolution of Apostolic Mission in the Context of New Spain Conquests.* Bloomington, IN: iUniverse, Inc., 2012.

Trask, Kerry A. *Black Hawk: The Battle to the Heart of America.* New York: Henry Holt and Company, Holt Paperbacks, 2006.

"Treaty of Paris, 1763." Avalon Project. Documents in Law, Diplomacy and History. Yale Law School. Lillian Goldman Law Library. 2008. http://avalon.law.yale.edu/18th_century/paris763.asp.

"Treaty of Paris, 1783." Avalon Project, Documents in Law, Diplomacy and History. Yale Law School. Lillian Goldman Law Library. 2008. http://avalon.law.yale.edu/18th_century/paris.asp.

"Trial of Brigadier General Hull." *The American Weekly Messenger* 2, no. 7 (May 7, 1814): 101–21.

Trowbridge, Charles Christopher. *Meeārmeear Traditions.* Edited by Vernon Kinietz. 1825. Ann Arbor: University of Michigan Press, 1938.

Trowbridge, Charles Christopher. *Shawnese Traditions.* Edited by Vernon Kinietz and Erminie W. Vogelin. 1824–1825. Ann Arbor: University of Michigan Press, 1939.

"True Character of General Jackson." *Truth's Advocate and Anti-Jackson Expositor* (June 1828): 216.

Tucker, Spencer C., ed. *American Revolution: The Definitive Encyclopedia and Document Collection.* 5 vols. Santa Barbara, CA: ABC–CLIO, LLC, 2018.

Tucker, Spencer C., ed. *The Encyclopedia of the Wars of the Early American Republic, 1783–1812: A Political, Social, and Military History.* 3 vols. Santa Barbara, CA: ABC–CLIO, LLC, 2014.

Turner, Frederick W. *Beyond Geography: The Western Spirit against the Wilderness.* New Brunswick, NJ: Rutgers University Press, 1994.

Twyman, Bruce Edward. *The Black Seminole Legacy and North American Politics, 1693–1845.* Cambridge, MA: Harvard University Press, 1999.

"The Union and the States." *North American Review* 37, no. 80 (July 1833): 190–249.

United States (US). *State Papers and Publick Documents of the United States.* 2nd ed. 10 vols. Boston: T. B. Wait and Sons, 1817.

"United States Army." *The Niles Weekly Register* 10, no. 250 (June 15, 1816): 351–53.

United States Bureau of the Census (USBC). *Negro Population, 1790–1915.* Edited by John Cummings and Joseph A. Hill. Washington, D.C.: Government Printing Office, 1918.

United States Bureau of Indian Affairs (USBIA). *Letter Book of the Indian Agency at Fort Wayne, 1809–1815.* Edited by Gayle Thornbrough. Indianapolis: Indiana Historical Society, 1961.

United States Congress (USC). "An Act for Establishing Trading Houses with the Indian Tribes." Avalon Project. The Statutes of the U.S. Yale Law School. Lillian Goldman Law Library, 2008. http://avalon.law.yale.edu/subject_menus/statutes.asp.

United States Congress (USC). *Acts Passed at the First Session of the Twenty-Second Congress of the United States.* Washington, D.C.: Francis Preston Blair, 1832.

United States Congress (USC). *Appendix to the Congressional Globe, for the First Session, Twenty-Ninth Congress: Containing Speeches and Important State Papers.* New Series, No. 1, 1845–1846. Washington, D.C.: Blair and Rives, 1846.

United States Congress (USC). *Congressional Globe: Containing Sketches of the Debates and Proceedings of the Twenty-Fifth Congress, Second Session,* vol. 6. Washington, D.C.: Blaire and Rives, 1838.

United States Congress (USC). *Congressional Globe: New Series, Containing Sketches of the Debates and Proceedings of the First Session of the Twenty-Sixth Congress, First Session*, vol. 8. Washington, D.C.: Blair and Rives, 1840.

United States Congress (USC). *Congressional Globe: New Series, Containing Sketches of the Debates and Proceedings of the First Session of the Twenty-Sixth Congress, Second Session*, vol. 9. Washington, D.C.: Blair and Rives, 1841.

United States Congress (USC). *Congressional Globe: New Series, Containing Sketches of the Debates and Proceedings of the First Session of the Thirty-first Congress*, vol. 9 Part I. Washington, D.C.: John C. Reeves, 1850.

United States Congress (USC). *The Debates and Proceedings in the Congress of the United States*. Ninth Congress, Comprising the Period from December 2, 1805, to March 3, 1806, Inclusive, vol. 15. Washington, D.C.: Gales and Seaton, 1852a.

United States Congress (USC). *The Debates and Proceedings in the Congress of the United States*. Tenth Congress, First Session, Comprising the Period from October 26, 1807, to April 21, 1808, Inclusive, vol. 17. Washington, D.C.: Gales and Seaton, 1852b.

United States Congress (USC). *The Debates and Proceedings in the Congress of the United States, with an Appendix Containing Important State Papers and Public Documents*. Fifteenth Congress. Second Session, Comprising the Period from November 16, 1818, to March 3, 1819, Inclusive. Washington, D.C.: Gales and Seaton, 1855.

United States Congress (USC). *Debates and Proceedings in the Congress of the United States with an Appendix Containing Important State Papers and Public Documents*. Thirteenth Congress, First and Second Sessions, Comprising the Period from May 24, 1813, to April 18, 1814, Inclusive. Washington, D.C.: Gales and Seaton, 1854.

United States Congress (USC). *The Debates and Proceedings of the Congress of the United States*. Eighth Congress. Washington, D.C.: Gales and Seaton, 1853.

United States Congress (USC). *Debates and Proceedings of the Thirty-Sixth Congress, Also of the Special Session of the Senate*. Washington, D.C.: Office of John C. Rives, 1860.

United States Congress (USC). *Executive Documents*. Twenty-Fifth Congress, Third Session. House of Representatives. Doc 177, vol. 4, 1–8. "Balances Due by Receivers, etc.," February 9, 1839.

United States Congress (USC). House of Representatives. *House Documents: Reports, Motions, Etc., Nos. 49–97, 3th Congress, 2nd Session, Jan. 31–April 16, 1814*, vol. 2. Washington, D.C.: R.C. Weightman, 1814.

United States Congress (USC). "An Ordinance for the Government of the Territory of the United States, North-West of the River Ohio." In *Laws of the Territory North-West of the United States, North-West of the River Ohio*, edited by Joseph Carpenter and Jonathan S. Findlay, vol. 1, 247–56. Cincinnati: Carpenter & Findlay, 1800.

United States Congress (USC). *Proceedings and Debates of the United States, at the First Session of the Eighth Congress, Begun at the City of Washington, Monday, October 17, 1803*. Washington, D.C.: Gales & Seaton, 1834.

United States Congress (USC). *Public Statutes at Large of the United States of America, from the Organization of the Government in 1789, to March 3, 1845*. Sixth Congress, Session I. Chapter 41. May 7, 1800, vol. 2. Boston: Charles C. Little and James Brown, 1845.

United States Congress (USC). *Public Statutes at Large for the United States of America, from the Organization of the Government in 1799 to March 3, 1845, et seq.* Edited by Richard Peters. 18 vols. Boston: Charles C. Little and James Brown, 1845–1875.

United States Congress (USC). *Register of Debates in Congress, Comprising the Leading Debates and Incidents of the First Session of the Twenty-fourth Congress. Part IV,* vol. 13. Washington, D.C.: Gales and Seaton, 1836a.

United States Congress (USC). *Register of Debates in Congress, Comprising the Leading Debates and Incidents of the First Session of the Twenty-fourth Congress, Together with an Appendix Containing Important State Papers and Documents and the Laws, of a Public Nature, Enacted during the Session, with a Copious Index to the Whole,* vol. 9. Washington, D.C.: Seaton and Gales, 1833.

United States Congress (USC). *Register of Debates in Congress, Comprising the Leading Debates and Incidents of the First Session of the Twenty-fourth Congress, Together with an Appendix Containing Important State Papers and Documents and the Laws, of a Public Nature, Enacted during the Session, with a Copious Index to the Whole,* vol. 12. Washington, D.C.: Seaton and Gales, 1836b.

United States Congress (USC). *Register of Debates in Congress, Comprising the Leading Debates and Incidents of the Second Session of the Twenty-Second Congress,* vol. 12. Washington, D.C.: Seaton and Gales, 1836c.

United States Congress (USC). *Report of the Select Committee to Investigate Matters Connected with Affairs in the Indian Territory with Hearings November 11, 1906–January 9, 1907.* Fifty-Ninth Congress, Second Session. Report 1013. Parts 1 & 2. 2 vols. Washington, D.C.: Government Printing Office, 1907.

United States Congress (USC). *Statutes at Large and Treaties of the United States of America, from December 1, 1845, to March 3, 1851.* Edited by George Minot. 18 vols. Boston: Little Brown Company, 1862.

United States Congress (USC). *Treaties and Conventions Concluded between the United States of America and Other Powers since July 4, 1776.* Washington, D.C.: Government Printing Office, 1871.

United States Congress, and Sam Baldwin (USCSB). "An Act Ascertaining the Bounds of a Tract of Land Purchased by John Cleves Symmes," approved April 12, 1792. In *Acts Passed at the Second Congress of the United States of America: Begun and Held in the City of Philadelphia, in the State of Pennsylvania, on Monday, the Twenty-Fourth of October, One Thousand Seven Hundred and Ninety-One.* Chapter XIX, 83–84. Philadelphia: Francis Childs, Printer of the Laws of the United States, 1795.

United States Department of Commerce, Bureau of the Census (USDC). *Population of States and Counties of the United States: 1790–1990.* Compiled and edited by Richard L. Forstall. Washington, D.C.: Government Printing Office, 1996.

United States Department of the Interior (USDI). "Report of the Commissioner of Indian Affairs." In *Annual Report to the Secretary of the Interior on the Operations of the Department for the Year Ended June 30, 1880,* vol. 1, 83–404. 3 vols. Washington, D.C.: Government Printing Office, 1880.

United States Department of the Interior (USDI). *Report on Indians Taxed and Not Taxed in the United States (except Alaska) at the Eleventh Census, 1890.* Washington, D.C.: Government Printing Office, 1894.

United States Department of the Interior, Census Office (USDI). *The Five Civilized Tribes in Indian Territory: The Cherokee, Chickasaw, Choctaw, Creek, and Seminole Nations.* Extra Census Bulletin. Washington, D.C.: Government Printing Office, 1894.

United States Department of the Interior, National Parks Service (USDI). *Underground Railroad, A Special Resource Study: Management Concepts, Resource Study.* Washington, D.C.: Government Printing Office, 1995.

United States Department of State (USDS). *Calendar of the Miscellaneous Letters Received by the Department of State from the Organization of the Government to 1820.* Washington, D.C.: Government Printing Office, 1897.

United States Federal Courts (USFC). *The Trial of Col. Aaron Burr on an Indictment for Treason, before the Circuit Court of the United States Held in Richmond (Virginia), May Term, 1807.* 3 vols. Washington City: Wescott & Co., 1808.

United States Senate (USS). *Documents, Otherwise Publ. as Public Documents and Executive Documents during the First Session of the Thirty-first Congress, 1849–'50.* 14 vols. Washington, D.C.: William M. Belt, 1850.

United States Senate (USS). *Journal of the Executive Proceedings of the Senate of the United States, from the Commencement of the First, to the Termination of the Nineteenth Congress.* 3 vols. Washington, D.C.: Duff Green, 1828.

United States Senate (USS). *Journal of the Senate including the Journal of Executive Proceedings of the Senate,* Seventh Congress, Second Session, December 1802–March 1803, vol. 2. Washington, D.C.: Government Printing Office, 1804.

United States Senate (USS). *Public Documents Printed by Order of the Senate of the United States during the Second Session of the Twenty-ninth Congress, Begun and Held at the City of Washington December 7, 1846.* 3 vols. Washington, D.C.: Ritchie and Heiss, 1847.

United States Senate (USS). *Public Documents Related to the First Fourteen Congresses, 1789–1817.* Compiled by Adolphus Washington Greeley. Washington, D.C.: Government Printing Office, 1900. Congressional Serial Set.

United States Senate (USS). "Treaty of San Lorenzo" ("Pickney's Treaty"). As "Treaty of Friendship, Limits, and Navigation Between Spain and The United States." October 27, 1795. Avalon Project. The Statutes of the United States. Yale Law School. Lillian Goldman Law Library. Accessed December 4, 2018. http://avalon.law.yale.edu/18th_century/sp1795.asp.

United States Supreme Court (USSC). *Dred Scott v. Sandford.* Roger Taney. "Opinion." 60 U.S. 19, How. 393, 1857, 399–454.

United States Works Project Administration (USWPA). Federal Writers' Project. Writers' Program of the Works Project Administration in the State of Illinois. "The William Henry Harrison Mansion." The WPA Guide to Indiana, The Hoosier State. 1945. San Antonio, TX: Trinity University Press, 2014.

Upham, Charles Wentworth, and Nathaniel Silsbee. *Eulogy on the Life and Character of Zachary Taylor, President of the United States.* Salem, MA: W. Ives and G. W. Pease, 1850.

Valencius, Conevery Bolton. *The Lost History of the New Madrid Earthquakes.* Chicago: University of Chicago Press, 2013.

Van Blarcom, Ralph. *Seminole War Artifacts & a History of the Forts of Florida.* Bloomington, IN: Xlibris, 2011.

Van Deusen, John G. "Detroit Campaign of Gen. William Hull." *Historical Society of Northwest Ohio Quarterly Bulletin* 5, no. 3 (July 1933): 1–9.

Vandervort, Bruce. *Indian Wars of Canada, Mexico and the United States, 1812–1900.* New York: Routledge, 2006.

Varner, John Grier, and Jennette Johnson Varner. *Dogs of Conquest.* Norman: University of Oklahoma Press, 1983.

Vaughn, William Preston. *The Antimasonic Party in the United States, 1826–1843.* Lexington: University Press of Kentucky, 2009.

Voegelin, Charles F. "The Shawnee Female Deity." In *Yale University Publications in Anthropology,* 8–13, 3–21. New Haven, CT: Yale University Press, 1936.

Voegelin, Erminie Wheeler. *Mortuary Customs of the Shawnee and Other Eastern Tribes*. Prehistory Research Series. 1944. Reprint. New York: AMS Press, 1980.

Wait, Eugene M. *Opening of the Civil War*. Commack, NY: Nova Science Publishers, Inc., 1999.

Wakefield, John Allen. *Wakefield's History of the Black Hawk War*. 1834. Reprint. Chicago: Caxton Club, 1908.

Wakula County Chamber of Commerce. "Forts of Wakula County." 2013. Accessed December 2, 2018. http://wakullacountychamber.com/about-the-chamber/about-wakulla-county/history/.

Waldo, Putnam. *Memoirs of Andrew Jackson, Major-General in the Army of the United States; and Commander in Chief of the Division of the South*. 5th ed. Hartford, CT: J. & W. Russell, 1820.

Walker, Adam. *A Journal of Two Campaigns of the Fourth Regiment of U.S. Infantry, in the Michigan and Indiana Territories under the Command of Col. John P. Boyd and Lt. Col. James Miller during the Years 1811 & 12*. Keene, NH: Sentinel Press, 1816.

Wallace, Anthony F. C. *The Death and Rebirth of the Seneca*. New York: Vintage Books, 1972.

Wallace, Anthony F. C. *Prelude to Disaster: The Course of Indian-White Relations Which Led to the Black Hawk War of 1832*. Springfield, IL: Illinois State Historical Society, 1970.

Wallace, Anthony F. C. "Revitalization Movements." *American Anthropologist* 58, no. 2 (April 1956): 264–81.

Wallenstein, Paul. "Indian Foremothers: Race, Sex, Slavery, and Freedom in Early Virginia." In *The Devil's Lane: Sex and Race in the Early South*, edited by Catherine Clinton and Michele Gillespie, 57–73. New York: Oxford University Press, 1997.

Wandell, Samuel H., and Meade Minnigerode. *Aaron Burr, A Biography Written in Large Part from Original and Hitherto Unused Material*. 2 vols. New York: G. P. Putnam's Sons, 1925.

Waselkov, Gregory A. *A Conquering Spirit: Fort Mims and the Redstick War*. Tuscaloosa: The University of Alabama Press, 2006.

Waselkov, Gregory A., Brian Mark Wood, Joseph M. Herbert, and James W. Parker. *Colonization and Conquest: The 1980 Archaeological Excavations at Fort Toulouse and Fort Jackson, Alabama*. Montgomery, AL: Auburn University at Montgomery, 1982.

Waselkov, Gregory, and Raven Christopher. *Archaeological Survey of the Old Federal Road in Alabama: Final Report Prepared for the Alabama Department of Transportation*. Project No. STEMTE–TE09(925). Montgomery, AL: Center for Archaeological Studies, University of Alabama, 2012.

Washington Constitution. "The Winnebagoes and the Black Hawk War." In *Collections of the State Historical Society of Wisconsin*, vol. 5, 306–9. Madison: State Historical Society of Wisconsin, 1907.

Washington, George. *The Writings of George Washington from the Original Manuscript Sources, 1745–1799; Prepared under the Direction of the United States George Washington Bicentennial Commission and Published by Authority of Congress*. Edited by John F. Fitzpatrick. 39 vols. Washington, D.C.: Government Printing Office, 1931–1944.

Watts, Florence G. "Fort Knox: Frontier Outpost on the Wabash, 1787–1816." *Indiana Magazine of History* 62, no. 1 (1966): 51–78.

Wayne, Tiffany K. "Enslaved Women." In *The World of Antebellum America: A Daily Life Encyclopedia*, edited by Alexandra Kindell, vol. 1, 213–16. 2 vols. Santa Barbara, CA: Greenwood, an Imprint of ABC-CLIO, LLC, 2018.

Webb, William Snyder, Charles E. Snow, and James B. Griffin. *The Adena People.* Knoxville: University of Tennessee Press, 1988.

Webster, Homer J. *William Henry Harrison's Administration of Indiana Territory.* Indiana Historical Society Publications, vol. 4, no. 3. Indianapolis: Sentinel Printing Co., 1907.

Welter, Barbara. "The Cult of True Womanhood, 1820–1860." In *The American Family in Social-Historical Perspective*, edited by Michael Gordon, 224–50. New York: St. Martin's Press, 1973.

West, George A. "Aboriginal Pipes of Wisconsin." *Wisconsin Archaeologist* 4, no. 1 (1904): 47–171.

Western Historical Company. *History of Lafayette County, Wisconsin, Containing an Account of Its Settlement, Growth, Development and Resources: An Extensive and Minute Sketch of Its Cities, Towns and Villages, Their Improvements, Industries, Manufactories, Churches, Schools and Societies; Its War Record, Biographical Sketches, Portraits of Prominent Men and Early Settlers; the Whole Preceded by a History of Wisconsin, Statistics of the State, and an Abstract of Its Laws and Constitution, and of the Constitution of the United States.* Chicago: Western Historical Company, 1881.

Wheatcroft, Andrew. *Infidels: A History of the Conflict between Christendom and Islam.* New York: Random House, 2005.

White, Charles. *An Account of the Regular Gradation in Man, and in Different Animals and Vegetables; and from the Former to the Latter.* London: C. Dilly, 1799.

White, Richard. *The Middle Ground: Indians, Empires, and Republics in the Great Lakes Region, 1650–1815.* New York: Cambridge University Press, 2011.

"White Slavery! or Selling White Men for Debt!" Pamphlet. Lexington, KY, 1840.

Whitman, James Q. *Hitler's American Model: The United States and the Making of Nazi Race Law.* Princeton, NJ: Princeton University Press, 2017.

Whitney, Ellen M., ed. *The Black Hawk War, 1831–1832.* Vols. 1 and 2. Parts I & II. Springfield: Illinois State Historical Library, 1973–1975.

Whittlesey, Charles. "Recollections of a Tour through Wisconsin." In *Collections of the State Historical Society of Wisconsin*, vol. 1, 64–85. Madison: State Historical Society of Wisconsin, 1903.

Wickar, J. Wesley. "Shabonee's Account of Tippecanoe." *Indiana Magazine of History* 17, no. 4 (December 1921): 353–63.

Wiecek, William M. "Somerset: Lord Mansfield and the Legitimacy of Slavery in the Anglo-American World." *University of Chicago Law Review* 42, no. 1 (Autumn 1974): 86–146.

Wilkinson, James. *Memoirs of My Own Times.* 3 vols. Philadelphia: Abraham Small, 1816.

"Wilkinson Paternal Family Line." In *Papers of Mark Aldrich*, 9. Lafayette, NY: Rick Grunder Books, n.d. http://www.rickgrunder.com/AldrichCollection.pdf.

"Will of Benjamin Harrison." *Virginia Magazine of History and Biography* 3, no. 2 (October 1895): 124–31.

"William Henry Harrison." In *The Presidency, A to Z*, edited by Michael Nelson, 220–21. 2nd ed. New York: Routledge, 2013.

Williams, Jai, and Charlene C. Gianetti. *Plantations of Virginia.* Guilford, CT: Globe Pequot, 2017.

Williams, Samuel Cole. *History of the Lost State of Franklin.* Rev. ed. New York: Press of the Pioneers, 1933.

Williams, Samuel. *Sketches of the War between the United States and the British Isles.* Vols. 1 & 2 in one. Rutland, VT: Fay and Davidson, 1815.

Williams, Thomas John Chew, and Folger McKinsey. *History of Frederick County, Maryland.* 2 vols. 1910. Reprint. Baltimore: Genealogical Pub. Co., 1997.

Willig, Timothy D. *Restoring the Chain of Friendship: British Policy and the Indians of the Great Lakes, 1783–1815.* Lincoln: University of Nebraska Press, 2008.

Willoughby, Lynn. *Flowing Through Time: A History of the Lower Chattahoochee River.* Tuscaloosa: University of Alabama Press, 2012.

Wilson, Clyde W. "Taylor, John." In *The New Encyclopedia of Southern Culture*, vol. 10: *Law & Politics*, edited by James W. Ely Jr., 393–94. Chapel Hill: University of North Carolina Press, 2014.

Wilson, Frazer E. *History of Darke County, Ohio, from the Earliest Settlements to the Present Time.* 2 vols. Milford, OH: The Hobart Publishing Co., 1914.

Wilson, James. *The Earth Shall Weep: A History of Native America.* New York: Atlantic Monthly Press, 1998.

Winn, Ed. *Early History of the St. John's River.* Maitland, FL: Winn's Books, 2003.

Wisconsin Historical Society. "Old Fort Hamilton Recalled as Wiota Celebrates." *Wisconsin State Journal*, July 22, 1828. Accessed June 3, 2019. https://www.wisconsinhistory. org/Records/Newspaper/BA13090.

Woehrmann, Paul. *At the Headwaters of the Maumee: A History of the Forts of Fort Wayne.* Indiana Historical Society Publications, vol. 24. Indianapolis: Indiana Historical Society, 1971.

Wood, Eleazar D. "Journal of the Northwestern Campaign of 1812–1813, under Major-General William Henry Harrison." In *Campaigns of the War of 1812–15 against Great Britain, Sketched and Criticised, with Brief Biographies of the American Engineers*, edited by George W. Cullum, 362–412. New York: James Miller, Publisher, 1879.

Wood, William, ed. *Select British Documents of the Canadian War of 1812.* Champlain Society Publications, nos. 13, 14, and 15. 3 vols. Toronto: Champlain Society, 1920–1926.

Wright, Albert Hazen. *The Sullivan Expedition of 1779: Contemporary Newspaper Comment.* Studies in History, nos. 5, 6, 7, and 8. Four parts. Ithaca, NY: A. H. Wright, 1943.

Wright, J. Leitch. *Creeks and Seminoles: The Destruction and Regeneration of the Muscogulge People.* Lincoln: University of Nebraska Press, 1986.

"Zachary Taylor Home, Springfield, Kentucky." U.S. Department of the Interior; National Parks Service. Accessed October 10, 2018. https://www.nps.gov/nr/travel/ presidents/zachary_taylor_springfield.html.

Zee, Jacob Van der. "Early History of Lead Mining in the Iowa Country." *Iowa Journal of History and Politics* 13, no. 1 (January 1915): 3–52.

Index

About the Author

Barbara Alice Mann, Ph.D., is Professor of Humanities in the Jesup Scott Honors College, University of Toledo. Author of thirteen books and over 200 articles and chapters, she recently published *Spirits of Blood, Spirits of Breath* (2016) and the *Matriarchal Studies Bibliography* (2019, 2015), along with several books for Praeger's Native America: Yesterday and Today series.